USA

A SYNOPTIC HISTORY OF AMERICA'S PAST

GERALD BAYDO
Grossmont College
El Cajon, California

John Wiley & Sons, Inc.
New York · *Chichester* · *Brisbane* · *Toronto*

Designer: Judith Fletcher Getman
Cover Tapestry: Helena Hernmark
Production Supervisor: Elizabeth Doble
Copy Editor: Deborah Herbert
Photo Research: Rosemary Eakins, Research Reports
Photo Editor: Stella Kupferberg

Library of Congress Cataloging in Publication Data:

Baydo, Gerald, 1942-
  USA, a synoptic history of America's past.

  Bibliography: p.
  Includes index.
  1. United States—History—Sources. 2. United
States—History—Addresses, essays,
lectures. I. Title.

E173.B32   1981b   973   80-19567
ISBN 0-471-06432-7

Printed in the United States of America

10 9 8 7 6 5 4 3 2 1

Preface

All instructors of the American history survey course have at one time or another searched for the ideal history text. Often their search ends with a weighty volume that is a veritable encyclopedia. The style is invariably dull, and student interest soon wanes. Another choice is an outline of American history that is the skeleton text; the instructor decides that his or her lectures will put the required meat on the frame. But the end result of the course is too little meat and a lot of bone. Another choice is a book with a novel approach; the novelty, however, wears off fast, and the instructor turns again to the traditional text.

Although there is no such thing as an ideal history text for either students or faculty, there is a definite need for a book that contains more than the mere essentials of American history, keeps student interest, includes material on minorities and women, and portrays the human side of history. I wrote this book to fulfill this need. My first priority was to make it short, concise, and readable. Rising inflation plus diminished student reading levels encouraged me in that direction. Although the result is more than an outline of American history, it does not profess to be an encyclopedic study. Much effort was spent in making the writing style interesting and clear, and readers, students and instructors alike, will find that this end has been accomplished.

Throughout the emphasis is on political, economic, and social history. Recent critics note that the discussion of minority and women's history has been overdone. Still, these groups have played an important role in the history of our nation, and their contributions should be included. Hence, in this text special emphasis is placed on their involvement in American history and on certain aspects of our social and cultural development that are seldom placed in proper perspective.

Some useful features add to the book's attractiveness. Each chapter begins with a *time line* that places the important events of the chapter in a chronological framework. There is a short *biography* of each president that aids in understanding that individual as a person. Finally, each chapter ends with a short *essay* that gives insight into certain topics that are usually ignored in more traditional presentations.

Instructors who look for essential names, dates and facts, the newest interpretations, maps, illustrations, and suggested readings, will find them included. In addition, there is a detailed index, and a teachers' guide is available to accompany the text.

In summary, this book is a short, readable history of the United States that presents the story of the American people from the pre-Columbian Indians to the present. Since it appears in both a one-volume and two-volume edition, it can be used in schools with either the semester or quarter systems.

I am grateful to the members of the Community College Social Science Association who offered their opinions and suggestions during the writing of this book. Special thanks go to Wayne Anderson, his staff, and reviewers, for helping to guide the finished product. The input of my students at Grossmont College was invaluable in writing a book that would meet their needs. Finally, much deserved appreciation goes to my wife, Julie, for her support and to Robbie, Brian, and Monica for their welcome and even unwelcomed help in the hallowed space of my home office. And a quiet thank you must go to the newest Baydo, Colleen.

It is my hope that this book will find a place in many history classrooms across the country and make a genuine contribution to the study of America's history as a nation.

El Cajon, California   *Gerald Baydo*

CONTENTS

Photo Credits

CHAPTER 1

North America:
The Indian, The European

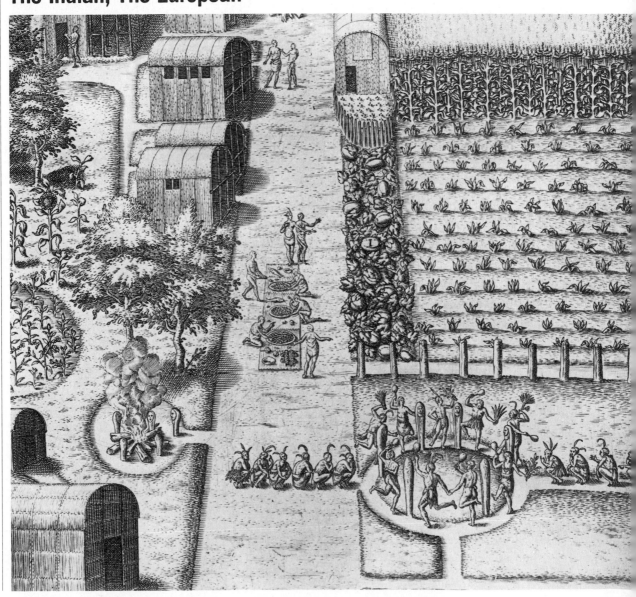

Time Line

?–10,000 B.C.	Migration of Native Americans to North America
A.D. 1000	Leif Ericson's exploration of eastern North America
1492	Christopher Columbus lands on San Salvador in the West Indies
1513	Ponce De León "discovers" Florida
1534–1541	Jacques Cartier explores eastern Canada
1540–1542	Francisco Coronado explores Southwest
1607	First permanent English settlement at Jamestown
1620	Pilgrims establish Plymouth Colony
1630	Puritans found Noble Experiment at Massachusetts Bay
1637	Pequot War
1675–1676	King Philip's War
1682	William Penn founds Quaker colony of Pennsylvania
1732	James Oglethorpe establishes the debtors' colony of Georgia

1776	Declaration of Independence
1789–1797	Presidency of George Washington
1812–1815	War of 1812
1816–1824	Era of Good Feelings
1846–1848	Mexican War
1861–1865	Civil War
1865–1877	Reconstruction
1877–1900	Industrialization and urbanization
1900–1916	Progressive Era
1917–1918	World War I
1930s	Depression and New Deal
1941–1945	World War II
1945–1960	Post-war politics
1950–1953	Korean War
1950–1960	Civil rights movement
1961–1973	Vietnam War
1976	Bicentennial celebration

?–A.D. 1492	Migration and evolution of American Indian societies
1492	Christopher Columbus lands in West Indies—beginning of European exploration
1607–1732	Establishment of 13 English colonies
1775–1783	American Revolution

North America: The Indian, The European

In 1492 Christopher Columbus sailed the ocean blue, no more courageous a sailor was there than he. With a tear running down his cheek, Little George Washington confessed that he had chopped down the cherry tree. After Abe Lincoln returned home through the snow, he discovered that he had been given too much money, so he charged out into the storm again to return the ill-gotten gain to the shopkeeper. The Battle of Wounded Knee in 1890 ended the resistance of the American Indian and brought an era of peace to the West. Here is the stuff that American history is made of, or is it?

For many Americans, American history is an innocuous story of heroes and heroic deeds that took place a long time ago. This tale is filled with an abundance of names, facts, and dates, but it happened in the past and has little influence today on our modern technological society. Columbus is no Neil Armstrong. George Washington and Abraham Lincoln are not as human as Jimmy Carter. The American Indian is a vanishing American.

But wait. There is much more to it than that. American history can have relevance to the present. Some writers even believe that the present is only a direct reflection of the past. American history should not be a tale told about hollow men, but about real human beings who came from Asia, Europe, and Africa and settled a vast land. It is the recreation of the evolution of a nation from its early days to its bustling present. The tale contained happiness and woe, bloodshed and conquest, greedy men and altruistic men, presidents and farmers. The story that will unfold in these pages is the story of a people who came together from the far reaches of the globe, forged a nation, mixed progress with goodness, and became one of the strongest powers in the world. Some obvious mythology and legend will appear here, too, but mythology is not bad as long as it is recognized as mythology.

One important element that frequently is forgotten is the stage on which the tale or play unfolds. This particular stage called North America is a vast continent with a wide variety of climates and terrains. As with most plays, the physical stage does much to help guide the direction of the cast.

Geography of North America

It is with North America that American history begins. Here was a land replete with natural resources—a virgin paradise. This paradise, however, was not uniform in climate or terrain, so a brief sketch of the continental United States is in order. The major geographic sections of the country include the Atlantic and Gulf Coastal Plain, Appalachian Highlands, Central Lowlands, Great

Plains, Rockies, and Pacific Borderlands. Although each of these land regions has a great deal of uniformity, the geographic variety of the continental United States appears endless.

The Atlantic and Gulf Coastal Plain, or East Coast, is the lowland bordering the Atlantic seaboard of the United States from Maine in the north to Florida in the south. This plain is extremely narrow in the north but broad in the south. Relatively short rivers and excellent deep water bays are also characteristic of this region. In the past, the narrow plain in the north accentuated the stony soil and short growing seasons. It was natural for early residents to turn to other productive pursuits such as commerce, industry, and fishing. The continental shelf—a broad, submerged plain off the northern coast—held one of the world's richest fishing grounds. In the south the broad coastal plain and fertile soil lent itself to a plantation economy. While drainage problems from the level terrain and thin soil, which was exhausted quickly, caused numerous headaches, still large farms with their dependence on a single cash crop prospered.

On the western edge of this area is the fall line where falls or rapids were created by the seaward rivers. Many early industrial cities such as Raleigh and Richmond were established near the waterpower the falls provided. Many other important cities grew up as ports along some of the excellent bays. By the time of the American Revolution nine out of every ten Americans lived along this coastal plain. Here was England's frontier in North America and the eventual foundation for an American nation.

The Appalachian Highlands run in a southwesterly direction from New England to central Georgia and include the Piedmont region east of the fall line and two mountain chains—the Appalachians and Alleghenies. Here is found a region dotted by valleys with fertile soil and possessing rich beds of coal and deposits of petroleum. Industrial cities such as Pittsburgh sprang up within the area. The Appalachian and Allegheny mountain chains traverse the length of the highlands, and the obstacle these chains presented to travel delayed migration westward by concentrating early settlers on the Atlantic plain. Eventually the colonial settlers found three trails—the Wilderness Road, the Pennsylvania Road, and the National Road—that gave them access into the Trans-Appalachian area and the Central Lowlands.

The Central Lowlands was the great interior valley of North America, known today as the Middle West. It includes an expanse of land from the Appalachian Highlands on the east to the Rocky Mountains in the west. Glaciers during the Ice Age left nearly level land, with rich soil and abundant rainfall, making it an excellent agricultural area and eventually the Corn Belt of America. Water, timber, and minerals combined to make it an industrial

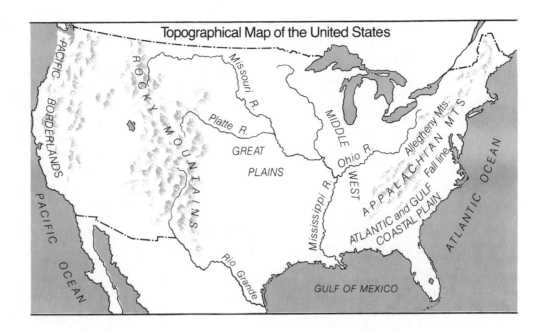

Topographical Map of the United States

center as well. The main artery of the region is the mighty Mississippi River that cuts through the interior and provides a water highway. This river, along with its important branches, the Ohio and Missouri, provided an easy form of transportation for the pioneers. This relatively flat area was quickly settled, but settlement slowed substantially at its western edge—the Great Plains.

Also called the Great American Desert, the Great Plains, a semiarid belt, was an area long considered unfit for cultivation and habitation. Over the years the view of the plains has changed little. But much of the area has been given over to wheat and corn, and even the arid high plains were brought under cultivation by a process called "dry farming." Life here, both animal and human, has been shaped by the lack of water. Found here also is the "dust bowl" region, where terrific wind storms literally remove the top soil over-night. This is the land of sodhouses, cowboys, and cattle drives—a land characterized by a deficiency in water.

The Rocky Mountains comprise the western border of the Great Plains and stretch from northern New Mexico through Canada into Alaska. In the same way that the Appalachian Highlands became a barrier to expansion in the east, the Rockies blocked further expansion in the west. But the Rockies

Overland travelers crossed the Great Plains and
saw a formidable obstacle before them—the Rockies.

were a much more forbidding barrier, with their rugged terrain and majestic peaks which can rise more than 14,000 feet above sea level. Pioneers spent much time and effort getting through them. Today, interest in the Rockies centers on its mineral deposits and its vacation potential.

The Pacific Borderlands stretch from the Rockies to the Pacific Ocean. The region is a jumble of mountains, arid plateaus, and basins with well-watered mountains and valleys. Between the Rocky Mountains and the Sierra Nevada and Cascade ranges, which extend the length of the Pacific Coast, a series of western plateaus and basins are found with extremes in temperature and few cities. Yet the natural landscape is panoramic, for example, the Grand Canyon, the Great Salt Lake, and Death Valley, the lowest point in the United States, 280 feet below sea level. Protected from the harsh inland environment by the Sierra Nevadas and Cascades, a series of broad coastal plains and valleys border the Pacific Coast. Here were built the important cities of the Far West. Due to its location, the Pacific Borderlands is frequently looked upon as the last frontier, as well as the land of golden opportunity. This vision of the Far West as utopia is only slowly changing.

Origins of the American Indian

It was to this land of environmental variety that the first humans came. But they were not of English origin, Spanish, or French; they were ancestors of the peoples that we today call American Indians.

Relatively little is known of the early people who were the real discoverers of America. There is, of course, little doubt that the first humans to reach America were not Norse or Italian. But how and when they got to America is one of history's puzzles that may never be solved. It is generally agreed that the first Americans came from northeast Asia and entered the New World in the general area of Alaska. Yet the oldest remains of humanity in the New World have not been found in Alaska but in California. This "La Jolla Man" resides in a museum in San Diego and has been dated to a period around 50,000 years ago. Recent archaeological finds have pushed back the date of early human life in America even further.

The most popular answer to how the ancients came to the Americas is by way of land. From 40,000 to 10,000 B.C. a land bridge existed between Asia and Alaska. It appeared when the glaciers of the last Ice Age were at their peak which caused the level of the Bering Sea to lower more than 300 feet. It was across this land bridge, which may have measured more than 1000 miles wide, that the Asian hunters traveled in search of food. One of the newer theories concerning these migrations is that the land bridge was not open during the entire 30,000 year period but only accessible to foot traffic twice: once from about 32,000 to 36,000 years ago, and again from about 13,000 to 28,000 years ago. Another problem complicating travel was that, at the time the land bridge was open, much of North America was ice-covered. It is still not certain whether the peopling of North America stemmed from a single migration or from successive waves of immigrants over a long period, but generally it is agreed that all land travel ended between 10,000 and 9000 B.C..

The end of land travel does not mean that all migrations came to an end; there are theories about other migrations. It is plausible that a Japanese or Chinese fishing craft, or even a Polynesian outrigger canoe, may have drifted across the Pacific to the New World. Some believe that Asians continued to come by way of an island-hopping process or along the Japanese Current from the east. The Norwegian Thor Heyerdahl, in particular, has attempted to prove the migration of peoples from the Pacific and even from Egypt. His raft *Kon-Tiki* successfully sailed across the Pacific from South America to show that Indians could have reached the islands of Polynesia. His voyage of *Ra II* across the Atlantic tried to explain the numerous cultural parallels between Egypt and Central America by linking them through ancient sea travel.

Due to the imagination of man, there have been other legends or popular beliefs about these Native Americans (the name "Indians" was given them by Columbus, who believed he had reached the Indies). Some of the earlier beliefs were really no more wild than some of the most recent. In 1512 the Pope declared officially that the New World Indians were true descendents of Adam and Eve and had come originally from the Garden of Eden. The biblical interpretation of the origins of the American Indians has been an intriguing one. According to one Christian theory Indians were aboard Noah's Ark, while according to the Book of Mormon the Indians are descended from the Lamanites, who it describes as a degenerate element of the Jews that migrated to the New World prior to the Christian era. American Indians have also been linked to many other races—Egyptian, Chinese, Phoenician, Greek, Roman, Welsh, Danish, and even Trojan. Viscount Kingsborough, a nineteenth-century Irish nobleman, spent many years and a fortune trying to prove that the Mayas of Middle America had descended from one of the Lost Tribes of Israel. Other investigators have insisted that the Indians came to the Western Hemisphere via the supposedly Lost Continents of Atlantis in the Atlantic Ocean or Mu in the Pacific, making their way across from the old World safely before the continents sank beneath the oceans. An even more sensational theory contends that Indians were either inhabitants of space ships who landed here or were visited themselves by travelers from beyond the earth. Such speculation will continue as long as there is mystery concerning the Indians' arrival in North America.

Present Native Americans, however, spend little time pondering their origins. Their own oral traditions indicate that they were created here as the offspring of nature.

Indians Before Columbus

From their first encounters with white men to their everyday life in contemporary America, numerous myths and stereotypes about Indians have existed. These concepts arose primarily from contact and conflict between white and red. Indians initially were described by early writers as a race of happy people who were children of nature. These inhabitants of the virgin wilderness were pictured as innocent, childlike persons who had not yet been tainted by civilization. Of course, this idea was particularly popular when Indians outnumbered whites. The most enduring concept, however, was that of the Indian as a bloodthirsty savage who understood little of white values and who lived on blood and gore. Both of these notions were perpetuated by writers who depicted noble savages such as Meek Wolf (the Puritan Indian who knew enough to build a Christian church in the wilderness), Tonto (the invisible companion of the Lone Ranger), and savages such as the Hurons in James Fenimore Cooper's *Last of the Mohicans*. The savage stereotype was and is perpetuated through Wild West shows, dime novels, movies, and television. Added to these stereotypes was the mistaken notion that all Indians were alike; a notion easily disproven by a brief description of the cultural diversity of the pre-Columbian Indians.

The noble savage stereotype initially pictured the Eastern Indians as simple children of nature.

Western Tribes

The white men who first arrived in North America would have had a far more difficult time finding an "average Indian" than would a Hollywood producer of cowboy-Indian epics. Wide differences existed between Indian societies, and these cultural variations depended to a great extent upon the environment. The Indians of Southern California and much of Nevada lived a seemingly simple, nomadic existence. They frequently subsisted on nuts, berries, seeds, roots, insects, small game, and fish; yet their religious practices were quite complex. Referred to for years as simple "Diggers", these Indians had practices which were unique to their culture, such as their interest in a very complex religion concerned with death and dying. The culture among the Pacific Northwest Indians revealed a different emphasis. These Indians lived along the Pacific coast from northern California to southern Alaska and were skilled in fishing and hunting. Acquiring food from the land was so easy that these natives never did become farmers. The wealth of their culture was evident in their elaborate wood carvings, totem poles, slaves, and institution of the *potlatch*. The potlatch was a great feast in which the host would prove his worth by giving away his material possessions or, occasionally, even destroying them. One Northwest Indian saying goes, "We do not fight with weapons, we fight with property." These Indians were the most materialistic of all North America.

Southwestern Tribes

The Indians of the Southwest were much different from those of the Pacific coast and southern California. In this semiarid region wild game was not plentiful, and there were not enough streams to provide adequate fishing. The ancestors of these southwestern tribes, the Hohokam with their ingenious irrigation projects and the Anasazi with their impressive architecture, set the pattern for survival in this bleak environment. Many of the tribes of this area turned to farming and lived in adobe apartment houses built into cliff walls situated on the top of plateaus or along the few rivers. The making of pottery, weaving of baskets, and spinning of cotton cloth were important parts of their culture. Religion played a dominant role in their lives, and tribes frequently devoted much of their time to performing rituals with brilliantly colored prayer sticks and feathered masks. These ceremonies were directed toward healing the sick, bringing good harvests or rain, and ensuring peace. Individualism was usually frowned upon, and the tribal community had the highest priority.

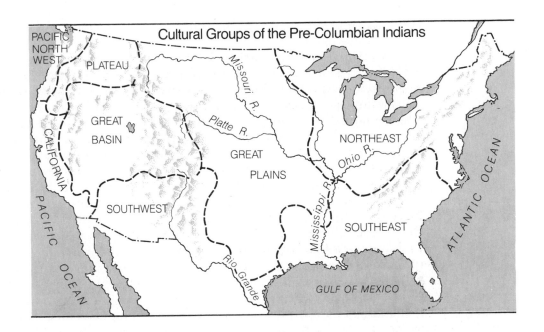

Cultural Groups of the Pre-Columbian Indians

Southeast Tribes

The natives of the Southeast had the benefit of a relatively mild climate in which to develop a complex social system with distinct social divisions. These inhabitants of the southern coastal plain utilized the fertile soil to maintain the best-balanced farm economy in all of North America. The relative ease in maintaining a stable food supply allowed the development of leisure time activities such as arts and crafts, sports, and complex religious practices, such as the green corn ceremony.

Plains and Northeast Tribes

The Indians of the Great Plains and of the Northeast were again different from other tribal groups. The Plains Indians were nomadic hunters who followed the buffalo herds. Prior to the arrival of the horse, they were forced to hunt on foot with dogs. Because of their nomadic existence, they spent little time on arts and crafts except for buffalo-hide painting and beadwork. With their great reliance on the environment, nature was uppermost in their culture—

particularly in their religion, in which they depicted the sun as being at the center of the universe.

The Indians of the Northeast developed a much more settled way of life than did the Plains Indians. The Northeast Indians usually lived in villages in rectangular longhouses covered with bark or in cone-shaped wigwams. They farmed, hunted, and fished. Their government structure was characterized by a matriarchal system in which women were the decision makers. One group among the Northeast tribes, the Iroquois nation, even developed a workable confederacy. The feminist movement today has looked with favor upon such a system, and our founding fathers used the Iroquois government as a model for our constitution.

Cultural Differences and Similarities

The major differences between tribal groups include differences in language; there were more than 200 identifiable languages among the Indians of North America. Generally, pre-Columbian Indians neither looked like each other nor lived in the same manner. From the tall Crow to the short, stocky, Ute, from the Sioux bow and arrow to the Seminole dart gun, from the Pueblo apartment house to the Kiowa tepee, the cultural diversity of these peoples was quite apparent.

Yet, amid this diversity, there was highly significant unity, too. For example, the Zuni tribe spoke a language that was unique, but their general culture was the same as many of their neighboring southwestern tribes. Three tribes in northern California spoke different languages, but their baskets and tools are so similar in pattern and structure that even experts cannot tell the difference. Among Indians, there was also a uniform way of looking at the world which was decidedly non-Western. The statement "Our land is more valuable than your money, it will last forever" is not one that is heard frequently today. Indians were truly nature's children. The world about them was their church, and they practiced their religion constantly. Spirits, great forces beyond the power of man, inhabited nature; Indians developed prayers, dances, and songs to please the friendly spirits and soothe the evil ones. But this religion of animism was not the only similarity among the natives. Although chiefs of war and peace often emerged as dominant leaders, the major decisions of the tribes still were made by councils of advisors. Because of the deep faith in supernatural forces, a holy man or shaman—the link with the spirit world—was essential to all societies. The shaman's powers ranged from curing to prophecy, and such a role in the tribe could be a dominant one. Marriages frequently were arranged by parents or an older brother, and gifts often were exchanged for the bride. Polygamy, especially the marrying of one man to sisters, was common. Divorce even existed. The belief in an afterlife (not necessarily "the happy hunting ground") was also universal. But the burial practices meant to send the dead off to that afterlife varied greatly: Some Indians "buried" their dead in caves, others buried them in the ground, while still others practiced cremation.

Although the highest levels of civilization emerged among the Aztecs of Mexico, the Mayas of Central America, and the Incas of Peru, many advanced types of primitive culture also were evident in what eventually became the United States. Archaeological work being done among the remains of the Mississippi culture of the Mound Builders is revealing the sophistication of these peoples and their pyramid-type structures. The Cherokee of the Southeast developed their own alphabet and written language, and most Cherokee tribes had developed a workable political structure. The Five Nations of the Iroquois even formed an alliance system that was studied openly by the founding fathers when they gathered in Philadelphia to frame the Constitution of the United States. The Indians of the Plains, particularly the Comanche and the Sioux, became some of the most remarkable horsemen the world has ever known. Surely the path of American history would have been different if the continent of North America had been uninhabited when the first white people arrived.

White and Indian Interaction

When Europeans initially arrived in the New World, it is estimated that there were a million or more Native Americans in the region that is known today as the United States. What was the major effect of these two civilizations coming together? Which society was to gain and which one was to lose? The Indian tribes were developing their cultures at a rate much different from that of Europe when the first white people stumbled upon them. It is erroneous to believe that Indian tribes had never undergone rapid cultural changes before— they fought wars, and even drank alcohol before the arrival of "the white man." But everything accelerated after 1492. And such sudden change makes it difficult to judge whether the benefits of European society outweighed the drawbacks.

White technology, which included items such as metal tools, firearms, and copper kettles, simplified and eased life. Arts and crafts, and even practical items such as utensils, could be produced at a much faster pace. And there is no doubt that the Spanish introduction of the horse brought a real revolution to the New World, especially to the Plains Indians. The dog as a beast of

The clash between white and Indian cultures usually
broke out into open war.

burden (and a source of food) ended, as did foot travel. The horse made raids
and war more feasible. Mobility expanded the tribe's world: Not everyone in
the tribe now had to be a producer; definite roles began to appear, and new
religious practices emerged. The horse brought a revolution of vast dimensions
to the North American Indian.

But not all European gifts produced positive results. Guns not only increased wars and tension among tribes, but they accelerated the inevitable
clash between white and Indian as well. Liquor had a truly debilitating effect,
the results of which are evident today among twentieth-century Indians. Eu-

ropean diseases were among the most devastating "gifts." Tuberculosis, measles, syphilis, and smallpox swept through Indian settlements, virtually annihilating tribes. Not only were these diseases contracted innocently from Europeans, infections sometimes were spread intentionally by whites who gave Indians disease-filled blankets—an early use of biological warfare.

Did the Indian have a similar effect on the white settler? Could the whites have survived without the Indians? Look around you today. What you may be eating and wearing—and even where you may be living—often has a direct connection with the early natives of North America. One of the most enduring gifts was the range of foods that have become commonplace to us. Foods grown by Indians included corn—the first basic staple of white America—as well as peanuts, tomatoes, squash, beans, chocolate, pumpkin, and turkey. Indians helped many of the early settlers to grow these crops (without which they would have perished). The Indians also taught many whites the ways of the forest—hunting, fishing, and marking trails. Such useful objects as canoes, snowshoes, sleds, and hammocks were designed by Indians; and approximately 60 drugs, including those from which cocaine, novacaine, and quinine were derived, originated here. Further, our map is covered with their picturesque words. More than half of the 50 states and scores of counties, towns, rivers, mountains, valleys, and other geographic features have Indian names. Today, Indian heroes such as Red Cloud and Chief Joseph are found on best-selling posters. Indian jewelry is on display at many stores. Many writers rate Indians as the first ecologists and would like us to treat nature the same way they did. Still, the tragedy of cultural clash—from the first voyage of Columbus to the reservation life of today—lingers on. A better understanding of this clash of cultures will be possible after we have examined the history and motives of European exploration.

Pre-Columbian Explorers

Most Americans accept the year 1492 as the date of the discovery of America, but this is actually the date of the "rediscovery," or effective discovery, of America. There is some evidence that Irish or Welsh monks may have been the first non-Indian discoverers of the New World. There is also evidence that between the years A.D. 450 and 500 Buddhist monks under the leadership of Hwui Shan traveled eastward from China to a land they called Fu-Sang. There they planted a mysterious tree—a possible explanation for the origin of the

California redwood or Monterey cypress. They also tried to convert local Indians to Buddhism but failed and returned home. Hwui Shan has been called "the Inglorious Columbus." Although he may have been first, his voyages caused no rush from the Orient to this new land. But even Hwui Shan's voyages may have been predated by others. A stone uncovered from an ancient grave site at Bat Creek, Tennessee, has recently been proved to contain ancient Canaanite letters that date the inscription on the stone to the period between A.D. 70 and 135. The mystery of the first non-Indian discoverers of America perhaps will remain unsolved for many years to come.

Norse Exploration and Settlement

The best-known of the pre-Columbian explorers were of Nordic origin. From Icelandic sagas we learn of early Viking voyages to Iceland, and then to Greenland. About A.D. 985 Eric the Red visited and colonized Greenland; this conclusion is supported by the discovery of numerous ruins, for the Norse remained there for several centuries. About A.D. 1000 Leif, the son of Eric, driven by adventure and strong winds, sailed again and arrived at land in the West. This wooded area was called Vinland. During the next few years a Greenland trader named Thorfinn Karlsefni attempted to establish a colony there. Exactly where the colony was established is not known, but in 1963 positive remains of a Norse settlement were found on the northern tip of Newfoundland. Evidence indicates that Karlsefni's wife and the natives, whom they called *skrallings* ("dwarfs"), were too difficult to manage, and the colony was abandoned.

Besides the sagas, three other objects may substantiate the early Norse voyages. In 1898 a Kensington rune stone was discovered in the roots of a tree on a farm in Minnesota. This stone appears to relate the misadventures of a Norse party that entered Hudson Bay and traveled into central Minnesota. This stone, however, is rejected by many today as fake. In 1965 Yale University acquired a Vineland map, drawn between A.D. 1400 and 1450 by a European cartographer, that details a group of islands in the West, including Vinelandia Insula. While this map helps to substantiate a Norse settlement in Vineland, it gives little assistance in pinpointing its exact location. In recent years many experts also have felt that this map was a well-conceived forgery. A Norse coin found in Maine, which dates back to the year A.D. 900, raised serious questions about the time of Norse exploration and settlement, as well as questioning the extent of Norse expansion. Although the Norse indeed may have reached the east coast of the United States, they were forced to abandon their settlements. Nor is there any evidence that Columbus ever heard of these discoveries or that they inspired his plan for reaching the Indies.

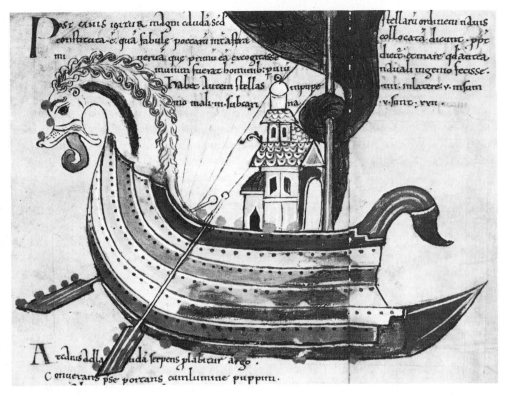

This Norse longship from a tenth century English chronicle pictures the vessel that carried the Norsemen to America.

European Expansion

Actually, Europe in the year 1000 was not prepared for the discovery of America. Numerous changes were to take place in Europe by 1492 that would make it more open to such a development. Because of these changes, Columbus would be the effective discoverer of America.

With the fall of the Roman Empire in the fifth century, Europe was thrown into chaos and entered a period referred to as the Middle or Dark Ages. This was a period of very localized authority with no national governments or kings. The main occupation was agriculture, and farms were centered around small independent communities, called manors, usually with a castle at the center. Life was generally immobile. Weaker lords owed their allegiance to stronger lords, and peasants and serfs were tied to the land. If a person was born a serf, he or she generally died a serf. The opportunity to move up in society was practically nonexistent. One of the worst differences between then and now was the lack of sanitation. Garbage gathered in the moats; the stench was quite obvious.

This society changed drastically after 1100. A commercial revolution occurred that created new classes, such as traders and bankers. Small towns began to grow near the older manors; and then trade began to develop, first between the towns and manors, and eventually between the towns themselves. Towns broke the monopoly of the castle lords and provided a growing market for the rising business class. The merchants of the towns became interested in acquiring wealth—initially trading outside their local areas with other parts of Europe, and eventually trading with distant lands outside the bounds of Europe itself. Early on, the merchants of the city-states of Italy were dominant in controlling the trade of Europe and the lands beyond.

These city-states profited handsomely from the military expeditions—known as the Crusades—called by Pope Urban II in 1096, which attempted to reconquer the Holy Land from the infidel Moslems. Militarily, however, the Crusaders profited little. In one military encounter a European leader drunk, fell into a stream and drowned. The Moslems were the ultimate victors. But the Crusades did force the Europeans out of their isolationist shells and into contact with a new culture, one with such valued products as spices, precious stones, and silks. Because of the lack of refrigeration, most of the meat Europeans ate was either salted or partly spoiled. Spices made food more edible and left Europeans dissatisfied with their own products. The Crusades brought a demand for expanded trade.

In the 1200s travelers such as Giovanni de Plano Carpini, Willem van Rujsbroek, and Marco Polo traveled deep into Asia and returned with stories of the wealth of the Orient. Polo wrote, "The Lord had a great Palace which is entirely roofed with fine gold just as our churches are roofed with lead." Polo's stories stirred the avarice and taste buds of Europeans. They could imagine dabbing fine perfume on their bodies, wearing fine silk, and lying on Persian carpets while preparing to eat food that they knew would taste good. Trade in general, and with the East in particular, increased. By the end of the 1200s the Italian merchants had gained a monopoly on eastern trade by controlling overland routes. By the mid-1400s many parts of Europe hoped to break this monopoly by finding a new route to the Orient.

The rise of Nation-States

Another change that influenced the discovery of America was the rise of national monarchies. By the end of the Middle Ages kings were regaining their power from the feudal lords, and nations were forming that shared a political organization under one ruler. By the 1400s France, England, and Spain were ruled by ambitious kings and queens. Once national boundaries had been secured, these monarchs looked to expand their powers. These ambitions frequently were met by expeditions on the unknown seas. In one instance, the financing of Columbus's expedition by the monarchs of Spain led to a most positive result.

Renaissance and Reformation

The discovery of America also was influenced by the Renaissance and the Reformation. The former was an intellectual and artistic movement, a revival of learning, that expanded the European citizen's self-knowledge and understanding of the surrounding world. Rabelais, a Renaissance writer, said that people formerly "drank, ate, worked, and slept," but now they had become curious and adventurous. The Renaissance led to the invention of certain instruments that were essential for the exploration of the area beyond the Mediterranean; among these were the compass, the astrolabe, and the cross-staff. Printing presses began to publish books, which spread new ideas about the world. Of course, curiosity frequently was intertwined with the desire for precious metals or wealth. Actually, Mammon and God worked hand in hand to encourage exploration.

In 1517 a monk named Martin Luther led a successful revolt against the Catholic church, the dominant Christian church in Europe during the Middle Ages, and the Protestant Reformation began. Other religious revolts soon followed, such as those led by John Calvin and by King Henry VIII of England. With the single-church idea disappearing, religious persecution heightened. Many churches, such as the Church of England, became nationalized. Today it is difficult to understand how religion could so permeate the lives of the citizens of Europe during this period. In many ways Columbus regarded his discovery of the New World as a triumph for Christendom; and popes were so powerful they could assign entire continents to nations they favored. Even before the finding of the New World, many Protestants wished to leave Europe for a sanctuary where they could practice their new faith in peace. Many Catholics also wished for a new land where they could practice their old faith

Martin Luther was greatly responsible for the religious revolt against the Catholic Church.

without having dissident Protestant voices to contend with. The discovery of America answered the prayers of many.

The reasons others had for taking part in exploration are less clear. Why, for instance, would ordinary seamen wish to venture beyond the known seas? Most of the money to be made would go to the kings or the captains. Also, most Europeans were illiterate and influenced little by the Renaissance. But it must be remembered that this was an age when the average life expectancy was about thiry years and life on land was hard and uncertain. Statistics show that more farmers and tradesmen died of plague then did seamen of scurvy. For some, sea exploration was a chance to get a little more money and to change their luck.

Influence of Legends

One of the most important motivating factors in the discovery of America was legend. Numerous fantasies influenced explorers: somewhere, people thought, there was a land studded with treasures that were guarded by dragons and hovered over by legless birds who spent their entire lives in the air; there was a popular belief in a river of gold that emptied into a seething tropical sea; somewhere there were sheep as great as oxen, giants who could wade into the ocean and seize a ship in the grip of one hand, and women whose eyes—made of precious stones—could slay an intruder with a single glance. The Spaniard Ponce de León, who was beginning to feel his age, was driven to explore by a story of a Fountain of Youth. When he arrived in America, Indians told him that such a fountain existed, but they warned him to be cautious—too long a bath would erase too many years. Today, de León is considered to be the discoverer of Florida, where the search for the fountain still continues. Inspired by legend, many Spaniards explored the Southwest looking for the Seven Cities of Gold. There were also many stories told of wild women warriors, such as the Amazons. Somewhere there was believed to be a golden island peopled by large, powerful women known as Amazons, who hoarded enormous fortunes. But where were these things in legends to be found? In America? Across the sea to the west?

One of the most influential legends was that of the Northwest Passage—a water route through North America to the Pacific. During the first few centuries of European exploration, many sailors searched for this waterway to the wealth of the Orient. They did not find it, but they did map and discover much of the coastline of North America.

Some of the legends seem foolish today, such as the one that told of people who lived in trees, slept standing up, lived on the smell of food, and had feet so large they used them as umbrellas. Foolish or not, all these tales contained two basic elements: (a) the main characters in them were heroic (people you really would like to get to know), and (b) all of the heroes possessed fabulous wealth. Such legends could exist because little was known about Asia, Africa, and the oceans west. They caused many a careful man to throw caution to the wind in search of gold, Amazon women, or both.

One popular misconception concerning the period prior to the voyage of Columbus is that all Europeans believed the world was flat and believed that if they sailed too far they would fall off. Educated persons like Columbus, however, were taught that God created the world in the form of a sphere—the most perfect shape. Still, many of the uneducated did believe that the world was flat and that monsters inhabited the West. Another prevalent notion was that, if one sailed south toward the equator, one would find the sea to be on fire from the oppressive heat—the unknown always has caused the human imagination to be most active.

But by 1492 Europe finally was ready for the discovery of America. In the year 1000, when Leif Ericson came to the North American continent, the time had not been ripe for expansion westward. Now Europeans were ready for a land in the West where they could search for their legends, satiate their greed, and satisfy their need for adventure. From our modern perspective it seems surprising that the country that led the way was Portugal.

Portugal Takes the Lead

Portugal, well positioned on the Atlantic Ocean, became the first country to launch voyages of exploration. Tall and muscular Prince Henry, third son of the king, established in 1451 an academy dedicated to geographical studies. Prince Henry had two goals in mind: One was to find new sources of gold; the other was to find the legendary King Prester John with his enormous riches and to expel the Moslems from North Africa and the Holy Land once and for all. By the time of Prince Henry's death his men had explored the Madeira, Azores, and Canary islands. By settling western Africa, they also had disproved the legend that near the equator the sea was boiling and visitors were turned black by the blazing sun. In 1487 Bartholomeu Dias continued the adventurous spirit by rounding the southern tip of Africa, only to be turned back by his mutinous men who still feared the unknown. Eleven years later Vasco da Gama sailed around Africa and arrived in India, where he was nearly murdered. On the return trip the majority of his men died of scurvy. The cargo that da Gama brought back stimulated further voyages, and during the next few years Portugal established a trading empire in India and on the east and west coasts of Africa.

Christopher Columbus

On the morning of October 12, 1492, a sailor on the ship *Pinta* yelled, *Tierra! Tierra!* ("Land! Land!")—America was discovered. The man most responsible for this achievement was Christoforo Colombo, better known as Christopher Columbus. There is a great deal of uncertainty about the early background of this man. It generally is accepted that he was born in Genoa, although some authorities have claimed that he was either French, German, Greek, Corsican, or Armenian. He first worked on sailing ships out of Genoa; later, he worked on Portuguese ships for nearly nine years. While in the pay of the Portuguese, he proposed a plan to find a direct ocean route to the Indies. His calculations were based on those of Greek writers, who he misread and misinterpreted. To

Columbus the world was 25 percent smaller than it really was, and the distance to the Orient was off by more than 10,000 miles. By sailing a mere ten days, Columbus believed Europeans would arrive at the riches of the Orient—referred to as the "Indies." The Portuguese king, relying on advisers who reported that the world was much larger than Columbus believed, rejected his plan. Columbus then approached Queen Isabella and King Ferdinand of Spain, and, after many years of petitions and court intrigues, they agreed to finance a small fleet for his westward expedition. The commission given to him made him "Admiral of the Ocean Sea" and "Viceroy and Governor" of any islands or countries—excluding Japan and China—that he might occupy or possess. He was also to receive 10 percent of all wealth. He even carried letters of introduction to the Chinese emperors, a Latin passport, and sailors who could speak and write Arabic.

He sailed from Palos in southern Spain, stopping first in the Canary Islands. He then crossed the Atlantic, and after six long weeks, his ship arrived at San Salvador in the Bahamas on October 12, 1492. Columbus, of course,

Christopher Columbus was sure he had discovered the Indies; today he is looked upon as the discoverer of America.

did not proclaim that he had found America, for he believed that this was part of the Indies and that the inhabitants should be called "Indians." He spent the rest of his trip attempting "to go and see if I can find the Island of Japan." Although he did not find the Orient, he did discover many islands of the Caribbean. Before returning to Spain, he decided that he would need to put on an impressive sales exhibition there if he was to acquire financing for future voyages—so he brought back samples of the "Orient" with him: an alligator, some gold, colorful parrots, plants, and natives. The Spanish monarchs were convinced, and Columbus made three subsequent voyages. On his three trips he saw natives smoking cigars, eating people, turning their backs when they spoke, chewing herbs that rotted their teeth, and living on pineapple wine and sardines. He and his men also tasted such new foods as sweet potatoes, pineapples, and nuts. He also touched Yucatán, the eastern side of the Isthmus of Panama, and the mouth of the Orinoco River. He still believed he had found part of the Orient. The pressure of travel, plus his lack of skill as an administrator, took its toll. His men mutinied, and he was shipped back to Spain in disgrace. He died in Spain, a discredited and disappointed man. Just before his death he revised his geography and said that the earth "had the form of a pear . . . upon one part of which is a prominence like a woman's nipple." His end was as obscure as his beginnings. Today, two locations share his remains. It is believed the more important you are in this world, the more burial places you will have. This was Christopher Columbus—a man who did not know what he had discovered and who is celebrated today as the discoverer of America. History evolves in many strange ways.

Spanish Exploration

After Columbus the Spanish expanded from the Carribean islands to the mainland. Explorers again were the forerunners of this growth, but, taken as a group, they were a tragic lot. Ponce de León, an Indian-slave hunter, searched for that fabled Fountain of Youth, and his search led him in 1513 to Florida, which he named after the Easter season. There he brutally "pacified" the Indians with the help of savage dogs. His career, however, was short lived, for in 1521 the Calusa Indians of the region planted an arrow in his back, which led to his speedy demise. Vasco Núñez de Balboa, a stowaway, in 1513 hacked his way across the Isthmus of Darien and is considered to be the first European to gaze upon the Pacific Ocean. He thought he had found the Indian Ocean,

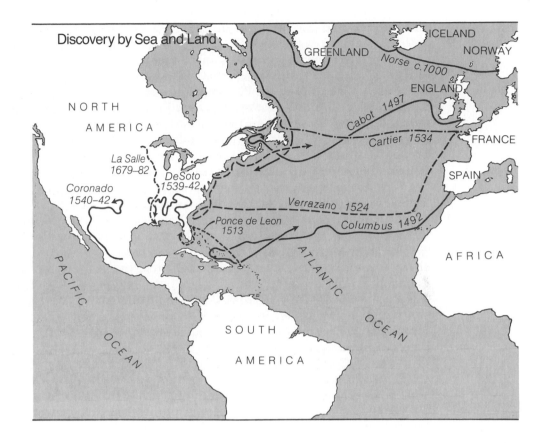

Discovery by Sea and Land

and he rushed into its waters, claiming all lands that it touched for Spain. His discovery led to much jealousy among his colleagues and to his being beheaded for treason—hardly a fitting end for the discoverer of the Pacific Ocean.

Balboa's discovery of this new body of water led to a renewed search for the Northwest Passage—that elusive waterway through America. The Portuguese sailor Ferdinand Magellan believed one could reach the riches of the Spice Islands (modern Indonesia) by sailing west through that passage. The Portuguese king disagreed, but the Spanish outfitted five ships. In 1519 Magellan sailed around the tip of South America by way of the strait that today bears his name. He was a strict disciplinarian, and on his voyage around South America he brutally punished one mutinous captain after another. He had one skinned alive and another put in irons. But his strict discipline gave way to bad luck, and he traveled for 14 weeks across the Pacific and missed island after island. Hunger became the main problem: "We used sawdust for food and rats were such a delicacy that we paid half a ducat apiece for them." Eventually he arrived in the Philippine Islands where he was killed by a jealous husband. Only 18 out of several hundred men finally returned to Spain. Magellan is regarded as the first man to have sailed around the world, but this is technically not true, although his body did make it home. But his voyage proved that the East could be reached by sailing west—and that unknown dangers lie across the uncharted seas.

The Spanish attempt at controlling the Philippine trade routes seemed merely a diversion, for the Spaniards immediately concentrated their efforts on the conquest of Central and South America. In 1519 Hernando Cortés left Cuba for Mexico to establish a trading station. His arrival was well timed. Not only were many local tribes restless because of Aztec domination, but there was also a belief among the Indians that their absent god Quetzalcoatl, depicted as a tall, bearded man of fair complexion, was soon to return. The Aztecs assumed that Cortés was the god. Montezuma, king of the Aztecs, showered Cortés and his followers with riches and gifts in the hope that they would leave. But this was not to be. Cortés eventually captured Montezuma's capital and became master of Mexico. However, even after a prolonged torture of the king, Cortés and his men found no fabulous wealth.

The advanced empire of the Aztec Indians was gone. Mexico was now in the hands of the Spanish, and it became the base of operations for expansion both south and north. The American Southeast and Southwest lay open for Spanish exploration and eventual colonization.

Disaster, however, continued to plague the Spanish adventurers. In 1528, one-eyed Captain Pánfilo de Narváez attempted to transport 400 colonists to Florida. After navigation problems, attacks from hostile Indians, and a hurricane, only 4 of the 400 were left. These survivors, led by Álvar Núñez Cabeza de Vaca, traveled for eight years as medicine men from one Indian tribe to another and wandered through Texas, New Mexico, and Arizona until they arrived in 1536, in northern Mexico. De Vaca wrote that the Spanish cavalry which encountered them "stood staring at me a length of time, so confounded that they neither hailed me nor drew near to make an inquiry." De Vaca's reports of the legendary Seven Cities of Gold led one of their members, Estevanico, a black, to return with Fray Marcos de Niza. Estevanico demanded too much from the Zuni Indians and was killed, while Fray Marcos reported of "a very beautiful city." Although his accounts were almost completely imaginary, they did stimulate further exploration—especially by Coronado.

Coronado and De Soto

Francisco Vásquez de Coronado was the leader of the greatest Spanish frontier expedition—a veritable parade through the American Southwest. In his search for the Seven Cities, Coronado took with him 225 cavalrymen, 60 foot soldiers, 5 friars, 1000 Indians, mules, and horses, and nearly 1500 head of cattle. He is considered by many to be the most important explorer of the Southwest, for his party explored the Colorado River and discovered the Grand Canyon. He traveled from New Mexico to eastern Kansas. Along the way he encountered numerous adobe Indian pueblos and seized many of them. The Coronado National Monument today is located along the Rio Grande north of Albuquerque near the site of the former Indian pueblo of Tiguex where Coronado wintered. Needless to say, Coronado found no gold. His expedition was considered a failure, and out of frustration he hung the native who had guided him safely into the interior. Although his treatment of Indians was less than enlightened, it is ironic that his expedition may have introduced horses to the Plains Indians. With the Coronado expedition, the search for the Seven Cities abated, but the Southwest still was destined to be the northern frontier of the Spanish Empire.

Meanwhile, in the Southeast, the exploration of the region and the exploitation of the natives was continuing under the command of Hernando de Soto.

Hernando de Soto was the Spanish explorer of the Southeast; his search for wealth caused him to mistreat the native population.

De Soto reached the Mississippi in 1541 after an arduous journey from the Florida coast into Georgia, across the Great Smokies into Tennessee, and southwest almost to the Gulf of Mexico. He crossed the mighty river to reconnoiter the Ozark country and pressed as far west as Oklahoma before he returned to the Mississippi to die of a fever in 1542. One contemporary described him as rich, handsome, and "fond of this sport of killing Indians." Along his path of exploration he looted and burned Indian villages, tortured and murdered native leaders, and massacred thousands of people. He also collected Indian women, and at one time he had six. De Soto and Coronado are usually described as adventurous individuals who pioneered in the exploration of the southern section of the United States—it seldom is mentioned that they left behind a legacy of Indian animosity.

The final boundaries of the Spanish northern frontier were drawn by sea explorations. In 1542 Juan Rodríguez Cabrillo was sent north from Mexico to find the Northwest Passage. His ships entered the future harbor of San Diego and continued northward as far as Fort Ross in California. His description of the Santa Monica area was apt; he called it the "Bay of Smokes"—Indian fires and inversion factors already were creating smog conditions. In 1602 Sebastián Vizcaíno followed the path of Cabrillo, visited many of the points described by the earlier explorer, and renamed them. He left behind many familiar place names, such as San Diego, Santa Catalina Island, Santa Barbara, Monterey, and Carmel. His maps were also invaluable guides to later colonization of California.

The Spanish Empire

In the Spanish realm exploration soon was followed by settlement. From Florida to California the Spanish Empire in the United States emerged. Of course, the empire also spread throughout Central and South America. The mission system, first under Jesuit and then under Franciscan control, became a civilizing agent in Texas, Arizona, and California. This was an empire based on Spanish culture, the Catholic church, and exploitation of black and Indian slaves. The Spanish *encomienda* system of forced labor bound the Indian to the land and continued the harsh treatment that they had received earlier at the hands of the explorers. Spain soon found that she had overexpanded in the Americas and had created a society there with little mobility. Although it is true that there was virtually no self-government in Spanish America and much inhuman treatment of the natives, a Spanish heritage, nevertheless, sprang up in all of Spain's areas of colonization. The Spanish language, architecture, Catholic church, mission system, ranching practices, and horse raising are reminders that the Spanish were the first Europeans in North America. Of course, the belief that Indians and padres lived in perpetual happiness within the walls of the missions and that the Indians were content with their white conquerors is far from the truth. The Pueblo Revolt of 1680 in New Mexico is testimony to Indian unrest. Under the leadership of a medicine man, Popé, and other key individuals, the Pueblos staged a concerted uprising, killed more than 400 Spaniards, and drove the rest completely out of Pueblo country for 14 years.

The exploitation of the Indians, lack of mobility, poor self-government, and overexpansion of the empire—these were only a few of the factors that weakened Spain's American possessions from within. In 1588 the defeat of the Spanish Armada by the English signaled the weakening from without. Spain's power was now on the decline, and other European nations were prepared to challenge her New World dominance.

French Exploration

The French had learned of the potential riches of the New World from the Spanish, and in 1524 King Francis I sent Giovanni da Verrazano, an Italian, to search for the Northwest Passage. Verrazano sailed along the Atlantic coast from Cape Fear to Maine, vainly searching for the passage; and although he failed, he is known today as the first European to have sailed into the New York harbor. When he returned to France, his brother drew a map of his journey that pictured a large inland sea, a notion probably derived from the Indians' description of the Great Lakes. This mistaken notion lasted well into the 1700s.

Ten years later Jacques Cartier made the first of his three expeditions to the Gulf of St. Lawrence in search of the Northwest Passage. This "Columbus of Canada" opened the St. Lawrence to eventual settlement and paved the way for future expansion down the Mississippi to the Gulf of Mexico, as well as westward to the Great Lakes. His dealings with the Indians were quite unusual. He offered the Huron Indians hardtack and red wine, which they refused, thinking the French were eating wood and drinking blood. But they did tell Cartier some intriguing stories: of an interior waterway; of a land of gold; and of people who had only one leg, flew like bats, and never ate. Cartier never found the one-legged bat-people or the golden kingdom in Canada, but he did return with "diamonds"—which turned out to be quartz crystals. Although his findings generally were disappointing, his early exploration led the way to the formation of the empire of New France.

It was Samuel de Champlain, however, who actually pioneered the French empire. Champlain made 11 trips of exploration to America. In 1608 he erected a fort at Quebec, which soon became the permanent center of a French trapping and trading empire. Champlain and his followers continued to explore the interior of Canada, and his discoveries eventually guided the explorations of other Frenchmen, such as Pierre Esprit Radisson and Médard Chouart, who penetrated far into the Great Lakes region and probably beyond the Mississippi. Further trips were made by trader Louis Joliet and Jesuit Father Marquette, who were searching for "mitchee seepee"—great flowing waters. They traveled down the Mississippi to the mouth of the Arkansas River and were amazed at the size of the catfish which "struck our canoe with such violence that I thought that it was a great tree about to break the canoe to pieces." Their arduous canoe trip was completed by former Jesuit René Robert Cavelier, Sieur de La Salle, who reached the mouth of the Mississippi in 1682 and claimed all the area along the river and its tributaries for France. Two years later he led an expedition from France to establish a colony and secure control of the Gulf of Mexico, but he missed the mouth of the Mississippi and was forced ashore near the Brazos River in Texas. His men were so enraged at his plan to march to Canada that they murdered him. Today the search for his burial place continues.

The French Empire

The French Empire in America covered a vast amount of area in the New World. This empire was strictly controlled from France, and it was mostly Catholic. Although the huge land area, the European control, and the Catholic church made France's American empire similar to that of Spain's, in most ways the two empires were different. For example, New France's treatment of the Indians was very different from the Spanish *encomienda* system. The French did not attempt to enslave the Indians or even to assimilate them into their society. The French policy emphasized trade with Indians, and gift giving. It is true, however, that French diseases frequently decimated many Indians and that Indians fought Indians in their rivalry to win French friendship and material goods. Champlain even armed the Hurons in their fight with the Iroquois, hoping to reap benefits in furs and other goods.

In the first years of New France, private investors tried to discover gold and to establish a lucrative trade with the natives. These ventures proved unprofitable, so the king took over the jurisdiction and management of the colony. Under his direction a planned colonial society emerged, with strict controls. Immigrants to New France were screened carefully, and even those who passed the test found the highly disciplined and structured society not much to their liking. This explains why New France grew physically in leaps and bounds but was populated thinly with only 3000 colonists by the 1650s. With the two Catholic countries of France and Spain establishing empires in America, England could not be far behind.

English Exploration

Although the English were last to colonize the New World, they had not been last in voyages of exploration. In 1497 Giovanni Caboto, a Genoese sailor better known as John Cabot, sailed west to try to discover the Northwest Passage. He landed somewhere near Cape Breton Island—the first authenticated landing on the North American continent. He then sailed southward along the "bareen shore" and returned to England where he reported rocks, codfish, and little other wealth in North America. Cabot may have been the first to discover the mainland of America, but his voyages caused little immediate stir in England. England was a fairly weak agricultural nation in the 1500s and was interested more in local politics than in discovery and settlement of distant lands. This does not mean that voyages of exploration stopped, but they were frequently trading voyages, such as those of Albert de Prado and John Rut, who sailed to the West Indies and Newfoundland, or those of pirates Francis Drake and John Hawkins, who chased Spanish galleons in both the Pacific and the Atlantic. Drake was one of the most famous "seadogs," or pirates. On one trip in 1577 he traveled as far north in the Pacific as the present American-Canadian border and was then driven by weather to a bay just north of San Francisco, now referred to as Drake's Bay, where he left a plate as evidence of discovery. By the late 1500s motives for the English colonization of America were becoming obvious.

English Settlement

The English knew from the French and Spanish experience that exploration alone would not create a successful empire in the New World. Settlement and colonization were the next logical steps. In the struggle for the control of the Americas, England was the last and poorest of the exploring and colonizing powers. But during the reign of Queen Elizabeth (1558–1603), the English in

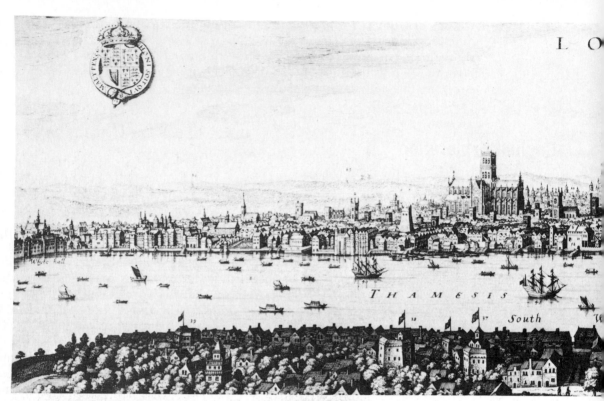

London in the 1500s was becoming increasingly overcrowded.

growing numbers concluded that the New World was their best opportunity. But why would the English really want to settle in that unknown, forbidding land? To the rising merchant class, overseas colonies offered vast economic opportunities. Trading companies were beginning to carry on a worldwide trade. These companies were granted a trade monopoly from the king or queen for trading in a particular region. America seemed to fit well into the plans of these merchant-capitalists. Goods could be sold to the settlers, and in return natural resources could be sold in England and Europe. Of course, religion also played a major role. To zealous English Protestants, a colony in America would offer a bulwark against Catholic Spain and France; to English dissenters, it would offer a bulwark against English Protestants. God and money went hand in hand.

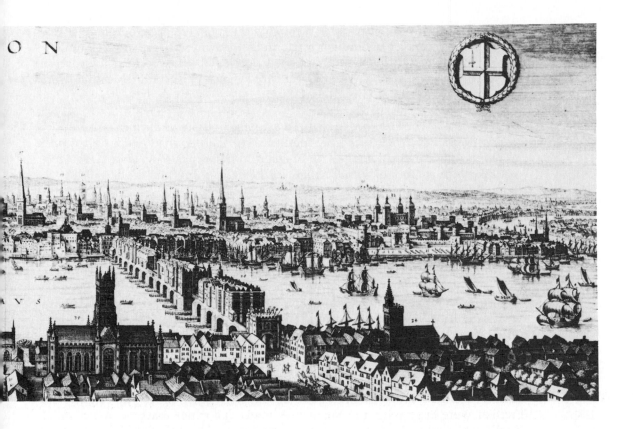

The Enclosure Movement of the 1500s also stimulated English colonization. This was a movement by large landowners to turn agricultural fields into sheep pastures, for sheep raising was more profitable than growing staple products. This agricultural shift led to thousands of farm workers' losing their jobs and to an increase in the urban population. The cities, in particular London, became overcrowded. An Elizabethan nursery rhyme reflected the urban problem: "Hark, hark, the dogs do bark; the beggars are coming to town." Where would be a good place to send this excess population? Why, to America. Others wanted to come to America to leave oppressive political institutions, to escape burdensome church duties, to acquire large landholdings, or merely to change their general pattern of living. Of course, material gain was a common factor. One enthusiast wrote of the new life in America, "Why man, all their cooking pans are pure gold." Probably the most effective public relations man for the founding of English settlements in America was an Oxford clergyman, Richard Hakluyt, who published a series of essays on the foundation of western colonies. His writings reflected many of the motives that were prevalent in England at this time.

> *Yea, if we would behold with the eye of pity how all our prisons are pestered and filled with able men to serve their country, which for small robberies are daily hanged up in great numbers. . . . If we first seek the kingdom of God, all other things will be given unto us. . . .*

Early Attempts

In 1578 Sir Humphrey Gilbert acquired a charter from Queen Elizabeth to settle "remote heathen and barbarous land." His initial attempt failed, but in 1583 he sought to establish a colony in Newfoundland. Due to the coldness and desolation of the land, his men mutinied. On the return trip in his ship the *Squirrel*, Gilbert fell overboard and was drowned. The first English attempt at colonization was hardly a booming success; the second was not much better. Gilbert's attempts were carried on by his half brother, Sir Walter Raleigh. After an exploratory expedition to the area around North Carolina, and an unsuccessful attempt at settlement, Raleigh sent out 117 men, women, and children to establish a colony on Roanoke Island, off the coast of North Carolina. For three years Raleigh sent no supplies or ships to the island; the English were busy with the Spanish Armada and other matters. When relief finally was sent in 1590, no survivors were found. The only trace of the colony was the word *Croatoan* the native word for the island carved on a tree. Theories today hold that the members of the colony starved to death, were killed by Indians, left the island for the mainland, had a mass drowning, or were eaten by native cannibals. The Lumbee Indians of southeastern North Carolina today believe that the blood of Roanoke colonists runs in their veins. The mystery probably never will be solved. Although Raleigh lost a great fortune, spent much of his later life in prison, and finally lost his head to a royal ax, he did lead the way to the eventual settlement of Virginia, although today Americans are more inclined to connect him with a tobacco product than with "The Lost Colony."

Jamestown

When Queen Elizabeth died in 1603, King James I (remembered today by the American Medical Association as the first antismoking critic, who detested

The lost colony of Roanoke Island was an ill-fated example of early English settlement.

"that foul weed") began to sponsor a joint stock company. He felt the major cause of failure of earlier colonization attempts was the lack of money. The Virginia Company of London was formed, a charter was given, and in April 1607 Jamestown was founded on the lower reaches of Chesapeake Bay on a low, swampy island. The location of the settlement itself led to much hardship and disease, and within the first 6 months the population of 104 was cut in half. Not only was the environment less than salutary, but many of these early settlers expected to "dig gold, wash gold, refine gold, load gold." But no gold was to be found. Early relations with the Algonquin-speaking Indians of the region were generally peaceful. Powhatan, chief of an Indian confederacy of some 200 villages, believed that it would be to his benefit to trade peacefully with whites. According to John Smith, soldier, explorer, and author, Smith was about to have his brains beaten out by Powhatan when Powhatan's daughter, 11-year-old Pocahontas, threw herself upon Smith and saved his life. Whether spared by Pocahontas or not, he became one of the dominant leaders in the early years of the colony. The problem in Virginia, however, stemmed less from Indian attacks in the early period than from disease, starvation, and unwillingness to work. In 1609 an influx of 600 new settlers came to Jamestown and encountered a real "starving time." Smith described the extent of the suffering.

> *Nay, so great was our famine that a savage we slew and buried, the poorer sort took him up again and ate him. . . . And one amongst the rest did kill his wife, salted her and had eaten part of her before it was known, for which he was executed, as he well deserved. Now whether she was better roasted, boiled, or broiled, I know not. . . .*

Reorganization of the colony and substantial economic and social changes finally brought success to Virginia.

In 1614 John Rolfe, who married Pocahontas, brought a blend of tobacco to England, and England went tobacco mad. The economic foundations of Virginia were laid firmly in smoke; tobacco was even grown in the main streets of Jamestown. Pocahontas also made a success in English society, although she soon died of smallpox—a white man's disease. The career of Pocahontas is indeed a confusing one. To some writers she was the patron saint of Jamestown, to others she was a typical Indian woman abused by whites. It does appear that she was held hostage during one of the struggles between whites and Indians. Tobacco and Pocahontas were not alone in bringing the colony notoriety. In the early years private property was nonexistent, and even tools were owned in common. This led to a lack of incentive, and eventually, in order to change this pattern, every man who came to Virginia was given 50 acres of land—a real enticement. Another problem was the lack of women. Those women who initially did go usually did not survive the hardships. The Virginia Company actually recruited "young, uncorrupt maids" and sold them in Virginia for 150 pounds of leaf tobacco—not the last example of mail-order brides in American history. Finally, the slowness of communications from England, and need for local government administration, led to the establishment of the House of Burgesses—a local assembly—in July 1619 for the purpose of local self-government. Affairs were improving for the Virginians, but not for the Algonquin-speaking Indians.

Because of the scarcity of land for growing tobacco, Indian land was needed and some Indian cornfields were seized. With the death of Powhatan in 1618, good relations permanently came to an end. His successor, Opechancanough, felt that the English posed a threat to the remaining lands held by the Indians and decided to strike before the settlers became invincible by numbers alone.

Ætatis suæ 21. Aᵒ. 1616.

Matoaks als Rebecka daughter to the mighty Prince Powhatan Emperour of Attanoughkomouck als Virginia converted and baptized in the Christian faith, and Wife to the Worᴸᴸ Mʳ Tho: Rolff.

Pocahontas, daughter of Powhatan, became an unwilling pawn in the struggles between the English settlers and the Indians in Virginia.

In March 1622 Indians attacked the settlement and killed more than 347 whites. One white wrote, "They basely and barbarously murdered, not sparing either age, or sex, man, woman, or child." This attack sparked reprisals against Indian villages. Fighting continued until Opechancanough was captured in 1644 and killed by one of the settlers ordered to guard him. The confederacy was smashed; most Indians moved or were sold into slavery. A few powerless remnants, however, did remain. The pattern of Indian friendliness followed by war and extermination was common in the development of colonial America.

Virginia then, founded in 1607, became the first English colony. Unlike the French and Spanish, English America developed into semiautonomous colonies. From 1607 to 1732 thirteen colonies, bordering the Atlantic Ocean and stretching from Maine to Georgia, were founded. A brief review of their origins not only will help to explain the variety of English experience in America but also will help to clarify the discussion of colonial culture that follows in Chapter 2.

Maryland

The colony of Maryland, founded in 1633, learned from Virginia's trying experiences but stumbled unwittingly into some of its own. Lord Baltimore (George Calvert), a friend of King Charles I, acquired a charter from him for land in northern Virginia. The King's lack of geographic knowledge was revealed in the charter that granted Baltimore the entire Potomac river (both banks). This ignorant decision led to the oldest local dispute in American history, (which even involved a killing as late as 1959). The charter given to Baltimore made him the proprietor, or controller, of the colony; he had almost absolute power, with only two limitations—that two Indian arrows were to be given yearly to the King and that laws passed had to be approved by the people living there. The first Lord Baltimore died before actual settlement; it was the second Lord Baltimore that sent the vessels *Ark* and *Dove* to found Maryland in 1633. The Baltimores had envisioned Maryland as a haven for English Catholics who suffered persecution in England. These dreams never were realized. The Protestants were always in the majority, although the Catholic aristocrats frequently held the power. Although Maryland avoided the "starving time" of Virginia, planted its first city on a hill rather than in a swamp, encountered few Indians, and found immediate economic success with tobacco, it did experience constant religious strife between Catholic and Protestant. In 1649 an Act of Toleration was passed to guarantee religious liberty for all Christians; actually, this act was an attempt to protect Catholicism. In the 1650s a civil war broke out, and more than 50 men were killed or wounded. By 1689 Lord Baltimore had given his control over the colony to the king, and it became a Protestant stronghold. However, while religion was quite significant in the early development of the Maryland colony, it was even more so in the settlement of the New England colonies.

New England Colonies

The influx of Calvinism—with its emphasis on the universal priesthood and salvation only for the elect—into England in the 1600s led to the growth of two factions within the Anglican Church. A group of separatists, better known as Pilgrims, believed that salvation could be found only outside the officially established Church of England; these were the founders of the Plymouth colony. Another group, the Puritans, believed that salvation could be found within the Anglican Church but that the Church had to be purified substantially of any traces of Roman Catholicism; these were the founders of the Massachusetts Bay Colony.

The Pilgrims were the first of the two groups to come to America. After finding England and Holland unfit places for the practice of their religion, they purchased land from the Virginia Company of London (or London Company) to settle in the northern part of the Virginia colony. In the fall of 1620 a group of 35 Pilgrims and 70 non-Pilgrims set out on the ship *Mayflower* for northern Virginia. However, when the ship reached North America this group of saints and strangers found themselves at Cape Cod, obviously far from their destination. Knowing they were now outside of any legally constituted government, the Pilgrims drew up the famous Mayflower Compact, which stated they would make "just and equal laws . . . for the general good." The Mayflower Compact is considered by some historians to be the first American constitution, although to the Pilgrims themselves it was merely a temporary agreement that would suffice until a legal charter had been obtained from England.

The bad luck of the Pilgrims continued for the next few years. After the first winter more than half the colony had perished from starvation and disease; and the next ship to arrive brought 35 more people but few supplies. It was the Pilgrims' good fortune that relations between them and the Indians were peaceful.

Although it is said sarcastically that the Pilgrims first fell upon their knees and then upon the Indians, this is not entirely the case. But it is true that white traders brought disease, probably plague to the Wampanoag Indians of the area, exterminating more than two-thirds of them. It may be surprising that Massasoit, the *sachem*, or chief, believed that peaceful relations with the

The Pilgrims celebrated a feast of thanksgiving in the fall of 1621.

whites was the best policy to pursue. It also may be surprising that one Indian, Squanto—who had been enslaved earlier by English traders—taught the Pilgrims how to grow Indian corn and where to hunt and catch fish. After the Pilgrims harvested a good crop in the autumn of 1621, a feast of thanksgiving was held. It is indeed difficult to picture this first thanksgiving, for elementary-school Pilgrim plays and American mythology have obscured the reality of the incident. Some authorities believe that a simple feast of thanks took place and that Indians, such as Massasoit, participated. Others believe the feast was a weeklong celebration, in which the Indians brought most of the food, such as eel, and ate apart from the whites. Also, games and prayers enlivened the festival. Although the Pilgrims frequently are considered to be the spiritual ancestors of the American people, their colony remained small and weak and actually had little effect, even on the formation of other colonies. Eventually they were absorbed into the Puritan Massachusetts Bay Colony.

The Pilgrims were hardly the first to come to the coast of New England. Trading and fishing companies explored and mapped the area, and Thomas Morton established a community north of Plymouth. Usually left out of textbooks, Thomas Morton was a happy-go-lucky individual who decided to found a colony in the New World that would consist of ex-servants who were interested in living for the moment. He and his settlers provided themselves with a large supply of liquor and built an 80-foot maypole that became the center of their merrymaking. Here was built the settlement of Merrie Mount— a real scandal to the Pilgrims nearby. When the Pilgrims could take no more, they sent Miles Standish (nicknamed "Scrimp") to arrest Morton. Morton was sent to England, but he returned with more liquor. Morton was arrested again, and this time his maypole was chopped down (a real psychological blow). Morton spent the rest of his life in England, and, according to some tales, died not with his boots on but with liquor on his breath.

Morton and the trading and fishing companies soon were followed by the Puritans who, unlike the Pilgrims, came from the upper-middle-class gentry of England. With much money and planning, they founded the Massachusetts Bay Company and obtained a charter from King Charles I, who may have been relieved to see these religious dissenters leave England. In 1630 they sailed from Salem, Massachusetts, where they were met by 400 Puritans connected with earlier trading companies who already had prepared the way. The Puritans, who experienced little suffering or starvation in their new settlement, wished to govern themselves. In fact, they wanted so much to be independent from England that they carried their charter with them to ensure complete, independent self-government. By 1640 the colony numbered some 20,000 people. The most influential leader in the early years was John Winthrop, a man chosen governor 12 times during the 19 years he spent in New England.

Why did the Puritans come to America? They came not merely to worship in their own way but also to demonstrate that the Puritan life was the ideal way. It appears that they initially did not intend to settle permanently in the New World but planned to establish a Puritan model state for the instruction of all true Christians, believing that the English would be forced to call them back to England to be taught Puritan beliefs. They were going to create a "city on a hill," a New Jerusalem in America based on their interpretation of the Bible. Whether, in the Massachusetts Bay Colony, there was a distinction between church and state is unclear, for the church and state both were based on the *covenant*—a voluntary association of the elect. Only church members could vote for civil officials, and both magistrates and ministers were chosen by God and had divine sanction. Although the strict Puritan experiment failed by the 1700s, the Puritans left an indelible mark not only on Massachusetts but on the whole of New England—particularly the native population.

Puritans and Indians

The Wampanoag Indians continued their peaceful policy but found the Puritan view of Indians increasingly difficult to accept. The Puritans believed they had religious justification for Indian extermination. They had not tried to enslave the Indians; instead, they had tried unsuccessfully to civilize and Christianize them. Removal seemed the best answer to this failure. The Puritans felt that the Lord had given them the New World and that the Indians were trespassers. The Puritans also preached that the Indians who lived in the darkness of the woods, blinded by the wilderness, were actually agents of Satan. Eventually, land greed and cultural misunderstanding on both sides led to an inevitable clash. Christianity and Indian animism could not coexist side by side. The Puritans explained the resultant Indian wars in terms of God's plan for the Puritan elect. Thus Indian extermination became part of the early American heritage.

A pattern was evident between whites and Indians from the beginning: initial friendship was soon followed by mutual animosity and physical conflict, which usually led to the ultimate destruction of the Indians. This pattern was present in the early days of the Virginia and Massachusetts colonies and lasted until the Massacre of Wounded Knee in 1890. It was never more evident than in the Pequot War and in King Philip's War.

The Pequot tribe was one of the fiercest and most brutal of New England and was resented by many of the weaker tribes. Taking advantage of this jealousy, in 1636 Connecticut colonists attacked the Pequots in retaliation for the alleged murder of a white trader. The major "battle" of the war was not really a battle at all. The Pequot village of Mystic Fort was surrounded, and more than 600 Indian men, women, and children were killed or burned to death. The survivors were sold into slavery. The Puritans confidently justified their action in the name of God. One captain wrote that the Indian cries of torture were so pathetic that "if God had not fitten the hearts of men for the service, it would have bred in us a commiseration towards them."

The Pequot War and the death of Massasoit further strained relations between whites and Indians in New England. Massasoit's successor, Metacomet, better known to the colonists as King Philip, tried in vain to form an alliance with other Indian tribes to fight the white menace. In 1675 the killing of 11 English settlers in retaliation for the murder of an Indian was the im-

King Philip, who had plans for Indian unity, was a formidable challenge to the Puritans in Massachusetts.

mediate cause of a second Puritan war known as King Philip's War. Although King Philip has been considered the first true Indian leader to organize Indian resistance against whites, neither his alliance nor his military tactics were noteworthy. Early in 1676 he was shot and killed, drawn, and quartered. His hand was given as a reward to the Indian informer who had betrayed him; the Indian preserved Philip's hand in a bucket of rum. Meanwhile Philip's skull remained on view on a pole in Plymouth as late as 1700. King Philip's War ended the serious resistance of the New England tribes.

The other colonies of New England also were established by Puritans. New Hampshire and Maine, for example, were settled by devout Puritans who began to move north from Massachusetts. On the other hand, Rhode Island and Connecticut were established by dissatisfied Puritans. Roger Williams was a young minister who came to Massachusetts but found little acceptance there. His beliefs that Indians actually owned the land and that Puritans should make a clearer distinction between church and state were hardly popular ones. He was deemed a heretic, and since the Puritans felt they had a monopoly on the truth and could accept no other opinions, they banished him in 1635 from the colony. Moving south, Williams purchased land from the Indians and founded the town of Providence, in what was to become Rhode Island. Williams's belief in religious tolerance led Rhode Island to become the first colony to offer complete religious freedom. Thomas Hooker, a Puritan minister, also believed that individuals should be able to choose their own religion, and he boldly said so: "Forced worship stinks in God's nostrils." Leaving Massachusetts, Hooker and his followers also traveled south and established settlements that became the nucleus of the Connecticut colony. But even in Rhode Island and Connecticut, the Puritan mark was obvious.

Later Colonies

From the 1630s to the 1660s English efforts to settle outside New England were limited for England was involved in civil war and political upheavals. In the period that followed, from the 1660s to the 1730s, the rest of the colonies were founded. During this time the English settlements were not extensive along the Atlantic seaboard. The Dutch had established the lucrative colony of New Amsterdam, and the Swedes had founded New Sweden and erected log cabins along the Delaware River. In 1664 the English sent four warships to take over New Amsterdam and met little opposition; the colony of New York was born, and with it East and West Jersey. Since the Dutch previously had captured the Swedish colony, the English takeover also included the area soon to become the Delaware colony. About this time the king of England gave a grant of land south of Virginia to eight noblemen, who founded the colony of Carolina. Here developed a plantation economy based on slave labor. Subsequently, the eight noblemen found that the enterprise was not lucrative enough and turned over their interests to the king, who in 1729 divided the colony into North Carolina and South Carolina.

The colonies of Pennsylvania and Georgia were last but hardly least. The colony of Pennsylvania is said to reflect the ideals of one person more than any other colony—that person was William Penn. William Penn, a rich, powerful man, originally had been an Anglican but had become influenced by the teaching of George Fox, founder of the Society of Friends, better known as the Quakers. Fox preached that every human being possessed a spark of divinity and was predestined for salvation. The Quakers that Fox led called everyone "thee" and refused to pay taxes or serve in war. Hundreds of Quakers were arrested, including William Penn, who spent two years in jail. King Charles II owed Penn's father a large debt and decided to repay it by granting the family land in America. In 1682 William Penn arrived in America on the ship *Welcome* and soon established one of the most liberal colonies, Pennsylvania,

The Thirteen Colonies

Lake Superior

Lake Michigan

Lake Huron

Lake Ontario

Lake Erie

Ohio R.

Mississippi R.

NEW HAMPSHIRE

MASSACHUSETTS

Albany

Boston

Plymouth

NEW YORK

RHODE ISLAND

New Haven

CONNECTICUT

New York

PENNSYLVANIA

Philadelphia

NEW JERSEY

Annapolis

DELAWARE

MARYLAND

VIRGINIA

Williamsburg

Jamestown

NORTH CAROLINA

SOUTH CAROLINA

Charleston

GEORGIA

Savannah

ATLANTIC OCEAN

GULF OF MEXICO

with its Quaker emphasis on religious and civil liberty. His promotional literature brought such a diverse population from Europe that his settlement was known as "the melting pot." Although the colony prospered, Penn himself did not, and he returned to England where he died in a debtor's prison—an institution that stimulated the founding of the last English colony, Georgia.

In the 1700s England was becoming much more aware of the growing power in America of the Spanish Empire in the south and of the French Empire in the north. A barrier was needed between the colony of South Carolina and the Spanish settlement of Florida; such a barrier also could satisfy a social need in England itself. A common practice at this time was to imprison a person for debt. These debtors' prisons were disease-ridden places where sadistic jailers applied thumbscrews and strangled prisoners until blood flowed from their noses and ears. James Oglethorpe, a reformer and idealist, was moved deeply when one of his friends died in such a jail. He decided to organize a group of English philanthropists to form a colony in America that would serve as a barrier against the Spanish; the colony would be populated by prisoners. A charter was obtained from King George II, and in 1733 Georgia, the criminal colony, was settled. This Noble Experiment was both too noble and too restrictive. If you had lived in early Georgia you would have found no Catholics, no self-government, little private property, a price-wage freeze, no slavery, no hard liquor, mandatory military service, and a curfew. The goals of Oglethorpe and his friends were high minded, but not too realistic. Gradually the restrictions were lessened, and the king took control of the colony.

By the 1750s the character of the 13 colonies was beginning to take shape. And by that time the three elements—North America, the Indian, and the European—were coming together into what has been termed the American experience. North America, with its great variety of terrains and environment, greatly helped to mold this experience, as did the American Indian and the European. It is a great tragedy that the Indians and Europeans could not live together and that one race virtually had to destroy the other. First Spanish settlers, then French, then English came to America and slowly developed a culture that was no longer strictly European. The way these people thought and lived and even the games they played will be the subject of Chapter 2.

The Anasazi: Ancient Dwellers of the Southwest

Today the ruins of a once-thriving civilization are scattered across a barren region known as the "four corners" area, where the states of Utah, Colorado, Arizona, and New Mexico come together. In this semiarid land, cliff cities and apartment complexes stand as silent monuments to an ancient people who are called the Anasazi, a Navajo word for "the ancient ones." Their entrance into the Southwest and their sudden disappearance are cloaked with mystery and present a puzzle that probably never will be solved. In a relatively short period of time, they attained a high level of civilization, long before Columbus ever touched upon America's shores.

They first appeared in the Southwest around the year 100 B.C. as a basketmaker society. Their knowledge of agriculture and of arts and crafts was limited. Their houses were often temporary

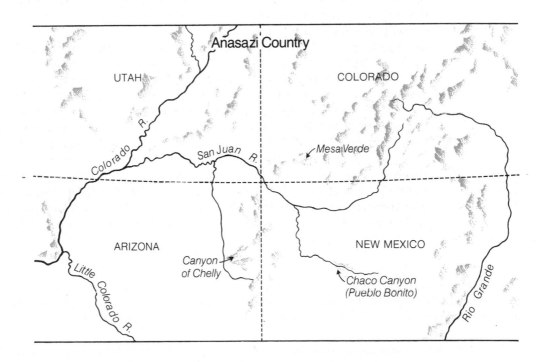

Anasazi Country

and crude, but some of them were circular, domed dwellings with clay floors. The men and women wore fiber sandles and wove robes of fur and feathers. While their villages were small, with little government, they did develop an advanced form of basketry. During the next few hundred years they moved into a period known as the modified basketmaker period.

By the year A.D. 400 they began to occupy permanent dwellings, which were in the form of pit houses. These residences had stone slab walls, fire holes in the ceiling and actually were built as pits in the ground. In virtually every house was found a small hole in the floor to symbolize the hole in the earth from which they believed all humans emerged. During this period their villages grew in size, and their knowledge of agriculture became evident. But they never irrigated their lands like their neighbors to the south; they practiced a form of dry farming that depended upon a fairly long rainy season. While their basket weaving continued, they also developed the art of pottery. In fact, they were the first people in the Southwest to make pottery of all shapes and sizes.

By A.D. 700 they entered the Pueblo stage, which led to the high point of their civilization. Their pit houses now became above-ground dwellings. The pit houses, however, remained as male-gathering places known as kivas. Since most of their communities appeared to have been formed along female lines, the kivas were a sanctuary for the men. The Anasazi of this period even looked different than their ancestors, but they did continue the weaving of baskets and the making of pottery.

Their population grew, and they began to live in small villages concentrated around regional centers, such as that of Pueblo Bonito located in the Chaco Canyon area of New Mexico and Mesa Verde located in Colorado. In Chaco Canyon they built 12 towns characterized by one or more apartment buildings, which usually rose 4 to 5 stories high. Pueblo Bonito was the best known of these towns with its 800 apartments that spread over 3 acres. It has been estimated that it took over 150 years to develop this apartment complex, which held a population of about 1200 and which remained the largest apartment building in the United States until the 1920s. Central to these settlements were large outdoor kivas, with their pit houses leading to the world of the spirits—a world which men alone could enter.

They also formed large villages on the tops of mesas. Here is where they farmed; at the bottom of the mesa they gathered water and wood. But eventually cliff dwellings, such as Cliff Palace at Mesa Verde, replaced the open villages on top of the mesas. Cliff Palace was actually a city built into the sloping side of a cliff with 200 rooms and 23 kivas. The only way into the city was down the side of the cliff by a series of difficult hand- and foot-holds. To say that this was an extremely defensive location is an understatement. Like Pueblo Bonito to the south, Cliff Palace was a regional center with numerous small- and medium-sized settlements close by.

All the Anasazi ruins, which date from A.D. 700–1300, particularly those at Pueblo Bonito and Mesa Verde, are a tribute to the architectural and building skills of these people. Out of rough natural stones with mud mortar, untold dwellings were built; their permanence is evident, since so many of them still remain standing. A detailed description of this ancient civilization never will be written, for they had no written language; it is known, however, that they continued to refine their pottery into a fine artform and also wove cotton cloth. Ornaments of turquoise and rock art also reveal their creativity.

By the year 1300 they began to decline and

Cliff Palace at Mesa Verde represented the peak of Anasazi culture.

to leave their cities. What caused this decline will never be known for certain. Numerous theories have been advanced, including overpopulation and enemy attacks. The most acceptable explanation of their demise involves a drought that hit the Southwest from 1276 to 1299. Since they had not developed an elaborate irrigation system and depended upon the seasons for their crops, the drought hit them particularly hard and forced them to move north and south. Whether they became the Pueblo Indians, who lived along the Rio Grande and who the Spanish encountered in the 1500s, is uncertain. It is possible that the Anasazi were the Pueblos' spiritual ancestors.

Today a large power plant dominates the landscape in the four corners region, and many an Anasazi building is now only the home of the rattlesnake or scorpion; it is difficult to imagine a group of simple basketweavers emerging over the centuries to become such ingenious builders. Yet urban America burst full blown in the Southwest, built by a race of nameless Indians who rose and fell in one of the most hostile environments in all of North America. ∎

Suggested Readings

Two excellent studies of the origins of Native Americans and their precolumbian societies are *Indians of North America* by HAROLD E. DRIVER, (1961) and *The Indian Heritage of America* by ALVIN M. JOSEPHY, JR. (1969).

Studies of the period of European exploration are quite numerous. Some of the best include: *The Age of Reconaissance* by J. H. PARRY, (1963), which discusses both the motivations for exploring and the explorations themselves; the classic *Admiral of the Ocean Sea* (1942) by SAMUEL E. MORRISON, a study of Columbus, and the newer *European Discovery of America: Southern Voyages, 1492–1616* (1974) by the same author; *Spain in America* by CHARLES GIBSON, 1966) traces the rise of the Spanish Empire in the Americas; and *The English People on the Eve of Colonization* (1954) by WALLACE NOTESTEIN, which describes the English push for exploration and colonization.

The evolution of the 13 English colonies is described well in *The Formative Years, 1607–1763* (1964) by CLARENCE L. VER STEEG.

Two new studies of the interaction of Puritans and Indians are *The Invasion of America* (1975) by FRANCIS JENNINGS and *Puritans, Indians, and Manifest Destiny* (1977) by CHARLES M. SEGAL and DAVID STINEBACK.

CHAPTER 2

Living in Colonial America:
The Birth of Modern Culture?

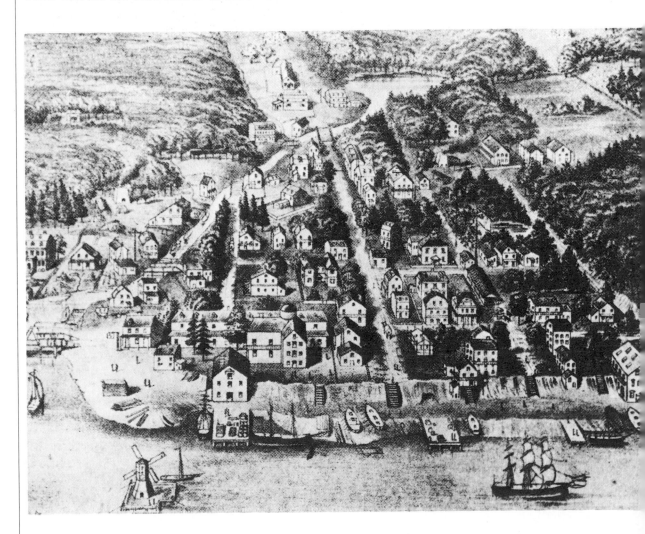

Time Line

?–A.D. 1492	Migration and evolution of American Indian societies
1492	Christopher Columbus lands in West Indies—beginning of European exploration
1607–1732	Establishment of 13 English colonies
1619	Blacks first arrive in Virginia
1631	*Blessing of the Bay* launched in Massachusetts Bay Colony
1636	Harvard College is founded
1639	The first printing press in America is operational
1647	Massachusetts General Education Law is passed
1665	First American play, *Ye Bare and Ye Cubb,* is performed
1692	Salem witchcraft trials are held
1704	*Boston Newsletter* becomes first American newspaper
1735	Zenger Trial takes place
1739–1740	Great Awakening sweeps the 13 colonies
1741	New York slave revolt breaks out
1790	First federal census takes place
1775–1783	American Revolution
1776	Declaration of Independence
1789–1797	Presidency of George Washington
1812–1815	War of 1812

1816–1824	Era of Good Feelings
1846–1848	Mexican War
1861–1865	Civil War
1865–1877	Reconstruction
1877–1900	Industrialization and urbanization
1900–1916	Progressive Era
1917–1918	World War I
1930s	Depression and New Deal
1941–1945	World War II
1945–1960	Post-war politics
1950–1953	Korean War
1950–1960	Civil rights movement
1961–1973	Vietnam War
1976	Bicentennial celebration

America today obviously is different from America in the 1600s and 1700s. But the early origins of our culture—the way we think and act—can be found in the people who came to the shores of North America and even in the people who were here before the Europeans. It is true that the European colonists brought with them a developed and fairly rigid culture; but the American wilderness caused immediate changes in their way of life. In fact, during most of the 1600s, survival was uppermost in the colonial mind. Periods of starvation and Indian wars did not lend themselves to the development of a complex culture.

Americans of today would not have had only a difficult time surviving, but also would have had problems relating to the general cultural environment. Ninety percent of colonials were farmers; urban America was a late phenomenon. The 13 colonies saw a mixture of races, yet one-fifth of the population was composed of black slaves who were outside the cultural mosaic. The slave heritage of colonial America is one of our history's great tragedies. Both colonial farmer and free laborer worked long and hard. The roles of women and men in society were as a producer not a consumer. Colonial industry was tied to the land rather than to assembly line production. And permeating all of colonial life was religion. From the established Anglican Church to the Puritan "New Jerusalem" in Massachusetts, religion was highly visible. Education was primarily the responsibility of the parent and, like farming, varied from colony to colony. American literature grew slowly but became very evident by the 1700s. Even in such a work-oriented culture, mass amusements did appear. Although they were much different from today's mass spectator sports, they filled a real leisure-time need. Last—but hardly least—were the urban dwellers, who comprised less than 10 percent of the population, yet who included the leading politicians and capitalists. Colonial city life was often a hazardous existence, but one which frequently set the pace for the development and expansion of a colonial culture.

The Immigrant Mix

By the mid-1700s the majority of settlers in the 13 colonies were non-English. The English in 1763 constituted only 49 percent of the population, with 20 percent of the population being made up of black slaves. The Dutch, Swedes, Scots, Irish, French, and German added to the ethnic mixture. Yet even though there was this racial mix, early America was not a "melting pot"; it was more like a mosaic, with the dominant design being English. The English had arrived first, had established their institutions and social values, and had kept control in terms of wealth and power. And the lines between cultural groups were clear and distinct.

Until the early 1700s the colonies were overwhelmingly English, and the population numbered only 200,000. A few minorities were present, including Sephardic Jews who came from Spain and Portugal. By 1763 the population numbered more than 2 million, and the immigration of diverse nationalities added greatly to this total.

Excluding the blacks, the largest non-English group—and also the most tenacious of the minorities in clinging to their native cultural ties—were the Germans. German immigrants had left war, starvation, excessive taxation, and religious persecution behind in their native land and had settled in Pennsylvania and on the frontiers of Maryland, Virginia, and North Carolina. Although they became separated from the dominant English culture because of their ethnic background, they contributed a number of valuable elements to the American heritage. Referred to as the Pennsylvania Dutch, they became some of the best farmers in America; their gunsmiths pioneered the Pennsylvania rifle, and their wagonmakers developed the Conestoga wagon, the forerunner of the prairie schooner. Their folk arts and music also added enrichment.

The Scotch-Irish, or Ulster Scots, came to America pressured by financial motivation, and they settled the backcountry of Pennsylvania, the Appalachian valley, and the Carolina wilderness. These people not only were the pioneers of frontier expansion but were also in the forefront of the American Revolution. The tombstone of one hardy pioneer sums up the early experience of the Scotch-Irish: "Here lies the remains of John Lewis, who slew the Irish lord, settled Augusta County, located the town of Staunton, and furnished five sons to fight the battles of the American Revolution."

Among other groups of immigrants were the Highland Scots, who left Scotland for political reasons and became prominent as merchants, ministers, lawyers, and schoolmasters. The French Protestants, or Huguenots, found life in Catholic France to be quite trying, so they began to trickle into the English colonies. Although numerically they made up only one percent of the population, they assimilated well into the English culture and provided early America with some outstanding social and political leaders. It is wrong to assume, however, that the English in America welcomed the immigrants with open arms, for *nativism*—protection of Americans from foreigners—was evident early. The Scotch-Irish were referred to as "rabble," while the Germans were "Palatine boors." Benjamin Franklin reflected these nativist sentiments when he asked, "Why should Pennsylvania, founded by the English, become a colony of aliens, who will shortly be so numerous as to Germanize us instead of our Anglifying them, and will never adopt our language or customs any more than they can acquire our complexion?'' Of course, not all non-English were distrusted, and America still remained the land of promise and plenty. Franklin himself even wrote that America was a place "Where the sick stranger joys to find a home, where casual ill, mam'd labor freely come." However, there was one very important immigrant group who came to the shores of America against their will. These were the blacks.

Colonial Slavery

"About the last of August came in a Dutch man of warre that sold us twenty negars." So went the report of the first importation in 1619 of black slaves from Africa to Virginia. It is unclear whether these blacks were servants or slaves, but it actually makes little difference, because by 1640 most of the imported blacks became servants for life. Actually, it is unfair to look upon these early-American blacks as immigrants, because they came involuntarily from Africa. Much of the white justification for black slavery in colonial America arose from the argument that Africa had no culture. This belief still is held widely today. Most people's knowledge of Africa is filled with misconceptions; Africans are believed to be backward and superstitious, to live in isolated primitive villages, and to rely on witch doctors and voodoo ceremonies for medicine. While this is a simplistic view, for many people an accurate picture of Africa both then and now is virtually nonexistent. Black Africans, however, did not lack culture. The television special *Roots* provided an insight into the culture of West Africa and the trauma of enslavement. The government system ranged from empires, such as the Songhay Empire, to local village chiefdoms. Although subsistence economics varied from region to region, there was a clear economic pattern: in the fertile areas farming and cattle raising were commonplace; the river people were fishermen and boatmakers, while hunting and gathering of fruits and nuts were also common.

African chemistry was evident in antidotes for poison and in the process of embalming. Geometry was used to locate and measure irrigated land. Education was practiced. Men taught boys the way of life as a man, while girls learned from the women. Roles were definite and distinct in African society. Belief in the world of spirits and in ancestor worship were essential parts of African religion. Often there was a supreme spirit corresponding to the Christian God.

This example of African art reveals the high level of African culture.

The highest level of African culture was found in arts and music. African carvings and sculptures of wood, stone, and ivory displayed creativity and personal expression. They were made frequently for religious purposes and were used during ceremonies. Africans also invented many types of musical instruments, such as drums, harps, and guitars. These people, with their rich cultural heritage, became the black slaves of colonial America. The absence of any significant African culture among American blacks today shows how successful Europeans were in stripping Africans of their history and culture.

Although modern slavery began with the Portuguese in 1441, the concept of slavery is not a new one. Ancient civilizations had slaves; yet ancient slavery was very different from modern slavery in that slaves were frequently of the same color and race as their masters. Although Portugal initially had a brief monopoly over the slave trade, soon all the expansionist nations of Europe—including the English and their colonies—would join in this profitable enterprise. Initially, slaves were used as laborers in Europe, but it was only a matter of time before slaves would be brought to the New World. With the discovery of America came a great demand for cheap labor, and this demand could be best met by slaves. The first slaves were brought to the island of Hispaniola (today the Dominican Republic and Haiti). By the 1550s there were 10,000 blacks being imported each year into the Spanish colonies. By the end of the 1700s more than half of the blacks in Spanish America were found on the sugar plantations of Puerto Rico and Cuba. These islands were the training grounds for slavery, where Africans were stripped of their culture and forced into an alien work system.

It already has been mentioned that English colonial slavery began with a Dutch ship arriving in Jamestown, Virginia, in 1619. The first blacks to be imported to the colonies were treated as bound servants and were freed when they had earned their passage, giving them a chance to make their own way in a fairly egalitarian society. But there were probably not more than a few hundred of these cases. The 1640s marked the beginning of the practice of selling imported blacks as servants for life, and *black* became synonymous with *slave*. By the 1600s, statutes in Virginia and Maryland provided a legal basis for permanent enslavement. Slavery seemed to be the answer for the large-scale production of tobacco and rice, and, by the 1700s, slaves could be found in all colonies, both North and South.

Of course, the number of slaves in a given colony was primarily determined by economic necessity. The bulk of the black population was in the Middle and Southern colonies, where the tobacco, rice, and indigo plantations were best suited to slave labor. In the New England colonies the number of slaves was small. There they often were used as unskilled labor, but many were engaged in such skilled occupations as printing and carpentry, as well as being farmers and house servants. The lack of white artisans, both in the North and the South, forced whites to train their slaves as artisans. Although New Englanders owned a smaller percentage of blacks, they still had a part in the growth of slavery, for the demand for slaves made the slave trade a profitable commercial activity.

The Slave Trade

The practical operations of the slave trade were much the same for all nations. The American slave merchants described the trade as "triangular trade," because ship passage initially went from the colonies to the African coast and then to the West Indies or the South in the shape of a triangle. With rum, guns and gunpowder, utensils, textiles, and food, the trader left Boston, Salem, Providence, or Newport—the leading slave ports of North America—and arrived at a trading post in Africa. There he contacted the chief trader, who discussed price and arranged for an auction to be held. Frequently, not enough slaves were available, and expeditions were made into the interior. Slaves were purchased at auctions with rum. While the prices varied, women with child-bearing potential received the highest price. Slave trade involved much more than sailing into a port, loading up with slaves, and sailing away. In addition to the various courtesy visits and negotiations expected of a trader, it often was difficult to find enough satisfactory slaves to fill a ship. Many ships put into several different ports or had to wait in one port for a month or more. Once filled, the ships and slaves faced the most arduous part of the trip.

The sixty-day voyage, or "middle passage," from Africa, which ended in the West Indies or the American mainland, was a living hell for the slaves and one of the cruelest aspects of colonial slavery. The human cargo was packed

On the voyage of Middle Passage black Africans were victims of cruelty and miserable conditions.

aboard ship and chained together by twos, with hardly any room to stand, lie, or sit down. There between decks unbelievable atrocities occurred. One captain wrote, "The Negroes are so incident to the smallpox that few ships that carry them can escape without it." According to one eyewitness:

> *The surgeon upon going between decks in the morning to examine the situation of the slaves frequently finds several dead, and among the men, sometimes a dead and living Negro fastened by their irons together. When this is the case, they are brought upon the deck, and being laid on the grating, the living Negro is disengaged and the dead one thrown overboard.*

Traders were not saddened by the loss of their cargo, for they had insurance that covered cargo loss. They simply had to keep the hands of the dead slaves to receive damages when they returned home. Not only cargo insurance but also "revolt insurance" was carried by the traders for financial protection. Many slaves were driven to suicide, some by self-starvation; in many cases forced feeding by means of a "mouth-opener" containing live coals was considered necessary. There were instances where more than two-thirds of the slaves on a ship were dead by the time it arrived at the West Indies; the loss of half was not at all unusual.

It is impossible to determine the exact number of slaves brought out of Africa, but it is estimated that some 50 million Africans died in transit; the countless millions who were seized in Africa will never be known. Ten million, however, did survive to make it to Europe and to America—the New World. The trade system was a profit-making enterprise. Profits varied from 20 to 30 cents for every dollar invested. In the West Indies, traders first sold their slaves, usually for gold and silver, and then purchased a large supply of molasses and sugar with which to make rum. By the 1700s traders were avoiding the West Indies, and slaves were carried directly to the mainland.

Slave Conditions

The treatment of blacks in colonial America varied from colony to colony. By 1775 there were more than a half-million blacks, and more than three-fifths of them were in Virginia and the Carolinas. Each colony had to make its own rules defining not only who were slaves but how slaves should be treated. With the growing population of slaves (South Carolina's slave population actually exceeded the white), stringent slave codes were passed to lessen the danger of slave insurrection. Generally, codes provided that slaves could not carry arms, own property, or leave their plantation without a written pass. In New England, as might be expected, the slaves were given more freedom; there they had certain rights and were entitled to trial by jury, to sue and be sued, and to testify against whites. Punishment was confined to whipping, and laws primarily were concerned with regulating behavior. There is a popular myth that during the colonial period the slaves were quite happy and that there were no slave revolts until the period just before the Civil War, and then only in the South. Actually, the two most significant slave rebellions during the colonial period took place in New York City in 1712 and 1741. In 1712 a group of 23 blacks killed 9 whites, and the blacks in turn were executed by burning and hanging—one was broken on the wheel. In 1741 a plot involving both whites and blacks was uncovered, for which 13 black leaders were buried alive, 18 hanged, 80 deported, a white family executed, and a Catholic priest hanged as an accomplice. Even with the rebellions and the obvious cruelty of the system, there only were scattered voices that cried out against slavery.

Many Quakers opposed the practice from the beginning. John Woolman, a New Jersey Quaker leader, warned that the consequences of slavery would be "war and desolation," while his friend Anthony Benezet became the leading antislavery propagandist and believed that blacks could be prepared for freedom by teaching them how to read and write. Such prominent Puritans as Cotton Mather and Samuel Sewall became concerned with the spiritual welfare of the slave. Mather established charity schools for Bible instruction, while Sewall, whose pamphlet *The Selling of Joseph* in 1701 was the first direct attack on slavery in New England, urged religious training for slaves. Although there was little opposition to slavery outside of these religious groups, a few blacks were attracting attention on their own.

The first widely read black writer in America was an elderly slave named Jupiter Hammon, whose poems reflected in verse on his religious faith, the evils of slavery, and the hope for freedom. Phillis Wheatley, the most famous black writer of colonial times, won international acclaim. Her poems expressed the entire range of human experience. A number of prominent Americans, including George Washington, praised her for her artistry. Still, she remained a slave during most of her lifetime and only received freedom a few years before her death. By the 1770s other Americans slowly were beginning to question the right to hold another person in slavery, but radical social changes would not come until after the American Revolution. Although slaves made up the majority of the work force in colonial America, they were not the only laborers.

Colonial Labor

Many of the early white migrants to the New World dreamed of finding there "rubies and diamonds" and "dripping pans of pure gold." Instead, they found a great deal of hard work. Since land was cheap and abundant and many farmers preferred to work for themselves rather than someone else, labor was extremely scarce. In fact, during part of the colonial period, more than two-thirds of the laborers were legally bound servants, and less than one-third of the remainder were free labor. At least 50 percent of the entire white population came to the colonies as servants. Of bound labor, indentured servitude was the most common: men and women, in return for ship passage, bound themselves by indentures to serve for a specified period of years, usually not more than seven. These indentures often were held by shipmasters, who sold them in America to pay the costs of transportation. Some bound laborers were redemptioners, who agreed to reimburse shipmasters for their passage money by selling their labor in the colonies. There generally was no social stigma attached to this form of servitude.

Contract servitude, whether by redemption or indenture, was by no means slavery but still was far from satisfactory. Servants frequently came to America in poor physical condition. After being auctioned, they became the private property of their masters for an average term of four years. During this time they could be bought and sold, leased, or hired out with almost no restrictions. The servant's contract required that he or she be given adequate food, clothing, housing, and medical attention during the servant's time of service and, at the end, perhaps a freedom grant, which meant tools and clothing, and occasionally a small tract of land. Often these contracts were not met completely by the masters. The law also gave masters full authority to administer corporal punishment for refusal to work. In the Southern colonies severe penalties, such as whipping or branding, were imposed on servants who refused to work or who deserted. The servant's lot was hard, and conditions occasionally led to organized revolts, such as in the Virginia counties of York and Gloucester, in 1661 and 1662. Individual runaways were common. Frequent advertisements concerning runaway servants appeared in colonial newspapers. Special rewards were offered for the return of skilled laborers, such as shoemakers. The main difference between the white servant and the black slave was that the former's rights as a person were recognized. The white servant could sue or be sued, testify in court ,and the servant's children did not inherit the indentured condition. Of course, once freed, the white worker, particularly if he or she were skilled, could be sure of receiving the highest wages in the world. Although authorities believe that many former servants eventually became squatters and crude laborers, others became skilled artisans and achieved a high place in society.

Skilled Artisans

Skilled artisans were specialists in certain facets of production. These people were necessary in the emerging society of colonial America and were always in demand. The wealthy colonials were writing constantly to their agents in England to produce for them an able brickmaker, a skilled shoemaker, or a good barrelmaker. Because of the scarcity of skilled workers, the artisan often performed many functions, such as both barrelmaking and shoemaking. Artisans were a welcome addition to early America. Among those who com-

Skilled craftsmen were always in demand in colonial America.

Living in Colonial America: The Birth of Modern Culture?

manded wide respect were cabinetmakers, such as John Alden of Plymouth and William Savery of Philadelphia, who was famous for his furniture in the later colonial period. Because of the isolation of many settlements, a craftsmaker often would move from settlement to settlement. This traveling artisan was welcome everywhere, not only for products or service but also as a source of news.

Today, with career planning and professional schools, it is relatively easy to educate oneself for a trade-oriented career. During the colonial period the main method of training was a practical one—apprenticeship. According to this system, a master agreed to teach a youth "the art and mystery of his craft" in return for the youth's labor for a specified period of years. Children were bound out as apprentices when they were very young and usually served until they were 21. Because child labor was legal and socially accepted, there were many abuses of the apprenticeship system. Isaiah Thomas, aged six, was apprenticed to a rascal printer. He remembered setting the broadside ballad "The Lawyer's Pedigree" to the tune of "Our Polly Is a Slut" while still a youngster. As compared with today, the lot of an apprentice was hard, dreary, and monotonous. The apprentice was expected to work from dawn to dusk and to keep busy in the evenings if duties in the household required it. Once the apprenticeship had been completed, the apprentice went out into the colonial world where free laborers were in great demand.

As desired as free laborers were by employers, they did not have absolute freedom. All colonies attempted to control free laborers by the use of English industrial codes, which regulated workers' conditions and masters' profits. All colonies also enforced compulsory labor; laws punished idleness and required that men between the ages of 16 and 60 labor part of the time on public work projects. The shortage of laborers often led to high wages, which created severe economic problems. This crisis was most apparent in New England, where there were relatively few indentured servants. In 1630 the General Court of Massachusetts established a wage ceiling of 2 shillings a day for carpenters, bricklayers, thatchers, and other artisans and a ceiling of 18 pence for all-day laborers. Three years later Massachusetts passed a comprehensive wage law. Eventually, the colony tried to establish price controls and to regulate workers' dress. According to the dress code, workers were not to be seen "wearing gold or silver lace or buttons, or points at their knees, or to walk in boots, or women of the same rank to wear silk or tiffany scarfs." Colonial Americans believed that work itself was good therapy and that low wages and long hours were benefical working conditions.

During the colonial period, with the unusual situation involving labor—free and unfree—there were no unions. There were attempts to transplant the

English guild to the colonies, but these failed. There was actually little reason for wage earners to organize in colonial America, because markets were local and wages and prices could be controlled easily. Still, glimpses of unionization can be seen even at this time. In 1636 a group of Maine fishermen mutinied when their wages were withheld. In 1677 the licensed cartmen of New York "combined to refuse full compliance when ordered to remove the dirt from the streets for threepence a load." In 1741 the bakers of New York City agreed "not to bake bread but on certain terms." In 1768 a group of journeymen tailors walked out because their wages had been reduced. While these were isolated examples, they boded well for the future of workers' organizations.

Colonial Agriculture

In 1790 the first federal census found less than 3 percent of the population in towns of more than 10,000. Colonial America was essentially agricultural. And, except for a few large plantations which were mainly in the South, small farms abounded. Although most farms produced enough food for the inhabitants and a nearby market, farming varied from region to region. Initially colonial farmers were backward in both method and technology. Superstitions were prevalent, such as plowing by the light of a full moon or leading a pig backwards into a stile. Most farmers were wasteful, and because of the abundance of land they paid little attention to talk about crop rotation and the use of manure. In many ways the tools used by colonial farmers were not much better than those used by Indians. Wooden plows were common, and farmers cut grain with sickles or scythes, threshing it by using wooden flails or by having oxen trample it out, methods little advanced over those of biblical times.

Farming in the New England colonies was difficult. New England farmers had to cultivate boulder-strewn land where the soil was thin and poor. The long winters and short summers made plantation agriculture there unthinkable. Corn, rye, oats, and barley were the most popular crops of the area, but with the dominance of small farming and transportation to market difficult and expensive, little income could be made solely from farming. The New England Yankee farmer was forced to become a jack-of-all-trades and usually worked part time during the winter season. The area from New England to Virginia, frequently called the Middle Colonies, became the most productive area for general farming. This colonial breadbasket produced wheat and potatoes as the major staple. By the early 1700s German farmers brought their

Living in Colonial America: The Birth of Modern Culture?

Rice was one of the cash crops of the colonial South; here slave laborers toil on a rice plantation in Georgia.

improved agricultural techniques there. In both regions, many of the crops were used in making liquors.

Even though plantation farming was not the only type of farming to develop in the South, it is true that a one-crop economy did arise. Farmers usually raised a specialized crop for export: in Maryland and Virginia, tobacco; in South Carolina, rice and indigo. More than in any other part of the country, the Southern farmers looked to the urban and export markets for the sale of their cash crops. Out of this system emerged the Southern planter, who held sway over a large farm based on the exploitation of black slaves. Not only did this planter's world revolve around the success of one crop, but it became dependent largely on credit. Credit was needed to purchase new land and more slaves and to uphold the high standard of living that the planter's social position dictated. Generally, whether in the Northern, Middle, or Southern colonies, farming reflected self-sufficiency. One farmer wrote: "All sorts of grain, all that we plant and sow gives us plentiful returns, so that we are richly supplied with meat and drink...." Farms even contained early industry.

Industry as we know it today was nonexistent during the colonial period. There was no factory production, and distribution methods were primitive. The most practical industry was household manufacturing, where farm families made the necessities of life. Their work included the production of food, tools, clothing, and furniture. All members of the family participated in these essential tasks. Women were responsible for curing meat, making bread, drying and preserving fruits and vegetables, and making candles and soap. Women also took part in the processing of various alcoholic beverages. Men were responsible for the heavy work, such as building homes, manufacturing tools and furniture, sowing and harvesting the crops. The production of textiles was also largely a household industry, for every home had its handloom and spinning wheel. By the 1700s, however, the production of goods gradually was shifting; more and more of the household manufacturing was performed by skilled craftsmakers or artisans, and, by the time of the Revolution, more than half of all manufactured products in America were made by them.

The Colonial Woman

Household manufacturing was greatly dependent on the dedication of colonial women. The place of the woman in colonial America was considerably better than her counterpart in Europe, but she still was handicapped greatly by education, the legal system, and local customs.

Marriage was the basic career of American women, and marriage was not difficult to come by because men outnumbered women six to one. Once married, the real work began. It was quite usual for a woman to go through eight or nine childbirths. This, coupled with their essential household duties, frequently led to an early grave. Men then outlived women; this was a sad commentary on the colonial woman's difficult lot in life.

Education was male dominated, for it was believed that women merely had to learn household duties. One colonial wrote that women needed only "sufficient geography to find their way around the house." Women also had limited privileges under the law. The husband was the sole guardian of the children. He was also the unquestioned judge and jury in his home. Physical abuse of women was legal in most areas. While divorce was not a viable route of escape from marriage for the colonial woman, running away was; advertisements for runaway women appeared in colonial newspapers.

The colonial woman was the main laborer in the household industry; her many tasks even included assisting in the construction of the dwelling.

While the woman's lot was not ideal, it was better than the British woman's. In Britain a woman had no legal identity at all; in America the courts upheld a woman's right to own property and allowed her to make contracts and sue. While few women ever left their household duties, some did become skilled artisans; others were planters and managers of large estates. One of the most remarkable colonial women was Eliza Lucas Pinckney, who not only managed Southern plantations but also undertook significant agricultural experiments. Household industry, which greatly relied upon female deligence, was not the only colonial industry.

Colonial Industry

The sea and land also provided the colonials with the basis for the growth of extractive industries. Initially, forests were only barriers to settlement, but soon their real potential came to be realized. The industries of lumbering and shipbuilding burgeoned. New England, with its lush forests, was a forerunner in the milling industry. At the rapids of the full line sawmills were set up. Lumber had numerous uses. It was necessary for wooden barrels—universal colonial containers. Barrels stored food and alcohol, and barrel staves and hoops became important articles of commerce. Lumber also was essential in ship and house construction and in the manufacture of furniture. Although the English in the colonies made futile attempts at conservation by marking certain trees for naval use only, colonial America generally made no provision for conservation.

Shipbuilding became an extremely profitable colonial venture and was centered in the New England and Middle colonies. The industry had its greatest success in Massachusetts: in 1631 the *Blessing of the Bay*, the first American-built ship, was launched. Shipbuilding was substantially less expensive in the colonies than it was in Europe; by 1760 the colonies were building between 300 and 400 ships a year. While New England kept its early lead in shipbuilding, New York and Pennsylvania also had their shipyards. Virginia and the Carolinas, with their fine supply of live-oak timber, became important centers of the industry in the late 1700s.

The colonial forests also provided the setting for another important industry: fur trading. Fur trading was important both as an economic activity and as a practical means of learning about the unknown lands to the West. Trapping and trading furs eventually became a thriving business, employing what were, by colonial standards, large amounts of capital. Of course, the English fur traders were in direct competition with Indian, French, and Spanish traders, and this often limited their success. Ultimately, the role of fur traders in exploring virgin wilderness was more important than fur trading itself.

Shipbuilding worked hand in hand with the other sea-born industry of fishing. Primarily restricted to the Northern colonies, fishing and whaling were of major importance in the development of the early colonial industrial economy. While Europeans were finding that their coastal supply of fish had disappeared, New England colonists were finding that they had an ample supply of fish, a proximity to the fishing grounds, and an increasing market. The fishing industry of New England outstripped all other commercial activities in the first century of settlement. Cod and mackerel were the main fish of commercial value. Although the New England fisheries were of prime importance, there was also profitable fishing along the coast of the Middle and Southern colonies.

By the 1700s whaling also became a profitable industry in New England. Whaling actually started on land. Whales, of course, could not be lured by

Whaling was an important colonial industry
dominated by New Englanders.

placing bait strategically along the beaches, but whales often were stranded accidentally on them. In fact, Plymouth in 1654 enacted a law specifying that a whale cast up on any person's private land was the property of the landowner. Eventually, lookouts were stationed on cliffs above the beaches. When they sighted whales, crews would row out to harpoon them and drag them onto the shore. Such pursuits were often worthless. Eventually whalers shifted to small sailing ships from which boats could be lowered to pursue the whale; these became commonplace. Once the whale skillfully had been harpooned, a crew put out in a small boat and allowed themselves to be dragged on a "Nantucket sleigh ride" by their injured captive. Such trips were dangerous but exciting;

often a whale would sound and drag the men under or turn on the small boat and crush it like an eggshell between its jaws. A captured whale was indeed a worthy prize, for all parts were used: blubber for soap, spermaceti for candles and ointments, whalebones for women's garments, and ambergris for perfume. Raw whale oil also was used by some colonial women as a perfume.

The only mineral colonials used in any industrial pursuit was iron. The origins of an iron industry date from early settlements. The early days of Massachusetts and Virginia saw small bloomeries and forges erected to utilize the bog ores in those colonies. Eventually, sizable furnaces appeared in all the colonies. By the time of the American Revolution, the colonies were providing more pig and bar iron than England. The most extensive industrial enterprise anywhere in English America was the work of a German ironmaster, Peter Hasenclever. Located in northern New Jersey and founded in 1764, it operated with a labor force of several hundred and included furnaces and forges, as well as sawmills. The colonial iron industry must have been successful, for the process was quite simple and charcoal was abundant. The economic life of colonial America varied from region to region and from city to farm. But economics generally played a subservient role to religion in the formative years of American culture.

Colonial Religion

It is difficult for us today, in our materialistic world, to understand the influence of religion upon the early settlers. Religion affected everyone and influenced laws and customs in all the colonies. Particularly in New England, religion was responsible for directing even the minor details of everyday life. This religious fervor was not born in the New World—it was carried from Europe.

At one time it was the practice of Protestant ministers in the United States to speak of the discovery and colonization of America as a providential event. This seemed true since only 25 years after Columbus's voyage Martin Luther nailed his 95 theses to a church door in Germany. The Protestant revolt and the discovery of America were contemporaneous events—God appeared to have created America for Protestantism.

With the Reformation came the birth of numerous church groups and individual sects. The Lutheran ideas of justification by faith, the authority of the Bible, and the priesthood of all believers eventually found their way to America. Calvinism, with its emphasis on predestination and the virtues of industry and thrift, justified business leadership and legitimized business prosperity, making it quite popular among the rising middle classes of Europe and America. The Reformation in England, under the direction of Henry VIII, gave birth to the Anglican Church—also called the Church of England. The Puritans believed in the necessity of an official Church of England, but they wanted to eliminate such Catholic vestiges as the altar, the vestments, Christmas, the cross, and formalized church government. The Puritans believed that they were the elect and that they could follow God's will only by setting up the perfect religious community in America, which would serve as an example to the world. Many individualistic church groups placed importance on the religious experience. The Anabaptists believed that infants should not be baptized and that the rite should be administered only to adults after their conversion. The Friends, or Quakers, stressed the importance of the mystical experience of God's inner light. All the varieties of European religion were, in one form or another, transplanted to American soil during the first century of colonization.

During the age of exploration, European nations brought with them to the New World their culture, which of course included their religion. In fact, seaborne religion was quite prevalent at this time. Many explorers' ships carried chaplains as a kind of insurance against disaster. Sir Francis Drake ordered regular prayers said on shipboard and forbade swearing lest it bring down the wrath of heaven. Fearful of the danger of the uncharted seas, many hard-boiled sailors fell on their knees to seek God's help. Once in the New World, Europeans continued to place great emphasis upon the religious experience.

The Spanish and French carried Catholicism to their American empires. The dominance of Catholicism was particularly evident in Spain, for just prior to the voyages of Columbus she had driven the Moslems out of her boundaries and had become the leading Catholic country in Europe. This religion was carried to America by the mission system. Under the guidance of the Jesuits and Franciscans, the Spanish mission system was carried throughout the southern regions from the Atlantic to the Pacific. While the heritage of Catholicism is still evident in these areas, the missionaries' approach has become the subject of much criticism. Often religious Spaniards were imbued more with love of empire than of God; and there is no doubt that the mission system mistreated the natives. But the Spanish mission system also served in many places to assimilate aboriginal races, religions, and cultures, helping to create a new civilization. In France, there was less religious unity, but the French mission system was an integral part of the French Empire in America. Jesuit priests and explorers carried Catholicism from eastern Canada to the Great Lakes and the Mississippi valley. Frequently, French priests were just as destructive of native religion as the Spanish, but their intent was different. They boldly lived among the natives and taught their religion of salvation. Their preaching was a unique blend of Roman Catholicism and native religion. Both France and Spain established a close alliance between church and state in America, and even after the decline of their New World empires a heritage of Catholicism remained.

Religion also occupied a prominent place in the settlement of English America. Initially, English propagandists for settlement expressed a desire to Christianize the Indians. It was believed widely that the conversion of these heathen would rebound to the credit of England and ensure a blessing upon the colonial enterprise. Clergyman Richard Hakluyt, an early public-relations representative for English settlement, expressed the desire to colonize in order to evangelize: "Now the Kings and Queens of England have the name of Defenders of the Faith. By which title I think they are not only charged to maintain and patronize the faith of Christ, but also to enlarge and advance the same." These sentiments were evident in English colonization attempts in the 1600s.

The Anglican Church in the Colonies

Although the Anglican Church was the official church of England, no single religious denomination ever was able to control all 13 English colonies. Although predominantly Protestant, the religious groups remained fragmented. Of 2.5 million Americans in 1776, no more than one-fifth were Anglican, and more than double that number belonged to various Calvinist groups consisting of Puritans, Presbyterians, and Dutch and German Reformed. There were also Quakers, Lutherans, Pietists, Methodists, Huguenots, and Baptists in the colonies. More than 25,000 Catholics and 2000 Jews added to the religious mixture. However, of all the religious groups that came to the English colonies, the one that received the most support from the government was of course the Anglican Church.

The Anglican Church came with the foundation of the first permanent English colony in Virginia. On June 21, 1607, Anglican Chaplain Robert Hunt held services; the English religious experience in America had begun. The worship of God and the propagation of the faith became essential to the growth of the colony. The colonists were required to visit Hunt's newly erected church twice daily and four times on Sunday. Religious guidelines were set down clearly. People could be whipped for missing daily prayers, and those who gamed on the Sabbath or missed services could be executed. John Rolfe, the "Father of Tobacco," married the beautiful Indian maid Pocahontas more from religious than from romantic reasons. He wrote: "But Almighty God, who never faileth him that truely invoke his holy name, hath opened the gate and led me by the hand that I might plainly see and discern the safe path wherein to tread." When self-government arrived with the establishment of the House of Burgesses, religious functions had civil backing and the Anglican Church eventually became the official church of Virginia.

Although the Anglican Church was officially linked to the government in Virginia, it had numerous problems to overcome. Clergymen were given land and had their salaries paid by the state, but their lot was a difficult one. Many families lived too far from the church, and, since there were no local bishops, colonial congregations felt free to run their churches and fire their spiritual leaders as they chose. With the only training for the ministry being in England, the quality of the ministers was another problem. In 1632 a law was enacted that prohibited ministers from "excess in drinking, or riot, spending their time idly by day or night, playing at dice, cards or another unlawful game." With the growth of frontier settlements, Anglican ministers were forced to travel into the backcountry. One such minister reported that a group of Presbyterians hired troublemakers with 57 dogs to disturb the meeting. The commotion immediately ceased when the minister thanked the "fifty-seven Presbyterians" for attending his sermon. Although the Anglican Church remained the established church in Virginia until the Revolution, it was not the only one, and eventually Presbyterian, Baptist, Methodist, and other churches also were founded in the colony.

By 1692 the Anglican Church had emerged from the struggle between Catholics and Protestants to become the established church of Maryland as well. The Church of England also was established officially in North Carolina, Georgia, and four counties of New York. During the 1700s Anglicanism made significant gains in the Northern and Middle colonies, where the Anglican Church became the church of the aristocracy and the well-to-do. In New England, however, Anglicans had difficulty in combating the Puritan heritage.

The Puritan Experience

In the 1600s the Puritans were the major challenge to the Anglican Church. They believed the Church of England to be a loose federation of congregations, each receiving its authority directly from God. The state was responsible for the union of these congregations, enforcement of church and civil law based upon the scriptures, and suppression of all heretical movements. The hostility of the government of England prevented them from realizing their dream, so they looked to America. The Separatist Puritans, or Pilgrims, believed that

John Winthrop served for many years as governor of the Puritan Massachusetts Bay Colony.

salvation existed outside the established church. Plymouth Colony, their settlement in America, remained small, weak, and generally uninfluential.

The mainstream of American Puritanism came in 1630 with the settlement of Massachusetts Bay Colony under the leadership of John Winthrop. There the Puritans attempted to show the world that their way was the ideal way; they planned to recreate in America a society that bore a close resemblance to the original community of Christ and his followers. Over the years there have been so many differing interpretations about these people that it is difficult to describe the Puritan experience. Were Puritans repressed people who wore dark clothing and constantly looked for witches? Did they enjoy sex and drinking to excess? Or were they merely English people forced to adapt to the American wilderness? Puritans did believe in the voluntary formation of a church by the elect or God's chosen. These elect drew up a church covenant, or agreement, that became the foundation for church government. Ministers and elders then were appointed. It also was true that the Puritan church was an elitist fellowship of true believers who planned to show the world the Christian way of life.

In Massachusetts Bay Colony the relationship between church and state was a close one. In the early years of the Colony only male church members were eligible to become "freemen," that is, citizens with a right to vote. And to become a church member, an individual had to testify that he had experienced conversion; he then had to be approved by the minister, the church officers, and the congregation. The ministers of the church attained a prominent position in the community. Since church and state worked so closely together, often the distinction between civil and religious authority was blurred: church synods influenced law making, while civil magistrates restrained or punished "idolatry, blasphemy, heresy, venting corrupt and pernicious opinions, and profanation of the Lord's Day." A pious minority dominated the early days of the colony.

A description of the Puritan people must include their church, for it was at the center of their physical universe. The church was situated at the center of the Puritan town. Here the people gathered to express their thanks for being chosen the elect. Early Puritan churches were hardly places for rest and relaxation. Within, there were rough wooden benches without backs. Men sat on one side, and women, on the other; all were to keep their eyes trained on the minister. There was no heating in the churches, and in some cases the cold was so severe that the communion bread froze. Sermons often lasted more than two hours, and prayers, more than an hour. Generally, Puritans found it hard to keep warm in winter and to keep awake in summer. To maintain their attention, a church official, holding a long rod with foxtails, walked around the church and poked and prodded people who were nodding. Life outside the church also reflected the Puritan way.

The Puritan religious community demanded a strict observance of God's laws; this was not always an easy task. Although some church leaders looked upon marriage as an obligation and not a pleasure, love and emotion could not be totally suppressed. The same stern religious outlook governed the rearing of children. Any idle time was devil's time, so children were discouraged from playing. Each adult in the community had a "calling"—an occupation chosen for him or her by God; children between the ages of 9 and 13 were expected to discover this calling for themselves. The typical child then moved into the home of a village artisan to become an apprentice. Such rigid regulations as these led to increasing frustration; it may be no surprise that adultery and drunkenness were the two leading sins of the colony. The Puritans found out the hard way that human nature could not be suppressed completely.

By the 1700s the Puritans found that their struggle against heretics—religious dissenters—and traders, who were bringing more wealth into the colony through commerce, was becoming more and more futile. In 1691 Massachusetts received a new charter from the king permitting religious toleration for all Protestants. Second- and third-generation Puritans found themselves unable to cope with the standards their fathers and grandfathers had set. The Half-Way Covenant in 1662, which allowed unregenerate members to transmit church membership and baptism to their children, watered down the faith.

The witchcraft hysteria climaxed with a series of witchcraft trials.

Living in Colonial America: The Birth of Modern Culture?

One of the last gasps of dying Puritanism was the witchcraft hysteria. Puritans now combined fear of the supernatural with religious frustrations. In 1692, at Salem, Massachusetts, 20 persons and 2 dogs had been executed. The court that investigated the hysteria accepted as evidence the testimony of the victims, who reported supernatural happenings. The trials did not end until the governor of the colony himself had been accused. The Salem trials actually had a minimal effect on colonial America. However, they did reveal a real antagonism toward the aristocratic leaders, and they also signaled the death of the Puritan experiment. By the end of the colonial period, Puritans were fighting not only their people's growing tendency to worldliness and material gain but also desertions to other faiths, especially the Anglicans.

Of all the early religious groups, the Puritans are said to have had the greatest influence upon the American work ethic. The notion that idleness is sin is deep in the American character—an idea that emerged full blown after the Civil War. The Puritans' emphasis on education also has become part of the American way. The Puritans were convinced that they were the chosen of God; later this idea was applied to the American belief that our way is the ideal way and that Americans are a special people in the world. The Puritans also left a heritage of town planning; the concept of life set around a town square at the center of a settlement originated with them and has been adopted in many sections of the country. Finally, the idea of the *covenant* is a significant one. Students of government readily point out that the American Constitution was based on this idea. And today the communes of the Jesus People and of the Amish contain many elements that are similar to the Puritan experience.

By the 1700s the American religious scene was one of great variety, ranging from Anglicans, Puritans, and Dutch Reformed to Huguenots, Mennonites, Moravians, Amish, and Lutherans. Yet it was also at this time that religious fervor was declining and wealth was increasing. Most religious groups were finding that their members were taking an indifferent attitude toward church rituals and formalism. A stimulus was needed to rekindle faith and was found in a religious awakening that spread from Europe to America, where the spark was ignited by Theodore Frelinghuysen, the Tennents, and Jonathan Edwards.

The Great Awakening

The origins of the Great Awakening are to be found among the local revivals in the Dutch Reformed and Presbyterian churches. In the 1720s, Theodore J. Frelinghuysen took his emotional preaching to the Dutch Reformed church in New Jersey, while John and Gilbert Tennent preached their emotional experience to the Presbyterians of New England. Puritan Jonathan Edwards carried the spirit of the revival throughout New England. He was an exceptionally bright youth who decided that the salvation of mankind was the major goal of his life. As a Puritan minister in Massachusetts, he was appalled at the "licentiousness" that prevailed among the youth of the town. "Many of them were very much addicted to night walking, and frequenting the tavern and lewd practices . . . and indecent in their carriage at meeting," he wrote. He believed Christians must become aware of their sinfulness and actively feel their conversion to God. To deliver this message, he traveled throughout New England where he presented his hell-and-brimstone sermons, which even caused some church members to have heart attacks. Edward's spiritual revival spread throughout New England and led the way for George Whitefield.

Whitefield was a famous English evangelist who visited the colonies in 1740. He too preached the necessity of a conversion experience, as well as the love of God. His antics included the acting out of the Bible, which caused his listeners to cry, yell, prostrate themselves on the floor, and beg for forgiveness.

The tour of the colonies by evangelist preacher George Whitefield created a Great Awakening in 1740.

It was said that Whitefield could make hell so vivid that you could locate it on a map, and that, by merely pronouncing the word "Mesopotamia," he could bring tears to the eyes of his listeners. His being cross-eyed too was an asset, because when he stared down at the audience no one could tell where he was looking. Ben Franklin was so moved that he emptied his pockets into the collection plate. Whitefield's preaching was the climax to a "general, great awakening," and he made the movement nation-wide.

This emotional movement, which touched both city and farm dweller, rich or poor, eventually led to excesses, such as those of James Davenport. Churchgoers were seeing members cry out, weep, sob, faint, swoon, and even bark—a sign of salvation. Davenport's methods included all of these plus screaming and indiscriminate denunciations of ministers. He often conducted noisy and unrestrained revivals and pronounced as converted all who could join in his wild emotionalism. Because of Davenport and others like him, the Great Awakening subsided.

All this emotional outpouring had many effects: the more emotional churches, such as the Baptists and Methodists, increased their membership; some churches, such as the Presbyterian, divided into two camps. During this time religion generally became more sensitive to the common man and stimulated more interaction among various religious groups. Evangelism was born and would continue to appear time and time again—as it does today in the Jesus Movement. Humanitarianism extended to black slaves, Indian missions, and orphanages. Most importantly, the Great Awakening helped prepare the American mind for the American Revolution by forming a national consciousness among people in the colonies, whose primary ties before had been with Europe. Localism was giving way to nationalism. The powerful influence of religion in the colonial period was helping to make the transition to independence.

Colonial Education

A Puritan writer reflected upon the importance of education, "Unless school and college flourish, church and state cannot live." In today's world of mass education, this statement appears true. In the colonial period, it was true of New England but not of the rest of the colonies. Actually, differences in regional culture were quite evident at this time. Education, science, and literature varied not only from region to region but also from century to century. The period of the 1600s was generally a period of beginnings, with little sophistication or material wealth. By the 1700s the times were changing, and wealth and leisure gave birth to a culture that was becoming more American than European.

In education, for example, the early American ideas were transplanted European ones. In England education was the parents' responsibility. If parents were wealthy enough, they would send their children to school. If parents were not wealthy, children often remained uneducated and illiterate. In the early Southern colonies, the belief that education was solely the responsibility of the parents was widely held. It is interesting to note that the first educational enterprise in Virginia was a school for both Indians and whites; the Indian wars, however, killed the enthusiasm for this project. Most early Virginians were well educated and dedicated to learning, but this dedication often diminished as settlers moved into the American wilderness. Those who wished to have their children educated often hired private tutors, who moved in with the family and taught the children at home. A few Southern planters attempted to set land aside for the education of poor children, but these attempts were usually futile. The "old field system" also sprang up in the South. Since the Southern plantation system did not lend itself to large population centers, a group of families would get together, construct a shelter in an abandoned tobacco field, and hire someone to instruct their children. The itinerant schoolmasters who ran the schools were often unqualified and afraid to impose much discipline. To many Southerners, this educational system was no better than a lack of education. Some wealthy planters, unhappy with private tutors, decided that the only place for their children to be educated was back in England, where they sent them. In the South of the 1600s there was no universal system of education. Governor William Berkeley of Virginia reflected the attitude of the South with this statement: "I thank God we have no free schools." William and Mary College, founded in 1693 at Williamsburg, Virginia, was the only Southern institution of higher learning during the entire colonial period. The demand for formal education was much greater in New England.

Puritan Education

The belief that children must learn to read and study the Bible was most prevalent in the Northern colonies. Education was felt to be essential to every citizen, for religion and education went hand in hand. Responsibility again lay with the parents, and most parents accepted it. Township government also began to provide for schools. Since the population was fairly concentrated, pupils could go to centrally located schools. In 1642 the General Court of Massachusetts passed a law concerning education, which instructed officials

Living in Colonial America: The Birth of Modern Culture?

of every township to see that parents—and masters of apprentices—gave their children enough education to ensure "their ability to read and understand the principles of religion and the capital laws of the country." In 1647 the court passed a general education law, which required towns with 50 or more families to have a school that taught children to read and write, while towns with 100 families or more were to maintain schools where boys could prepare for college. Although this would appear to be the birth of public school concept in America, the law was not completely followed; some parents balked at universal education or refused to pay for schooling if their own children were not

Harvard College is America's first institution of higher learning.

being schooled. Although universal public education did not start in New England in the 1600s, the Puritan system did provide for the best education in the colonies at that time.

In New England an educational pattern was emerging that would eventually become the American model. Children were taught the rudiments of reading and writing at home or in a "dame" school, often operated by widows. With that knowledge they continued to grammar school—a combination elementary and secondary school—where they prepared for college education. Grammar-school education emphasized learning of the classics and was administered through strict discipline. Some teachers actually believed in "beating learning" into students. In some schools parents were expected to help pay for a child's education by supplying firewood; when parents failed to supply wood, their children were placed farthest from the fire in the coldest part of the room. Once finished with the classic curriculum of the grammar

This page from the *New England Primer* shows how Puritans blended religion with learning.

Living in Colonial America: The Birth of Modern Culture?

school, students prepared to enter Harvard at the age of 14 or 15. Harvard, founded in 1636, was the first college in America and remained the leading educational establishment throughout the century. Before entering Harvard, students had to have an expert knowledge of Latin, for all lectures and books were in Latin, as were all arguments in class and all questions. The normal curriculum consisted of grammar, rhetoric, logic, Latin, Greek, Hebrew, mathematics, and astronomy. Harvard, as well as the other schools in Massachusetts, attempted to train religious leaders. Separation of church and state was not practiced in education. For example, the first American alphabet focused on Adam and Eve. *The New England Primer*, the first American reader, had as its intent the teaching of the Bible and of reading at the same time; in it, the letter *a* was learned through the verse "In Adam's Fall we Sinned all."

In the 1600s, Southern education was sketchy at best; while in New England, education moved toward a public school system. Meanwhile, education in the Middle Colonies ranged from good to bad. There, parents again bore the major responsibility. The least enthusiasm for education was shown by the German sects of Pennsylvania, who believed that too much "book learning" was dangerous. The Quakers, on the other hand, insisted on practical education and set up schools that taught such useful subjects as navigation, bookkeeping, and surveying. The Dutch in New York also attempted to set up a public-school system. During the 1600s there were no colleges in the Middle Colonies, but a number of good grammar schools were developed.

Colonial Science and Literature

Religion and education went hand in hand during much of the 1600s. Early science and literature were also under the control of religious leaders; these branches of learning, however, were both fairly primitive. Some clergymen expressed scientific interest through theology; Cotton Mather investigated astronomy, while others tried to explain the witchcraft phenomenon scientifically. John Winthrop's son dabbled in chemistry and constructed the first American telescope. Most of the literature of this time also was found in New England. Puritan clergymen, such as John Cotton, Richard Mather, and Thomas Hooker, wrote sermons and books that were religious in nature. The most ambitious writer was Cotton Mather, who viewed life in biblical terms; before his death he had published more than 450 works. The best seller of the 1600s was poet Michael Wigglesworth's *Day of Doom*, a long epic poem that described the end of the world and the agony of the damned: "Where day and night, without respite, they wail and cry and howl." Two other Puritans, Anne Bradstreet and Edward Taylor, also were poets. Bradstreet viewed the human experience in religious terms, while Taylor wrote poems of mysticism and nature. He, therefore, was not well accepted; his works were generally ignored until the twentieth century. The best-selling prose work of the time was Mary Rowlandson's *Narrative of the Captivity and Restauration of Mrs. Mary Rowlandson*, an early-American adventure tale of Puritans and Indians. It told the story of Mrs. Rowlandson's capture, torture, and eventual escape from "red savages"—events described entirely in terms of God's destiny.

Outside of New England there was less education and fewer writers. Robert Beverly and William Byrd wrote early histories of Virginia and of the frontier, while Ebenezer Cook's *Sot-Weed Factor* described early Maryland in poetry. Daniel Denton's view of life in provincial Manhattan and the Dutchman Jasper Danckaerts's description of his voyage to New York and New England in 1679–80 were New York's literary contributions. Considering the arduous task of establishing colonies in the American wilderness in the 1600s, one is surprised to find as many writers as there were. In general, these writers viewed the settlement of the colonies and the struggle for survival in terms of God's relationship to man. By the 1700s, the wilderness was being conquered, material wealth was on the rise, the religious colonial mind was becoming the secular colonial mind, and, finally, the European Enlightenment was affecting English colonists.

The Enlightenment and Its Effects

The European Enlightenment was a philosophical movement that took a rationalistic and scientific approach to humanity and the world. Man was a rational creature, who could direct his reason, by use of the scientific method, to achievements in science and related fields. In Europe, Sir Issac Newton and John Locke were the leaders of this movement. The Enlightenment reached America more than a century after its initial impact in Europe, but when it arrived, during the 1700s, it stimulated a new secular interest in education, science, and literature.

Secularization in education caused the Puritans to lose their dominance and was responsible for the decline of the public-school idea in New England. Private academies, with emphasis on practical subjects, began to challenge Latin grammar schools. Even in the Latin grammar schools such secular subjects as English grammar and geography were becoming standard fare. Southern education continued to lag, although more charity schools were set up. The middle colonies now introduced education for their growing minorities. The Germans were eager to establish their own schools to emphasize German heritage and German language, while the Scotch-Irish Presbyterians wanted to establish parochial schools.

Many colleges were founded during the 1700s, and older colleges expanded their curricula. Harvard added professors of natural science, literature, and mathematics. William and Mary College became the center of colonial culture. Yale, Princeton, and the College of Philadelphia were founded and soon became popular colleges. Despite the rise of secularization, most colleges remained traditional and religious in their curriculum. Few courses prepared graduates for careers other than the ministry. No American college taught law or medicine.

Although colleges did teach science and mathematics, the great colonial scientific achievements in the 1700s were in no way connected with schools. Practical science was a hobby for wealthy gentlemen. The most oustanding colonial scientist was Benjamin Franklin, who is best known for his kite experiments in electricity. However, his invention of the Franklin stove, which caused a revolution in heating, was his most practical achievement. Another colonial scientist was David Rittenhouse, a self-taught mathematician and astronomer, who made notable contributions to the study of the planets. Cadwallader Colden, John Morgan, and Benjamin Rush tried to understand the causes of diseases and to treat them in a scientific way. Lewis Evans and Dr. John Mitchell drew maps of America that were popular in Europe and led to further geographical study. All these men were leading participants in the American Enlightenment and helped to stimulate interest in reading and writing.

Colonial Newspapers

Newspapers, books, and other publications also existed in the 1700s. More than 50 years earlier, in 1639, the first printing press in America had been set up, while others were built later in the century. These presses were used primarily to print the Bible and other religious material. Colonial newspapers were virtually nonexistent until the 1700s. In 1704, America's first successful newspaper, the *Boston News Letter*, was published. This newspaper was merely a digest of news without any editorial comments; it was more like a modern newsletter. More than 43 newspapers were published in the colonies by 1765, but editors were forced to be careful because freedom of the press was not yet a well-accepted principle. Newspapers were also without such

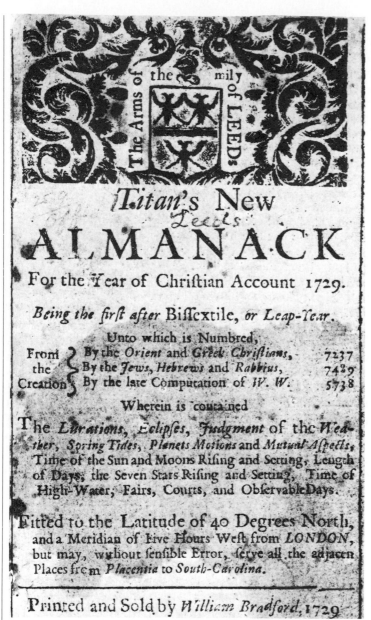

The Arms of the [Fa]mily of LEEDs

Titan's New *Leeds*

ALMANACK

For the Year of Christian Account 1729.

Being the first after Bissextile, *or Leap-Year*.

Unto which is Numbred,

From the Creation
- By the Orient and *Greek Christians,* — 7237
- By the *Jews, Hebrews* and *Rabbius,* 7429
- By the late Computation of *W. W.* 5738

Wherein is contained

The *Lunations, Eclipses, Judgment* of the *Weather, Spring Tides, Planets Motions* and *Mutual Aspects*, Time of the Sun and Moons Rising and Setting, Length of Days, the Seven Stars Rising and Setting, Time of High-Water, Fairs, Courts, and Observable Days.

Fitted to the Latitude of 40 Degrees North, and a Meridian of Five Hours West from *LONDON,* but may, without sensible Error, serve all the adjacent Places from *Placentia* to *South-Carolina*.

Printed and Sold by *William Bradford*, 1729

Early American literature often mixed religion and practical affairs.

modern essentials as comics, sports pages, and classified ads. They were no more than a collection of trite sayings, literary jokes, announcements of meetings, business notices, and other general news. And there was no particular organization to a newspaper, so one did not know what to expect, or where.

In 1735 Peter Zenger gave a great boost to freedom of the press. Zenger, a New York printer, had assailed the corrupt royal governor of New York in his newspaper and was tried for criminal libel. Zenger's able attorney Andrew Hamilton reasoned that anything that could be proved true could be printed in the newspaper. Zenger's acquittal was an important landmark victory for freedom of the press; newspapers became much more immune to libel suits. But even by the time of the American Revolution, although newspapers placed more emphasis on politics and local news, their general format was cautious and quite formal; complete freedom of the press still was unknown.

The number of books available to colonials also increased considerably. Most colonists still received their books from England, but the larger towns now had bookstores that did a thriving business. The wealthy began to amass impressive personal libraries; William Byrd of Virginia owned 4000 books. Public libraries also were founded in many towns, but they were actually subscription libraries; those who wished to borrow books had to pay a small fee. Many writers still dealt with religious themes. Jonathan Edwards wrote religious literature expressing an emotional relationship between God and man. In 1710 John Wise wrote a rousing defense of Puritanism, *The Churches Quarrel Espoused*. The leading secular writer was Ben Franklin, who wrote *Poor Richard's Almanac* and an autobiography. A sad commentary on colonial culture is that no American was able to support his or her career on literary earnings. The dearth of colonial culture also was evident in the scarcity of colonial amusement.

Colonial Amusements

It is difficult for us today to imagine a time without radio, television, movies, sports, and other aspects of mass entertainment. In the colonial period, the struggle for survival, plus the influence of religion, left little time for leisure activities. Still, some recreation was available. The notion that colonists had no time at all for fun and play is incorrect. A governor of Virginia in 1611 found the starving colonists playing lawn bowling. The first Thanksgiving at Plymouth involved both food and games. At Merrie Mount, Thomas Morton, a lively precursor of the Puritans, supervised over numerous celebrations, and

Lawn bowling was a popular pastime for men, especially in the summer.

he and his group were said usually to be found "dancing and frisking together like so many fairies." Of course, these activities were not daily events, but the fact that they took place at all is noteworthy.

Many colonial laws enacted in the 1600s reflected the religious belief that play was the handmaiden of the devil. Laws prohibited merriment and discouraged leisure. The Virginia assembly in 1619 decreed that any idle persons should be put to work; it also outlawed gambling with dice or cards, excessive drinking, and "excess of apparel." Puritan New England tried with mixed success to limit amusements. In these colonies dice, cards, and bowling were all illegal. Even the game called "Shuffle Board" was outlawed; and one could not smoke in public. Laws such as these were hard to enforce; vigilant ministers often went out at night to catch sinners—or to sin themselves. Drinking was a popular pastime in all the colonies, even in New England. The popularity of taverns led to the problem of drunkenness, which was particularly troublesome to the Puritans. By the 1700s religious restraints were weakening, and sports and games became more prevalent.

Hunting and fishing were two popular amusements that were found in all colonies, for early America was a sportlover's paradise. "Bundling," a widely practiced form of courtship, was another colonial pastime. When a man visited a woman, he was often invited to get into bed with her, "but without pulling off their undergarments, in order to prevent scandal." The reasoning behind this practice was the conservation of light and heat. As one can imagine, this practice led to problems—and sometimes pregnancy. While some colonials eventually frowned upon this practice, "bundling" may have been no more harmful than the buggy or automobile ride of later centuries.

Many amusements were regional ones. Southern amusements concentrated on horse racing, cock fighting, and boxing matches, horse racing being the favorite. Rich planters were proud of their racing stables and prouder still of their winnings. Cock fighting, as well as horse racing, involved heavy gambling, with some planters losing more than they could afford. Some authorities have called gambling the major vice of the colonial South. In the Middle Colonies ice skating and lawn bowling thrived. New York, in particular, became well known for its tavern life, ice skating and, coaching parties. Taverns also functioned as the local theater. New England amusements were legally restricted during most of the colonial period, but hunting and fishing did remain popular.

Traveling shows similar to modern circuses began to appear in time. These shows exhibited bizarre creatures, such as "a creature called a Japanese about two feet high, his body resembling a human body in all parts except the feet and tail." Music, painting, and the theater also began to attract attention. Music strongly reflected regional tastes. In New England, Cotton Mather and other ministers condemned mixed dancing as lustful, and musical instruments were kept out of church services; songs were sung with no musical accompaniment until the Revolution. In the South slave music was evident. Plantation music often reflected the misery of the slave experience. Blacks sang and also were allowed to play musical instruments. The most sophisticated colonial music was found inthe Middle Colonies. By the American Revolution public concerts had been held in New York and Philadelphia. The Pennsylvania Germans also had brought with them a rich musical tradition, which was obvious in their folk songs and hymns. Original American composers were scarce. Francis Hopkinson wrote nostalgic ditties, William Billings composed "swinging tunes," and James Lyons, the most innovative, put psalms to Ukrainian folk music.

Colonial painters attempted to capture every aspect of American life—but in a very amateurish way. There were few trained painters in America and little work of artistic greatness. John Copley and Benjamin West are considered the two great portrait painters of the colonial period, but they spent most of their time studying and painting in Europe. The theater, on the other hand, flourished in the 1700s. It was born even earlier. The first play presented in America was *Ye Bare and Ye Cubb*—a version of *Goldilocks and the Three Bears*—seen in 1665. This fairly mild drama was taken before the courts for scrutiny and finally deemed acceptable. By the 1700s touring companies traveled throughout the colonies. Still, actors and actresses faced much opposition from local authorities. Plays were presented in barns, in taverns, and finally in theater buildings. Actors were considered socially unacceptable and often were beaten before and after the performance—and sometimes during it. The leading actor of the colonial period was the Shakespearean actor Lewis Hallam, who traveled from town to town with a London company. By the time of the American Revolution, music, painting, and the theater were well established.

Chart 2–1
Population Statistics 1790

Total Population 3,929,000
Urban Population 202,000
Rural Population 3,728,000
White 3,172,000
Nonwhite male and female 757,000 (19% of total population)
  Male white 1,615,000
  Female white 1,557,000

Colonial Cities

Today America is urban America. Colonial America was rural America, but the origins of urbanism were evident. Most English colonists came from an urban setting, usually from London, where people had become aware of cities as centers of politics and culture. These ideas were transferred to America, where the incipient cities continued as political and cultural centers. While these cities were not initially industrial settlements, many of them were products of careful planning. William Penn, who planned Philadelphia, and James Oglethorpe, who planned Savannah, were forerunners of later urban designers; they each took great care in laying out a city in rectangular grids along a port area. Colonial cities were at the hub of a commercial network, and their character varied from region to region.

The New England towns reflected the Puritan experience. The Puritans expected all settlers to live in a close religious community, building their houses within a mile of the meeting house (church), which served as a focal point for the area. In Massachusetts, Boston became the largest city and the early leader of the colonies. Physically, Boston was situated on the Charles River with good harbor facilities and natural barriers. Most New England towns had a strong sense of community and a pattern of living closely together, yet some towns still had loose organization, scattered farms, and little sense of community.

In the Middle Colonies, New York and Philadelphia were the dominant towns. Born of Dutch and English influences, New York originally was located on the southern tip of Manhattan Island, and early emerged as the chief port and political capital of the New York colony. Philadelphia was a river city with excellent port facilities and fertile land nearby. By 1750 Philadelphia had

At the time of the American Revolution, Philadelphia
was the largest American city.

replaced Boston as the major colonial town. Southern urban development was
slower, due to the plantation economy. The only Southern cities of any consequence were Charleston and Savannah. Charleston, the cultural center of
the South, became the home of rich planters. Located at the junction of the
Ashley and Cooper rivers, it also became a leading trade port. Savannah,
planned by Oglethorpe in 1732, only had begun to develop as a commercial
center by the time of the Revolution.

Other colonial cities emerged for various cultural and economic reasons.
Williamsburg, Virginia, the cultural capital of the colonies, remained small
because it was geographically isolated. Baltimore never developed as a tobacco
port but led in the exportation of colonial wheat. Norfolk, Virginia also became
an important port for exports from Virginia and North Carolina. The larger
colonial cities were port cities and greatly depended on commerce for their
existence. While port cities are not the only urban centers today, modern
America still experiences many of the problems of the colonial cities.

City Problems

Crime, fire, and police protection were three leading problems of the colonial cities. Philadelphia had only 30,000 residents by the time of the Revolution, so urban problems were on a much smaller scale than today. In fact, the cities we see in Hollywood westerns are more like colonial cities than anything else we can imagine. Fire was a major problem, because most houses were made of wood, and fire departments were initially nonexistent. In 1711, for example, Mary Nors of Boston got drunk and set a house on fire, which spread flames throughout the city. It was not until 1717 that a Boston volunteer fire department was set up; this idea was adopted in other cities.

The leading crimes of colonial cities were homicide, theft, and assault. Times have not changed much. Criminals usually are more active at night. This was much truer for the colonial cities. Police were only police by day. During the night, urban dwellers really had to be wary. Eventually a nighttime volunteer police force was established, but weary volunteers would sometimes fall asleep, and others turned to crime themselves. Finally, money was allotted for fire and police protection, and, by the time of the American Revolution, such services existed in many cities. While early cities did not have pollution and traffic problems, the garbage disposal problem was a major one. Citizens were so frustrated by garbage that it often ended up in the streets. Garbage collection and other municipal services were late arrivals in urban America.

Early Colonial Government

Much of the life of the 13 colonies reflected European culture. This was particularly true in the early period of colonial government. Generally, colonial government was similar to the British system. In both America and England voting rights were restricted to property owners, taxpayers, or in some cases to master craftworkers. Colonial America was hardly democratic. With the pattern of monarch and Parliament as a model, the colonial governments usually consisted of a governor and a two-house legislature. The governor had the power to veto all legislation, and, ultimately, all colonial laws had to be approved by Parliament in England. By the 1700s, due to a prolonged period of English neglect toward her subjects in America, the colonies were becoming increasingly self-governing. It was this fact of colonial independence that would cause a split between England and America and lead to the American Revolution.

Origins of "American" Culture

The differences between colonial and modern America are so pronounced that it is sometimes difficult to discover the origins of today's America in its past colonial period. It was in that period, however, that European colonists began to think of themselves as Americans and began to do things uniquely American. It was a transitional time: America—the land of many races—appeared more as a cultural mosaic than a melting pot; amusements were evident but played a secondary role in the overall culture; religion dominated many levels of society; land, labor, and industry were partners in developing a successful economic base; the meager beginnings of public education were noticeable; the problems of the cities, crime, garbage, fire, and police, were being dealt with slowly. The origins of what we consider to be American culture were found in those taverns, meeting houses, cities, and farms. The emergence of an American way, rather than an English way, eventually led to harsh words, gunfire, and a fight for independence.

Essay

Evangelicalism and American Religion

Sinclair Lewis, in his book *Elmer Gantry,* written in 1927, pictured a salesman who turned to religion and became an overnight success. His brand of emotional preaching moved his listeners to fill huge tents with their shouts of joy and public confessions of sin. While this book revealed the shallowness and salesmanship of Midwestern evangelism, it also focused on a brand of American religion that first rose in the New England countryside, spread from colony to colony, and eventually was found coast to coast. Its permanence is evident today in the halls of Oral Roberts University and in the mass appeal of Billy Graham.

Evangelicalism first appeared during a time of public apathy with religion both here and in Europe. Religion seemed interested more in faith and rationalism than in keeping members in church. Formal religion was leaving churchgoers cold. Ministers such as Theodore Frelinghuysen and William Tennent began to preach a religion of feeling: one must vividly experience conversion and feel salvation. This belief reached new heights with the Congregational minister Jonathan Edwards, who carried his fire-and-brimstone sermons throughout New England in the 1730s. By 1740, newspapers reported that the visit of famous English evangelist George Whitefield, with his crossed eyes and theatrical gestures, had caused a real "Great Awakening." Evangelicalism as an American phenomenon was born; colony after colony experienced the same emotional uplifting.

But the American Revolution caused this movement to slowdown and religion reached a new low. But the Great Awakening had made inroads into established churches, and some of the churches had even split into groups, emphasizing either faith and reason or feeling and emotion. With the conclusion of the American Revolution, truly American religion came onto the scene and evangelicalism was again evident. In 1801 in Cane Ridge, Kentucky, thousands gathered to preach and sing, swept up by this religion which now had great attraction for frontier people. For three days preaching, weeping, shouting, jumping, jerking, and even some sinning took place. The wilderness shook with the power of the religion of emotion. But evangelicalism was evident in places other than Cane Ridge, Kentucky.

Two of the most popular religions of the 1800s showed the effects of evangelicalism. The Baptists and Methodists both incorporated some elements of evangelicalism in their churches and found these elements to have mass appeal. Members of communal or utopian communities, such as those of Mother Ann Lee, who established the religious community of the Shaking Quakers, or Shakers, in New York or those of George Rapp, who established his Rappite community in Pennsylvania, talked of feeling God and emotionally draining oneself of sin. Charles Finney was the person who made evangelicalism urban, leaving the frontier and bringing prayer meetings and tents into an urban environment.

The Civil War brought a real crisis to American religion by splitting the North and South and

Revivalism was evident in early America in mass camp meetings.

causing many major churches to form Northern and Southern branches. After the Civil War, American religion had to face major challenges from rising industrialization and urbanism. New challenges came from the writings of Charles Darwin, who applied science to the Bible and who described the evolution of humans from lower animal forms. Evangelicalism now entered a phase of American religion referred to as the period of the social gospel. Churches became leaders in social change; revivalist-church preachers now began to establish city rescue missions, which offered derelicts both food and salvation. The Young Men's Christian Association and the Salvation Army offered the same, with the latter adding a little music to the scene.

The Jonathan Edwards and George Whitefield of the late 1800s were Dwight Moody and Billy Sunday. Moody made the transition from shoe salesman to city missionary preacher. He talked of a relevant religion that would bring about solutions to the problems of the growing cities. Billy Sunday carried the preaching of Moody to new emotional heights; being a former baseball player, Sunday used the mass appeal of baseball to win thousands of converts to his revivalist team—the team of God. He personally carried the evangelical campaign into the twentieth century and led the way for a mass religion of feeling.

World War I and World War II, coupled with the Korean War and the Vietnam War, have provided profound crises for modern American religion. By the 1960s a New Morality was also very evident, and Sunday was becoming anything but a day of rest and meditation. In the midst of this turbulent period evangelists again made an appearance. During the 1940s and into the 1950s, the National Association of Evangelicals and Youth for Christ pushed hard for good, fundamental Christianity—of course, with an emotional flavor. One of the best young traveling preachers was Billy Graham. Graham became a media preacher, exploiting his expert use of radio and television and his wisely orchestrated meetings. By the 1970s his mass meetings not only became television productions but filled huge sports complexes with newly born Christians.

Though possibly the most successful, Billy Graham is not the only evangelical preacher of modern America; Brother Bob Harrington of Bourbon Street, A. A. Allen, and of course, Oral Roberts continued the fire-and-brimstone of Jonathan Edwards and frequently offered sinners the gift of faith healing. Turn on your television set early Sunday morning and view American evangelicalism today.

The Great Awakening rose to offer early American colonists an alternative form of religion; the popularity of this form of religion has risen and fallen during the 1800s and 1900s. But today the permanence of evangelicalism is more than apparent. The traveling tents have been replaced by temples, schools, and in some cases even hotels. The fiscal empires of evangelicalism reach out through radio, television, and newspapers to touch Americans seeking an answer in these uneasy times. While the crossed eyes of Whitefield have been replaced by the selling ability of Graham and the Christian lyrics of the Pat Boone family, the same theme that was being preached and shouted in the 1740s is with us today. ∎

Suggested Reading

LOUIS B. WRIGHT offers an excellent general survey of colonial culture in *The Cultural Life of the American Colonies* (1957), while JOHN C. MILLER in *The First Frontier: Life in Colonial America* (1966) gives a much briefer view.

The mechanics of slave trading are well covered by Philip D. Curtin in *The Atlantic Slave Trade* (1969), while the origins of racial attitudes and descriptions of colonial slavery are found in Winthrop D. Jordan's *White Over Black: American Attitudes Toward the Negro, 1550–1812* (1968).

The Americans: the Colonial Experience (1968) by DANIEL BOORSTIN analyzes the Puritan experiment and its adjustment to the American wilderness. PERRY MILLER presents a classic two-volume study of the Puritan intellectual tradition in *The New England Mind* (1939). Other aspects of Puritanism are expressed in EDWARD S. MORGAN's *The Puritan Family* (1966) and HERBERT W. SCHNEIDER's *The Puritan Mind* (1930). The witchcraft hysteria is well documented in *Witchcraft at Salem* (1969) by CHADWICK HANSEN.

The roots of American education are analyzed in BERNARD BAILYN's *Education in the Formation of American Society* (1960).

CARL BRIDENBAUGH presents a complete picture of colonial urban development in his two books *Cities in the Wilderness, 1625–1742* (1938) and *Cities in Revolt, 1753–1776* (1955). KENNETH LOCKRIDGE, in *A New England Town: The First Hundred Years* (1970), shows the development of a New England town and its government.

CHAPTER 3

The Birth of a Nation
A Revolution Is Fought

Time Line

?–A.D. 1492	Migration and evolution of American Indian societies
1492	Christopher Columbus lands in West Indies—beginning of European exploration
1607–1732	Establishment of 13 English colonies
1756–1763	French and Indian War
1763	Pontiac's Rebellion
1763	Proclamation Act
1765	Stamp Act
1767	Townshend Acts
1770	Boston Massacre
1773	Boston Tea Party
1774	First Continental Congress meets
April 1775	Battles of Lexington and Concord
July 1776	Declaration of Independence
October 1777	Battle of Saratoga
1781	Yorktown: the defeat of Cornwallis
1783	Treaty of Paris: Britain recognizes American Independence
1775–1783	American Revolution
1776	Declaration of Independence
1789–1797	Presidency of George Washington
1812–1815	War of 1812
1816–1824	Era of Good Feelings
1846–1848	Mexican War
1861–1865	Civil War
1865–1877	Reconstruction
1877–1900	Industrialization and urbanization
1900–1916	Progressive Era
1917–1918	World War I
1930s	Depression and New Deal
1941–1945	World War II
1945–1960	Post-war politics
1950–1953	Korean War
1950–1960	Civil rights movement
1961–1973	Vietnam War
1976	Bicentennial celebration

With the Vietnam War now "past" history, modern war seems confined to television news and to distant parts of the globe. Violence is another story; it appears in America in many forms—the street gang in your neighborhood, the demented sniper, hand-to-hand combat on television shows. War and violence are not new here. In fact, our nation was born out of strife—a strife that has been interpreted in biblical terms by some and demonic terms by others. The War for Independence just did not appear suddenly in 1775–76. It was a child of the colonial experience. The British imperial policy, the wars between France and England, and finally the policies and events of the 1760s and 1770s led to an almost inevitable struggle. This war was our first war and one that was for the independent survival of the 13 colonies as 13 united states. It was not a fight of a strong America against a strong Britain. It was a fight of a weak group of colonies who had decided that war was preferable to any other choice they had. An understanding of this war begins with the concept of mercantilism.

The British Imperial Policy

Despite variations in local government from colony to colony, the colonists formed suprisingly similar governmental bodies. Colonial assemblies, councils, and governors guided provincial politics. Of course, these governments were supposed to be subservient to imperial administration. In the end, however, colonists achieved a large measure of self-government in practice, if not in principle. England attempted to govern its colonies according to a set of ideas that are known as *mercantilism*. According to mercantilism, a major purpose of any colony is to increase the wealth of the mother country. Colonies are desirable both as markets for the products of the homeland and as sources of essential raw materials. The rules and regulations imposed on the 13 colonies were designed to promote British interests rather than those of the colonies.

At the heart of British imperial policy were the Navigation Acts. The first such act, passed in 1651, specified that no goods could be shipped to England from America except in English or colonial ships and that foreign goods brought to England or her possessions from other areas must be carried either in English ships or in ships of the country producing the goods. In 1660 this act was strengthened by the stipulations that all exports and imports of both England and her colonies had to be carried in English or colonial ships and that all colonial exports of sugar, tobacco, cotton, indigo, speckled wood, and various dyewoods had to be shipped directly to England. It would appear that these stipulations should have damaged colonial trade, but they did not. In fact, the colonials prospered in spite of such restrictions because of their favorable trade position within the British mercantile system. The 13 colonies, for example, had a monopoly on the production and sale of tobacco within the British Empire. In addition, it was no secret that smuggling had become a fine art. On the other hand, the English government frequently proceeded on the assumption that its imperial laws were essentially unenforceable and that the situation was all right as it was. This was the spirit behind "salutary neglect," the policy associated with England's first prime minister, Robert Walpole (1721–42). Under this rule colonists obeyed or violated regulations pretty much as it suited them.

English rule of the colonies also applied to politics. The English Board of Trade and Plantations, which was created in 1696, issued instructions to the colony's royal governors, reviewed laws passed by colonial assemblies, proposed legislation of Parliament, and generally supervised all colonial affairs. In addition, the Bureau of the Treasury Board collected customs duties, the Admiralty Courts retained jurisdiction in matters relating to the laws of trade, and the Privy Council approved legislation and made appointments in the name of the king. Despite the policy of salutary neglect, English interference in colonial affairs by the mid-1700s seemed to be increasing. When Virginia attempted to prohibit the slave trade to save the tobacco industry from overproduction, the decision was overruled. When colonies attempted to issue paper currency to alleviate the shortage of money, Parliament passed the Currency Act in 1764, which prohibited the printing of paper money. Although colonial Americans resented British meddling in internal affairs, they also assumed that England would handle all foreign affairs for them. Actually, it was in the area of international relations that certain events took place that placed the colonials on the path of revolution. These events centered on a series of four wars with France.

Early Wars

During the 1600s France and England were becoming powerful nations with territorial ambitions. All the ingredients were there for a struggle for dominance not only of Western Europe but also of North America. Prior to 1688 European conflicts had little direct effect on either the French or English colonies. The French had formed a highly structured colony, New France, in Canada and were expanding down the Mississippi River and its tributaries. Meanwhile the English were struggling to establish colonies along the Atlantic seaboard. As the French and English bases of power in America began to expand, a rivalry became evident. Both countries vied for Indian trade and better boundaries. The Protestant British and the Roman Catholic French mistrusted each other. British and French fur traders and fishermen were coming into conflict. This growing tension burst into the open in 1688 and was not resolved until 1763.

In 1688 King William's War began with a series of inconclusive border raids. The French raided upper New York and New England, while the New England colonists captured Port Royal in Nova Scotia. The end of the war (1697) resulted in the restoration to both parties of all occupied territory. The high point of American involvement in this struggle was an unsuccessful expedition against the French stronghold of Quebec led by Sir William Phips of Massachusetts, referred to as "Lucky Bill," who was the twenty-first child in his family. In 1702 another inconclusive war began.

Both Queen Anne's War (1702–13) and King George's War (1740–48) accomplished little. In the first war the French instigated Indian attacks on the Massachusetts frontier, which resulted in the Deerfield Massacre. The Americans again seized Port Royal, Nova Scotia. At the end of the war, the French lost Nova Scotia, New Foundland, and Hudson Bay to England. In the second war, a New England military effort was climaxed by the successful seizure of Fort Louisbourg, a strategic French fortress. Great was the resentment in New England when the British-French peace treaty returned all property to France. The London government did attempt to appease the colonies by substantially reimbursing them for their expenses in capturing Louisbourg. Although the first three wars accomplished little in America, they did serve to increase the growing hostility between the two European powers.

The French and Indian War

In the 1750s the Ohio Valley became the battlefield for a war that eventually would involve all of North America as its prize. The French now were building a string of forts from Canada to New Orleans. At the same time land speculators from Virginia were moving west to stake their claims in the wilderness. In 1752 a French and Indian force wiped out a Virginia land company's trading post. Further conflict seemed unavoidable.

Lieutenant Governor Robert Dinwiddie of Virginia, a land investor, took action in 1753 by sending a young, inexperienced surveyor named George Washington to warn the French that they were trespassers and must leave. At

George Washington was a young surveyor who saw action against the French in the early stages of the French and Indian War.

the French fort he was told that "it was the absolute design to take possession of the Ohio, and, by God, they would do it." Although this mission was futile, it was memorable to Washington, because on the return trip he almost lost his life three times. Not only did an Indian shoot at him, but his raft collapsed, he almost drowned, and then, almost froze to death from his surprise dunking.

Promoted to lieutenant colonel, Washington went back into the wilds in the spring of 1754 to help construct a fort at the forks of the Ohio River. Easily defeating a French scouting party, Washington and his men then met the main French troops from behind crude defensive stockades called Fort Necessity. After a spirited fight, Washington and his men surrendered. The French tricked Washington, who could not read French, into signing an admission that he

The Birth of a Nation: A Revolution is Fought

Fort Duquesne was a French stronghold which did not fall until the later stages of the French and Indian War.

had murdered the leader of the scouting party. Then they permitted him and his men to march off. This seemingly insignificant event led to an international conflict.

Dinwiddie, who some historians think was aptly named, now sought help from England. The British were officially at peace with France; but believing that France was preparing for a major American war, they sent two inferior regiments of British regulars under the command of 60-year-old General Edward Braddock. In July 1755 Braddock decided to move against Fort Duquesne, a French fort located at present-day Pittsburgh. But things began to go wrong. It was difficult to build a road through the wilderness to the fort. Indian allies and anticipated colonial money did not arrive. In addition, friction between the colonial "buckskins" and the English professional soldiers developed. About eight miles from the fort, the two sides met in an encounter that surprised the British. Braddock not only had trouble with his retreating soldiers, but he had not taken Washington's advice about fighting in America. European military tactics involved the lining up of forces on opposite sides of a field, and then, after one commanding general bowed to the other, the fighting began in a very orderly fashion. In the ambush on July 9, known as the Battle of the Wilderness, Baddock and many of his men were killed. Before the battle he had stated, "These savages may, indeed, be a formidable enemy to your raw American militia, but upon the King's regular and disciplined troop, sir, it is impossible they should make any impression." But the French made a lasting impression on Braddock, for his last dying words after the battle were, "We

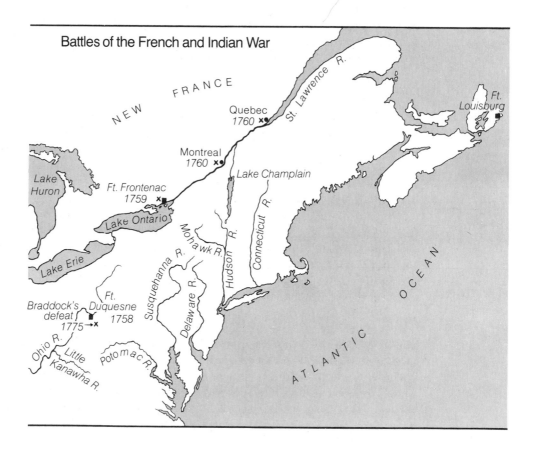

Battles of the French and Indian War

shall know how to deal with them another time." There was, of course, no other time for Braddock.

The Battle of the Wilderness was the Pearl Harbor of the French and Indian War, a war which began badly in North America and would continue to go badly for the English for the next few years. Becoming a world war, the French and Indian War in America (1756–63), known as the Seven Years War in Europe, initially revealed British weaknesses and lack of colonial support. Defeat followed defeat, and by 1757 it appeared that the English would lose the battle for North America.

In England, however, emerged a military and political genius, William Pitt, who, as prime minister, gave a new sense of direction to the struggle. Pitt, an extremely moody individual, believed that an overall strategy was needed for the war. He supposedly announced, "I am sure I can save this country and that no one else can," and he proceeded to fulfill his boast. He concentrated men and money in America, while blockading the coast of France. Old political generals were replaced with young, competent ones. And at the heart of his grand strategy was the capture of Quebec.

British Victory

The tide slowly turned. Fort Louisbourg, Fort Frontenac, and Fort Duquesne fell to English forces. By 1759 the British were at Quebec. Youthful, red-headed General James Wolfe attempted month after month of futile seige operations until he led most of his army up a narrow ravine that was un-guarded. On the Plains of Abraham near the city the crucial battle of Quebec was fought; both Wolfe and the noted French commander Marquis de Mont-calm fell in battle, but the English captured Quebec. Montreal was taken the following year. By 1760 the war was just about over in America. The Treaty of Paris of 1763 gave England a virtual monopoly over North America; France lost her Canadian possessions to England and her Louisiana territory to Spain, an English ally. France retained only a few small islands in the West Indies and off the coast of Canada. The French threat to the English colonies was gone. England had won the struggle for North America.

With the end of the war, Britain became the most powerful nation in the world. While the war appeared to finally settle the problem of the ownership of North America, it had engendered new problems and tensions that led to the American Revolution. In the colonies, news of British defeats and American victories led to a newfound faith in colonial military skill. The war marked the first time British and American soldiers had come into close con-tact with each other, and the result was mutual contempt. One English officer called the Americans "broken innkeepers, horse jockeys, and Indian traders." The colonials also resented impressment into the navy and forced enlistment into the army. One observer wrote that "to see a drunken man lugged through the streets on a soldier's back guarded by others . . . must certainly give a strange impression of the method of enlisting and certainly have an ill effect on an inflamed mob." The war also brought the Americans into closer contact with each other and resulted in a spirit of cooperation and incipient nationalism. One contemporary writer said that for the first time he noticed "a feeling of nation." It was still surprising, however, how much indifference there was for the war throughout the colonies. The colonials had agreed to support the war only after London offered to reimburse them substantially for the expenses involved.

New Imperial Policy

The French and Indian War marked the end of the era of salutary neglect and the beginning of active imperial policies toward the colonies. Administration of the enlarged English Empire now cost five times more than before the war. The financial burdens of war on the English taxpayers had been heavy. Would they continue to bear the responsibility of the defense and administration of distant colonies?

This was not the only burning question in the minds of the English leaders. The old trade and navigation laws had proved ineffective for so many years. Should they remain mere symbols of mercantilism? There was also the question of the American West. For the colonists the war opened a new era in land speculation. The French threat was gone. They also saw little justification in disrupting their freewheeling trade system or checking the burgeoning power of the local assemblies. From 1763–76 there was little agreement between England and the colonies over the administrative course of action. The British attempt to manage rationally an empire in America was seen as a threat to a system that had emerged gradually over the years. The initial tension involved British policies in the American West.

Western Policy

In the West the British not only had to dictate policy for the English colonists but had to control Indian tribes, many of which had fought with the French during the war. In fact, during the war both sides had used Indian allies. The League of the Iroquois had aided the English, while most of the Algonquin-speaking tribes had helped the French. Also during the war the English had formulated a uniform Indian policy, which established a single office of Indian affairs with responsibility divided between two superintendents, William Johnson in the North and Edmund Atkin in the South. This arrangement improved Indian affairs to such an extent that it was used as the basis for American-Indian policy after independence had been achieved. Of the two superintendents, Johnson was the more dedicated. A former fur trader who had married a Mohawk woman, he worked to become a trusted friend of the Iroquois and, after the war, worked to assure them preferential treatment.

Pontiac

The interior tribes feared the loss of their French ally and the movement of the English into the French forts. Lord Jeffrey Amherst lived up to their worst

Pontiac, an Ottawa, led an uprising in the Great Lakes region in 1763.

expectations. Amherst, commander in the West, believed that the French practice of giving gifts to the Indians should be abandoned; if the Indians became aggressive, he believed they should be knowingly infected with disease by the English (using smallpox) in order to kill them off. Pontiac, an Ottawa warrior who had fought on the French side (and who is believed to have drunk the blood and eaten the heart of many a slain enemy to absorb their courage), tried to form an alliance of the Great Lakes tribes in order to attack the British forts. He joined forces with a Delaware prophet who preached that dependence on white materialism had destroyed the Indians and that if they gave up white materialism, they would regain strength and power. In 1763 Pontiac planned to first capture Fort Detroit and then sweep through the West. He carefully scrutinized the fort during a ceremonial dance, but just before his surprise attack an informer told the British of Pontiac's plans. Pontiac still laid seige to the fort, but for eight months was unable to capture Detroit. His alliance of 18 tribes, however, met with much success; every British post in the region except for Forts Detroit and Pitt were seized and occupied. But the unity was only a temporary one; Pontiac himself abandoned his seige by 1764. The end of this conflict, referred to as Pontiac's War, brought an uneasy peace to the interior. Pontiac's brillant military tactics, however, must be given full credit. Today historians still refer to him as a great Indian unifier and strategist. It is ironic that he was killed near St. Louis by an Indian.

Formulating an imperial policy for the western territories was in many ways a much more difficult task for the British than controlling the Indians. To avoid further tension between white settlers and Indians and to limit the English colonists to the Atlantic seaboard, the British issued the Proclamation Act of 1763. This act forbade colonists to move west of a line drawn along the crest of the Appalachians; the land west of the line was to be reserved for Indians. The negative reaction among fur traders, land speculators, and settlers was immediate. However, the act was unenforceable. British soldiers hardly could monitor all mountain passes. And what of settlers already in the West? In actuality, many colonists ignored the act. Even George Washington advised his fellow colonists to stake claims in the West. The governor of North Carolina estimated that in 1765 as many as 1000 emigrant wagons crossed the Proclamation Line to the west. This defiance of British law foreshadowed future events.

After years of investigation, the British solved the problem of French Canada with the passage of the Quebec Act of 1774. This act authorized a permanent government for Canada, established French civil law, and recognized the rights of the French-speaking inhabitants there. Official recognition of those "damnable" French customs and sanction of the Roman Catholic

Church in Quebec further antagonized the colonists, much more so than the Proclamation Act of 1763. But the most criticized feature of the Quebec Act was the extension of the boundaries of the province of Quebec to include the territory between the Ohio and Mississippi rivers south of the Great Lakes. The claims by seaboard colonies to this land, therefore, would be negated. Although the Proclamation Act and the Quebec Act angered the colonists, these acts alone would not have caused a revolution. It was the new British policy of enforcing old acts, combined with new taxation, that led to war.

The Coming of the Revolution

The new imperial policy actually stemmed from the enormous debt that Britain had incurred during the war. Taxes were soaring so much that British taxpayers were paying a fifth of their income to the government. Officials predicted that more than 10,000 troops would be garrisoned permanently in the colonies for defense. The British felt that the Americans should begin to help raise money for their own defense. This seemed reasonable, since the colonials would be required to pay only one-third of the cost of defense. However, to the colonists who were used to the policy of salutary neglect, the paying of taxes was as repugnant as the enforcement of old trade acts.

George Grenville, the British finance minister, felt that trade laws, which originally had been passed to regulate trade rather than revenue, should be enforced so that revenue would be increased. He also felt that other trade laws could be introduced to increase revenue. To accomplish his first goal he ordered strict enforcement of the dormant Navigation Acts and especially of the Molasses Act of 1733, which attempted to prevent the importation of foreign molasses by a prohibitory import tax. This enforcement included the use of writs of assistance—general search warrants permitting British officers to search without the owner's permission or knowledge. Colonials reacted angrily to this new policy. They were opposed to the searching of ships, the seizure of cargo, and the numerous arrests. They felt that, as British citizens, the writs violated their right to protection from search and seizure of private property. They were English citizens and they should have the rights of the English. This line of thinking was typical of colonials during the period prior to the Revolution.

The first British act for the purpose of raising colonial defense revenue from the colonials themselves was the Revenue Act, or Sugar Act, of 1764. This act imposed a tax on such foreign imported luxury goods as sugar, silk, wine, and coffee and provided new methods of enforcement to stop smuggling. From an American perspective, the right of local assemblies to levy taxes had been taken away, while the basic English right to trial by jury also was being violated. The American response, one that would be utilized frequently over the next few years, was a boycott. American merchants refused to import taxed goods, while American colonials avoided buying them. Even the students of Yale University agreed to abstain from the use of foreign liquor. As one newspaper wrote, "The gentlemen of the College cannot be too commended for setting so laudable an example. This will not only greatly diminish the expenses of education, but prove very favorable to the health and improvement of the students." Colonials also complained that they were being taxed without their consent. Grenville replied that they had consented to the tax, since the tax was passed by Parliament: Americans were not directly represented but were virtually represented, as were all Englishmen. This meant that American opinions were at least considered by members of Parliament. The American slogan that emerged from these constitutional debates was "No taxation without representation." While few Americans actually understood the constitutional theories behind the slogan, it did become a rallying cry against the new taxes. The Sugar Act became the first in a series of challenges that led both sides to war.

Stamp Act

Revenue from the enforcement of the trade acts and the Sugar Act was meager, so the British levied a direct tax with the passage of the Stamp Act. The Stamp Act was the first direct tax ever to be imposed on the colonies. Colonists were to pay a tax to register every legal document; taxes also were levied on newspapers, pamphlets, almanacs, playing cards, and even on dice. The Sugar Act had not been well received, but at least it had seemed part of the mercantile system. The Stamp Act was solely a revenue measure; Britain seemed to be making the transition from mercantilism to imperialism. The colonists actually were less concerned with the financial aspects of the act than with the way the act was constructed. As with other acts, the Stamp Act had been passed by a body in which the colonies were not directly represented. Two forms of protest emerged. The most immediate was a violent one. In every seaport there formed a group of "Liberty Boys," citizens who called themselves "Sons of Liberty" and took direct action. They pressured stamp collectors into resigning their positions, burned stamped paper, and stimulated mob violence. Records were destroyed; some stamp collectors were tarred and feathered, and others were hanged in effigy. The *Boston Gazette* offered George Grenville a

This scene depicts American feeling toward taxation.

suggestion: "To make us all Slaves, now you've lost Sir! the Hope, You've but to go hang yourself—We'll find the Rope." Another response was legal. Nine colonies sent representatives to New York to discuss the Stamp Act. This Stamp Act Congress began a spontaneous movement toward colonial union. The congress issued a declaration of rights and grievances, which stated that "No taxes ever have been, or can be constitutionally imposed on [colonial citizens], but by their respective legislatures." It further petitioned the king and Parliament to repeal the Sugar and Stamp acts. Merchants again banned the importation of British goods. Lawyers turned out pamphlets attacking the Stamp Act.

With the end of the Grenville ministry and the rise of the Marquis of Rockingham, a new policy appeared. British merchants had suffered under the colonial boycotts, and the Stamp Act appeared to be completely unenforceable. Meanwhile, many members of Parliament were agreeing with William Pitt, who issued such statements as "I rejoice that America has resisted" and "Why should they submit voluntarily to be slaves?" The Stamp Act had stirred up a hornet's nest. In March 1766 both the Stamp Act and the Sugar Act were

SUPPLEMENT to the PENNSYLVANIA JOURNAL, EXTRAORDINARY.

PHILADELPHIA, *May* 19, 1766.

This Morning arrived Capt. WISE, in a Brig from POOL in 8 Weeks, by whom we have the GLORIOUS NEWS of the

REPEAL OF THE STAMP-ACT,

As paffed by the *King, Lords* and *Commons.* It received the ROYAL ASSENT the 18th of March, on which we moft fincerely congratulate our Readers.

The repeal of the Stamp Act caused much rejoicing in the colonies, but it was merely a temporary victory.

repealed. Americans rejoiced at the news (one victory celebration even offered free grog and food), but they soon realized that on the same day that Parliament had repealed the Stamp Act it also had passed a Declaratory Act. This act clearly reasserted Parliament's right to make laws without colonial approval; Parliament could "make laws and statutes of sufficient force and validity to bind the colonies and people of America . . . in all cases whatsoever." This act did not bode well for future imperial relationships.

The euphoria created by repeal of the Stamp Act was short lived. Charles Townshend, nicknamed "Champagne Charlie" because of his frivolous habits, became chancellor of the exchequer. When Ben Franklin testified before Parliament that the colonials disapproved of internal taxes, Townshend responded by giving the colonies another dose of external taxes. Grenville, the finance minister, dared him to again tax America, Townshend replied, "I will, I will"; and he did. In 1767 The Townshend Act taxed certain English manufacturers entering America, such as paper, lead, glass, paint, and tea. A new collection system was instituted; taxes were to be paid only in gold and silver, and part of the revenue would pay the salaries of royal officials—a real threat to colonial self-government. Massachusetts took the initiative and sent a circular letter to all colonies demanding repeal of the new tax. The colonists also decided to boycott English goods once again. Imports fell off by over 50 percent, and England was spending more to collect the taxes than it was gaining in revenue. The Townshend Act produced more tension and little financial success. By 1770 all the Townshend taxes had been repealed except the tax on tea. Repeal was another psychological victory for the Americans, and it appeared to some that peace would return permanently.

The Boston Massacre

But even before the taxes had been repealed, a clash occurred between civilians and British soldiers. Two British regiments had been sent to Boston to keep peace in that unruly colony. There, on March 5, 1770, a group of people made up of "Negroes, Mulattoes, Irish teagues, and outlandish jack-tars [delinquents]" began pelting a redcoat guard with snowballs; ice chunks and clubs

Colonial newspapers pictured the Boston Massacre as a senseless attack of savage British soldiers against peaceable Americans.

also were thrown. Other soldiers were called out, and after being stoned and taunted for more than half an hour, an order to fire was given and five citizens were killed. This incident, known as the Boston Massacre, was described in a colonial newspaper as "the wanton killing of peaceable citizens by a brutal and licentious soldiery." Colonials were incensed. The captain in charge and his men were brought to trial. Two leading colonial lawyers, John Adams and Josiah Quincy, bravely defended the soldiers. Eventually all were acquitted except for two, who were branded on the hand and then released. No direct consequence followed, but tension continued to build.

1770–1776: The Critical Period

From 1770 to 1776 certain crucial events occurred that would lead to a revolution. In June 1772 the customs schooner *Gaspee* ran aground near Providence, Rhode Island. A rich Rhode Island merchant led an attack on the ship in which the captain was shot, the crew removed, and the ship set afire, Rumors prevailed that the suspects in the attack would be tried in England, not in the colonies. American rights again were being flaunted. About the same time, the governor of Massachusetts announced that he would be paid by the British crown instead of by appropriations from the Massachusetts legislature; this action would make the royal executive much more independent. Also, under the leadership of Samuel Adams, a Boston lawyer, Committees of Correspondence were established to keep citizens informed of happenings in Massachusetts and elsewhere in the colonies. Soon similar committees sprang up in other colonies, and an underground news system was established.

By 1773 the only section of the Townshend Act that remained in force was a tax on tea; but this was only a minor source of discontent, for colonists smuggled most of their tea in from Holland. In that year Parliament attempted to save the near-bankrupt British East India Company through passage of new legislation known as the Tea Act. This act authorized the East India Company both to secure a monopoly over colonial tea and to ship its tea directly to its agents in America. Actually, this new system allowed tea to be sold in America more cheaply than it could be in England or than it could be by smugglers of Holland tea. The British felt the law benefited the colonials by providing a lower price of tea—and at the same time that it saved the East India Company from bankruptcy. Americans, however, were rather outraged. Colonial merchants were no longer used. If a monopoly could be granted for tea, why not for other products? Letters such as the following were sent to captains of tea-bearing ships: "What think you, Captain, of a halter around your neck—

ten gallons of liquid tar decanted on your pate—with the feathers of a dozen wild geese laid over that to enliven your appearance? Signed the committee of Tarring and Feathering." Warnings were sent to the East India Company not to send the tea, but the warnings were not heeded. When the ships arrived, mass demonstrations were held to stop the tea from being unloaded. In most cases, the tea returned to England. In Boston, New York, and Annapolis, "tea parties" occurred.

On the evening of December 16, in Boston, a group of some 50 men "dressed like Mohawks" boarded the company ships, ripped open 342 chests of tea valued at $90,000, and threw the contents into the harbor. John Adams reflected, "Many Persons wish, that as many dead Carcasses were floating in the Harbour, as there are Chests of Tea." A few months later, a group of Sons of Liberty in New York, also disguised as Indians, dumped a cargo of tea into the harbor. In Annapolis, the entire ship *Peggy Stewart* and the cargo of tea on board were burned by a howling mob.

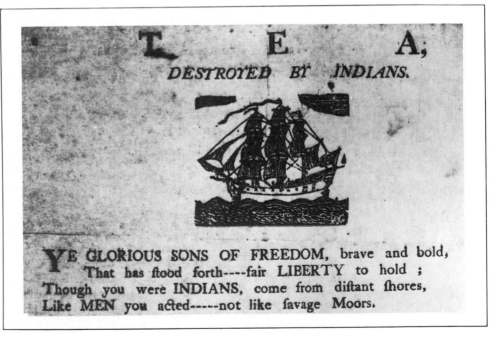

The Boston Tea Party inflamed the British to action—The Intolerable Acts were the results.

These tea parties, the Boston one in particular, brought a strong reaction from Britain. The British deplored the wanton destruction and decided that action must be taken. The tea parties brought to a head the controversy over British authority. George III announced, "We must master them or totally leave them to themselves and treat them as aliens," while his minister, Lord North, "a great, heavy, bobby looking fellow," realized that these "haughty American republicans" must be dealt with severely. Under his direction, Parliament passed four punitive laws, which the American called "the Intolerable Acts," directed at Boston and Massachusetts. These laws included the closing of the port of Boston until the tea was paid for, the restructuring of Massachusetts' government to give more power to the royal authority, and requisitioning of more buildings as housing for the increased number of British troops. The Quebec Act, which has already been mentioned, was passed at this time and was considered one of the Intolerable Acts. Americans interpreted these acts as a threat to colonial liberty. Colonial radicals began to take up the cause of independence; even a moderate like George Washington wrote: "The crisis is arrived when we must assert our rights, or submit to every imposition, that can be heaped upon us, till custom and use shall make us as time and abject as slaves, as the blacks we rule over with such arbitrary sway."

To Lexington and Concord

In the crisis, Massachusetts called for a meeting of all colonies, a meeting now known as the First Continental Congress. Here representatives from all colonies except Georgia met in what has been called a "nursery of American Statesmen." Barely defeating a pledge of loyalism to the crown, Congress issued a petition to the British government denouncing the Intolerable Acts as cruel and vicious and denying the Parliament authority of legislature over the colonies. In addition, a complete boycott of British goods was adopted. Before retiring, the delegates agreed to meet again if the American wrongs had not been redressed.

The king and Parliament rejected a suggestion to withdraw troops from America and answered the challenge by increasing the number of troops and warships. The king wrote, "The New England governments are in a state of rebellion, blows must decide whether they are to be subject to this country or independent." Blows were soon to come. More and more British troops were pouring into Boston, coming under the command of General Thomas Gage. Their presence caused colonial militiamen to begin training; bands of "minutemen" were organized, ready to march at a minute's notice to meet a British attack. General Gage learned that colonial munitions were being stored

The opening shots of the American Revolution took place at Lexington and Concord.

at Concord and that two important colonial leaders were hiding at Lexington, so, on the night of April 18, 1775, Gage sent a force under the command of Major Pitcairn to Concord and Lexington. It was on this night that Paul Revere rode around the countryside shouting his warning of the British approach. At Lexington, Pitcairn found the colonial militia ready to halt his progress. Of course, 70 militiamen against 700 British soldiers was not very good odds. No one today knows who fired the first shot, but when the smoke cleared, eight Americans were dead and ten wounded. The soldiers then marched on to Concord, destroyed colonial munitions, and encountered hundreds of armed Americans. On the return march, the British troops faced the guerilla fire of the colonials, and by the time Pitcairn arrived back in Boston, more than 247 of his men had been killed or wounded. The "shot heard 'round the world" had been fired, and an armed conflict was underway.

The Second Continental Congress now rushed to meet and decide upon a course of action. The king had rejected the First Continental Congress's petitions; Americans had been killed at Lexington and Concord; British artillery and ammunition at Fort Ticonderoga had been seized by Ethan Allen and his Mountain Boys—little course of action was open. George Washington was appointed commander in chief of the Continental army, which initially consisted of the militia surrounding Boston. Washington, a wealthy Southerner well known for his service in the French and Indian War, was the unanimous choice for the job. Congress also authorized the outfitting of a navy and assumed power in Indian affairs. King George III refused the Olive Branch Petition—a conservative attempt to preserve peace—declared the colonies in a state of rebellion, and ordered more troops to America. Independence was very near.

Causes of the Revolution

The events from 1763 to 1776 did not make the revolution inevitable; there was no single incident or event that can explain the coming of the Revolution. As with most wars, the causes were many and complex. Prior to 1763 the English colonies had benefited from both their political and economic roles within the British Empire. After 1763 new policies challenged the political and economic freedoms, and the Americans felt that the old days were surely better than the new ones.

The Revolution was not merely a struggle of the good guys against the bad guys, of freedom versus tyranny. King George III, "The royal brute of Britain," was generally a poor administrator, but he had compromised many times. The Boston Tea Party, however, was too much for him to take. The Intolerable Acts were not merely his doing, they reflected the sentiments of the English public at that time. In short, political and economic leaders on both sides of the Atlantic were responsible for the war. Over the years historians have pondered the causes of the American Revolution, and they will continue to do so. But whatever view one holds, the Revolution came, lasting until 1783.

Military Action

With the opposing armies ready to strike, a general survey of the military action is in order. In 1775 the war opened with fighting at Lexington and Concord and with the fall of Fort Ticonderoga. The British in Boston, afraid they would be isolated by the Americans, fought the Battle of Bunker Hill in June. Remember the slogan, "Don't shoot 'til you see the whites of their

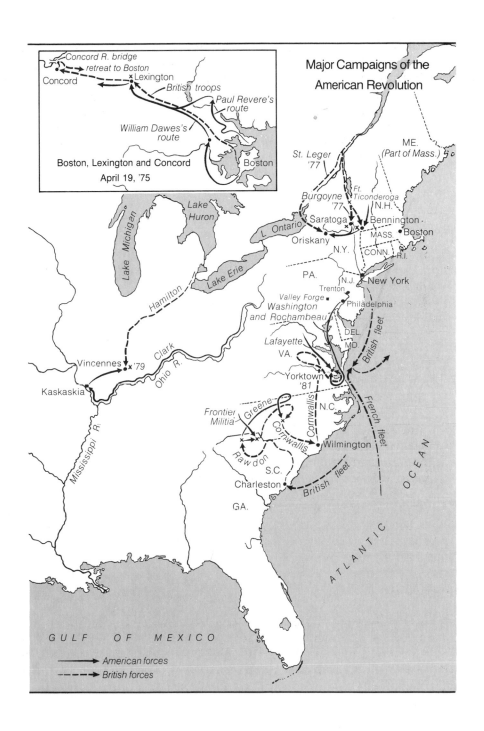

Major Campaigns of the American Revolution

Concord R. bridge
retreat to Boston
Concord
Lexington
British troops
Paul Revere's route
William Dawes's route
Boston, Lexington and Concord
April 19, '75
Boston

Lake Michigan
Lake Huron
Lake Erie
L. Ontario

St. Leger '77
Burgoyne '77
Ft. Ticonderoga
N.H.
Saratoga
Bennington
Oriskany
Boston
ME. (Part of Mass.)
N.Y.
MASS.
CONN.
R.I.
PA.
Trenton
N.J.
New York
Valley Forge
Washington and Rochambeau
Philadelphia
DEL.
MD.
Lafayette
VA.
Yorktown '81
Cornwallis
N.C.
British fleet
French fleet
Frontier Militia
Greene
Cornwallis
Wilmington
Rawdon
S.C.
Charleston
British fleet
GA.

Hamilton
Clark
Vincennes '79
Ohio R.
Kaskaskia
Mississippi R.

ATLANTIC OCEAN

GULF OF MEXICO

American forces
British forces

eyes"? It came out of this battle, which ended with more than 1054 British casualties out of 2600 troops. The Americans lost 400 of their 1500 soldiers here. The victory actually was a hollow one, for by March 1776 the British left the city, deciding to make their stand elsewhere.

Having left Boston, the British troops concentrated on the Middle Colonies. William Howe, a tall, handsome, and indecisive general, chased George Washington's forces across New York and through New Jersey. Thomas Paine wrote of these crucial times: "These are the times that try men's souls." And they were. Washington's army was in retreat, and the British occupied New York. One observer wrote, "Many of the rebels who were killed were without shoes or stockings and several were observed to have only linen drawers . . . without any proper shirt or waistcoats." The year 1776 was so good for the British that at the end of the year Washington was forced to try a desperate ploy. On Christmas night he crossed the ice-filled Delaware River and defeated the Hessians at Trenton; he then moved to Princeton, where he forced Cornwallis, the British commander, to retreat. The ebbing American morale received a much needed boost.

In commemorating the American bicentennial, numerous television specials and public celebrations have focused on 1776 not as the year of Washington's victory over the Hessians at Trenton but as the year of the Declaration of Independence and the birth of a nation. From our modern perspective, independence seems to have been the goal of most colonials for a long period. This was hardly the case. Even with the fighting at Lexington and Concord and the decision of the Second Continental Congress to take an armed stand, most Americans were not committed to independence. It must be realized that the Second Continental Congress met in May 1775, while independence was not declared until July 1776. What was the delay? With independence, the colonials actually were rebelling against their English heritage; this was not easy to do. Not only were many Americans uncommitted, but many supported the king—and the Loyalists created novel problems. Of course, the events in 1775 and 1776 caused most Americans to agree in wondering about the future.

The Declaration of Independence

During the Second Continental Congress, Richard Henry Lee of Virginia offered the motion that "these United Colonies are and of right ought to be free and independent states." After much debate the resolution carried on July 2, 1776—not July 4. It was on July 4 that Congress accepted the Declaration of Independence, which was the document that explained the reasons for independence. This document, written by Thomas Jefferson with the help of Ben-

With the signing of the Declaration of Independence Americans were committed to the cause of complete revolution.

jamin Franklin and John Adams, listed 27 grievances. It is interesting to note that the king rather than Parliament was blamed throughout the document (Parliament was not mentioned directly). The document also contained a description of the general principles of government, and this first section is today considered the most important: "We hold these Truths to be self-evident, that all Men are created equal, that they are endowed by their Creator with certain unalienable Rights, that among these are Life, Liberty, and the Pursuit of Happiness." This is considered one of the great statements of liberty in the Western world, and Thomas Jefferson is deemed a great equalitarian (even though he was a slave owner). Actually, there was nothing new or unusual in the Declaration of Independence; it was only a statement of what had happened in the past, what was happening in the present, and why. It was a statement of a rebel Congress at war, and by signing the document every delegate was risking his life. Franklin wrote, "We must all hang together or assuredly we shall all hang separately." Still, in 1776, even with the victories at Trenton and Princeton, it seemed inconceivable that independence would ever become a reality.

How could a strong imperial power be defeated by a weak, disorganized group of 13 colonies? The colonists had few advantages, and even viewing the situation from our modern perspective, it is difficult to see how the war was won. The Continental army was poorly trained and badly staffed. One critic wrote that it was merely, "a receptacle for ragamuffins." Throughout the war the army was plagued by critical shortages of ammunition, food, clothing, and medical supplies. The colonies also lacked a strong central government to direct and successfully finance the war effort. Inflation and more than 14 different currencies in circulation were among the most obvious economic deficiencies. And the Continental navy was not strong enough to cut the English off from their supply lines or to break the blockade of American ports. Despite such major disadvantages, the colonies possessed some advantages. The Americans were defending their own land; the English had to fight a war more than 3000 miles from home—one which was becoming increasingly unpopular there. Most of their supplies had to be shipped across the Atlantic. Much of the British strategy during the war was based on overconfidence and miscalculation; also, most British leaders were weak and cocky. Among the British commanders was Lord George Germain, who had been court-martialed for cowardice in 1760; he was placed in charge of the army in the field. When William Pitt heard who the commanders were, he remarked, "I do not know what effect these names have on the enemy, but I confess they make me tremble." The British blunders, coupled with the American determination to fight, eventually led to American victory. However, by 1777 the end was not yet in sight.

1777: Year of Decision

By 1777 the British had formulated a master plan. General John Burgoyne was to lead a large army down the St. Lawrence, via Lake Champlain and the Hudson, to Albany; Lieutenant Colonel Barry St. Leger was to travel with a smaller force from Lake Ontario to Albany; finally, General Howe was to move from New York to Albany. The offensive failed. Howe, who decided that he would join the other two armies at Albany later, first planned to move against Philadelphia. Howe had acquired a mistress in New York—Mrs. Joshua Loring, the beautiful wife of one of his officers. To him, the move against Philadelphia, a short distance from New York, made much more sense. St. Leger also hesitated to move his army, and when he did he was defeated at

French General Marquis de LaFayette was one of the most famous foreign officers of the American Revolution.

the bloody battle of Oriskany. "Gentlemen Johnny" Burgoyne moved slowly down the St. Lawrence with more than 7000 men, accompanied by over 1000 women. His huge caravan moved so slowly that it was an easy target for American snipers. On October 17, 1777, Burgoyne was forced to surrender to General Horatio Gates at the Battle of Saratoga after suffering very heavy losses.

The Battle of Saratoga is considered the turning point of the war. It changed the American mood to optimism but more importantly it caused action abroad. The secret support that the French had been providing the Americans now became public, and in 1778 the French signed a treaty of alliance. European historians have called this aid crucial. Some American historians have acknowledged that it helped but have felt that the Americans really won their own revolution. In some ways the treaty was more of a liability than an asset. American forces relaxed as they waited for the trained

French army to take the field, while British attitudes toward the Americans hardened. Spain entered the war both as a French ally and to keep alive its claims to the Trans-Appalachian area. Since the Americans had been involved in earlier colonial wars against the French, it was not always easy to accept them as allies.

During the winter of 1777–78 Washington and his beaten army encamped at Valley Forge. Tradition has deeply engraved this incident in the minds of many Americans, who picture Washington kneeling in the snow at Valley Forge, praying. Although many soldiers did suffer from lack of food, clothing, and medicine, the winter of 1777–78 was no worse than earlier winters. Much of the suffering was due to the greed of American farmers, who felt that British silver and gold were more valuable than worthless Continental currency. Also, recent archaeological investigations have revealed that while the men in the barracks were eating horse and mule meat, the officers were eating rather well. New disclosures concerning Washington's expense account lead one to further question the motives of Washington and his officers.

Victory

From 1778 to the end of the war much of the military action took place in the South. Sir Henry Clinton became the new British commander and moved from Philadelphia to New York, where he remained the rest of the war. Fighting took place in the colonies of Georgia, North Carolina, and South Carolina. After the Americans drove the British army out of these colonies, General Charles Cornwallis was ordered to attack and conquer Virginia. In October 1781, at Yorktown, Cornwallis was defeated by a combined French and American force. The American victory was at hand, and the bands played "The World Turned Upside Down." In 1783 the Treaty of Paris was signed.

During the Revolution, Ben Franklin, John Jay, and John Adams had been sent to Europe to obtain assistance and to negotiate a peace. Formal negotiations began in April 1782, and much talk involved quibbling over the words "the thirteen colonies" and "the United States of America." Once this matter was resolved, negotiations proceeded quickly. Pressure from England and news of recent American military victories moved the British negotiators to agree to the Treaty of Paris in 1783. This treaty was on the whole a generous one for the United States. Britain acknowledged the independence of the United States and fixed its boundaries along the line of the St. Lawrence-Great Lakes system to the north, the Mississippi River to the west, and the thirty-first parallel to the south. Both sides possessed free navigation of the Mississippi. British creditors were to meet "no lawful impediment" in recovering their

The surrender of Lord Cornwallis at Yorktown brought
an end to the American Revolution.

debts. Loyalists were to be immune from persecution and were to have their
property restored. What was sorely lacking in the treaty was a trade agreement
between the United States and Britain, a country who now possessed a near
monopoly of world trade. Franklin had hopefully written to the English: "What
would you say to a proposition of a family compact between England, France,
and America? America would be as happy as the Sabine girl if she could be
the means of uniting in perpetual peace her father and her husband." But this
was only a future hope. The United States was now on her own.

Indians in the Revolution

It is true that the War of Independence was a war in which two Anglo-Saxon peoples fought each other. But it is also true that both Indians and blacks fought in the Revolution, and on both sides. Initially, both the British and the colonists avoided the use of Indians, but allies became necessary. The English openly recruited the Creek and the Cherokee, while the Iroquois League of Six Nations supported both sides. Many tribes were racked by dissension between Pro-American and Pro-British factions, so by the conclusion of the war many Indian nations were crumbling from within.

Mohawk Joseph Brant was England's most capable ally in the frontier campaigns.

Exploitation of the Indians occurred on the frontier where General George Rogers Clark and General John Sullivan were active. Clark used psychological warfare against the Indians, such as tomahawking four bound Indians in full view of an Indian settlement. Sullivan believed in "civilization or death to all American savages"; his atrocities included the flaying of Indians and the making of boot tops for his troops from their skins. Of course, historians have called Mohawk warrior Joseph Brant the most savage fighter of the Revolution. Joseph Brant, adopted by Indian agent William Johnson, became the first member of his tribe to read and write English. He also became a convert to Anglicanism and worked to translate the Bible into the Mohawk language. As a British colonel, he led devastating attacks on the settlements of Cherry Valley, New York and Wyoming, Pennsylvania. The success of his raids led patriots to describe him and his men as "robbers, murderers, and traitors." With the conclusion of the war, Brant attempted to further the land claims of the Six Nations, but his efforts were in vain; the Treaty of 1783 made no mention of Indian rights. During the war, however, Congress had set up Northern, Middle, and Southern, departments to handle Indian affairs. The United States now inherited from the British jurisdiction over Indian affairs and a responsibility for protecting Indian rights.

Land in the West was thrown open to settlement, and many pioneers reflected the belief that "animals vulgarly called Indian had no natural right to the land."

Blacks in the Revolution

Most colonies had laws excluding blacks from militia service, but with a confrontation approaching, these laws were overlooked. Crispus Attucks, an unemployed black, was killed in the Boston Massacre of 1770. Black minutemen were at Lexington and Concord in 1775. Washington, a plantation owner, eventually agreed to enlist free blacks, but he continued to push for the exclusion of slaves. By 1777 the Continental army needed all blacks—slave or free. Slaves who served in the military usually were promised their freedom. During the war 5000 blacks fought in the Continental army and participated in all military action. Peter Salem and Salem Poor, for example, were cited for acts of outstanding heroism at the Battle of Bunker Hill, while Oliver Cromwell and Prince Whipple were with Washington in 1776 when he crossed the Delaware. Blacks also served admirably in the American navy. The British also actively recruited blacks to fight against the colonists. Lord Dunmore,

Crispus Attucks was a black colonial killed during the Boston Massacre.

British governor of Virginia, used blacks in his Ethiopian regiment. He also used biological warfare by sending diseased blacks into the American lines. When the war ended, the British were determined to keep the blacks who had come into their military service. While thousands of blacks had been given freedom, many others had become the personal property of British officers and soldiers. With the conclusion of the war they removed their slaves with practically no American interference.

Was the Revolution a true revolution? Some historians today say that the Revolution was merely a conservative movement, with Americans trying to preserve what they claimed was their property. In terms of the results, the war was a true revolution. Economic democracy developed as a result of the redistribution of property. More than 100,000 Tories (those who supported the king) left America; their land was confiscated, divided into smaller units, and sold to farmers.

Social equality also made great strides. Freedom was granted to blacks who had served in the armed forces. And after the war a number of abolitionist societies emerged; by 1792 all states from Massachusetts to Virginia had antislavery societies dedicated to the abolition of the slave trade and to gradual abolition of slavery itself. Northern state legislatures were providing for gradual emancipation. A Northern court upheld these sentiments with the Quock Walker case in Massachusetts, which declared that slavery was inconsistent with the new state constitution's stipulation that all men were free and equal. Property qualifications also were lowered for voting and officeholding. Americans of the 1780s hardly believed in popular democracy, but they were letting more Americans vote and hold office than ever before. Emphasis was given also to state-supported education, while separation of church and state continued apace.

In 1763 the Americans were part of a powerful British empire; in 1776 the Americans had asserted their right to govern themselves; and in 1783 they were given complete independence. The growing feeling of nationalism had been impossible to contain, and the 13 states went on their own course. The course would have to include a central government, but the form and direction of that government was surely unclear in 1783. Trial and tribulation would eventually lead from the Articles of Confederation to the Constitution and, finally, to George Washington as first American president.

Essay

Blacks in the American Revolution

During the 1600s each English colony was responsible for raising its own militia to maintain domestic order and defend its borders against Indians. While every available man in the colony was supposed to serve in the militia, the arming of blacks, even free ones, presented a special problem. Eventually every colony passed laws barring blacks from military service. But these restrictions did not last, for wartime necessity lent itself to the use of free blacks and slaves. In many cases slaves were offered freedom as a reward for outstanding performances. Black service was most noticeable during the French and Indian War, when they served in many capacities from soldier to scout to servant. Generally they served in unsegregated units and received equal pay with whites.

Blacks were also evident in the events leading to the American Revolution. Crispus Attucks, for example, a runaway slave, was the first American killed during the controversy known as the Boston Massacre. Blacks also served with the Massachusetts Minutemen and were involved in the fighting at Lexington and Concord. Lemuel Haynes, one of Ethan Allen's Green Mountain Boys, participated in the capture of Fort Ticon-

Peter Salem pictured as shooting Major John Pitcairn at the Battle of Bunker Hill.

deroga. Peter Salem is said to have fired the shot that killed John Pitcairn, leader of the British forces at the Battle of Bunker Hill, while Salem Poor was officially recognized for bravery.

It would seem that their extraordinary action in the early stages of the Revolution would have won them a permanent place in the military; this was not the case. Fear was raised, particularly by slaveowners; George Washington, commander in chief of the Continental army, prohibited the enlistment of blacks. His decision agreed with most slaveholders, who felt that they would lose their human property and that the revolution would serve the slaves as a road to freedom. George Washington, among many other revolutionary leaders, also assumed that black soldiers would be cowardly and inferior to white soldiers.

While the Continental army outlawed the use of blacks, the British army was openly recruiting them to overcome an immediate manpower shortage. This British policy, plus an American manpower shortage of its own, caused Washington by 1776 to recommend the use of free blacks as soldiers. But no slaves were to be used. The continuation of the war caused a critical shortage of men for the American army. State quotas were established to meet these new needs, but white men were still reluctant to sign up for extended service. More and more states turned to free blacks to meet their quotas. Some states even turned to the enlistment of slaves with a promise of eventual freedom and with a plan for compensating their masters. The states of Rhode Island and Connecticut went so far as to organize black battalions of slaves, offering enlistees freedom, equal pay with whites, and remuneration to slave owners up to $400 for each slave. In addition, whites could avoid service by providing a substitute; many Northern slaveholders sent their slaves in their place.

While many Northern states eventually allowed military service for both free blacks and slaves, the state of Maryland was the only Southern state to follow this practice. Even when the British army seized Georgia and invaded South Carolina, these states remained adamant in their refusal to enlist blacks, fearing insurrection. Meanwhile thousands of slaves joined the British army in hope that they would receive freedom. The basic fear of a slave revolt and the widespread belief that blacks were inferior to whites limited their use in the Southern Continental army.

Both Britain and America were less reluctant to employ blacks in their respective navies. Blacks were used widely in the Continental navy and on state naval vessels and privateers. They served as gunners, pilots, sailors, and cooks. Whether it was in the army or navy, blacks participated in virtually every military engagement from Lexington to Yorktown. They usually served in integrated units, although certain jobs such as fifers and drummers were almost always black. They served admirably in the war effort, and some even emerged as war heroes. But they are today the forgotten men of the American Revolution.

It is true that some blacks did make specific gains from the war. Some slaves received freedom, as promised. But many white masters attempted to reenslave their property at the conclusion of the war, while Virginia sold the blacks who had been in its navy back into slavery. In fact, it appears that more blacks received their freedom by serving with the British army than with the Continental army. These liberated blacks eventually settled in the West Indies, Florida, and Canada. The position of blacks in the North was substantially improved after the war and eventually slavery was outlawed there. This does not mean, however, that political, social, and economic equality was gained; that was hardly the case. In the South few slaves participated in the American cause, so few received their freedom. The slave system continued to prosper there, and the cotton gin soon would give slavery new economic meaning. While there were few black heroes and fewer black monuments honoring them to emerge from the Revolution, black Americans should be commended for their valiant efforts in our Revolutionary War. They helped to achieve a lasting independence. ∎

Suggested Reading

A good general survey of the revolutionary era is *The Birth of the Republic, 1763–1789* (1956) by EDMUND MORGAN.

A detailed series on the evolution of British imperial policy is found in LAWRENCE H. GIPSON's 15-volume study, *The British Empire before the American Revolution* (1936–1970).

Two differing interpretations of the coming of the revolution are *Origins of the American Revolution* (1943) by JOHN MILLER, and *The Origin of the American Revolution, 1759–1766* (1956) by BERNARD KNOLLENBERG.

EDMUND and HELEN M. MORGAN, in *The Stamp Act Crisis: Prologue to Revolution* (1962), discuss this critical piece of legislation from the American perspective, while B. W. LABAREE in *The Boston Tea Party* (1964) and H. B. ZOBEL in *The Boston Massacre* reveal the importance of these events.

The circumstances surrounding the signing of the Declaration of Independence are detailed in CARL L. BECKER's *The Declaration of Independence* (1922).

Indian affairs are covered by JACK SOSIN in *The Revolutionary Frontier 1763–1783* (1967) and by BARBARA GRAYSON in *The Iroquois in the American Revolution* (1975).

Military events are well documented in HOWARD H. PECKHAM's *The War for Independence* (1958).

CHAPTER 4

Creating a Nation

Time Line

?–A.D. 1492	Migration and evolution of American Indian societies
1492	Christopher Columbus lands in West Indies—beginning of European exploration
1607–1732	Establishment of 13 English colonies
1775–1783	American Revolution
1776	Declaration of Independence
1777	Articles of Confederation are drafted
1781	Ratification of Articles of Confederation
1785	Land Ordinance
1786	Shays' Rebellion
1787	Northwest Ordinance Constitutional Convention
1789	George Washington becomes first president
1791	National Bank Act
1792	Reelection of George Washington to presidency
1794	Whiskey Rebellion
1795	Jay's Treaty
1796	Election of John Adams
1797–1800	XYZ Affair and Undeclared War with France
1798	Alien and Sedition Act
1800	Election of Thomas Jefferson
1803	Louisiana Purchase
1803	*Marbury* v. *Madison*
1789–1797	Presidency of George Washington

1812–1815	War of 1812
1816–1824	Era of Good Feelings
1846–1848	Mexican War
1861–1865	Civil War
1865–1877	Reconstruction
1877–1900	Industrialization and urbanization
1900–1916	Progressive Era
1917–1918	World War I
1930s	Depression and New Deal
1941–1945	World War II
1945–1960	Post-war politics
1950–1953	Korean War
1950–1960	Civil rights movement
1961–1973	Vietnam War
1976	Bicentennial celebration

Today critics of national policy point to Watergate, the energy crisis, and inflation as symptoms of decaying government and lack of presidential leadership. But a time when there was no president to lead at all, a Congress without power to tax or regulate commerce, and no judiciary is unthinkable. If there were no government at all and you had to start one, what would you do? Would a king be preferable to a president? How about two presidents? Would a court system really be necessary? Doesn't the power to tax seem unfair, even ridiculous? The government can survive on contributions. But how much would you voluntarily contribute?

The Americans of the revolutionary period found themselves with 13 independent states and a fear of a powerful central government, for they had rebelled against a strong imperial system. So Congress adopted the Articles of Confederation. The dangers of a strong executive and central government were avoided, but other pitfalls were encountered. Another framework of government was necessary; delegates came to Philadelphia, and the Constitution was written. With this vague document as a guide, Washington launched the ship of state, and it continued to sail under the command of John Adams and Thomas Jefferson.

Forming a Government

The nation emerged from the Revolution deeply scarred. It is not easy to fight a war in your own country. Many colonial cities had been occupied, while the surrounding countryside mirrored the past struggle. But independence had been achieved. Cheering crowds and booming guns made Americans forget the fight that had just ended and look to the future. One patriot wrote, "I look forward to the happy days our children will see." The future, however, of 13 *united* states looked dim indeed.

With the signing of the Declaration of Independence, the states and the Second Continental Congress were forced to create new forms of government. Most Americans demanded that government guidelines be in written form in order to limit and define the powers of government. States were accustomed to colonial charters, and most Americans felt that the lack of a written British constitution had been a handicap. State constitutions were written now by relatively young men, such as Thomas Jefferson (33) and James Madison (27), who were well grounded in political theory and who attempted to set up a practical framework of government. These new constitutions hardly were drawn up in the most democratic way. They usually were drafted by legislative bodies and became effective without consulting the voters; the Massachusetts constitution of 1780 was an exception. Generally, all state constitutions featured a government that emphasized a weak executive branch and a strong legislative branch. After the colonial experience with the king of England, this is no surprise. The constitutions also reflected the past experience of freeborn English citizens by setting down their basic rights and liberties. The writers of these documents attempted to balance liberty with authority by placing power in the hands of the legislatures. While the state constitutions were being written, Congress struggled with the difficult problem of federalism—the relationship between the states and the central government.

The Articles of Confederation

It generally was believed that a central government was necessary to protect American rights, coordinate action between states, and deal with Indians and foreign countries. In 1777, under the direction of John Dickinson, the Articles of Confederation were adopted and sent to the states. This first American constitution created a "league" of states in which each state retained "Its sovereignty, freedom, and independence, and every Power, Jurisdiction and rights, which is not by this confederation expressly delegated to the United States, in Congress assembled." The Articles formed a very loose union of states within the framework of a central government; actually, there was little unity between the states (today it still is not unusual for people to say "The United States are acting in league" rather than refer to the United States as an entity).

These Articles, however, were not ratified immediately by the states because the question of ownership of western lands was unsettled. Many of the colonial charters, such as those of Virginia and New York, gave sea-to-sea grants. Because of these charters, many states claimed ownership to land in the West. Other states had fixed charters and felt that the states with western claims should relinquish them to the central government. Many states refused to ratify the Articles until the claims question was settled. But this was easier said than done. Many of the claims involved a background of lengthy and bitter disputes. For example, long before the Revolution, Virginia and Pennsylvania had struggled over land in the Ohio Valley. Pennsylvania said that it had purchased land there from Indians, while Virginia quoted its colonial charter. However, on March 1, 1781, the first constitution of the United States finally went into effect, and "the evening was ushered in by an elegant exhibition of fireworks and ushered out by a washtub or two of liquor."

In many ways the celebration was premature, for the years under the Confederation were trying ones—wrought with problems and pitfalls. In es-

ARTICLES

OF

Confederation

AND

Perpetual Union

BETWEEN THE

S T A T E S

OF

NEW-HAMPSHIRE, MASSACHUSETTS-BAY, RHODE-ISLAND AND PROVIDENCE PLANTATIONS, CONNECTICUT, NEW-YORK, NEW-JERSEY, PENNSYLVANIA, DELAWARE, MARYLAND, VIRGINIA, NORTH-CAROLINA, SOUTH-CAROLINA AND GEORGIA.

L A N C A S T E R:
PRINTED BY F R A N C I S B A I L E Y.
M,DCC,LXXVII.

The Articles of Confederation became the first American Constitution, yet were only a temporary government framework.

sence, the Articles made little noticeable change in the framework of government that had evolved under the First and Second Continental Congresses. The Continental Congress now became the Congress of the Confederation. Under the Articles, very limited power was given to the central government. The independence and sovereignty of the states—preserved by the Revolution—were the guiding principles of the Articles. In turn, the powers of Congress were limited. In that body, each state was represented by not less than two nor more than seven members, but each state had only one vote. The approval of 9 of 13 states was required for important decisions, such as waging war or raising an army, and no major changes could be made in the Articles unless there was unanimous approval. Congress did reserve the power to appoint executive departments, but there was no provision for a national court system. Due to the revolutionary experience, Congress was given no power to tax imports, to regulate domestic and foreign commerce, or to raise money. Congress could requisition money from the states, but the states easily could refuse the requisitions. Nor did Congress have the power to maintain a standing army; it had to request troops from the states. Congress was so handicapped by many of these restrictions that eventually some states no longer bothered to send representatives. And John Hancock, president of the Congress, even stopped attending sessions. With these weaknesses, it is no wonder that the period from 1781 to 1789 appears "critical."

The Critical Period

The period of the Articles of Confederation (1781–89) was both critical and creative. In fact, the most creative aspects of the period involved the problem of western lands. Should the British policy toward the West be followed? Should the West be opened to settlement or sold to greedy land companies? These were only two of the questions that were being discussed in the 1780s. It seemed virtually impossible to stop the flood of land speculators and settlers into the West, so Congress decided upon a policy that would dispose of western lands, provide orderly government in them, and at the same time acquire needed income. It must be remembered that the Congress did not have power to tax and that large debts had been incurred during the Revolution. The passage of the Land Ordinance of 1785 provided for the distribution of the public domain, including the surveying of land before settlement and eventual sale. Land was surveyed into townships 6 miles square, each containing 36 sections of 640 acres (1 mile square). In each township, Section 16 was reserved for the maintenance of public schools. After the land was surveyed it was sold at public auction, with even-numbered townships being sold by sections and odd-numbered sections as a whole. While the ordinance favored speculators rather than small farmers, the concept of selling the public domain continued until 1862, when the Homestead Act climaxed the movement for free land. Without specific authority from the Articles to dispose of the public domain, Congress had established a rational system of land distribution.

A group of land speculators then approached Congress and voiced a need for government in the western area. Congress responded with the Northwest Ordinance of 1787. This law created the Northwest Territory, an area north of the Ohio River, where civil liberties were ensured, slavery was prohibited, and education was encouraged. This area would be divided into three to five states. Statehood was to be attained in three stages. Initially, a governor, a secretary, and three judges were to be elected by Congress. When the district contained 5000 free white males, a local assembly could be established; when it contained 60,000, it could apply to Congress for admission as a state. This outstanding law established a model that was followed many times in America's seemingly inevitable expansion west.

The settlement of the Northwest Territory, however, did not always go smoothly, for the area already was inhabited by Indians. The early policy of Congress was to warn settlers against purchasing or squatting on Indian land. But enforcement of such regulations was virtually impossible, so the government formally negotiated with tribes for title to their land through a series of agreements, better known as treaties. According to the treaties, tribes agreed to cede land title in return for goods, money, the right to continue to hunt and fish, and other benefits of white society. This became the legal way to acquire Indian land and to open the West to settlement. A series of treaties, such as the Treaty of Fort Stanwix and the Treaty of Fort McIntosh, paved the way for the eventual occupation of the Great Lakes region. Most of the tribes of the Northwest, however, were not anxious to negotiate treaties, for during the 1780s there were few settlers there. But the treaty process that began under the Articles would set the pattern for Indian relations until 1887.

While Congress's policy toward western land may have been creative, its policy toward foreign countries was handicapped severely. The United States under the Articles of Confederation commanded little respect abroad. John Adams noted the cold shoulder he received in London: "They [the European powers] will be pleased to see us weakened, and our growth a little retarded." Also, though Congress could negotiate treaties with foreign countries, it lacked the power to hold those foreign nations—or individual states, or even American citizens—to any agreements it made. The British took the United States so lightly they did not even send a delegation to America. And the British reneged on their promise to evacuate frontier posts inside the American boundary in the Great Lakes area; the British argued that the United States had not lived up to its obligations to collect private debts and return Loyalist property—this was all true. British officials also discouraged trade with America by placing heavy import taxes on goods from America and by closing the West Indies. Other nations were also reluctant to trade. The United States owed money to France and Holland for money borrowed during the Revolution; but with Congress unable to tax, raising money was a difficult task. Trouble existed not only abroad and along the northern borders but in the

South where the Spanish were making life difficult. The Spanish now were settled in the Southwest, and there was fear that they might cross over the Mississippi or even begin to claim part of the Trans-Appalachian West. Foreign matters were hardly in fine shape, but the country was new and the Articles of Confederation were still in their infancy. Ultimately, it was neither the West nor foreign affairs that brought the Articles to a critical stage, but general economic matters arising between states and within states.

Shays' Rebellion

Congress did not have the power to regulate commerce, so individual states regulated their own commerce. This frequently led to interstate squabbles and jealousies. States began to tax produce and imports from other states. States also suffered from lack of gold and silver; in fact, money was so scarce that some debts were paid in salt pork, whiskey, and tobacco. Congress faced similar problems; Continental money was supposed to be redeemed by gold and silver, but little of either was to be had—the "worthless Continental" was exactly that. Out of frustration, more than seven states began to print their own money, but this money was usually worthless even within the state's own boundaries. A depression followed the war, land values were shrinking, and industry was on the decline. While it is true that by the late 1780s conditions were improving—the depression was ending and industry was improving again—in the mid-1780s days were dark, particularly in Massachusetts.

> My name is Shays, in former days in Pelham I did dwell, Sir; but now I'm forced to leave the place because I did rebel, Sir; within the state I lived of late, by Satan's foul invention, in Pluto's cause against the law; I raised an insurrection.

And he did—an insurrection that reflected the growing frustration with the government under the Articles and with the state of Massachusetts.

The post-war depression hit the state of Massachusetts particularly hard, for the state legislature was controlled by wealthy Bostonians. In the face of mounting debts and increasing foreclosures, the legislature refused to print more money or pass other relief measures. Jails were jammed with farmers who were unable to pay their debts. According to a report from one town: "We are almost ready to cry out under the burden of our taxes as the children of Israel did in Egypt when they were required to make bricks without straw, for we cannot find that there is money enough in the town to pay." The discontent mounted until in 1786 a veteran of the Revolution, Daniel Shays, along with Samuel Ely and Luke Day, took direct action. Shays tried to in-

Shays' rebellion revealed the inherent weakness of
the Articles of Confederation and spurred government
leaders to demand a change.

terfere with the courts, and some 400 men demonstrated against the state
legislature. When the rebels attacked the federal arsenal at Springfield, state
troops were called out and quickly put down the rebellion. The government
captured 150 farmers, and Shays fled to Vermont. The importance of Shays'
Rebellion is not that it caused the Massachusetts legislature to change its
direction and accede to some of the demands but that it caused many Americans to seek a revision of the Articles. Washington wrote, "We are fast verging
to anarchy and confusion." The Articles were referred to as a "rope of sand."

Thirty nine delegates to the constitutional convention approved the final document; a difficult ratification fight, however, lay ahead.

The Constitutional Convention

In March 1785 representatives from Virginia and Maryland gathered at Washington's home to discuss a dispute involving the use of the Potomac River. After this dispute was settled, they talked generally about the Articles of Confederation and proposed a meeting the following year in which all states would be present. The meeting at Annapolis was a disappointment, however—only five states sent delegates. One delegate suggested that Congress send invitations for a meeting to propose changes "necessary to render the constitution of the federal government adequate to the exigencies of the Union. . . ." Congress reluctantly agreed, and in May 1787, 55 men met in Philadelphia and wrote the Constitution of the United States. The Articles, however, had not been a complete failure. They were a by-product of the Revolution and reflected the desires and apprehensions of a new republic. But a more permanent framework of government seemed to be needed.

Who were the men that came to this Philadelphia meeting, and why did they vote to rewrite the constitution? Generally, these delegates represented the best of America in 1787. They were well educated and fairly young; the most common profession among them was law. These men were not demigods but young aggressive Americans with a desire to create a nation. In 1913 Charles Beard wrote the sensational book *An Economic Interpretation of the Constitution of the United States.* In it he attempted to prove that the Constitution was a document written exclusively by wealthy men for the good of wealthy men and that it had been forced on an unwilling population. While it is true that most of the delegates were men of wealth, it is erroneous to conclude that they were motivated purely by selfish motives. Since these were the cream of the crop in postrevolutionary America, it is not surprising to find that they were men of property.

Many of these delegates did come to the meeting to create a document that would protect property, but not necessarily their own. Many of them came to create a stable central government, to build a basis for a permanent foreign policy, to stem the anarchy that was growing out of incidents such as Shays' rebellion. While one is unable to measure or test the motives of individuals precisely, many of these men had risked their lives in the Revolution and surely did not want that Revolution to have occurred in vain. This is why, in May 1787, the delegates voted—contrary to their instructions—not merely to revise the Articles but also to write, in secret meetings, an entirely new document. While they generally approved of a stronger central government than that authorized under the Articles, they found themselves divided on numerous major issues.

Those attending included such noteworthy men as George Washington, hero of the Revolutionary War and much respected, Ben Franklin, now 81, in ill health, the ancient patriarch of the meeting, James Madison of Virginia, whose meticulous journal is the major source of information on the convention, and Alexander Hamilton, a fiscal genius with a sharp mind and a sharp tongue to match. But even these leaders could not stop the bitter clashes between north and south, large and small states, and certain key individuals.

The weather was hot and humid and the debates were hotter. Most delegates agreed that the proposed new national Congress should make laws, but they did not agree on the composition of the legislature. Some suggested that states have one vote as under the articles, others suggested that representation be based on population. The large-state delegates found their sentiments expressed in the Virginia Plan, which held that larger states should have a larger representation. The small states' sentiments were expressed in the New Jersey Plan, which proposed that a small state should have the same voting power as a large state. At one time this disagreement threatened the entire meeting. Finally, in July, a compromise was reached. Congress would consist of two houses: a Senate in which each state would have two senators and a House of Representatives in which each state would have at least one representative, with the number of other representatives to be determined by population. One compromise was hammered out, but it was only one of many.

Delegates also had to solve the problem of balancing power between the central government and the states. Obviously, the Articles had handicapped the federal government, but there was a feeling that too powerful a central government would lead to another revolution. Areas of authority eventually were defined. The central government was given power over national matters, such as war and peace, taxation, commerce, and foreign relations. The states were given jurisdiction over local matters, such as roadway construction. In some areas, such as taxation, their authority overlapped. Here were the seeds of our present federal system.

The delegates further agreed that one person—the president—should be made chief executive and that the president would be elected for four-year terms, not for life. Since many of the delegates feared direct election of the executive by all the people, they agreed upon a system of presidential electors,

Benjamin Franklin had been active in the formation of the early government system and urged swift acceptance of the federal constitution.

who would be chosen by the states. To ensure a system of checks and balances, the Congress would inaugurate laws, the president would execute them, and the court system would interpret and apply them. Finally, South and North compromised by having only three-fifths of the slaves count in Southern representation and by extending the life of the slave trade until 1808. After that date the importation of slaves would be illegal. The convention had opened on May 25, and by September 12 the final draft was submitted for approval. The work of writing a Constitution had been done, but it had not been an easy job. Compromises were evident throughout the document, while many parts were vague. When the final document was read, Ben Franklin, weak from age and unable to stand, said, "So I hope each of you will join me . . . and show your approval of the whole effort by signing it and supporting it before the people." Thirty-nine of the delegates signed the document, and it next went to Congress and then to special state ratifying conventions, not to the state legislatures. Meanwhile, the delegates retired "to the City Tavern." The easiest part of the job was finished, now approval of nine states had to be secured for the document to be approved. The writers had violated their instructions by writing a new Constitution instead of merely submitting proposals to change the old one. The fight for ratification was on.

The Ratification Fight

Those who stood for the Constitution were referred to as Federalists; those who opposed it were called by their opponents Anti-Federalists. The most outstanding Federalists were Alexander Hamilton, James Madison, and John Jay, authors of *The Federalist,* a collection of 85 essays, which has become the classic commentary on the federal system of government. However, all the capable and able men in America at that time were not necessarily Federalists. Orator Patrick Henry, George Mason—author of the *Virginia Declaration of Rights*—and New York Governor George Clinton all opposed ratification. The arguments against the Constitution varied, but they revolved around the issue of a strong central government versus individual liberty. The Anti-Federalists spoke out for a bill of rights, a one-house legislature, no standing army, no taxing power, and a weak executive branch. It is believed today that if the Constitution had been put to a direct vote of the people, a majority would have opposed it. But the ratification struggles took place within state conventions.

The small states were first to ratify the document. The main battles against the Constitution took place among the larger states, but Federalist unity began to show, and by June 1788 New Hampshire became the ninth state to ratify. Still, New York and Virginia had not ratified, and without these important states there was little hope of success. In both these states ratification barely carried, requiring the guarantee that a bill of rights would be added to the Constitution. North Carolina and Rhode Island waited until the government went into operation before ratification. Now a new government began to function. Would it be better than the government under the Articles? Would the Anti-Federalists' fear of tyranny under a strong central government be justified? Would another "rope of sand" lead to nationwide Shays' rebellions? The nation now looked to one man for answers to many of their questions and doubts—that man was George Washington.

The Presidency of Washington

The first election followed precisely the letter of the Constitution. States selected electors, and each group of electors voted and sent the returns to Congress where the results were to be announced. March 4, 1789 was to be the date for the meeting of the first Congress in New York City, the capital. Travel, however, was difficult. When that day came and passed, one congressman wrote, "The people will forget the new government before it is born." By April 6 a quorum was assembled, and the results were announced. George Washington was elected unanimously to be president, and John Adams was elected vice-president.

The Myth of Washington

Americans know that George Washington was the first president. But people today readily assume that Washington was elected by a popular vote and confuse his term as president with the myths that surround him.

Who was the real George Washington? Even today we don't know for certain. It is difficult to separate the man from the myth. The person who was most responsible for the myth was the Reverend Parson Weems; he wrote, in 1799, a biography of Washington, which pictured him as a man for the ages. Weems made famous the cherry tree story and related the incident of Washington scolding his classmates for fighting: "You shall never, boys, have my consent to a practice so shocking! Shocking even in the slaves and dogs; then how utterly scandalous in little boys at school, who ought to look on one another as brothers." The strength of youthful Washington was revealed by his throwing a stone across the Rappahannock; this feat caused Weems to

THE LIFE

OF

GEORGE WASHINGTON;

WITH

CURIOUS ANECDOTES,

EQUALLY HONOURABLE TO HIMSELF AND
EXEMPLARY TO HIS YOUNG COUNTRYMEN.

A life how useful to his country led!
How loved! while living!—how revered! now dead!
Lisp! lisp! his name, ye children yet unborn!
And with like deeds your own great names adorn.

EIGHTH EDITION—GREATLY IMPROVED.

EMBELLISHED WITH SEVEN ENGRAVINGS.

BY M. L. WEEMS,
FORMERLY RECTOR OF MOUNT-VERNON PARISH.

PHILADELPHIA:
PRINTED FOR THE AUTHOR.
1809.

Parson Weems' biography of George Washington has been most responsible for the Washington myth.

remark, "It would be no easy matter to find a man, now-a-days, who could do it." Washington luckily escaped death at the Battle of the Wilderness in 1755. An Indian there reportedly exclaimed, "Washington was not born to be killed by a bullet! For I had seventeen fair fires at him with my rifle, and after all could not bring him to the ground." Another melodramatic episode described a Continental soldier discovering Washington praying at Valley Forge: "As he approached the spot whom should he behold but the commander in chief of the American armies on his knees at prayer." This ideal man is the Washington of American history and of Weem's biography, which by 1825 had gone through 40 editions; another 40 were to appear over the years. The Washington myth was in full bloom.

While the cherry tree story and other facets of the myth remain, the reality of this man has become more and more obscure. To some Americans he was the inventor of ice cream, to others he was a direct descendent of William the Conqueror. To many, Gilbert Stuart's portrait on the one-dollar bill is the real Washington. He has become a statue, a monument, a name, a saint. But recent critics have questioned his reputation as a faithful husband, as well as boldly asserting that he died from syphilis rather than natural causes. True, the man known as The Old Fox and The Father of His Country was not a genius; nor was he particularly creative, innovative, or a man of the people. He was without a college education; he was an aristocrat and a military hero; and he was the nation's overwhelming choice as the first president.

Washington's Life

Washington was born and raised among the plantation gentry of colonial Virginia. His early education was practical rather than academic, including experiences as surveyor, plantation manager, and soldier in the Virginia militia. After his marriage to the wealthy widow, Martha Curtis, he served in the Virginia legislature, was a county court judge, and became one of the largest landowners in Virginia. His service in the American Revolution is legendary. But his revolutionary exploits today are treated with both praise and contempt. His frequent retreats, his aristocratic air, and his expense accounts are balanced against his administrative skills and perserverence in the face of overwhelming odds. Even before the Constitution was adopted, public opinion had fixed upon him as the living embodiment of the American republic. Although his role in the Constitutional Convention was not essential in the making of important compromises, he helped hold the convention together. At the age of 57, having been elected to the presidency, he reluctantly left Mt. Vernon, his home, with the feeling that he had no "wish beyond that of living and dying an honest man on my own farm." He also wrote, "My movements to the chair of government will be accompanied by feelings not unlike those of a culprit who is going to the place of his execution." Before he traveled to his inauguration in New York City, he borrowed money to clear up local debts and pay traveling expenses. On April 30, 1789 Washington, the Virginia landowner, became Washington, the first president.

On the balcony of Federal Hall, Washington raised his right hand and, with his left hand on the Bible, he took the oath of office. He then delivered his first inaugural address, which assured the listeners of his "pursuit of the public good." He was, however, not a public man. One spectator wrote a description of his address.

> *This great man was agitated and embarrassed more than ever he was by the leveled cannon or pointed musket. He trembled and several times could scarce make out to read, though he must have before. He put part of the fingers of his left hand into the side pocket of his breeches and then tried to take them out without much success. When he came to the words "all the world" he made a flourish with his right hand which left rather an ungainly impression. This first of men had read off his address in the plainest manner. I felt hurt he was not the first in everything.*

George Washington was a human being. He has been called "first in war and first in peace." But his talents were limited. Yet he brought perserverence and administrative skills to the office of the president. He knew he had no tradition to follow, for he reflected, "I walk on untrodden ground."

Washington's Traditions

Was Washington's task to create an American king? No. He definitely believed in the separation of powers and the balance of responsibilities among the executive, legislative, and judicial branches. He rejected the proposal that he be addressed as "His Highness the President of the United States, and Protector of Their Liberties." Yet he did believe in pomp, circumstance, and formality. He was not a commoner; he lived in prestigious houses in New York and Philadelphia, with large staffs of servants and slaves. One congressman wrote that Washington was surrounded constantly by "satellites and sycophants." He and his wife entertained constantly and frequently returned home to Mt. Vernon, where he often resided for three months of the year when Congress was not in session.

He followed his belief in the separation of powers very carefully. Among his ideas on the president's role were several key ones: The president should never propose or even favor pieces of legislation while they were being debated. The legislature made laws and the courts upheld them; the president's role was to administer laws and keep the ship of state afloat. The president should veto legislation only if it was obviously unconstitutional.

While Washington's view of the presidency appeared to be a passive one, this was hardly the case. His niche in history has been measured by the durability of his important decisions and the precedents he established. He organized the executive office in the British traditon by appointing individuals to head each executive department—war, treasury, and state. Congress also provided for the offices of attorney general and postmaster general. These department heads were to be responsible only to Washington. Yet he never tampered with their autonomy and did allow them to influence legislation before Congress.

Washington's choices for these positions were noteworthy. Henry Knox, Washington's Chief of Artillery during the revolution, was a military genius (though once, on a duck-hunting expedition, he did lose two fingers from a gun explosion). He became secretary of war. Thomas Jefferson had served with Washington in the Virginia legislature; one of the most experienced diplomats, he was presently minister to France. He became secretary of state. Alexander Hamilton had been one of Washington's military aides. He understood finances and economics, was a demon for work, and was a logical choice for secretary of the treasury. Attorney General Edmund Randolph and Postmaster General Samuel Osgood were also Washington's friends.

Washington now began to establish tradition and precedent for future presidents to follow. His department heads were to report not to Congress but to the president. While these appointees were confirmed by the Senate, once installed, they were to be removed by the president alone. Initially, these advisers did not meet together as a group, but eventually Washington began calling the group together for meetings and the "cabinet" idea emerged.

Frustrated with the "advice and consent" that the Senate gave him in negotiating an Indian treaty, Washington decided that the Senate would have the ultimate vote on treaties but would not be directly involved in negotiations. The concept of territorial waters also was developed in a very practical way under his direction. The office of the president was taking shape and Washington was anxious to work with Congress to get the government in motion.

First Term as President

One of the most important problems of the new government was financial, and many of the chief items of early legislation had to do with related matters. Under the Articles of Confederation, Alexander Hamilton had presented a finance bill that called for a 5 percent duty on all imports, but the Confederation had been crippled by its inadequate power to tax. On the advice of Hamilton, Congress started the federal revenue system with the passage of a tariff act that placed taxes on enumerated items that varied from 7 to 15 percent. The purpose of this act was merely to raise revenue rather than to protect American industry—such protection was needed later. It was not until

Alexander Hamilton, the first Secretary of the Treasury, was responsible for putting the new government on a sound fiscal foundation.

March 1791 that the first excise tax was created, being a tax on liquor. Responding to the call of New York and Virginia for a new Constitutional Convention to write a supplement to the Constitution that would safeguard rights and liberties, Congress, under the leadership of James Madison, drew up a series of amendments that were ratified by three-fourths of the states in 1791 and became the Bill of Rights. With the significance today of separation of church and state, freedom of speech, the right to bear arms, and due process of law, the Bill of Rights has become one of the most important parts of the Constitution and one of the most closely scrutinized and interpreted documents in our history.

Congress also organized the judicial branch of the government with the passage of the Judiciary Act of 1789. This act established a federal system of 13 district courts and 3 circuit courts. The Supreme Court became the highest federal court; John Jay served as the first chief justice along with five Supreme Court associate justices. The Supreme Court's hallowed sanctuary in Washington, D.C., did not exist in the early days of the republic. The justices brought the Court from region to region. Jay eventually resigned to accept a more prestigious position—governor of New York.

Washington's first term of office primarily was concerned with getting the government in gear and putting it on a sound fiscal course. Here he relied on Alexander Hamilton. Hamilton believed in a strong central government that favored the wealthy and wellborn, for they had the largest stake in government. He had come to mistrust the common people, even though more than 90 percent of the Americans at that time were farmers. While his economic program was a brilliant one, it favored the wealthy and led to a growing split between him and Thomas Jefferson, champion of the common people. With the nation owing more than $50 million and the states, another $25 million, Hamilton proposed the Funding and Assumption Acts. The funding plan proposed the funding, at face value plus interest, of certificates given to soldiers of the Revolution and to merchants. While Hamilton did not profit directly from the funding act, news of the plan leaked to a few rich speculators, who purchased the seemingly worthless certificates and in turn made considerable profits. After much debate, Congress funded the national debt.

The assumption plan proposed that the federal government assume the states' debts. The major problem with the plan was that Northern states owed most of the debts, while the Southern states had paid off most of their borrowing. After Hamilton supported Thomas Jefferson's desire to locate the American capital in a federal district composed of land taken from both Maryland and Virginia, the assumption of state debts also became law. It is interesting to note that in comparison with modern finances Hamilton was dealing only with petty cash. During Washington's administration it cost $600,000 to run the government, while the annual interest on the national debt was only $2.2 million. The government required only $2.8 million yearly in revenues to be financially stable. Hamilton's fiscal policies went a long way toward achieving this goal.

Hamilton's most controversial proposal was the creation of a United States National Bank, modeled after the Bank of England, which was an institution that was privately owned but publicly controlled. One-fifth of Hamilton's bank, however, would be owned by the federal government. Northerners and men of wealth and property agreed with Hamilton. They argued the need for a national bank that would provide a sound currency, control state banks, and give the mercantile community a vested interest in the government. While the Bank Bill passed Congress with 39 votes for and 20 against, Washington worried about its constitutionality and asked the opinion of his cabinet. The debate over the constitutionality of the bank further intensified the philosophical split between Jefferson and Hamilton concerning the role and function of government and went a long way toward pushing American politics into warring camps.

Jefferson and Madison argued that the federal government could only take an action specifically provided for by the Constitution. This "strict-construction" view claimed that such a bank did not fall within the power granted Congress by the Constitution and, further, would be monopolistic. Hamilton took the "loose-construction" view, claiming that the Constitution was a vague document that outlined the general boundaries of government. He believed the Constitution could be interpreted to mean what it only implied. After listening to both sides, Washington signed the Bank Bill. Chartered for 20 years time, the bank was capitalized at $10 million; the government held one-fifth of the stock and appointed one-fifth of the directors. Wealthy citizens received 8.5 percent interest from their investment. The bank proved to be a very successful fiscal venture and helped the nation to move away from the chaotic days of the Confederation.

Indian Policy

The first administration of Washington saw not only the leadership of Hamilton in economic matters and the growing split between Hamilton and Jefferson but also the birth of the government's Indian policy. In 1783, the treaty establishing independence from Britain had made no mention of the American Indian. Still, the Congress in 1786, in creating the Ordinance for the Regulation of Indian Affairs assumed complete jurisdiction over all Indians east of the Mississippi and established two Indian superintendents for a Northern and a Southern district. The Northwest Ordinance of 1787 attempted to set the tone for Indian affairs: "The utmost good faith shall always be observed towards the Indians; their land and property shall never be taken from them without their consent; and in their property, rights and liberty, they shall never be invaded or disturbed, unless in just and lawful wars. . . ." The Constitution gave little direction for the Ordinance only noting that "Congress shall have power . . . to regulate commerce with foreign nations and among the several states, and with the Indian tribes. . . ."

In Washington's administration Indian affairs were placed in the Department of War under Henry Knox. Knox believed that Indians were the true owners of the land in America by the right of prior occupancy—simply put, they were here first. The only way, therefore, to acquire legal title to their land was to draw up agreements between Indian tribes and the federal government in which the tribes consented to give up their titles. This treaty-making process, which had evolved under the Articles, would go through various stages but would remain basic to Indian policy until 1887. Under this system a tribe agreed to cede title to land in return for payment, such as goods, education, money, or the right to hunt and fish "as long as the grass shall grow and the sun shall shine." According to modern critics of Indian policy, treaties became legal ways to drive Indians from their lands. While this may be an extreme view, it did become easy to negotiate treaties that took advantage of Indians. Lack of interpreters, alcohol at treaty councils, and the manipulation of pro-white Indians were only some of the ways agents got Indians to sign illegal documents. But treaties should be viewed only as stopgap measures, for eventually settlers moved into Indian land and forced Indians out.

Treaties were broken, and the onrushing white tide moved the Indians west. "Just and lawful wars" went hand in hand with the treaty process.

The Northwest Territory was the locale of the first Indian wars of the new republic. Treaties in this area north of the Ohio River were not being negotiated fast enough to meet the needs of the settlers, and they sought help from their new government. In 1790 General Josiah Harmar led a punitive expedition, but Little Turtle of the Miamis and Blue Jacket of the Shawnees drove back his poorly trained and equipped army. In 1791 Harmar was followed by Arthur St. Clair, who encountered the same problems as Harmar and whose army suffered 900 casualties out of 1400 men; it was one of the worst defeats of the United States Army at the hands of the Indians—far worse than that of Custer, but hardly as well known. It even caused Washington to exclaim of St. Clair, "He is more than a murderer! How can he answer to his country?" While the victories over Harmar and St. Clair were renewing confidence and unity among the tribes of the Northwest, another expedition under the leadership of General "Mad Anthony" Wayne was being outfitted.

Wayne earned his nickname "Mad Anthony" from daring tactics during the Revolutionary War. In August 1794, with a well-trained and well-equipped

General Anthony Wayne's victory at the Battle of Fallen Timbers was a death blow to the resistance of the tribes in the Northwest territory.

army that included Chicksaw and Chocktaw scouts, Wayne met the fading forces of Little Turtle and in two hours defeated them at the Battle of Fallen Timbers. With the fighting braves defeated, Wayne continued to demoralize the natives by burning Indian villages and destroying fields of Indian corn. Out of hunger and disillusionment, negotiations opened and tribes reluctantly signed the Treaty of Greenville in 1795. This treaty forced them to cede a large parcel of the Northwest Territory—specifically, most of the present state of Ohio, a small area in Indiana, and small pockets of land beyond the ceded area for American posts. The Northwest Ordinance of 1787 had promised fair treatment of the Indian, but a "just and lawful war" had taken place to take their land and would many more times in the future.

While battles between soldiers and Indians raged on the Northwest frontier, verbal battles between Hamilton and Jefferson continued to rage in Washington's cabinet. These quarrels greatly disturbed Washington, and he planned in the spring of 1792 to announce his retirement and to return to the peace and tranquility of Mount Vernon. But Hamilton, Jefferson, and Madison persuaded him to serve another term. In the fall of 1792 Washington and Adams were reelected. Washington now moved into a term filled with foreign intrigues and pitfalls.

Washington's Foreign Policy

Washington's first term as president primarily was concerned with creating a government. While domestic issues were a first priority, foreign affairs now slowly were reaching a critical stage. The British still occupied forts in the Great Lake area and appeared to be inciting Indians there to attack. The Spanish were in the Floridas and were a real threat to American control of the Mississippi. As usual, war clouds hung over France and England. The direction of foreign policy led to some bitter clashes within Washington's cabinet.

Jefferson, as secretary of state, viewed Great Britain as the main enemy and France as a devoted ally. He, as well as most Americans, initially was pleased with the French Revolution (1789) because it seemed similar in many ways to the American Revolution. The revolutionary experience seemed to be repeating itself there. Hamilton, on the other hand, had deep respect for the English political system. He and his supporters were alarmed by the anarchy and revolution in France and described Jeffersons supporters as "hog-eating, man-eating, blood-drinking baboons." Hamilton also saw to it that the United States became closely tied economically to Britain and could only suffer from a trade war. He went so far as to feed highly confidential information to Major Beckwith, a British agent in New York, and to establish a close relationship with George Hammond, the first British foreign minister to the United States.

To Hammond, Hamilton indicated that Jefferson really did not speak for the United States in foreign affairs and that Jefferson's views on such issues as forts, trade, and neutral rights were not representative of the American people. Hamilton's meddling and his great influence on President Washington finally caused Jefferson to resign his position in 1793, but not before Washington issued his Proclamation of 1793.

When the French revolutionary government went to war with Great Britain and its allies in 1793, the United States found itself in the midst of a diplomatic crisis. Many Americans believed the United States was obligated by the Treaty of 1778, which formalized French involvement in the American Revolution, to help its ally France defend the West Indies and enter the war. Hamilton and Jefferson both recommended a policy of neutrality but for different reasons. Washington compromised by recognizing the French government and at the same time announcing the intention of the United States to remain at peace. This Proclamation of 1793 has been viewed as a neutrality statement, even though the word neutral was not used in it. Washington spoke instead of "conduct friendly and impartial toward the belligerent powers." The next year his Proclamation was confirmed by an act of Congress.

Many of Jefferson's adherents resented the apparent violation of the French treaty, and one of them commented, "Let not the little buzz of the aristocratic few and their contemptible minions, of speculators, Tories, and British emissaries, be mistaken for the exalted and general voices of the American people." Washington was described as defying "any man on earth to produce one single act of his since he had been in government which was not done on the purest motive." His anger, however, soon abated because he had to withstand a direct challenge to American neutrality.

In 1793 youthful French minister Edmond Genêt arrived in America and threw caution to the wind. He outfitted ships as privateers for the French; in Philadelphia he planned an invasion of Spanish possessions in the South. Genêt had been received warmly in America, which he interpreted as complete acceptance of his actions. "I live in a round of parties, Old Man Washington can't forgive my success." Washington and Jefferson both agreed that Genêt was a threat. Washington demanded his recall to France. With a more radical government now in control in Paris, however, Genêt knew he probably would lose his head if he returned. Granted asylum, he lived to a ripe old age with his American wife on a Long Island farm. Neutrality had withstood its first challenge.

The next challenge came from England. As a neutral, America was subject to having its ships seized by both France and England in international waters.

The English also "impressed," or seized, numerous American sailors and forced them to serve in the British Navy. Further, the British still were occupying forts in the Northwest and apparently inciting Indians to make raids on settlers. Talk of war along the Canadian border intensified. A temporary embargo on trade with England was secured, but war remained a real possibility. The war crisis forced Washington to act. He sent John Jay, in 1794, to England to settle the issue of neutrality in the Northwest, and to secure a new commercial agreement.

Jay was a skilled negotiator, but not a miracle worker. In 1794 he signed a treaty in which the British merely agreed to evacuate their frontier forts within two years and to grant a few trade concessions. There was nothing in the treaty about neutrality, impressment of sailors, or arming and inciting Indians. In fact, the treaty stipulated that Americans had to pay damages to English citizens for debts incurred before the Revolution (a settlement of $2.6 million was finally agreed upon in 1802). When terms of the treaty were revealed in the United States, Americans were incensed. Jay noted that he could walk at night from Philadelphia to New York and have his way lit by burning effigies of himself. "Damn John Jay. Damn everyone who won't damn John Jay." Even Washington disliked the treaty, but it did prevent war at a time when the United States was following a course of neutrality. So Washington supported the treaty, and it was ratified eventually by the Senate, but only by one vote. Washington's popularity was evaporating quickly. Still, a tragic war was postponed, and in the light of history the unpopular Jay Treaty was a success.

John Jay, the first Supreme Court chief justice, negotiated a very unpopular treaty with Britain in 1795, known as the Jay Treaty.

In fact, the Jay Treaty succeeded in causing Spain to enter into fruitful negotiations with the United States. Before the treaty, Spain had been reluctant to settle differences, but it now felt that Great Britain would support the American takeover of Louisiana and Florida. Thomas Pinckney, the United States minister to Spain, was able in 1795 to negotiate a favorable treaty in which Spain acceded to all the demands of the United States, including placement of the southern boundary at the 31st parallel, free commercial use of New Orleans for three years, and unrestricted navigation of the Mississippi River. Pinckney's Treaty climaxed Washington's second administration—a period that was primarily involved in foreign affairs, but not completely devoid of domestic troubles, too.

The Whiskey Rebellion

In 1791 an excise tax on several domestic products including whiskey was passed by Congress to help raise money for the assumption of state debts. In the West, especially backwoods Pennsylvania, whiskey was a cherished commodity. It was one of the only ways the backwoods people could profitably transport their corn and rye to market. In many cases it was used as money in exchange for other goods. The whiskey tax caused protests among western farmers and rioting in 1794 in western Pennsylvania. Some government agents were tarred and feathered, and the home of one was burned. Washington saw this as a threat to the system. He wrote, "Shall the majority govern, or be governed? Shall the nation rule, or be ruled? Shall the general will prevail, or the will of a faction? Shall there be government or no government?"

Hamilton advised Washington to crush this uprising, which became known as the Whiskey Rebellion. In turn, Washington called out 13,000 militiamen, putting Hamilton at the head. The army marched over the Alleghenies, but could not locate the rebels. Jefferson critically noted, "An insurrection was announced, but could never be found." Two men were finally arrested, found guilty of treason, and later pardoned as being "simpleton" and "insane." Washington, under the influence of Hamilton, had clearly shown his contempt for organized opposition to the government.

At the end of his second term, Washington decided he would not seek reelection. He was dismayed by the growing rivalry between the factions of Hamilton and Jefferson, and he too was becoming more of an object of abuse. His refusal established the two-term presidency as a tradition in American politics (which was made into law in 1951 by the twenty-second amendment to the Constitution). Before leaving office, Washington issued a document based on his experiences as president that has been referred to as his Farewell

Address. He did not present this address orally but delivered it to a newspaper that published it. More than two-thirds of this message dealt with domestic policies and contained a strong warning against political parties. Other sections of the document dealt with foreign affairs.

> It is our true policy to steer clear of permanent alliances with any portion of the foreign world, so far, I mean, as we are now at liberty to do it. For let me not be understood as capable of patronizing infidelity to existing engagements. . . . But in my opinion it is unnecessary and would be unwise to extend them.

This has been interpreted as the classic American statement of isolationist policy. Actually, Washington was warning of the pitfalls of permanent alliances, but he saw that temporary alliances could be useful. Specifically, he was commenting on America's relationship with France in light of America's refusal to honor the Alliance of 1778, and he also was giving support to the election of John Adams in 1796. When he left office, Washington wrote: "I now compare myself to the wearied traveler who seeks a resting place, and is bending his body to lean thereon. But to be suffered to do this in peace is too much to be endured by some." Even after his address, abuse increased. One newspaper said, "If ever a nation was debauched by a man, the American nation has been debauched by Washington." And on the day of his retirement, another commented, "This ought to be Jubilee in the United States, for the man who is the source of all the misfortune of our country is this day reduced to a level with his fellow citizens." Three years later Washington would be dead.

Washington's place in the hierarchy of great American presidents rests not on his legend but on his skillful administration of the federal government. He had followed deftly the line between dictatorship and revolution. He used good, firm judgement and set government on a fair, moderate course. He was the first in the office and so lacked a model to follow. He had to create one and did, proving himself to be a capable first president. The office of the presidency had taken shape; now it would be modified.

The Adams Presidency

The election of 1796 was really the first presidential contest in our history. Washington, the unanimous choice, was now gone. A two-party system was

John Adams won the election of 1796, becoming the second president of the United States.

taking form. The Federalist party of Hamilton nominated Vice-President John Adams, while the Democratic-Republicans (as they were coming to be known) nominated Thomas Jefferson. John Adams was elected to succeed Washington, but only by a margin of three electoral votes. Thomas Jefferson, who had the second highest number of votes, became the new Vice-President. For 4 years "3-vote president" Adams found himself between Hamilton, who was disgusted at Adam's "egotism," and Jefferson, who feared that Adams would increase the power of the central government even more than Washington had.

Who was this man John Adams? Born on the family farm in Quincy, Massachusetts, he achieved early success in the village school and continued on to graduate from Harvard College. After a brief period of teaching school, he studied law and became one of the leading attorneys in colonial Boston. After his marriage to Abigail Johnson, he took a leading part in the coming of the Revolution and the drive for independence. He was instrumental in writing the Massachusetts state constitution, which included a Bill of Rights, and in handling negotiations that led to the end of the Revolution. He was elected vice-president under Washington, although he felt the position was "the most insignificant office that ever the invention of man contrived. . . ."

Physically, he was short and stout, with a ruddy complexion. He had helped to create a nation and appeared to have earned the office of the presidency. Yet his personality was unfit for such a position. He had few friends; he was impatient, cantankerous, and vain. His cabinet was manipulated by Alexander Hamilton, who had just returned to private life. And his vice-president was from the opposition party. The split between Adams and Jefferson increased as time went on. Finally, Adams paid less attention to his duties than any of his successors. He was absent from the capital 385 days in 4 years, partly because his wife loved their farm in Quincy and was not always in the best of health. The tragedy of Adam's presidency lies in both his personality and his policies.

Upon assuming office, Adams faced a precarious foreign policy. The French were angered by the Jay Treaty and began to seize American ships and treat American sailors harshly. By the time of Adam's inauguration more than 300 American ships had been seized, and the American ambassador had been forced to leave France. War seemed likely unless the Adams administration could settle the difficulties. In an effort to avert war, Adams sent a diplomatic mission to bargain. The three commissioners were met by French agents, referred to by Americans as X, Y, and Z, who demanded a loan for France and a bribe of $250,000 for French officials. Legend has it that the commissioners were scandalized by the mere mention of a bribe and one of them screamed, "No! No! Not a sixpence!" This slogan later became "Millions for defense, but not one cent for tribute." When news of this XYZ Affair reached America, hostile feelings ran high and patriotism abounded; "Hail Columbia" became the popular song. Congress reacted by creating the Department of the Navy and by reestablishing the Marine Corps. Adams was riding a wave of popularity, and he answered the people's outrage with an undeclared naval war against France, which lasted from 1798 to 1800.

Adams immediately cut off all trade with France, abrogated the Treaty of 1778, and authorized seizure of French ships on the high seas. Washington even left Mt. Vernon to command the army. Warships for the new navy were constructed. This new navy soon gave a good account of itself. American warships won a number of duels with French vessels and captured a total of 85 ships, including armed merchant vessels. But Adams, contrary to the wishes of Hamilton and most of his party, felt that this undeclared war might burst full blown into a real European conflict, so in 1799 he pushed for peace. Hamilton's plan for a war against Spain in the South was dashed. After prolonged negotiations, a peace treaty was signed in 1800. Later Adams wrote, "... I desire no other inscription over my gravestone than: 'Here lies John Adams, who took upon himself the responsibility of the peace with France in the year 1800.'" While Adams's foreign policy and the coming of peace caused internal tension in his own party, most of his domestic policies tended to alienate Jefferson and his followers.

Alien and Sedition Acts

As a domestic leader, Adams acted as a partisan Federalist and strongly opposed the Democratic-Republican party. When the naval war began, Congress passed four laws, known collectively as the Alien and Sedition Acts, which definitely handicapped the party of Jefferson. The acts dealing with aliens raised the residency requirement for citizenship and empowered the president to deport undesirable aliens who were considered "dangerous to the peace and safety of the United States." The Sedition Act prescribed fines and imprisonment for saying or writing anything "false, scandalous, or malicious" about the president or Congress. It was one of the most repressive measures ever directed against political activity in the United States. It appeared to be an obvious violation of the free-speech amendment, but the Supreme Court had not assumed as yet the power to judge legislation constitutional. Certain Fed-

This 1798 cartoon shows Matthew Lyon fighting it out with a rival congressman.

eralist opponents became political martyrs by challenging this act. Lyon of Vermont, who spat in the faces of his Federalist opponents in Congress, was jailed under the Sedition Act, as were three Jeffersonian editors.

Thomas Jefferson and James Madison felt these laws would severely cripple their party and lead to a one-party dictatorship. They issued strongly worded constitutional protests, which were adopted by the legislatures of Virginia and Kentucky. These two resolutions claimed that the central government jeopardized the rights of its citizens and that individual states had the right to step in to protect those rights. In fact, the Kentucky Resolutions mentioned possible "nullification" of the acts, but Jefferson really looked to the national election of 1800 to bring about a change of policy. Meanwhile, Adams was splitting his party and alienating many others by his connection with the Alien and Sedition Acts. The times just did not seem right for Adams; his personality was not suited for the office of the presidency, and, of course, he followed Washington. And that was a hard act to follow. The election of 1800 would leave him a one-term president.

Thomas Jefferson as President

The Alien and Sedition Acts were primarily responsible for Adams's defeat in the election of 1800, but internal disputes within Adams's party plus high taxes were also factors. The election of 1800 was truly a strange one because Jefferson and his running-mate for vice-president, Aaron Burr, tied in electoral college votes. It was possible at that time for a tie to take place between candidates of the same party. After 33 ballots in the House of Representatives, neither candidate had won a clear majority. A decision had to be reached, for without a duly elected president the system would crumble. Rumors arose of bribery in the Congress and of state militias being called out to settle the presidential deadlock. Thanks to Hamilton, who disagreed philosophically with Jefferson but hated Burr, and a few blank ballot votes, on the thirty-sixth ballot Thomas Jefferson became America's third president.

Thomas Jefferson viewed the election of 1800 as a "revolution"—a new political party came into power for the first time. Many Federalists initially agreed with him, for a party of farmers with a leader opposed to a strong national government threatened to bring much change. Would all traditions be destroyed? Would a "real revolution" take place? No. The new party brought with it a new emphasis but no drastic changes in government. In his inaugural address, Jefferson calmly noted, "We are all Republicans, we are all

Thomas Jefferson here dismounts from his horse to attend his inauguration in the newly created District of Columbia.

Federalists." Jefferson spoke in the spirit of compromise, but he was still a Democratic-Republican.

Jefferson planned to continue the national bank, to cut taxes, and to attempt to balance the budget. He eventually filled 60 percent of government positions with members of his party, and he let the Alien and Sedition Acts expire. He also found that the office of the presidency was an awesome one, whose powers sometimes had to be exerted.

Thomas Jefferson was born in the Virginia tidewater region. Educated at William and Mary College, he studied law and spent much of his early life in the rolling hills of Virginia's backcountry. His writing skills helped the cause of the colonial rebellion, but he had no interest in military life, serving instead as a member of the Virginia legislature and as Virginia governor. Today he is best known as author of the Declaration of Independence. After the Revolution, he became ambassador to Paris and first Secretary of State. He was truly a remarkable American, with his talent for foreign affairs and his skills as an architect, farmer, inventor, and musician. Physically, he was tall with red hair and a long face. His wife had died in 1782, so he was a widower president.

Although Jefferson was a cultivated gentlemen with expensive tastes in food and drink, his clothing was an object of ridicule. Often his clothing did not match or fit. Despite his sophistication, he emphasized plainness and informality. His annual messages to Congress were read by the clerk, and he tried to avoid formal dinners and meetings. Still, his wine bill for a single year was $2800—a princely sum for that time. He walked to his inauguration, but he had a mansion at Monticello with scores of slaves. Jefferson was, indeed, a complex individual.

Jefferson believed in a nation of farmers, yet he also believed that top government positions should be staffed by the most capable. His cabinet was composed of educated, experienced followers. His secretary of state was his close friend from Virginia, James Madison, a mild-mannered individual with much political experience and an extraordinary sense of humor. His secretary of treasury was Albert Gallatin, a Swiss aristocrat with a keen financial sense. Gallatin devised a plan for the gradual extinction of the national debt and earned the respect of both parties. On the other hand, Madison frequently was frustrated by the growing tension between England and France.

Jefferson's eight years as president (he was overwhelmingly reelected in 1804) involved problems with the Barbary pirates, the acquisition and exploration of Louisiana, a struggle with the Supreme Court, and an uneasy neutrality with France and England. For years the North African nations of Morocco, Algiers, Tunisia, and Tripoli had acquired substantial wealth by preying on Mediterranean commerce, while leading maritime countries, including Britain and the United States, had been spared Barbary piracy only by paying tribute. Under Washington and Adams more than 2 million dollars were spent. When the Barbary rulers felt that the United States navy had weakened, they demanded an increase in tribute and began to seize American ships and hold sailors ransom. Although Jefferson favored peace, he was so angered that he ordered the small United States Navy to attack the greedy pirate states. In 1805 the ruler of Tripoli stopped demanding payments, but war dragged on with the other nations until 1816. During Jefferson's presidency, outmanned American forces achieved a number of surprising victories, and the Barbary rulers acquired a wholesome respect for the power of their distant enemy.

The Louisiana Purchase

The Barbary pirates were a relatively simple problem in comparison to the Louisiana question. News had reached America that Spain had given the region of Louisiana to France. Jefferson feared that this was a move by Napoleon to reestablish a French empire in America. The Mississippi River was the main artery of the West. Free navigation of the river plus use of New Orleans as a shipping center was essential to the West's economy. Jefferson himself wrote, "The cession of Louisiana by Spain to France works most sorely on the Unites States." He also noted that a French Louisiana would make France "our natural and habitual enemy" and would compel America to "marry ourselves to the British fleet and nation." This hardly sounds like Jefferson; it is difficult to believe that he took seriously an alliance with Great Britain. In 1802 the crisis worsened. Before France took over, the Spanish governor of New Orleans suspended the free use of that city's port. Westerners were no longer able to get their goods to market. Federalists again might have a war with France.

Wanting neither war nor foreign alliances, Jefferson decided that creative diplomacy was the answer. Robert Livingston, minister to France, was authorized to offer $2 million to purchase New Orleans and West Florida. He made little progress. Jefferson then sent his special minister, James Monroe, to join Livingston and to offer $10 million for the same territories. If they failed, they were to cross to England and negotiate a treaty of alliance with the British. To their great surprise, Monroe and Livingston found that Napoleon was willing to sell all of Louisiana for a total of $25 million. Why did Napoleon wish to sell? First, Napoleon's expedition to Haiti to begin his New World empire had proved a failure; second, war with Great Britain was imminent; and third, Napoleon needed money and foreign friends. It also is rumored that Napoleon himself declared, "We helped them to be free; now let us help them to be great." After some haggling, the American ministers reduced the price to $15 million. This was a great bargain: the United States acquired title to 828,000 square miles of land for about three cents per acre. Livingston wrote, "We have lived long, but this is the noblest work of our lives." One major obstacle lay in the path of ratification—President Jefferson.

Jefferson had major doubts about the legality and constitutionality of the purchase. His earlier view had been that powers not expressly conferred on the central government by the Constitution were reserved to the states. And since the Constitution did not mention the annexation of foreign territory and incorporation of its citizens into the Union, the purchase would be unconstitutional. He thought of drawing up a constitutional amendment, but this would take time, and he feared that Napoleon might change his mind. Ultimately, the advantages of the purchase were too numerous. "Is it not better that the opposite bank of the Mississippi be settled by our own brothers and sisters?" Jefferson wrote. The Mississippi would be annexed; doubling the land area of the United States. He submitted the treaty and urged its swift acceptance. The Louisiana Purchase may have been the high-water mark of Jefferson's presidency. It is interesting then to note that Jefferson wanted the inscription on his tombstone to include his achievements concerning the Declaration of Independence, the Statute of Virginia for Religious Freedom, and the University of Virginia, but not the Louisiana Purchase. Despite his

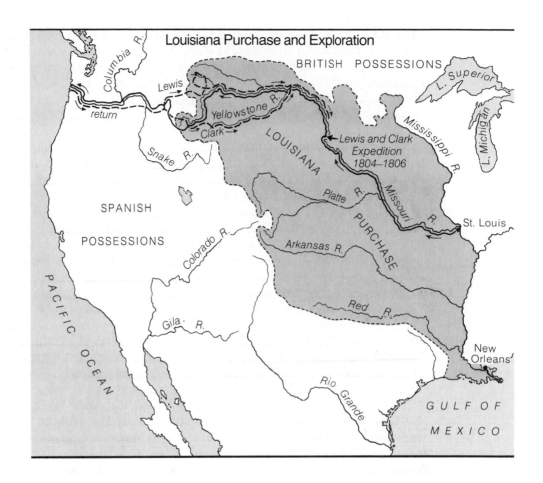

Louisiana Purchase and Exploration

constitutional scruples, however, Jefferson stimulated the exploration of the region even before the final agreement had been reached.

Lewis and Clark Expedition

In 1803, before the Louisiana transaction, Jefferson persuaded Congress to secretly allot $2500 for a military expedition to explore the Louisiana region. His private secretary, Meriwether Lewis, was chosen to lead the expedition. In Philadelphia Lewis learned mathematics, astronomy, botany, zoology, and practical medicine in preparation for the trip. To protect the health of his men, he advised them to wear flannel next to their skin in wet weather and shoes without heels; they should wash their feet in the mornings in cold water and rely on "opening pills" for digestive troubles. With Jefferson's consent, Lewis chose William Clark as coleader of the enterprise. With similar backgrounds, both of these men worked well together.

Lewis and Clark's instructions were clear: follow the Missouri River to its source and seek a water route to the Pacific. Along the way they were to make careful studies of animal and vegetable life, and of the soil, minerals, and terrain. They were also to gather facts about the rivers and learn about the fur trade. Well equipped, the expedition left winter camp near St. Louis in May 1804 and traveled up the Missouri to their winter camp at a Mandan village, near present-day Bismarck, North Dakota. Traveling at a rate of nine miles per day, they were bothered by "ticks, mosquitoes, and gnats" and met with numerous friendly Indian tribes that usually asked for a drink of "Great White Father's Milk"—whiskey. They built Fort Mandan as their winter quarters. It was there that they hired a French trapper, Toussaint Charbonneau, and Sacajawea, his Shoshone wife whom he had won in a card game, as interpreters. Except for these two and York, Clark's black servant, the expedition was composed of a detachment of the United States Army on special mission.

The expedition set out again in April 1805, first by boat to Three Forks, where the Missouri River forms, and then by foot up the Jefferson River and through the Beaverhead country to the Continental Divide. They were now low on food and their horses were weakening, so Lewis led a scouting party to look for help. He crossed Lemhi Pass, persuaded a group of Shoshones to return with him, and found that the leader of the band was Sacajawea's brother. The Shoshone provided them with horses and food, and eventually the expedition reached the forks of the Clearwater. The arduous journey of crossing over difficult mountain trails had been accomplished primarily through the aid of friendly Indians. Once over the mountains Clark wrote, "I have been wet and as cold in every part as I ever was in my life, indeed I was at one time fearful my feet would freeze in the thin Mockirsons which I wore."

They then continued to the Columbia River in dugout canoes and on November 7, 1805, arrived at the Pacific Ocean. Here they built their winter quarters, named Fort Clatsop, on the south side of the Columbia River, near present-day Astoria, Oregon. The five months at Fort Clatsop were made difficult by the constant rain, fleas, and local Indians. One of the high points of the winter travail was finding a whale cast up on the beach; they mixed whale meat and oil with elk meat and feasted. Winter cold, food poisoning, and minor accidents also had to be faced. On March 23, 1806, the weary travelers left for home.

Indians provided valuable assistance to Lewis and Clark on their famed expedition; here they are seen on the Columbia River.

On the return trip they decided to explore new routes. Lewis attempted a shortcut to the east, reaching the great falls of the Missouri six days after crossing the Continental Divide, and he explored the Marias River, where he was shot by a nearsighted French hunter who mistook him for a bear. At the Mandan village the two groups were reunited, and from there they followed the Missouri to St. Louis. The Lewis and Clark expedition had come to an end.

The Lewis and Clark expedition is one of the best-reported and scientifically valuable explorations in American history. Four detailed records of the expedition remain. While the explorers did not find a waterway to the Pacific, they did return with maps, skins, plants, and Indian artifacts, which became objects of scientific investigation. Not only did they explore the Louisiana country, they carried their discoveries beyond to the Pacific Northwest. Today they are remembered as the foremost explorers of the American wilderness, while many transcontinental highways and historical markers are continual reminders of their exploits. And two modern-day explorers offered them an apt tribute by traveling along the Lewis and Clark route in a four-wheel drive vehicle and describing in detail their arduous trip.

Jefferson and the Supreme Court

If the acquisition and exploration of Louisiana was the high point of Jefferson's presidency, his attack on the independence of the Supreme Court was one of the low points. As president, Jefferson resented the Federalist-controlled judiciary and decided to challenge the court system in order to "sink Federalism into an abyss from which there shall be no resurrection from it." When John Adams was leaving office, 16 new federal judgeships and 52 justices of the peace—all Federalists—had been created. William Marbury was one of these justices, serving in the District of Columbia, but his papers of appointment had not been delivered. Jefferson planned to block this appointment by keeping the documents undelivered and making another appointment. Marbury brought suit against Secretary of State Madison to force him to deliver his commission. The Supreme Court heard the case of *Marbury* v. *Madison* in 1803, and its ruling had profound consequences. Chief Justice John Marshall, a distant and disliked relative of Jefferson, knew that he could not force Jefferson to deliver the papers, but he could berate Jefferson for not following his duty. Most importantly, Marshall ruled that Congress, in the Judiciary Act of 1789, had exceeded its authority. What did this mean? It meant that a portion of that act had been declared null and void. But, far more importantly, it meant that the Supreme Court had ruled for the first time on the constitutionality of an act of Congress. Although Jefferson had attempted to change the direction of the Court, he had inadvertently helped to strengthen its powers. It is ironic that the main criticism of the decision at the time was not that the Supreme Court had gained the power of judicial review but that Chief Justice Marshall had violated the balance of powers by lecturing the President and the Secretary of State.

Angered by this obvious criticism, Jefferson continued his attack by trying to use impeachment as a partisan political weapon. He initially used it successfully against John Pickering, a district judge of New Hampshire, who was incapacitated for office because of drunkenness, profanity, and fits of insanity. One story told of his appearance in court virtually naked. But later trials, such as that of the strong Federalist Justice Samuel Chase, became an embarrassment; Chase was a competent judge, and "high crimes and misdemeanors" were not in evidence. The trial of Chase lingered on, and he was finally acquitted. After the trial even Jefferson admitted it was a "farce" and that impeachment should not be used as a political weapon. The independence of the judiciary was challenged again in the Burr trial of 1807.

Aaron Burr, has been remembered chiefly for killing Hamilton in a duel on July 11, 1804, but he was also an unsuccessful candidate for president in 1800 and for governor of New York. Frustrated in politics, he became involved in a bizarre plot to establish an independent empire in the West. When Jefferson learned of his intent, he ordered that Burr be charged with treason and conspiracy. Jefferson, feeling deep hatred for his former vice-president, wanted the Court to find Burr guilty, but again Jefferson was stymied. Not only was Jefferson subpoenaed, which he refused on grounds of executive privilege (President Richard Nixon in 1974 used similar arguments), but he suffered further embarrassment when Chief Justice Marshall's rigid interpretation of the Constitution defeated his plans. Marshall insisted that a conviction for treason required "the testimony of two witnesses to the same overt act of war or an open confession by the accused." The witnesses failed to prove Marshall's definition of treason and after a 25-minute deliberation the jury found Burr innocent. This decision not only set the precedent for future treason trials but also gave Marshall another judicial victory over Jefferson. Jefferson had failed to break the independence of the judiciary and had set precedents for many presidents in the future. And events continued to surround him. He now found the United States again between the two antagonists, France and England. His foreign policy helped to lead the way to the War of 1812, which will be discussed in Chapter 5.

From our modern perspective, much time elapsed from the Revolution to the presidency of Jefferson. But what is seventeen years! In that short time many events took place: The Articles of Confederation were created—the first constitution, but not the last. Maybe this constitution failed because it had not been given a chance, but much more patience with it might have brought tyranny and ruin. The second Constitution has withstood the test of years, and it is easy today to say, "Damn, that is a great document." Washington surely would have liked your hindsights when he took the oath of office and tried for eight years to get the ship of state afloat and keep it afloat. He did a capable job, not because he was a hero from a myth but because of his determination and sincerity as first president. But all presidents were not Washingtons; Adams proved that. In 1800 Jefferson brought into government a new party. What did that mean? It meant that a new party would give the government a different slant, not a revolutionary one. By the time of the presidency of Jefferson, the government of the United States was leaving its infancy. From the time of Jefferson to that of Andrew Jackson that country would undergo another war with Britain, a period of unrivaled peace, and the birth of Jacksonian Democracy.

Essay

The Presidential Veto

Article I, Section 7 of the Constitution refers to the president's power to kill a law that the legislative branch already has passed.

> Every Bill which shall have passed the House of Representatives and the Senate shall, before it becomes a Law, be presented to the President of the United States; If he approve he shall sign it, but if not he shall return it, with his Objections to that House in which it shall have originated, who shall enter the Objections at large on their Journal, and proceed to reconsider it. If after such Reconsideration two thirds of that House shall agree to pass the Bill, it shall be sent, together with the Objections, to the other House, by which it shall likewise be reconsidered, and if approved by two thirds of that House, it shall become a Law.

This is the veto power of the president, which can be overridden by a two-thirds vote of both houses of Congress.

In the early years of the Constitution Alexander Hamilton noted that the presidential veto should be used with great caution. While some presidents did exercise due caution, others were not so careful. The first veto was cast by George Washington on April, 5, 1792. A bill was presented to him that would have set the number of members for the House of Representatives permanently at 120. In his veto message Washington made it very clear that the Constitution based representation in the House on population, not a fixed number. The bill, therefore, was clearly unconstitutional. Washington's successor

Andrew Jackson used the presidential veto twice as often as all the preceding presidents combined.

John Adams, who served four years, never vetoed a bill, nor did the first Democratic president Thomas Jefferson, who served for eight years.

Andrew Jackson, who served as president from 1828 to 1836, had seen his predecessors use the veto only 10 times; during his two terms he ignored their collective lead and employed it 12 times. His most famous veto was that of the Second Bank of the United States Recharter Bill, which would have kept the National Bank alive. His message in 1832 not only revealed that he felt the National Bank to be unconstitutional but also revealed that he personally disliked banks and felt that many of his constituency shared his antipathy. The "moneyed monster" was now dead; the veto did it in.

Andrew Jackson's hatred of the National Bank surprisingly was shared by a president from a rival party. The Whig party had risen in opposition to Jackson and his common-American policies. They took the steam away from Jackson's successor, Martin Van Buren, by nominating a man in the mold of Jackson, the old dirt farmer William Henry Harrison, who was elected in 1840. His sudden death placed Vice-President John Tyler in office. Whig-party leader Henry Clay now saw an opportunity to resurrect the National Bank; Congress passed a bank bill but Tyler vetoed it on economic grounds similar to Jackson's. Newspapers began to question the veto power. A similar bill was passed, but another veto was exerted. "Executive Ass" Tyler, as he was called by many members of his party, had once again revealed the power of the veto.

While Congress does have the authority to override the presidential veto, rarely has Congress done it. But there are some exceptions. Six bills became law over Woodrow Wilson's vetoes, and seven bills over Grover Cleveland's vetoes. Congress has overridden Calvin Coolidge four times, Herbert Hoover three times, Theodore Roosevelt and William Howard Taft once each, Franklin Delano Roosevelt nine times, Harry Truman twelve times, Dwight Eisenhower twice, and Richard Nixon twice. One president much frustrated by the power of Congress to override the veto was Andrew Johnson (1865–1868), the man who became president after the assassination of Lincoln. Johnson was a believer in the power of the president to reconstruct the South after the Civil War; Congress did not adopt this point of view, feeling they should take the lead in the reconstruction process. The tension between Johnson and Congress was evident in his liberal use of the veto power and the frequent successes Congress had in overriding him. "Sir Veto," as he was sarcastically called, was a knight without a kingdom.

In his four terms as president, Franklin Roosevelt used his veto power more than any other president.

Many students of government have noticed that Richard Nixon vetoed 43 bills and Gerald Ford, 66; they may seem to be this century's veto leaders. This is far from being the case. Since presidents are now limited to 2 terms in office and since Franklin Roosevelt served for 12 years, it is unlikely that his record of 635 vetoes will ever be broken. While Roosevelt worked closely with Congress on his New Deal legislation, his record number of vetoes reveals that he and Congress did not always see eye to eye.

One of the more unusual vetoes involved President Rutherford B. Hayes, who vetoed a bill authorizing the coinage of the standard silver dollar. Woodrow Wilson vetoed a bill repealing the Daylight Saving Law. Franklin Roosevelt's vetoes included a bill that authorized the use of War Department equipment for the August 1938 American Legion Convention in New York City and another bill that would have safeguarded homing pigeons. Reflecting on these vetoes, one would wonder whether these presidents were following Hamilton's advice in using great caution.

The presidential veto over the years has been one of the chief executive's strongest weapons in the struggle with Congress. Some presidents have used it sparingly or not at all; other presidents have felt it their prerogative to shift government leadership away from Congress to the president. This power still remains; it is one that sometimes reveals the president's personal bias—often for a very good reason. ∎

Suggested Reading

A fine study of the Confederation period and the development of the Constitution is in FOREST MCDONALD's *E Pluribus Unum: the Formation of the American Republic, 1776–1790* (1965).

One of the most detailed and readable studies of the Constitutional Convention is *1787: The Grand Convention* (1966) by CLINTON ROSSITER.

MARCUS CUNLIFFE's *The Nation Takes Shape* (1959) and JOHN MILLER's *The Federalist Era, 1789–1901* (1960) are two excellent books on the formation of the national government.

The Presidency of George Washington (1974) by FOREST MCDONALD and *George Washington and the New Nation, 1783–1793* (1969) by JAMES T. FLEXNER provide insights into the foreign and domestic policies of the first president. NOBLE E. CUNNINGHAM, in *The Jeffersonian Republicans, 1789–1801* (1957) traces the evolution of the two-party system.

FATHER FRANCIS PAUL PRUCHA, in *American Indian Policy in the Formative Years* (1962), traces the evolution of American Indian policy.

STEPHEN G. KURTZ, in *The Presidency of John Adams: The Collapse of Federalism, 1795–1800* (1957), and PAGE SMITH, in *John Adams* (1962), reflect upon the failures and foibles of the Adams presidency.

An excellent four-volume biography describing the life and times of Jefferson is found in *Jefferson and His Times* (1948–74) by DUMAS MALONE.

CHAPTER 5

The Evolution of National Policy: From Jefferson to Jackson

Time Line

?–A.D. 1492	Migration and evolution of American Indian societies
1492	Christopher Columbus lands in West Indies—beginning of European exploration
1607–1732	Establishment of 13 English colonies
1775–1783	American Revolution
1776	Declaration of Independence
1789–1797	Presidency of George Washington
1804	Reelection of Thomas Jefferson
1807	*Chesapeake* Affair
1807	Embargo Act
1808	Election of James Madison
1811	Battle of Tippecanoe
1812	Reelection of James Madison
1812–1814	War of 1812
1814	Battle of Lake Champlain
1815	Battle of New Orleans
1816	Election of James Monroe
1816–1824	Era of Good Feelings
1820	Missouri Compromise
1823	Monroe Doctrine
1825	Election of John Quincy Adams
1828	Election of Andrew Jackson
1832	Nullification Crisis
1832	National Bank Veto
1838–1839	Trail of Tears: Forced removal of the Cherokee Nation

1812–1815	War of 1812
1816–1824	Era of Good Feelings
1846–1848	Mexican War
1861–1865	Civil War
1865–1877	Reconstruction
1877–1900	Industrialization and urbanization
1900–1916	Progressive Era
1917–1918	World War I
1930s	Depression and New Deal
1941–1945	World War II
1945–1960	Post-war politics
1950–1953	Korean War
1950–1960	Civil rights movement
1961–1973	Vietnam War
1976	Bicentennial celebration

The Evolution of National Policy: From Jefferson to Jackson

"These are the best of times; these are the worst of times." When has there ever been any real agreement about the state of the country among Americans of a particular era? Today, professional athletes occupy a heroic status in society, yet many of them hold out for more money or more prestige. Scientists research a cure for cancer, while countless thousands die from that dreaded disease. Homemakers complain about the rising cost of food. Workers threaten to strike for higher wages. Republicans continue to condemn Democratic party policies, while Democrats are equally critical of Republican leadership. There has never been an idyllic period in our history. Actually, the period from Thomas Jefferson to Andrew Jackson was as filled with political ups and downs as any in our history. President Thomas Jefferson found his neutral position between England and France leading directly to war. He tried an economic weapon that had worked during the American Revolution, but this time it failed. James Madison, Jefferson's successor, tried to avoid war but could not. The War of 1812 accomplished little, but it did lead to a period of relative peace that for a time was filled with "good feelings." But by the election of John Quincy Adams in 1825, an era of ill will had developed. In 1826 John Quincy Adams and Andrew Jackson struggled for political power, while John Adams and Thomas Jefferson struggled unsuccessfully for life, both dying that year. The election of Andrew Jackson in 1828 brought a "common man" to the presidency, or at least it appeared so. Jackson gave the people what they wanted: an end to the National Bank, the removal of the Indians, and a strong stand on nullification. Jackson could not please everyone, and his opposition came to be known as the Whig party. By the end of his presidency new troubles were brewing: Indians were being pushed further west, the country's economic picture was confused, and the state of South Carolina was getting ready for another round of conflict with the national government.

Jefferson's Foreign Policy

On assuming office, President Thomas Jefferson found that he had inherited the problems of commerce with England and France that had plagued the administrations of Washington and Adams. Since the American Revolution, America had had a great deal of difficulty in foreign affairs, because England and France were almost constantly at war. During Jefferson's first administration, America found itself again the leading neutral between the warring powers. In 1806 and 1807 France and England issued a series of bewildering orders and decrees aimed at controlling oceanic trade. Great Britain had issued orders known as the Orders in Council in an attempt to blockade the French coast and force neutral ships to pay fees to England. Napoleon in France issued the Berlin and Milan decrees in an attempt to blockade Britain. At first these orders and decrees seemed to threaten the commerce of the United States with ruin, but eventually prices of commodities and shipping rates rose so high that American merchants continued to prosper in spite of losses. Both France and England harassed American commerce, but since Britain was virtually master of the sea, the British mistreatment was more effective. The British also practiced *impressment*—the seizure of American citizens from American ships as supposed deserters from the British navy. The English claimed that naturalization was illegal; "Once an Englishman, always an Englishman," they reasoned. It is estimated that between 8000 and 10,000 American citizens were impressed into the Royal Navy, in addition to citizens from Sweden, Denmark, and Portugal. This practice incensed Americans much more than the mere seizure of property, and by 1807 Jefferson found the nation on the brink of war with Britain.

In June of 1807 the frigate *Chesapeake,* under the command of Commodore James Barron, left Norfolk, Virginia, for the Mediterranean; she soon encountered the British warship *Leopard.* Barron refused to allow the crew to be searched for four deserters. The *Leopard* then fired 3 broadsides into the *Chesapeake,* killing 3 men and wounding 18. Barron was unable to resist because his guns were unmounted, so the British boarded the ship and seized four "deserters." The *Chesapeake* then limped back to Norfolk with the dead men lashed to the bow. This unprecedented attack incensed the American public. War fever swept the country. Jefferson wrote, "Never since the battle of Lexington have I seen this country in such a state of exasperation as at present, and even that did not produce such unanimity." If Congress had been in session, surely war would have been declared. Jefferson, aware of the weak status of the American navy, issued a proclamation denouncing the seizure of American ships and outlawing British warships from American waters. The English response was reflected in newspaper references to America as "an insignificant and puny power" that could not be allowed to "mutilate Britain's proud sovereignty of the ocean." War seemed the only alternative.

The Embargo

Instead of immediately declaring war, Jefferson used a tool that had been successful before the Revolution: economic coercion in the form of a boycott called the Embargo Act. The Embargo Act prohibited all American exports and further restricted imports of certain British manufactured goods. Amer-

This cartoon pictures the Embargo Act in action, which stopped all American exports and created an economic depression.

ican ports were virtually closed. Jefferson reasoned that if vital supplies were withheld from England (and France as well), these countries would be forced to cease violating American neutral rights. It was a noble experiment to avoid war, but it backfired. The principal effect of the embargo was not British submission but an American economic depression, particularly in the Northeast. American ships rotted at anchor, and merchants went bankrupt. One man wrote, "The streets near the waterside were almost deserted; the grass had begun to grow upon the wharves." To avoid financial ruin, many traders reverted to smuggling. While the embargo did hurt a segment of the British economy, it created too much hardship in the United States. Jefferson was blamed for the misfortune. One writer even suggested that he return to the "sable arms" of his alleged mulatto mistress. Before Jefferson left office, Congress repealed the act and replaced it with the Nonintercourse Act, which banned trade only with Great Britain and France. While the Embargo Act was an immediate failure, it did cause capitalists to invest in American manufacturing and helped pave the way for the American Industrial Revolution. Jefferson left the presidency amid the storm of controversy surrounding the Embargo Act; the frustrations of international affairs had caused him to follow Washington's two-term tradition. To the presidency, Jefferson had brought a new democratic philosophy with emphasis on the common people, yet he did little to change the precedents started by Washington. Although a believer in decentralized government, he found himself sponsoring federal expeditions to the West, agreeing to the Louisiana Purchase, and resorting to the Embargo Act. While he was frustrated in his court fights and foreign policy, he kept America out of war. His leadership of Congress and his conversion of the office of the presidency into a political one are also noteworthy. Although he was leaving the arena of politics, he personally intervened to obtain the presidential nomination for his secretary of state, James Madison, who won the election of 1808 by a sizable majority.

James Madison as President

James Madison, the oldest of 12 children, was born and raised in Virginia. He excelled in school and finished Princeton University in two years. A frail and sickly individual with a weak voice, he pondered taking up a career as a minister but instead turned to politics. He helped to write the Virginia state constitution and the Virginia Declaration of Rights. As a member of the Virginia House of Delegates, he became good friends with Thomas Jefferson—a friendship that lasted all his life.

Madison frequently is called "The Father of the Constitution." As a delegate to the Constitutional Convention, he took a leading part in the fight for a strong central government, and his notes are the only full record of the constitutional debates. During the ratification struggle, he was one of the authors of *The Federalist*, a brilliant defense of the new constitution. As a member of the first House of Representatives, he was largely responsible for drafting the Bill of Rights, the first ten amendments to the Constitution. As an opponent of Alexander Hamilton's philosophy of government, he was a

"Little Jimmie" Madison was frustrated for eight years by foreign affairs; his wife Dolly, meanwhile, added a real flare to Washington society.

major force in organizing the Democratic-Republican party. Jefferson, as president, appointed Madison secretary of state. The Louisiana Purchase was Madison's greatest personal success.

"Little Jimmie" Madison, as many of his friends called him, was elected president in 1808 and faced the same frustrations in foreign policy he had encountered as secretary of state. He brought to the office a rich background of government service and a keen insight into the workings of government. Still, he was physically ill and indecisive as president. His lovely wife, Dolly—a true social leader—and his sense of humor were his greatest assets. He was the first president to have cabinet choices forced upon him by Congress. His immediate problem on assuming office, however, was American neutrality on the high seas.

The Nonintercourse Act authorized Madison to reopen trade with France or with England if either of them ceased violating neutral rights. Pro-American British minister David Erskine promised that the British would withdraw the Orders in Council; Madison then lifted the embargo against the British, but his actions were premature. The London government rejected the agreement, and a new anti-American minister, who described Madison as a "plain and rather mean-looking man" and Dolly as "fat and forty," was sent to replace Erskine. Madison now turned to Macon's Bill No. 2, which opened American commerce with Great Britain and France but authorized the president to prohibit trade with either country should the other power withdraw its orders against American commerce.

Napoleon immediately took advantage of the new law by professing his love of America and promising that France would withdraw the Berlin and Milan decrees. A careful check, however, would have revealed that Napoleon's navy was still seizing American ships and destroying American property. Madison, nevertheless, accepted the French position and stopped trade with Great Britain. The British still did not withdraw their Orders in Council, however; and on June 1, 1812, Madison sent a message to Congress reviewing "the injuries and indignities which have been heaped on our country [by Great Britain] and asking for war. Congress did not unanimously respond. With a close vote in the Senate and a divided vote in the House, war was declared. Meanwhile, the British, in the grip of an industrial depression, were feeling the effects of the Nonintercourse Act; they suspended the Orders in Council. But when news of the repeal reached America, war already had been declared.

"Free Trade and Sailors' Rights" was a popular slogan of the time, which would appear to explain the causes of the coming war. The violation of neutral rights, as the major cause of the war, is questionable, however, in view of the intense opposition to the war from the New England area. In his war message President Madison had listed British encouragement of Indian efforts to forestall American settlement as one of the causes. Actually, the American pioneers moving west into Indian land incited the Indians more than the British did. By the early 1800s more settlers were moving into the Great Lakes region and demanding more of the Indian land. Under Jefferson the treaty process, which relieved natives of their land and moved them west, continued. Jefferson wrote: "I am myself alive to the obtaining of lands from the Indians by all honest and peaceable means . . . I trust and believe we are acting for their greatest good."

Jefferson also conceived of a plan that would alleviate all Indian and white problems. He hoped to have Indians purchase goods from government trading posts and in doing so accumulate large debts that they could only pay off by ceding land. The government would settle Indians on agricultural reservations where they would learn to farm and become like their white neighbors. This idea obviously indicated a lack of understanding of Indians and their culture. Before leaving office, Jefferson talked of removing the Indians to land west of the Mississippi: "We shall be obliged to drive them with the beasts of the forest into the stony [Rocky] mountains." While neither of these plans reached fruition, treaty making was becoming a fine art.

Tecumseh

William Henry Harrison, who served as governor of the Indiana Territory from 1800 to 1812, used treaties as weapons against the Indians. He was responsible for 15 treaties that gave the government title to what today is Indiana, Illinois, and parts of Ohio, Michigan, and Wisconsin. Harrison's most formidable opponent was a Shawnee brave named Tecumseh, a leader much like King Philip or Pontiac. His father and brother had been killed by whites, and Tecumseh refused to sign the Treaty of Greenville. He knew that an alliance of tribes was necessary to stop the white movement west. But he pushed the alliance idea one step further and proposed organizing a permanent Indian nation. He tried to instill in all Indians a national rather than a tribal consciousness. To him, treaties were illegal because land belonged to all tribes and none of them could rightfully cede any of it without the consent of the rest. Said Tecumseh, "The Great Spirit gave this great island to his red children."

To make his idea a reality, Tecumseh began to travel from the Great Lakes to the Gulf of Mexico to preach his doctrine of nationalism. He also joined with his half brother, a one-eyed, epileptic medicine man known as Prophet. The Prophet was responsible for a religious revival among the Indians, and his union with Tecumseh was the basis for a spiritual and political alliance. Harrison tried to disgrace Tecumseh and the Prophet and push for more treaties. But the Prophet's accurate prediction of a total eclipse caused thousands of Indians to flock to his side. In 1808 Tecumseh and the Prophet began to gather their followers at Prophet Town, near the fork of the Wabash and Tippecanoe rivers. This was to be the center of Tecumseh's confederation. Tecumseh continued to raise the ire of Harrison by protesting Harrison's treaties and personally confronting him at a treaty council. Harrison even admitted that Tecumseh was "one of those uncommon geniuses" but insisted that the Indian confederation must be destroyed.

In 1811 Tecumseh journeyed south to gather more support. During this absence, Harrison marched against Prophet Town with more than 1000 soldiers. Even though Tecumseh had left instructions to avoid war, the Prophet became overly anxious and attacked. The Indians were driven from the town, and it was burned to the ground. Although the white soldiers suffered as many

Tecumseh, with his concept of Indian nationalism, provided a real challenge to the federal government in the early 1800s.

losses as the Indians, this Battle of Tippecanoe has been considered one of the great military victories over the Indians. After the battle many Indians became disillusioned with the Prophet's magic, and the dream of an Indian confederacy began to crumble. Tecumseh returned to find his town destroyed. He almost killed the Prophet, and the alliance between the two men ended. By 1812 many of Tecumseh's braves were taking justice into their own hands through bloody border raids.

After the Battle of Tippecanoe, British rifles were found on the battlefield. This confirmed the American suspicion that the British had been supplying Indians with arms from Canada and that the Indian trouble was due to the British. While it is true that the British traded Indians guns for furs and would have liked to have had an Indian nation in the West, the British feared eventually causing a war that might lead to the occupation of Canada. American land greed better explains the Indian antagonism. This land greed became united with patriotism in the minds of a group of congressmen who were known as the War Hawks.

Causes of the War

In the congressional election of 1810, a group of young men from the South and West were elected who desired an all-out war with Britain to prove the independence of the American republic. Young, nationalistic, and proud, these so-called War Hawks took control of the House of Representatives. Henry

Henry Clay, as speaker of the House, was one of the leading War Hawks in the quest for war with England.

Clay, who had favored war earlier, was elected speaker of the house. He appointed other War Hawks to key positions there. John Calhoun of South Carolina and Felix Grundy of Tennessee joined Clay's push for war. These congressmen turned a deaf ear to the pleas of equally hawkish but eccentric—and probably unbalanced—John Randolph, who felt that war with France would be as just as war with England. But war with France would not satisfy land greed. War with England would make an excellent excuse to seize Canada in the north and Florida in the south; one War Hawk wrote, "It appears that the Author of Nature has marked out limits in the south by the Gulf of Mexico, and on the north by the regions of eternal frost." Expansion, Indians, impressment, seizure of ships, a national depression, and the War Hawks were all responsible for the coming of the war in 1812. Apparently at the heart of the matter, however, was the American feeling that the United States could not remain self-respecting among nations if it allowed impressment to continue. Andrew Jackson of Tennessee asked, "Shall we, who have clamored for war, now sulk into a corner?" No, sulking was not necessary. War with Britain soon came.

Reason for War of 1812

The War of 1812

In general, the War of 1812 was a military disgrace. The Americans were lucky that the British had Napoleon as their major enemy at the time. In 1812

America had only a small navy and an army of 7000 ill-trained and poorly supplied men. Madison asked for 50,000 volunteers, but only 5000 responded. The boast of the War Hawks about taking Canada and Florida was just that, a boast. The American General Hull crossed into Canada but then retreated when he received a false report that his troops were outnumbered. A few days later he surrendered Detroit. At Lake Ontario General Van Rennselaer planned to cross the lake to invade Canada, but the first rowboat carried all the oars and no one could follow. Troops under one American officer, Captain Dearborn, resisted orders, while forces under a Captain Wood deserted and watched the annihilation of Wood and the rest of his band. Frequently, militiamen refused to travel too far from home. Secretary of War William Eustis (sometimes referred to as "Useless") was another obvious incompetent, but he was not replaced until 1813.

On the positive side the American ships *Constitution* and *United States* did defeat several British vessels. And in 1813 American hopes were buoyed by a brilliant victory on Lake Erie. In September of that year Captain Oliver Hazard Perry captured a British squadron on Lake Erie and secured American control over the Great Lakes. His victory was reported with the well-known words, "We have met the enemy and they are ours." This victory was soon followed by William Henry Harrison's success at the Battle of Thames, in which Tecumseh was killed. When the war started, Tecumseh and his allies joined the British cause, for they believed that the English supported the idea of an Indian state. Tecumseh became a brigadier general in the British army, and with his Indian allies provided invaluable assistance. When Harrison moved to invade Canada, Tecumseh persuaded the English commander to stand and fight. During the ensuing melee, Tecumseh was slain. Gone was one of the greatest Indian leaders in our history. His belief in Indian nationalism placed him far ahead of his time and made him one of the most relevant historical figures for the Indians' struggle today. Before his death, he accurately foretold future tension between the races when he said, "Who are the white people that we should fear them? They cannot run fast, and are good marks to shoot at. Our fathers have killed many of them. We are not squaws and we will stain the earth red with their blood." The War of 1812 lasted two years, but the Indian wars would last until 1890.

1814: Year of Crisis

By 1814 a major crisis had emerged. British blockade of the American coastline was becoming much more effective, and Napoleon had been defeated, which meant the British now could focus all attention on the American war. A three-pronged attack was planned; the British were to implement an invasion from

The Evolution of National Policy: From Jefferson to Jackson

Major Campaigns of War of 1812

Lake Superior

Lake Michigan

Lake Huron

Lake Ontario

Lake Erie

MAINE (Part of Mass.)

Plattsburg — Battle of Lake Champlain

VT.

N.H.

NEW YORK

MASS.

CONN.

R.I.

Battle of the Thames

MICHIGAN TERRITORY

ILLINOIS TERRITORY

INDIANA TERRITORY

OHIO

PENNSYLVANIA

Ft. McHenry

N.J.

Baltimore

DEL.

Washington D.C.

MD.

VIRGINIA

KENTUCKY

TENNESSEE

NORTH CAROLINA

British Blockade

ATLANTIC OCEAN

SOUTH CAROLINA

MISSISSIPPI TERRITORY

GEORGIA

Horseshoe Bend (Jackson defeats Creeks)

LA.

New Orleans

FLORIDA (Spain)

GULF OF MEXICO

→ American forces
⇢ British forces

the North, the South, and directly at the American capital. The British first landed at Chesapeake Bay and marched against Washington, D.C. They burned the Capitol, the White House, and other government buildings. James Madison and his wife Dolly were forced to flee. From there the British moved to Fort McHenry, near Baltimore, where they were met by American forces and defeated. In the rain and drizzle at Fort McHenry, Francis Scott Key wrote "The Star Spangled Banner," which was set to the tune of a racy old English drinking song, "Anacreon in Heaven." It was not until 1931, however, that Congress officially designated this song as the national anthem. From Fort McHenry the British went to the West Indies. The first invasion had been successfully repulsed.

The British also had planned to invade the United States from Canada. They decided to enter upper New York by way of Lake Champlain, a waterway essential to the transporting of soldiers and supplies. Here, in September 1814 the British forces of General Sir George Prevost met the forces of a young American naval officer, Thomas Macdonough. The battle of Lake Champlain, the decisive naval engagement of the war, ended in American victory—a stunning blow to the British. Invasion from the north was stalled and eventually dissolved. Soon after news of the battle reached Europe, terms of a peace treaty were drawn up. Actually, peace overtures had begun almost as soon as the United States declared war. But early negotiations failed, so the British focused their attention on war rather than peace. Having defeated Napoleon in Europe, the English turned their military might on America, while peace negotiators still met at Ghent, Belgium. Initially, the American commissioners—Henry Clay, John Quincy Adams, and Albert Gallatin—demanded the abandonment of impressment as an absolute prerequisite to peace. The British negotiators, meanwhile, had come to Ghent prepared to make sweeping demands, which included the annexation of American land along the Canadian border and the creation of a separate Indian nation. One British journal asked for "peace such as America deserved, and British generosity may bestow." When news of the failure of the northern and central invasions of America reached Europe—and with the example of the Duke of Wellington, who refused to fight in America—it became obvious to London that a massive military effort would be necessary before extensive territorial gains could be obtained. Meanwhile the heavily burdened British taxpayer was losing enthusiasm for prosecuting a distant war against the United States. Signed on December 24, 1814, the Treaty of Ghent formally recognized that neither side had won the war. All the heroism and valor, the bloody and costly sacrifices of both belligerents, seemed in vain; the treaty simply restored peace. The war was formally over, but fighting continued, for the invasion from the south was still underway.

The Battle of New Orleans, which occurred after the signing of the Treaty of Ghent, was remembered as a great American victory.

Victory and Peace

The only smashing American triumph on land during the war occurred at New Orleans two weeks after the peace treaty had been signed. The Battle of New Orleans was an encounter in which the forces of British General Edward Pakenham met a ragtag army under Andrew Jackson, which consisted of Kentucky and Tennessee riflemen and of blacks, sailors, Indians, and even Jean Laffitte's pirates. This army met a frontal attack of the redcoats, and in less than half an hour more than 2000 British were killed or wounded and the battle was over. According to some reports Americans lost only eight men in the conflict—one by accidental discharge of his own gun. So the war ended with a rousing victory—one that would obliterate the memory of military defeats, retreats, and mutinies. Still, the treaty that ended the war was only a peace treaty. Neither side acquired territory, and both sides returned to the state of things that existed at the start of the war. However, internally the war did cause changes in America: it created an antiwar movement in the New England area; it tarnished James Madison's image as a creative statesman. And it caused the virtual death of the Federalist party.

New Englanders saw the war as a threat to their economy and referred to it as "Mr. Madison's War." In the election of 1812, New England Democratic-

Republicans opposed the candidacy of James Madison and put up their own candidate, De Witt Clinton. Although Madison was reelected, Clinton carried all of New England and the Middle Atlantic states, except Vermont and Pennsylvania. American losses during the war's early stages did nothing to decrease New England opposition, and trade actually continued with the English. In fact, Massachusetts and Rhode Island, both friendly to the British, were not blockaded through most of the war.

In 1814 the Massachusetts legislature called for a convention to choose a course of action—possibly secession from the Union. Late in 1814 some disaffected Federalists met in Hartford, Connecticut, to talk. The moderate representatives retained control, and the convention only issued a set of resolutions that criticized the war and attempted to protect states' rights. Three representatives were sent to Washington D.C. to present the demands, but they arrived just as news of the victory at New Orleans reached the capital. The delegates left Washington in disgrace, cries of treason being raised against them. The Hartford Convention not only destroyed the myth that the nation was united during the War of 1812, but also virtually killed the Federalist party. To many Americans, the Hartford Convention was a treasonous act of the Federalist party.

While the United States neither won nor lost the War of 1812, the war was not completely in vain. In 1815 the war between Britain and France was over, so impressment and harassment of ships stopped. The United States had proved to itself that it could fight to vindicate national honor. The Treaty of Ghent actually closed one period of American history and opened another. Europe was not to experience another general war until 1914, ample time to free the United States from serious foreign threats and to enable it to concentrate on its own internal development and expansion. The war saw the rise of new military heroes, specifically William Henry Harrison and Andrew Jackson. The war, however, did little for President Madison's career. By October 1814 he was described as "miserably shattered and woebegone—heartbroken. His mind full of New England sedition." This great statesman (of small stature—only five feet, four inches) faced a nation that had been unprepared for war and was now virtually bankrupt; he himself had been seriously ill during much of the war. Just before he retired from office in 1816, he signed a bill that provided for a new bank, the Bank of the United States, and for trade controls, the Tariff Act of 1816, to protect American "infant industries" from British competition. The Democratic-Republicans now began to adopt strong nationalist policies. Madison was a two-term president, but he was not to be remembered as a great one. Foreign affairs and his personality hampered any creative domestic plans he may have had.

James Monroe and the Era of Good Feelings

The election of 1816, like the election of 1820, was virtually a one-party affair. James Monroe, Madison's secretary of state, was the choice of the Democratic-Republican party, while the Federalists did not have an official candidate (Rufus King of New York did receive 34 electoral votes). James Monroe received 183 electoral votes, becoming the fifth president of the United States.

At age 61, Monroe came to the presidency after 40 years of government service. He had fought in the American Revolution, had served both in the Virginia assembly and in Congress under the Articles of Confederation, and had been a United States senator. He had been foreign minister to France, Spain, and England, and under Madison was both secretary of state and secretary of war. Tall and dignified, he was not the intellectual equal of Jefferson and Madison. Jefferson described him as "so honest that if you should turn his soul inside out there would not be a spot on it." His style of dress reminded Americans of the old days of the Founding Fathers, yet he stood at the threshold of an emerging nationalism.

After election, Monroe made a goodwill tour of the country; no president had done it since the days of Washington. Everywhere he was greeted by cheering crowds, even in New England, the Federalist stronghold. One Boston newspaper observed that an "Era of Good Feelings" had arrived. This phrase became popular, and it became synonymous with the presidency of Monroe. Actually, the term "Era of Good Feelings" is misleading. Not all was bliss in foreign and domestic affairs during Monroe's eight-year presidency.

Chief Justice John Marshall influenced the Supreme Court by making numerous decisions that strengthened the national government.

It was true that during this period the party of Monroe went virtually unchallenged. It seemed that the two-party system was gone. Nor were there any European wars of consequence to involve the United States. The national economy was growing, the Industrial Revolution was on, and American trade was on the upswing. The Indian danger appeared to be over in the West, and thousands of Easterners packed their bags and headed for the wilderness. Patriots still remembered the beating the Americans had given the British at the Battle of New Orleans, and Congress discussed and acted on measures that would build a strong nation. A powerful National Bank and a protective tariff were two measures that strengthened the nationalism of the period. Even the Supreme Court under Chief Justice John Marshall seemed to reflect the national mood, which was both patriotic and sympathetic to the protection of business enterprise. But there has never been a time in American history when all of the people were happy—or even when most of the people were happy. Sectionalism was on the rise, as was revealed by the Missouri Compromise crisis in 1820. The Panic of 1819, the first national depression, revealed that most of the prosperity of the period was false prosperity. The South was growing restive with rising tariffs, while the West squabbled over land sales and internal improvements, such as roads and canals. This "happy" period ended with the Monroe Doctrine—a warning to foreign powers—and with the election of 1824, in which five major candidates decided to compete for the office of the presidency. However, in his first message to Congress, Monroe noted that the country was "prosperous and happy." Certain Supreme Court decisions, influenced by Marshall, contributed greatly to this prosperity and happiness.

The Marshall Court

John Marshall, a "midnight" appointee of John Adams, had emerged victorious from his judicial battles with President Jefferson. In fact, as chief justice his influence over the other justices was such that writers referred to the Supreme Court as "the Marshall Court." There is no doubt that Marshall was a dyed-in-the-wool Federalist; he was no friend of the common people. His friends were land speculators and businessmen. As chief justice he attempted to steer the country along nationalist lines that would strengthen the central government, often at the expense of state governments. During Monroe's presidency, Marshall made four decisions of nationalistic consequence. In *Gibbons v. Ogden* (1824) Marshall ruled that the state of New York did not have the power to grant monopolies to the steamboat industry because certain steamboats were involved in interstate commerce and Congress alone held power to regulate interstate commerce. Marshall had sided earlier with the federal government in _McCulloch_ v. _Maryland_ (1819). The state of Maryland had sought to tax the Baltimore branch of the Bank of the United States, hoping in the long run to drive it out of existence. Marshall ruled that the state of Maryland could not tax an agency of the federal government; he further ruled that the federal government had the power to create the Bank of the United States. Two other decisions Marshall made were favorable to the business community. _Dartmouth College_ v. _Woodward_ (1819) saw the sanctity of contracts upheld; _Sturges_ v. _Crowninshield_ (1819) declared unconstitutional a New York law that relieved debtors of their obligations. It has been written that Marshall had greater influence on the future direction of government than any other man in this early period. While Marshall was pushing for a strong central government, many other forces were pushing in an opposite direction.

Depression and Missouri Crisis

The first national depression in our history—the Panic of 1819—made many Americans question the economic policies of the central government. Actually, the Panic of 1819 was a logical outgrowth of the unrestricted expansion that followed the War of 1812. After the war, overexpansion was prevalent, particularly in the Western lands, where pioneers could even buy land on credit. Western banks sprang up and offered easy loans; at first the United States Bank went along with the expanding economy, but in 1819 it underwent new management and a financial squeeze took place. Loans were recalled, and mortgages were foreclosed. Banks began to close, and businesses failed. The poor and the Western farmers were hit especially hard. This panic created a wave of resentment among Westerners against the Eastern establishment in general and banks in particular. During the 1820s the supporters of Andrew Jackson would remember well the Panic of 1819. The panic was soon followed by another sectional struggle of major proportions that involved proposed statehood for Missouri.

In 1819 Missouri asked to be admitted to the Union as a slave state. To many, slavery there was acceptable, but the admittance of Missouri to the Union would give the South control in the Senate, which now held an equal number of slaves and free states, and this was controversial. Representative James Tallmadge of New York, called "one of nature's bad bargains," offered an amendment to the statehood bill declaring that no more slaves could be brought into Missouri and that the children of those already there must be freed upon reaching the age of 25. Southerners saw in the amendment a threat to their "peculiar institution,"; Northerners saw Missouri as a threat to the Senate balance and dangerous because it would be the first state carved from the Louisiana Purchase to be a slave state. Economic, political, and moral questions were debated, and an uproar followed. Disunion began to be spoken openly in the South. And a small group of antislavery agitators began to raise their voices in loud protest.

The issue was settled in Congress in 1820. To add to the confusion of statehood for Missouri, the House of Representatives had just moved into new quarters and over half of the House was composed of newcomers. The compromise that was reached—thanks to Senators Jesse Thomas of Illinois and Henry Clay of Kentucky—allowed Missouri to be admitted as a slave state, while Maine was to be admitted as a free state. So the balance between slave states and free states still was preserved in the Senate. In addition, an imaginary line across the Louisiana Purchase territory at 36 degrees north was drawn; the further spread of slavery was to be prohibited "forever" north of the line. Of course, the compromise did not settle permanently the issue of slavery, nor did it completely please either side. A compromise usually pleases few. John Quincy Adams called this struggle, "a title page to a great tragic volume," while Jefferson called it "a firebell in the night." By 1860 the truth of their statements would be clear to all. But in 1820 the Missouri Compromise postponed further tension between North and South for a few years. This controversy had a further dampening effect on the Era of Good Feelings, but it did not severely hurt the popularity of President Monroe. In the presidential election of 1820 the Federalist Party was noticeably absent, and Monroe received all electoral votes but one. Today he is remembered best for an event that occurred late in his second term, an event that turned out to be more important for later presidents than for Monroe; this was the Monroe Doctrine.

The Monroe Doctrine

Actually, Monroe's foreign policy was marked by little trouble. The Canadian-American boundary line was extended from the Great Lakes to the Rocky Mountains, and the Floridas were acquired from Spain through the Adams-Onis Treaty of 1819. By the 1820s America was increasingly becoming concerned over affairs in its hemisphere. Most of Spain's colonies in the Americas had revolted and established themselves as independent republics. In 1823 rumors were circulating in Europe that the powers known as the Holy Alliance—Russia, Austria, Prussia, and France—were planning to restore direct Spanish control in the old Spanish colonies. British Foreign Secretary Canning, fearful that these valuable markets would be lost to British merchants, pro-

Russian settlements in North America such as this one at Fort Ross in Northern California provided the basis for Monroe's warnings in the Monroe Doctrine.

posed to the American minister in London, Richard Rush, that the United States and Britain issue a joint warning against foreign intervention in Spanish America. Ex-president Jefferson strongly supported this stand: "With her [Great Britain], then, we should most sedulously cherish a cordial friendship; and nothing would tend more to knit our affections than to be fighting once more, side by side, in the same cause."

John Quincy Adams, Monroe's secretary of state, distrusted Britain's motives. Adams was not interested in helping England's Latin American trade, nor was he about to limit possible American expansion south. He also was aware of the Russian threat on the Pacific coast. The Russians had been moving south from Alaska and now were claiming all the coastal area north of the fifty-first parallel. Adams finally concluded it would be more desirous for the government to speak out on its own instead of following along like "a cockboat in the wake of a British man-of-war." Adams and Monroe collaborated on an official pronouncement, which the United States would stand by alone.

On December 2, 1823, Monroe sent his annual message to Congress, which contained three important statements on foreign policy. First, the doctrine of noncolonization proclaimed that "The American continents, by the free and independent condition which they have assumed and maintain, are henceforth not to be conceived as subjects for future colonization by any European powers." Second, Monroe noted that "The political system of the allied powers is essentially different in this respect from America." The Old and New Worlds were decidedly different. Finally, he stated that the United States would respect any existing European colonies in the Western hemisphere, but it would regard any attempt by any European powers to oppress or control the newly independent Latin states "as the manifestation of an unfriendly disposition toward the United States." Furthermore, the United States would not interfere in the affairs of the Eastern hemisphere, but the European powers should not interfere in the Americas.

This nationalistic pronouncement had little immediate impact. It made clear to the world that the United States intended to stay out of the affairs of Europe and that Europe should do the same with the affairs of the Western hemisphere. It is interesting to note that the doctrine did not limit action by the United States within the Western hemisphere. Monroe expressed open sympathy for the Latin American republics and laid the basis for a foreign policy that would make the United States the economic and political leader in the West. While Americans cheered this egotistical pronouncement, Europe did not take it too seriously, for America had little military might to back up its words. During the next few years the doctrine was rarely used or even referred to, but by the end of the 1800s the doctrine would be resurrected to become a major instrument of United States foreign policy and to justify intervention in the affairs of Latin American countries.

With the Monroe Doctrine, the presidency of James Monroe fast came to an end. He followed the two-term tradition and did not stand for reelection in 1824. He had been a popular president, but a rather colorless political figure. He was connected with an Era of Good Feelings that was more often than not an era of hostile feelings. He faced few crises in foreign affairs, and he reflected the national mood rather well in domestic affairs. The Virginia Dynasty of Jefferson, Madison, and Monroe as presidents from the state of Virginia came to an end with the exit of Monroe. He had administered the country well but was unable to stem the rising tide of sectionalism. The election of 1824 not only marked the end of the Era of Good Feelings but the end of a brief period of political unity.

The Election of 1824

In 1824 five men stood for the presidency. They included Secretary of State John Quincy Adams, who had served the nation well for 30 years and was the son of the second president, and Andrew Jackson, who was senator from Tennessee and the hero of the Battle of New Orleans. The others were William Crawford of Georgia (secretary of the treasury and official candidate of the Democratic-Republican party's congressional caucus), John Calhoun (secretary of war and favorite son of South Carolina), and Henry Clay (former War Hawk and ardent nationalist and the "favorite son" of Kentucky). Due to the number of candidates and factional feuds, no candidate obtained a majority in the electoral college. According to the Constitution the final choice was to be made by the House of Representatives, with each state entitled to one vote. The Constitution also indicated that the election had to be made from among the top three candidates, which meant Jackson, Adams, and Crawford.

Jackson had more states than Adams, while Crawford had suffered a crippling stroke and was now a paralytic. The key to the final decision was Henry Clay. Clay, old "Harry of the West," disliked Jackson but was not wildly fond of puritanical Adams either. One night Clay met with Adams and pledged him his support. On the first ballot, Adams was elected president. It was a legal election, but an unpopular one. Jackson and his supporters immediately exclaimed "We was robbed!" Four days after the election, Adams appointed Clay secretary of state, an office regarded as a stepping-stone to the White House. Jackson and his forces called the whole election "a corrupt bargain." Jackson, who received the largest percentage of the popular and electoral votes, had lost to the second-place man. Jackson wrote, "You see the Judas of the West has closed the contract and will receive the thirty pieces of silver. His end will be the same." Although there was no evidence of a "a corrupt bargain," the political maneuvering hurt the careers of both Adams and Clay.

John Quincy Adams as President

Short and plump, with a massive bald head, shifting eyes, and a loud, shrill voice, John Quincy Adams was the sixth president of the United States. Born in Massachusetts, his early life involved education on both sides of the Atlantic. Under Washington and under his father, John Adams, he served as foreign minister. After a brief tenure in the United States Senate, he became minister to Russia under Madison and participated in negotiations at Ghent that led to the conclusion of the War of 1812. Monroe called Adams home to serve as secretary of state and followed his advice in issuing the Monroe Doctrine. Personally, Adams had few friends for he was an aloof, lonely man. Through his long public service, he had earned the office of the presidency, but he was out of touch with the time.

John Quincy Adams was unfortunately out of touch with his times and is rated one of our weaker presidents.

In his first annual message he noted that "the great object of the institution of civil government is the improvement of those who are parties to the social compact." He wished to expand the scope of the national government by enlarging the navy, building national roads and canals, financing expeditions to the Far West, establishing institutions of learning and research, and making Washington D.C. the national cultural center. He was preaching a strong nationalism, but the Era of Good Feelings was over and a new sectionalism was emerging. Actually, Adams talked a better game than he played, for he believed that the president should not interfere unduly in the affairs of the legislative branch. A natural leader Adams was not; in fact, some of the policies connected with his presidency stirred up latent antagonisms.

Adams had more experience in foreign affairs than any other president before or since. To secure cooperation with Latin American governments, he appointed two delegates to attend an international conference in Panama in 1826, which was called by Simón Bolívar. But Adams made a mistake when he sought confirmation of the two men from the Senate and requested expense money from Congress. Jackson's followers saw an opportunity to handicap the president; they were joined by Southerners who hated to think of white Americans mingling in Panama with colored delegates from Haiti while discussing the issue of slavery in the United States. Congress delayed the Panama mission so long that the eventual trip became futile and ridiculous. One of the American delegates died on the way to the conference, and the other arrived too late. American politics had handicapped Adams's effort to seize an upper hand in Pan-American politics. British influence was still dominant in Latin America. Adams's failure in foreign affairs also was marked by his lack of agreement with Great Britain over the right of free navigation on the St. Lawrence River and the opening of ports in the British West Indies.

His failings also extended to domestic policies. Adams tried to stem widespread speculation in Western land and incurred the undying antagonism of that region. His term is connected with the Tariff of 1828, commonly called the Tariff of Abominations. By 1828 the Northwest and Middle Atlantic states, with their new industrial products, seemed to be benefitting from higher tariffs, while the Southern states, with their cotton exports, were being hurt by them. The South was becoming more frustrated by national politics, in particular tariff legislation, and, in turn, Adams's popularity suffered.

The Election of 1828

In 1828 the national issues of the tariff, the National Bank, and internal improvements were lost in the bitter personality clash between Adams and Jack-

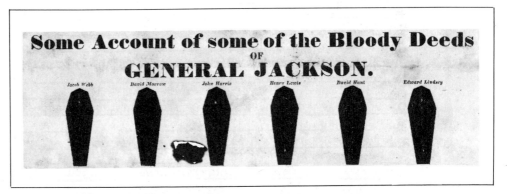

The Coffin Handbill was propaganda distributed by the followers of Adams that told of Jackson's brutal shooting of six militiamen.

son. Modern politics was being born. Adams was pictured as a compulsive gambler who had furnished the White House with a billiard table at public expense and who had pimped for one of his servants. Jackson supporters even charged that while in office Adams had written a dirty poem. Adams's followers hardly were quiet themselves. Jackson's illicit love affairs were listed and a "coffin handbill" was distributed that told of Jackson's shooting of six militiamen for insubordination. Jackson also was called a gambler, a brawler, and a slave trader. Even his mother was described as a prostitute. It was a personality contest and one of the dirtiest elections in our history—though not the last of its kind. Jackson received 65 percent of the popular vote; the electoral college voted him president; and "the era of the common man" began.

The Presidency of Andrew Jackson

Who was this man Jackson, whose election climaxed the rise of the common American? Raised in the Carolina wilderness, Andrew Jackson was the first president born in a log cabin. Basically self-educated, he early earned a reputation as a fighter and not as a scholar. During the American Revolution, at age 13, he joined the mounted militia of South Carolina. After the Revolution he received a substantial inheritance from his grandfather, which he wasted on horse races and cockfights. Becoming a lawyer, he established a successful practice in Nashville, Tennessee, and began to make money by selling land to new settlers. During the next few years he served in the House of Representatives and the United States Senate, became justice of the Tennessee Supreme Court, managed two plantations, speculated in land, and ran a general store. His quick temper in those days caused him to engage in many duels.

With the War of 1812 Jackson's military career burst into full bloom. A major general in the Tennessee militia, he earned his reputation as an Indian fighter in 1814 by defeating a group of rebellious Creeks at the Battle of Horseshoe Bend. His victory over the British at New Orleans earned him national honor. After the war he led an expedition into Florida, then Spanish territory, and became provisional governor of Florida. By the 1820s Jackson had retired to his large plantation home, the Hermitage, and had begun to enjoy the life of a country gentleman. The Tennessee legislature had other ideas and nominated him for president in 1824. Seemingly robbed of victory in 1825, he and his followers worked hard, and, in 1828, he won a sweeping victory.

Andrew Jackson was not a "common man"; he was a landed aristocrat. His stand on major issues was unclear. Still, he appealed to almost everybody:

Andrew Jackson was the symbol of the common man and became one of the most popular presidents.

the urban poor, the Western farmer, the factory owner, and the Southern aristocrat. He was the symbol of the self-made man who had risen from humble beginnings; he was the citizen soldier who led a rag-tag army to a victory over the mighty British army; he was the man the people knew as "Old Hickory." The truth about him and his democracy lay partly in his personality and partly in the image people had created.

Physically, Jackson was an imposing figure. Sixty-one-years-old, 6-feet-1-inch tall and weighing 145 pounds, he was long and lean, with a mane of white hair. His face was wrinkled from age and his frequent illnesses. He suffered more from painful illnesses than any other president. Two bullets that were lodged in his body continued to poison his system; his constant cough was from tuberculosis. Severe headaches, dysentery, and dropsy also plagued him. But these physical illnesses seemed forgotten in the euphoria that surrounded his inauguration.

Nearly 10,000 supporters came to Washington, D.C., to see their "Andy." One spectator noted, "It was like the inundation of the northern barbarians into Rome." His inaugural address was not particularly noteworthy, but that made little difference. The crowd followed him to and into the White House. The whole scene was chaos. His followers stood on satin chairs in muddy boots, fought their way to the refreshment table, broke glasses, and even pinned Jackson against a wall. Daniel Webster wrote, "People have come five hundred miles to see General Jackson, and they really seem to think that the country has been rescued from some dreadful danger." With this inauspicious beginning, Jackson—the man of the people—entered his career as president.

Jacksonian Democracy

Jackson's philosophy of government was based on the principle that any ordinary American can serve in government and even be president. He also was willing to reward many of his followers by putting them into government positions. This "spoils system" goes back to the roots of the Republic, but it wasn't used to such an extent before or after Jackson. More than 10 percent of federal officials were replaced with Jackson's men. Along with the spoils system, Jackson used the principle of rotation. "No man has any more intrinsic right to official station than another," he wrote. By "rotating" officeholders, more Americans could participate in government. His philosophy attempted to reduce the government "to that simple machine which the Constitution had created." He felt that the president was the voice of the people and must play a powerful role in the determination of government policy. Jackson's early reforms initially were overshadowed by a political scandal and a growing rift with his vice-president.

The O'Neale Scandal

Peggy O'Neale Timberlake was a married woman in Washington, D.C., whose husband was a naval purser and thus frequently was away at sea. It was said she "drove the young men of Washington wild and some of the old ones, too." John Eaton, a wealthy senator from Tennessee and a close acquaintance of Jackson, expressed an excessive interest in her, even helping finance her father when he went broke. Rumors spread of their relationship. At the time of Jackson's election, her husband died at sea and Eaton married her. This incident would have caused little stir if Jackson had not appointed Eaton secretary of war and if the cabinet wives had not forced their husbands to literally "boycott" the "hussy." This public humiliation of the Eatons caused internal dissension in the Jackson administration. Martin Van Buren brought matters to a head by revealing that Vice-President John Calhoun was attempting to make political gain of the circumstances. Van Buren and Eaton resigned from Jackson's cabinet, as did the followers of Calhoun. As a final consequence of this scandal Van Buren gained the inside track, eventually becoming Jackson's successor; Calhoun was the loser.

The Nullification Struggle

The split between Jackson and Calhoun continued to grow with the tariff crisis. During the 1820s the South became more and more critical of the tariff because they felt that the tariff discriminated against their one-crop economy and favored the industrial North. This feeling was particularly strong in South Carolina, where economic depression and soil exhaustion brought the tariff issue to a critical point. The high tariff, South Carolina reasoned, was responsible for all their problems. The "favorite son" of South Carolina, John Calhoun agreed with this thinking. In an unsigned essay, "The South Carolina Exposition and Protest," Calhoun argued that a state has the power to nullify an act of Congress. Jackson favored a low tariff and states' rights, but he could not accept a direct attack on federal power. At a dinner in 1830, the split between Jackson and Calhoun reached its climax. Jackson proposed a toast, "Our Federal Union—it must be preserved." Calhoun followed with, "The Union—next to our liberty, the most dear!" Calhoun had become the chief defender of the South and its interests.

A new tariff bill in 1832 reduced tariff rates, but the South saw little progress in it. A special convention in South Carolina drew up a document, the Ordinance of Nullification, which declared that the recent tariff act "was unauthorized by the Constitution of the United States, null, void, and no law, not binding upon these states, its officers, or citizens." The collection of tariff duties within the state was forbidden and funds began to be raised to finance an army for protection "from invasion." Privately, Jackson was angered; he threatened to hang Calhoun and the nullifiers. Publicly, he took a firm, rational stand by issuing a proclamation to the people of South Carolina that was a brilliant defense of the Union. Jackson reasoned that nullification was "incompatible with the existence of the Union, contradicted expressly by the letter of the Constitution, unauthorized by its spirit, inconsistent with every principle on which it was founded, and destructive of the great objective for which it was formed." In short, the Union must be preserved; but South Carolina was not immediately convinced.

Jackson went to Congress and asked for a force bill that would give him authority to raise an army and navy, and, at the same time, he asked for a lower tariff. Both laws were passed. Under Henry Clay's leadership, a compromise tariff was engineered that pleased Calhoun and South Carolina. The state's nullification ordinance was repealed, and the force bill was nullified, too. Both sides declared victory. Calhoun now continued as the voice of the South and lost any chance of national support. Jackson's response to this crisis had been personal, yet effective; a believer in states' rights, he had seen the need for a strong, nationalistic position. This position was not always popular, but his actions to support it were quite courageous.

Indian Removal

Critics of government Indian policy would hardly say that Jackson's Indian policy was a courageous one, or even a humane one. Although the treaty process was continued after the War of 1812, Indian affairs were becoming more systematized. And in 1824 the Office of Indian Affairs was created within the War Department, with the head of the bureau in 1832 being designated "Commissioner of Indian Affairs." The inauguration in 1828 of Andrew Jackson, frontiersman and Indian fighter, brought a new emphasis to the Indian-land cession process. In 1830 the Indian Removal Act empowered the president to negotiate treaties to exchange Indian land east of the Mississippi for territory west of the river, territory which was considered by some explorers to be mostly desert. Jackson was a veteran Indian fighter, and he was anxious to clear the Southeast of Indians. It was those powerful nations of the Southeast—the five civilized tribes, the Choctaw, Chickasaw, Cherokee, Creek, and Seminole—that were most affected. The implementation of forced removal produced one of the darkest chapters in American history.

The Choctaw, Creek, and Chickasaw were forced to accept a treaty of removal, an initial step in the removal process. Due to the severity of the weather and the shoddy contractors that the government used in moving the tribes to their new homes, all tribes suffered. Of the Choctaw, for example, 1000 perished on the trail. The Cherokee Indians, however, presented an unusual challenge.

The Cherokee were one of the most successful tribes in the United States in using the white race's skills for their own benefit without becoming completely white. The argument that Indians were savages who had to be moved west in the face of advanced civilization did not apply to the Cherokee, for their civilization was a sophisticated one. Not only did they have a written language and a bilingual newspaper, but their literacy rate was higher than that of the whites. The Cherokee nation, located within the State of Georgia, had made remarkable progress. It had schools, large herds of cattle, sawmills, blacksmith shops, well-cultivated fields, and a ferry system. The tribe believed the land belonged to the Cherokee people and could not be bought or sold. Yet the Georgians lusted for their well-developed land; this land greed was whetted by the discovery of gold.

Between 1828 and 1831 the Georgia legislature abrogated a federal treaty and brought the Cherokee nation under state law by confiscating all Cherokee land and nullifying all Cherokee laws. Cherokees even were denied the right to testify in court. In 1832 the Cherokee mixed-blood chieftain, John Ross, took their cause to the Supreme Court. In *Worcester* v. *Georgia,* Chief Justice John Marshall ruled that federal law, not Georgia law, took precedence over the Cherokee tribe. This victory was short-lived. The State of Georgia ignored the court, and Jackson is supposed to have said, "John Marshall has made his decision, now let him enforce it." The federal removal policy joined with Georgia harassment. In 1835 an unrepresentative group of Cherokees signed a treaty of removal in return for some blankets. Once rounded up and herded into stockades like animals, the Cherokee prepared for their trek west. A small group of Cherokee hid in the mountains and avoided removal; today this group

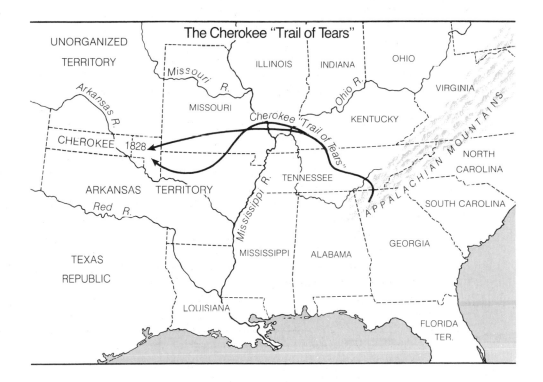

is known as the Eastern Cherokee. In 1838–39 the majority of the Cherokee people were removed forceably from their lands and driven to Oklahoma; this trek west was called the "Trail of Tears." Troops and government contractors pushed the Indians across the South to Oklahoma in the dead of a bitter winter, and nearly a fourth of the Cherokee died of disease, starvation, and hardship. In Oklahoma, then Indian territory, the Cherokee nation regrouped and rebuilt its civilization. But the Civil War and later white settlement of Oklahoma were to provide two more disruptive challenges to their way of life. While the tragedy of Cherokee removal is a dark blot on our past history, to the Americans then it was a popular policy and a tragic success.

Another group that avoided removal was a remnant of the Seminoles, who resisted the United States army with guns and poison darts in the Florida Everglades. More than 2000 American soldiers died, and more than $60 million was spent before the majority of the tribe agreed to remove to Oklahoma. Osceola, the leading Seminole chieftain, was tricked into surrendering, but a remnant led by leaders named Wildcat and Alligator held on. (Until recently this group of Indians was still at war with the United States government. During the Vietnam War a Seminole who had been drafted boldly declared that he was a citizen of the Seminole nation, not of the United States, and did not have to serve in the army.)

With the exception of a few scattered Cherokee and Seminole people, the tribes of the East had been forced upon the tribes of the West. But Indian removal was merely a stopgap measure in white expansion west.

The Bank War

By the 1830s a common enemy of the people and of President Jackson was the National Bank of the United States. The Second Bank of the United States had been rechartered in 1816 for a 20-year period. Its early policies were fairly unrestrictive, but with the Panic of 1819 it began to be described in such terms as "the Monster" and "the Octopus." Many Westerners, including Jackson, had lost large sums of money in banks that went broke, and a substantial portion of the population began to distrust all banks and financial monopolies. During the 1820s, under the control of Nicholas Biddle, the bank followed a fairly conservative monetary policy. When Jackson became president he looked with a jaundiced eye at the bank in general and at Biddle in particular. To him, Biddle represented the more conservative financial interests of the Eastern seaboard. Biddle disliked the loose fiscal policies of state banks and used the Second Bank to control them. Personally, Biddle was ambitious and was linked to certain questionable financial deals. Whether he also was trying to benefit the country by creating an institution that would provide controls for gradual economic growth is unclear.

In 1832 the issue of Biddle, Jackson, and the National Bank came to a head. Jackson seemed to indicate that he would not oppose the bank's recharter if he was reelected in 1832. A few opponents of Jackson, particularly Biddle, were not satisfied with this neutral stand and tried to bring the issue to a head before the election. Jackson's political opponents persuaded Biddle to let them introduce a bill for recharter immediately, thus making the bank a political issue in the ensuing campaign. The Bank Bill passed Congress but was vetoed by Jackson. "The Bank is trying to kill me, but I will kill it," he wrote. And he did. He argued that the bank was undemocratic, unconstitutional, and was a monopoly for the wealthy. His message reflected not only his personal bias but also the sentiments of many Westerners and factory workers who preferred a loose money policy. The veto message was also good political propaganda for Jackson's reelection fight. Congress was unable to achieve a two-thirds majority to override the veto. Jackson's reelection in 1832 demonstrated the popularity of his stand on the National Bank. Now Jackson was going to help "the Monster" die a painful death.

During the next four years government expenses were paid from existing deposits while deposits of new government funds were placed in 89 state banks, popularly called "Pet Banks." Biddle responded by tightening credit, but that only caused more hostility toward the dying bank. When Jackson was asked if he had an answer to the tight credit problem, he retorted, "Go to Biddle." In 1836 the bank died and unrestricted speculation was in full bloom. Jackson himself feared the effects of such rapid economic growth and in 1836 issued a Specie Circular, which required all public lands to be purchased with "hard" or metallic money. While inflation continued, the Specie Circular was the beginning of an economic decline. Jackson would not see the effect of his killing of the National Bank within his presidency, but his hand-picked successor, Martin Van Buren, would face a national depression.

Rise of the Whig Party

By Jackson's second term, a two-party system had emerged again in the form of the Democrats and the Whigs. Under Jackson's leadership, the Democratic party was a coalition of Eastern workers, frontier farmers, plantation owners, and the wealthy. The Whigs, led by Henry Clay, who was soundly defeated in the presidential election of 1832, were composed of all who opposed Jackson. While many of Jackson's policies were popular, their long-term effects were often disastrous; still, Jackson had kindled the public's imagination. Before he left office at the age of 70, old, thin, and tired, he picked Martin Van Buren as his successor. Today, Jackson is considered "the president of the people" and a symbol of democracy, since he stirred the popular mind as no president has before or since. True, he was too personal in his approach to problems and used the veto at will. His appointments were not always the best, but he made reasonable changes in government and broadened participation in governing. He emerged from the office having strengthened the presidency. He did leave unsolved problems (as his successors would find out), but he had done his best to handle his immediate problems. Considering his deteriorating physical condition, he did a truly remarkable job.

The period that spanned the Jefferson and Jackson administrations was a period filled with war, political unity and disunity, dirty political campaigns, nationalism, sectionalism, spoils systems, Indian removal, rotation in office, uneasy foreign policy—in other words, no different from today. It was a period that marked the careers of two great men as president; Thomas Jefferson and Andrew Jackson. Both Jefferson and Jackson were human, and their democratic tendencies were tempered by their respective biases against the court system and the National Bank. A second war with Britain was fought; nothing concrete was decided, but America had shown the world that it was part of the world community. An Era of Good Feeling (mixed with much bad) took place during the presidency of James Monroe, a man who personally offered little leadership. With the election of John Quincy Adams, partisanship returned to politics; and by 1836 a two-party system was again to be part of the political scene. It was during this time that a way of life was forming that was a product of an emerging nation. A national culture was being born that reflected the variety of the American experience. The many facets of this burgeoning culture will be examined in Chapter 6.

Essay

The Burning of Washington, D.C.

War Hawks in Congress wanted expansion into Florida and Canada and revenge against the British. Westerners complained of the alliance between the Indians of the Great Lakes and the British in Canada. An economic decline in 1811 was blamed on the British disruption of our trade with Europe. President Madison told Congress that war was necessary because of Britain's Orders in Council, which interfered with American commerce and took American seamen and forced them to serve in the British navy. Whatever the reason, in 1812 we entered a war against Britain, one which many newspapers called "Mr. Madison's War" but which members of his party described as America's "Second War of Independence."

The bravado, however, disappeared quickly with defeat after defeat. The American invasion of Canada was a fiasco at best. Meanwhile the British fleet began a successful blockade of the New England coast. Fortunately, while the first two years of war were hardly glorious ones for the United States, the British army and the British public were much more concerned with Napoleon. But the defeat of Napoleon was at hand, and soon first-class soldiers could be sent across the sea to conquer the upstart Americans. A plan was instituted for a threefold invasion of the United States with the major maneuver to be directed at the capital itself—Washington, D.C.

Fifty-six-year-old Vice-Admiral Alexander Forrester Inglis Cochrane became commander of the British fleet for the Chesapeake Bay operations. A veteran of amphibious warfare, he had accumulated considerable experience in Egypt and was ready to coordinate a land and sea attack. He worked closely with 48-year-old Robert Ross, a veteran of numerous European land battles. His insistence on rigid discipline and relentless drill kept his men in readiness. In August 1814, the invasion was underway; Ross' professional soldiers had been transported up Chesapeake Bay to Benedict on the upper Patuxent River. They were now ready to strike at the city of Washington.

In 1813 rumors of a threatened invasion of Washington had circulated widely. But no attack materialized, so military preparedness ceased. By 1814 the defensive system for Washington was nonexistent except for a few troops near the city and a weak naval force. Month after month Congress had voted down resolutions to place the capital in a defensive posture, while the secretary of war kept concentrated on his invasion of Canada. The best plan for defense came from the cabinet in July, when it proposed to defend Washington with an army of volunteers from all the states. The result was inadequate at best. Some of the men that reported for duty were told to go home and get better shoes and to bring back a butcher knife if they could not get a musket. On August 18 news reached the capital that a British fleet had sailed into the Patuxent River. The city was put on immediate alert.

As the British army marched closer to the capital, 38-year-old Brigadier General William Henry Winder was entrusted with defense of the city. His frustrations were many. Secretary of War

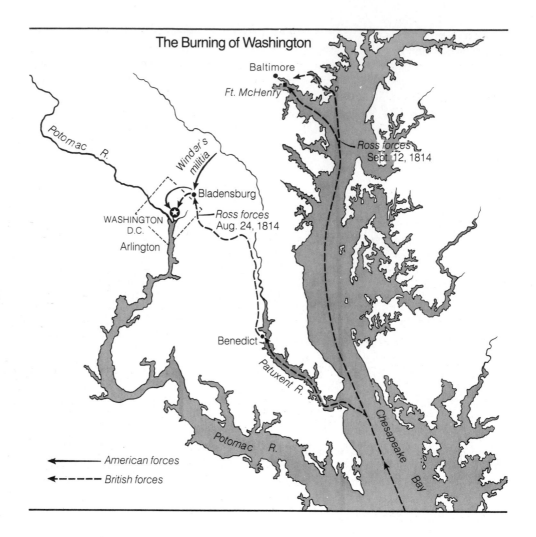

The Burning of Washington

Baltimore

Ft. McHenry

Potomac R.

Winder's militia

Bladensburg

WASHINGTON D.C.

Arlington

Ross forces
Aug. 24, 1814

Ross forces
Sept. 12, 1814

Benedict

Patuxent R.

Potomac R.

Chesapeake Bay

⟵ American forces

⟵----- British forces

John Armstrong, new to his office, still believed that the British force would not attack Washington; the quartermaster of the army was unable to supply axes for cutting trees to impede the enemy advance; and Winder's own troops were untrained, volunteer militiamen. In addition, he got little consistent help from his superiors, who included President James Madison and Secretary of State James Monroe. His was an indefensible position, which led to one of America's darkest days—that of August 24, 1814.

This was the situation: A British army of nearly 10,000 veterans was marching on Washington, which was defended by about 5000 un-

The Evolution of National Policy: From Jefferson to Jackson

trained, raw volunteers. The confrontation took place at Bladensburg, just northeast of the capital. It was one of the few battles in American history in which the president was in reality a commander in chief. With his musket strapped to his side, President Madison rode to the battlefield to help with coordination. He was joined by many citizens from Washington who came out on horseback and in carriages to view the action.

While the British forces expected the encounter to be a mere skirmish, fighting continued for three hours. Eventually the action at Blandensburg developed into two separate battles. The British use of skyrockets gave their army little advantage but did panic and demoralize the untrained American troops. The American militiamen could hold out no longer; Winder gave the order for retreat. He then joined Monroe

General Robert Ross and his troops are pictured here burning many government buildings in their attack on Washington, D.C.

and Armstrong and rode to Washington. While the British troops under Ross rested, the capital was evacuated. Men, women, and children were seen running through the streets with personal possessions, while government officials packed up documents, which included the Declaration of Independence, the Articles of Confederation, and the Federal Constitution. Ross and his invading army now marched down Maryland Avenue with a white flag raised high. He had come to talk surrender but no one came to greet him. After waiting awhile and debating the various possible courses of action, Ross agreed to burn all public building. The Capitol Building was already burning as the British set torch to the White House, known then as the President's House, and the Treasury and War offices. So ended the day—a day long remembered in early American history.

Although the eventual defeat of the British at Fort McHenry nullified the effects of their central invasion, and although the burning of Washington was of little military significance, it did reveal America's weakness in its lack of a standing, professional army. It was a stunning moment in our history when the President and the First Lady were forced to ride into the countryside while the nation's public buildings, including their home, were burned to the ground by an opposing army. Such was the tragedy of that fateful day in August 1814. ■

Suggested Reading

The causes of the War of 1812 are covered by JULIUS PRATT in *The Expansionists of 1812* (1925), while the war is described by HARRY L. COLES in his *The War of 1812* (1965).

Two studies of Madison include *James Madison: a Biography* (1971) by RALPH KITCHAM and *James Madison, The President, 1809–1812* (1956), which is part of a six-volume work by IRVING BRANT.

The Era of Good Feelings and the coming of Jacksonian Democracy are described in two books by GEORGE DANGERFIELD, *The Era of Good Feelings* (1963) and *The Awakening of American Nationalism, 1812–1828* (1965).

DEXTER PERKINS in *The Monroe Doctrine* (1927) discusses the complex motives behind the doctrine.

Indian policy from Jefferson to Jackson is examined in *Expansion and American Indian Policy, 1782–1812* (1967) by REGINALD HORSMAN and in *Indian Policy in the Jacksonian Era* (1975), by RONALD SATZ.

Many studies of Jackson and his democracy include as references the following books: *The Election of Andrew Jackson* (1963) by ROBERT REMINI, *The Age of Jackson* (1945) by ARTHUR SCHLESINGER, JR., *Andrew Jackson: Symbol for an Age* (1956) by JOHN W. WARD.

CHAPTER 6

The Nation Develops a Personality: Emerging National Culture

Time Line

?–A.D. 1492	Migration and evolution of American Indian societies
1492	Christopher Columbus lands in West Indies—beginning of European exploration
1607–1732	Establishment of 13 English colonies
1775–1783	American Revolution
1776	Declaration of Independence
1789–1797	Presidency of George Washington

1791	Hamilton's "Report on the Subject of Manufacturers"
1800	Gabriel Prosser Revolt
1806–1807	Zebulon Pike Expedition
1825	Completion of Erie Canal
1830	Joseph Smith founds Mormon Church
1831	Nat Turner Revolt
1833	Formation of American Anti-Slavery Society
1842	*Commonwealth* v. *Hunt*
1846	Congress establishes Smithsonian Institute
1848	Seneca Falls meeting for women's rights

1812–1815	War of 1812
1816–1824	Era of Good Feelings
1846–1848	Mexican War
1861–1865	Civil War
1865–1877	Reconstruction
1877–1900	Industrialization and urbanization

1900–1916	Progressive Era
1917–1918	World War I
1930s	Depression and New Deal
1941–1945	World War II
1945–1960	Post-war politics
1950–1953	Korean War
1950–1960	Civil rights movement
1961–1973	Vietnam War
1976	Bicentennial celebration

The crowd stands just before the kickoff at a football game and sings the national anthem. The American flag is floating in the breeze from its position on the front porch; it must be the Fourth of July. Critics of American foreign policy talk about this "Uncle Sam" who has given too much to nations around the world. The nation's seal pictures a bald eagle (not a wild turkey, as Ben Franklin would have preferred). It is Washington's birthday: Children and government officials alike enjoy the holiday. On this day many Americans are shopping at the nearby shopping center, taking advantage of the tremendous bargains of a Washington's Birthday Sale. The national anthem, the flag, "Uncle Sam," the bald eagle, Washington's Birthday—these are all symbols of the emergence of a national culture, a culture that really took root during the American Revolution. But it is not only a culture that smacks of nostalgia, it is also a culture that reflects racism, inhumanity, intellectual progress, women's rights, mass amusements, and urban growth. It is a culture that, in its founding era, attempted to bind people of states and regions together during a period when states and regions did not always get along. It was not only a national culture but also a culture for the masses. And it went a long way in making constant change an essential part of the American heritage.

Immigration

From 1790 to 1850 the United States had more than tripled its land area, and its population had increased eightfold: from 4 million to over 23 million people (see Chart 6-1). Although the nation still remained overwhelmingly rural, the percentage of urban population was rising (to over 13 percent by 1850), with more than 7 cities claiming 100,000 residents or more. The population was aging but was still very young. In 1840 the median age for Americans was 17.8 years. One of the major reasons for the rapid growth in population was the growth of immigration. By 1850 the foreign born represented 10 percent of the total population. From 1820 to 1850 more than 2.4 million people came to the United States, and the majority of them were from Ireland and Germany. Strong incentives to migrate came from both Europe and the United States. The fear of overpopulation, low wages, oversupply of agricultural workers, and rising demand for land were just some of the motivating factors in Europe at this time. But stronger than the forces pushing people out of Europe were those magnetic ones pulling them to the United States. While there was no Statue of Liberty to greet them to this "land of opportunity," there was the unofficial open door policy that seemed to welcome all to this prosperous

Chart 6-1
Population Growth in the National Period

1790	3,929,214
1800	5,308,483
1810	7,239,881
1820	9,638,453
1830	12,866,020
1840	17,069,453
1850	23,191,871
1860	31,443,321

place. The opportunity for better wages and cheap land were two major motives. Enterprising Americans attempted to sell land in the West to immigrants; others went to Europe and began to sell travel books about America. "American Letters"—letters that the immigrants sent home to report what they found—told of the freedom and advantages. These people often were impressed with the most prosaic items: "We now get beef and pudding, tea and rum"; "The poorest family adorns the table three times a day."

Nativism

All Americans, however, did not welcome these people with open arms to the "American melting pot." Once Americans began to look upon themselves as Americans, a strong protective movement called *nativism* arose. One writer sarcastically reflected the feelings of the nativists: "All men are created equal, except Negroes, and foreigners, and Catholics." To native-born Americans the immigrants seemed to be a threat. These foreigners were beginning to gather in separate communities in the cities, which began to be referred to as ghettos. Here violence, crime, and poverty abounded. Since many of the early immigrants were Irish, much of the antiforeign reaction was also anti-Catholic. During the 1830s nativism reached ugly proportions. Native American political parties were formed in the larger cities; these parties attempted to exclude foreigners from political office and to change naturalization laws. Some zealots also destroyed homes of Catholics and burned churches and convents. In 1834 a mob burned an Ursuline convent in Charlestown, Massachusetts, while

The Irish immigrants were the first European victims of American nativism. They are pictured here leaving Ireland for the land of opportunity.

similar episodes were occurring elsewhere. These actions were stimulated by anti-Catholic writings, such as Samuel F. B. Morse's *Foreign Conspiracy*, which pointed out that the immigrant-filled slums were breeding places of crime and immorality and that the Catholics were trying to seize the government for the pope. A similar work was Maria Monk's *Awful Disclosures of the Hotel Dieu Nunnery*. Allegedly written by an ex-nun, the book confirmed every Protestant suspicion of life in a convent.

In 1852 a secret organization calling itself the Grand Council of the United States of North America was formed. This group commonly was referred to as the Know-Nothing party. As with earlier groups, it was directed against immigrants, particularly Irish Catholics. And it was to be a secret organization composed only of native-born American citizens who professed Protestantism. Secret signs, passwords, and rituals were all part of the group's trademark. Not only did Know-Nothings indicate their strength by electing in the campaign of 1854 nine governors and filling state legislatures and Congress with their supporters, but they also involved themselves in mob violence. The appointment of James Campbell, a Catholic, to the position of attorney general opened the floodgates; many mobs staged demonstrations in which they hung the pope in effigy. In 1855 there were anti-Irish riots in New York City. This explosion of bigotry was retarded by the coming of the Civil War, but this was not the last time that foreigners were victims of the nativism movement. The Irish immigrant was the first victim, but another victim of bigotry was an unwilling immigrant—the black.

Black Americans

It has already been pointed out that more than 5000 blacks participated in the American Revolution and that the slave system came under severe criticism with the end of the war. By 1792 all states north of Virginia had antislavery societies dedicated to the abolition of the slave trade and to the gradual emancipation of the slaves. These societies petitioned state legislatures and Congress for action. Eventually Northern state legislatures provided for gradual emancipation. The Quock Walker case in Massachusetts hastened these sentiments. A slave, Quock Walker was freed on the grounds that, since the preamble to the new state constitution of 1780 proclaimed that all men were born free and equal, slavery was illegal. The courts were confirming what the legislatures were enacting. Congress climaxed the trend with the passage of the Northwest Ordinance in 1787, which specifically prohibited slavery in the Northwest Territory. Even in the South, many state legislatures were beginning to outlaw the importation of slaves. It appeared that slavery was on the way out.

What appeared to be the imminent demise of the slave system was reflected in the Constitution itself. The Founding Fathers, however, were concerned less with equality than with property rights. Slaves were counted as only three-fifths of a person in determing both a state's representation in Congress and a state's taxes. The importation of slaves was outlawed after 1808, but neither Northern or Southern representatives at the Constitutional Convention were eager to take a position on freedom for the slaves; many delegates felt that slavery was already on the decline and that the prohibition of foreign slave trade would cause its natural death. This was not the case.

The growing textile industries of France and England were demanding an increased supply of cotton. During the colonial period Southern farmers found indigo, tobacco, and rice to be their major cash crops. With cotton, on the other hand, there seemed to be no easy and inexpensive method of separating the seeds from the fiber. In essence, cotton production was unprofitable. The growing demand for cotton in Europe and the invention in 1793 of the cotton gin by Eli Whitney, a device which easily separated cotton seeds from fiber, made the expansion of the cotton kingdom possible. A new demand for slave labor arose, while the cotton growers looked to the fertile, bottom land of Alabama and Mississippi for their incipient empires. Slavery did not die a natural death in the South. In fact, by 1860 more than four million slaves were found there, primarily on cotton plantations.

Plantation Slaves

Life in the antebellum South varied from plantation to plantation and from city to city. A general picture of slavery in the days of the cotton kingdoms is very difficult to draw. The majority of Southern farmers did not own slaves; many were classified as poor white trash. Statistics reveal that the plantation owners comprised a small percentage of the total population, but they dominated the economic life of the area. In reality only 10 percent of the plantation owners had more than 20 slaves. Slaves on small plantations performed a much larger range of duties, from cooking to carpentry to harvesting to tending animals; they had a closer relationship with their owners and were treated better than blacks on the large plantations.

On large plantations slave owners were farther removed from their slaves, while slaves were much more specialized in their work. But generally they were divided into "household" and "field" slaves. The field slaves worked in gangs from sunrise to sunset; their immediate masters were white or black overseers who monitored their work. Each slave was considered to be an expensive piece of property, or *chattel*; their lot in life was a difficult one. But since they were looked upon as expensive machines, the smart slave owner usually did not abuse his human property—by 1860 each slave was worth as much as $1600.

The house slaves usually performed the domestic chores for the master. They were nurses, maids, cooks, drivers, and butlers. Since they usually lived in the same house with the owners and ate their food, their conditions were much better than the field slaves. In fact, many of these house slaves eventually learned to read and write. Since their conditions were superior to those of their counterparts in the field, they often considered themselves superior, and a real animosity arose between the two groups.

It is false to believe that no slaves were whipped or beaten, yet physical punishment was not the prime motivation in slave labor. The threat of beating was found to be much more effective and less damaging to the labor force than whipping itself. Many slave owners rewarded their best workers with money, food, goods, bonuses; others withheld privileges. The *task system*, offering artificial incentives, was used often with much success. When a field slave completed a specific task, he or she was given a reward; but the assigned task was usually impossible to complete in one day. Since the slave system was primarily a work system, much care was taken in getting the most out of one's property.

While some writers have pictured the positive features of the black subculture, emphasizing singing, dancing, hunting, fishing, and other amusements, the cruelties of slavery were numerous. General conditions were often inhumane. Slave houses were crude shanties with dirt floors. Here slaves slept and ate their meager meals, which usually consisted of salt pork, corn bread, and molasses. One wrote of his food, "The pork was often tainted and the fish were of the poorest quality." Slave clothing consisted of old rags and worn-

Most Southern slaves in the pre-Civil War days were field hands on cotton plantations.

The Nation Develops a Personality: Emerging National Culture

out items from the master and his family. Medical attention was provided but medicine at this time was still more of an art than a science.

Although importation of slaves still continued after the 1808 ban, slave population further increased through the use of breeding farms, which used fertile females who were referred to as "good breeders." The large number of mulattos were an obvious sign of the frequent sexual abuses that occurred. Slave conditions did not allow for normal family living. In fact, slave marriages were not recognized by law, so many slaves began to adopt a very casual view of marriage. One of the greatest fears was of being separated from one's family. Slave traders frequently justified these fears.

Slave Trading

Slave traders were an essential part of slavery as an economic system; they were businessmen who bought and sold slaves. Many were independent merchants who worked on a commission basis. Some hunted runaway slaves, while others merely housed slaves and sold them by auction. With the increasing demand for slave labor, slave trading could be a very profitable venture. Slave markets were found in all the Southern cities, especially in New Orleans, Mobile, Natchez, and even in Washington, D.C. It was not until 1850 that a law was passed that prohibited the buying and selling of slaves in the

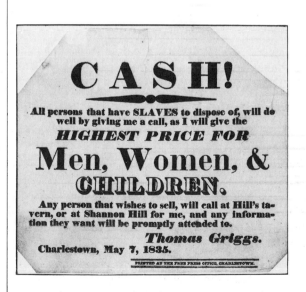

Slave traders bought and sold slaves as property.

District of Columbia. The Southern legal system protected slave owners and traders, while the slaves themselves fell under the jurisdiction of state laws known as "slave codes."

Slave Laws

Although there are some instances of slaves suing their masters for damages and pleading in court for freedom, slaves were legally outside the laws. Southern state legislatures, however, passed a series of laws to regulate their behavior. These slave codes (or "black codes") forced slaves to live in an inferior position, while it assured owners that slave rebellions could never take place. Any slaves connected with a rebellion or alleged rebellion were immediately put to death. Slaves were forbidden to leave their plantations or to assemble without a written note. They could not own animals, guns, musical instruments, such as horns or drums, or liquor, and in many cities they were denied even cigarettes. They were not allowed to be educated, although many house slaves did learn to read and write. If they were taken to church they were only allowed to sit in the rear of the building or in the loft, where they learned the virtues of being a good slave. These state laws attempted to instill respect in blacks for their white masters. Adult slaves were called "boy" or "girl" to constantly remind them of their inferior status. In some states blacks were supposed to step aside when a white passed them. Individual and group resistance to these laws and to the entire slave system took place in the form of slave rebellions.

Slave Revolts

The cruelties of slavery were numerous, still, many Southern writers pictured the happy blacks working and singing in the fields for their "white folks." These contented slaves desired nothing more than to live on a plantation and work from sunrise to sunset. This romantic portrait of slavery was propaganda used to rationalize the general conditions, but it did not adequately portray the underlying discontent that was obvious from slave revolts. From 1619 to 1865 it has been estimated there were over 250 organized slave rebellions in both the North and South. The most noteable Southern slave rebellions were those of Gabriel Prosser in 1800 and Nat Turner in 1831. Prosser and Turner were both inspired by the biblical struggle of the Israelites held captive in Egypt. Prosser viewed himself as a latter-day Moses leading his people to freedom, while Turner had received God's message and become God's agent to lead the slave out of the house of bondage. Gabriel, in the summer of 1800, organized more than 1100 slaves and marched them toward Richmond, Virginia, to seige an arsenal. Word leaked out of the rebellion and the uprising failed. Hysteria swept Virginia, and Gabriel and 35 followers were put to death. Although few whites were killed, this attempted revolt spread terror through the South. On August 21, 1831, Nat Turner took direct action against his captors, and more than 60 whites were killed before the rebellion was put down. Again white reaction was swift: Turner and more than 19 followers were hanged. According to one story, after Turner was hanged, his body was cut apart and parts of it were auctioned to slave owners to display as a deterrent to rebellions. Slave rebellions were the great threat to the Southern plantation system.

While no organized rebellions were completely successful, many individual acts of revolt caused a real challenge to the slave system. Blacks knew that if they did not work they would be causing economic harm to their owners; so many feigned illness or even maimed themselves. Some committed suicide. Destruction also included burning of cotton bales, killing of livestock, and destruction of equipment. The house slaves were much closer to the master and his family and their protests, which included putting ground glass in food, or even strangling, were much more direct. "This troublesome property" caused many a plantation owner to question whether slavery was profitable or not. Meanwhile Southern writers provided very persuasive arguments in their vigorous defense of their "peculiar institution."

Southern Writers

By the time of the Civil War slave investment represented more than $4 billion; slavery had become a system that permeated the economic life of the South. Southern intellectuals first described it as a necessary evil but eventually defended it as a positive good, even going so far as to use resources such as the United States Constitution and the Bible to defend their positions. Writer William Harper provided one basic rationalization for slavery when he reasoned that the blacks from Africa merely had undergone a change of masters and that their Southern masters were much better to them. Another defender, Thomas Dew, a history professor, used the historical argument to show how the rise of all great civilizations, such as Greece and Rome, depended on slave labor. He also argued that God had allowed his chosen people such as Moses and Abraham to have slaves; therefore, it was established by divine authority. One of the most persuasive arguments was presented by William Grayson in a long poem, *The Hierling and the Slaves.* He pictured the long hours and low wages of the Northern factory workers and then showed how the slaves, provided with food, shelter, and clothing, had much more security. The Northern factory worker, however, had freedom.

Urban Slaves

Twelve percent of all Southern slaves lived and worked in the cities of the South. Most of them were skilled craftworkers who were given much more freedom than plantation slaves. Their occupations, such as shoemaker, cobbler, barrelmaker, and dock worker, were essential to the life of the city, so the slave codes that so strictly regulated the plantation slaves often were not followed. Instead, segregation began to develop. Blacks and whites were separated; some blacks lived in the back lots of their master's property, others lived in early ghettos on the edge of the city. With the increasing demand for field hands, more and more urban slaves were forced out of the city.

Free Blacks

Another group of blacks found in both North and South were the free blacks. Forty-six percent of them lived in the North, while the rest were found throughout the South. In the South their position was extremely precarious, for they were only quasi-free. Most Southern blacks were slaves, so the free blacks were kept under close scrutiny. These blacks were also victims of segregation and were in constant fear of being put back into slavery. Each had to carry a certificate of freedom and a registration number. Many state laws stipulated that if a slave failed to pay fines or taxes, he or she could again be put into slavery. Although free, they were not allowed to be citizens or to exercise all the privileges of citizenship. The free black's place in the life of the South was uneasy at best.

Freedom had come to the Northern slaves, but not equality. Racial bigotry pervaded race relations; most free blacks work as unskilled laborers. Blacks were considered inferior even to immigrants, while their general presence was a constant threat to white society. Most states denied them citizenship and the right to vote. Generally social and economic opportunities were limited severely. They could not even join state militias. Still, few blacks desired to return to their ancestral home in Africa. Groups like the American Colonization Society, which was formed in 1816 to transport blacks back to Africa, were greeted with little enthusiasm. America was now their home, and they lived the best they could considering their inferior status. But this did not mean that they had to be passive and avoid challenging the system. The origins of black protest run deep in American history.

The free Northern blacks did have the freedom to protest. They initially did this through the "convention movement." This movement attempted "to devise ways and means for the bettering of our condition." Beginning in Philadelphia in 1830, it had spread throughout the North by 1860. Conventions met regularly. Black activists there such as David Walker attempted to call attention to the conditions of free blacks and slaves alike in emotional speeches and stirring protests. They accomplished relatively little change, but they did vent the frustrations of free blacks in their struggle for equaliy.

One of the most famous free blacks to lead the movement for freedom was Sojourner Truth. This former slave was born Isabella Baumfree, but she changed her name because she believed that her mission in life was to travel, *sojourn* (stay briefly) in a place, and preach the truth. The truth she spoke was that blacks were not inferior to whites and that slavery, the cruel system, should be abolished. Her deeply religious speeches described her past life as a slave and her future life as a free American. While she was one of the outstanding free blacks before the Civil War, she was not alone.

Despite restrictions in both North and South, some talented blacks received recognition. Benjamin Banneker was the first American black to achieve fame. Self-educated, he became proficient in science and mathematics; Thomas Jefferson recognized his ability and appointed him to a commission to plan the District of Columbia. Later in his life Banneker urged adoption of a plan for world peace. Thomas Fuller made notable mathematical achievements; Norbert Rilleux revolutionized the processing of sugar. Lewis Temple designed a toggle harpoon which transformed American whaling. Black writers included George Moses Horton, Frances E. W. Harper, and William Wells Brown. James Derham won acclaim as a pioneer physician. The accomplishments of these gifted blacks made even more poignant the cruelties of the slave system.

Sojourner Truth was a free black in the North who traveled and preached the abolition of slavery and equality for blacks.

The Abolitionist Movement

Black voices were joined by a growing number of white voices, which demanded either gradual or immediate abolition of slavery. Many Northerners had expected that with the abolition of slavery in the North and the prohibition of the slave trade slavery would eventually disappear. This was not the case. But it was not until the 1820s that whites began to again urge the abolition of slavery. In 1821 a Quaker, Benjamin Lundy, began printing a newspaper that sought gradual emancipation for slaves and eventual colonization in some foreign land for all blacks. For some Northerners this appeal did not go far enough. In 1831 William Lloyd Garrison shattered the aura of moderation by demanding "immediate abolition."

Garrison, the highly emotional son of an alcoholic father, demanded in his newspaper *The Liberator* "immediate abolition." He appealed, "I will be heard . . . the apathy of the people is enough to make every statue leap from its pedestal and to hasten the resurrection of the dead." Other Northern extremists began to flock to the Garrison cause. The New England Anti-Slavery Society was organized in 1832 and the American Anti-Slavery Society in 1833. These groups were composed primarily of the followers of Garrison—radical abolitionists who composed only a small part of the antislavery movement in the North. Many Northerners demanded a gradual emancipation, which would include compensation for slave owners. One voice of the abolitionist movement was John Greenleaf Whittier; another was abolitionist-novelist Harriet Beecher Stowe, author of *Uncle Tom's Cabin.* Many abolitionists felt that success would only come through political activity; they became involved with the Liberty party and then the Free Soil party. While abolitionists pushed for an end to slavery, they allowed few blacks to participate openly in their movements.

Although Garrison did not represent all the abolitionists, his antics and shrill voice caused him to be seen and heard above the others. Due primarily to Garrison, the abolitionist movement was cursed in the South and looked upon with much suspicion in the North. Abolitionists appeared too radical. They frequently were interrupted, heckled, and sometimes stoned at public meetings. Garrison was even dragged through Northern city streets. White workers felt that the freeing of more blacks would jeopardize their job security. The American Anti-Slavery Society withstood attacks around the country, but it could not withstand disputes within its own ranks. Garrison began to attack all those who disagreed with him, be they Northern or Southern, male or female, or even the clergy. After 1840 the power of the antislavery societies declined, but national politics now caused many Americans to continue their concern with the issue of freedom versus slavery. Slavery as a political and

Harriet Beecher Stowe's book *Uncle Tom's Cabin* revealed to many Northerners the evils of Southern slavery.

moral issue would enter national politics by the 1850s and help to lead the nation to a civil war.

The American Industrial Revolution

One of the difficulties in the slave system was the slave's dual role as person and property in an age when property was becoming more valuable in America's transition from an agricultural to an industrial country. During the period after the American Revolution, the limited methods of the colonial industrial economy were still in vogue. By 1860, however, the United States was fast becoming a manufacturing nation, and the groundwork was being laid for the rise of big business. While it is pleasing to think of American ingenuity as being responsible for the rise of industry, the technology and talent necessary for an industrial revolution were essentially English in origin. About 1750, British inventors developed machines for the mass production of textiles, and thus began the English Industrial Revolution. In this revolution power-driven machines were substituted for hand labor, and the steam engine became central to factories and transportation. Britain quickly realized the value of increased production and tried to maintain complete control of this mechanization. In 1781 Parliament imposed drastic penalties for attempting to export any "machine, engine, tool, press, paper, utensil, or implement used for silk manufacture." And in 1785 a law was passed prohibiting the exportation of tools, machinery, engines, or plans of machines used in the iron industry. Britain's attempt to monopolize the Industrial Revolution failed, and it was not long before the factory system spread from England—"the world's workshop"—to Western Europe and then to the United States.

The American factory system followed the English pattern but developed much more rapidly. Following the American Revolution, industrial experimentation and concurrent promotion had become popular. In 1775 the United Company of Philadelphia for Promoting American Manufactures was established and became the model for other, similar societies. Their purpose was to promote manufacturing through literature, prizes, and direct financial aid. The Pennsylvania Society for the Encouragement of Manufactures and the Useful Acts went one step further and set up its own textile shops. On the national level Alexander Hamilton, the fiscal genius in Washington's cabinet, was most responsible for promoting industrial growth. In 1791, in his famous "Report on the Subject of Manufactures," Hamilton recommended protective duties and every other possible aid to stimulate manufacturing. He felt that manufacturing would increase the national income and stop the dependence on foreign goods, but he received little support from Congress, which provided only a small increase in tariff duties. Hamilton futilely attempted to establish factories in New Jersey. He came to realize that America would be slow in developing its industrial potential since labor was generally scarce, money was limited, and the population was sparsely sprinkled along the Atlantic seaboard. Yet these handicaps did not completely retard industrial experimentation.

Slater and Lowell

Textile plants were established in New England, but all of them failed. It was not until the arrival in America of Samuel Slater, "the Father of the Factory System," that the first successful spinning mill began operations. Slater was a young English textile worker who was enticed by American advertisements that offered prizes for innovations in textile machinery. Disguising himself as a farm boy, with plans for spinning machinery tucked away in his brain, he traveled to New York. Once in America he formed a partnership with William Almy and Moses Brown, who had unsuccessfully attempted to spin cotton yarn on poor equipment. This partnership represented the first step of the textile revolution in America. Reconstructing the spinning machines and water frames from memory, Slater put their mill into operation in Rhode Island, on the Blackstone River, and produced the first machine-made cotton warp in America. Other factories modeled themselves on the Slater idea, but they all encountered numerous difficulties. Competition with English markets and lack of capital caused most of these plants to close. By the 1800s there were only eight factories based on the Slater model: one in Massachusetts, four in Rhode Island, and three in Connecticut.

The initial growth of the factory system was slow, but it received a substantial boost from 1807 to 1815. This period of the trade embargo, the Nonintercourse Act, and the War of 1812 caused an interruption in importation of English manufactured goods. Americans were forced to turn to their own resources. It was during this time that Francis Cabot Lowell brought a radical change to textile manufacturing. Lowell was a Yankee trader who had been severely handicapped by the commercial policies of Jefferson and Madison. In England he made a detailed study of machinery, particularly the power loom. When he returned to America, he tried to reconstruct the machine but failed. With the aid of Paul Moody, a mechanical genius, Lowell designed and constructed both a spinning machine and a power loom, which were set up at Waltham, Massachusetts, in 1814. They had built a factory that united under one operation an integrated process for yarn spinning and cloth weaving. This Waltham model soon was copied in other New England towns and gave rise to the American Industrial Revolution. A necessary change gradually came about when water power was supplemented by steam power. By the Civil War both steampower and waterpower were common in the cotton textile factories of the North.

This Rhode Island mill was part of the early stages of the American Industrial Revolution.

229

As the factory system expanded, it embraced other industries. Cyrus McCormick, for example, brought about a dramatic change in the reaping of grain. In America, farm labor was generally scarce, and most harvesting tools were crude. In 1834 McCormick patented a mechanical power reaper that completely replaced the sickle and scythe. By the time of the Civil War the machine had revolutionized harvesting. In general, industrial activity had sky-rocketed: in 1860 there were 140,053 factories in the country, capitalized at over $1 billion; and patents were being registered at a record pace. (It is ironic that, in 1838, the clerk of the Patent Office had resigned because he felt that all workable inventions had already been invented.) The American Industrial Revolution had made tremendous advances during the national period, but most Americans were still farmers. One major impact of industrialization was its concurrent social effects, which were most evident in the early factories.

Factories and Labor

In the industrial "sweathouses," hours were long, wages were low, and workers' lives were controlled to a great extent by the factory owners. The factories utilized two different systems of labor: the Fall River system and the Waltham system. The Fall River system, used in southern New England and in the Middle Atlantic states, was based on farming methods, which meant complete family employment in the factory—men, women, and children. Child labor was particularly evident. In Rhode Island in 1853 there were 1857 children

New England factories employed men, women, and children for long hours at low wages.

working in factories; 59 of them were under the age of 9. This was a common occurrence. The Massachusetts Act of 1842, which forbade the employment of children under the age of 12 for more than 10 hours a day, was considered progressive. One young worker recalled: "I worked fifteen hours a day. I used to go in at quarter past four in the morning and work till quarter past eight at night, having thirty minutes for breakfast and the same for dinner." For this long and difficult work, wages averaged about 90 cents a day for a male worker, 40 cents for a woman, and 25 cents for a child. Many workers were paid in script redeemable only at the company store; this usually kept employees constantly in debt to the company.

The Waltham system originated in Waltham, Massachusetts. The Waltham textile mill employed young, unmarried girls from farms; most girls worked there as a temporary way to get money for marriage. The girls who moved to the town lived in boardinghouses under strict supervision. Here they were required to sleep, eat, and be in their quarters by 10 P.M. They were also subject to dismissal for immoral conduct. This system proved so successful that it was used in other mills in northern New England. During the 1820s and 1830s most factory girls accepted their miserable plight. One observer wrote that "the lot of working women in mills like those of Lowell seem idyllic in contrast with the plight of women who work in the British mills . . ." Actually, in comparison with their farm homes, the factory surroundings were not that objectionable. By the 1840s, however, discontent became evident. Competition had stiffened. Moreover, wages were reduced and hours lengthened. For a workweek of 75 hours, the girls earned an average of $1.50. One factory manager demanded his workers come to work without breakfast because that way he "got 300 more yards of cloth a week made." Conditions in the company dorms were overcrowded. Long after the 10-hour day became common, factory employees were still laboring from 11 to 13 hours a day. However, with worker dissatisfaction growing, it was becoming difficult to recruit and hold factory workers, so by the 1850s factory managers turned to a new class of workers, the immigrants, who had little choice in hours and wages. By 1860 Irish workers accounted for over half the labor force in the New England mills. Factory conditions continued to decline.

Labor in the Age of Jackson

The working conditions of this period led to attempts at unionization. The origins of unionization lie in the chartered companies for craftworkers that developed during the colonial period. But since markets were local and wages and prices could be regulated fairly easily, there was little need for organization. After the American Revolution, expanding market conditions forced skilled artisans to form into unions. The main goal of these early unions was maintaining wage levels. Employers, however, were beginning to limit wages. Artisans were forced to organize to meet this challenge. The first trade union was founded by Philadelphia shoemakers in 1792, but it only survived a year. In 1794 the shoemakers were reorganized and their new union, the Federal Society of Journeymen Cordwainers, lasted for more than a decade. This group also initiated the first organized strike in 1799, which lasted ten weeks. Eventually printers organized in New York and Philadelphia and shoemakers in Baltimore and Pittsburgh. By the early 1800s most of the skilled trades were unionized. While these craft unions remained local and small, they bore the seeds of unionization. Their goals were shorter hours, better pay, and improved working conditions. These unions also attempted to establish the principle of the "closed shop," by refusing to work alongside nonmembers and "untrained workers." In 1799 the Philadelphia shoemakers even struck in sympathy with Philadelphia bootmakers, who were striking for higher wages. Strike benefits were also paid during this time, but in the form of loans that had to be repaid. The origins of collective bargaining were also apparent. It was quite common for skilled craftsmen to submit a chart of wages and prices to their masters, which was then negotiated.

There were many early strikes, even some violent ones. Six "scab" shoemakers who worked during a strike in Philadelphia were beaten severely one night in a neighborhood tavern. In 1800 in New York, a group of striking sailors tried to board a vessel in the harbor and suffered broken heads and bloody noses. Of course, many artisans felt that violent confrontations were unbecoming to their skilled crafts. These early unions often broadened their functions by providing sickness and death benefits whenever possible. In response, many owners formed employer associations. And often, employers felt that the best weapon against these incipient unions was the court.

A series of conspiracy trials from 1806 to 1842 provided the greatest challenges to the early growth of unions. In 1806 a group of Philadelphia shoemakers was prosecuted for striking for higher wages. The court ruled that the workers were guilty and established the doctrine that a "combination" of workers for the purpose of raising wages was a criminal conspiracy and hence illegal. Other cases yielded similar verdicts. While these cases did not completely kill unionization, they did severely hurt the workers' legal cause. In 1842 the doctrine of criminal conspiracy was overturned in the case of *Judicial Commonwealth* v. *Hunt*; in it the chief justice of the Massachusetts Supreme Court dismissed a conspiracy indictment against the Boston Bootmakers So-

The Nation Develops a Personality: Emerging National Culture

ciety. While employers were no longer able to turn to the courts as a weapon for criminal conspiracy cases, they still found some solace in the legal system.

Incipient unions in the early 1800s actually were hurt more by depressions than by the conspiracy cases. During these dark days craftworkers lost their bargaining power and were concerned most about keeping their jobs. The depression of 1819, for example, hit them particularly hard. But when prosperity returned in the 1820s, unions continued to grow in strength and power. Workers now were beginning to feel that the answer to their problems lay not in unions but in politics. This belief gave rise to the workingmen's parties of the 1830s. From 1828 to 1834 workingmen's parties—local political groups—sprang up in every state and demanded a political voice for working people. Laborers felt that political change would improve their working conditions. Many workers felt that the wealthy controlled politics and that they must get their own people elected to public office. The climax of this movement came with the election of Jackson—the symbol of the common people. But by 1834 most of the parties had disbanded, partly because of internal strife and partly because the Democrats and Whigs were beginning now to cater to the worker. Many Americans, including party members themselves, felt that the labor parties were too idealistic and too radical. Their leaders often had to guarantee that they had "no desire or intention of disturbing the right of property of individuals, or of the public." But workingmen had raised their political voices and shown their potential power. After this political experiment laborers turned back to labor unions to solve their immediate problems.

During the 1840s reform movements attempted to stop the tide of industrialization by proposing utopian schemes. The *cooperator* movement, for example, offered producer and consumer cooperatives in the Eastern cities. *Associationists* sought to create an ideal community in which the evils of industry were nonexistent and workers had no reason to organize. The *agrarianist* movement believed that land was the solution to all the workers' problems; they wanted land and property to be equally divided and shared. Needless to say, these reform movements were not successful, nor did they stem the impetus for national unions. These national unions, however, would have to wait until the smoke had cleared from the Civil War.

Religion

While the period after the American Revolution provided an environment for the emergence of an American Industrial Revolution and a change in the role of the worker, it also allowed for great variety in the American religious experience. The American Revolution that brought separation from the mother country affected some churches in a negative way, others in a positive way. Agitation against the established churches, particularly the Anglican Church, had begun during the Revolution and continued after its conclusion. First Virginia and then other states terminated their official connection with the Anglican Church. The Methodists, who considered themselves Anglicans, shared in the unpopularity of their parent church, while the Quakers, Mennonites, and Moravians, who all opposed war generally, also were persecuted. Since most of the Anglican Church leaders were Loyalists and had been driven from the states—one leading minister had cow dung thrown in his face—the church was forced to reorganize. An American bishop was elected in 1789, and the Anglican Church eventually changed its name to the Protestant Episcopal church. The American Methodists revolted under the leadership of John Wesley in England, chose their own bishops, and formed the Methodist Episcopal church. The Roman Catholic church petitioned the pope for a superior in America, and this plea was answered by the appointment of John Carroll, America's first Catholic bishop.

The states were now beginning to legislate the separation of church and state, but, at the national level, this separation already had been written into the Constitution. The Constitutional Convention actually paid little heed to religion. The only direct reference to it in the body of the Constitution is in Article VI, which provides that "no religious Test shall ever be required as a Qualification to any Office or public Trust under the United States." Many religious groups, however, felt that further amending must be done to preserve religious liberty. The First Amendment to the Constitution, adopted in 1789, provided that "Congress shall make no law respecting an establishment of religion, or prohibiting the free exercise thereof; or abridging the freedom of speech, or of the press; or the right of the people peaceably to assemble, and to petition the Government for a redress of grievances." The federal government had taken the lead in separating church and state and guaranteeing religious liberty.

Second Great Awakening

The period after the Revolution was one of the low points in American religion. A marked reduction in spiritual zeal was characterized by two popular antichurch books: Ethan Allen's *Reason, the Only Oracle of Man*, which attacked organized religion, and Thomas Paine's *The Age of Reason*, which attacked both the Bible and orthodox religion. A new faith was needed to stem this tide of religious indifference. This faith was to be found during the Second Awakening. The Second Awakening, like the First Awakening, was characterized by the rise of revivalism. It appears that this movement started almost simultaneously in many places and spread from the Atlantic states to the frontier, where it reached its greatest potential. Here in the wilderness the evangelical institution known as the camp meeting was born. Frontier camp meetings usually lasted for several days; frontierpeople gathered around a clearing where they heard and felt the word of God. This movement reached its climax in August 1801 at Cane Ridge, Kentucky, where the greatest frontier revival took place. At this meeting, which was highlighted by the impassioned preaching of James McGready, there may have been as many as 25,000 people in attendance—at a time when the largest settlement in the state contained only a few thousand inhabitants. Preachers of every denomination preached from makeshift platforms. People would wander from wagons to preaching stands in small groups to hear recent converts relate their experiences. Everywhere there were outbursts of weeping and shouts of joy, and frequently men and women were swept into "physical exercises—rolling, running, jumping, and jerking," evidence of the power of the Almighty. These meetings were

Methodist camp meetings brought religion to the frontier.

examples of unrestricted emotionalism. Some people sang, others screamed, and many cried for mercy. One man wrote, "My heart beat tumultuously, my knees trembled, my lip quivered, and I felt as if I must fall to the ground. A strange supernatural power seemed to pervade the entire mass of mind there collected." Such unbridled emotionalism frequently attracted dissolute souls. Ironically, when so many souls were being saved, others were being lost through drunkenness and seduction.

The groups that benefited most from the Second Awakening and became the largest churches were the Baptists and Methodists. The American spirit of democracy entered into the Baptist religious life: the only requirements necessary to become a Baptist preacher were evidence of conversion and an ability to preach. Most preachers were also farmers. Individual churches were even permitted to dictate their own beliefs. These democratic tendencies won them a wide following in the West. Baptism by total immersion, even in the dead of winter, was also practiced. The Methodists, however, were even more successful. According to one frontier jingle: "The devil hates the Methodist because they sing and shout the best." By the time of the Civil War this denomination had nearly 1.5 million members. Their doctrine of salvation to all believers and their frontier circuit riders were their greatest assets. The circuit riders were Methodist preachers who rode a six-week circuit of frontier settlements. When a circuit rider came to a settlement, he preached and attempted to organize converts into a Bible class. Since the circuit rider visited the settlement infrequently, much responsibility was in the hands of lay preachers. This method of using lay preachers enabled Methodists to expand along with the Western frontier.

Charles G. Finney carried the emotionalism of the frontier and the Second Awakening to the city. Six feet two inches in height, with hypnotic eyes, he was an imposing figure in the pulpit. He first preached in the backwoods and then took his revivalism to New York City. There he conducted a subdued urban awakening. His great innovation was to use prayer meetings in much the same way as camp meetings. The revivals, both agrarian and urban, led to further experimentation in religion and to the rise of a variety of religions, including numerous communal societies seeking the utopian dream.

Utopianism

All the utopian experiments were motivated by the search for an ideal life. The Shaker community of "Mother" Ann Lee sought such a goal. Mother Ann Lee arrived from England, where she had been leader of a small group of Shaking Quakers who believed that Christ's second arrival was near. Her followers were called Shakers because their worship involved "violent vibrations of the body, running and walking on the floor, with singing, shouting, and leaping for joy." They believed God had revealed to Mother Lee that marriage was the source of all sin and evil in the world. This belief may have been more than revelation because her relationships with men were failures. Persecuted in England, she and her followers relocated in America. The Shakers followed Mother Lee's insistence upon celibacy and found salvation in strange, rhythmic dancing and singing. By 1860 they numbered about 6000, living in 19 different communities. A simple Shaker dance song reveals the Shaker ritual:

> Leap and skip ye little band
> Shaker faith will fill the land
> O the comfort life and zeal
> Little Shaker children feel
> Shaking is the work of God
> And it has to spread abroad
> Till the wicked feel and know
> God Almighty reigns below.

The ways of the Shakers caused them to be social outcasts. They did become, however, prosperous farmers, and they produced some of the best handicraft in early America. With the loss of fervor, the abandonment of celibacy, and the decline of rural revivals, the Shakers fell in population and virtually disappeared.

While the Shakers were seeking the ideal life in celibacy, others were looking for perfection through "complex marriages." The self-acclaimed leader of a community dedicated to perfection was John Humphrey Noyes. Noyes, a revival preacher, planned to create a society in Oneida, New York, dedicated to perfectionism. Here one would be free from sin by practicing primitive Christian communism. According to his "complex marriage theory," every person in the community belonged to everyone else. Critics immediately screamed "free love"; but Noyes retorted that sexual intercourse was "organized" rather than promiscuous and that it was inspired by Christian spirituality. This experiment was so contrary to the morality of the 1800s that it was eventually abandoned, but the Oneida community prospered as a conventional business, manufacturing silver products.

The Mormon Church

Utopian community groups were not the only example of religious experimentation to appear during this experimental age; other groups such as the

Mormons and the Millerites also were evidence of the religious variety. The Mormon church, also known as the Church of Jesus Christ of Latter-Day Saints, appeared in the 1820s. Tall, blue-eyed Joseph Smith reported that an angel named Moroni had given him golden plates, upon which a mysterious book had been written in a strange language. With the aid of mystic glasses, he began their translation. The book told of the wanderings of the Lost Tribes of Israel and the recollections of the prophet Mormon. Despite the seeming incredibility of his story, Smith's book won many converts. He and his believers eventually moved from New York to Missouri, and Illinois, where, in the town of Nauvoo, the church established its headquarters in 1840. Almost immediately Smith's religious oligarchy encountered difficulties with its neighbors, who detested Mormon economic success and the Mormon practice of polygamy. In 1844 Smith and his brother were murdered by a mob in Carthage, Illinois; the church then dissolved into splinter groups, and it appeared that Smith's dream had ended. But there emerged a determined leader, Brigham Young, who continued the teachings of Smith and led his followers away from persecution to isolated Utah. The Mormons survived in this barren environment and soon made the desert bloom by means of ingenious methods of irrigation. In 1848 hordes of crickets threatened to destroy their crops but flocks of sea gulls appeared, as if by a miracle, and gulped down the invaders. A monument to the sea gulls stands today in Salt Lake City. While Salt Lake City became a model of civic planning, the Mormon practice of polygamy brought them trouble with the gentiles. Young himself married 27 women and begot 56 children. In 1857 the federal government sent an army against the Mormons, but serious bloodshed was avoided. The Mormons ran afoul of the antipolygamy laws passed by Congress in 1862 and 1882; in fact, their peculiar practice delayed statehood for Utah until 1896.

The Variety of Religion

The idea of millennialism—the imminence of Christ's second coming—was a very popular belief during this period. The Millerite movement, for example, accepted millennialism and predicted the exact date of Christ's coming. William Miller, a simple farmer, was a firm believer in the literal truth of the Bible. One day he calculated that Christ would return "about 1843." During the early 1830s he began to share his findings with his neighbors and friends, and suddenly the news spread. Publication of his calculations helped give the movement momentum. Eventually 50,000 followers from all faiths began to prepare for the Messiah's arrival. As the fateful year approached, the heavens were watched for celestial signs. Some disciples went insane in anticipation;

others waited anxiously, in poverty after selling all their worldly goods. When 1843 and 1844 came and went, disillusion set in and the Millerite movement disappeared. In 1849 Miller died a broken man. A few recalcitrants believed that Christ's failure to appear was due to a neglect of the proper Sabbath observance, and they created what is today known as the Seventh Day Adventist church.

The Millerite excitement tended to add to the already active concentration on supernatural happenings. The Fox sisters, Maggie and Katie, reported that they could communicate with the spirits of the dead through mysterious "rappings," which were later discovered to be their cracking toe joints. The belief in spiritualism was just coming into vogue, and hundreds of Americans, including Horace Greeley, participated in seances, convinced that the spirits of the dead could be contacted by the living. By the time of the Civil War interest had declined, but there remained a substantial legacy of spiritualism. Religion during this period closely paralleled the rapid changes of a growing, dynamic agricultural nation. It was also a time when rapid changes and advances were taking place in education, science, and literature.

Education

After the American Revolution, educators found that the belief that education was primarily the responsibility of the parents hindered the development of the system of public schools. While tax-supported schools were relatively rare, private institutions were fairly common. These private institutions and many spirited individuals argued long and loud against the spread of public education, but support continued to grow. Many state constitutions provided public support of education, as did the federal government in the Northwest Ordinance of 1787. The demand for public education increased with the rise of Jacksonian Democracy. The passage of "free school" laws in the New England states allowed residents to choose between private or public school systems. But even when schools were public, this did not ensure universal education; parents could keep their children out of school, for no compulsory attendance laws were passed until the pioneer Massachusetts Act of 1852. While a developing system of both private and public education was emerging in the East and the West, private education alone continued in the South until after the Civil War.

The need for more general education forced educators to directly confront two problems: the separation of church and state and the structure of the district schools. The growth of public schools gave birth to a movement for completely secular education. Noah Webster's *American Spelling Book* and

An old log hut.
A new log hut.
Is it for me?
Is it for you?
Why do you ask?

I see a tub.
The tub is big.
Can you use it?
O yes, I can.
I can use it.

Is it a bed?
It is a bed.
Is it for you?
It is for me.
Kit is on my bed.

Old Tom, our cat.
He is ill in bed.
Tom saw a rat.
The rat saw Tom.
The rat ran off.

McGuffey's Primer taught young Americans to read without the teaching of religion.

Lindley Murray's *Grammar* became the standard texts. "In Adam's Fall We Sinned All" became "*A* was an Apple Pie made by the Cook." Secularization and Americanization went hand in hand. Dick, Jane, and Spot were not far behind. In the 1800s states began to outlaw the teaching of religion in public schools. This not only hastened a complete secularization of the schools but also created a need for religious schools. Denominational schools sprang up everywhere, but state aid for them was not allowed. By the time of the Civil War, education was well on a secular course.

As a rule, district schools were one-room schools, with one teacher teaching all eight grades. Beginning and advanced students were taught together in an ungraded situation with a poorly paid teacher. Often there was little learning because the teacher was a mere babysitter; the same lessons might be taught year after year. Discipline was usually the number-one priority in these schools, where attendance was irregular, standards were low, and the entire situation was begging for change. The picture of boys and girls giggling, throwing spitballs, and dipping pigtails in inkwells was not far from the truth. Schooling here consisted of the three R's—"readin', 'ritin', and 'rithmetic." Little else was taught.

Horace Mann

Horace Mann was the educational reformer who was needed. As state superintendent of education in Massachusetts he had issued a series of reports that revolutionized elementary education. His philosophy was: "If we do not prepare children to become good citizens, if we do not enrich their minds with knowledge . . . then our republic must go down to destruction, as others have gone before it." He felt that children should be viewed as individuals, but within a rigid structure, which featured compulsory attendance, high teaching standards, and a graded system. While many of his ideas were labeled "radical," they eventually won acceptance. Today his name remains inscribed in the foundation stone of many a city school.

While elementary education was widespread by the time of the Civil War, secondary education lagged. Private religious academies monopolized secondary education. These schools concentrated on preparing only boys for college. The concept of state support for secondary schools was slow in winning acceptance. Massachusetts once again led the way. The nation's first public high school opened in Boston in 1832; a Massachusetts law in 1827 had stipulated that towns with more than 500 families had to provide for secondary education. This concept, however, grew very slowly; a truly universal secondary system did not emerge until the twentieth century.

Educational innovation paralleled religious innovation. For example, followers of progressive education, who believed that a child's inherent talents were frustrated by traditional education and that learning could occur only when a child was happy, experimented to prove their theories. Although this idea failed in America, it would reappear. The Prussian emphasis on high academic achievement and scholarship was coming into vogue at the university level but would not be widespread until the establishment of graduate schools in the late 1800s. Educational democracy was most evident in the burgeoning of state universities. The first state-supported universities were started in the late 1700s in North Carolina and Georgia. The University of Virginia, chartered in 1819, and the University of Michigan, chartered in 1837, became leading citadels of public education. Such institutions provided a combination of outstanding professors, quality curriculum in science and the classics, and academic freedom.

Actually, little similarity exists between college life then and college life today. Children entered college at age 14 or 15 and graduated at age 18 or 19. The normal day went from five in the morning till nine at night. The religious colleges added to this rigid schedule large doses of spiritual instruction and prayer. With no athletics and little time for amusements, students sometimes shot at teachers, brought cattle into church services, threw food in the halls, and actually raised a lot of hell. The faculty often was occupied less with learning than with fines, suspensions, and disciplinary problems. In general, however, education was becoming more universal and of a much higher quality. With increased education came a growing desire for scientific achievements.

Science and Western Exploration

The rise of science was linked closely to the federal government. During the 1800s the government sponsored military expeditions for the exploration of the West. The Lewis and Clark expedition had stimulated further interest in the Louisiana Territory and the land beyond. So Congress continued to grant appropriations for scientific military expeditions to investigate the Red and Arkansas rivers. The Thomas Freeman expedition in 1806 traveled more than 635 miles up the Red River and reported on animals, plants, and minerals. In 1806 Zebulon Pike and his party traveled as far west as Colorado and unsuccessfully tried to climb the peak that now bears his name. "I believed no human being could have ascended to its pinical [pinnacle]," he wrote. In the spring of 1807 he crossed through the Royal Gorge of the Arkansas River, the Sangre de Cristo Mountains, and the San Luis valley to emerge on the upper Rio Grande, where he ordered his men to erect temporary quarters. There in Spanish territory Pike and his men were arrested and taken to Santa Fe, the New Mexican capital. Ultimately they were escorted to Chihuahua, Mexico, through Texas and released at Natchitoches on the Louisiana border in July 1807. From memory and notes hidden in his men's rifles, Pike wrote a report of this semiarid region that was published in 1810. This report was the origin of the popular belief that America's Southwest was nothing but a great, uninhabitable desert. This report also brought national attention to Pike. Major Stephen H. Long followed the route of Pike's expedition and explored the area of the Canadian and Arkansas rivers. He also gave the area between the Rockies and the Mississippi its name: the Great American Desert.

In 1838 the Army Corps of Topographical Engineers was created to conduct scientific and mapping expeditions. The Corps' most important military explorer was John C. Fremont, "the Pathfinder of the West." On his first trip in 1842 Fremont surveyed and marked the Oregon Trail as far west as South Pass in the Rockies. While this expedition revealed nothing new, the report was written so glamorously by Fremont's wife that he was given another expedition the following year. This second expedition in 1843–1844 included such notables as topographer Charles Preuss and Kit Carson, the latter as principal guide; the party traveled through South Pass to the Great Salt Lake, along the Snake River into Oregon, then south to Nevada, across the Sierra Nevadas into California, eventually returning to St. Louis from there. It had been one of the most important expeditions to the Far West. Fremont had surveyed and mapped some of the wildest and most desolate country in North America. He destroyed the Spanish myth that told of a river which connected the Great Basin to the Pacific, and he also created a real interest in Mexican California. For years Fremont's published reports proved to be a major source of information for travelers. This Army Corps expedition expanded knowledge of the trans-Mississippi West and led to eventual settlement of the Pacific Coast region.

The government also sponsored other scientific ventures. Civilian geologists, biologists, ethnologists, and botanists attached to military expeditions returned with so much valuable material that Congress created the United States National Museum and the United States Botanical Garden to collect them. In 1844 the Naval Observatory was founded to conduct astronomical studies; their findings would aid navigation. Sometimes the scientific advancement came in strange ways. Wealthy James Smithson decreed in his will that a large sum of money be given to the federal government to advance knowledge. In 1846 Congress used this money to establish the Smithsonian Institution as the center of scientific research. The Smithsonian, with its library and museum, eventually became the leading institution for scientific work in America.

Many college instructors in the physical sciences and in biology made important finds. Benjamin Silliman and Willard Gibbs, for example, were noteworthy academic scientists. The rise of American science often was coupled with the rise of national culture. American plants and flowers were examined to see if they were superior to their European counterparts. By 1850 it was proclaimed, with some credence, that American scientists had cut ties with their European teachers. Medicine witnessed some scientific advancements, but by modern standards it was still quite primitive. Medical schools had opened and medical journals were being published. In 1847 the American Medical Association was established. Scientists who investigated the origins of diseases still found themselves frustrated repeatedly when epidemics of cholera, typhoid fever, typhus, and smallpox raged in the cities. And prior to the 1840s the only anesthetic used in surgery was a stiff drink of whiskey.

American Women

The period between the Revolution and the Civil War saw the status of women change in a number of ways. More and more professions were closed to women, while the belief that "a woman's place is in the home" grew in acceptance. Since employment opportunities were limited, many women found themselves working in factories or in the schools as teachers. Woman participated in various reform movements, and this impetus, plus the growing frustration with their subservient roles in society, led to the birth of the women's rights movement.

The belief that women's education should consist of cooking and sewing continued into the 1800s. But the founding of women's colleges, such as Troy Female Seminary, Georgia Female College, and Mount Holyoke, were breaking this tradition. One of the pioneers in womens' education was Margaret Fuller. She was a leading intellectual of the time; her activities involved her as writer, lecturer, reporter, and literary critic.

In the late 1700s and in the 1800s a number of magazines appealed to the female reader. At this time many notable women also took up literary pursuits. Lydia Maria Child pioneered in establishing a children's magazine and espoused the cause of abolition. Louisa May Alcott's novels, such as *Little Women,* have endured the test of time. Jane Swisshelm was a frontier journalist who owned and edited a Minnesota newspaper. The most famous of the pre-Civil War female writers was Harriet Beecher Stowe, whose *Uncle Tom's Cabin* sold 2.5 million copies in its first year of publication. Her book, which appeared in 1852, brought the horrors of slavery to the Northern public and helped flame antislavery sentiment. Female writers of this period made significant contributions to American literature.

Women led the way in the field of relief work, serving orphans, prisoners, and the handicapped. The real leader in humanitarian reform was Dorothea Dix. In ill health and forced to abandon teaching, she turned her energy to an

The Seneca Falls meeting signaled the beginning of the women's rights movement in America.

exposé of the penal system. Her detailed reports were classics, which led to penal reform and to the establishing of more than 100 institutions for the insane.

While many Americans in general were questioning the old values in religion, education, and work, many women wondered about their roles in society. In 1848 Elizabeth Cady Stanton and Lucretia Mott called for a "public meeting for protest and discussion" of women's rights. At Seneca Falls more than 300 persons gathered and adopted a declaration of women's rights, which stated that both men *and* women were created equal. The women's movement was making progress.

National Literature

Great achievements in literature were taking place, too. Literature after the Revolution reflected emerging nationalism. Many patriotic plays and novels began to appear. While most works were not literary gems, they served a need for a growing nation. For example, Parson Weems's *Life of Washington* was a best-seller. More serious writers were beginning to challenge their European counterparts. In poetry the Hartford wits, John Trumbull, Timothy Dwight, and Joel Barlow, expressed an enthusiastic American patriotism in British poetic style. The outstanding poet of the early Post-Revolutionary period was Philip Freneau, who was less interested in the current political changes than in the beauty of the American landscape. His poems on bees and butterflies remain as noteable tributes to American nature. In 1789 William Hill Brown wrote the first American novel, *The Power of Sympathy*, a tale of seduction and suicide. Other novelists of this period were Charles Brockden Brown, whose novels were Gothic horror tales, and Hugh Henry Brackenridge whose books studied democracy in its unbridled state. These literary works marked the birth of American literature, though at the time they were no challenge to the work of the European writers.

Washington Irving became the first American writer of international repute. He entertained readers with a subtle satire of New York State; he is remembered today chiefly for his stories "Rip Van Winkle" and "Legend of Sleepy Hollow." At the time, these stories did not bring him national or international fame, but his other works displayed him as a literary genius who made the initial step in gaining respect for American literature. James Fenimore Cooper and William Cullen Bryant were also part of the New York Knickerbocker school of writers. Cooper was best known for frontier tales. His classics *The Last of the Mohicans* and *The Pathfinder* firmly placed the theme of red man versus white man in the American mind. William Cullen Bryant was famous for his lyric poems "Thanatopsis" and "To a Waterfowl," works which reflected his penchant for the mystic symbolism of nature. Once an English edition of his poetry had appeared, his reputation as America's leading poet was established. American literature was definitely on the rise.

By the 1840s the New England Renaissance was blooming; writers such as Ralph Waldo Emerson, Henry David Thoreau, Nathaniel Hawthorne, Herman Melville, Edgar Allen Poe, and Henry Wadsworth Longfellow were part of a new golden age of American literature. Emerson and Thoreau subscribed to the Transcendental school of thought, which believed in a reality that transcended the physical world. Emerson tried to show that a divine unity existed which permeated nature and morality. Thoreau, the social critic, was more of a literary rebel than Emerson. Thoreau also tried to show that a special relationship existed between man and nature; in *Walden* he intimately pictured his day-to-day life in a rural retreat. He was a literary dissenter and today is considered a leader in the tradition of social protest. Hawthorne and Melville wrote novels that explored the psychological struggles within man. In *The Scarlet Letter* Hawthorne examined Puritan frustration and sin, while in *The House of Seven Gables* he showed Puritan guilt inherited as a family curse.

In *Moby Dick* Melville wrote both a sea adventure and a tale of good versus evil. This novel, once rejected and scorned, now is considered one of the world's great novels. Longfellow, the most enduring of all American poets, wrote poetry on universal themes. In *Hiawatha*, *Evangeline*, and numerous other works, he wrote poems with mass appeal. Children today are still compelled to memorize lines from Longfellow's works; he is recognized as one of the truly great American poets. Poe, however, was not strictly part of the New England Renaissance, because he was a product of the Southern aristocracy. His poems and stories appeal to the bizarre and macabre; his personal life was a tragic one. These writers moved toward more philosophical and psychological themes, which used Americans and the American landscape as their source of inspiration.

Poet Walt Whitman climaxed the age of literary nationalism with his works that praised the greatness of America. In 1865 he published *Leaves of Grass*, his most outstanding work. Whitman's focus on patriotism and democracy appealed to all Americans: "It is the broad show of artificial things, ships, machinery, politics, creeds, modern improvements, and the interchange of nations, all for the average man of today." By the time of the Civil War, cultural pursuits were engaging more Americans of every background and taste. And much of that culture involved popular culture, with its emphasis on mass amusements.

The Rise of Mass Amusements

The changes in popular culture during the national post-Revolutionary period reflected the rapid transformation of society in all areas. Urban America was growing. Cities and the working class created a new demand for popular entertainment. Interest in the theater grew, and other forms of entertainment emerged. During the 1800s the theater became an established feature of American life. The trend was away from Shakespeare and toward melodrama and variety. The people drawn to the theater wanted to be entertained. In comparison with modern theaters, theater buildings were huge; many housed more than 2500 spectators. Such buildings, with their extremes of temperature and bad acoustics, were dreaded by most actors. Women usually remained at home; newspapers of the period reveal the violence often connected with theatrical performances. Early actors were a mediocre lot. Initially most of them were English, but by the time of the Civil War actors such as Edwin Forrest, James Hackett, and Edwin Booth led the list of home grown products.

By the 1850s circuses, concerts, variety acts, and minstrel shows also were found in most large cities. The leading promoter of popular culture was Phineas T. Barnum. He gave Americans what they wanted, or what he thought they wanted. His traveling collection of curiosities included the Feejee mermaid, General Tom Thumb, the Bearded Lady, and a dog that ran a sewing machine. Barnum's American Museum was established in New York as a permanent exhibition. Here on display were three living serpents, Porter the Giant, whose ankle was three feet five inches in circumference, and Joyce Heath, who was supposedly George Washington's former nurse. Even as the whitewash on the famous white elephants of Siam began to fade, the public demanded more. When public interest in his freaks began to wane, Barnum turned to variety acts and the promotion of the singer Jenny Lind, "the Swedish Nightingale." Barnum's tour with Jenny Lind brought fiscal success and provided the basic idea for modern traveling rock concerts and other touring shows. The American desire for the unusual was further stimulated at Niagara Falls, where thousands of spectators gathered to watch "Noah's Ark"—a boatload of animals that rode over the falls. If any animal survived the plunge, it had a spot reserved on the next boatload.

In the 1840s minstrel shows became popular, for they offered a unique form of entertainment with their timely songs and jokes. The Christy Minstrels became the most popular group. These shows filled the need for mass amusement with simple jokes that were laughed at by all and such popular songs as "Stop da Knockin' at My Door" and "Root, Hog, or Die." The song "Dixie" was first presented in a minstrel show, as were many of the other Stephen Foster favorites. Circuses, with their traveling menageries and variety acts, also had national appeal. By the 1850s traveling circuses performed for both farm and city folks. Barnum now entered the circus business and outdid all his rivals. The age of mass entertainment was underway, and it was an age that catered more and more to an urban population.

It was this urban population that demanded a shift away from active participation in sports. Vicarious participation replaced actual competition. Horse racing became the major spectator sport of the post-Revolutionary period. The race between Sir Henry and Eclipse in New York in 1823 attracted a crowd of more than 50,000. Critics of the sport condemned the increase of gambling, but its popularity continued. Foot races with competitive betting were first run through city streets, but their popularity soon led to their being moved to race courses, where admission was charged. Boxing was still socially unacceptable. Often fighters boxed until one contestant died or was unable to continue. Some fights lasted for more than three hours. Yielding to social pressure, one championship fight in 1849 was held in seclusion in the Maryland woods. The most significant sports development was the birth of baseball,

The Nation Develops a Personality: Emerging National Culture

Baseball as an American pastime had its origins in
the pre-Civil War era.

the first team game. Actually it was a form of an English children's game
called "rounders" rather than being the brainchild of Abner Doubleday of
Cooperstown, New York. The belief that Doubleday was the Father of Baseball
was part of the nationalistic heritage of the 1800s. In 1845 a group of professional men and merchants formed the Knickerbocker baseball club. The
Knickerbockers tried to keep the game restricted to the upper classes, but this
failed. Rich and poor alike played, and by the 1850s it was called "the national
game." In 1858 the first convention of baseball players voted to conclude a
game after 9 innings instead of playing until one team had scored 21 runs.
Professional baseball was in its infancy. Much of the growth of mass amusements and spectator sports was due to the growing cities.

The Rise of the City

While America was still overwhelmingly rural by the time of the Civil War,
urban culture was making itself known. At the time of the American Revolution, only 5.1 percent of all Americans lived in cities, but with the expansion
westward, cities became the spearheads of the frontier. The major Western
cities frequently were established in remote areas; gradually the land around
them was settled, too. Cincinnati, for example, was a city of early financial

speculation—typical of a great many cities developed by speculators who hoped to make money from them. Actually, the town and its location were well planned, and its future growth lay as a river trading center for farm and industrial products. Lexington, Kentucky, was also a planned Western city, but with the expanded use of steamboats the city declined in importance. St. Louis was formerly a center for fur trading and by the 1820s had become the gateway to the West and one of its most prosperous urban centers.

While Western cities were being planted, the metropolitan centers of the East were experiencing fantastic growth (see Chart 6-2). In 1860 New York had a population of one million and was the dominant city. Much of the history of Eastern urban growth during the post-Revolutionary period is the story of the rapid maturity of New York City. After the Revolution, New York and Philadelphia were about equal in size. Both cities were hurt by the disruption of trade during the War of 1812, yet both recovered. New York had always wanted to cut a waterway between the Hudson River and the Great Lakes to open the trade potential of the West. Political deals financed the building of a canal, and in 1825 the Erie Canal was opened. This canal tied New York to the West, and virtually overnight that city became the leader in the export trade. New York not only began to monopolize exports, but also became the leading port of entry for the European immigrant. Other Eastern cities, jealous of New York's supremacy and fearing that New York would monopolize the inland trade, contemplated canals and railroads that would connect them to the West, too.

New York City, as seen here in 1840, was fast becoming unsanitary and overcrowded.

Chart 6-2
The Rise of the City; 1790–1860

City Population	1790	1800	1810	1820	1830	1840	1850	1860
500,000–1,000,000							1	2
250,000–500,000						1	—	1
100,000–250,000				1	1	2	5	6
50,000–100,000		1	2	2	3	2	4	7
25,000–50,000	2	2	2	2	3	7	16	19
10,000–25,000	3	3	7	8	16	25	36	58
5,000–10,000	7	15	17	22	33	46	85	136
2,500–5,000	12	12	18	26	34	46	89	163

The settlement of the Great Lakes region created regional urban centers. Chicago, an early fort, was the western terminus of a canal that connected Lake Michigan with the Illinois River. Chicago grew slowly in population, but by the 1850s shrewd promotion and railroad construction made Chicago the hub of a transportation network. Cleveland was also the product of promotion and railroads. Favorably located along the Cuyahoga River on Lake Erie, it was connected by canal with the Ohio River and southern Ohio. During the post-Revolutionary period, much of the urban successes were caused by a combination of politicians, promoters, and businessmen and by rapid expansion of such transportation facilities as the steamboat and the railroad.

Urban Problems

While American cities seemed much cleaner than European cities, problems still were evident. Slums were growing in the major cities of the East. By the time of the Civil War, visitors described filth and overcrowding in New York. While the slums of New York and Boston were notorious, all cities had some negative features. Mud streets were common, and wallowing in that mud were herds of wild pigs that ate the garbage thrown there by the residents. Not having a garbage collection agency, residents threw their garbage out into the streets and waited for denizens to eat it. One New York resident noted that after a snowfall the mud, garbage, and manure were mixed together in one huge mess and "left for weeks together on the sides of the streets." The lack of sewage facilities also created problems. Cesspools were common, but often urine and fecal material were deposited in ditches along the streets. Inadequate sanitation obviously led to disease in the cities, such as outbreaks of dysentery and typhus.

By the 1840s overcrowding was the major ailment of urban America. Poverty and crime accompanied overcrowding, and it was only a matter of time until gangs of young delinquents ran wild through the streets. In 1849 the New York chief of police commented, "of the young children in the denser part of our city, one in ten is doomed to a life of inevitable vice, misery, and degradation, doomed to be ground to powder in the vortex of infamy and shame." Early reformers tried to organize groups to assist the poor and the children, but no real headway was made. Philadelphia, Boston, and other cities did establish municipal services, such as police departments, fire departments, and water control districts. Urban leaders attempted to keep up with the changing urban scene, but most were unable to keep pace.

Rapid change was at the heart of the culture of the national post-Revolutionary period. The slave system was becoming more firmly entrenched in the South, while in the North nativism was on the rise. America became an industrial nation, and with that status came concurrent social evils and labor problems. Religion became highly Americanized and innovative. Women were demanding an equal place in society. Experimentation became more and more a major American characteristic. While thousands were moving west, other thousands were crowding into urban centers. America had now forged an identity—and also an ego. It was this ego that burst forth during the era of Manifest Destiny and grew until it exploded in a bitter and bloody Civil War.

P. T. Barnum:
Father of Mass Amusements

Phineas Taylor Barnum (1810–1891) served as a member of the Connecticut legislature and was a temperance lecturer. But his fame lay in his showmanship and his promotional ability. Those who are involved in the merchandising of twentieth century mass entertainment owe a real debt to P. T. Barnum.

Barnum read the times almost better than any promoter in American history. American cities in the first three decades of the nineteenth century were beginning to grow in size; the factory system was taking hold, and the restless urban masses were beginning to search for a form of popular entertainment. President Andrew Jackson, who had been elected in 1828, represented the rise of the common people in politics; there was room for common people in entertainment, too. There was a need for unsophisticated, mass amusements, which would offer escapism but would be strictly moral. This was an age of high morality—at least on the surface. Most religions still looked upon amusements with a jaundiced eye. Barnum now stepped into center stage. His idea was to offer a form of entertainment that would be educational, moral, and of course profitable. He recognized the new urban market and attempted to satisfy it.

In the late 1830s he decided to collect real and fake oddities and display them to the public. Take, for example, his publicity of Joyce Heath, an elderly black woman who he claimed was the nurse of George Washington. In 1841 he opened in New York City the American Museum, which was said to have housed "six hundred thousand curiosities." People came from all over the Eastern United States and even from foreign countries to view his collection of freaks. Displayed there was a real model of Niagra Falls, Porter the Canadian Giant, who weighed 619 pounds, the Bearded Lady, the Wooly Horse of the West, and the White Elephants of Siam. Wax figures were found throughout the museum. In the early days of the museum the Feejee mermaid was the greatest attraction, but she soon gave way to one of Barnum's enduring finds—Charles S. Stratton, better known as Tom Thumb. This midget even charmed Queen Victoria on Barnum's foreign tour in 1844.

Certainly the visitors wondered whether Barnum's collection was genuine or not. But it seemed to make little difference. Even when the Wooly Horse appeared less wooly and the White Elephants of Siam began to fade, they returned in larger numbers. Now they could see bell ringers and a dog that operated a sewing machine or view Chang Fong, the Chinese juggler. When the exhibitions began to lose appeal, Barnum added melodramas such as *Uncle Tom's Cabin* in the lecture room of the museum. And all the time he continued his mass advertising, which was paying off in huge profits.

Near mid-century Barnum sponsored the tour of the idol of the American masses, Jenny

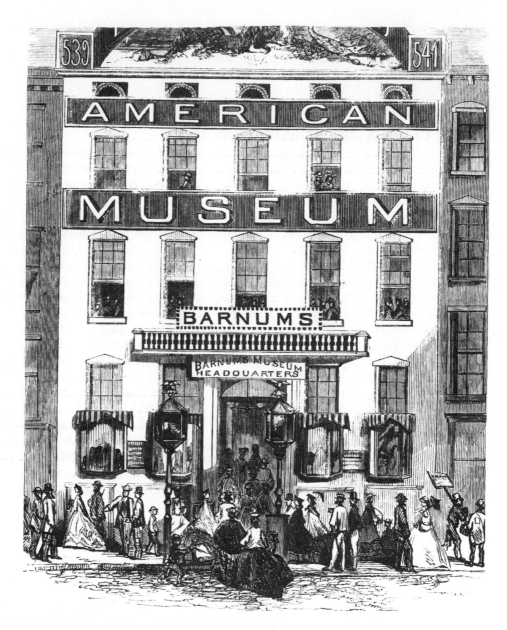

P. T. Barnum's American Museum in New York featured oddities from all over the world.

The Nation Develops a Personality: Emerging National Culture

Lind, "the Swedish Nightingale." He presold and prepackaged her so adeptly that *Lindomania* had swept the Eastern cities even before her first public concert. There were reports of people paying 25 cents to kiss the outside of her glove and 50 cents to kiss the inside of it. Products appeared, such as "Jenny Lind" hats and dresses. With this promotion her first concert in New York before 7000 screaming people was a fantastic success. Barnum had achieved a new level of promotion. He had created a market for Jenny Lind before she had warbled her first note. Popular amusements were becoming big business. The concert tour was reaping fantastic profits.

Barnum also saw the circus as a growing form of popular entertainment and believed that it too could be highly profitable. The American circus had evolved out of traveling shows that initially had played in colonial taverns, but by the 1800s they were playing for rural audiences who felt left out of the growing city entertainment. By the 1830s some 30 circuses were touring the country on a fairly regular basis. During the next few decades the circus would begin to take on the flavor that it exhibits today. The circus came to town and put on a parade, revealing just some of the sights and sounds which would be taking place under the big top. The "big top" itself began as the arena for the traveling shows. More and more wild animal acts were added, then riding acts and clowns.

When Barnum entered the circus business he vowed to make it the Greatest Show on Earth, and he did much to live up to that vow. The circus gave him an opportunity to centralize many of his earlier successes; freaks, curiosities, plays, and concert performers were all presented under one tent. He eventually joined with William Cameron Coup, who helped Barnum to switch the circus from travel by wagon to travel by railroad cars. Also joining them was James A. Bailey, who saw a foreign market for the circus and instituted foreign tours. By the 20th century the Barnum and Bailey Circus had achieved a near monopoly on the circus business. The keen showmanship of Barnum again appeared when he imported a giant African elephant named Jumbo. He was always looking for a new product to merchandise.

The death of P. T. Barnum in 1891 brought to a close the career of America's greatest showman. He opened the way for the mass advertisement of the 1920s and even for the rock concerts of today. Tom Thumb and Joyce Heath live no longer, and Ringling Brothers has merged with the Barnum and Bailey Circus. But the memory of P. T. Barnum as the Father of entertainment will linger on. ■

Suggested Reading

Two excellent general studies of national culture are RUSSELL BLAINE NYE's *The Cultural Life of the New Nation, 1776–1830* (1963) and J. A. KROUT and D. R. FOX in *The Completion of Independence* (1944).

HERBERT APTHEKER, in *American Negro Slave Revolts* (1943), traces the slave rebellions from the earliest times to emancipation, while LOUIS FILLER, in *The Crusade Against Slavery* (1960) describes the abolitionist campaign. Studies of Southern slavery are numerous; they include KENNETH STAMPP's, *The Peculiar Institution* (1956), JOHN BLASSINGAME's *The Slave Community: Plantation Life in the Antebellum South* (1973), which describes slave culture, and ROBERT W. FOGER and STANLEY L. ENGERMAN's study of the slave business in *Time on the Cross: The Economics of American Negro Slavery* (1974).

DOUGLAS C. NORTH, in *The Economic Growth of the United States* (1961), describes the coming of the American Industrial Revolution; factory conditions are ably documented in NORMAN WARE's, *The Industrial Worker, 1840–1860* (1924).

BERNARD A. WEISBERGER, in *They Gathered at the River* (1958), presents a view of the evangelical religious experiences.

RICHARD C. WADE, in *The Urban Frontier* (1959), describes how Western cities spearheaded the growth of the frontier.

ELEANOR FLEXNER in *Century of Struggle* (1975) depicts the rise of the womens' movement.

CHAPTER 7

Act One: War with Mexico
Act Two: War Between
North and South

Time Line

?–A.D. 1492	Migration and evolution of American Indian societies
1492	Christopher Columbus lands in West Indies—beginning of European exploration
1607–1732	Establishment of 13 English colonies
1775–1783	American Revolution
1776	Declaration of Independence
1789–1797	Presidency of George Washington
1812–1815	War of 1812
1816–1824	Era of Good Feelings

1836	Election of Martin Van Buren to presidency
1837	National Depression
1840	Election of William Henry Harrison to presidency
1841	Vice-President John Tyler assumes presidency upon death of Harrison
1844	Election of James Polk to presidency
1846–1848	Mexican War
1848	Treaty of Guadalupe Hidalgo Election of Zachary Taylor to presidency
1850	Vice-President Millard Fillmore becomes president upon death of Taylor
1850	Compromise of 1850
1852	Election of Franklin Pierce to presidency
1854	Kansas-Nebraska Act

1856	Election of James Buchanan to presidency
1857	Dred Scott Decision
1858	Lincoln-Douglas Debates
1859	John Brown raid
1860	Election of Abraham Lincoln to presidency
1861	Battle of Fort Sumter opens the Civil War

1846–1848	Mexican War
1861–1865	Civil War
1865–1877	Reconstruction
1877–1900	Industrialization and urbanization
1900–1916	Progressive Era
1917–1918	World War I
1930s	Depression and New Deal
1941–1945	World War II
1945–1960	Post-war politics
1950–1953	Korean War
1950–1960	Civil rights movement
1961–1973	Vietnam War
1976	Bicentennial celebration

"Van, Van, he's our man." "Remember the Alamo." "Fifty-four Forty or Fight." These slogans were from the period before the Civil War; they relate to specific past incidents, yet they bear present and future implications. Van Buren was the man elected in 1836, but who will be elected in our next presidential election? Political slogans frequently have revealed the intensity of the campaign and even have helped bring victory. "Remember the Alamo" recalls the fall of the Alamo, the Texas Revolution, and the Mexican War—a period of American expansion. Today, critics of American policy suspect expansion is still in the minds of many of our leaders. War, on the other hand, is a part of our heritage that most Americans would like to forget. "Fifty-four Forty or Fight" recalls problems in foreign affairs. Today we worry about world oil, the Middle East, Russia, and China. What will our worries be tomorrow?

Beginning with the presidency of Martin Van Buren, the United States went through a period that is often called the Age of Manifest Destiny. The American character was emerging full-blown. Many young men were following advice and moving west; others were thinking of American expansion to Alaska, Mexico, the Carribbean, and beyond. It was a time when America fought an expansionist war with Mexico and claimed what is today the American Southwest. But this new land acquisition opened a can of worms that could not be easily contained. Slavery and its expansion emerged as a national issue and led directly to the conflict of the Civil War. While the Age of Manifest Destiny is often pictured favorably as a time of nationalistic pride and expansionism, it was a time of generally weak presidential leadership, imperialistic war, and sectional conflict. The aura of "complete democracy" evident during the presidency of Andrew Jackson was soon lost with the election of Martin Van Buren in 1836 and the depression of 1837.

President Martin Van Buren

Andrew Jackson described his successor Martin Van Buren as "a true man," while Davy Crockett, a product of Jacksonian Democracy, wrote "Van Buren is secret, sly, selfish, cold, calculating, distrustful, and treacherous." Who was the real Van Buren? He entered the presidency with high expectations. He was Jackson's hand-picked successor—a skilled political manipulator and an experienced statesman. The public felt that Van Buren, "the Little Magician," would carry on the policies of Jackson and lead to even greater prosperity. This was hardly the case.

Born in the Dutch community of Kinderhook, New York, near Albany, Van Buren became the first president born under the American flag. At an

Martin Van Buren was Jackson's hand picked successor but he never lived up to Jackson's expectations.

early age he studied law, was admitted to the bar, and practiced in his home town. Impressed with the ideas of Thomas Jefferson, he joined Jefferson's party and entered politics as a New York state senator, later serving as attorney general of New York and eventually United States senator. During his political rise he earned the title of "Little Magician" and "the Wizard of the Albany Regency" through his skilled use of political manipulation and patronage. He resigned as governor of New York to become Jackson's secretary of state. The developing rift with Calhoun caused Van Buren to resign and to lose confirmation of his appointment to Great Britian by one vote. In 1832 Jackson chose him as his vice-president and probable successor. During Jackson's second term, Van Buren actively supported his bank policies. The fierce debates in the Senate even raised the possibility of his assassination, so he carried a loaded pistol with him when he presided there. Small in stature, with a bald head and fringes of red hair, Van Buren became the eighth president of the United States in 1837.

The Depression of 1837

President Van Buren's first major problem was the Depression of 1837, which he inherited from Jackson. Jackson had killed the National Bank in 1832, and by 1835 the national debts had been paid off. Prosperity and economic expansion were in vogue. More and more state banks were opening and making sizeable loans, some without adequate collateral. There was also wild land speculation in the West at this time, based largely on rapid investment, and overexpansion of credit. To slow the runaway economic overexpansion Jackson had issued in 1836 the Specie Circular, which directed that only specie (gold and silver) should be received in payment for public land. By the time of this order the system as a whole was dangerously overextended, and many banks had almost no reserves. The collapse came in the spring of 1837 and resulted in a general depression that lasted for several years. Not only did hundreds of banks collapse, but prices dropped, land sales diminished, and unemployment rose.

It was Van Buren who bore the brunt of this fiscal panic, but he seemed unwilling to use any government action to slow down the depression. Van Buren's political philosophy (a philosophy that generally prevailed until the 1930s) was that the national government should deal primarily with political issues and that economic matters were the domain of states and local governments. Van Buren did not believe it was the job of the federal government to act in this matter. He wrote, "The less the government interferes, the better for general prosperity." While unemployment and hunger continued, Van Buren waited for the economic blizzard to run its course. Van Buren's answer was not a new National Bank, nor a massive relief program, but an independent treasury system, which was eventually adopted by the Congress in 1840. According to this system, government funds were no longer to be deposited in state-chartered banks for them to invest as they say fit, but instead were to be housed in government subtreasuries, located in various cities. This would divorce the federal government from banking entirely. This measure was Van Buren's most constructive accomplishment, yet it was repealed in 1841. In 1846 it was reintroduced and lasted until the days of the Federal Reserve System instituted in 1913. Van Buren's bad luck as president was also evident in foreign affairs. In 1837 Canadian insurgents rebelled against English rule. Many Americans sympathized with the rebels and furnished them with material aid. The rebels employed a small American steampship, *The Caroline*, to carry supplies across the Niagara River from New York. One night when the ship was on the American side of the Niagara, Canadian forces loyal to the British captured and burned her, killing one American in the process. There were rumors of war on both sides of the border and Congress appropriated money for defense. While Van Buren urged caution, a new dispute arose further east. A boundary dispute between Maine and New Brunswick led to the Aroostook War of 1838–39. Canadian lumberjacks moved into Maine. Authorities on both sides of the border mobilized militias; 50 Americans were captured. Congress appropriated $10 million and authorized the president to raise 30,000 troops. Both incidents were smoothed over through tricky diplomacy and with the signing of the Webster-Ashburton agreement of 1842 which gave 60 percent of the Maine-New Brunswick area to the United States and made minor changes in the international boundary in the area of Lake Champlain and the area from Lake Superior to Lake of the Woods. Financial and foreign turmoil spoiled the presidency of Martin Van Buren and did not allow him to use his talents for political organization to further expand Jacksonian policies.

Election of 1840

Although Van Buren had been an unpopular president, the Democratic party reluctantly nominated him again in 1840 to face the military hero of Tippecanoe, General William Henry Harrison. Harrison was the choice of the Whig party, the party that had been formed to oppose Jackson and continued to oppose Jackson's man Van Buren. The Whigs did not choose their ablest candidates, such as Henry Clay or Daniel Webster, but instead chose a popular Western hero as their nominee, who would poll lots of votes and win the election. Harrison, with varied political experiences, was still without political enemies. Harrison and his vice-presidential nominee, John Tyler from Virginia, made popular the slogan "Tippecanoe and Tyler too" in their campaign. Harrison pictured himself in the image of Jackson. Harrison let people know he had lived in a log cabin, had been a simple Ohio farmer, and was a military hero. One Democratic journalist wrote that Harrison would be content to live forever in a log cabin as long as he had some hard cider with him. This was a mistake, because it caused the Whigs to stress Harrison's background in the campaign which became in essence a "log cabin" campaign. There were log cabin badges, songs, newspapers, and parties. Political rallies were held in log cabins, where cider would be liberally dosed with whiskey. The Democrats attempted to show that Harrison actually was an aristocrat, living in a 16-room mansion. But it was Van Buren Americans thought of when they remembered the difficult days of the depression. Van Buren's aristocratic habits, such as dousing his whiskers in French cologne, sleeping in a Louis XV bed, and riding the countryside in an expensive carriage hurt his image, as did his lack of a vice-president on his ticket. "Van, Van is a used-up man" was quite

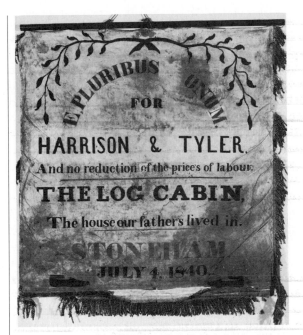

The election of 1840 featured the log cabin campaign of Whig William Henry Harrison.

accurate. Although the popular vote was close, Harrison was swept into office by a sizeable majority in the electoral college; "Sweet Sandy Whiskers" Van Buren left office. This campaign of personalities, not issues, set the stage for many others that would follow. The Whigs had beaten the Democrats at their own game.

Harrison and Tyler

William Henry Harrison was born of the planter aristocracy in Virginia, where he studied law and medicine. After a brief career in the army, he became governor of Indiana Territory and one of the ablest treaty negotiators in Indian affairs. In 1811 his defeat of Tecumseh's Indians brought him national recognition. During the War of 1812 he served as a major general and after the war as a United States Representative, Senator, and first United States minister to Colombia. In 1836 he ran unsuccessfully for president on the Whig ticket, but Whig antics and popular appeal won him the presidency in 1840.

On a bitterly cold inaugural day Harrison showed his strength by not wearing a hat or coat. The cold he caught that day developed into pneumonia, complicated by a liver disorder. Once the physicians of the day got hold of him his condition deteriorated rapidly. They bled and blistered him and gave him crude petroleum and snakeweed as medicines. On April 4, 1841, the old Indian fighter died after only 30 days in office. Little known John Tyler, called "His Accidency," now became the first vice-president to ascend to the office of president.

Born a Virginia aristocrat, John Tyler attended William and Mary College, became a lawyer, and served in the Virginia state house. Elected to the House of Representatives in 1816, Tyler displayed his propensity for a strict interpretation of the Constitution; he opposed all measures that extended the power of government. A former Democrat, he was nominated for vice-president in 1840 to attract Southern states' rights votes. Once he was president, his philosophy of government did not conform to the ideas of his party, particularly to those of Henry Clay. President Tyler blocked Clay's attempts at internal improvements, such as federally financed roads, high tariffs, and a new national bank. His entire cabinet, except for Daniel Webster, resigned in protest. The House of Representatives unsuccessfully tried to pass a resolution to impeach him. Tyler was literally a man without a party. But was not a complete obstructionist. Under his leadership a general preemption act was passed that gave settlers first chance to buy lands in the public domain and a needed reorganization of the navy was undertaken. He also tackled the touchy Texas question.

The Texas Revolution

Since the early 1800s Americans had long desired the wilds of Texas, then under Spanish rule. With Mexican independence in 1820 an agreement was reached with Americans, such as Moses Austin, that would allow Americans to settle a certain number of families in Texas. Stephen Austin, following in his father's footsteps, attempted to bring in more than 300 American families. The Texas province always had been underpopulated and the Mexican government felt it could solve its problem by immigration from the United States. By the mid-1830s Austin's colony numbered about 30,000 inhabitants, including such notable men as Davy Crockett, Jim Bowie, inventor of the large Bowie knife, and Sam Houston, formerly called "Big Drunk." These American "gringos" came more and more into conflict with the Mexican "greasers." Culturally there was a great deal of mutual misunderstanding involving issues such as religion and slavery; further, the Americans were becoming increasingly restive with administration from Mexico City. Once Antonio López de Santa Anna, "the Napoleon of the West," became president of Mexico and overthrew the liberal constitution of 1824, the Americans in Texas felt they had little choice but to rebel. On March 2, 1836, independence was declared and the war for Texas began.

With about 6000 men Santa Anna advanced into Texas and destroyed a band of 200 American rebels at the Alamo. Later stories tell of how Davy Crockett was found riddled with bullets and how Jim Bowie was shot while lying sick in bed. But in the eyes of the Mexican government these insurgents had challenged their government. Soon after this incident at the Alamo, a band of American volunteers surrendered at Goliad on the south bank of the San Antonio River. Acting on Santa Anna's orders, the Mexican commander butchered all the Americans in cold blood. "Remember the Alamo" and "Remember Goliad" became American rallying cries, but for a long time there

The battle of the Alamo ended in the destruction of the American rebels at the hands of the Mexican army.

seemed little to rally around. Sam Houston, commander of the Army of the Texas Republic, was retreating eastward across Texas, pursued by the army of Santa Anna. But he and his troops managed to surprise the Mexican army during a siesta, rushing into their camp yelling "Remember the Alamo" and capturing their leader. At knifepoint, Santa Anna agreed to the Treaty of Velasco, by which Mexico agreed to withdraw its forces from Texas and to recognize the Rio Grande as the southwestern boundary of Texas. The independent Texas Republic was born.

Now independent, Texas submitted a formal proposal for annexation to the United States but found a chilly reception. Andrew Jackson, then president, knew that Texas annexation would reopen the problem of slavery extension, so he avoided the issue. His successor Van Buren mostly followed the same policy, for there was now suspicion in the North of a "slave plot," which involved annexation of Texas. Texas had been settled mainly by slaveowners; this is not surprising, for most of the Americans had come in the traditional pattern of direct westward movement from the South. So while the United States waited, Texas governed itself as an independent republic. The Texas republic was forced to defend itself and even to send foreign diplomats abroad. Some of the European countries, particularly England, saw a great advantage in an independent Texas. But the pull of the United States was too strong, and President Tyler felt that the objections of the North could be overcome. When the Senate rejected the Texas treaty of annexation, Tyler proposed a joint resolution of both houses, which only needed a simple majority for passage, and the plan worked. Just before he left office in 1845, Texas was offered statehood. John Tyler is hardly remembered today. A Whig president, he was a Democrat at heart, and, in 1844 even attempted to acquire the Democratic nomination. Actually he was a study in frustration, particularly for the Whig party, which attempted to regroup and put in one of their own in 1844.

Polk and Manifest Destiny

The election of 1844 has been known as the election for Manifest Destiny. By this time sentiment was building for the belief that the American system of democracy should be spread throughout the entire continent, even to South America. Americans were destined by God to be the chosen race and were destined to be "the guardians to preserve [freedom] for the human race." This general philosophy was used to justify American ambitions in California and Oregon. Henry Clay was the candidate of the Whig party, while James Polk, a dark-horse candidate from Tennessee who was nominated on the ninth ballot, was the Democratic choice. Democrats were yelling for "reannexation of Texas" and "Reoccupation of Oregon," while the Whigs were shouting "Clay, Union, and Liberty." Both parties also tried to portray the opposing candidate as a slaveowner and Southern sympathizer. Polk took a strong stand on expansionism, while Clay strattled the fence, particularly on the issue of Texas. When the ballots were counted, Polk had been elected by a small margin.

The first "dark horse," or little-known presidential candidate, Polk was not a virtual unknown. Born in North Carolina, he lived most of his early life in Tennessee, where he entered law and state politics. He became so close to Andrew Jackson that Polk was called "Young Hickory." Elected to the House of Representatives, he eventually became Speaker of the House. After serving as governor of Tennessee, unusual political circumstances won him the Democratic nomination in 1844 and eventually the presidency. Personally, Polk was a humorless individual with a secretive bent; physically, he was a sickly, small man with a thin face and piercing gray eyes.

After his inauguration he is supposed to have said to his secretary of the navy that he wanted to achieve four things: lowering of the tariff; reinstitution of the Independent Treasury System; settlement of the Oregon question; and acquisition of California and the Mexican Southwest. While the first two goals were relatively easy to attain with Congressional help, the last two were much more difficult and involved both domestic and foreign intrigues.

James Polk became the president of Manifest Destiny with his policies concerning Oregon and Mexico.

The Oregon Question

The vast wilderness known as the Oregon Territory, lying west of the Rocky Mountains and north of California, had previously been claimed by as many as four nations: Spain, Russia, Great Britain, and the United States. But by the 1820s only England and the United States continued to push their claim. In 1818 the two powers had agreed to joint occupancy of the area. Both countries based their claims on discovery and settlement, but Britain's claims seemed more realistic. British explorers had arrived first in the region and had gone in greater number. While both American and British fur trappers had settled the area, the British fur companies began to exert a monopoly. By the 1820s the English Hudson Bay Company virtually controlled the region and American claims seemed relatively weak.

During the 1830s, however, Protestant missionaries were being lured to Oregon by free soil and Indian souls. Their glowing reports encouraged an "Oregon Fever," which gave rise to substantial American settlement. By the mid-1840s American settlement was concentrated in the Willamette Valley of Oregon. Few Americans lived north of the Columbia River in what today is the state of Washington. Polk's platform in 1844 had contained a statement on the "reoccupation of Oregon"; in his inaugural address he also asserted that America's claim to Oregon was "clear and unquestionable." Democratic slogans such as "Fifty-four Forty or Fight", a demand for all land south of the parallel along the Alaska border, indicated the national desire for all of Oregon. Polk, however, was willing to compromise. He proposed that the present Canadian border be extended to the Pacific. The British minister refused the compromise.

While Westerners were continuing to shout, "all of Oregon or none," Polk himself was now more convinced than ever that the "only way to treat John Bull was to look him straight in the eye." Negotiations were reopened. Britian approved the compromise, and in 1846 the Oregon Treaty was signed. Conditions of the treaty were that the international boundary at the forty-ninth parallel be extended to the Pacific and that Vancouver Island remain British. Had Polk forced the British into yielding? Hardly. Politics in Britain were in a state of chaos; in addition England depended on American wheat, and free trade was more important than a distant war. In 1845 the Hudson's Bay Company had moved their main headquarters from the Columbia River to Vancouver Island. The value of Washington as a fur area had diminished, as had the value of the Columbia River. The British compromise had been proposed only ten days before Britian learned of war between the United States and Mexico. Polk was lucky to settle the Oregon dispute in a favorable manner; in regard to war with Mexico, little luck was involved there.

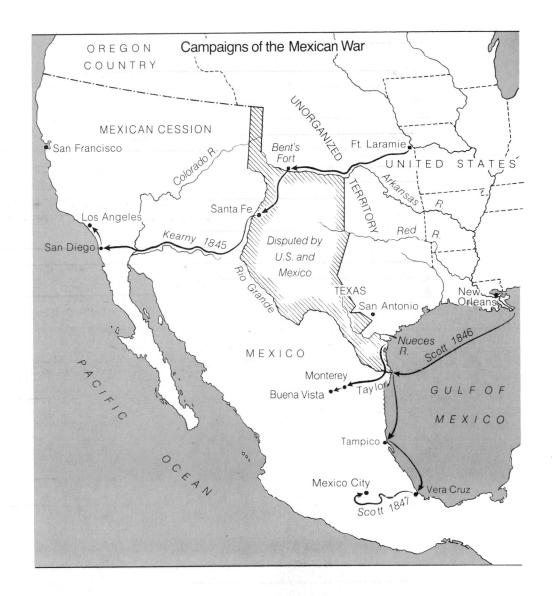

Campaigns of the Mexican War

OREGON COUNTRY

MEXICAN CESSION

San Francisco

Colorado R.

UNORGANIZED TERRITORY

Bent's Fort

Ft. Laramie

UNITED STATES

Arkansas R.

Santa Fe

Los Angeles

Kearny 1845

San Diego

Rio Grande

Red R.

Disputed by U.S. and Mexico

TEXAS

San Antonio

New Orleans

MEXICO

Nueces R.

Scott 1846

Monterey

Buena Vista

Tay lor

GULF OF MEXICO

PACIFIC OCEAN

Tampico

Mexico City

Scott 1847

Vera Cruz

The Mexican War

Relations had been strained with Mexico ever since the days of the Texas Revolution. Once Texas was admitted to the union, Mexico broke off diplomatic relations and even talked of possible war. Problems were further complicated by a boundary dispute. Polk and the expansionist Texans had wanted the southern boundary of Texas to be the Rio Grande, but Mexico had long accepted the boundary as the Nueces, a river 150 miles to the north. Polk further reflected the spirit of Manifest Destiny by his desire to acquire the lush province of Mexican California. He was beginning to believe—or at least profess to believe—rumors that the British were about to buy or seize California and that he must act soon.

In 1845, Louisiana diplomat John Slidell was sent to Mexico to discuss the boundary dispute and to offer up to $20 million for Mexico and California. When Polk now learned that the Mexican government refused to speak with Slidell, he felt that "aggressive measures" were necessary. General Zachary Taylor already had been sent to occupy the banks of the Nueces River. Polk now ordered Taylor to instead occupy the bank of the Rio Grande—in Mexico's eyes an invasion of Mexican territory. When the Mexican army responded by attacking—leading to 16 Americans killed or wounded—Polk sent a war message to Congress that emphasized the shedding of "American blood on American soil." He announced that a state of war existed "notwithstanding all our efforts to avoid it." The patriotic Congress did not avoid the opportunity for war, and the Mexican War began. Since the Nueces had long been the southern boundary of Texas, Taylor's occupation of the Rio Grande further south appears to have been an act of war. But it must be noted that both sides were anxious for a struggle. The Mexicans wanted to once and for all put down "the gringos," while Americans wished to rescue California from the hands of "the greasers."

Polk had been determined to acquire California, even if he had to go to war. He saw the acquiring of a Pacific Coast frontage as essential to the commercial interests of the United States. He was actually writing his war message before the Mexican attack. New England, however, viewed the war as part of a slaveholding conspiracy to build "bigger pens to cram in slaves," and many Northerners criticized it as an aggressive war, picturing Polk as a War Hawk. Whig congressmen, including Abraham Lincoln, insisted that Polk show the exact "spot" on which American blood had been shed. Still the war was accepted with enthusiasm and slogans arose such as "Ho for the Halls of the Montezuma." More than 23,000 volunteers almost immediately signed up for duty. Polk later wrote: "We have just as good a reason for it [war] as a strong nation ever had against a weak one." Here was a precise expression of Manifest Destiny.

General Taylor, "Old Rough and Ready," fought his way across the Rio Grande into Mexico and won the Battles of Monterey in 1846 and Buena Vista in 1847. The second battle was close, and even to this day Mexican historians claim that the battle was won by the army of Santa Anna. Polk viewed Taylor as an indecisive leader and entrusted command of an invasion of Mexico City to General Winfield Scott. General Scott, "Old Fuss and Feathers," now launched an amphibious assault on Vera Cruz with the help of the United States Marines. From Vera Cruz the forces of Scott marched through mountain passes and across difficult terrain, singing "Green Grow the Lilacs" all the way into Mexico City, which they seized after a spirited fight. Scott's efforts won him the recognition as the most capable general in the period between the War of 1812 and the Civil War. Mexico was now his.

Meanwhile military forces were seizing California and New Mexico. Before the war, Polk had sent representatives to California to stir up an independence movement; with the outbreak of war, General John C. Fremont joined with a group of American rebels to set up a Republic of California under the "Bear Flag."

After victories in northern California, Fremont and his forces moved south against the Mexican army. Colonel Stephen W. Kearney invaded New Mexico, in 1846, capturing Santa Fe, then marched to southern California, where he joined Fremont in putting down scattered resistance near Los Angeles and San Diego. New Mexico and California were now American possessions.

This war of conquest was reflected also in the diplomacy of conquest. At the start of the war Polk decided that he would not actively block European involvement. Britain and France both viewed the war as imperialistic, but neither country desired to become involved. At the start of the war Polk had wanted to acquire New Mexico and California, but with repeated military successes he began to side with his advisors in pushing for more land, possibly even "all Mexico." The United States commissioner, Nicholas Trist, who was with the army under Scott and who tried to negotiate a peace, did not agree with Polk's desires. Polk learned of Trist's negotiations and ordered him back to the United States. Trist refused and instead signed the Treaty of Guadalupe Hidalgo, which limited the new Texas boundary to the Rio Grande and ceded only New Mexico and Upper California. The United States agreed to pay Mexico $15 million and to pay the claims of its citizens against the Mexican government. Although Polk was enraged at the limited treaty, he knew there was considerable opposition to the war, so he submitted the treaty to the Senate, which proceeded to ratify it. Nicholas Trist subsequently was dismissed from office and denied back pay. It was 25 years later that Congress finally rectified that wrong. The Treaty of Guadalupe Hidalgo completed the formation of the continental United States, except for land along the southern boundaries of New Mexico and Arizona, which was acquired from Mexico for railroad development in 1853 in the Gadsden Purchase.

The Mexican War was indeed a successful one for the United States and the high point of the Age of Manifest Destiny. While more than 13,000 soldiers died, only 172 died in battle, the rest succumbed to disease. The war cost about $100 million. This war has received bitter treatment from both contemporary writers and later historians and has been the most condemned American war before the Vietnam War. On the positive side, the United States's lust for territory was satiated temporarily with the acquisition of Mexican land. On the negative side, the war led to a serious questioning of America's foreign policy and to an eventual clash of cultures between Americans and Mexican-Americans. The treaty clearly noted that all Mexicans living in the newly acquired area had the option of retaining their Mexican citizenship or becoming American citizens. Whatever their decision, they were to be allowed to exercise their full civil and political rights. The treaty also stipulated that all Mexicans would retain full title to their property and that valid Spanish and Mexican land grants would be upheld. These guarantees were not honored in the period after the Civil War.

The lowering of the tariff, the adoption of the Independent Treasury System, the settlement of the Oregon question, and the acquisition of California and New Mexico were the major victories of President James Polk. As a domestic leader, he again strengthened the office of the presidency, through use of White House interference and executive veto. A strong believer in the separation of powers, he wrote, "Any attempt to coerce the president to yield his sanction to measures which he cannot approve would be violation of the spirit of the Constitution." He was, however, much more dynamic in foreign diplomacy. His handling of the Oregon question, the Texas problem, and the Mexican War brought him both severe criticism and lavish praise. While he felt he had accomplished his avowed goals as president, he also knew his sickly physical condition could stand no more than one term as president. He reflected in his diary, "This day closed my third year in the presidential office. They have been years of incessant labor, anxiety, and responsibility." He died three months after leaving office, never to know the problems stemming from the new territory in the West. Slavery again became a national issue, and it opened a sectional struggle that led in 1861 to the Civil War.

The Civil War exploded at the end of a long period of growing tension between North and South. In 1820 North and South fiercely debated the admittance of Missouri to the Union as a slave state. The Missouri Compromise of 1820 solved the immediate tension but did not permanently end the power struggle between North and South. During the presidency of Andrew Jackson in the 1830s, South Carolina challenged the government's tariff power. In that nullification drive, a Southern state had directly confronted the federal government. It was a tragedy that both sides declared a victory. Newly acquired land in the West again created a struggle between North and South.

The Coming of the Civil War

The acquisition of Mexican land in 1848 reintroduced the question of slavery into national politics. Congress now debated the extension of slavery into New Mexico and California. Two years earlier Polk had asked for $2 million to be used in negotiations for Mexican land. In the House of Representatives, Democrat David Wilmot from Pennsylvania introduced a resolution, which passed, proposing that slavery should be prohibited in any territory acquired from Mexico. This free-soil resolution failed in the Senate, and two doctrines now began to emerge. The North took the stand that Congress must limit slavery to the South, while the South felt that Congress must allow its expansion and must protect it wherever it existed. There seemed to be no immediate resolving of these differences. The election of 1848 did little to help the situation.

Election of 1848

Both parties attempted to avoid the major issue of slavery, nominating fairly uncommitted individuals. The Democrats chose Lewis Cass, a pompous individual with much diplomatic experience, who tried to placate both North and South by campaigning on the doctrine of popular sovereignty, in which the people of a territory decided themselves whether they wanted slavery or not. Lewis Cass, referred to as "Gass" by his enemies, tried to take a middle-of-the-road approach, and the Democratic platform avoided slavery completely. This led to the birth of a third party. The Free Soilers opposed the extension of slavery; they nominated Martin Van Buren. The Whigs followed their winning formula by nominating a military hero, Zachary Taylor. Taylor was a career military man with no political experience. In fact, he even admitted that he had never voted in a presidential election. His party offered no political platform at all, but, in a close election, Taylor carried the day, and the military hero and slave-owner became the fourth popular military officer elected to the presidency.

Born among the planter aristocracy of Virginia, Zachary Taylor spent much of his early life on the family farm in Kentucky. Tales of his father's service in the American Revolution lured him into a military career. He par-

Career military man Zachary Taylor became president in 1848.

ticipated in the War of 1812, the Black Hawk Indian War in Illinois, and the Seminole Indian War in Florida. He played a major role in the early campaigns of the Mexican War, until President Polk doubted his ability and picked Winfield Scott to lead the invasion of central Mexico. He was a reluctant Whig candidate in 1848, but was elected. As a political babe in the woods, his leadership was hesitant and weak. He wasn't prepared to take a decisive role in the growing crisis over slavery in the territories.

The discovery of gold in California once again brought the issue to a boil. In January 1848, a workman in the Sacramento Valley discovered gold at Sutter's Mill and word spread like wildfire. In a few months all America was dreaming of the fortunes that could be made by merely separating gold from

The discovery of gold in California hastened California's admission into the Union.

sand. The gold rush was on; within a year California had a population of 100,000. Towns like Polker Flats and Grubber Gulch reflected the turbulence and violence of the period of the "forty-niners." The growth of California could not be controlled by a military government. In late 1849, with the encouragement of President Taylor, California drew up a constitution outlawing slavery and applied for admission to the Union. The balance between slave and free states in the Senate would be destroyed, probably forever. The Utah and New Mexico territories were waiting to be organized as free areas. The future of the South was seriously in doubt, as was the fabric of the Union. Only another compromise would preserve the Union in 1850, and the "Great Compromiser" Henry Clay would have his final day.

The Compromise of 1850

Aging Henry Clay, who had been responsible for the Compromise of 1820, came to the fore. In the Senate he introduced a series of resolutions that included immediate admission of California as a free state, the organization of territorial governments in New Mexico and Utah without mention of slavery, a new and stringent fugitive-slave law, and the abolition of domestic slave trade in the District of Columbia. These resolutions sparked one of the greatest debates in the history of the Senate; it was the last time some of the fiery old leaders would be heard. Of course, Clay, old, weakened, and faltering in voice, spoke in favor of his resolutions; he argued that the Union must be preserved and that the spirit of compromise must carry the day. John C. Calhoun, dying of tuberculosis and unable to speak, listened while a fellow senator read his speech demanding Southern rights. "The Federal Union can be saved only by satisfying the South," he wrote. The debate continued, but Calhoun never knew the results, for he died before the decision was made. On his deathbed he said he believed the South's fate now lay in the hands of God. The crucial speech was that of Daniel Webster, also sick and dying, who argued in favor of concession. "I speak today for the preservation of the Union. Hear me for my cause." This speech on March 7 seemed to turn the tide. Still dissension reigned supreme. Senator Stephen Douglas of Illinois, "the Little Giant," decided to gather support for each section of Clay's package. This strategy worked, and the measures passed separately. With congressional approval the only hurtle that remained was President Taylor, who had earlier indicated he would veto the measures. Just before he had to make that decision, he died, probably of an acute intestinal disorder, and Millard Fillmore, a strong advocate of compromise, became president.

Millard Fillmore

Millard Fillmore was the second "vice president" to assume the presidency. Born in New York state, he was a poor boy who became a clothmaker's apprentice. Later he became a Buffalo lawyer, a state representative, and he served in the United States House of Representatives. He was chosen as Taylor's running mate to balance the ticket. He had presided over the compromise debate, and, as president, now supported the compromise. While he provided little leadership during his two years as president, he did enforce the compromise, including the provision for the return of runaway slaves. This lost him Northern support and the nomination in 1852.

The Fugitive Slave Law

With the passage of the Compromise of 1850, Americans were talking of a Second Era of Good Feelings. But this talk was premature. Both North and South wondered which side had been the victor in 1850. In the midst of this wondering, the North became more and more antagonistic over the new Fugitive Slave Act. This act stipulated that harsher penalties would be imposed for harboring or aiding a fugitive slave and that citizens could be forced to serve in posses to hunt escaped slaves. The harshness of the law was met by stern resistance in the North. Writers such as Ralph Waldo Emerson expressed their sentiments: "I will not obey it, by God." Mobs impeded the Southern "man-hunters," while many Northern states passed laws that denied the use of local jails or prisons for holding fugitives. The Underground Railroad, which helped to lead slaves to freedom, stepped up its activites. One Southerner noted that over the previous forty years more than 50,000 slaves had been abducted by Northern sympathizers. The Fugitive Slave Act helped to dramatize the issue of slavery at a time when thousands of Americans were reading, in Harriet Beecher Stowe's *Uncle Tom's Cabin*, the story of little Eliza, a slave girl, crossing the ice-bound Ohio River as she was being pursued by a slave trader. The passage of the Fugitive Slave Act may have done more harm than good for the South.

Pierce and Compromise

Even with growing reaction to the Fugitive Slave Law, a spirit of moderation and compromise prevailed in the election of 1852. The Whigs had won in 1840 and 1848 by nominating military heroes; in 1852 they tried again with Winfield Scott, "Old Fuss and Feathers" of Mexican War fame. After 49 ballots the Democrats turned to a dark-horse candidate, Franklin Pierce, a New Hampshire lawyer-politician, who never formally compaigned in the election. While the Whigs emphasized Pierce's fondness for the bottle, the Democrats were yelling "We Polked 'em in '44; we'll Pierce 'em in '52." The disorganization of the Whig party, plus Pierce's lack of scandal, led to his election in 1852. This election marked the last time that the Whig party participated in national politics. The great leaders Webster and Clay were dead; the party divided into sectional components, and it finally disappeared into political limbo.

Franklin Pierce at age 48 became the youngest president up to that time. Born in New Hampshire, he studied law, then entered politics. Elected to the

United States House of Representatives and the United States Senate, he resigned his seat because his wife disliked Washington and its social activities. After serving as brigadier general in the Mexican War, he returned to law. He was the compromise candidate for president for the Democrats in 1852.

President Franklin Pierce was a true compromiser. He tried to please everyone, but he actually pleased few. As president, he watched in frustration as the slavery issue became more and more pressing and the strands of Union became less and less permanent. Slavery as a political issue was even affecting foreign affairs. The island of Cuba had long been considered a natural area for American expansion. In the late 1840s and early 1850s Southern demand for the island grew intense. Many Southern planters viewed Cuba, with its slave population of 200,000, as a potential Southern state. American soliders of fortune tried a series of unsuccessful expeditions to get control of the island. When these failed, the United States government tried diplomatically to obtain the island from Spain. Both presidents Polk and Pierce offered to buy the island, but Spain refused. In 1854 United States minister to Spain Pierre Soulé conferred with James Buchanan and John Y. Mason, United States ministers to Great Britain and France, in Ostend, Belgium, to discuss how Europe would react if America seized the island. Their confidential report, known as the Ostend Manifesto, proposed that if Spain refused to sell Cuba for $120 million "Then by every law, human and divine, we shall be justified in wresting it from Spain." Details of their report became public, and Northerners screamed of a Southern plot. The tension over the Ostend Manifesto was mild compared to the controversy that arose over the building of the transcontinental railroad and the formation of the territories of Kansas and Nebraska.

The Kansas-Nebraska Act

With the acquisition of Oregon and California, improved travel to the Pacific Coast was a necessity. Travel across the Isthmus of Panama and around South America was too long, while overland travel was often too laborious. For years some Americans had dreamed of a railroad that would link the Pacific Coast to the Atlantic Coast, tying America together. In the early 1850s Congress made a series of surveys to find out the best overland route. The southern route seemed to have the most geographic advantages, but Northerners opposed it. Stephen Douglas, the "Little Giant," proposed the route through the central regions. His dealings in real estate made his interest in a central route a questionable one. And critics exclaimed that the central route was impossible since there was a lack of organized government there. His answer was the Kansas-Nebraska Bill of 1854, which stipulated that Kansas and Nebraska were to be organized as territories, with the question of slavery to be settled by the territories' people themselves according to the principle of popular sovereignty. The passage of this act nullified the compromise of 1850 and created a furor of unrealized proportions. "Bleeding Kansas" was the result. Slaveholders poured into Kansas to make it a slave state, while Northerners moved in to make the territory free. Many Southerners had expected that Kansas would become a slave state and Nebraska would become a free state. They now saw Northerners intentionally trying to limit slavery from both areas. It was here in 1856 that shooting first started, mirroring the Civil War struggle of five years later. Here also greybearded, crazed John Brown came from Ohio and personally took his antislavery vengence out against Southerners. The bleeding of Kansas also took place on the floor of the Senate.

Charles Sumner of Massachusetts was a leading abolitionist. After learning of the increasing tension in Kansas, he made a two-day speech in the Senate describing the miscarriage of justice in Kansas and referring to Southern slave owners as the "vomit of an uneasy civilization." He also personally attacked the reputation of Senator Butler from South Carolina. Butler's cousin Preston Brooks, a young congressman, was infuriated by the speech and wanted revenge. Instead of challenging Sumner to a duel, which he probably could have, and unable to confront Sumner outside the Senate chambers, one day he entered the Senate and broke a heavy cane over the head of Sumner, who was sitting at his desk. The senator fell bleeding to the floor; his nervous system was shattered. Brooks became a Southern hero. For three years Sumner was incapacitated. This incident showed how emotional issues were becoming between North and South.

Republican Party and Buchanan as President

During Pierce's presidency the Whig Party had disappeared and was replaced by a new party named the Republican party, which had regional appeal because of its stand on the limitation of slavery. This party, which embodied Northern sentiments, did not work to disrupt Southern slavery where it already existed or to bring equality to the blacks but worked to prohibit the expansion of slavery. In 1856 this new party nominated John C. Fremont for president, the "glamour boy" and military explorer; the Democrats turned to James Buchanan, an overweight politician with much experience in government work. The Republican party stood firm against the Kansas-Nebraska Act and the spread of slavery. Since its appeal was primarily Northern, James Buchanan was elected president in 1856.

At age 66 James Buchanan was the choice of all Southern states except

James Buchanan, the only bachelor president, was in office when the lower South seceded from the Union.

Maryland and of four Northern states; he became the fifteenth president of the United States. Born in a log cabin in Pennsylvania, he worked hard in his father's store, studied law, fought in the War of 1812, then entered politics. An unhappy love affair caused him to devote his energy to government work. After ten years in the United States House of Representatives, Jackson appointed him minister to Russia, where he negotiated the first trade treaty between the two nations. Under Polk, Buchanan served as secretary of state and, under Pierce, as minister to Britain. In 1856 he was an uncontroversial figure with much government experience. Once elected, he became the only bachelor president. Despite his long career in public service, Buchanan did not bring real leadership to the presidency. He constantly wavered on important issues and seemed at times to be pro-South. Personally he opposed slavery, but he believed that the Constitution protected it. Only two days into his presidency a legal bombshell exploded—the Dred Scott decision.

Dred Scott Decision

Dred Scott was a slave who had been taken by his master to the North and had lived there for several years. When his master died, Scott sued for his freedom in the Supreme Court on the basis that he had once been in free territory. Chief Justice Roger Taney and four Southern associate justices saw in this case an opportunity to settle the issue of slavery extension once and for all. The Supreme Court ruled that Scott was a Negro and, thus, not a citizen of the United States; hence he could not sue in a federal court. Further, even though Scott was taken to free territory, he was taken as property and should remain property. Finally, and most importantly, the Court ruled that the Missouri Compromise of 1820 was unconstitutional because it deprived Southerners of property without due process of law. This decision clearly stated that slavery could not be restricted to the South. The doctrine of popular sovereignty seemed no longer valid. Some Northerners argued that this decision could not be enforced, while others argued that it was not really a decision but merely an opinion. President Buchanan urged acceptance of the decision; his stand caused the Democratic party to begin to split. The Dred Scott decision was the greatest legal victory for the South in the pre-Civil War days and a real psychological shock to the North. Neither side could stand many more crises, but they continued to occur.

The passage of a lower tariff in 1857 and the national depression that same year further added to the inflamed feelings. The lower tariff was regarded by the cotton-producing South as a godsend, while the North tended to blame it for the national depression. This fiscal panic hurt the urban, industrial North much more than the South. Churches were even being rent asunder. To many major religious groups in America it seemed impossible to reconcile statements like "All slaveholding is a sin against God" with others like "We believe that the Holy Scriptures do unequivocally authorize the relation of master and slave." The Methodists and Baptists had divided into Northern and Southern churches in the 1840s; the Presbyterians held out until 1857.

John Brown

Near hysteria swept the South with the activities of John Brown in 1859. Brown, who had butchered Southerners in Kansas, decided to set up a black state in the South. Initially slaves must be armed, so Brown and his followers raided the federal arsenal at Harper's Ferry, Virginia, in October 1859, killing seven people and wounding ten more. Captured, Brown was given a trial; in his defense, he refused to plead insanity, even though there was an obvious history of insanity in his family. Found guilty, Brown was hanged. To many Northerners he became "Saint John," joining the ranks of martyrs to the cause of freedom. "John Brown's body lied a-mouldering in the grave, But his soul goes marching on," went the words of the song. To Southerners he was a typical Northerner trying to destroy the Southern way of life. How could the South live with those mad Northerners like Brown! There were probably thousands of Browns just waiting to kill more innocent Southerners and stir up the slaves!

In 1860 sectional strife had intensified hysteria even more. At the national convention the Democrats split over the issue of slavery in the territories. Stephen Douglas of Illinois became the choice of a Northern Democratic convention, while the Southern Democrats, at Richmond, Virginia, nominated John Breckenridge of Kentucky. John Bell was the presidential candidate of the Constitutional Union party, which advocated peace and union. The Republican party, which supported restriction of slavery to the South, also proposed free land through a Homestead Act, as well as a higher tariff and liberalized naturalization laws. On the third ballot, compromise candidate Abraham Lincoln of Illinois became the Republican nominee.

The Election of 1860

The election of 1860 was as sectional as the candidates. Lincoln's name did not appear on most ballots in the South, where Breckenridge was the clear winner. The race between Lincoln and Douglas in the North was fairly close, but Lincoln emerged the victor. In fact, he became the overall winner with 39 percent of the total vote and 180 electoral votes.

The election of Lincoln was the final straw for most Southerners. He represented an unacceptable threat to their way of life. In December 1860, South Carolina formally withdrew her ratification of the Constitution and seceded from the Union. It was closely followed by Mississippi, Florida, Georgia, Alabama, Louisiana, and Texas. President Buchanan believed that secession was illegal, but he felt he could not force the South to remain in the Union. So as the Southern states left the Union, Buchanan protested but avoided confrontation. Lincoln, a sectional president, now faced the greatest internal crisis in American history.

Lincoln: Man and Myth

Who was this man Lincoln—a hero of both folklore and history? Year after year he has been rated the greatest American president. In America, there have been more words written about him than any other individual except Christ. He appeals to conservatives and liberals alike. His name and image are even found in such unlikely places as banks and Disney World. Lincoln the man and Lincoln the myth are most difficult to separate.

Born of a frontier family in Kentucky in 1809, at age 7 he moved to Indiana where he lived for 14 years. In Indiana he received little formal education, so he was basically self-educated. He was tall, gangling, and strong, and was employed in many odd jobs, such as cutting wood, plowing fields, and rowing passengers to steamboats. During this time he gained a reputation as a speaker and storyteller. Moving to Illinois, he lived and worked in a general store in

Lincoln, the man, and Lincoln, the myth, are difficult to separate.

THE LAST RAIL SPLIT BY "HONEST OLD ABE."

New Salem. In 1832 he served for 90 days as a militia captain during the Black Hawk Indian War but saw little action. After failing at his first attempt to enter politics and losing much money as an owner of a store, he was appointed postmaster of New Salem.

In 1834 he was elected to the state legislature as a Whig. From politics he turned to law and became a moderately successful lawyer in Springfield, the state capital. Elected to the House of Representatives, he became a harsh opponent of the Mexican War and alienated many of his Illinois patriots. Defeated for reelection, he again returned to law. With the passage of the Kansas-Nebraska Act, Lincoln became one of its strongest critics and unsuccessfully attempted to run for the United States Senate in 1854. Once the Whig party died, Lincoln joined the new Republican party. Before 1858 Lincoln was well-known in Illinois but was not a familiar figure outside the state. It was his debates with Stephen Douglas for the senate seat from Illinois that brought him national prominence.

While the Lincoln-Douglas debates focused on many local issues, they also addressed many national questions and gave birth to some of the best verbal encounters in our history. During these debates Lincoln reminded his listeners of his belief that slavery was morally wrong but that the federal government could not interfere where it existed. Although Lincoln lost to Douglas, the debates won him national support and made a strong impression on influential Republicans. His moderate views on slavery and his humble origins contributed to his winning the party nomination on the third ballot. In 1861 he became president of a sorely divided nation.

When inaugurated, Lincoln had decided upon his course of action. Unlike Buchanan, Lincoln was not about to compromise with the South and allow the extension of slavery. He felt that if slavery were limited permanently it would die out. Lincoln also believed that secession was illegal because it destroyed the Union. The Union was more than just a loose compact of states. Lincoln saw federal troops and property in the South as symbols of the Union. He was not about to give in and withdraw them. When the Southern attack came on April 12, 1861 at the federal fort in the Charlestown harbor—Fort Sumter—the Civil War began.

Causes of the Civil War

The causes of the Civil War are complex and the interpretation of these causes has varied from era to era. For many years Northerners referred to the War as

Act One: War with Mexico/Act Two: War Between North and South the War of Rebellion, while the Southerners called it the War between the States.

By the turn of the century historians saw the war in economic terms, as a struggle between the industrial North and the agrarian South. Twentieth century analysts have blamed the capitalistic North and slavery in the South for the struggle. Sectionalism tops the list of causes, for it encompasses many of the professed causes. The North and South were developing as distinct sections of the country. Economically, socially, religiously, and intellectually, they were moving farther and farther apart. It appears doubtful that the North went to war solely for the blacks. But slavery had been a political issue over the years, deeply dividing North and South. Specific incidents—from the Missouri Compromise in 1820 to the election in 1860—further hastened the crisis. Of course, a cause that is difficult to document is the emotional one. North and South viewed each other in negative, almost psychotic, terms. War in 1860, for a variety of reasons, seemed the only possible solution.

The period from 1836 to 1860 was one of expansionism; the Mexican War was over and the Civil War was on the horizon. The spirit of Manifest Destiny burst forth in the 1830s and reached its climax with the presidency of James Polk. The Mexican War was a war of aggression, filled with partisan criticism, which resulted in the acquisition of the Southwest. It was also a war that reopened the slavery question and led to its ultimate solution in the bullets of the Civil War. The coming of the Civil War was more than just a struggle over whether slaves should be brought to California or Kansas. It was a struggle over two differing life styles and thought patterns. Looking back, one wonders whether Northerners and Southerners in 1861 were both truly "American" in the same way. The tradition of the Revolution, the Constitution, and the federal system were under great stress. Now the nation entered a four-year conflict that would pit brother against brother and American against American.

Essay

Blacks and the Supreme Court

The United States Constitution was intentionally vague when it came to the composition of the national court system. It was necessary for Congress in 1789 to pass the Judiciary Act, which set in motion the system of the Supreme Court and lesser courts. While it is true that the genesis of judicial power can be found in the 1790s, the Supreme Court did not come into its own until the era of John Marshall, who influenced decisions such as *Marbury* v. *Madison,* stipulating the Supreme Court's power of judicial review. Since black Americans possessed no legal status for many years of our early history, the ultimate judge of slavery, civil rights, and freedom and later of desegregation and discrimination was the Supreme Court.

The Massachusetts Supreme Judical Court, in the 1790s, ruled in the Quock Walker case that damages were due this slave and that slavery was inconsistent with freedom; however, two most significant United States Supreme Court rulings on slavery rejected this Massachusetts decision. Article IV, Section 2 of the Constitution provided for the return of fugitive slaves; in 1793 Congress implemented this provision by outlining certain procedures for recovery. But growing abolitionist pressure in the North by the 1830s caused many Northern states to pass personal liberty laws that made it virtually impossible for slaveowners to recover their property. In the Supreme Court case of *Prigg* v. *Pennsylvania* (1842) a direct challenge was made to a Pennsylvania liberty law. The Supreme Court upheld the constitutional provision that guaranteed the return of fugitive slaves and noted that states could not legislate in an area which had already been preempted by the federal government.

The most significant ruling of the Supreme Court on slavery came in 1857 with the case of *Dred Scott* v. *Sanford.* By this time the burning question between North and South was whether the federal government had the right to limit the extension of slavery. The Missouri Compromise of 1820 had tried to resolve that issue by setting up an arbitrary boundary between North and South. But by the 1850s a new doctrine of "popular sovereignty" emerged with the passage of the Kansas-Nebraska Act. The background for the Dred Scott case seemed simple enough. Dred Scott had lived for more than five years with his master in Illinois and Wisconsin territory; he now sued for freedom because he had lived on free soil. Under the leadership of Chief Justice Roger Taney from the slave state of Maryland, the Court initially ruled that Dred Scott was a slave, (that is, property), and could not sue in court. In part, the decision said:

> They had for more than a century before been regarded as beings of an inferior order; and altogether unfit to associate with the white race either in social or political relations; and so far inferior that they had no rights which the white man was bound to respect.

But the Court went one step further and ruled that the Missouri Compromise of 1820 was unconstitutional because it gave Congress the

Slave Dred Scott in 1857 lost in his appeal to the Supreme Court for freedom. In fact, the court told him that he was not a person but merely property.

power to limit slavery. This was an unconstitutional power because it deprived slaveowners of their property without due process of law. The Supreme Court had legitimatized the property status of black slaves and at the same time gave its approval to the extension of the Southern system. Four years later the North and South would be at war, and this Court decision hastened that confrontation.

With the end of the Civil War came freedom, citizenship, and the right to vote for all black Americans. But public sentiments in both North and South were against racial equality. In a series of Civil Rights cases the Supreme Court frequently reflected these sentiments. In the case of *United States* v. *Reese,* the Supreme Court took a very limited view of the fifteenth amendment, which extended suffrage to blacks. Another major setback took place in 1883 when the Court ruled that the Civil Rights Act of 1875, which had prohibited racial segregation in transportation, inns, and theaters and required racial equality in selecting juries, was unconstitutional. Yet in the case of *Strauder* v. *West Virginia* the Court had ruled that a West Virginia law requiring all-white juries was invalid for it denied blacks in the state equal protection of the law. This victory was a hollow one for in *Virginia* v. *Rives* the Court upheld the Virginia practice of excluding blacks from juries and ruled that they must prove systematic and deliberate exclusion. This was nearly impossible.

During Reconstruction the Louisiana legislature had prohibited racial discrimination in any form of transportation; attacks were made on the law on the grounds that it interfered with interstate commerce. In the case of *Hall* v. *De Cuir* the Court agreed with these attacks and voided the law. By the 1890s "Jim Crow" legislation, which embodied the doctrine of segregation, reigned supreme. Discrimination was widespread and obvious. In 1896 the Supreme Court issued a far-reaching decision in *Plessy* v. *Ferguson* when it ruled on whether Louisiana legally could require separate railroad accommodations for the races. Plessy challenged the law as a violation of the thirteenth amendment, which gave him freedom, and the fourteenth amendment, which made him a citizen and guaranteed him equal protection under the law. The Court's decision said:

> We consider the underlying fallacy of the plaintiff's argument to consist in the assumption that the enforced separation of the two races stamps the colored race with a badge of inferiority. If this be so, it is not by reason of anything found in the act, but solely because the colored race chooses to put that construction upon it.

"Separate but equal" became the established doctrine, justifying segregation for many years to come.

By the late 1930s the Supreme Court slowly began to reverse its stand on segregation and equal rights. And in 1950 in *Sweatt* v. *Painter* the Court ruled that a separate law school provided by Texans for blacks violated their equal protection and was illegal. This led the way to the historic decision of 1954 in the case of *Brown* v. *Board of Education of Topeka*. The Court, under Chief Justice Earl Warren, ruled: "We conclude that in the field of public education the doctrine of 'separate but equal' has no place. Separate educational facilities are inherently unequal." Jim Crow was dealt a death blow. But death was fairly slow in coming, requiring more prodding from the Court. In *Cooper* v. *Aaron* in 1958 the Court had to reaffirm the *Brown* decision, and it talked of the need for implementing its earlier decision.

In the last century, The Civil Rights Cases of 1883 had invalidated the Civil Rights Act of 1875; almost a century later, with the passage of the Civil Rights Act of 1964, new assaults were made through the courts. But the reaction was decidedly different. In 1964 in *Heart of Atlanta Motel, Inc.* v. *United States* the Court ruled in support of Title II of the Civil Rights Act, which prohibited racial discrimination in public accommodations. In that same year, in *Jones* v. *Alfred H. Mayer Co.*, the Court supported prohibition of racial discrimination in all sales and rentals of property.

Historically, the Supreme Court frequently has reflected the sentiments of the white majority toward American blacks. But there have been some exceptions. Over the centuries the Supreme Court has been a battleground for blacks' struggle for civil rights; this will continue to be the case. ■

Suggested Reading

The philosophy of Manifest Destiny is well described in FEDERICK MERK's *Manifest Destiny and Mission in American History* (163).

W. C. BINKLEY, in *The Texas Revolution* (1952), describes the split between Texas and Mexico. The Mexican War is well covered in K. J. BAUER's *The Mexican-American War, 1846–1848* (1974) and OTIS A. SINGLETARY's *The Mexican War* (1960).

The general events of the 1850s are detailed in R. F. NICHOLS's *The Stakes of Power, 1846–1877* (1961). HOLMAN HAMILTON focuses on the Compromise of 1850 in *Prologue to Conflict: The Crisis and Compromise of 1850* (1964). The general causes of the Civil War are outlined in AVERY O. CRAVEN's *The Coming of the Civil War* (1957), while KENNETH STAMPP, in *And the War Came* (1950, analyzes the immediate causes. The differing views on the causes of the Civil War are presented in THOMAS J. PRESSLEY's *Americans Interpret their Civil War* (1962).

CARL SANDBURG's *Abraham Lincoln* (1926–1939) (6 voumes) discusses the reality of Lincoln. B. P. THOMAS, in *Abraham Lincoln* (1952), and R. H. LUTHIN, in *The Real Abraham Lincoln* (1960), also present excellent pictures of this complex man.

CHAPTER 8

Blood, Bullets, and Jim Crow

Time Line

?–A.D. 1492	Migration and evolution of American Indian societies
1492	Christopher Columbus lands in West Indies—beginning of European exploration
1607–1732	Establishment of 13 English colonies
1775–1783	American Revolution
1776	Declaration of Independence
1789–1797	Presidency of George Washington
1812–1815	War of 1812
1816–1824	Era of Good Feelings
1846–1848	Mexican War
1861–1865	Civil War

April 1861	Civil War begins with fighting at Fort Sumter
July 1861	First Battle of Bull Run
November 1861	*Trent* Affair
March 1862	The *Merrimack* versus the *Monitor*
April 1862	Battle of Shiloh
September 1862	Battle of Antietam
July 1863	Battle of Gettysburg Fall of Vicksburg
November 1864	Reelection of Lincoln
April 1865	Lee surrenders to Grant at Appomattox Courthouse Assassination of Lincoln; Andrew Johnson becomes president

1866	Civil Rights Bill
1867	Military Reconstruction Act
1868	Impeachment trial of Andrew Johnson
1877	End of Reconstruction

1865–1877	Reconstruction
1877–1900	Industrialization and urbanization
1900–1916	Progressive Era
1917–1918	World War I
1930s	Depression and New Deal
1941–1945	World War II
1945–1960	Post-war politics
1950–1953	Korean War
1950–1960	Civil rights movement
1961–1973	Vietnam War
1976	Bicentennial celebration

The military is an active part of contemporary American life: veterans protest the late delivery of their checks and the conditions in Veterans' hospitals across the country. Members of Congress debate the newest defense budget. Crippled veterans appear on college campuses. Recruiters advertise the new all-volunteer army. And toy soldiers, tanks, and guns are still popular children's toys. Evidence of the military in American society is with us every day. But imagine a time when war was being fought not in far-off Vietnam but just down the street, or over the nearest hill. The Civil War era was much different than today, but many elements of war then echo the present and even the future. Soldiers were young, some of them mere boys. Military food was bad, and so was medical treatment. A draft system existed, for an all-volunteer army could not provide adequate manpower. The Civil War was the only American war in which Americans fought against each other—and for a truly American cause. In this savage encounter more than one soldier in five lost his life. It was truly a modern conflict, deploying massive armies, large numbers of men and heavy equipment. Every citizen, in both the North and South, became involved in military or civilian capacity; the energies of the entire nation were poured into a struggle in which one side must lose and one win. When the smoke cleared and the whites, blacks, and Indians who had fought put down their guns, the Union was no longer the same Union that had been created in 1776 and which had burgeoned during the post-Revolutionary National period; it was a Union that barely hung together. After the war the North attempted to reconstruct the South, but Reconstruction was not easy, for the war had not determined the precise relationship of the South to the Union nor of the free blacks to the rest of the Americans. Out of the struggle emerged an industrial, urban America that waved good-bye forever to the young, agrarian nation and looked ahead to the hazy future. The Civil War was a watershed in the evolution of the American nation.

North Against South

When Abraham Lincoln rose to deliver his inaugural address, no one knew what course of action he would take nor what would happen to the nation. Seven Southern states had already left the Union. Lincoln was not prepared to undertake a holy war, as demanded by the abolitionists, but he wanted uppermost to preserve the Union. His inaugural address reflected these sentiments: "We are not enemies, but friends. We must not be enemies." It was just one day after this address that he received a note from Major Anderson of Fort Sumter, in the Charleston harbor. Anderson wrote that he needed more men and provisions. But if Lincoln supplied the fort, he might be provoking an act of war; if he did not, public support for his administration might be lost. Acting against the counsel of the majority of his cabinet, Lincoln authorized reinforcements. On Jefferson Davis's advice, the Southern commander ordered Anderson to surrender. When he did not, on April 12, 1861, a bombardment of Fort Sumter began. The first shots of the war had been fired.

With the attack on Fort Sumter, Lincoln called for 75,000 volunteers and a naval blockade of the South. The states of North Carolina, Arkansas, Tennessee, and Virginia left the Union and joined the Confederacy. Both sides

With the firing on Fort Sumter in the Charleston harbor, the Civil War began.

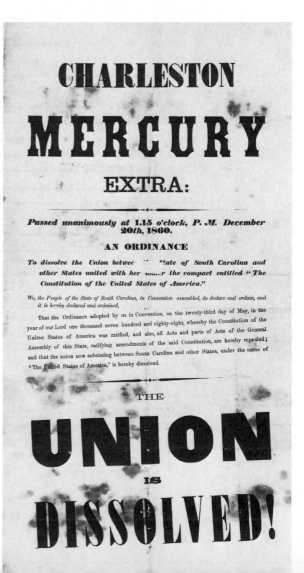

CHARLESTON
MERCURY

EXTRA:

Passed unanimously at 1.15 o'clock, P. M. December 20th, 1860.

AN ORDINANCE

To dissolve the Union betwee⁓ ⁓⁓⁓tate of South Carolina and other States united with her un⁓⁓r the compact entitled " The Constitution of the United States of America."

We, the People of the State of South Carolina, in Convention assembled, do declare and ordain, and it is hereby declared and ordained,

That the Ordinance adopted by us in Convention, on the twenty-third day of May, in the year of our Lord one thousand seven hundred and eighty-eight, whereby the Constitution of the United States of America was ratified, and also, all Acts and parts of Acts of the General Assembly of this State, ratifying amendments of the said Constitution, are hereby repealed; and that the union now subsisting between South Carolina and other States, under the name of " The United States of America," is hereby dissolved.

THE
UNION
IS
DISSOLVED!

began to mobilize their material resources for the impending war. The North had obvious superiority in manpower and economic resources. The North had a population of 22 million, the South 9 million. More than 2 million Americans fought for the Northern cause and about 800,000, for the South. While the Southern slaves indirectly assisted the Southern effort, the Union army counted 180,000 black soldiers in the ranks and the Union navy, 20,000 black sailors. Initially both sides utilized a volunteer army, but a draft system became necessary. The Northern manpower superiority became more obvious during the later stages of the war. In many of the early encounters the opposing armies were about equal in size.

Most of the Northern volunteers were young with no previous military experience.

Evaluating The Opponents

The economics of war overwhelmingly favored the North. The plantation economy of the South had retarded manufacturing. The North had about six times as many factories as the South, and with its industrial workers, the North was able to expand manufacturing production to meet the needs of a nation at war. The South was forced to turn to Europe for manufactured goods. But with little capital and an effective Union blockade of its coast, the South lacked essential supplies. By 1863 the lack of certain items became a real morale problem. Food, medicine, uniforms, and ammunition were some of the items in short supply. Sacrifice was common: church bells were cast into cannons; clothing was used for bandages. To add to the Southern disadvantages, the North possessed an extensive railroad network, which gave it superiority in transportation.

In comparing the material factors on both sides, one must conclude that the South was fighting a lost cause. But this was not really the case. The South had able military leaders in Robert E. Lee and Stonewall Jackson and a strong military tradition. The Northern task was to invade the South (an area larger than Western Europe) and occupy it. This would not be easy, for it involved more than just recruitment of an army; it included the establishment and maintenance of supply and communication lines. The South also believed the North and West would eventually turn against Lincoln and his invasion of the South. And Southerners were fighting to defend their own soil—which gave them a great psychological boost. Still, without European intervention the possibility of a sustained Southern victory seemed slim.

The Civil War was fought on four fronts: The East, the Mississippi West, the Trans-Mississippi West, and the Atlantic Ocean off the Southern coast. The crucial fighting took place in the region between the Union capital of Washington, D.C. and the Confederate capital of Richmond, Virginia. Since the Confederate army adopted defensive tactics, the Union strategy was to capture Richmond and in the process defeat the defending army. Along the Mississippi and its major tributaries, the Union army attempted to stop all commerce and isolate the lower South. In the Far West only minor action took place. Since Europe was the major source of Southern manufactured goods, it was essential for the Confederacy to break the coastal blockade which the North had imposed.

The Early Years

After isolated struggles in Missouri and West Virginia in which the North was successful, the first major battle of the Civil War was fought for the control

General Robert E. Lee became the most capable military commander for the Confederacy.

of Richmond and was known as the First Battle of Bull Run, or Manassas. Neither side was prepared, but the cry "On to Richmond" was being raised throughout the North. With 30,000 troops, General Irvin McDowell marched against a smaller Southern army. Both sides were confused, and the troops were green. The unreality of the early stages of the war was revealed here by the spectators who brought their picnic lunches to view the battle. After being pushed back by Confederate reinforcements, General McDowell ordered an orderly retreat but his men panicked and ran back to Washington, while some Confederate soldiers were sure they had lost "until they saw the Yanks running." The Southern victory here was a hollow one, for the tough fighting had taught both sides that the war would be a prolonged struggle and not merely a "picnic."

By 1862 the war had spread to all fronts. The South attempted to break the Union naval blockade by use of an ironclad vessel, the *Merrimack*. When it first engaged Union warships, it destroyed two large Union vessels with ease. There was panic in the Northern coastal cities, and the entire Union fleet seemed in danger. The North countered with its own ironclad, the *Mon-*

The Northern ironclad *Monitor* repulsed the Southern ironclad *Merrimac* and helped secure the Northern naval blockade.

itor. In March 1862 the *Merrimack* met the *Monitor* in the battle of the ironclads, and the *Merrimack* was forced to withdraw. While this was no decisive victory for the North, the battle helped to ensure the permanence of the sea blockade.

In the West, Union forces moved on the Mississippi from two directions. General Donald Buell and Ulysses Grant moved down the Mississippi, while David Farragut tried to lead a naval force up the Mississippi. In February 1862, Grant won battles at Fort Henry on the Tennessee River and Fort Donelson on the Cumberland River, where he asked for "an unconditional and immediate surrender." Surprised by General Albert Sidney Johnston, commander of the Southern army of the West, Grant regained his composure and won the important Battle of Shiloh in April 1862. Much of Tennessee and Kentucky was now occupied. More Americans had been killed at Shiloh than had been killed in the entirety of any past American war. The reality of war was beginning to be recognized. That same month Farragut, nicknamed "Old Salamander," captured New Orleans with the help of General Benjamin "The Beast" Butler and General E.R.S. Canry. Farragut then proceeded up the Mississippi. At year's end the Union forces were moving toward the Confederate stronghold of Vicksburg, Mississippi.

In 1862 Union forces in the East were commanded by General George McClellan, who was constantly plagued by his overcaution and insecurity. During the peninsula campaign, May–July 1862, McClellan tried to advance on Richmond but was driven back by Confederate General Robert E. Lee and his right-hand man General Stonewall Jackson. Criticism of McClellan began to mount; even Lincoln accused McClellan of having the "slows." (Some contemporaries claimed that in private Lincoln called McClellan "the baboon.") Lee now felt that a victory on Northern soil was necessary to secure European assistance. So in September 1862, he advanced into Maryland and was met by McClellan at the Battle of Antietam. Here at Sharpsburg, on Antietam Creek, 23,000 men were killed in the bloodiest single day of the war. Tactically the fight was a draw, but Lee was forced to withdraw into Virginia; his Northern invasion had failed. McClellan was criticized highly for not pursuing the Confederates after the battle and was removed from command for the last time. Lincoln had said of McClellan, "If he will bring me victory, I will hold his horse." This was one promise Lincoln was never forced to keep.

1863: The Turning Point

1863 was the year of decision. In the spring of that year, General Grant, in the West, found that he was unable to seize Vicksburg on the Mississippi, the

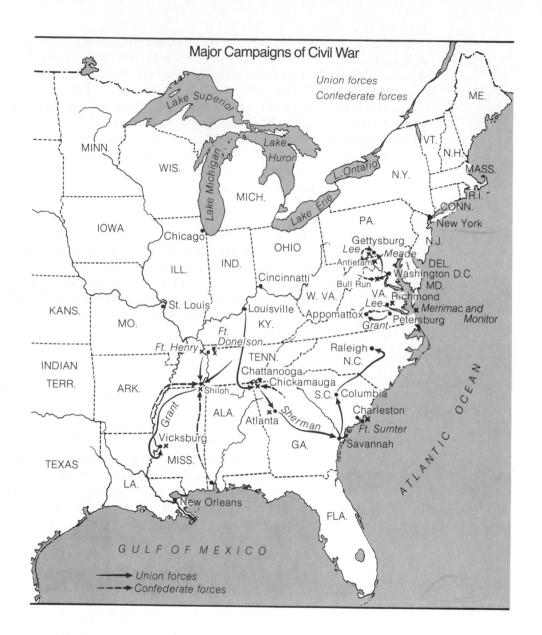

Major Campaigns of Civil War

Union forces
Confederate forces

Union forces
Confederate forces

Blood, Bullets, and Jim Crow

"Gibraltar of the Confederacy." So he marched south of the city and laid siege. After six weeks, with rats and mules as their available food supply, the Southern forces at Vicksburg surrendered on July 4, 1863. The Mississippi was in Union hands. The Southern forces in the Trans-Mississippi region now found themselves cut off from their main source of supply. Meanwhile the attention of the North was focused on Lee's advancing army.

After Southern victories in Virginia at Fredericksburg in December 1862 and Chancellorsville in May 1863, Lee decided again to try for a Northern victory and invaded the North through Pennsylvania. On the hills near Gettysburg, Pennsylvania, the Confederate forces of Lee met the Union army of General George Meade. For three days in July the outcome of the war seemed to hang on the 168,000 soldiers engaged in bloody combat. When the smoke cleared Lee's Southern forces had been repulsed, and Lee once again returned to Virginia. Many historians consider this battle the turning point of the war. It occurred just about the same time as Grant's victory at Vicksburg. Never again would Lee feel strong enough to invade the North. After 1863, the Confederacy knew it had no chance to win its independence by a military defeat of the North. Now it could hope to triumph only by exhausting the Northern will to fight.

The End of the War

In 1864 General Ulysses Grant was appointed supreme commander of the Union army. He now undertook the defeat of General Lee in Virginia and of General Joseph E. Johnston in Georgia. General William "Tecumseh" Sherman, one of Grant's subordinates in the West, was sent against Johnston, who provided Sherman a formidable opponent. Johnston frustrated Sherman repeatedly, but Sherman finally fought his way into Georgia and captured Atlanta in September 1864. Sherman's army then marched "from Atlanta to the sea." Sherman, considered by many to be the precursor of modern warfare, believed in total war; on his march he cut a 60-mile path of destruction. Sherman's march cut the South to the quick; here was a Northern army moving virtually unopposed through the heart of the South. From Savannah, Sherman moved north to join the forces of Grant, who had not yet inflicted the mortal blow on Lee's army.

Grant, "the Butcher," lost more than 50,000 men in the Wilderness campaign of early May 1864. Lee did remarkably well with his depleted army, winning battles such as Cold Harbor in June 1864, but he was losing men, and by April 1865 he saw that further fighting was useless. On April 9, 1865, Lee surrendered to Grant at Appomattox Courthouse, Virginia; the rest of the

At Appomattox Courthouse, General Lee surrendered to General Grant; the Civil War then formally came to an end.

Confederate army finally surrendered on May 26, 1865. The Civil War was over. The Richmond *Evening Whig* published the following obituary notice: "Died: Confederacy, Southern. At the late residence of his father, J. Davis, Richmond, Virginia, Southern Confederacy, aged 4 years. Death caused by strangulation. No funeral."

Blacks in the Civil War

While the military action of the Civil War may appear to have involved only the forces of the white North meeting the forces of the white South, this was not completely true. Blacks and American Indians participated in the war, too. When the war began, free blacks were not accepted for military service. Generally, blacks were seen as unfit to be soldiers; there was also a fear that military service would cause blacks to rise in society. During the first years of the war, Lincoln spent much effort attempting to purchase Chiriqui, a province in Panama, and also the island of Haiti, both to be used as colonies for voluntary emigration of American blacks. In September 1862, he had decided that the war effort needed a morale boost. He knew that freed slaves would swell the thinning Union army, and liberating the slaves would also win support in Europe for the Union cause. Lincoln's resultant proclamation freeing the slaves did not apply to slaves in border states or to slaves in those areas already under the control of the federal government. Still, the Emancipation Proclamation frequently has been described as a magnificent document, and Lincoln has been called "the Great Emancipator." On the one hand, the document was a wise political move, which put new life into the war effort and preserved European neutrality. On the other hand, the effect of the proclamation would have been very limited without the passage of the Thirteenth Amendment, ratified in 1865, which formally freed the slaves. Lincoln made his sentiments on the Proclamation very clear:

> *If I could save the Union without freeing any slave, I would do it; and if I could save it by freeing all the slaves, I would do it; and if I could do it by freeing some and leaving others alone, I would also do that.*

This document did, however, open the door to black military participation.

Blacks were encouraged to join in the war effort by one of their most vocal leaders (and the first nationally known one), Frederick Douglass. Born as a slave, he escaped from slavery to the North, where he educated himself and became a leading voice for abolition. During the 1850s he participated in antislavery politics, and with the outbreak of the war he worked hard for freedom and black recruitment. But he was not about to accept Lincoln's plan for colonization (or any form of Northern bigotry). His goal was to win freedom and social equality now. Time after time he was frustrated in his nonviolent search for equality, but he established a civil rights tradition that would last well into the twentieth century.

Black recruitment went well. By the end of the war more than 180,000 blacks had served in the Union army, and 20,000, in the Union navy. Regular black troops took part in more than 450 engagements and received 22 Congressional Medals of Honor. More than 39,000 blacks died for the Northern cause. Douglass had been "authorized to assure" his fellow blacks in 1863 that all black soldiers serving in the Union army would receive "the same wages, the same rations, the same equipment, the same protection, the same treatment, and the same bounty secured to white soldiers," but these were empty promises. Blacks usually were given the most degrading work available, and, regardless of rank, blacks all were paid the same paltry salary. Southerners were

Black soldiers served admirably in the Union army and helped secure victory.

particularly harsh with captured black soldiers. In April 1864, at Fort Pillow, nearly 250 black soldiers were murdered. The black soldiers held inferior positions in the war, but were a major factor in the Northern military victory.

Indians in the Civil War

Little has been written of the American Indian's participation in the Civil War. Since Jackson's Indian removal policy had been so successful, there were few Indians left in the Eastern theater or the Mississippi valley. The main Indian involvement in the war occurred in the Trans-Mississippi West, an area of less strategic importance. Many of the members of the "Five Civilized Nations" (Cherokee, Chickasaw, Choctaw, Creek, and Seminole), who were now located in Indian Territory in Oklahoma, owned slaves and supported

American Indians in Indian territory in Oklahoma fought on both the Northern and Southern side in the Civil War.

Southern secession. In fact, there were four Indian regiments in the Confederate army and one Indian brigadier general, Stand Watie, a full-blood Cherokee, who was the last Southern general to surrender. But these tribes were hardly united in their support of the South; this divisiveness hurt both factions. Many pro-South groups renegotiated treaties with the Confederacy, which allowed them more control of trading, plus taxing and police power. The defeat of the South, of course, did not help the standing of these tribes in the eyes of the federal government. The Civil War marked the arrival of the reservation system and the final Indian wars of the West.

The War in North and South

What occurred on the battlefield explains why the South militarily lost the war. But the behind-the-scenes manipulations of men and materials by Abraham Lincoln in the North and Jefferson Davis in the South really provides an insight into the Southern defeat. In February 1861, the seceding states met to draw up a new government. This confederation followed almost exactly the model of the federal government, with some major exceptions. There was no Supreme Court; the central government could not issue tariffs and control slavery; and the sovereignty of the states was paramount. The delegates in Montgomery, Alabama, appointed Jefferson Davis as provisional president and Alexander Stephens as provisional vice-president for six years. An eventual election confirmed the delegates' choices. Jefferson Davis was a West Point graduate with congressional experience. He had major faults, however; he was petty, egotistical, and opinionated. He felt he could be both president and commander in chief. Since he seldom listened to others' opinions, his cabinet was one of shifting personnel and mediocre men. During the life of his cabinet 14 different men were chosen to fill 6 cabinet posts. Davis began acting almost immediately on the assumption that the Confederacy was an established nation. This was hardly the case. Davis' job was to create a nation. His failure to view the Confederacy as country in its infancy hurt his cause.

Abraham Lincoln, on the other hand, did not lead a politically united North. There was much jealousy and factionalism even within his own party, while many Democrats criticized the war effort, and some, referred to as Copperheads, even favored a negotiated peace. Lincoln believed that he must use extensive executive power to bring the war to a fitting conclusion. This policy earned him the title of "Dictator," "Tyrant," and "Despot." From the start of the war Lincoln delegated to himself powers hitherto reserved to Con-

This anti-Lincoln cartoon pictures the signing of the
Emancipation Proclamation as a compact with the
devil.

gress. And his disregard for civil rights angered others. Examination of the
federal mails was commonplace, and in some areas military courts took precedence over civilian courts. In September 1862, he issued a proclamation
authorizing the arrest of those who discouraged enlistments, resisted the draft,
or committed other disloyal acts. More than 15,000 Americans were held
under this order (many until the end of the war). Often they were not told of
the charges against them. Lincoln did support congressional measures that
would win him continued support. The Homestead Act granted many Westerners 160 acres of land for a nominal fee. The Morrill Tariff raised the tariff

from the 1857 levels and pleased Northern industrialists, who were also happy with the National Bank Act of 1863, which created a centralized system of banking and money production. Lincoln was a much maligned president, yet his popularity was proved in the election of 1864. The Republicans, now called the Union party, were split over the question of Reconstruction but supported Lincoln, while the Democrats, on a peace platform, nominated the war hero George McClellan. Lincoln was 55 percent of the popular vote, near unanimous support in the electoral college, and was returned to office.

Wartime Problems

The North and South at war did face similar problems. The South began the war with little capital. It failed to secure European loans, and its taxes were usually on a volunteer basis. Near the end of the war taxes were even paid in goods rather than in money. To raise money for the war, the Confederacy began to issue paper money. This move backfired and inflation ran rampant. Shoes sold for $245 a pair, chickens were $35 apiece, and by the end of the war a breakfast for three in Richmond cost $141. Eventually more than one billion dollars in Confederate money was printed with little gold backing.

The North also had little money on hand when the war began, but it was much more successful in securing needed capital. The tariff was raised, an income tax was levied, and war bonds were sold. The North also put more money into circulation by printing "greenbacks," but Northern inflation was less disastrous.

With the first shot of the war, both sides filled their armies with enthusiastic volunteers. This initial enthusiasm, however, did not take long to wear off. So both North and South turned to a wartime draft. In March 1863, the Northern draft law enlisted unmarried men between the ages of 20 and 45 and married men between 20 and 35; enlistees served three years. While there were no deferments under this law, one either could hire a substitute or pay $300 to get out of the draft. "A rich man's war and a poor man's fight" expressed the belief that the draft favored the rich. Public criticism of the system reached a peak in July 1863 when draft riots hit New York City and hundreds were killed. Still the draft provided the needed manpower for the Northern army.

Jefferson Davis also found himself resorting to the draft system to offset the heavy loss of men and the rising desertion rate. Through 4 laws the South extended the draft so that it eventually included all men from ages 17 to 50— "from the cradle to the grave," wrote one Southerner. Just before the wa ended Davis extended the draft to include black slaves. Davis and Lincoln als faced problems from Europe.

Savage anti-draft riots in New York City in 1863
indicated Northern resistance to the wartime draft.

The Diplomacy of War

Diplomacy was the main hope of the South. Europe would have to be persuaded, or even forced, to recognize the South as an independent nation; Europe would then break the Union blockade and actively enter the war on the Southern side. The way to achieve such involvement was by "cotton diplomacy." The Southern argument reasoned that cotton was essential to the textile industries of England and France. Without it, both countries would face economic collapse. So European intervention on the Southern side would be necessary to restore prosperity. Cotton diplomacy made a great deal of sense to Southern leaders, but it assumed too great a role for the textile industry in the economies of England and France and did not take into consideration the strong aversion to slavery the general populace had in both of these countries.

The North as a diplomatic nation had the benefit of a trained and established foreign service. The goals of the Northern diplomats were to prevent recognition of the South as a separate country and, of course, to direct European aid and involvement to the North. The Northern diplomats met the

Southern challenge very ably, while the Southern diplomats were never able to overcome their parochial viewpoints or completely understand the protocol of European diplomacy.

The loss of cotton did hurt the economies of France and England; the South had been correct. But the damage was not so severe that either country would risk war. In addition, Britain was dependent on Northern wheat and did not wish to lose that valuable commodity. One of the major reasons for the continued neutrality was the military situation in America. The defensive tactics of the South did not encourage the prospects of Southern victory. And after 1863 Southern defeat seemed inevitable. While Napoleon III of France did not intervene directly, he took advantage of the situation and seized Mexico. Maximillian of Austria became the dictator of Mexico. Secretary of State Seward issued a strong warning against the seizure, but the North was in no position to take action. In 1866 an American army of 50,000 veterans was sent to the Rio Grande, and the French army returned home. Maxmilian remained, but only to face a firing squad.

While neither France nor England succumbed to cotton diplomacy, the North faced certain crucial diplomatic problems with England, the leading neutral. In 1861 two Confederate diplomatic agents, John Slidell and James Mason, were traveling aboard the English steamer *Trent* for England when the ship was stopped by an American frigate *U.S.S. San Jacinto* under the command of Captain Charles Wilkes. Wilkes seized the two diplomats and returned them as prisoners to the North. In the North, Wilkes was a hero; in England the public was outraged. The rights of a neutral had been violated. England demanded the release of the two men and an apology, or the English threatened action. Lincoln hated to give in to England, but war was a distinct possibility. After much deliberate delay, the two men were released, and an indirect apology was given. The *Trent* affair was not the last example of tension between the North and England.

Once the *Merrimack* had been defeated, the Northern blockade became virtually unbreakable. To draw ships away from the blockade, the South decided to prey on Northern ocean commerce. Since the Confederacy had no shipyards, raiders and ironclads were to be built in England and were to sail from English ports. Six raiders were built—the most famous being the *Alabama* and the *Florida*—and used English ports as their home bases. The North constantly criticized England for violating neutrality, but the raids continued and gradually took their toll. After the war an international court charged that England was liable for damages and $15.5 million was awarded to the United States.

The South also contracted with the Laird shipyards in England for two powerful ironclad ramming vessels to break the blockade. The raider tactics had not worked completely, but these two vessels were another matter. At this point in the war, Southern victory looked slim. But the Laird rams could change the whole disposition of the war. Northern minister Charles Francis Adams pointedly warned the English of their dangerous course. If the rams sailed, war might occur between the North and England. The English were not about to risk war, so the rams were detained and diplomatic relations smoothed.

The Vanquished South

Why did the South lose the war? There is no easy answer to that question. The most obvious reply is that the South lost militarily and was forced to surrender. The Southern loss, however, involved a variety of factors. Jefferson Davis did not have the personality or leadership qualities necessary to create a nation; he could not even allow his generals freedom to control the military. He failed to finance the war or gather adequate manpower. But Davis was not the scapegoat of the Southern loss. The South did not make the transition quickly enough from a land of plantations and slaves to a land of factories and factory workers. The Northern blockade handicapped the war effort and cotton diplomacy failed. The defensive tactics were abandoned too late in the war. And, of course, one of the major reasons for the Southern loss was the leadership of Abraham Lincoln, who was assassinated on Good Friday (April 14) 1865, not long after the end of the war.

The bullet of a crazed actor, John Wilkes Booth, ended the life of a great president. For most of his presidency he had presided over a divided nation. His formidable task of preserving the Union was made more formidable by cabinet squabbles, political opponents, and incompetent military leaders. Still, he rallied the North behind him and molded a successful Northern army. His cabinet appointments were excellent, and his legislative leadership gained valuable Northern and Western support for the war. He saw the necessity for a powerful president and became one. His Emancipation Proclamation was a brilliant political move, which led to the eventual freeing of the slaves. While he did not believe in the equality of the races, he had done more for the blacks than any other president before him. In 1865 the Union was restored. Much credit must be given to Lincoln for this accomplishment. Yet his untimely death caused a shadow of uncertainty to hang over the nation; the process of reconstructing the shattered Union had begun.

SURRAT. BOOTH. HAROLD.

War Department, Washington, April 20, 1865,

$100,000 REWARD!

THE MURDERER

Of our late beloved President, Abraham Lincoln,

IS STILL AT LARGE.

$50,000 REWARD

Will be paid by this Department for his apprehension, in addition to any reward offered by Municipal Authorities or State Executives.

$25,000 REWARD

Will be paid for the apprehension of JOHN H. SURRATT, one of Booth's Accomplices.

$25,000 REWARD

Will be paid for the apprehension of David C. Harold, another of Booth's accomplices.

LIBERAL REWARDS will be paid for any information that shall conduce to the arrest of either of the above-named criminals, or their accomplices.

All persons harboring or secreting the said persons, or either of them, or aiding or assisting their concealment or escape, will be treated as accomplices in the murder of the President and the attempted assassination of the Secretary of State, and shall be subject to trial before a Military Commission and the punishment of DEATH.

Let the stain of innocent blood be removed from the land by the arrest and punishment of the murderers.

All good citizens are exhorted to aid public justice on this occasion. Every man should consider his own conscience charged with this solemn duty, and rest neither night nor day until it be accomplished.

EDWIN M. STANTON, Secretary of War.

DESCRIPTIONS.—BOOTH is Five Feet 7 or 8 inches high, slender build, high forehead, black hair, black eyes, and wears a heavy black moustache.

JOHN H. SURRAT is about 5 feet, 9 inches. Hair rather thin and dark; eyes rather light; no beard. Would weigh 145 or 150 pounds. Complexion rather pale and clear, with color in his cheeks. Wore light clothes of fine quality. Shoulders square; cheek bones rather prominent; chin narrow; ears projecting at the top; forehead rather low and square, but broad. Parts his hair on the right side; neck rather long. His lips are firmly set. A slim man.

DAVID C. HAROLD is five feet six inches high, hair dark, eyes dark, eyebrows rather heavy, full face, nose short, hand short and fleshy, feet small, instep high, round bodied, naturally quick and active, slightly closes his eyes when looking at a person.

NOTICE.—In addition to the above, State and other authorities have offered rewards amounting to almost one hundred thousand dollars, making an aggregate of about TWO HUNDRED THOUSAND DOLLARS.

The assassination of Lincoln on Good Friday, April 14, 1865, ended the career of the man who had guided the North to vistory in the Civil War.

Reconstructing the South

With the end of the war the South was in shambles. The war had been fought there, and war has a tendency to ravage a land. But by war's end it was not clear what the new South would look like. The question of Reconstruction had been debated from the beginning of the war until the end, but there was still no agreement. Three of the most significant questions being debated were: should the South be punished for secession? who should lead Reconstruction, the president or congress? what role should free blacks play in the reconstructed South? Of course, this Reconstruction was not merely to be a political one; reconstruction would occur in economic, social, and cultural areas. Congress and President Lincoln had struggled many times during the war over Lincoln's supposed dictatorial use of power. They also struggled over Lincoln's policy of Reconstruction.

Reconstruction

Lincoln had maintained from the early days of the war that the Confederate states had never actually left the Union; they had merely been in rebellion. He also believed that the sooner the South was restored to the Union by the president the better, so he offered pardon on generous terms. His plan permitted the reestablishment of a state government whenever the required oath of Union had been taken by a number of persons equal to 10 percent of that state's voters in 1860. This 10-percent plan was opposed vehemently by a group of Congressmen who wished to radically reconstruct the South. These opponents of presidential Reconstruction such as Benjamin Wade of Ohio became known as the Radical Republicans. Their plan was embodied in the Wade-Davis Bill of 1864. This bill disenfranchised all who had voluntarily taken up arms against the United States; it also raised the oath requirement to 50 percent, making it harder to create a state government. Of course, the whole measure implied that Congress, not the president, should dominate the process of Reconstruction. Lincoln answered the challenge with a pocket veto, and before his assassination state governments had been set up in Tennessee, Arkansas, and Louisiana. With Lincoln's death, generous Reconstruction suffered a mortal blow. The "tailor president" now took office.

Born in North Carolina, Andrew Johnson spent most of his early life in Tennessee as a tailor. Taught to read and write by his wife, he became an avid Jacksonian Democrat. After serving in local politics in Tennessee, Johnson was elected to the United States House of Representatives, where he fought for the small farmer. During the next few years he became governor of Tennessee and United States senator. When his state of Tennessee seceded from the Union, Johnson became the only Southern senator who refused to secede with his state. Although he was a slave owner, he put the Union ahead of slavery and supported Lincoln and the Union cause. Once Tennessee came under control of the Union army, Johnson was appointed military governor of

Andrew Johnson, who succeeded Lincoln as president, was nearly impeached from office.

the state. He became the most prominent unionist Democrat and was chosen as Lincoln's running mate in 1864. A loner basically, he was often handicapped by his humble origins. It is true that he was drunk when he took the oath of office for vice-president; he, however was not a drunkard. On assuming the presidency, Johnson indicated to Congress that he was an ally willing to allow a harsh policy of Reconstruction in the South. But Johnson, surprising Congress, continued to follow Lincoln's 10-percent plan and, going even further, began to issue state pardons quite liberally; by December 1865 all of the Southern states except Texas had taken steps toward readmission into the Union.

Congressmen, and Northerners in general, were not too happy about the fact that many leading ex-rebels were seeking seats in Congress; in addition, white Southern legislatures now began to pass "black codes" that attempted to keep the black in their place in society. These codes smacked of the slave codes of an earlier era; some required blacks to be sold into forced labor for breach of contract, debts, or vagrancy. The system of slavery seemed to be reinstated. The Freedman's Bureau, organized in 1865 by the War Department, had not done an adequate job of feeding and educating the blacks, and it had fallen into severe disfavor with Southern whites. The voices of Radical and moderate Republicans alike were now raised in protest against the lenient treatment the South received and the actions the South was taking.

The leading Radicals were Thaddeus Stevens of Pennsylvania and Charles Sumner of Massachusetts. Stevens argued that with secession the Southern states had committed suicide, while Sumner reasoned that the Southern states were like conquered provinces. Both men believed Congress was the only power that could direct a thoroughgoing Reconstruction. With clubfooted Stevens as the driving force, an alliance of moderate Republicans and Radical Republicans began to pass legislation that would take away the impetus of presidential Reconstruction. The Civil Rights Bill of 1866 gave blacks citizenship and struck at the "black codes." This measure was passed over Johnson's veto (during much of his presidency he would be referred to as "Andy Veto" or "Sir Veto"). Radicals now sent the Fourteenth Amendment to the states. It brought citizenship to blacks and forbade states to abridge the privileges or immunites of any United States citizen. The final decision as to who would control Reconstruction—the president or Congress—would be decided in the congressional election of 1866.

Radicals tried to make the main issue of the campaign a choice between the loyal Republicans and the disloyal Democrats or between national patriotism and treason. Before the election Johnson embarked upon a speech-making tour to urge the election of anti-Radical Congressmen. But the public was in an ugly mood. Ex-president Jefferson Davis was still untried and unhanged, and a recent antiblack riot in New Orleans had resulted in some 200 casualties. Johnson, "The Tailor of the Potomac," also reverted to yelling at his audience and hurling insults. "Notwithstanding the subsidized gang of hirelings and traducers in Congress, I have discharged all my duties and fulfilled all my pledges . . . ," he exclaimed. The dignity of the presidential office was hurt badly. The election of 1866 brought overwhelming success to the Radicals. Now congressional Reconstruction moved ahead.

Congressional Reconstruction

From 1863 to 1867 presidential Reconstruction dominated the restoration process. Now, with the passage of the Military Reconstruction Act in March

1967, control passed to Congress. This act, and subsequent ones, was based on the idea that legal government in the South was nonexistent; the new Southern governments were to be formed on the basis of thoroughgoing disfranchisement of Confederate leaders and full enfranchisement of blacks, and the process was to be under military control at all stages.

The period of Reconstruction (1867–1877) is referred to by some historians as the darkest days in our history. The mechanics of reconstruction were the following: ten states of the South were divided into five military districts, each under a commanding officer. This officer was to oversee the formation of new governments. Voters were to be registered without distinction of race or color, but ex-Confederates were disqualified. Constitutional conventions were to draw up new frames of government embodying black suffrage. These constitutions were to be adopted by the new electorates and approved by Congress. Legislatures then elected on this basis were to ratify the Fourteenth Amendment, and readmission to the Union would be followed by congressional action. As one final step in 1869, Congress passed the Fifteenth Amendment, which stated that the right to vote shall not be restricted in any way because of "race, color, or previous condition of servitude."

Tradition has pictured the era of Reconstruction as one filled with carpetbaggers and scalawags who took advantage of the newly freed blacks. There was some truth in this statement. Many Northerners did move South to become political leaders; others moved in with money and began industry. The *scalawags* were those Southerners who supported the North and followed Reconstruction policies. They were not really traitors; they were realists who were accepting the inevitable. These people helped soften the blow of military occupation. Nor is it true that the carpetbaggers and scalawags completely manipulated the blacks. Many blacks were elected to state legislatures. Johnathan J. Wright and William G. Brown were two of the outstanding black officeholders. Also during this time 22 blacks were sent to Congress. They had little influence on a national level, but they worked hard and represented their areas well. Despite white fears, blacks never dominated any state legislature nor were these legislatures corrupt or inept. The new state constitutions passed by black-white regimes, with their new emphasis on voting rights and public education, were marked improvements over old documents. While the corruption of the Reconstruction period disillusioned many blacks and whites alike, the overwhelming number of blacks served the South well. Much progressive legislation became the model for future social advances. Even so, the Southern reaction to black participation was a predictable one.

White Southerners bitterly resented black political power, and some of them reacted with a campaign of terror. Secret societies like the White League

Congressman John Willis Menard was the first black
politician to address the House of Representatives.

and the White Camilia were organized. The best known was the Ku Klux
Klan, born as a joke among a group of drunken college students in Pulaski,
Tennessee. By 1867 the Klan was a popular terrorist movement under the
control of an ex-Confederate general, Nathan Bedford Forrest. Its tactics in-

cluded whipping, tar-and-feathering, castration, lynching, and other violence against the recently enfranchised blacks. In the late 1860s and early 1870s the Klan, protected by Southern laws and law enforcement officers, was most effective in minimizing the black vote.

While Radical Republicans had been moderately successful in achieving black political participation during Reconstruction, their policies were generally a failure in the social and economic arenas. The Freedman's Bureau was only of temporary value. So, with little direction and virtually no money, the landless blacks often returned to their former masters to work as share tenants or sharecroppers. (Share tenants and sharecroppers both paid a portion of the crop they produced to the landowners, but share tenants provided their own tools, while sharecroppers paid a larger portion of the crop.) Local storekeepers sold food and other supplies to the black farmers on credit until harvest time, but high interest rates and unfair contracts forced most blacks into permanent economic slavery. Debt slavery had replaced the old slave system. The blacks that tried to work for salary were little better off, and urban blacks had trouble finding any jobs except those typically black, such as in domestic service. Political rights for blacks were not concurrent with social and economic opportunities, and a Jim Crow system of legal segregation was being born. Free blacks found themselves with little else but their freedom.

Impeachment of Johnson

Even though congressmen now controlled Reconstruction, they continued to badger President Johnson, and were even referring to his dealings with immoral women. Their ultimate punishment for Johnson would be impeachment. An impeachment victory would give Congress control of the presidency, and this could have important future consequences. The House voted to impeach on the grounds that Johnson had violated the Tenure of Office Act by removing Edwin Stanton as secretary of war. Stanton was sympathetic to the Radicals. Johnson charged that the act was unconstitutional, but this charge was merely a disguise for the real reasons. During the Senate trial in 1868 it became obvious that Johnson was not guilty of "high crimes and misdemeanors" and should not be found guilty. But the Radicals came close, falling short by only one vote of acquiring the two-thirds majority necessary to convict. Johnson served the rest of his presidency quietly and calmly, afterward retiring to private life. He is remembered as the first president to nearly have been forced out of the office.

By 1870 all of the Southern states had reorganized their governments, had been accorded full rights, and were now controlled by conservatives. But it was not until 1877 that military occupation ended completely and Reconstruction technically came to an end. Over 600,000 men had died in the Civil War. Lincoln fought the war for the Union, but it would take long for the Union to heal itself from the internal struggle. With the conclusion of the war slaves became free, but not completely free; Southern blacks, in particular, gained politically but gained little economically and socially. The Civil War was a watershed in American history; it ended the American myth of internal peace and tranquility and began the decline of agrarian America. Industrial-urban America would benefit most from the war; industrialism and urbanism would soon capture the imagination of the American mind. Meanwhile, politics became increasingly intertwined with business; great presidents would not appear again until the twentieth century.

Essay

The Birth of the Ku Klux Klan

The small town of Pulaski, Tennessee, was named after a young and daring Polish count who died in the War for Independence. It was there in that town, in December 1865, that six college men, former Confederate officers, formed a club. Deciding they needed an outlet for their restless spirits, they formulated a secret initiation, had secret meetings, put on various disguises and outfits, and took the Greek word *kuklos* for their name. So began the organization that became known as the Ku Klux Klan. Their horseplay had an unexpected effect; it frightened the blacks of the area. Here seemed to be a way to control the newly enfranchised blacks and their carpetbagger friends from the North.

From 1865 to 1867 Klan groups spread throughout the South. There was some loose organization of the movement, but most groups

The Ku Klux Klan was the self-proclaimed savior of the South; action was directed at blacks and white sympathizers alike.

worked on a completely independent basis. In April 1867, representatives from these groups met in Nashville and drew up a Klan constitution, which vowed to uphold the Constitution of the United States and to protect the poor, downtrodden Southerners. Former Confederate General Nathan Bedford Forrest became Grand Wizard, ruling over an Imperial Empire that was divided into regions and subregions, which were referred to as realms, provinces, and dens. Leaders of these areas were given titles such as Grand Dragon, Cyclops, and even Ghoul.

The main thread of unification between Klan groups, was the belief that the Klan, as a self-appointed police organization, was to be the major enforcer of laws in the South. Secrecy and the white sheet became the Klan's symbol of courage and protection. The organization included a great many former Confederate officers plus many leading Southern businessmen and politicians. Although pledged to uphold the law, they frequently broke it in outbursts of hanging, mutilating, and shooting.

The introduction of Congressional Reconstruction in the South in 1867 and the overthrow of the state governments that had been set up by Lincoln and Andrew Johnson gave the organization a needed boost. These new "Radical governments," as they were called, relied upon state militias, which included blacks, for military support, as well as relying on blacks for votes. The state militias and the black electorate were two of the major targets for Klan harassment. Militiamen were frequently whipped and murdered, while blacks were constantly frightened away or physically kept from the ballot boxes. It is not surprising that few blacks fought back against the Klan in the highly racist South. For example, in 1871 in Mississippi a Klan-led riot was directed against some black leaders who were

trying to gather support for a black anti-Klan movement. Many blacks were killed, and those who fled into the woods were tracked eventually down and shot. The safest defense against Klan activity was to go into hiding.

Klansmen felt the greatest dangers to white society came from black voters, politicians, and from education. Remember that during the plantation days teaching a black to read and write had been in violation of most slave codes. This feeling was carried on into the post-war era. Many school teachers had come from the North. They were also the victims of Klan harassment and violence. The Klansmen also were called "night riders," but they did not limit their activi-

Lynching of blacks was one of the violent activities of the Ku Klux Klan.

ties to night alone; in many parts of the South they marched down the streets of small towns in daylight parades.

The Klan had some of its most noticeable success at the polls. Radical governments and black economic and political power were synonymous with the Republican party. With Klan backing, Democrats began to win elections in many Republican areas. But the strict discipline that had held the Klan together in the early days was now breaking down. Ordinary lawlessness was being done in the name of the Klan; poor whites now joined and used it to justify their criminal activity. Although the rural South of the late 1860s viewed the Klan as the savior of the white race—many conservative newspapers even condoning and praising their acts of violence—internally the society was having serious problems.

This secret society with semi-autonomous units was virtually impossible to control. In January 1869, Imperial Wizard Forrest ordered the dissolution of the Klan and the burning of all its records. The better citizens were now dropping out of the organization, and the quality of membership was rapidly declining. Some dens immediately followed orders; others were reluctant to disband and cease activities. By 1871 the Ku Klux Klan, which had grown out of a social club to become a potent force in Southern Reconstruction, was only a memory. The Klan had lasted only a few years. It had served as one of the most prominent anti-black groups, rising to quell the fears and channel the frustrations of white Southerners. Over the next few decades its mythology as the romantic savior of the South would grow and lead to its rebirth in the early 1900s. ∎

Suggested Reading

A good general study of the period studied in Chapter 8 is *The Civil War and Reconstruction* (1969) by J. C. RANDALL and DAVID DONALD.

The American Civil War (1968) by PETER J. PARISH provides a one-volume study of the war; a multi-volume study with much more detail, *The Civil War* (1958-1974), has been written by SHELBY FOOTE.

Military aspects of the war are described in T. HARRY WILLIAMS's *Lincoln and His Generals* (1952) and in the many books by BRUCE CATTON, such as *Glory Road* (1952), *A Stillness at Appomattox* (1953), and *This Hallowed Ground* (1956). The politics of the Union are explored in GEORGE M. FREDERICKSON's *The Inner Civil War* (1965). The black involvement in the war is documented in D. T. CORNISH's *The Sable Army: Negro Troops in the Civil War* (1956). M. COULTER, in *The Confederate States of America* (1950), describes the Confederacy.

Two excellent studies of Reconstruction are *The Reconstruction of the Nation* (1967), by RICHARD W. PATRICK and *Reconstruction After the Civil War* (1961), by JOHN HOPE FRANKLIN. E. M. COULTER, in *The South During Reconstruction 1865–1877* (1947), discusses the South during Reconstruction.

CHAPTER 9

Politics and Race Relations in an Industrial Age: From Grant to McKinley

Time Line

?–A.D. 1492	Migration and evolution of American Indian societies
1492	Christopher Columbus lands in West Indies—beginning of European exploration
1607–1732	Establishment of 13 English colonies
1775–1783	American Revolution
1776	Declaration of Independence
1789–1797	Presidency of George Washington
1812–1815	War of 1812
1816–1824	Era of Good Feelings
1846–1848	Mexican War
1861–1865	Civil War
1865–1877	Reconstruction
1867	Oliver Kelley forms the Grange
1868	Election of Ulysses Grant
1872	Reelection of Grant
1876	Defeat of Custer at Little Big Horn
1877	Rutherford Hayes wins disputed election and becomes president
1878	Lincoln County War
1880	Election of James Garfield
1881	Vice-President Chester Arthur becomes president upon assassination of Garfield
1882	Chinese Exclusion Act
1884	Election of Grover Cleveland
1887	Dawes Act
1888	Election of Benjamin Harrison
1890	Sherman Silver Purchase Act Sherman Anti-Trust Act McKinley Tariff
1891	Court of Private Land Claims
1892	Second election of Grover Cleveland Formation of Populist party
1896	Election of William McKinley
1877–1900	Industrialization and urbanization
1900–1916	Progressive Era
1917–1918	World War I
1930s	Depression and New Deal
1941–1945	World War II
1945–1960	Post-war politics
1950–1953	Korean War
1950–1960	Civil rights movement
1961–1973	Vietnam War
1976	Bicentennial celebration

In our modern society politicans live and die by polls that assess their relative popularity. Polls are applied also to past presidents. The questions Who is the best president? and Who is the worst president? are often asked in classrooms. Certain names appear year after year: Washington, Jefferson, Lincoln; but other names almost never appear: Rutherford Hayes, Chester Arthur, Benjamin Harrison. The fact that these men are forgotten presidents can be explained by the period in which they lived and by their mediocre careers.

The period from the Civil War to the beginning of the twentieth century was a period of rapid industrial growth and urban development. Unrestricted business expansion grasped the American imagination; politics played a secondary role. There were few important differences on major issues between Democrats and Republicans. In fact, presidential contests frequently boiled down to a personality clash between two uninspiring candidates. Once elected, these men allowed the free enterprise system to remain free, for government regulation was considered unnecessary and even immoral. Political reformers were out of the mainstream. It was a time when our open-door immigration policy was closed to the Chinese; in the Southwest the Mexican-Americans saw their land and power being taken from them. And the Indians of the West were making their last stand, being put on reservations, and, in 1887, being pressured to assimilate by legislation. The list of presidents of this industrial era begins with the election of Civil War hero Ulysses S. Grant.

General Ulysses Grant as President

Born in Ohio, Grant worked hard in his father's tannery until he was appointed to West Point. After graduation he served well in the Mexican War and was stationed in the Oregon Territory, but he also acquired a drinking problem. Rctiring from the army, he failed at one occupation after another: farming, real estate, and storekeeping. At the onset of the Civil War Grant joined the Union army and rose rapidly in ranks. His successful campaign in the West led to his being appointed supreme commander of the Union army in 1864. His victory over Lee brought him great popularity in the North and made him the foremost military hero of the Civil War.

In 1868 the Radical Republicans felt this popularity would win him the election, so they nominated him for president. Actually, he just as easily could have been the nominee of the Democratic party, for he was a political babe in the woods without any prior party commitments. He accepted the nomination with the innocuous words, "Let us have peace." The Democrats, torn by factions, turned to former New York governor Horatio Seymour, a reluctant candidate who did not choose to decline the nomination as he had five times earlier. Most Americans looked upon the Republicans as the party of victory; the Democrats were labelled rebellious because of their repudiation of the Reconstruction acts. "Vote as You Shot" was indeed a successful campaign slogan, and Grant was elected by an impressive margin in the electoral vote, although the popular vote was surprisingly close. The West Pointer now entered the White House.

The presidency of Ulysses Grant is one of the most remarkable tragedies of our past history. With no political experience, he believed that the president should merely make certain the laws were being followed. He believed that the will of the people was embodied in the Congress and that it was the American people, not the president, who should be the main watchdogs of Congress. The role of the president, to Grant, was primarily an administrative

Ulysses Grant, the military hero of the Civil War, was hurt by his political inexperience during his two term presidency.

one. The only true reality he knew was the military, so he turned the White House into an army camp. He appointed many of his old army friends to office. He accepted gifts and naively returned favors. During his two terms, corruption and greed reigned supreme on both national and local levels. Grant was not responsible for the corruption of this post-war period, but he did create an atmosphere as president that allowed it to fester. His election opened the era known as the Gilded Age.

The Scandals of the Grant Era

Grant's first term was characterized by his expansion of the spoils system, continuation of congressional Reconstruction, the Credit Mobilier, and the Good Friday scandals. Grant believed his political appointments should go to those men who supported him and did him favors. So his choices frequently included incompetents and greedy friends. The shining light of his cabinet was Secretary of State Hamilton Fish, who had earlier wined and dined Grant. While Grant talked of Civil Service reform, neither he nor Congress did much to bring it about. Meanwhile, his words. "Let us have peace," were lost in the bitter political struggles surrounding Congressional Reconstruction. In essence, Grant's achievements were few, while his mistakes were numerous.

Jay Gould and Jim Fisk, two notorious business manipulators, took advantage of Grant's willingness to accept gifts. In 1869 these men attempted to corner the gold market and used Grant as their victim by having him promise to stop the sale of treasury gold. Grant's brother-in-law was even involved in the scheme. The stock market plummeted on "Black Friday" (September 24), when news leaked out that gold was in limited supply. The Treasury once again began selling gold, and Grand disavowed any knowledge of the plot. A congressional investigation later proved that gullible Grant had not been involved.

Grant was further hurt by the Credit Mobilier scandal that surfaced in 1872. The Credit Mobilier was the construction company of the Union Pacific Railroad. This company had been created by the directors of the Union Pacific, and shares were sold "where they would do the most good"—to congressmen and even to the vice-president. The railroad then awarded a favorable contract to the construction company, and all shareholders reaped enormous profits. The company was eventually disbanded, after directors of the Union Pacific had run the railroad so far into debt that it was forced to charge exorbitant freight and passenger rates. This was another abuse of the public trust.

The corruption and graft that surfaced during the first term of Grant's presidency were not sufficient to prevent his renomination in 1872, but were sufficient to create a liberal branch of the Republican party. The Liberal Republicans, led by able men such as Carl Schurz of Missouri and Lyman Trumbull of Illinois, rejected Radical Reconstruction and Grant with it; choosing to nominate their own candidate. Having much difficulty in drafting a platform, they continued their problems by nominating Horace Greeley, known today for his immortal statement, "Go West, young man, go West." Greeley would have done much better if he had taken his own advice before the presidential election of 1872. He was a man totally unfit for the office of presidency; he was eccentric and espoused various causes, such as vegetarianism, that seemed strange to the public. He had been particularly critical of the Democrats during his career, but still they nominated him for president. The campaign of 1872 was one of personalities, not issues. Greeley was pictured as an out and out nut who had even helped bail out unpopular ex-Confederate President Jefferson Davis. Greeley himself admitted that he did not know whether he was running "for the presidency or the penitentiary." While Grant was also assailed as a drunk and loafer, he stood on his personal appeal and that carried the day. The strain of campaigning took its toll on Greeley, and he died within a month after the election.

Grant's reelection in 1872 marks another four-year period in which graft and corruption ran rampant. William Tweed controlled New York politics through his infamous Tweed Ring; the Brooklyn Bridge and phony gold bricks were sold time and time again. Shares were even sold in pay toilets. The "fast buck" was being made and city slickers were being taken in by the "old shell game." Congressmen even voted themselves a sizeable increase in salary.

Scandals continued to surround Grant himself. The Whiskey Ring was a combination of Treasury officials and distillers who had conspired to avoid payment of internal revenue taxes, thus robbing the government of millions in revenue. Grant first insisted that the guilty should be punished, but his tone became much milder when he found that his private secretary, Orville E. Babcock, was indicted. After personal intervention by Grant, Babcock was acquitted. Grant's Secretary of War, William W. Belknap, was nearly impeached after being connected with bribery in Indian affairs. Grant accepted Belknap's resignation with deep regret. In the midst of this wrongdoing, in 1873, the first economic panic since 1857 broke loose and caused much financial suffering. Yet despite the panic, the first world's fair was held in Philadelphia, where merriment reigned supreme. Although Grant talked of the possibility of running for an unprecedented third term, he became more and more bitter over politics and looked to the day when he could be an ordinary citizen again.

Grant was a president without political experience, yet he was not a complete failure. He was anxious to reunite the North and South and hastened to

"WHO STOLE THE PEOPLE'S MONEY?" — DO TELL. N.Y.TIMES. 'TWAS HIM.

The corruption among Boss William Tweed's cohorts is revealed in this Thomas Nast cartoon.

end military occupation. He vetoed an inflationary money measure in 1874 and attempted to change the direction of Indian policy. A Peace Commission in 1867 recommended that new directions be taken in Indian affairs. Grant tried to bring some improvements by upgrading the quality of agents, doing it by turning to the churches. If reservations were distributed among the major religious denominations, it would remove them from army and political domination and reduce corruption. Execution of this "Quaker Policy" was hurt by too few competent people. Some religious groups were even forced to go to college campuses to recruit volunteers. Many missionaries were more eager to serve in Africa or the Orient than with the Indians. And the Catholics felt that they had been discriminated against. Actually, Grant's policy provided little improvement in the quality of agents, for many of those who readily volunteered were religious fanatics who attempted to crush Indian culture.

Agents such as John Clum, who had a positive effect among the Apaches on the San Carlos reservation were an exception. In the long run Grant's "peace policy" brought little peace to the tribes, but it was an honest attempt to upgrade Indian services. During his lifetime Grant had reached the apex of the American experience: a three-star general and a two-term president. Yet his presidency stands as an outstanding example of incompetency. His was, indeed, a political tragedy.

Hayes: A Disputed Election

In 1876 both the Democrats and Republicans renounced corruption in government and nominated two untainted men. Samuel J. Tilden, bachelor governor of New York, had broken Boss Tweed's control of New York City; he was the choice of the Democrats. Tilden, known as "Whispering Sammy," was hardly a physically impressive individual, but he won the nomination on his spotless record. The Republicans turned to the reformist Governor Rutherford B. Hayes of Ohio, who was a Civil War veteran and an honest administrator. Both parties presented reform platforms, and the Republicans continued to remind the public of their Civil War record. Thanks to the corruption of the Grant era, known as "Grantism," Democrat Tilden received a majority of the popular and electoral votes, but the states of Oregon, Louisiana, South Carolina, and Florida had disputed returns. The fact that Tilden had 184 of the 185 votes necessary for election made him the overwhelming choice. In 1877, a 15-member electoral commission was established. Voting along partisan lines, the commission ruled all of the disputed votes to Hayes and he became the legal choice, but hardly the popular choice, for president. Hayes now entered the presidency, as had John Quincy Adams, with a dark cloud over his head. Yet threat of a Democratic filibuster still stood in Hayes' way. As a compromise, Southern Democrats threw their support to Hayes in return for the end of Reconstruction, awarding of federal offices to Democrats, the appointment of a Southern Democrat to the cabinet, and the financing of federal improvement programs in the South. After his inauguration Hayes lived up to some of the bargain. He removed federal troops from South Carolina and Louisiana, thus ending military occupation and congressional Reconstruction. He also appointed a former Confederate colonel, David M. Key of Tennessee, to the office of postmaster general. And he tried to sweep away the atmosphere of the Grant era.

Rutherford B. Hayes became the nineteenth president of the United States by one electoral vote. Born in Ohio, he excelled in school and eventually

Chart 7-1
Electoral Commission 1877

	Republicans (Hayes)	Democrats (Tilden)
House	2	3
Senate	3	2
Supreme Court	3	2
Total	8*	7

* Election won by Republican Rutherford Hayes by one Commission vote.

graduated from Harvard Law School. Winning much attention in two widely publicized murder trials, he was elected city solicitor of Cincinnati—an influential political position. He served in the Union army during the Civil War and was also elected to Congress. But he continued in the military, for he declared that any soldier who would "abandon his post to electioneer for a seat in Congress, ought to be scalped." After the war, he took his place in the House of Representatives and was elected governor of Ohio three times. As governor he worked hard for economy in government and civil service reform. A compromise candidate of the Republicans on the seventh ballot, Hayes won the disputed election of 1876.

Hayes, referred to as "His Fraudulency" or "Old 8 to 7," had a hard time living down the election of 1877 and its taint of corruption. Although he tried to strike against the spoilsmen who controlled the graft of the Grant presidency, he found himself not completely above reproach. He appointed some Republicans, who had been responsible for awarding the disputed votes to him, to federal jobs. He also was handicapped greatly by the Democratic majority in the House and Senate. But he and his prohibitionist wife, "Lemonade Lucy," restored faith in the integrity of the national government. He openly defied Senator Roscoe Conkling of New York, one of the greatest spoilsmen of them all, by attempting to clean up the New York Customs Office. Two of Conkling's men were replaced by those of Hayes. His ideas for reform, however, were often hurt by the turbulent economic and social conditions of the time. The depression of 1873 had caused widespread unemployment, the effects of which surfaced with labor violence in 1877. He also was pressured by a demand for free coinage of silver, which some thought was an answer to the tight money conditions. In 1878 Congress passed over Hayes' veto the Bland-

Allison Act, authorizing the Treasury to purchase not less than $2 million and not more than $4 million worth of silver each month and coin it into dollars at the ratio of 16 to 1. And Hayes soon felt himself face to face with a movement to restrict Chinese immigration.

The Chinese Issue

The first Chinese to come to the United States arrived in San Francisco in 1848 and were welcomed with open arms. California needed cheap labor, and these immigrants seemed willing to work hard for low wages. From San Francisco they spread through the gold fields and began to compete with white miners. The Foreign Miners' Law of 1850, which was originally passed to limit Mexican miners, was applied to Chinese miners and caused many to return to San Francisco. Californians feared economic competition so the state charged $50 a person for each foreigner, especially Chinese, entering California. These two laws, however, did not restrict the enterprising Chinese quickly enough. Violence became the next response.

In the late 1850s race riots drove the Chinese out of the mining regions of northern California. "Not a Chinaman's chance" became a popular but tragically true statement. More and more restrictions were placed upon them. In 1854 the California Supreme Court decided that no people of color could testify in court against whites. At the time, Mark Twain observed, "Any white man can swear a Chinaman's life away, but no Chinaman can testify against a white man." The next step was complete exclusion of the Chinese from entering the United States.

California Governor John Bigler took the first public stand on Chinese exclusion. He reasoned that the flood of Chinese immigration was disastrous to the United States and must be stopped completely. But public sentiment in California did not yet support such a drastic measure. And by the 1860s the Chinese had found employment in the construction of the transcontinental railroad. Referred to as "Crocker's pets," after Charlie Crocker who directed construction, they worked long hours for low wages and were essential in the completion of the Central Pacific line from Sacramento to Promontory Point, Utah. In San Francisco, in the mines, and in the railroad crews, they earned a reputation as hard workers, but racial hostility against them grew. They were out of the mainstream of American culture, excluded by their strange language and customs. They also remained isolated in their own communities, such as Chinatown in San Francisco. And newspapers began to circulate stories of a "yellow peril" that would arise out of the East to overwhelm white America.

Chinatown in San Francisco became the largest
settlement of Chinese in America.

In the late 1860s "anti-coolie" clubs attempted to keep the Chinese in
their place and at the same time drive them out of California. Mob violence
increased, while law enforcement officials stood idly by. The situation was so
bad in San Francisco that a Chinese Protective Society was formed to protect
the Chinese from San Francisco's hoodlum gangs. This society "for the pre-
vention of cruelty to Chinese," composed of special policemen, yielded to
public pressure and disbanded after only one year. The violence continued; in
1871 a fierce race riot in Los Angeles saw large numbers of Chinese injured
or killed. Many Californians had thought that once the transcontinental railroad was completed the Chinese would leave. This was hardly the case. By
1876 more than 116,000 Chinese were living in California.

In San Francisco local ordinances reflected the racial hatred that was
building. A Cubic Air Ordinance decreed that all adults must have a least 500
cubic feet of living space. This ordinance, applied to overcrowded Chinatown,
led to numerous arrests. The Queue Ordinance decreed that all prisoners in
city jails were to have their hair cut within an inch of their scalp. This hit
hard at the Chinese, who wore pigtails, or *queues*, which were symbols of
their religious beliefs. Further, a laundry ordinance that charged a license fee
on horse-drawn vehicles forced many Chinese to run laundry businesses without a horse.

The Panic of 1873 brought further hardship because the unemployed laborers blamed the Chinese for their problems. When fiery Irish agitator, Denis Kearney, raised the cry, "The Chinese must go," mobs gathered behind him, ready to act. Kearney eventually became president of the Workingman's party in California, which was devoted to the complete exclusion of the Chinese. Anti-Chinese feeling hit a new high when the vast majority of California voters cast their ballots in favor of exclusion. The voice of white California was being heard.

With the end of railroad construction and with a job shortage due to the Panic of 1873, Chinese began to move out of California to other parts of the West. They continued to be met, as in California, with hostility and violence. More and more Western states turned to the federal government for action. In 1876 a Joint Special Committee of Congress to investigate Chinese immigration heard testimony both for and against Chinese exclusion. The majority of the testimony followed these lines, "The Chinese are inferior to any race God ever made."

Chinese Exclusion

In 1878 a House of Representatives resolution requested President Hayes to seek a change in the 1868 treaty with China that permitted unlimited Chinese immigration. At the same time Congress acted by passing the Fifteen-Passenger Bill, which restricted the number of Chinese passengers on any ship entering the United States to 15. Hayes felt the law "inconsistent" with American treaty obligations and vetoed it. But he did negotiate a new treaty with China that gave the United States power to limit Chinese immigration but not to completely stop it.

Still anti-Chinese sentiment continued and increased. In 1882 Congress finally yielded to public pressure, passing the Chinese Exclusion Act which stopped Chinese immigration for a ten-year period. By 1902 exclusion became permanent. America, the land of opportunity, closed its doors for the first time—on the Chinese. The racial hostility against them was channeled into political action. But the Chinese were not the only ethnic group that was having a difficult time living in America in the post-Civil War period.

Mexican-Americans

With the conclusion of the Mexican War and the signing of the Treaty of Guadalupe Hidalgo more than 75,000 Spanish-speaking people in the Southwest came under American domination. During the period after the Civil War there was a gradual erosion of their land holdings and civil rights. In New Mexico, the Mexican-Americans, as these people began to be called, found themselves in the middle of ranch wars and real estate deals. The most famous of the ranch wars was the Lincoln County War of 1878. Mexican vaqueros were exploited by ranchers on both sides. Elfego Baca and Sostenes L'Archeveque emerged out of the range-war tension as two folk heroes. Baca gained a reputation as a gunfighter and sheriff. L'Archeveque, in retaliation for his father's murder, took direct action and killed 20 whites. He was killed in turn, not by white ranchers, but by Mexican-Americans, who feared his continued violence would lead to retaliation against them.

The land situation in New Mexico was a particularly frustrating one. The Treaty of Guadalupe Hidalgo specifically guaranteed Spanish and Mexican land grants, but this treaty was not being lived up to. Railroad and cattle interests pushed for more land, and territorial politicans were frequently sympathetic to their pleas. The situation came to a head in 1891, when Congress created the Court of Private Land Claims for New Mexico, Colorado, and Arizona, which would investigate land claims. The court negated most of the original land grants. The loss of land stimulated Mexican-American resistance.

Two vigilante groups, Le Mano Negro ("the black hand") and Las Gorras Blancas ("the white caps"), emerged in the 1880s to terrorize American ranchers, cattlemen, and other American business interests. Of the two organizations, Las Gorras Blancas was the most successful, claiming a membership of 1500 and dedicated to "protect the rights and interests of the people in general and especially those of the helpless classes." Destruction of railroad property and fence cuttings were typical of its activities. While these organizations did not stem the tide of American capitalism, they did vent the frustrations of many Mexican-American citizens of New Mexico. Under increased pressure from established Mexicans and law enforcement officials, the organizations dissolved. By the twentieth century the position of the Mexican-American in New Mexico had changed considerably; this change was also evident in California.

Mexican-Americans in California

The *Californios,* or Spanish-speaking people of California, came under American military rule after the Civil War and in 1850 under the state government of California. The same desire for Mexican land that existed in New Mexico existed early in California, too. The Land Law of 1851 forced Mexican land owners to prove title to their land. The legal process of proving title was a lengthy and costly one. While three-fourths of the landowners won their court cases, they had incurred such large debts that they usually had to sell anyway.

Joaquin Murieta, motivated by revenge, became the famous Mexican-American bandit of California.

While the loss of land continued, Mexican rights were being restricted. The Foreign Miners' Tax, which has already been mentioned as an economic tool used to restrict the influx of Chinese in the gold fields, was originally intended for Mexican miners. It was quite successful, and most Mexicans were forced to abandon their diggings.

As with the Chinese, mob violence accompanied legal restrictions. Hangings and whippings were common. Mexicans were looked upon as an inferior race and as a potential danger to the American way. One incident involved Juanita, a Mexican prostitute, whose lover had killed a white who had mistreated her. After a swift trial the lover and Juanita were hanged. Unlike the Chinese, the Mexicans in California frequently met violence with violence through bandit or guerilla action. Joaquin Murieta is the best known California bandit. After his wife had been raped, his brother hanged, and he himself beaten, he dedicated his life to the expulsion of the *gringo*. This Robin Hood of California became a hero in his own day. White sentiment caused the California legislature to create a special force to track him down. Although it is believed the special force killed him, there is still much speculation about his death. The activities of Murieta and of the bandit Three-Fingered Jack Garcia fueled the growth of anti-Mexican hostility.

Mexican-Americans in Texas

Francisco P. Ramirez, publisher of *El Clamor Publico* in Los Angeles, tried to help the Mexican cause through nonviolent means. But he was frustrated constantly and eventually driven out of business. The economic and political position of the Mexicans in California continued to deteriorate. This situation was no different in Texas. Sentiment toward Mexicans there had been getting worse since the days of the Mexican Revolution and the Mexican War. In 1857 jealousy over Mexican teamsters, who had been trading goods between the Texas coast and San Antonio, reached a boiling point. White teamsters began to attack and murder Mexican teamsters. The Cart War came to an end only after federal troops were called into action. The Mexican dissatisfaction again emerged in 1878. Mexicans near El Paso barely eked out a living by selling and transporting salt from nearby salt beds. But over the years more and more of their salt beds were taken from them, until, in the 1870s, Texas politican Charles Howard obtained final control of the beds. Mexicans now were charged for the salt they removed. In 1878 Howard went to the salt beds where he was captured and shot. The Salt War involved two days of rioting.

Vigilante action in Texas was climaxed by the activities of Juan "Cheno" Cortina. Cortina became famous in 1859 for his shooting of a sheriff who had been brutal to a Mexican worker. After the shooting he and his followers seized Brownsville and attempted to help Mexicans in need. After being chased for years by both Mexican and Texas troops, he eventually became a brigadier general in the Mexican army.

Individuals such as Baca in New Mexico, Murieta in California, and Cortina in Texas are looked upon today as precursors of the movement for Mexican-American liberation.

Throughout the Southwest after the Civil War Mexicans lost land and power; these losses led to the subjugated status of their descendants in the twentiety century. While the Chinese immigrants were being excluded from the country and the Mexicans in the Southwest were losing land, power, and prestige, the Indians of the West were fighting for their very survival.

The Indians' Last Days

By the 1850s the Bureau of Indian Affairs, which had been transferred to the Department of the Interior in 1849, found large numbers of whites living west of the Mississippi. These settlers caused the removal policy to gradually evolve into the reservation system, which attempted to place Western tribes on isolated parcels of land and restrict their movement. This system threatened the way of life of most mobile Western tribes, for, trapped on a fixed piece of land, their roaming and hunting days were ended forever. It was this policy, plus the movement of whites across the Mississippi to the Pacific Coast, which led to more than 950 separate violent engagements, known collectively as the Indian Wars of the West. The most notable encounters took place in the Pacific Northwest, the Southwest, and the Plains.

Isaac Stevens was appointed governor of Washington Territory and at the same time empowered to negotiate treaties with the tribes of that region. In 1854 and 1855 he negotiated a series of treaties with the tribes of western and eastern Washington, which placed them on selected reservations. However, the discovery of gold in eastern Washington, coupled with avarice for Indian land, led to the disruption of the reservation system and to war. This short-lived war, concentrated east of the Cascades, was typical of the perennial struggle between civilian and military authority over the direction of Indian policy. It also featured the widespread use of the citizen-soldier, the volunteer, who became a mainstay in the Western wars. By 1858 the war was over and the reservation system became a permanent fixture. The next war in the region involved the Modoc tribe.

The Modoc tribe lived near Tule Lake along the present Oregon-California border. By the mid-1860s, white farmers desired Modoc land, so the tribe was

The Modocs under the leadership of Captain Jack held out against hundreds of white soldiers in the lava beds of Northern California in 1873.

placed on a reservation with an enemy tribe, the Klamaths. Under the leadership of Keintpoos, known as Captain Jack, a group of Modocs left the reservation and returned to their ancestral home. Now tension began to build. White farmers reported incidents of harassment. Rumors told of Captain Jack killing a medicine man. The army was ordered to bring the rebellious Modocs back to the reservation. In 1873 the Modoc War occurred. It was an embarrassing war for the federal government. A force of about 75 warriors led by Captain Jack and Hooker Jim held out against as many as 1000 soldiers in the lava beds near Tule Lake. During a peace meeting, General E.R.S. Canby was shot and killed, the first United States general killed at the hands of Indians.

The public demanded an end to the war. More troops were sent in. Hooker Jim turned traitor, and the forces of Captain Jack surrendered. He was subsequently hanged, and the rest of his tribe were sent to Oklahoma, where their remaining descendants live today. Few whites presently live on Modoc land.

Nez Perce War

One of the great tragedies of the Western wars was that of the Nez Perce and Chief Joseph. The Nez Perce tribe lived in small bands that hunted and fished in southern Oregon and northern Idaho and had been friendly to whites since the days of the explorers Lewis and Clark. By the 1860s the government decided to apply the reservation system to this tribe. One group of Nez Perce, under the leadership of old Chief Joseph, lived in the lovely Wallowa Valley of eastern Oregon. This group refused to give up their valley and move to a reservation in Idaho. In 1873 President Ulysses Grant declared their valley public domain and open to settlement. General O. O. Howard was sent in to persuade young Chief Joseph to move to the reservation. Joseph refused to leave. War seemed imminent, but Joseph knew that most of his people would be exterminated in a direct action. So he and the other nontreaty bands headed for "grandmother's land"—Canada. The Nez Perce War was a war of flight. Generals Howard and Nelson A. Miles pursued a fleeing group of men, women, and children. Chief Joseph was a superb strategist; with the help of another tribe member, Lean Elk, he led his people on a 1300-mile trek, managing to elude his pursuers at the same time. This feat made Chief Joseph a legend. But the flight had taken its toll on Joseph's people, and, 20 miles from the Canadian border, he surrendered. His people were sick and dying. His speech of surrender sums up the feelings of the Indians in their final days, "Hear me, my chiefs, I am tired, my heart is sick and sad. From where the sun now shines, I will fight no more forever." With these words the struggle of the Pacific Northwest Indian for the preservation of his traditional culture ended.

Southwest Wars

The Navajo and Apache wars in the Southwest followed a different pattern. The Navajos were considered a threat to the farmers and cattle-breeders of New Mexico and Arizona. During the Civil War the army sent General James Carlton to apply the reservation policy to the Navajo. He, in turn, sent Kit Carson with Ute scouts to starve the Navajos into submission. Once rounded up, they were driven on "the long walk" to Bosque Redondo, a reservation near Fort Sumner in eastern New Mexico. Here they lived with the Mescalero Apaches in perpetual hunger and disease for four years; they then were sent back to a reservation in northeastern Arizona, where they remain today, the largest tribe with the largest reservation.

The Apaches proved a much greater challenge. They lived in small nomadic bands throughout Arizona and New Mexico. Their way of life involved raiding neighboring tribes as well as white farmers, ranchers, and travelers. The most adept guerilla warriors were the Chiricahua Apaches of southern Arizona. Under the leadership of Mangas Colorados and Cochise, bands of Apaches constantly harassed white settlers. Most of the Chiricahua eventually moved to the San Carlos reservation where they were allowed a measure of self-government by their Indian agent, John Clum. When Clum resigned and the military again took control of the reservation, a few radical Indians, such as Victoria, Nana, and Geronimo, renewed raids. Adept at guerilla warfare, these small groups continually frustrated the United States Army. It was not until 1886 that Geronimo surrendered and Indian resistance in the Southwest ended.

Sioux Wars

During the Civil War Little Crow led a Santee Sioux uprising in Minnesota, known as the Santee Sioux War, which saw the murder of hundreds of white settlers. Colonel John Chivington led a white force that slaughtered hundreds of defenseless Indian men, women, and children in an incident known as the Sand Creek Massacre in Colorado. Meanwhile, gold discoveries in Montana caused miners to rush into that area along a road known as the Bozeman Trail, which cut through the heart of the Plains Indians hunting area. The army was ordered to build forts along the trail to protect travelers from raids. This action precipitated a war in 1866 that is known as the First Sioux War. Oglala Sioux war chief, Red Cloud, and his Cheyenne allies used hit-and-run tactics effectively. The army units were under constant pressure for two years. The most famous incidents were the Fetterman Massacre and the Wagon Box Fight. Brash Captain William J. Fetterman, who had earlier stated that he could ride through the entire Sioux nation with 80 men, left Fort Phil Kearney in December 1866 to rescue a party that had left the fort in search of wood. Ignoring orders, he passed beyond the view of the fort and was surrounded; he and his entire force were killed. In the Wagon Box Fight a small number of soldiers with new repeating rifles held out against large numbers of attacking Indians and drove them away. The Fort Laramie Treaty of 1868 ended resistance with an unusual Indian victory. The army made a rare retreat by abandoning the forts and closing the trail. Red Cloud did agree to move to a large reservation and to retain hunting rights. But this was only a temporary victory.

The Plains Indian lifestyle was being further challenged. The railroad cut the Plains buffalo herd into northern and southern herds. For the Plains Indian the buffalo was not only the major food supply but was also at the heart of Indian lifestyle and culture. So the destruction of the buffalo by hunters and sportsmen, such as William "Buffalo Bill" Cody, was devastating to the Plains Indians. In the early 1870s gold was discovered in the sacred Black Hills of the Dakotas. Miners poured into the Black Hills and the federal government refused to uphold the Treaty of 1868. Government officials decided to limit hunting rights and to order all Sioux and Northern Cheyenne to reservations. The rebellious Sioux warriors were now led by Crazy Horse, an Oglala war chief, and Sitting Bull, a Hunkpapa warrior and medicine man. In 1876 the army sent three units to surround the rebellious Indians and force them to reservations. The winter of 1876 delayed government action, but by the spring the Second Sioux War was on.

General Alfred Terry proceeded from Fort Abraham Lincoln in the Dakotas and moved west. He learned of the movement of Sioux and Northern Cheyenne in the Little Big Horn River country, so he directed Colonel George Custer and his Seventh Cavalry to survey the situation and report back to him. Without knowing it, George Armstrong Custer was going to his final battle. Custer has become one of the most controversial figures in American history. A West Point graduate, "Boy General" in the Civil War, and Indian fighter in the West, he was gaining a national reputation. This suited his expanded ego well for he had plans to eventually be president. Recently, President Grant had rebuked him publicly for his testimony during an Indian affairs hearings. He had to attract national publicity, and get it fast, for the national political conventions were quickly approaching. His killing of northern Cheyenne in winter camp (1868) on the Washita River in Oklahoma had won him earlier notoriety. He needed one more great victory over the Indians, and he knew he would become a national hero. On June 25, 1876, he violated his orders, divided his forces, and attacked an overwhelming force of Sioux and Northern Cheyenne along the Little Big Horn River. What happened at the Little Big

This romanticized version of Custer's Last Stand reveals the feeling most Americans had toward General George Armstrong Custer.

Horn will never be known completely, but Custer and his men were killed. His subordinates were allowed to flee. While this victory had no effect on the course of the war, it shocked the nation and forced the army to redouble its efforts. Crazy Horse was captured and eventually killed, while Sitting Bull fled to Canada. The Plains wars were over forever, but the legend of Custer lives on.

The Ghost Dance

The Western Indians were now on reservations. Their culture had been crushed and their lifestyle had been drastically changed. The last hope was a messiah who would restore the old ways and drive out the whites. In the late 1880s a Paiute Indian known as "Wovoka" had a vision of the return of all the dead buffalo and dead Indians. The great day would arrive if certain dances and songs were followed. These beliefs created an excitement on the northern Plains. An Indian named Kicking Bear introduced a trancelike dance called the Ghost Dance and told of the powers of a magic shirt that would repel the

Those members of Big Foot's band who had been
killed at the Wounded Knee massacre here lie frozen
in the snow the morning after the massacre.

white man's bullets. The Ghost Dance belief caused the army to adopt a hard-line policy. Sitting Bull was killed during the crisis. A band of Hunkpapa Sioux led by Big Foot left the reservation in anticipation of the great day when dead Indians and buffalo would be resurrected. On December 28, 1890, at Wounded Knee Creek in South Dakota, the Seventh Cavalry rounded up Big Foot's band. A disturbance occurred while soldiers were searching for weapons. The troops started firing Hotchkiss rapid-fire cannons from the surrounding hillsides; men, women, and children were killed. In all, 300 Indians were killed or died of exposure. Mistakenly called the Battle of Wounded Knee, the Wounded Knee Massacre was the final defeat for the American Indian in a struggle that had lasted three centuries. "I shall not be there. I shall rise and pass. Bury my heart at Wounded Knee."

The Dawes Act

By the 1870s the treatment of Indians by white Americans came under careful scrutiny. National guilt was evident with the formation of organizations such as the National Indian Defense Association and the National Indian Rights Association. One crusader, Helen Hunt Jackson, put her feelings into words in the book *A Century of Dishonor*; published in 1881, it was an indictment of Indian treatment. It is interesting to note that this white-conscience movement arose when the American Indian was no longer a threat to white society. All these reformers sought an answer to the Indian's plight. Congress provided one with the passage of the Dawes Act in 1887.

The Dawes Severalty Act marked the end of treaty making and the beginning of Indian legislation. The act was based on the belief that the major problem with Indians was the fact that they were Indians and that the best way to help them was to make them white. Tribal land held in common was to be broken up, and each family was to be given an individual plot. According to the act the president had the power to survey reservation land, allot it to eligible Indians in 160-, 80-, or 40-acre parcels, and sell the surplus land at auction. Formal title to all Indian-occupied land, however, was only to be given after a 25-year period of government trusteeship. As amended by the Burke Act of 1906, at the end of the 25-year period citizenship would also be awarded. This act, which was in force from 1887 to 1934, saw the further deterioration of tribal culture and the loss of 90 million acres of Indian land through sale, lease, wills, and other methods. It was hoped the act would force Indians to become like white farmers, by giving Indians their own plot of land, but this simplistic solution to Indian problems did not work as planned. The end result was not a prosperous white farmer, but a poor Indian. So most Indians entered the twentieth century isolated from white society, living on individual plots of land scattered through the West.

The Chinese-exclusion policy, the treatment of the Mexican-Americans, and the Indian Wars of the West cannot be attributed solely to the administration of President Hayes. The dispossessionary policies inflicted on these minorities were standard during the terms of all the presidents in the years from 1868 to 1900, and even beyond. Hayes presidency saw the declining position of all three groups, but his main concern was to break from the days of Grant. Hayes brought honesty and a renewed prestige to the office of the Presidency, but, beyond ending Reconstruction in the South, he achieved little else that was concrete.

From Garfield to Harrison

In 1880, Hayes declined to run again, and the field was wide open. The Republican convention reflected the deep party divisions. The "Stalwarts," led by Roscoe Conkling of New York, were politicans most interested in the spoils system and patronage, whereas the "Half-Breeds," led by James Blaine of Maine, were party reformers; however, while they talked of change, they were little different from the Stalwarts. The Stalwarts now turned once again to the old war hero, Grant, who they hoped would release them from the frustrations encountered under Hayes. For 35 ballots Grant led the field, but the convention finally turned to a dark horse, ex-Congressman and ex-General James A. Garfield. To placate the Stalwart faction, second place on the ticket went to Chester A. Arthur, whom Hayes had dismissed as head of the New York Customs House. Samuel Tilden refused to try again, so the Democrats turned to a Civil War veteran, Winfield Scott Hancock. In the election there was little basic difference between Democrats and Republicans, because both parties reflected business sentiments. Garfield won by a 59-vote margin in the electoral college.

James Garfield was the last president to be born in a log cabin. Born in Ohio, he became a professor of language and literature and eventually became president of Hiram College. He was the youngest brigadier general in the Union army; later he was promoted to major general. Elected to the House of Representatives, he served for eight terms. He was one of several Congressmen accused of accepting gifts of stock from the Credit Mobilier company. Having served on the commission that settled the election of 1876, he became floor leader of the Republicans in the House. Winning a seat in the Senate (for Ohio), he then pursued the presidency. As the Republican nominee, he won a close election in 1880.

Garfield was a timid and vacillating president. He expressed his sentiments well when he exclaimed, "My God! What is there in this place that a man should ever want to get into it?" His struggles with Roscoe Conkling and the Stalwarts frustrated him. On July 2, 1881, Charles Guiteau, a mentally-disturbed man who was disappointed at failing to gain a minor office, shot and killed Garfield. Standing over the wounded President, he said, "I am a Stalwart and Arthur is president now." Guiteau never received his appointment but instead was executed for murder.

Arthur as President

The Stalwarts now saw their man as president. Chester Arthur, hardly a household word today, became the fourth vice-president to become president. Born in Vermont, he became a lawyer in New York City and was known as a defender of black rights. His skills at political manuevering won him the position of state quartermaster general during the Civil War. After the war he became aide to Roscoe Conkling, then head of the New York Republican organization. Grant appointed Arthur to be collector of the Port of New York; in this position he gave government jobs to party workers and helped to strengthen the Republican party. President Hayes forced Arthur to resign his position. Nominated for vice-president on the Garfield ticket, he helped to win Stalwart support. With the assassination of Garfield, this machine politician became president. But "Widower Arthur," who was known as a slick dresser, rose above his background as staunch Stalwart and actually gave the country a good administration. Under his leadership the Civil Service was reformed, postal frauds were investigated, and government spending was cut back. The United States Navy was modernized, funded by a Treasury surplus, and the White House was renovated. The enactment of the Pendleton Civil Service Act marked the passage of the first Civil Service reform legislation. The act, passed in 1883, authorized the president to establish an independent and bipartisan Civil Service Commission of three persons, who would conduct competitive examinations to determine candidates' qualifications for office. Initially this act made few changes because it only applied to 12 percent of federal positions. Yet it was a start, and subsequent presidents expanded it until, by the 1900s, the act affected 40 percent of all federal positions. Little more can be said about the presidency of Chester Arthur. He rose above his background and made an honest and fair president. He began to enjoy his role as president, but because he had alienated too many factions of the party he was refused the nomination in 1884. Two years later he died of a cerebral hemorrhage.

The "Plumed Knight" James Blaine, leader of the Half-Breeds, was the Republican choice in 1884, but his spotty political background so alienated the reformers, now called "Mugwumps," that they bolted the party. The Democrats tried to steal the support of the Mugwumps by nominating a relatively untainted individual, Grover Cleveland. A bachelor, Cleveland had been sheriff and mayor of Buffalo and then had been governor of New York. He had acted as a reformer and had earned the slogan, "We love him for the enemies he has made." The campaign of 1884 focused on the morality of the two candidates. Cleveland was pictured as a Southern sympathizer and as the father of an illegitimate son, a fact that he never denied. Critics wrote, "No decent man surely would think of victory for a horse thief; and for an equally good reason, no one should vote for the lecherous corrupter of womanhood." Blaine, on the other hand, was called the "tattoed man" who had "wallowed in spoils like a Rhinoceros in an African pool." The Mulligan letters incriminating correspondence, seemed to prove that Blaine had been involved in unethical dealings in regard to land grant railroads. One reformer suggested,

This cartoon pictures Cleveland and his illegitimate son; Cleveland's morality was an issue in the election of 1884.

"We should elect Mr. Cleveland to the public office he is so admirably qualified to fill and remand Mr. Blaine to the private life which he is so eminently fitted to adorn." The Democrats escaped with a narrow victory.

Cleveland, the Democrat

Cleveland's election in 1884 brought a Democrat to office for the first time since the Civil War. Born in New Jersey of a poor family, he worked hard in a general store, received little education, but did become a lawyer in Buffalo. During the Civil War he stayed on the home front and supported his mother and her family. The fact that he hired a substitute to fight in his place was used many times by his political enemies. After serving as sheriff of Buffalo, he returned to his law practice. As reform Mayor of Buffalo he became known as "veto mayor." His outstanding reputation for honesty won him the office of governor of New York in 1882. As governor he continued his reform propensities by keeping a balanced budget and attempting to reform the political machinery of New York City. Being accused of "rum, Romanism, and rebellion," an obvious reference to whiskey, Roman Catholicism, and Southern sympathy, Cleveland won a close election by a margin of only 37 electoral votes. Standing 5-feet-11-inches tall and weighing over 270 pounds, the bachelor now became President.

Cleveland came into office with the reputation of being a stolid, unimaginative reformer who "wore no man's collar." He had to please both the reformers and the regulars in his party; this was a difficult task. Frequently he took unpopular stands at a time when dedication and service to country were unusual. Financially he was a conservative and a defender of property rights. During his term as president he married 21-year-old Francis Folsom, in a quiet White House affair with no reporters present. Showmanship was not his strong point; he believed that "a public office is a public trust."

As President he faced the issues of Southern regionalism, the spoils system, and the tariff problem. He became less popular in the North when he allowed captured Confederate flags to be returned to the South. Further, he vetoed a general Civil War Pension Bill for Union veterans. Cattlebreeders were forced by his administration to move illegal fences. His stand on the spoils system was vague, for he both expanded the Civil Service Act and, at the same time, replaced thousands of Republican postmasters with Democrats. He broke with past presidential tradition by fighting for the reduction of the tariff. His lack of success here led to a stalemate in Congress. This deadlock caused the tariff to be the major issue in the election of 1888.

Although the Democrats were not overly pleased with Cleveland, they had no other outstanding leader, so they renominated him. Blaine still had aspirations for the presidency, but he bowed out of the race and the Republicans turned to Benjamin Harrison, grandson of "Old Tippecanoe" and a colorless Presbyterian elder. While sensational stories of Cleveland beating his youthful wife entertained the public, both parties turned to more sober issues, such as the tariff. The Republicans defended protection and Democrats advocated a reduction in duties. Both parties spent campaign money freely and historians today refer to this election as one of the most corrupt in our history. During the campaign Harrison, extremely pious and humorless ("Harrison sweats ice water," claimed one writer), conducted a series of "front porch" speeches under the direction of his adroit political manager, Matthew Quay. Although Cleveland won the popular vote, Harrison carried the electoral college and the election. Harrison had won (barely) on a platform of tariff protection and generous pensions; now the Republican Congress took control of his administration.

Harrison as President

Benjamin Harrison was the only grandson of a president to become president himself. Born in Ohio, he grew up on the family farm, studied law, and prac-

Politics and Race Relations in an Industrial Age: From Grant to McKinley

Benjamin Harrison defeated Cleveland in 1888 in his reelection bid. His term was connected with the Billion Dollar Congress.

ticed in Cincinnati. He served as city attorney in Indianapolis and during the Civil War commanded a unit of Indiana volunteers. After the war he won national publicity as a lawyer, was Mississippi River commissioner under Hayes, and was elected to the Senate. In the Senate he was particularly critical of President Cleveland's stand on the tariff and his veto of the pension bill. Winning the nomination in 1888, Harrison campaigned actively, lost the popular vote by more than 90,000 votes, but won in the electoral college. Nicknamed "Little Ben" because he was only five-feet-six-inches tall, he was a deeply religious man who rekindled respect for the American flag.

The Republicans had control of the presidency and both houses of Congress. The "Billion Dollar" Congress, under the leadership of Senator Nelson W. Aldrich of Rhode Island and House Speaker Thomas B. Reed of Maine, now began to act. In 1890 the Dependent Pension Act granted pensions to all Civil War veterans suffering from any disability. This raised the number of pensioners to over 970,000. The Silver Purchase Act of 1890 increased the amount of silver to be purchased by the treasury to 4.5 million ounces a month. This pleased the silverite faction by allowing the Treasury to purchase virtually all silver that was being mined. The Sherman Antitrust Act of 1890 seemed an answer to those who complained about the unrestricted power of industrial giants. This act outlawed "every contract, combination in the form of trust or otherwise, or conspiracy, in restraint of trade or commerce among the several states, or with foreign nations. . . ." The McKinley Tariff of 1890 raised the tariff levels to the highest peacetime rates ever and also protected more products than any previous tariff. Harrison's Republican Congress had handed out so much money that, in 1894, the Treasury surplus was gone, never to appear again.

The public response was hardly one of adulation, and in the congressional election of 1890 the Republicans were rebuked. President Harrison continued to offer little direction, standing mainly on his record as a supporter of business and patronage. Meanwhile, a new party of discontent was forming in the West—the Populist party.

Populism

At the heart of the Populist movement was the discontented farmer of the West and South. After the Civil War, America became increasingly an industrial nation, and the changes that accompanied this conversion hurt the dirt farmers of America. Farmers felt they were being victimized by monopolies, such as the railroads. In addition, they were hurting from sharp declines in agricultural prices and increased debts. Farmers also complained that they bore more than their share of the tax burden. Due to supposed government indifference and hostility, farmers began to organize.

In the 1860s, under the direction of Oliver Kelley, the Patrons of Husbandry, commonly known as the Grange, was formed to promote agricultural education and social fellowship. By the 1870s the Grange was attempting to solve farmers' economic problems through cooperative ventures. Some "Grangers" influenced state legislatures to pass favorable laws, but generally the organization did not solve the basic dissatisfactions. Eventually a coalition of rural political organizations—the Greenback Labor party, the Northern Farmers' Alliance, and the Southern Farmers' Alliance—grew into the Populist party.

In 1892 in Omaha, Nebraska, the Populist party formally was organized. It contained many discontented workers and, of course, dirt farmers. Its leaders, like religious revivalists, held their audiences spellbound with highflung oratory. Mary Ellen Lease ("Mary Yellin'") was an inexhaustible speechmaker; one person wrote that she could be heard from Kansas to New York without amplification. She wanted the people of Kansas to "raise less corn, and more hell." "Sockless" Jerry Simpson and Ignatius Donnelly were also two of the mainstays of the party. At this "mass meeting of maniacs", so labeled by the Eastern press, they adopted a platform listing their grievances and suggesting solutions. They wrote, "The fruits of the toil of millions are boldly stolen to build up colossal fortunes for a few. . . ." They felt that many of their ills would be reduced by having the government print more currency;

the inflation that would result would allow them to reduce their debts. They were equating inflation with prosperity. They also demanded free coinage of silver, a graduated income tax, government ownership of railroads, telegraphs, and telephones, restriction of immigration, election of United States Senators by popular vote, postal savings banks, and an eight-hour workday. Their candidate for president in 1892 was General James B. Weaver of Iowa, former presidential candidate on the Greenback party ticket. With the birth of the Populist party, a third party was on the rise.

Cleveland Returns

The Republicans continued to support Benjamin Harrison even though he was uninspiring and the party bosses did not like him. The Democrats again stayed with Grover Cleveland. So the election of 1892 was a virtual rematch of 1888, with the Populist party adding a bit of excitement to an otherwise quiet, respectable campaign. The tariff was again the major issue. Labor unrest in 1892 plus the voters' desire for change made Cleveland the "safe" candidate, and he won by a wide margin; the Democrats, however, took control of Congress. The Populists had polled more than one million votes and had carried four states. Their impressive showing revealed the feeling of dissatisfaction in parts of America at that time.

Cleveland now became the only president ever reelected after being defeated. If he had been able to foresee the problems of his second administration, he might have refused to stand for a second term. Cleveland spent much of his second term dealing with the Depression of 1893. The more urbanized America became, the harder the depressions hit. A European depression, coupled with a general agricultural slump, began to shake public confidence in business. During 1893, a worried public watched 600 banks and 74 railroad corporations pass into receivership. There were more than four million unemployed, coupled with strikes and general discontent. President Cleveland, like Van Buren earlier, did not believe it was his duty to use the federal government to combat the depression. But he did believe that the Silver Purchase Act had helped cause the depression, so he was instrumental in its repeal, an action which alienated silverites and inflationists alike. Next he tried to build up gold reserves, but no one was anxious to release gold. The Treasury was being depleted. So he was forced to deal with a group of bankers headed by financier John P. Morgan. The group was allowed to purchase government bonds for gold at a reduced price. This got Cleveland his gold and helped to stabilize the national economy and halt the inflationary trend, but this move tied Cleveland closer to the business interests. Cleveland was again making many enemies.

Cleveland failed with tariff reform. The Wilson-Gorman Act of 1894 was hardly an improvement over the McKinley Tariff Act of 1890. With more than 600 amendments tacked onto the original bill, the act changed the tariff rates only slightly and satisfied no one. Cleveland himself denounced the act, but he allowed it to become law without his signature. More than ever it looked as if he was on the side of big money and had given up the reform cause. For the rest of his term he continued to alienate the public by actions such as ordering federal troops to put down workers in the Pullman strike and snubbing an army of unemployed workers who marched to Washington to see him. By 1895 Cleveland himself was remarking, "Think of it. Not a man in the Senate [exists] with whom I can be on terms of absolute confidence." By 1896 he was booed at the party convention and called an "old bag of beef." One conservative wrote, "I hate the very ground that man walks on."

So in 1897 the career of Grover Cleveland came to an end. At times he took unpopular stands and refused to yield to public pressure, but he knew that support from both spoilsmen and reformers was essential. Frequently he tried to please both factions, but with little success. He never espoused the cause of the worker or the farmer, and he failed to achieve real tariff reform. Some historians today rate him as the best of the mediocre batch of post-Civil War presidents; but in 1896, even his own party was anxious to forget his second term.

In 1896 the Republicans nominated William McKinley for president, who had been the sponsor of the McKinley Tariff Act of 1890. He believed in government support of business interests but also showed great sympathy for the laborer. He was managed by a wealthy businessman named Marcus Hanna, who skillfully engineered his nomination.

The Democrats were in turmoil. Their convention repudiated the Cleveland programs and pushed for an income tax and free coinage of silver. Richard "Silver Dick" Bland of Missouri was the popular choice, but on the fifth ballot the nomination went to William Jennings Bryan of Nebraska, who had captivated the convention with his Cross of Gold speech. "You shall not," he exclaimed, "crucify mankind upon a cross of gold." The Democrats now turned to the radical cause of free silver as a panacea to all economic and social problems. Their saviour was Bryan, boy orator of the Platte, who promised to wrest control of America from big business.

The Populists could not avoid the lure of Bryan and the silver platform either, so they threw their support behind the Democrats. The campaign was

William Jennings Bryan won both Populist and Democratic support in 1896 with his stand on free silver.

now a two-man race. McKinley held to a low-key "front porch" campaign, which promised continued prosperity and support of the gold standard; meanwhile, business manipulations went on behind the scenes. Bryan made a whirlwind tour of 21 states, making more than 600 speeches. His emotional appeal frightened business leaders enough to contribute more than $16 million to Republican campaign chests. In addition, the press stood almost united against Bryan. One reporter wrote:

The Boy Orator makes only one speech, but he makes it twice a day. There is no fun in it. He simply reiterates the unquestionable truths that every man who has a clean shirt is a thief and should be hanged, and there is no goodness or wisdom except among the illiterates and criminal classes.

When the votes were counted, Bryan had lost by 600,000 popular votes and 95 electoral votes. He had failed to carry a single industrial or urban state. Labor did not support him. The coalition of farmers and workers had not succeeded. The fear of rampant inflation and economic chaos led to the defeat of the silver issue. Agrarian reform had been defeated. The principle of limited government, with slogans such as "McKinley and a full dinner pail," had won the day.

McKinley as President

McKinley lived up to his pledge to raise the tariff and continue prosperity. Gold discoveries and agricultural price increases helped the economic boom. The Dingley Tariff of 1897 raised duties to an average of 52 percent, the highest yet. The Gold Standard Act of 1900 ended the confusing controversy of gold versus silver by providing that gold remain the basis for the monetary system of the United States. Business and industry prospered. And the United States entered an era of world imperialism with its involvement in the Spanish-American War.

The election of 1900 was a virtual replay of 1896, with McKinley again facing Bryan. But this time Bryan's popularity was hurt by McKinley's vice-presidential running mate, Theodore Roosevelt, a "Rough Rider" and popular hero. Though Bryan's chances were dim, it was not because of enthusiasm for McKinley. One voter commented on the election: "It is a choice between evils, and I am going to shut my eyes, hold my nose, vote, go home, and disinfect myself." McKinley was overwhelmingly elected. Six months later in Buffalo, an anarchist named Leon Czolgosz shot and killed him. McKinley had brought America prosperity and imperialism. This devoutly religious man, who read the Bible to his invalid wife, lived till the end of the 1800s. If he had lived to see the presidency of that "damned cowboy," Theodore Roosevelt, he would have seen the first effective government regulation of business.

The politics of this industrial-urban era did not bring to the fore inspiring leaders or even inspiring issues. It was a time of domestic expansion, and frequently it appeared that there was no need for a president. Grant, Hayes, Garfield, Arthur, Harrison, and even Cleveland are not the most cherished nor the most well remembered presidents in our history. This does not mean that they were completely insipid individuals. But many of them believed in the business of politics and the politics of business. To best understand the mediocrity of politics in the late 1800s one must turn to the culture of this Gilded Age.

Essay

Selling the Candidate

In the bitter race for the presidency each party portrays an image of its candidate that will capture the popular imagination. From Presidents Washington to Carter a formula has emerged of what a president should be like. Whether they really do or not, candidates are pictured as meeting that formula. A look at some of the successful candidates will reveal the political skill involved in selling the presidential candidate.

George Washington was a military hero, a man of property, and an individual with a distaste for politics. There was little selling of this candidate. His wealth and military experience helped guarantee his selection. Wealth and military experience have become two of the most enduring qualities in the race to the White House. John Adams, the second president, was not a military hero, a man of wealth, or a popular figure. It is surprising that he was elected president, but remember that this was 1796; the political party system had not yet taken a definite shape. Adams had been fortunate enough to be Washington's vice-president, and this seemed enough to propel him into the presidency. But the office of vice-president would not always be such a successful stepping-stone; frequently it was the road to oblivion.

Thomas Jefferson read the voters well and became president in 1800. Even though only taxpayers could vote, he formed a successful grassroots campaign focused on small farmers and skilled workmen. He was pictured as the image of the American farmer, who stood against the wealthy gentry. His followers saw him as the savior of the downtrodden taxpaying masses, and he emerged as the first adept politician to become president. It is a tribute to this fine politician that the next two presidents would be more Jefferson's successors than candidates in their own right. A new road to the presidency, however, was emerging. Jefferson had been secretary of state; his two successors, James Madison and James Monroe, had also held that position. A pattern was emerging.

Andrew Jackson, who became president in 1828, could have taught Thomas Jefferson some lessons in politicking. The fact that Jackson was log-cabin bred and a self-educated frontiersman helped his image with the masses; in addition, he had the advantage of being a popular military hero due to his success at the Battle of New Orleans. Jackson's campaign tactics featured cleverly selling himself as one of the masses and also viciously slandering his opponent—John Quincy Adams. Connected with Jackson's victory was the slogan "to the victor belongs the spoils." Promises were made and, in many cases, kept; juicy rewards were given to Jackson's supporters. A new political morality was emerging. Jackson's campaign and image had earned him a permanent spot in the hearts and minds of the voters. His reelection was a foregone conclusion.

Humble roots and military success now seemed more important to presidential aspirants than having held the position of secretary of state. This was quite apparent in the election of 1840. It seemed to make little difference that William Henry Harrison was a Whig and not a

Democrat, for he inherited the same popular appeal which Jackson possessed. In 1840 a tactic had emerged: avoid controversial issues and appeal to the popular imagination. Harrison, the Virginia gentleman, posed as a dirt farmer, and his image carried the day. Politicians now seemed to care little for the future and prepared for one campaign at a time. In 1840, fundamental political differences between parties appeared to dissolve, never to return to what they had been in the past.

Abraham Lincoln was a party politician. He did not have the popular appeal of Harrison, nor did he even have national support; but he did his homework well and studied politicians before him. There is no doubt that the emotional sentiments connected with the election of 1860 worked both in his favor and against him. He became the symbolic embodiment of the Union. Lincoln the man will never be known; Lincoln the candidate was a reflection of the best of the Republican party in 1860. His success included his hard work, careful cultivation of party connections, and constant publicity of his virtues. He knew that he needed supporters in the worst way, and he was loyal to them. Once elected, Lincoln, the *candidate,* was transformed by the office into Lincoln, the *President*; the tremendous pressures of the Civil War helped mold him into a great president.

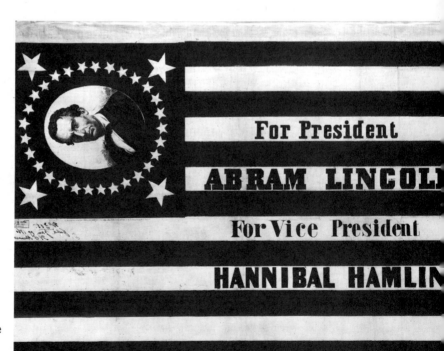

Abraham Lincoln stood for the presidency in 1860 on the cause of union.

Ulysses Grant followed the pattern of Andrew Jackson, stressing his image as a military hero and his dedication to the spoils system. But this political babe in the woods never took advantage of his overwhelming popular support. One of the strangest candidates for president in the period after the Civil War was Grover Cleveland, the bachelor candidate. In 1882 Cleveland had been mayor of Buffalo, two years later he was president. What was involved in the selling of this candidate? He was not a military man—he had no military background at all; he was not a family man, and this fact was made worse by the revelation that he had fathered an illegitimate child. He appeared to be an extremely vulnerable candidate; he was outside the presidential mold. But he had one overriding characteristic—honesty. The time was ripe for a president who would restore dignity to the office. Cleveland was that man. He was not a party politician; he was an independent at a time when being one was a virtue and not a vice.

In the twentieth century, military heroes such as Theodore Roosevelt and Dwight Eisenhower, "log cabin" men such as Harry Truman, party politicians such as Richard Nixon, and individuals with a cause such as Franklin D. Roosevelt have been successful candidates. Over the years a formula for the successful candidate has emerged, but that formula is quite elastic and changes with the times. While some Americans believe that anyone can become president, in reality the presidency is within the grasp of only a select few. Today another element has been added to the campaign success-formula—the media. The wrong media image can hurt a candidate. Nixon suffered in his debates with John Kennedy; televised news conferences of Jimmy Carter sometimes have given the impression that he lacks leadership and is indecisive. The correct media image can lead to success and national popularity. Franklin Roosevelt used his fireside chats to persuade the nation that his New Deal was to solve its ills. Presidents Gerald Ford and Jimmy Carter saw their ratings rise after their addresses to the nation on the energy crisis and inflation. In the election campaign of 1980, California Governor Jerry Brown not only used Hollywood producers in orchestrating his spot commercials, but even sought youth appeal through rock concerts and antinuclear rallies.

Every four years Americans prepare for a national election and for a prolonged ritual known as "the selling of the candidate." ∎

This campaign poster from the 1880 election reveals the different approaches used in selling the candidates.

Suggested Reading

A good survey of the presidents of this period is found in *From Hayes to McKinley* (1969) by H. WAYNE MORGAN.

The Chinese experience in California up to their exclusion is found in *Passage to the Golden Gate: History of the Chinese in America to 1910* (1962) by DANIEL and SAMUEL CHU.

The Mexican-American struggle is well documented in *North from Mexico* (1949) by CAREY MCWILLIAMS.

Numerous books exist on the Indian leaders and Indian wars of the West; two of the best surveys are RALPH ANDRIST's *The Long Death* (1964) and DEE BROWN's *Bury My Heart at Wounded Knee* (1970).

Some of the best studies of American politics from 1868 to 1900 are W. H. HESSELTINE's *Ulysses S. Grant* (1935), HARRY VARNARD's *Rutherford B. Hayes and His America* (1954), H. J. SIEVERS's *Benjamin Harrison: Hoosier President* (1959), HAROLD U. FAULKNER's *Politics, Reform and Expansion, 1890–1900* (1959), and HORACE SAMUEL MERRILL's *Bourbon Leader: Grover Cleveland and the Democratic Party* (1957).

CHAPTER 10

Return to the Gilded Age:
Culture of the Industrial Era

Time Line

?–A.D. 1492	Migration and evolution of American Indian societies
1492	Christopher Columbus lands in West Indies—beginning of European exploration
1607–1732	Establishment of 13 English colonies
1775–1783	American Revolution
1776	Declaration of Independence
1789–1797	Presidency of George Washington
1812–1815	War of 1812
1816–1824	Era of Good Feelings
1846–1848	Mexican War
1861–1865	Civil War
1865–1877	Reconstruction
1869	Formation of Knights of Labor
1870	John D. Rockefeller forms Standard Oil of Ohio
1873	National depression
1874	Formation of Women's Christian Temperance Union
1876	Alexander Graham Bell invents the telephone
1877	*Munn* v. *Illinois*
1882	Formation of Standard Oil trust
1886	Haymarket Square riot
1886	Birth of American Federation of Labor
1887	Interstate Commerce Act
1891	Invention of basketball
1892	Homestead strike
1893	National depression
1894	Pullman strike
1901	Formation of U.S. Steel Corporation
1877–1900	Industrialization and urbanization
1900–1916	Progressive Era
1917–1918	World War I
1930s	Depression and New Deal
1941–1945	World War II
1945–1960	Post-war politics
1950–1953	Korean War
1950–1960	Civil rights movement
1961–1973	Vietnam War
1976	Bicentennial celebration

Imagine a country with a public transportation system that can take you from one end of the continent to the other. Put yourself in a city with minority and slum problems. Walk into factories capable of mass production and plagued by all the concurrent social problems. Read the comic strips in the newspapers. Pick up the *Ladies' Home Journal* and browse through it. Listen to the talk on the streets about labor unions striking for higher wages. See women competing with men for jobs. Attend football and baseball games or boxing matches. Buy books and get involved in popular or serious literature—now stop a minute and reflect on where you are. It sounds a lot like the America of today, but actually you are in the America of the post-Civil War period— the Gilded Age. A time arrived then when the values and ideals of rural, agrarian America were changing. Industrial, urban America had been born, and with it came major cultural changes. The cultures of colonial and national America gave way to the real beginnings of the mass society of modern America. And at the heart of this transformation was the industrial boom.

The Rise of Big Business

The American Industrial Revolution was slowed by the Civil War. The nation's priorities turned to rapid production of certain essential wartime products, while general industrial growth declined. Yet the war did encourage mass production, the establishment of a national banking system, and the expansion of the railroad network. These factors helped to create a postwar boom. The rapidly growing population provided a market for products, while America's bountiful natural resources were widely exploited. Many innovative individuals, such as Philip D. Armour in meat packing, utilized organizational skills that they had acquired during the Civil War. Added to the burgeoning population, abundant resources, and organizational skills of key individuals were cheap labor and plentiful capital, including substantial foreign investment. All these factors combined to allow America to become one of the world's leading industrial nations. At the same time the American mind turned to individualism and the gospel of wealth.

Individualism encompassed the philosophy of self-achievement, while *the gospel of wealth* viewed wealth as the end-all and be-all of life. Taken together, these two ideas led to the belief that the American way was the making of money. The more money made, the higher the place in society. Added to this belief was the axiom that the wealthy should use their riches for the benefit of the community. The ideal held that government was to be a neutral party which neither helped nor hindered the accumulation of wealth. But this was hardly the case. In this free enterprise system, poverty was a fault—possibly even a sin. Wealthy men became heroes; individuals who went from rags-to-riches became legendary. One writer reflected this wealth-as-virtue philosophy:

> Even the poorest can be made to see this, and to agree that great sums gathered by some of their fellow citizens and spent for public purposes, from which the masses reap the principal benefit, are more valuable to them than if scattered among themselves in trifling amounts through the course of many years.

Intellectually, most Americans accepted financial success because it brought industrial growth. This industrial expansion was hastened by railroad building and consolidation.

Railroad Expansion

Phenomenal railroad growth occurred after the Civil War; by the early 1900s America possessed one-third of the world's railroad tracks. While early railroads were essentially local in service, the dream of a transcontinental line, which would link the Atlantic and the Pacific, was not new. During the 1840s, Asa Whitney dreamed of a railroad that would bring items from the Far East to the cities of the East Coast. His hopes were never realized. Gold discoveries in California, however, stimulated congressional action. After a spirited debate over location of the route, Congress passed two laws in 1862 and 1864 that authorized the Union Pacific and Central Pacific railroad companies to build a transcontinental railroad. Congress also offered the companies alternate ten-mile-square blocks of land along the tracks for each mile laid, as well as generous loans. By completion, the companies had received 54 million acres of public domain and $60 million in loans. The precedent of government assistance in the building of railroads had been set. On May 10, 1869, at Promontory Point, Utah, a golden spike was driven into the ground—the first transcontinental railroad had been completed. The transcontinental railroad was a reality, but railroad expansion had just begun.

With land grants and public loans, other railroads built west. The Northern Pacific railroad extended from St. Paul, Minnesota, to Portland, Oregon; the Atchison, Topeka, and Santa Fe railroad and the Southern Pacific railroad crossed the Southwest. Eastern lines also greatly consolidated their networks. By 1871 the federal government had given to the railroads more than 135

The joining of the Union Pacific and Central Pacific Railroads in May 1869 marked the completion of the transcontinental line.

million acres of land. This land, coupled with millions of dollars of interest-free loans, plus generous state policies, led to the creation of three transcontinental routes and eventual consolidation of smaller lines.

The rapid birth of a national railroad network led to overexpansion and financial disaster. By the 1870s hundreds of railroad companies had gone bankrupt. Too many lines were competing for the same markets. Many shippers had to constantly transfer goods from one short line to another. Out of financial necessity and convenience, consolidation became popular and eventually led to regional monopolies. With no competition, railroads would charge as much as the traffic would bear. Certain fiscal manipulators were responsible for the consolidations. One of the most successful was Cornelius Vanderbilt. In 20 years, "Commodore" Vanderbilt had created a railroad empire which included 4500 miles of track and $250 million in capital. Unscrupulous and power hungry, Vanderbilt purchased and consolidated railroads, and through deft stock manipulation and political bribery, extended his system from New York to Illinois. Other successful railroad magnates included James J. Hill, Collis P. Huntington, Leland Stanford, Edward H. Harriman, Jay Gould, and William

Vanderbilt. Most of these men viewed their railroad empires according to this philosophy: "The railroads are not run for the benefit of the dear public. Their cry is all nonsense. They are built for men who invest their money and expect to get a fair percentage on the same. . . . Let the public be damned."

Generous government policy plus increased consolidation led to frequent abuses. Corruption in the sale of railroad stock became a common practice, while discrimination in rates was also a fairly common practice. Rates were frequently lower for favored shippers. In fact, these shippers were also given part of their costs back in a practice known as *rebate*. It often cost a shipper more for a short trip, where competing lines were nonexistent, than a long one. To continue friendly government policies, the railroads gave free passes to influential people. These trips often resulted in lower taxes and favorable legislation.

The Credit Mobilier scandal, which surfaced during the presidency of Grant, exposed the extent of railroad abuses. During the 1870s and the 1880s stories of railroad manipulations frequently were circulated. In one year the Erie Railroad spent $70,000 for illegal practices and listed the amount in its books under an "India rubber account." While dishonest practices were often the exception rather than the rule, public sentiment began to turn against the railroads and demand government regulation.

While many groups were hurt by railroad abuses, farmers were hit especially hard. Through their Granges they pressured state legislatures to act. The result was a series of Granger laws that attempted to regulate railroad practices. The railroads now sought help from the courts. Initially, they received a major setback in the *Munn* v. *Illinois* case of 1877; in it, the Supreme Court ruled that the Illinois law which fixed maximum rates for grain storage was legal and that businesses involved with "public interest . . . . must submit to be controlled by the public for the common good." By 1886 justices sympathetic to the business community had reversed this decision in the case of *Wabash, St. Louis, and Pacific Railroad Company* v. *Illinois*. This case invalidated an Illinois law that regulated rates; the Court ruled that only the federal government could regulate interstate commerce.

Meanwhile, a Senate report that vividly described railroad abuses was made public. The time was ripe for national regulation. The Interstate Commerce Act of 1887 answered the public demand for federal action. This act forbade rate discrimination and provided that rates should be "reasonable and fair." Enforcement of the law was given to a five-man Interstate Commerce Commission, which listened to abuses and issued "cease and desist" orders. While this act seemed to bring effective regulation, it actually accomplished little because ultimate enforcement lay with the courts, and here the railroads had an advantage, for most justices believed competition was healthy. The

Return to the Gilded Age: Culture of the Industrial Era

Interstate Commerce Act was more important for future transportation control, but it did establish a precedent for government regulation.

While the unrestricted railroad boom often led to bankruptcy and monopoly, it did greatly benefit the national economy. Goods were now shipped from coast to coast. Natural resources were more easily utilized with the aid of railroads. Enormous amounts of materials and thousands of workers were employed in the building of the railroads. And the railroads brought settlers to the West and helped colonize America's last frontier. Certain key inventions such as the compressed-air brake and steel rails and bridges were essential to this boom. Other inventions also helped stimulate growth in certain industries.

Captains of Industry

Western Union, for example, utilized the invention of the telegraph. Western Union's alliance with the railroads made it one of America's prominent businesses. The invention of the telephone by Alexander Graham Bell in 1876 led to the development of nationwide communications. Guglielmo Marconi's experiments with the wireless and Thomas Alva Edison's invention of the stock ticker, phonograph, and incandescent lamp further changed the lifestyle of Americans and brought certain essential benefits to American industry. The typewriter and adding machine also changed business practices, while improved processes revolutionized the meatpacking and flour-milling industries. Refrigerator railroad cars made possible the nationwide sale of fresh meat. Edison, the "Wizard of Menlo Park," of course was the most productive inventor, and his inventions have served Americans well over the years. Utilizing these new inventions and techniques were shrewd business leaders. These men came from varied backgrounds, yet they shared an innate talent for organizing men and materials. They achieved success through large-scale production of goods. At times they appeared ruthless and ambitious, but this was an age of free enterprise and unrestricted competition. They lived according to the gospel of wealth, which equated success with the accumulation of money. While they became heroes of the age and were referred to as "captains of industry," they later became known as "robber barons," men of questionable morality who took advantage of poor laborers. Their names included Philip D. Armour, Gustavus Swift, Nelson Morris; others were Michael Cudahy in meatpacking, Cadwallader C. Washburn and Charles A. Pillsbury in flourmilling, and Gould and Vanderbilt in railroading. Dominant even among them were two industrial giants, John D. Rockefeller and Andrew Carnegie.

Certain changes in the oil and steel industries led to the rise of Rockefeller and Carnegie. Prior to 1849, petroleum oil was something that was noticed

Key inventions such as the sewing machine helped lead the way to the era of big business.

on the surfaces of springs and streams; it had been used by the Indians as a liniment and an illuminant, but it had few other uses. George Bissell, a New York lawyer, became intrigued with the strange substance, had it analyzed, and concluded that it would be valuable as a lubricant and for other uses. The great oil rush was on. Oil refineries sprang up in New York, Philadelphia, Pittsburgh, and Cleveland. The full potential of the oil industry, however, waited for John D. Rockefeller.

Meanwhile, the iron industry was unable to meet the needs of industrial America, yet the making of steel was too costly. In the 1870s and the 1880s, American William Kelley and Englishman Henry Bessemer developed a process that made the large-scale production of steel economically feasible. Steel plants, such as the Bethlehem Works, went up in Pennsylvania. The young steel industry was ready for a fiscal genius of the ilk of Andrew Carnegie.

John D. Rockefeller

Rockefeller rose from middle-class origins. One of five children, he learned excellent practical business training from his father, a wandering vendor of

John D. Rockefeller successfully used consolidation in his establishment of the Standard Oil Trust.

quack medicine and frequently a fugitive from the law. He was most influenced by his mother, who reared him with a rigid piety and stern supervision. At age seven he began raising turkeys for a living, but soon he learned that money could work for him by itself. "It was better to let money be my slave than to be the slave of money," said Rockefeller later. So he became a money-lender. As a person, he was extremely quiet, shy, and reserved. At age sixteen, he became a bookkeeper on the Cleveland docks and revealed his propensity for efficiency. On a salary of $15 per month, he saved $400 in 3 years. He took work seriously and had little time for social life. At night he frequently talked to his pillow and read the Bible, "These intimate conversations had a great influence on my life; not to get puffed up with any foolish notions. . . ." When he married, he did not take off one day of work. One of his great desires in life was to be wealthy. This desire would be realized.

Becoming a merchant in grain, hay, and meat, when the Civil War broke out, Rockefeller prospered with the sharp rise in prices. During the war he became interested in the oil industry and began investing in oil refining. By 1866 he was the largest refiner in Cleveland, and by 1872 he controlled 21 refineries there. His business practices consisted of efficiency, price-slashing, railroad rebates, and keeping ample cash in reserve. During the Depression of 1873 his ready reserves came in handy, and he began to buy out his competitors. And by the end of the decade he was master of an oil-refining monopoly. His price-cutting, thrift, price wars, and overall industrial efficiency made him master of the oil industry.

As a person, Rockefeller did not take advantage of his success; he continued to live a rather strict, disciplined life. Although he was wealthy, he was not part of the emerging wealthy society. His life was not simple, however; and oil refining caused him many legal problems. He had favored consolidation in industry, reaching the apex of consolidation himself in 1882 with the formation of the Standard Oil Trust. Nine trustees were given the capital stock of 27 competing oil companies and, in essence, were given control over these companies. Stockholders merely received stock certificates which in return entitled them to dividends. This final consolidation brought fantastic profits. The trust form of monopoly brought an end to price wars and competition, and new trust monopolies followed in the cotton, lead, sugar, whiskey, and cordage industries.

Andrew Carnegie

The dominance of Rockefeller in oil was paralleled by the empire of Carnegie in steel. In 1847 Carnegie came to America with his Scottish parents as an immigrant. As most immigrants, he saw America as the land of opportunity, yet opportunity did not seem to immediately avail itself to him. After working in a cloth mill for 12 hours a day at $1.50 a week, he found work as a telegraph clerk; then, at the age of 24, he became a division superintendant of the Pennsylvania Railroad. He was ambitious and hardworking and began to invest in stocks. He even mortgaged his mother's home to invest in American Express Company stock. He began speculating in Pullman sleeping cars, and then he turned to the iron industry.

By the early 1870s, when he moved to the steel industry, he had already become a millionaire. This small, charming man, who formed the Edgar Thompson Steel Works in 1873, decided to get vertical control of the steel industry. This meant he would control all aspects of the industry: natural resources, processing, and marketing. While he did not share Rockefeller's penchant for monopoly, he did follow Rockefeller's lead in efficient administration and organization. At the same time, Carnegie's partnership with Henry C. Frick gave him an associate who could run his business with extreme efficiency, freeing Carnegie's time for travel and promotion. Vertical integration was achieved, and, by 1892, the Carnegie Steel Company was formed and was producing over one-fourth of the nation's steel.

Andrew Carnegie, a Scottish immigrant, used vertical control of the steel industry to earn him the title of captain of industry.

Now that he was earning over $25 million per year he turned to travel and writing. His writings attempted to justify the moral role he believed the wealthy were obligated to fulfill in society. Before he died, he attempted to live up to his beliefs by giving away more than $400 million to libraries, universities, and other charities.

Finance Capitalism

But the day of the self-made industrialist was coming to an end, and the era of the banker-capitalist was becoming a reality. By 1900 the forming of large industrial giants involved huge sums of capital. A logical source of this capital were bankers, who were willing to invest as long as they received a sizeable benefit in return. This trend, known as "finance capitalism," gave birth to the dominance of Wall Street. At the heart of investment banking was John Pierpont Morgan. Morgan was born wealthy; the son of a Yankee banker, he soon became the New York agent for his father's firm. Once he had founded his own banking house with international connections, he entered a very successful career of money manipulation. Initially, he used his skills in reorganizing and consolidating railroads. Under his guidance, bankers began to control the financial affairs of railroad lines and then to serve in management positions. Morgan now turned to the steel industry; he decided to initiate new combinations rather than to manipulate old ones. After repeated failures, Morgan purchased Carnegie Steel for a half-billion dollars. This led the way to the formation in 1901 of that supercorporation the United States Steel Corporation, which controlled three-fifths of the steel industry and was capitalized at $1.5 billion dollars. Personally, Morgan was a homely man with a big, red nose and expensive tastes, but as a businessman he was unequalled. His use of finance capitalism led to more supercorporations in the early years of the twentieth century.

During this age of unrestricted competition and monopoly, business leaders believed that government had no right to regulate free enterprise. Government protection of the system was necessary, but government regulation was unnecessary. To help ensure this *laissez-faire* system, many businessmen

John Pierpont Morgan was a wizard at finance capitalism with its emphasis on the formation of supercorporations through manipulation of large sums of money.

participated directly in politics. The Senate became a "millionaires club," with a number of wealthy men in it. Both the Democratic and Republican parties were safe havens to businessmen, but the Republican party was the safest. And state and federal courts condoned business practices. Certain states, such as New Jersey, a home of lenient business laws, became popular places for incorporation. More and more industrialists invoked the name of God and the almighty dollar in the same breath. Rockefeller wrote of his trust, "God gave it to me." By 1890 corporations controlled half of all property in America. Were unrestricted monopolies necessary for the benefits of mass production?

For many Americans the evils of industrialization were beginning to outweigh the good. Public pressure began to build during the late 1800s. The Granger laws had failed to limit the railroads, but Congress had responded with the Interstate Commerce Act. Public pressure against consolidation led to the passage of the Sherman Antitrust Act of 1890. This act stipulated that "every contract, combination in form of trust or otherwise, or conspiracy, in restraint of trade or commerce among the several states, or with foreign nations, is hereby declared to be illegal." While this act appeared to answer the public's prayers, it did not. The wording in the law was too vague, and there were too many loopholes. The courts again interpreted the law in favor of businessmen. By the twentieth century, effective government regulation of big business had not yet occurred. In fact, one of the greatest challenges to the monopolies came not from government but from the workers themselves through national labor unions.

The Rise of Big Labor

The need for workers greatly increased after the Civil War. Yet their conditions did not improve. Employers believed that laborers were at their mercy and should work by their standards; they believed labor unions, like government, interfered with the free enterprise system and should not be encouraged or even allowed. Workers had experimented with national labor unions before the Civil War, but with little success. Government was in no mood to pass legislation to regulate labor conditions. Big business had built powerful "combinations" with great success, so workers also turned to national combinations as the only way to challenge big business.

The first attempt was undertaken by William Sylvis. Sylvis, son of a wagonmaker, first planned to bring all iron molders together in a National Molders' Union. His plans were temporarily delayed by the Civil War. He eventually formed the Iron Molders' International Union, which became one of the strongest unions in the country. Sylvis had a unique ability for organization; this talent was evident in this union. In 1868 the unions virtually disappeared after a prolonged strike; this strike caused Sylvis to become disillusioned with conventional labor activity, and he turned to a new reform union—the National Labor Union.

The National Labor Union, formed in 1866, was an attempt to bring all workers together in a common program. The new union believed that typical labor protest would not work and that the only answer to workers' needs was political reform. The National Labor Union included in its demands an eight-hour workday, the establishment of cooperatives, cheap currency, restrictions on immigration, and the creation of a National Department of Labor. While its goals were often idealistic, it became a powerful voice for labor when Sylvis became head of the union in 1868. Sylvis's administrative skills brought the union creative leadership and made him the most powerful labor leader in the country. At his death the following year, the organization entered national politics more actively than ever; and by 1872 the union had transformed into the National Labor Reform Party. However, the new workers' party eventually disappeared from the scene when labor turned away from political action and returned to strict labor organizing.

The depression of 1873, rising unemployment, and the growing power of the captains of industry caused the worker to enter a period of frustration, unrest, and even violence. The rise of unemployment caused workers to compete for jobs at lower pay and poorer conditions. Industrialists became acutely wary of union activity. Many unemployed even held demonstrations and organized protest. In 1874 in New York at Tompkins Square, a meeting of unemployed had been scheduled to demonstrate to city officials the need for help. Believing that radicals were to stir up the crowd, city fathers cancelled the meeting at the last minute. News of the cancellation did not reach the thousands of workers who gathered for the protest; they were surprised to find themselves attacked by mounted police. The *New York Times* noted that "the scrambles of the mob as the officers advanced were not unamusing." This incident, known as the Tompkins Square Riot, was described by the press as an example of foreign intrigue and radical meddling; the unemployed received little favorable sympathy from most Americans, who knew little of the labor situation.

Since many Americans distrusted immigrants coming to America, they began to blame all labor disturbances on them. In 1874 and 1875 the Miners' National Association became involved in a series of bloody strikes, which led to open war between strikers and the police. The public now blamed a secret organization composed of Irish immigrants, popularly known as the Molly

Maguires. They became the scapegoat for the miners' labor unrest; 14 "Mollies" were imprisoned and 10 were hanged. But foreign influence could not always explain labor unrest.

During the 1870s railroad workers found themselves working for long hours with low pay; many of them were even forced to leave labor unions. In 1877 railroad wages were cut arbitrarily and strikes broke out. One newspaper wrote, "It is wrong to call this a strike, it is a labor revolution." Strikes and, inevitably, violence occurred at all leading railroad centers, especially in Pittsburgh and Baltimore. In Pittsburgh most citizens sympathized with the workers. Ordered to action, the local militia refused. Troops were called in from Philadelphia to battle the striking workers and a real "war" ensued. The troops were pushed into a railroad roundhouse, where they defended themselves against bullets and burning railroad cars. After fighting their way out, they found themselves surrounded by a mob of approximately 5000 persons; the mob destroyed the railroad station and then turned on the town. The strike only ended after a wild weekend of looting—at a cost of millions. Nationally, the media was against the workers; the strike was described as "a revolution, an attempt of communists and vagabonds to coerce society, an endeavor to undermine American institutions." A preacher wrote, "I do not say that a dollar a day is enough to support a working man . . . . and five children if a man insists on smoking and drinking beer. But the man who cannot live on bread and water is not fit to live." A similar battle between strikers and the militia took place in Baltimore. The public was appalled by the violent strikes of 1877. Suspected foreign influences and violent strikes hurt the workers cause, yet workers began to realize their potential power and the need for organization. And labor violence was not to end with the 1870s.

During the 1870s and the 1880s certain foreign-born labor leaders interpreted labor problems in terms of revolution. Although they composed a small minority of labor leaders and had little appeal, they did attract a great deal of negative publicity. These radicals, or anarchists, often preached revolutionary violence and issued pamphlets, such as "A Manual of Instruction in the Use and Preparation of Nitroglycerine, Dynamite, Gun Cotton, Fulminating Mercury, Bombs, Fuses, and Poisons." They instructed workers to place dynamite, for example, "in the immediate vicinity of a lot of rich loafers who live by the sweat of other people's brows and light the fuse. A most cheerful and gratifying result will follow." It is too bad that many Americans connected them with the labor movement.

In May 1886 a national strike occurred in support of the eight-hour workday. In Chicago, a hotbed for the shorter-workday movement, four strikers died at the hands of police at the McCormick Harvester plant. Anarchists called for a meeting at Haymarket Square to protest police brutality. "To arms,

The Haymarket Square meeting in Chicago in 1886 broke into open violence with a bomb explosion.

we call you, to arms." Police and city officials attended to avert violence, but none occurred. This peaceful protest was just about over when 200 policemen ordered the crowd to go home. At that moment a bomb exploded; seven police were killed. The police then opened fire on the crowd and a full-scale riot was on. The public demanded justice. Eight leading anarchists were tried and found guilty on rather flimsy evidence. Four were eventually executed. Again, labor had lost another battle. The public viewed labor as a haven for revolutionaries and hence suspect. The one labor union that was hurt most by the Haymarket Square Riot was the one which was becoming the first national labor union—the Knights of Labor.

Knights of Labor

In 1869 a secret society of frustrated tailors was formed under the name of Knights of Labor. Since many employers were firing workers who belonged to

Return to the Gilded Age: Culture of the Industrial Era

labor unions, this group retained its secrecy and rituals for years. Although early members of the union were skilled workers, Uriah Stephens, its leader, planned to expand it into a union that would encompass skilled and unskilled workers alike. The unfavorable economic conditions of the 1870s hindered its growth. Still, the union experienced some increase in its local and district assemblies. In 1878 the First National Assembly of the Knights of Labor was formed. Although, as before, most members were skilled workers, the union welcomed all workers, skilled and unskilled, male and female. All were invited except bankers, stockbrokers, professional gamblers, lawyers, and "those who in any way derive their living from the manufacture or sale of intoxicating liquors."

The Knights voiced most of the traditional labor demands: an eight-hour day, cooperatives, a bureau of labor, better pay, and the adoption of a graduated-income tax. Aware of the public feelings toward labor violence and strikes, the organization took a very cautious attitude toward strikes. Uriah Stephens described the great dream he had for the union:

I do not claim any power of prophecy, but I can see ahead of me an organization that will cover the globe. It will include men and women of every craft, creed, and color. It will cover every race worth saving.

And blacks indeed were allowed in the Knights organization. This was a universal union for all workers. It seemed to fulfill a real need, for though it had fewer than 9000 members in 1878, by 1888 it could boast more than 800,000 members.

During the 1880s the Knights reached their high point. This was due greatly to the prosperity of the 1880s. It was also at this time that a new leader, Terence Powderly, took control of the union. Powderly, like Stephens, was a humanitarian, an idealist, and a social reformer. But Powderly did not appeal to the average worker. He was an immaculate dresser with impeccable manners and a devout teetotaler. His appeal to high ideals often moved no one to action. The fact that he was egotistical did not help his cause either. Powderly was known to brag, "The position I hold is too big for any ten men." While the union's strike policies were generally cautious, some successful strikes against railroads began to move them to greater activity. But an unsuccessful railroad strike in 1886 and an unsuccessful attempt to establish cooperatives hurt their cause. Nor had the Haymarket Square riot helped. Still, one of the greatest weaknesses of the union was the composition of the union itself. The presence of both skilled and unskilled workers led to disharmony; and both groups of workers wondered why they were in the same organization with farmers. By the early 1890s the union declined, turned to agrarian politics, and disappeared. No one factor—the leaders, social reform goals, failure of the cooperatives, rapid overexpansion, unsuccessful strikes, the Haymarket Square riot—can account for the union's demise. But the union had served a vital function, for it had filled a need for organization at a time when laborers had little bargaining power and less public sympathy. It had pressured the government to set up a Bureau of Labor Statistics, and it also led indirectly to the founding of the first permanent national union, the American Federation of Labor.

Gompers and the A.F.L.

The only national labor union to survive the labor turmoil in good shape was the International Cigar Maker's Union, which was under the leadership of Samuel Gompers and Adolph Strassar. Gompers and Strassar believed in the formation of independent craft unions within a national structure and in the practical approach to unionism. They were appalled by the political-reform movement of the National Labor Union and the mingling of skilled and unskilled workers in the Knights of Labor. Nor could they completely condone the cooperative experiment. Gompers and Strasser believed unions should strive for immediate, reasonable goals, such as shorter hours, better pay, and improved working conditions. The strength and durability of the craft union would come from its initiation fee and high dues, its system of sickness and death benefits, and its strict centralized administration. Strikes were not out of the question, but they would be undertaken very carefully and with specific, reasonable demands in mind.

This idea of a loose organization of independent craft unions (or trade unions) led in 1886 to the birth of the American Federation of Labor; Samuel Gompers was its first president. Born of Jewish parents in London, Gompers learned of unions from his father. Initially influenced by socialistic ideas, he later adopted a common-sense philosophy of labor. He believed labor must not strive for political reform but for legitimate goals within the capitalistic system. He was hardly an idealist, but, to Gompers, idealism had not seemed to work. Physically, he was short-legged, stocky, capped by a massive head, and wore large spectacles. He looked and acted tough; he spent much time in the beer parlors with the men and was considered "one of the boys." When representatives of 25 skilled-labor unions had decided to form the A.F.L., Gompers had been their logical choice for president.

Once in charge, Gompers immediately put his realistic philosophy into action. The A.F.L. did not believe in strong central control, as the Knights had. The central council ruled on matters of national concern but did not interfere in the affairs of the member unions. "Strict recognition of the autonomy of each trade" was observed. In the late 1800s both the Knights and the A.F.L. appealed to the skilled workers. The bitter disputes between these two national unions hindered their mutual growth. But the greatest blow to both came with the depression of 1893. In fact, this depression was the death blow to the Knights of Labor. The conservative policy of the A.F.L. led to its survival and growth; its membership reached the one million mark by the twentieth century.

The depression of 1893 brought increased frustration for workers. Labor violence, which paralleled that of the 1870s, began with a series of disastrous strikes, which first occurred in 1892. The dispute between the Carnegie Steel Company and the Amalgamated Association of Iron, Steel, and Tin Workers, known as the Homestead Strike, was the most noteable. Workers at Carnegie's Homestead Steel plant in Pennsylvania had assumed they would be sharing in the enormous profits of the plant. But events had gone differently. Wage cuts caused the Amalgamated Union to strike. Henry Frick, Carnegie's labor boss, called in Pinkerton detectives and strike breakers. Violence occurred; a running battle between workers and Pinkertons resulted in deaths on both sides. While the state militia was restoring order, many workers in Carnegie's other plants walked off the job. Public sympathy with the workers was brief, for in the midst of this dispute a crazed anarchist named Alexander Berkman burst into Frick's office and shot and stabbed him. This unrelated attack caused public furor against the strikers. The steel union was destroyed, and steel unionism would not appear again for many years.

The Pullman Strike

Labor suffered another setback with the Pullman Strike of 1894. Prior to the 1890s railroad workers had not formed a national union. The formation in 1893 of the American Railway Union, under the leadership of Eugene Debs, provided a union that encompassed all workers on trains and in the factories, such as the Pullman Palace Car factory. The workers in the Pullman factory lived and worked in Pullman's own town; in many ways their lives were in the hands of Pullman. With the depression of 1893 their salaries were cut four times, but the prices of necessities in the town were not reduced. Workers sought redress, but Pullman would have nothing to do with it. Debs was asked to arbitrate, but Pullman responded, "There is nothing to arbitrate." The Railway Union then asked other workers for a sympathetic boycott of all Pullman property in support of the striking Pullman workers. Thousands of workers left their jobs, and all rail lines west of Chicago were tied up.

The General Managers Association, representing the railroads, turned to Attorney General Richard Olney for help. Olney, a former railway lawyer and a member of the boards of several railroads, sympathetically requested that President Cleveland call out federal troops to end the strike. Cleveland refused; there was no good reason to call out federal troops. Olney sent more deputy marshals to Chicago; at the same time railroad officials won from the courts an injunction ordering all persons "to refrain from interfering with or stopping any of the business of any of the railroads in Chicago engaged as common carriers" on the grounds that such action was an unlawful restraint of commerce. Confrontation and violence occurred. In response, Cleveland sent in federal troops and wrote, "If it takes every dollar in the Treasury and every soldier in the United States to deliver a postal card in Chicago, that postal card shall be delivered." The 2000 troops sent in were supposedly there to "protect the mail." More violence occurred and thousands of railroad cars were destroyed. Debs was jailed for violation of the injunction. The strike was broken.

Debs, deeply disillusioned, became an apostle to the cause of socialism. Labor again had lost; a powerful union had been destroyed. The captains of industry again reigned supreme. And now they had been given the court injunction as a weapon to be used against labor unions, whose strikes were interpreted as restraints of commerce. Although a congressional commission eventually would blame the Pullman company for the strike, it was too late. The twentieth century dawned with business supreme and labor on the ropes. Only the A.F.L. survived the turmoil of the 1890s. Repeatedly Gompers praised the strikers and their leaders, but the A.F.L. stayed neutral and weathered the storm.

Urbanization

When the Civil War broke out, America was a rural nation with only 20 percent of the population living in cities. But, according to the census of 1920, by that year the majority of Americans lived in cities. There were many factors responsible for this change. Certain cities became key centers of industry and attracted thousands of workers. Cleveland became the center of the oil industry; Minneapolis became the flour-processing center; and Chicago and Kansas City became meatpacking centers. Industry not only provided cities with employment but also provided them with mass products and technological changes that made life in the cities easier. Indoor plumbing and electric lights were conveniences that lured people to the cities; the use of the telephone

Return to the Gilded Age: Culture of the Industrial Era

quickened communications; and the city physically kept pace through improved transportation facilities. While the pull of the city was very strong, the push from the farm was equally strong. Farmers were suffering from periods of economic distress and were losing battles with industrial giants, such as the railroads. To leave economic insecurity for a better job in an improved environment was the desire of countless thousands. But the growing urban population was not composed merely of disgruntled farmers; millions of immigrants were flooding in.

The New Immigrants

During the 1880s over five million immigrants came to the United States. These newcomers were different from the old immigrants because they came from Southern and Eastern Europe. Italians, Russians, Poles, Turks, Jews, and Rumanians were becoming citizens of urban centers. These new arrivals, who were so different from the immigrants from Western Europe, found much opposition. It was believed that they had come from backward lands and many of them were Catholic or Jewish. Everywhere they faced hostility, both from native Americans, who were beginning to lobby for limited immigration, and from the older immigrants, who were moving out of the central city and leaving places for these new immigrants. The word *mafia* began to be used to describe the Italian mobsters who controlled the new "Little Italies" in America with an iron hand. "Little Poland" and "Little Italy" were names of common ethnic ghettos in the industrial cities. Many urban problems were blamed on these people—and industrial cities did have a lot of problems.

Urban Problems

Cities literally expanded overnight; this rapid transition caused severe housing problems. Many newcomers moved into old, dilapidated buildings in the central parts of the cities. Many city planners believed that the best way to provide housing was not to build out from the inner city but to build *up*. So by the 1880s tenement buildings were being built rapidly; these buildings were five or six stories high and contained small apartments with inadequate ventilation and only one bathroom on each floor. Tenements became the blight of the city. By the twentieth century 430,000 tenements existed in New York City. The New York Tenement House Law, which required a window in the bedroom of newly built tenements, was considered quite progressive. These buildings led to overcrowded, squalid conditions that promoted crime and violence.

Public services also were lacking in most of the large cities. Many fire departments still were operated on a volunteer basis, so fire was a major fear.

The great Chicago fire of 1871 was a major example of the potential danger from fire. Sanitary conditions were pathetic. Human and industrial waste was poured into nearby lakes and rivers. Drinking water often was scarce and families were forced to share toilets. Garbage collection was sorely lacking, and piles of refuse accumulated in streets and vacant lots. Horse manure filled many of the streets, and sometimes even dead horses were left to rot in them. It is not surprising that diseases, such as small pox, cholera, and typhus, swept cities. To add to housing problems, fire danger, and poor sanitary conditions was the noise factor. Cities were noisy. Wagons and horses brought a constant clatter to the streets. Meanwhile thousands of homeless unemployed roamed the city avenues; in New York in 1890 there were more than 14,000 homeless paupers there, who drank stale beer, ate rolls at 2-cent restaurants, and slept in 10- or 15-cent flop houses. It is no wonder that cities were training grounds for criminals. "Robber's Roost" and "Murderer's Alley" in New York were names indicative of the rising crime rate. With all these problems it is not surprising that a reform movement appeared.

One of the most influential propagandists for reform was Jacob Riis, a newspaper reporter who made a detailed photographic study of the industrial

The life-style of a New York slum family is revealed in this 1910 photograph.

city. He diagnosed the problems of tenement life, and his photographs were a classic study of human degradation. Although he himself accomplished little concrete reform, he led the way for other humanitarians who made positive efforts to relieve urban conditions. Creative architects turned from designing tenements to designing skyscrapers and other projects to beautify cities. City parks began to appear. Public and private relief agencies sprang up. Youth clubs, such as the Boy Scouts of America, the Camp Fire Girls, and the Girl Scouts, had been formed by the 1900s.

One post Civil War institution to deal directly with the slum dweller was known as the settlement house. Based on a London model, the settlement house was a community center for the slum dweller that provided a variety of services from babysitting to education. The most famous example was that of Jane Addams's Hull House in Chicago, established in 1889. Here volunteers came "to share the lives of the poor." These houses helped slum dwellers to rise from their pathetic place in society and to begin to cope with city life. While settlement houses were early training grounds for social workers, they also served as centers where women reformers, who were very aware of discrimination in the male-dominated society, began to meet.

The Emerging American Woman

Technological advances in the period after the Civil War brought a real revolution to the role of the American woman. Sewing machines, washing machines, commercially prepared food, and improved cooking facilities released women from traditional household drudgery, allowed them leisure time to pursue creative work, and led the way to the reform movement of the twentieth century. One profession in which women had become accepted was that of teaching. By the 1900s over 80 percent of all teachers were female; this situation led to women's influence over many facets of education and to continued pressure on schools of higher education to admit women. A number of women's colleges such as Vassar, Smith, and Radcliffe met this need. Although discrimination also was weakening in most professions, still, few women turned to them because of strong social disapproval.

With more time to utilize their creative talents, many women became involved in organizations for social reform. The Woman's Christian Temperance Union was formed in 1874 by a group of Midwestern women. This organization was not just a haven for radicals, such as Carrie Nation who would enter saloons with an axe and proceed to smash the place. Its major guiding

With the arrival of the twentieth century the suffrage
movement was beginning to pick up steam.

spirit was Francis Willard, whose administrative skills turned the organization
into a very powerful one. Nor was temperance the only cause of the organization; Willard was very much interested in creating an organization that
would unite women across the country on such issues as women's suffrage.
Over 200,000 women were members of this organization by 1900. The death
of Willard caused the organization to turn exclusively to the issue of temperance.

Another training ground for female reformers was the urban settlement
house. Jane Addams, founder of Hull House, was touched by the helplessness

of the slum dweller and believed that charity work should involve direct action. She challenged the slum through her settlement-house work in the community. Not only did settlement workers provide a higher standard of living for the urban dweller, but they also challenged city officials to reform. Out of the settlement-house experiences emerged women reformers such as Florence Kelley, Mary Anderson, and Grace Abbott. Florence Kelley helped foster protection of consumers with the formation of the National Consumers League.

In this era of industrial growth the working woman was becoming much more commonplace. Statistics indicate that by 1900 women comprised more than 20 percent of the total work force. Most of these women were paid poorly and exploited constantly; and their working conditions were often pathetic. While women workers had been trying to organize since the early 1800s, the Knights of Labor was the first organization to accept women on an equal basis. Eventually 113 women's assemblies were chartered; Leonora M. Barry became one of the dominant leaders of this movement. But the Knights of Labor died out in the 1890s and the A.F.L. showed little interest in the cause of the woman laborer. It would not be for years that an interest in the plight of the working women would be shown again by organized labor.

Women's Suffrage

Suffrage had been one of the major goals of two female activists, Elizabeth Cady Stanton and Susan B. Anthony. After the Civil War, Lucy Stone, an avowed feminist, pushed for a feminist organization that would include both women and men and caused a real split in the suffrage movement. Of course, the liquor lobby was extremely active in the suppression of the women's vote because it believed that women would vote for prohibition. In addition, conservative males, a majority in society, feared the growing political power of women. But the fact that Wyoming and Utah had granted women suffrage indicated that suffrage could be delayed but not postponed forever. In this changing industrial-urban age women were making a significant contribution to society. Significant changes were taking place in American religion, too.

Religion in the Urban-Industrial Age

Cities with their social problems brought new challenges to the churches. The more traditional churches, however, were not the answer. Churches had to cope with urban problems on a daily basis, so new urban churches were born.

Nondenominational city missions were established on the pattern of the Water Street Mission of New York, which was founded shortly after the Civil War by Jerry MacAuley, a converted drunkard and burglar. These rescue missions offered food, shelter, and fervid preaching to guide derelicts to a useful life. In the same vein, the Young Men's Christian Association devoted itself to physical fulfillment with a Christian emphasis, while the Salvation Army brought ministry and music to the urban poor.

The Protestants responded to urban problems with the institutional church. Finding its origins among the Episcopal and Congregational churches of New York City, the institutional church offered practical programs as well as religious training. Gyms, reading rooms, and day nurseries were added to scriptural study. But new and reorganized churches were not enough; the entire philosophy of religion needed to be transformed. Churches not only needed to remedy the evils of society but needed to change the very direction of society so that these evils would not be possible. Thus was born the "social gospel."

Washington Gladden and Walter Rauschenbusch were the major proponents of this belief. Gladden, pastor of a Congregational church in Cleveland, believed that wealth dominated society and that workers must organize and strike. He also felt that churches must actively bring Christianity into society and accomplish social change. Rauschenbusch, a Baptist clergyman, preached social reform through income tax, public housing, and minimum wage laws. Theirs was a religion of social reform. While their criticism of contemporary society brought few changes, they did add their voices to a movement for reform that crystalized with the beginning of the twentieth century.

Darwin and Religion

Churches at this time also were being hit hard by the writings of many new sociologists and psychologists who tended to reduce religion to a mere social phenomenon. No other writer questioned traditional religion more than Charles Darwin in his book *On the Origin of Species.* The Book of Genesis stated that the earth and all living things were created in six days; but Darwin described the process as an evolution that lasted millions of years. Genesis pictured God's creation of Adam and Eve; Darwin postulated that the human being was a complex species who evolved slowly from more simple species. Genesis said that man was made in the image of God; Darwin said he was made in the image of an animal. Who was right, Darwin or the Bible? Could the Bible be literally believed? Crowds gathered to hear Robert G. Ingersoll, "the notorious infidel," who challenged the Bible with lectures such as "The

God," "Mistakes of Moses," and "Why I Am an Agnostic." Catholics and Protestants alike reacted to this challenge in two ways. The conservatives completely rejected this scientific heresy; the liberals attempted to reconcile religion with the new ideas.

Most of the conservative opposition to Darwinism, was based on the belief in the divine origin of the Bible. Charles Hodge became one of the ablest conservative theologians; he wrote of Darwinism: "A more absolutely incredible theory was never propounded for acceptance among men." Conservatives believed Darwinism had to be rejected because it led to a nonreligious explanation of mankind and to atheism.

Many articulate religious thinkers and writers defended the liberal position by attempting to reconcile Darwin and the Bible. Henry Ward Beecher, pastor of Plymouth Congregational Church, believed that an intelligent interpretation of the Bible was in order. Beecher, "a cordial Christian evolutionist," demonstrated how evolution merely reinforced Christian faith in the Bible. Lyman Abbott and others attempted to preserve God's word and at the same time restate the essential doctrines of Christianity in terms that would be intelligible. The liberals now had to reconcile the truth of the Bible with this new scientific approach. This "higher criticism," as the new approach was called, questioned certain parts of the Old Testament, no longer accepting the literal truth of such stories as the flood and the parting of the Red Sea. The application of science to religion led to an ongoing struggle between liberals and conservatives over the Bible. Heresy trials took place; new ministerial training schools were established and fundamental Bible schools were born. This struggle would last well into the twentieth century.

While American religion responded to changes and challenges certain trends continued. Revivalism, for example, was very much in evidence. Mentioned earlier was the evangelist Dwight Moody, a former shoe salesman who became interested in urban missionary work (see Chapter 2). In the 1870s he conducted a series of urban revivals in England. Returning to America, he applied his methods to urban dwellers. His revivals were not as emotional as the Western revivals, but they attempted to instill a sense of old-fashioned Christianity. This self-proclaimed preacher won thousands of converts with his keen power of salesmanship. Others tried to take advantage of the excitement generated by the Moody revivals, but only Billy Sunday in the 1890s was able to sustain the enthusiasm. Sunday was a former baseball player who conducted wild revivals. Many times in his preaching he had to pause because he felt faint or was about to fall unconscious. His use of baseball terms in his preaching had great appeal to athletic Christians: By "striking out the devil," and "sliding into salvation," Billy Sunday won thousands of converts. The

Former baseball player Billy Sunday preached a religion of emotion.

great upheaval connected with industrialism and urbanization not only brought changes to religion, but also to education, science, and literature.

Education, Science, and Literature

Urbanization and industrialization demanded new directions in education. Public education, once a dream, now became a reality. Education was forced to meet new social changes. American society was getting much more complex; literacy became more essential. Secondary education, which had been almost totally in the hands of private individuals up to the time of the Civil War, gradually became a public concern. By the early 1900s there were over 7000 high schools, totaling in an enrollment of over 1 million. Technological changes demanded more vocational training. Subjects such as bookkeeping, typing, agriculture, woodworking, and metalworking were introduced into the curriculum. American education finally was becoming universal.

Teaching methods also were changing. John Dewey introduced a system of progressive education, which allowed children to be put into challenging environments and to react to the best of their ability. Traditional learning by rote memorization and strict discipline came under attack. Practical education or "learning by doing" came into vogue. Compulsory attendance laws became more popular, but enforcement of them was spotty. By 1907 only about one-third of students who entered elementary school ever graduated (see Chart 10-1).

Higher education also responded to the need for more and different education. The Morrill Act of 1862 established state land-grant colleges that taught agricultural methods and vocational subjects. While curriculums included a large number of required courses during the first two years of college, more elective subjects were added during the last two years. In 1876 John Hopkins University instituted America's first graduate school for advanced study. In general, American education began to respond to the complexities of the industrial age and the need for a new focus in education.

New Developments in Science

Science and medicine kept pace with social change. Prior to the Civil War, American science had been concerned with practical research and immediate results. Research for the sake of research had been virtually nonexistent in America. After the Civil War drastic scientific changes occurred: practical research continued, but long-term research projects were established. Government assistance encouraged many scientific developments. The United States Weather Bureau and United States Geological Survey were founded. These bureaus became pioneers in their respective fields. Paleontology became a separate discipline, and Othniel C. Marsh became its first American professor. Henry A. Rowland and Albert A. Michelson were great American physicists,

Chart 10-1
High School and College Graduates, 1870–1910

Year	High school	College
1870	16,000	9,371
1880	23,634	10,353
1890	43,731	15,539
1900	94,883	27,410
1910	151,429	37,199

whose experiments in the measurement of light helped influence Albert Einstein's theory of relativity. Research also focused on the human mind and heredity. Humans and the universe around them came under close scrutiny.

The most important scientific achievements were in the field of medicine. American medicine had been a very weak art. Doctors were poorly trained; they had treated diseases rather than studied the causes of diseases. Medical training had been similar to the two-year training of apprentices in skilled labor. With little research and experimentation, America was far behind European medicine. In fact, many of America's best doctors had studied in Europe. Reform was demanded in medical schools. Harvard began to apply research and experimentation to American medical training. By the 1890s Johns Hopkins Medical School had instituted dramatic changes and had become one of the best schools in the world. Better medical training brought results, too, with the elimination of many dread diseases. Dr. Walter Reed was a pioneer in the study of yellow fever; Dr. Howard T. Ricketts and Theobald Smith brought the end to many dreaded animal illnesses. Typhoid fever and tuberculosis came under close scrutiny; a scientific approach to diet and sanitation was also introduced. Science and medicine made remarkable progress during the industrial era.

The rapid changes in American society caused many assumptions about humans and society to be questioned. Darwin had shocked the religious world; now certain writers began to apply this theory of "the survival of the fittest" to society. The new philosophy was known as Social Darwinism. During this age of unrestricted economic competition, the idea of the survival of the fittest seemed logical. The industrial giants Rockefeller and Carnegie seemed obviously to be among the fittest. Herbert Spencer, William Graham Sumner, and John Fiske were the ablest proponents of this theory, which helped to justify what was going on in the business world. They were strongly criticized by Lester Ward, often called the "father of sociology"; he wrote that unrestricted competition and the lack of government control actually handicapped American progress and led to frustration. Economist Thorstein Veblen also criticized Social Darwinism. He was especially distrustful of the wealthy, who he believed were social parasites. According to Veblen, technical rather than business leaders should run industry. In his *Theory of the Leisure Class* he argued that economists should adopt newer economic theories and more closely scrutinize economic facts.

Criticism of the establishment continued with the writings of Henry George and Edward Bellamy. George saw the great distance between rich and poor and argued that that gap must be narrowed. In his book *Progress and Poverty* he reasoned that poverty in the United States was due to the unearned

Henry George in his book *Progress and Poverty* suggested the single tax as the panacea for American poverty.

value of the land, since land was the stronghold of wealth. To end poverty he introduced the idea of a single tax on land that would make idle land unprofitable, would reduce the size of land holdings, and eventually would bring social equality. His book became a best seller, and his single-tax idea swept the country. Many single-tax clubs were formed, but no results occurred. His ideas stimulated discussion of the reasons for poverty and eventually led to property-tax reforms in the twentieth century.

Edward Bellamy offered a different challenge to the prevailing economics. His book *Looking Backward* described America from a viewpoint in the year 2000. Bellamy envisioned a future America in which government controlled all citizens; individuals between 21 and 45 served in an industrial army, socialism was dominant, and credit cards had replaced money. The year 2000 would begin in America an age of complete socialism with no financial worries, for each individual would share in the total production of the nation. Bellamy's book caused Americans in the late 1800s to analyze their society and question its direction.

During this time psychology and philosophy split into separate disciplines. John Dewey was greatly responsible for this split. Philosophers traditionally had studied ideas; Dewey now wanted to take ideas and experiment with them. He believed that many new ideas could come from continued experimentation and that one must apply experimental science to the task of improving society. In psychology, John Watson and Sigmund Freud were coming into their own. Watson was the pioneer in behavioral psychology. He believed man functioned as a machine and so must be studied in very mechanical terms. Freud, on the other hand, developed a study of psychology that emphasized sexual impulses as the source of both human suffering and human joy, depending on whether sexual impulses were suppressed or expressed. To many, Freud seemed to be propounding a philosophy of social hedonism.

The discipline of history also came up with new approaches. In the 1890s John Fiske applied the theory of evolution to historical writing. He showed how biological evolution explained historical evolution. Frederick Jackson Turner felt that the American West, not America's European origins, explained the development of American history. In 1893 in his essay "The Significance of the Frontier in American History," he argued that the American character was shaped by westward expansion. The validity of this theory was debated then and continues to be now. John Bach McMaster pioneered in the study of social history. Charles Beard in 1913 was applying an economic interpretation to history; he explained the writing of the Constitution in economic terms. In 1912 James Harvey Robinson introduced the idea that certain interpretations of history can bring social change. The complexities of American thought reflected the complexities of American society. This was also very noticeable in literature.

Trends in Literature

Realism became a major trend in American literature after the Civil War. This was evident in various regional writers, who attempted to portray the local color of their areas. Emily Dickinson was a New England poet who returned to the Puritan roots of the region for her themes. Sidney Lanier wrote about the demise of the plantation days and the birth of the urban South. Joel Chandler Harris reflected in his "Uncle Remus" stories the flavor of Southern-black folktales. Edward Eggleston, E. W. Howe, and Joseph Kirkland wrote of life in the Midwest. Bret Harte told of the mining camps of California. The only regional writer who acquired a national reputation was Samuel Clemens, better known by his pen name as Mark Twain. Twain's works reveal the roots of his own life along the Mississippi. His book *Huckleberry Finn* (1884) is rated a literary masterpiece because of its brilliant character portrayals. Twain's later works reveal his satire, wit, and pessimism. He was without a doubt the greatest artist of regionalism.

William Dean Howells and Henry James took realism beyond regionalism. Howells believed that literature should reflect the contemporary scene. In his books, such as *The Rise of Silas Lapham* (1885), he wrote of the evils of industrialization and middle-class America. An American disillusioned with his native country, Henry James wrote from a European perspective. His writings explore the confrontation between American and European values. Very elaborate and intricate, his works had little popular appeal but today are considered great works of an artistic genius. He and Howells did much to perpetuate the tradition of realism in literature.

Realism soon gave way to naturalism. Naturalism treated humans as the victim of their environment. Man was not the master of his destiny; he was without free will and hopeless. Stephen Crane in *Maggie: A Girl of the Streets* (1893) described how the evils of the city pushed a woman to suicide; and in *The Red Badge of Courage* (1895) he vividly portrayed the horrors of war. Jack London called upon the power of nature in many of his novels, such as *The Call of the Wild* (1903), in which a domestic dog reverts to wild behavior, and *Sea Wolf* (1904), the study of a ruthless sea captain. Theodore Dreiser is rated the greatest naturalist of them all. In his widely condemned *Sister Carrie* (1900) he portrayed the life of a girl who gained social position by exploiting her sexual attractiveness. This book represented the height of naturalism and a new literary approach to sex, which would continue well into the twentieth century.

While realism and naturalism dominated serious literature, most Americans were reading sentimental, popular books. Horatio Alger books told of the pauper who achieved riches. Lew Wallace's *Ben Hur* (1880) described the exciting days of Rome, with its wild chariot races. Ten- and 20-cent western adventures retold the days of the wild West, where cowboys defeated Indians time and again. Novels of pure romance such as Charles Major's *When Knighthood was in Flower* (1898) enjoyed great popularity. Magazines such as *Ladies Home Journal*, *Cosmopolitan*, and *The Saturday Evening Post* entered the mass circulation market. Newspapers, competing for readers, turned to "yellow journalism," emphasizing sensationalism, violence, crime, robberies, and rapes. Comics such as *The Yellow Kid* and lovelorn columns were added to daily newspapers. Popular literature opened the way to the industrial age's mass amusements.

The Rise of Popular Culture

Increased urbanization, changing technology, improvements in transportation, and improved communications produced new patterns of popular culture. This period saw the growth of clubs that catered to the wealthy, featuring sports that required expensive equipment, such as polo or golf. Tennis also was found first in such clubs. In the urban centers men's athletic clubs were started, but they were more than mere gymnasiums; they were both athletic and social in nature. The participant sports included golf, tennis, bicycling, and croquet. There also was renewed interest in hunting, fishing, hiking, and boating as well as the increased popularity of archery, target shooting, swimming, and track and field events. In 1891 Dr. James Naismith of Springfield, Massachusetts, invented the game of basketball, the first true American sport. Within a few years courts were set up all across America.

Urbanization caused spectator sports to become increasingly popular. Horse races still attracted many viewers and more gamblers than ever; by the 1890s it had formed into a circuit with prestige races such as the Kentucky Derby and Belmont Classic. Boxing became more acceptable. The worst boxing violence disappeared in the 1880s when the Marquess of Queensberry rules were accepted. But standardization of boxing did not tarnish its immense popularity. The champion heavyweight, "the Boston Strongboy" John L. Sullivan, became a national hero. Brawling Sullivan had survived a 75-round victory over Jake Kilrain. But boxing science replaced brawling and "Gentleman Jim" Corbett brought the science of boxing to new heights when he defeated Sullivan. But boxers rose and fell quickly. In 1897 Robert Fitzsimmon knocked out Corbett with the new "solar plexus" punch. Boxing was now more socially acceptable.

Football now became a mass-spectator sport. College football dominated the age. Ivy League schools such as Princeton and Harvard were the perennial champs, and the All-Americans were from Eastern schools. The popularity of the game spread, even though there were few scholarships and stadiums were small. Yet football was hardly a challenge for the true American pastime—baseball. Baseball development was slowed by the Civil War, but in 1869 the Cincinnati Red Stockings toured the country as the nation's first professional team. Other teams gradually were formed, and in 1876 the National League opened play with teams from Louisville, Cincinatti, St. Louis, New York, Philadelphia, Hartford, Boston, and Chicago. Although gambling scandals tarnished the game, its popularity continued. In the early 1900s the American League was established, and a two-league pattern became a tradition. Baseball then, however, was much different from baseball today. The heroes were George Wright, the bare-handed shortstop, Albert Spalding, the pitcher who won 52 games and lost 18 in one season, and Adrian Anson, who played major league ball for 27 years. Playing conditions and equipment were much different. One game ended with the score 201–11; another was stopped at the end of 24 innings with a scoreless tie.

Here are New York's baseball heroes in 1894.

The educated still attended the legitimate theater, which included few American products and many European imports. Shakespeare was still popular. The melodrama with heroes and villains was also common theater fare. Many dramas on life in the city such as *Nellie, the Beautiful Cloak Model* performed to large audiences. Western shows such as Buffalo Bill's Wild West Show also dazzled the Eastern dudes who knew little about the West. One of the most popular melodramas was *Uncle Tom's Cabin* with Simon Legree as the bad guy and Uncle Tom and Little Eva as the good guys. Melodramas even allowed audience participation; they cheered the heroes and booed and hissed the villains. When the mortgage was paid, the audience went wild. The Minstrel show slowly was giving way to vaudeville and burlesque. Vaudeville was truly family entertainment, with songs, dancing, and acrobatic acts. Burlesque also was popular but with a definite male bent. Marquees advertised their shows with promises of "50 pairs of rounded limbs, ruby lips, tantalizing torsos—*50*." Urban America offered something for everyone, from the saloons where you were served by scantily clad females to the beer bar where you could drink a five-cent beer for hours.

With the invention of the phonograph popular music became big business. The songs reflected the times: "The Sidewalks of New York" and "The Mulligan Braves" were two popular ditties. New Orleans jazz was more popular, and the "tin-pan alley" composers were becoming active. In the South, jazz greats such as King Bolden, King Oliver, Jelly Roll Morton, and Bunk Johnson were still accepted only in black clubs. Mass acceptance of jazz would have to wait until the twentieth century. Popular music like popular literature was moralistic and sentimental. Serious music was evident in symphony and opera associations, but this music was for the elite, not the masses. Meanwhile, for a nickel one could view a peepshow. Movies were just on the horizon.

Post-Civil War America saw the birth of American industrialization. With it came changes in all levels of society. Workers, frustrated by the control of big business, attempted to organize and challenge that control. The challenge was futile. The rise of the industrial city brought with it new technology and yet more social evils; churches tried to combat these evils, but frequently were occupied with internal doctrinal disputes. Education and science tried to cope with the changing times and progress was made in both areas. Literature, meanwhile, reflected upon the values of life in industrial America. In politics, a movement was burgeoning that demanded regulation of industry and a return to the simple dignity of the individual. These demands would see some satisfaction in the Progressive Era of the twentieth century.

Essay

The Rise of College Football

Whether the game of football was invented by the Eskimos or the Greeks or the Romans will never be known for sure. It is known, however, that during the 1500s in England a game of football, in which two sides kicked a ball back and forth, was played by the lower classes. It was not until the 1600s that football became an acceptable pastime for the upper classes. This game was transplanted to America by early English colonists; the Puritans were found playing football not long after they landed in New England. But the religious attitudes of the age kept such amusements to a minimum. Nor was football played in the early colleges, such as Harvard and Yale, for they were established as theological seminaries.

With the American Revolution attitudes toward leisure and recreation were changing; meanwhile colleges were becoming secular, with more freedom and more time for recreation. Interclass rivalries at Harvard and Yale now involved a game in which a ball was kicked, thrown, and carried. But this sport was more of a brawl than a game, and in some cases a ball was not used at all. These "annual games" turned into such wild affairs that they had to be held off-campus and were eventually outlawed just before the Civil War. Football, the college game, arose in America the hard way.

Just before the Civil War a new ball was introduced to the game. This round ball of heavy rubber made kicking and dribbling much more of an art. The end of the free for all game of football was fast approaching. Gerrit Smith Miller was a young man who played the freewheeling style of football well, but he saw that a team concept would be needed to bring real skills to the game. In Boston in 1862 he organized a group of friends and formed the Oneida Football Club of Boston—the first football organization in the United States. A team concept and rules of play began to emerge. There were now fifteen players to a side, but still the ball could not be carried. During the Civil War the club played all challengers but never lost a game. Red silk handkerchiefs tied to their heads were the first step toward a football uniform.

The first intercollegiate football game took place on November 6, 1869, and it was vastly different from modern college football. The ball could not be carried; it could only be kicked or butted with the head. There were 25 players to a side, and the first team to score 6 goals was declared the winner. The field was about 100 yards long. Some 250 spectators watched the day's game. Neither team wore special uniforms; they played in street clothes, merely removing their hats and coats before the game. The final score was Rutgers 6, Princeton 4.

By modern standards this game the students called football was basically soccer; the transition from soccer to Rugby football, where the ball could be picked up and transported, began to take place in the 1870s. Harvard was the first college to play this new form of the game, but initially Harvard found little acceptance from the surrounding schools, who preferred the old game. In 1874 Harvard battled

The first intercollegiate football game on November 6, 1869; final score: Rutgers 6, Princeton 4.

McGill in a game of Rugby football; the next year Harvard and Yale agreed to a game that was mostly Rugby mixed with a little soccer. This was the last year in which soccer was a major college sport; Rugby football now began to sweep the American colleges.

Walter Camp, the avowed father of American football, played the first Rugby game with 11-man teams when his Yale team faced off against Harvard in 1876. That same year Harvard, Yale, Princeton, and Columbia met to form the American Intercollegiate Football Associa-

tion. There was still no agreement on the number of players, but touchdowns now counted in the scoring. It was during these early days of football that Walter Camp excelled for six years on the Yale squad; he then turned to rulemaking and innovation. More than any other American, he was responsible for the evolution of the Rugby game into the American form of football.

He convinced the American Intercollegiate Football Association to adopt the 11-man team, to allow teams to line up differently, and to use the snapback. Camp eventually came up with

Under Walter Camp major rule changes occurred,
and the game began to assume its modern form.

the concept of the line of scrimmage, as well as the classic offensive formation. Camp then added another rule: if the offensive team did not gain five yards in three downs it had to turn over the ball. In 1912 this was changed to 10 yards in four downs. Camp's other additions to football included tackling below the waist, penalties, and numerical scoring. He also originated the selection of All-America teams. It was under his guidance that Rugby football became the exciting football game of today, with running attacks, passing, and kicking.

These changes caused attendance to increase. In 1891 over 40,000 spectators gathered to witness the rivalry of Yale versus Princeton. But the game of the late 1800s still bore little resemblance to the Sunday football wars of the National Football League. It was legal to stop the man with the ball by piling on, completely immobilizing the ball carrier. Some teams wore canvas jackets, which made tackling much more difficult. Cleated shoes and a rubber noseguard were eventually introduced, along with helmets. The heroes of the age included Alexander Hoffat

The Rise of College Football

of Princeton, who could boot the ball 65 to 70 yards with either foot, and Yale's Wyllys Terry, who made a 115-yard touchdown run. The brutality of the game did not end with Camp's rule changes, and this factor still limited its acceptance at the turn of the century.

A few decades later, however, college football was an established part of America and still was growing in popularity. Midwest schools now challenged Eastern colleges. New formations were tried; more sophisticated uniforms were used. And All-America teams received national publicity. Walter Camp would have been proud to view his creation in the twentieth century. ∎

Suggested Reading

General social and intellectual trends of the industrial era are covered in HOWARD MUMFORD JONES's *The Age of Energy: Varieties of the American Experience, 1865–1915* (1971), in HENRY STEELE COMMAGER's *The American Mind* (1950), and HARZER ZIFF's *The American 1890's: Life and Times of a Lost Generation* (1966).

MATTHEW JOSEPHSON studies the industrial giants in *The Robber Barons* (1934), while JOSEPH WALL, in *Andrew Carnegie* (1970), describes one of them in detail. GABRIEL KOLKO describes the challenge to the railroad monopoly in *Railroads and Regulation, 1877–1916* (1965).

A general study of the labor movement is found in JOSEPH RAYBACK's *History of American Labor* (1966).

The growth of the industrial city is well documented in *The Urbanization of America, 1860–1915* (1963) by BLAKE MCKELVEY.

The women's movement of the late 1800s is the subject of ELEANOR FLEXNER's *Century of Struggle* (1975).

LAWRENCE CREMIN, in *The Transformation of the School* (1961), shows the evolution of the universal school system.

JAY MARTIN, in *Harvests of Change: American Literature, 1865–1914* (1967), describes the writers of the late 1800s.

CHAPTER 11

Progressivism and
the Return to Normalcy

Time Line

?–A.D. 1492	Migration and evolution of American Indian societies
1492	Christopher Columbus lands in West Indies—beginning of European exploration
1607–1732	Establishment of 13 English colonies
1775–1783	American Revolution
1776	Declaration of Independence
1789–1797	Presidency of George Washington
1812–1815	War of 1812
1816–1824	Era of Good Feelings
1846–1848	Mexican War
1861–1865	Civil War
1865–1877	Reconstruction
1877–1900	Industrialization and urbanization
1900–1916	Progressive Era
1900	Robert Le Follette elected governor of Wisconsin
1901	Theodore Roosevelt becomes president after McKinley's assassination
1902	Roosevelt intervenes in coal strike Antitrust suit against Northern Security Company
1904	Reelection of Theodore Roosevelt
1905	Niagara Movement
1906	Pure Food and Drug Act and Hepburn Act become law
1908	Gentlemen's Agreement
1908	Election of William Howard Taft
1909	Founding of the National Association for the Advancement of Colored People (NAACP)
1910	Ballinger-Pinchot dispute
1910	Mann Elkins Act
1912	Election of Woodrow Wilson
1913	Underwood Tariff Federal Reserve Act
1914	Clayton Act
1915	Rebirth of Ku Klux Klan
1916	Reelection of Woodrow Wilson
1920	Election of Warren G. Harding
1923	Teapot Dome Scandal
1923	Vice-president Calvin Coolidge becomes president upon death of Harding
1924	Election of Coolidge
1928	Election of Herbert Hoover
1929	Stock market crash
1917–1918	World War I
1930s	Depression and New Deal
1941–1945	World War II
1945–1960	Post-war politics
1950–1953	Korean War
1950–1960	Civil rights movement
1961–1973	Vietnam War
1976	Bicentennial celebration

Within the last few years state governments and the federal Congress have been addressing themselves to the issue of ethics in politics. The three areas that they have become most concerned with are campaigning, conflict of interest, and lobbying. Many Americans feel that candidates are being bought by vested interests. Why should architects and developers be members of state planning commissions? Years ago, Colorado lobbying groups used to provide free beer by the caseload in the state capitol's press gallery; legislation eventually reduced the flow of the beer lobby. Today there is a growing dissatisfaction with the manipulations and malpractices of politicans. And this movement is similar to one that occurred in the first two decades of the twentieth century, one that has been called the Progressive Movement. It was initially a series of unrelated attempts to control evils created by advancing industrialism and its corollary, urbanism. Over time it became a comprehensive reform movement that tried to reconcile democracy with big business. It addressed itself to a variety of problems, such as the exploitation of women, the concentration of wealth, the rise of monopolies, the lack of responsive government, crime in the cities, and the plight of labor. It had no one leader. It spread from the cities and states to the federal government. It was a movement that used more government to make government more responsive to the people. By the 1920s progressivism slowed down, and Americans appeared less interested in reform and more interested in bathtub gin, the Charleston, and nostalgia. Meanwhile, big business once again was dominant, and politicans went along with the times. In 1929 the bubble burst, and America went on a downhill ride to the dark days of the Depression.

Origins of Progressivism

One important stimulus to progressivism came from a group of men and women who exposed the political and economic evils of the day in articles and books. These were the "muckrakers," a term which referred to those "who could look no way but downward with the muckrake in [their] hands." Between 1902 and 1906 these writers began to publish articles in mass-circulation magazines that exposed political and financial wrongdoing. Lincoln Steffens attacked graft in the cities; Ida M. Tarbell presented an accurate, well-balanced portrayal of the rise of Standard Oil; Ray Stannard Baker wrote on the railroads; Thomas Larson exposed the workings of high finance. Novelists also exposed the seedy side of American life. Frank Norris in *The Octopus* dramatized the railroad monopoly, while Upton Sinclair in *The Jungle* detailed the abuses of the meatpacking industry. These writers pricked the American conscience and exposed a multitude of sins.

The most important writer to give direction to the movement was Herbert Croly. In his book *The Promise of American Life* he pointed to America's past and then to the future. He believed that a large measure of government regulation was needed to keep the promise of American life intact. According to Croly laissez-faire economics and government noninterference were things of the past. This did not mean, however, that big business must be destroyed. No, it meant it must be regulated. Selective government action would preserve the dignity of individual Americans. Such an outlook greatly influenced progressivism and was carried on to the New Deal of the 1930s. But even before the book appeared, Croly's ideas were being followed on local, state, and national levels.

Lincoln Steffens had pointed out that city governments were no longer honest and efficient. Cities were being run by political machines, headed by a boss who had connections with business interests. Honest government must be restored. But this was not an easy task. Reform mayors began to get elected and to run their reform administrations on progressive lines. Samuel "Golden Rule" Jones of Toledo and Tom L. Johnson of Cleveland were two of the most successful reform mayors. Jones was elected mayor in 1897 and immediately rejected the awarding of a questionable railway franchise. He soon announced that he intended to run his administration guided by Christian principles from the Bible. He attacked political corruption through policies such as fighting for public ownership of utilities. Tom Johnson was elected mayor of Cleveland in 1901; his reforms were so successful that Steffens called him "the best mayor of the best-governed city in America." Johnson's actions included bringing street railways under municipal control and attacking tax-assessment abuses. While Johnson and Jones were the most spectacular leaders of municipal reform, they were not the only ones. The National Municipal League fought for local improvements, and the city-commission form of government, which took political control out of the hands of a single city officer, was an important reform. The reform of municipal government was extended eventually to the state level.

One of the early progressive leaders in state politics, and one of the great trendsetters of the Progressive Era, was Robert La Follette of Wisconsin. "Fighting Bob" put together a coalition of farmers, workers, and middle-class groups and won the governorship of Wisconsin in 1900. His plan for state reform became known as the "Wisconsin Idea." It included state regulation of railroads and industries, workmen's compensation, banking laws, and conservation of natural resources. He also used academic experts to help implement many of his ideas. These programs eventually were extended to other

Robert M. LaFollette, governor of Wisconsin, introduced progressive reform to his state.

states, where direct primaries and women's suffrage were also being introduced. In Arkansas, for example, Governor Jeff Davis, the "Karl Marx of the Hill Billies," fought successfully against business abuses; meanwhile Oregon and California were not far behind with the state reforms. While state reform moved ahead, a cry rose for national reform. That "damned cowboy" Theodore Roosevelt would be the catalyst for national progressivism.

Roosevelt: The Progressive as President

The assassination of McKinley brought to the presidency a real showman: Theodore Roosevelt, the youngest man, at age 42, ever to become president. Born to a wealthy New York family, he had an active childhood in spite of ill health and nearsightedness. His early interest in nature was evident in his collections of mice and birds. Ashamed of his puny frame, he worked hard at his family gymnasium to build up his physical strength and overcome chronic asthma. After graduating from Harvard College, he entered New York politics as a Republican and served in the New York state assembly. There he became interested in civil service reform. After the death of his wife and mother on the same day in 1884, he bought two ranches in the Dakotas and became a rancher. On the range he worked long hours, hunting buffalo and roping cattle. Leaving the Dakotas after a severe snowstorm destroyed most of his cattle, he unsuccessfully ran for New York mayor. Working for Harrison's election in 1888, he was rewarded by a position on the Civil Service Commission. In 1895 he was appointed president of the Board of Police Commissioners in New York City and fought against corruption in the police force. He was now gaining a national reputation and was appointed by McKinley to be assistant secretary of the Navy. With the outbreak of the Spanish-American War he resigned his position and recruited men for a calvalry unit. As lieutenant colonel, he lead his Rough Riders into battle and received national publicity for their heroic charge up San Juan Hill. A military hero, he was elected governor of New York and earned the reputation of being a mild reformer. After becoming Vice-President on the Republican presidential ticket with McKinley, in 1901 Roosevelt became the twenty-fifth president of the United States. He was an extremely popular individual (known affectionately as "Teddy" or "TR"). His early interest in nature and physical activities continued. His six children occupied a major place in his life. His face, almost a caricature with its bushy mustache, huge teeth, and rimless glasses, has become easily recognizable. In fact, because of him, toymakers started stuffing toy animals and calling them "teddy bears." Roosevelt followed his belief that the president is a "steward of the whole people, responsible to all people." During his seven-and-a-half years he enlarged the power and prestige of the presidency and focused attention on executive initiative. But at first he had to move very carefully, for Congress was dominated by conservatives, as was his cabinet. And in his first message to Congress he seemed to be taking a conservative stand. But by 1902 he was beginning to earn his title of "trust-buster." That year his attorney general, Philander C. Knox, instituted a suit against the Northern Security Company, a giant holding company of J. P. Morgan's, for violation of the Sherman Antitrust Act. This "thunderbolt out of a clear sky" did not signal the demise of the trust system but its regulation, for Roosevelt believed that government could distinguish between good and bad trusts. Two years later the Supreme Court ruled that the trusts were illegal and ordered them dissolved. Roosevelt had won his first big battle with monopolies.

This cartoon reflected on Theodore Roosevelt's ability to distinguish between good and bad trusts.

Attack on the Trusts

In the rest of his years as president, <u>Roosevelt started antitrust suits against 44 corporations and received 25 indictment</u>s. Some historians feel today that his role as trust-buster has been exaggerated. One cannot deny that <u>he breathed life into the dying Sherman Act and was responsible for the beginnings of government regulation of big business.</u> His actions in his first term as a friend of labor were also crucial ones. In <u>1903 the Department of Commerce and Labor was set up; ten years later the two were separated.</u> The <u>Department of Labor ran the business of labor statistics and of children labor and ran a conciliation service. In 1902 Roosevelt intervened directly in a coal strike.</u> Facing a coal shortage, Roosevelt threatened that the government would operate the

1903 Dept of Commerce & Labor

mines itself if the strike was not settled. The mine operators gave in, and the workers were granted a raise and a nine-hour workday. Roosevelt had exerted more pressure on employers than on employees and had become the first president to use his office impartially in a major labor dispute—especially one which seemed to favor labor. Later Roosevelt recommended the passage of child labor laws and workmen's compensation. He also helped to change the public view of workers.

Roosevelt had become a president through assassination, and in 1904 he wanted to be a president in his own right. His stand against the trusts and his intervention in the coal strike had increased his popularity; with the death of politican Marcus Hanna he became the unanimous choice of the Republicans. The Democrats passed over William Jennings Bryan and turned to conservative Judge Alton B. Parker. During the rather dull campaign Roosevelt emphasized his Square Deal, in which "there shall be no crookedness in the dealing." The only excitement in the campaign occurred when Parker accused Roosevelt of obtaining campaign funds by blackmail. But this accusation made little difference, for Roosevelt won by more than two million votes. He now planned to continue his reforms.

The railroads were now singled out as the major target. The Elkins Act of 1903 had attempted to eliminate rebates, but many other abuses still remained. The Hepburn Act of 1906 gave the Interstate Commerce Commission jurisdiction over railroads and all other forms of transportation. It made the Interstate Commerce Commission an effective agent by increasing its members from five to seven and giving it authority to nullify existing rates and establish maximum rates. The Hepburn Act was the strongest law yet passed to regulate big business.

In 1906 Upton Sinclair's novel *The Jungle* appeared. It was an indictment of the meatpacking plants; in it were descriptions of human fingers being ground up with the meat and other atrocious tales. It was said that Roosevelt, reading Sinclair's book one morning at breakfast, was so repelled that he threw his sausage out the window. Senator Albert J. Beveridge of Indiana introduced a bill requiring federal inspection of the meatpacking business. The Meat Inspection Act stipulated rules of sanitary meatpacking and allowed government inspection of meat products crossing state lines. The Pure Food and Drug Act curtailed the manufacture or sale of mislabeled or adulterated food or drugs in interstate commerce. The buyer now had to be less wary.

Conservation Politics

Roosevelt's greatest achievement was not in progressive legislation, but in conservation. He took a strong stand against the philosophy of waste and started conservation as a national policy. There were forerunners of the conservation movement before him, but they were usually voices in the wilderness. In the 1830s, Western traveler George Catlin had commented upon the natural beauty of the West and the need for a national park "containing man and beast, in all the wildness and freshness of their nature's beauty." Transcendental writer Henry David Thoreau constantly wrote about the importance of nature to man. Although he spent much of his life away from civilization, near the end of his life he proposed a plan to combine civilization with wilderness. He suggested that every Massachusetts township "should have a park, or rather a primitive forest, of five hundred or a thousand acres, where a stick should never be cut for fuel, a common possession forever, for instruction and recreation." This experiment in planned living remained only a dream.

The philosopher of conservation was George Perkins Marsh, who, in his book *Man and Nature or Physical Geography as Modified by Human Action*, explored the moral relationship between humans and their environment. He saw man as changing the delicate balance between himself and nature. These changes eventually would bring the destruction of civilization itself. Controlled use of nature was a necessity. This book was surprisingly well received and went through many printings, one of them just before the arrival of Roosevelt as president. Frederick Law Olmstead took the philosophy of Marsh and applied it to the park idea. He was mainly responsible in 1853 for the creation in New York's Central Park—"A specimen of God's Handiwork." This conservation pioneer eventually helped plan 17 major parks and had a role in the setting aside of Yosemite Valley in California as a national park. In 1864 Congress transferred title of the Yosemite Valley to California state; the valley was to be a park "for public use, resort, and recreation." This was the first step in the creation of a national park system. Although Olmstead did not accomplish the creation of Yosemite National Park himself, his pioneering role in conservation cannot be overstated.

Two other pioneers in the conservation movement were John Wesley Powell and John Muir. Powell, a one-armed veteran of the Civil War, explored the West and, in 1878, wrote *Lands of the Arid Regions of the West*, a book which in part proposed a reclamation program for the area. He could not see how the nation's land laws could apply to the West. He urged a drastic change in these laws, plus federal support of irrigation projects. This idea saw fruition with the Reclamation Act of 1902, which created the Bureau of Reclamation. John Muir, on the other hand, was responsible for the creation of Yosemite National Park. Muir had a real kinship with nature and spent countless hours roaming the Sierra Nevadas of California. He recognized civilization's future threat to the region and lobbied for a national park system that would include

1902 Reclamation Act

the mountain country around the Yosemite Valley. His efforts were finally successful, for in 1890 Congress created the Yosemite National Park (although the valley remained in state hands until 1906). Muir is also responsible for the creation of the Sierra Club, which today is a leader in preservation of America's dwindling natural resources. Powell and Muir made Americans aware of their natural environment.

The public slowly began to realize the need for conservation in the 1890s. The census of 1890 was an announcement that the last American frontier had disappeared. It shocked many Americans, who had moved from coast to coast, growing used to wasting the land and its resources and moving on. Several Congresses and presidents worked slowly, beginning to create a real conservation program. In 1891 Congress passed the Forest Reserve Act, which permitted the president to create "forest reserves" by withdrawing land from the public domain. In 1894 the Carey Act provided that public land should be turned over to Western states for reclamation by irrigation. Presidents Benjamin Harrison, Grover Cleveland, and William McKinley set aside 48 million acres of forest reserves, but none of them had developed a comprehensive conservation program that had yet seized the American imagination. This had to wait until the presidency of Roosevelt.

President Roosevelt's love for the outdoors and concern for nature was unquestioned; he could see the declining American wilderness was an obvious problem. Less than 200 million out of 800 million acres of virgin forest land remained. Roosevelt's ally in the conservation fight was a man who had knocked him down in a friendly boxing match and had taught him the hobby of woodcutting—Gifford Pinchot. Pinchot, the nation's first professional forester, was Roosevelt's head of the Forest Service. The Forest Service had been part of the Department of Interior, but in 1905 it was created as a separate bureau in the Department of Agriculture and given control of the national forests.

Roosevelt's first annual message set the tone for his conservation campaign: "The forest and water problems are perhaps the most vital internal problems of the United States." For eight years he lived up to this statement. Using the law of 1891, he set aside approximately 150 million acres of unsold government timberland as forest reserve. During his presidency the number of national parks had been doubled, and 16 national monuments and 51 wildlife reserves had been established. In 1907 he established an Inland Waterways Commission to study the problems of water-power development, water transportation, and water use. Following the commission's report, in 1908 he called a Conservation Conference of governors and congressional delegates to evaluate the restricted use of natural resources. This pioneer meeting further focused public attention on the need for conservation. During the meeting he restated his awarness of America's wasteful past and the need for future planning. "Neither the primitive man nor the pioneer was aware of any duty to posterity in dealing with natural resources." The conference urged further programs such as preservation of mineral lands, regulation of forest fires, limitations on timber cutting, and expanded irrigation projects. It also urged the creation of state and national conservation commissions. Eventually conservation commissions were set up in 41 states, and a national conservation association was established. Roosevelt further made Pinchot head of the National Conservation Commission, with a goal of calculating the nation's natural resources. But this was not enough. Roosevelt also sponsored a North American Conference on Conservation and even proposed a world conservation conference.

Roosevelt also undertook a federal commitment to irrigation projects. The Newlands Reclamation Act of 1902 provided that receipts from the sale of federal land in Western states would be utilized as a reclamation fund to survey, construct, and maintain irrigation projects in semiarid states. During the next few decades numerous dams, such as the Grand Coulee (1942) on the Columbia River, the Hoover Dam (1936) on the Colorado River, and the Roosevelt Dam (1911) in Arizona, were constructed. Roosevelt did more than give lip service to maintaining the delicate balance between humans and nature.

1902 Newlands Reclamation Act

Since his program challenged big businesses' use of natural resources, it caused much controversy. And Roosevelt also acted many times on his own without congressional approval, actions which made it appear he was making excessive use of executive power. Not only big business but many Westerners suprisingly opposed his programs, because they felt that he was retarding settlement of the West and was violating the power of states' rights. Although he was constantly hounded by opponents of conservation, he succeeded in making preservation of natural resources a national issue and inspired others to continue his fight. However, while he was fighting hard to make conservation a national policy, minority rights received many setbacks under his leadership.

Minority Rights

By the beginning of the twentieth century blacks had lost most of the gains made after the Civil War. Northern apathy toward black equality was reinforced by Supreme Court decisions. In 1883 the Supreme Court ruled that the

Civil Rights Act of 1875, which guaranteed equal rights at hotels, theaters, and other places of public amusement, was unconstitutional. In 1896 the Supreme Court ruled in the *Plessy* v. *Ferguson* case that the "equal but separate" doctrine, which was evident in the Jim Crow laws of the South, was legal. In the 1890s white violence helped enforce the Jim Crow segregation system. In 1892 alone, lynchings claimed 235 black lives.

Washington and DuBois

At the time of the turn of the century, the major spokesman for blacks was a moderate, Booker T. Washington. Once a slave, Washington was self-educated. In his early life he worked in the construction trades and excelled as a brick mason, but he felt that his gift lay in teaching. He was right. A success in teaching, he went on to help organize and then head Tuskegee Institute, which became one of the country's leading black institutions. He was able to attract both Northern and Southern white support for this trade school. His emergence as a national leader can be traced to his Atlanta Exposition Address in 1895. In this message he preached compromise: blacks, he argued, should not demand complete equality; they should work for such equality through economic successes. Although they were second-class citizens, they must accept their inferior positions until they excelled economically. He said, "The wisest among my race understand that the agitation of questions of social equality is the extremest folly, and that progress in the enjoyment of all privileges that will come to us in it be the result of severe and constant struggle

Educator Booker T. Washington believed in black equality through hard work and industrial education.

rather than of artificial forcing." Here was the black gospel of wealth: riches will make you free. Since he posed no threat to white supremacy, whites called him the greatest leader of his race and accepted him. In 1901 Roosevelt invited him to the White House for dinner. Later in his presidency Roosevelt realized that he had made a mistake in inviting Washington and invited no more black people to see him there. While Roosevelt did appoint some blacks to federal offices in the South, he personally believed blacks were inferior to whites and felt that the extension of suffrage to blacks was a mistake. He wrote, "I believe that the great majority of Negroes in the South are wholly unfit for suffrage." In August 1906 tension broke out between three companies of black soldiers and some white Texans. Violence occurred, the city of Brownsville was shot up, and one man was killed and a policeman was wounded. An investigation failed to establish the guilt of the black soldiers, so Roosevelt took the matter into his own hands and ordered that 160 blacks from the three companies be discharged "without honor." These companies had included many veterans and six men that held the Medal of Honor. No one ever was tried formally. (Many years later, in 1972, the secretary of the army reversed Roosevelt's decision and changed the discharges to "honorable.") Blacks considered this a racist act, though Roosevelt claimed he would have acted the same if they had been white soldiers. Since Roosevelt did little to extend his ideas of progressivism to blacks, they were forced to act on their own.

The leading black activist of the early twentieth century and the greatest critic of Booker T. Washington was William Edward Bughardt DuBois. The first black Ph.D., he felt that Washington was "leading the way backward." In his book *The Soul of Black Folks* he condemned Washington's program of industrial education, submission, and accumulation of wealth. Black Americans must receive a liberal education and demand complete equality immediately. He wrote:

> But so far as Mr. Washington apologizes for injustice—North or South— does not rightly value the privilege and duty of voting, belittles the emasculating effects of caste distinctions, and opposes the higher training and ambition of our brighter minds—so far as he, the South, or the nation, does this—we must unceasingly and firmly oppose them.

But DuBois felt that major gains could be achieved only through a national organization. He called for a meeting at Niagara Falls in 1905, which issued a document that called for freedom of speech and of the press, the abolition of discrimination based on race or color, and an acceptance of the principle of human brotherhood. This Niagara Movement, the first organized black protest in the twentieth century, remained small, exclusively black, and was labeled radical. Mob violence in Atlanta and Springfield during the next few years spurred white and black leaders to form an organization to "make 11 million Americans physically free from ignorance, politically free from disfranchisement and socially free from insult." This organization, known as the National Association for the Advancement of Colored People (NAACP), was controlled by whites. In its early years DuBois was an able publicity minister, but his disillusionment with its leadership and goals let to his leaving the organization and eventually the United States. But the black protest movement had gotten a start.

Japanese-Americans and Indians

Roosevelt's actions also reflected general American feelings toward the Japanese in America. Few Japanese came to America before the 1880s, but by the 1890s more than 1000 were arriving each year. Most of these were peasants who were content to work as farm laborers. They received low wages and were usually uncomplaining. After 1900 more middle-class Japanese migrated, often buying or leasing large tracts of farm land in California; they soon found themselves with a near monopoly in berries, potatoes, and flowers. They also were successful in restaurants and retail businesses in many cities and were active in the commercial fishing industry. They had come to the United States just after the Chinese immigration problem had been dealt with and anti-Oriental feelings were still very high. One area of controversy was school segregation. A California state law empowered local school boards to establish separate schools for Indians and Orientals. In October 1906 the San Francisco School Board ordered all Japanese to attend school with the Orientals in Chinatown. The Japanese government protested. President Roosevelt immediately put pressure upon the school board and they changed their decision.

Roosevelt, however, realized that the school board issue was symptomatic of a general anti-Japanese feeling in California and that continued Japanese immigration would cause more tension, so he decided to try to stem the flow. In 1907 he issued an executive order that outlawed immigration into the United States of Japanese from Mexico, Canada, and Hawaii. This order was mainly directed at the large number of Japanese coming from Hawaii. In 1908 he entered into a "gentlemen's agreement" with Japan which forbade the Japanese government to issue passports to the United States for either skilled or unskilled laborers. The number of immigrants was cut substantially.

Roosevelt believed in the principles of the Dawes Act, for he felt that the sooner the American Indians became part of the mainstream of life in America the better. While blacks should be segregated and Japanese immigration limited, Indians should be forceably assimilated. His feelings toward Indians were also revealed during his presidency when he wrote, "I wouldn't go so far as to say that the only good Indian is a dead Indian, but I would agree that it is true in nine out of ten cases, and I would have some reservations about the tenth."

While his minority policies were less than enlightened, Theodore Roosevelt was still one of the greatest presidents of the twentieth century. It is true that his administration ended on a sour note, for he was blamed for the financial depression of 1907. Yet he brought to the presidency new life and restored its power and vitality. He became the champion of the conservation cause and prepared the groundwork for the later ecology movement. But most importantly he brought progressivism to the national level. While his legislation was not extensive, he set the nation on a course of government intervention and regulation that would be continued long after he left the presidency. To many Americans, Roosevelt was a master showman and a real "teddy bear." He did have his critics, and while some do not consider him a great president, no one argues that he wasn't among the most vocal.

Taft: Roosevelt's Successor

Roosevelt enjoyed being president, and he had a difficult time deciding whether to run again in 1908. But he felt committed to an earlier decision not to run and to the two-term tradition, so he refused the nomination. He did, however, want a successor who would carry out his policies, so he turned to his secretary of war, William Howard Taft. The Republicans nominated Roosevelt's man and adopted a platform of progressive reform. That year the Democrats turned to William Jennings Bryan, who called for more progressive legislation and more power for the people. The campaign was lackluster, and Taft won the election by more than a million votes. It appeared that many of Roosevelt's ideas would now be carried out, but this was not to be. Taft not only failed to capitalize on Roosevelt's momentum, but in a four-year term he alienated much of his party and Roosevelt himself.

Roosevelt was a hard act to follow, and William Howard Taft, with his large frame and plainness of dress and speech, never emerged from Roosevelt's shadow. Taft would honestly admit, "When I hear someone say, Mr. President, I look around expecting to see Roosevelt." Born in Cincinnati, Ohio, his size earned him the knickname "Big Lub" by his playmates. He attended Yale College and received his law degree from the Cincinnati Law School. He served well as a lawyer, but his wife and father kept pushing him toward politics.

William Howard Taft, Roosevelt's hand-picked successor, caused a rift in the Republican party that led to Democratic victory in 1912.

Elected as a superior court justice, he was then appointed by President Benjamin Harrison to be solicitor general of the United States. He then became a circuit judge, dean of the Cincinnati Law School, and eventually chairman of a civil commission to govern the newly acquired Phillipines under President McKinley. He was the first civil governor of the islands. There, he established one of the best models of colonial government, but still he pressed for his great goal in life, to be Chief Justice of the Supreme Court. Roosevelt appointed him to his cabinet as secretary of war, and in 1908 Taft was Roosevelt's choice for president. Taft had served ably in judicial and legal capacities, but he had little practical political experience. While he was a progressive, he did not believe in Roosevelt's enlarged concept of the presidency. His lack of political savy left him bewildered in his new position as president. He wrote, "When I read in the headlines that the president and Senator Aldrich and Speaker Cannon have had a conference, my first thought is 'I wonder what they talked about?'" Such was the presidency of Taft.

Still the achievements of Taft were quite impressive. He instituted more antitrust suits during his four years than had Roosevelt in eight. He supported the Mann-Elkins Act of 1910, which increased the power of the Interstate Commerce Commission. And he supported the Sixteenth Amendment, which created the income tax. But his handling of tariff reduction and a conservation controversy lost him the trust of the public and of his own party. During the election campaign, Taft had promised a sizeable reduction in tariff rates. The

1910 Mann-Elkins Act

Progressivism and the Return to Normalcy

Payne-Aldrich Bill was supposed to be the answer to Taft's promise, but in actuality it either left the rates the same or increased them on many products. Taft appeared displeased with the act but he signed it into law. He now appeared to be the toy of big business and completely alienated the progressives in his party. His stand in the Ballinger-Pinchot controversy further alienated them.

Ballinger-Pinchot Controversy

Taft believed in the need for conservation, but he moved much more cautiously than Roosevelt. Taft publicly stated that Roosevelt had exceeded his authority in withdrawing lands from public sale; yet he withdrew more land than Roosevelt and put millions of acres into forest reserves. Taft also supported the Appalachian Forest Reserve Act, which allowed the government to purchase 1.25 million acres in the southern Appalachians. Interior Secretary Richard A. Ballinger, acting on Taft's advice, had restored to the public domain certain water-power sites that had been withdrawn by Roosevelt; Pinchot, who was adamently opposed to Ballinger's weak conservation stand, learned through Louis Glavis, a Department of the Interior agent, that Ballinger was responsible for the sale of a large tract of coal land in Alaska to the Guggenheims, mining industrialists. Pinchot now charged that Ballinger was giving in to business interests. Taft defended Ballinger and removed Glavis. Eventually a joint committee of 12 congressmen investigated the controversy and supported Ballinger. Meanwhile Pinchot took his case to the public and charged that Ballinger was submitting to private interests and weakening Roosevelt's conservation program. Taft was forced to fire Pinchot, a very unpopular stand. Once again the progressive Republicans who had supported Pinchot were defeated, and one of Pinchot's best friends, Roosevelt, was becoming increasingly disillusioned with his successor.

The Progressive Revolt

Taft's inept handling of crucial issues caused a progressive revolt to foment. Taft was being identified more and more with the conservatives in the Republican party. In 1911 the National Progressive Republican League was formed with Robert La Follette as their spokesman and presidential contender. Meanwhile Roosevelt had returned from his triumphant tour of Africa and had found Taft, like little boy blue in the nursery rhyme, "under the haystack fast asleep." Roosevelt's reforms were lying dormant. His administration's momentum was lost, and Taft even appeared to favor the conservatives. In 1910 Roosevelt made his famous New Nationalism speech, in which he urged the federal government to use its power to pass more legislation to curb social evils. He felt that the public welfare was uppermost. By 1912 Roosevelt had decided, "I will accept the nomination for President if it is tendered to me, and I will adhere to this decision until the convention has expressed its preference." Roosevelt now became the leader of the progressive Republicans and was ready to challenge Taft for leadership of the party and the nation.

The Taft-Roosevelt confrontation came to a head at the Republican convention. Roosevelt's disputed delegates were refused seats, and Taft was nominated on the first ballot. Roosevelt then left the party, even though the party adopted a fairly progressive platform. Roosevelt and his supporters then organized a new Progressive party, with the Bull Moose as its symbol. The platform called for outright progressivism, including measures such as direct primaries, direct election of senators, women's suffrage, prohibition of child labor, and an eight-hour day. The Democrats, meanwhile, found their opponents divided and hoped to take advantage. But it was not until the forty-sixth ballot that they agreed upon Governor Woodrow Wilson of New Jersey. The Democrats also adopted a progressive platform.

The campaign fight was between Wilson and Roosevelt and their two brands of progressivism. Both believed in exercising the power of the government but in different ways. Roosevelt's program, called New Nationalism, called for the expansion of federal power to curtail big-business abuses and bring more social welfare to ordinary citizens. Wilson's plans, called the New Freedom, rejected the expansion of federal-government powers and emphasized state action. He believed in making America again a land of "free enterprise." Trusts must be broken and competition again restored. Although Roosevelt fought hard and many Americans sang "The Moose is loose," expecting his victory, Wilson, with his united party, won the election. The "schoolmaster" now became president.

Chart 11-1
Election of 1912

	Popular Vote	Electoral Vote
Woodrow Wilson (Democrat)	6,293,454*	435
William Taft (Republican)	3,484,980	8
Theodore Roosevelt (Progressive)	4,119,538	88

* Wilson won with 41% of the popular vote.

Wilson: The Democrat as Progressive

Woodrow Wilson was born in Virginia into a deeply religious family. His father was a Presbyterian minister who stressed religious piety and the importance of education. He excelled in education and graduated from Princeton University. During his career there he actively participated in the debating society and was managing editor of the college newspaper. He saw his future in public service, so he received his law degree and practiced in Atlanta, Georgia. However, this occupation was not for him, so he turned to an academic career and received his Ph.D. in political science from Johns Hopkins University. During the next few years he taught at Bryn Mawr College and Wesleyan University, where he also coached football. Not only was he a successful football coach, but also a textbook writer. In 1889 his book *The State*, one of the first studies of comparative government, appeared. From Wesleyan, he became a professor at Princeton and, in 1902, the first nonclergyman to become the university's president.

His reputation as a reform president grew quickly. He wanted to change Princeton from a place "where there are youngsters doing tasks to a place where there are men thinking." But his educational reforms produced much controversy; he was moving against established traditions and constantly was frustrated. Still, he was earning the reputation of a reformer trying to bring more democracy into the educational system. Leaving education, he was convinced that politics would be his road to success. In 1910 he was elected governor of New Jersey and immediately became a progressive reformer. Under his leadership progressive laws were passed, including a primary-election law, a corrupt practices act, and a public utilities law. His reforms brought him national attention and serious consideration by the Democratic party for the presidential nomination in 1912. But the battle was long and hard. William Jennings Bryan's endorsement proved crucial, and on the forty-fifth ballot Wilson was nominated for president. With the Republican party badly split, his victory in the general election was almost certain. Thus Woodrow Wilson became the twenty-eighth president of the United States.

Woodrow Wilson, the scholar president, brought with him extraordinary talents. His speaking ability was unquestioned, while his intellectual abilities were outstanding. Wilson even had the physical appearance of a scholar with his thin build, glasses, and strong, jutting jaw. He brought to the presidency the philosophy of the New Freedom, which attempted to restore economic competition and to resurrect free enterprise. He was stubborn and sensitive to criticism, and he had an air of intellectual superiority. His strong religious background also influenced his thinking in moral terms. In his first inaugural address he noted, "This is not a day of triumph; it is a day of dedication." Wilson, the scholar-moralist, now rode the wave of progressivism to new heights.

Progressive Legislation

Wilson first attempted to keep his campaign promise by lowering the tariff. The Underwood-Simmons Tariff passed considerable opposition in the Senate and eventually became law. It was the first tariff reduction since the Civil War; and while it authorized lowering of the customs duties, it also included a graduated income tax, authorized under the Sixteenth Amendment. His demand for banking reform was met by the Federal Reserve Act of 1913. Up to that time the National Bank system, which had been instituted in 1864, was still in effect and made the currency very inelastic. In fact, this inelasticity had accounted for many of the depressions of the late 1800s. The Pujo committee in 1913 reported that there was a "great and rapidly growing concentration of the control of money and credit in the hands" of a very few men. The Federal Reserve Act was the progressive answer to banking problems, creating a decentralized banking system under federal control. It authorized the establishment of a national clearinghouse for bank checks, the creation of a flexible currency system, and the institution of an elastic credit system, one that could be adjusted to meet the needs of the American economy. Twelve Federal Reserve districts were created with one reserve bank for each district. The control was vested in a Federal Reserve Board consisting of seven members. All national banks were required to be members of the system, and state banks were also permitted to join. All member banks were required to keep part of their reserves in the Federal Reserve Bank of their district. Wilson now looked for new antitrust legislation.

In 1911 the Supreme Court, no longer responsive to the public's desire for reform, had ruled that the application of antitrust laws should "be determined by the light of reason." This was a subtly-worded victory for corporations. Congress reacted with the Clayton Act. The Sherman Act had outlawed trusts in vague terms; the Clayton Act prohibited specific practices. The new law outlawed unfair trade practices such as price discrimination and exclusive selling or leasing contracts; it also prohibited monopolistic tendencies such as interlocking directorates and combinations of corporate stock. These prohibitions allowed more competition and tended to undermine monopolies. The Federal Trade Commission was created to enforce the Clayton Act and prevent unfair competition. It specifically was authorized to investigate any "corporation engaged in commerce, except banks and common carriers...."

While the Clayton Act was designed specifically to strengthen antitrust laws, it also contained certain important clauses that defined the rights of labor. Section 6 stated that the "labor of a human being is not a commodity or article of commerce. Nothing contained in the antitrust laws should be construed to forbid the existence and operation of labor organizations, instituted for the purpose of mutual help. . . ." Section 20 prohibited the use of injunctions in labor disputes "unless necessary to prevent irreparable injury to property or to a property right." The law also upheld labor's right to strike, boycott, and picket. Samuel Gompers of the A.F.L. described the act as the "Magna Carta upon which the working people will rear their constitution of industrial freedom." The law, however, still was dependent upon court interpretation, which was not always beneficial to labor. By 1914 Wilson announced that his legislative program was complete.

Wilson was wrong; his program was not complete. His party wanted more progressive reform, which would be enforced by more government regulation; he also saw the need for more general support for his reelection in 1916.

This cartoon pictures Wilson the politician trying to make peace with the House and the Senate.

Wilson's New Freedom slowly became Roosevelt's New Nationalism. Political and public pressure had convinced him that a positive program of social legislation was necessary, so he now threw his support behind social welfare legislation. The La Follette Seamen's Act of 1915 improved sailors' working conditions and wages, established safety regulations, and made shipowners liable for infliction of corporal punishment on their ships. In 1916 the Adamson Act further increased congressional control of hours and wages; it specifically benefitted railway workers by establishing an eight-hour day and providing that there be no wage cuts for the shorter working day. The Owen-Keating Act of 1916 prohibited the interstate transportation of manufactured goods that were produced in factories employing children between the ages of 14 and 16 years who worked more than eight hours in one day. Wilson had answered the liberal demand for sweeping progressive legislation. But this legislation was only the start of government regulation. Many problems had not been touched. The year 1916 brought a real showdown to the Progressive Movement. By 1916 Wilson not only faced an election but faced a war in Europe as well.

The election of 1916 was held during a foreign crisis. The United States was being drawn ever closer to participation in the world war in Europe, which had been waged since August 1914. The Democrats again turned to Wilson, who ran on the slogan, "He Kept Us Out of War." Roosevelt declined to run for the Progressive party, so it died the death of many third parties. The Republicans did not turn to Roosevelt but to a justice of the Supreme Court, Charles Evans Hughes, who, with his evasive answers, managed to appeal to both progressives and conservatives. In spite of his fence-straddling and his poor campaign managers, he went to bed the night of the election convinced he was the next president-elect. But the Midwest and West supported Wilson, who barely was reelected. Progressivism was ignored during Wilson's second term, for the United States entered World War I in 1917 and Wilson's domestic policies were geared to mobilizing the nation. With the conclusion of the war, Wilson's energies were spent in trying to persuade the nation to accept the Versailles Treaty and to join the new League of Nations. The defeat of that treaty left him a broken man.

Woodrow Wilson was truly a progressive president. He joined the Progressive Movement, which attempted to restore individual dignity to American society, and brought it to new heights. He expanded both the office of the presidency and the role of the federal government. While initially he was committed to the philosophy of New Freedom, with its belief in state action and laissez-faire economics, he mixed the New Freedom with a New Nationalism and emerged with an effective progressive blend. The intellectual ability and moral purpose he brought to the presidency in his second term have been unequaled in modern times. While his idealism and energy focused on a plan for world peace and limited further progressive reform, the progressivism which he did institute brought real changes to American society.

Politics in the 1920s

The election of 1920 saw Americans attempt to return to the prewar times. The Republicans nominated handsome Warren G. Harding, who promised a return to "normalcy," and whose campaign slogan was "Less government in business and more business in government." The disorganized Democrats finally nominated James M. Cox on the forty-fourth ballot, and their platform pledged support for the League of Nations. The Republican platform was a collection of ambiguities that seemed to please everyone. The public was tired of war, internationalism, and the Democrats. When the results were in, the Republicans had won a smashing victory, the Democrats had lost, and Wil-

The politics of "normalcy" thrust Warren G. Harding into the presidency in 1920.

son's League had been repudiated. Wilson died three years later a broken and defeated man. He had carried the nation to the climax of progressivism but had exhausted much of his later energy in fighting "a war that would end all wars."

The Harding Years

Born on a farm in Ohio, Harding spent much of his early life working for a weekly newspaper. After graduating from college, he tried teaching and then turned to journalism. He became the editor of a newspaper, which he purchased, and also dabbled in state politics. His wife, known as "Duchess," pushed hard for him to enter national politics, and in 1914 he was elected to the United States Senate. His term as senator was uneventful; in fact, he missed more than half the roll calls. But he did vote with the Republican regulars, and party loyalty helped make him a Republican contender for president in 1920. Although he was selected by party leaders in "a smoke-filled room," he also had broad party appeal; his stirring oratory, with its vague statements, pleased many factions. While his campaign featured inconsistent stands on issues, it made little difference. The nation wanted a change and overwhelmingly elected Harding president.

"Nice Man" Harding, former director of a bank and a pillar of the Baptist church, was a charming individual with little intellectual ability, who brought his "Ohio Gang" with him into office. While he did make some worthwhile appointments, such as Secretary of State Charles E. Hughes, and Secretary of the Treasury Andrew Mellon, he placed more cronies into government positions than any other president since Ulysses Grant. Albert Fall, a man with his business interests in oil, became secretary of the interior; Charles Forbes, an army deserter, ended up head of the Veterans Bureau. Gaston Means, a known gangster and bootlegger, was given a position in the Department of Justice. If Grant's White House had a military-camp atmosphere, Harding's White House had a bar-room atmosphere. President Harding spent many night hours drinking and playing poker.

He understood politics little and economics less. Andrew Mellon, his secretary of the treasury who presided over the economy, was a multimillion-aire. Mellon believed that the wealthy were overtaxed and that lower income groups should share the tax burden. He also supported a higher tariff. The passage of the Fordney-McCumber Act of 1922 raised the tariff level to that of 1909. The prevailing philosophy of the time was that national prosperity depended on a friendly relationship between business and government. Laissez-faire economics began to return.

1922 Fordney-McCumber Act

Harding is not remembered for dynamic leadership but rather for the scandals that resulted from his appointments. Charles Forbes was accused of stealing millions of dollars from the Veterans Bureau; he resigned and eventually was convicted. Harding's Attorney General Harry Daugherty, who had been Harding's chief campaign manager, had been living with a known gangster; when the gangster was found dead, Daugherty, and indirectly Harding, was blamed. The most noteable scandal of the Harding years was the Teapot Dome scandal. Albert Fall had leased valuable petroleum deposits in California and Wyoming to oil companies. After a Senate investigation, Fall's connections with the oil companies were revealed; convicted of bribery, he became the first cabinet official to go to jail. These scandals involving the President's "friends" wore heavily on Harding, who looked increasingly tired and haggard. The economy was prospering but the scandals were destroying his credibility. During a West Coast trip in 1923, he became sick, and in San Francisco he died of a stroke. After his funeral, his reputation reached a new low with the publication of Nan Britton's book *The President's Daughter*, which told of Harding's mistress and of his illegitimate child. Rumors arose that his wife had poisoned him, but these stories were unfounded. Harding's shortcomings were quite obvious. He had below-average intelligence and trusted too many unreliable individuals. Although the United States did indeed return to "normalcy," Harding was and will be remembered chiefly for the scandals of his administration. On his death, Vice-President Calvin Coolidge became president.

From Coolidge to Hoover

Calvin Coolidge, "the Puritan in Babylon," was the shyest and most silent president in our history. Son of a Vermont merchant, he first practiced law and then entered politics. He worked his way up the ladder in Massachusetts politics and in 1918 was elected governor. He received national publicity for his firm stand against striking Boston policemen; it was then that he made the famous statement, "There is no right to strike against the public safety by anybody, anywhere, anytime." This statement won him the vice-presidency, and Harding's death thrust him into the presidency itself. When he learned of Harding's death he was vacationing at his father's farm in Vermont, where he took the oath of office by the light of a kerosene lamp. Calvin Coolidge was a mysterious individual. He rarely smiled and almost never laughed in public. He said and did little, while he slept a great deal. This man of few words was challenged to speak by a woman, who said that she could get him to say more than two words. He replied, "You lose." He often said that he had never been hurt by what "I have not said." He was a paragon of honesty and integrity, and he reflected even stronger probusiness sentiments than Harding. Stated Coolidge, "The business of America is business."

Since Coolidge became connected with continuing prosperity, the Republicans nominated him in 1924 on the first ballot. The Democrats were seriously divided, and it took 102 ballots to nominate John W. Davis, a New York corporation lawyer. The Republican slogan "Keep Cool with Coolidge" won the day, and the nation voted to continue prosperity by electing him president. The economic boom continued during his presidency, although Coolidge did little to help or hinder it. With less than 10 percent of the world's population, the United States now produced about 25 percent of the world's manufactures. One of the few stands he took as president was against the McNary-Haugen Bill, which attempted to help farmers. Coolidge easily could have run again for president in 1928, but his propensity for few words worked against him. He surprised the nation in the summer of 1927 when he announced, while wearing a half-cowboy, half-Indian costume, that "I do not choose to run for president." This ambiguous statement seemed to mean that the Republicans

Calvin Coolidge, here pictured with Secretary of the Treasury Andrew Mellon, rode the wave of prosperity in the 1920s and offered little in the way of positive leadership.

had to turn to another candidate, and they did. An evaluation of Coolidge's presidency can be as brief as his speeches. He rode the wave of prosperity; he was a man of few words and little action. The office of president was becoming less and less important. The Republican party now turned to an efficient administrator.

Herbert Hoover, the "Boy Wonder" of the Department of Commerce, was the Republican nominee in 1928, while the Democrats nominated the Irish Catholic governor of New York, Alfred E. Smith. Hoover stood for continued prosperity, promising "two chickens in every pot and a car in every garage." Smith and the Democrats also emphasized continued prosperity. The difference in the election was not between platforms but between individuals. Hoover was a successful businessman who had competed in the capitalistic system; Smith was Catholic, a product of urban immigrant America, and an opponent of prohibition. While Smith won many cities, his support was not broad enough, and Hoover won 58 percent of the popular vote.

Herbert Clark Hoover was the first president to have been born west of the Mississippi. Raised in Iowa, he was an orphan for most of his early years. Receiving his early education in Oregon, he graduated from newly established Stanford University with a degree in engineering. His work as a mining engineer caused him to travel to Australia and frequently to China. His success in engineering, in addition to making him wealthy, led him to establish an international mining firm in London. During World War I he headed a food-relief agency in Belgium and was given control of the United States Food Administration. After the war he helped direct the feeding of thousands in Europe. Harding named him secretary of commerce, a position Hoover also held under Coolidge. His skills as an administrator were revealed in his reorganization of the Department of Commerce and his sponsorship of numerous national conferences. Nominated in 1928, his stand on continued prosperity led him to the presidency.

Hoover brought with him an international background and a philosophy of "rugged individualism"; individuals, through hard work, inevitably become successful; government regulation limits individual initiative and eventually leads to socialism. He viewed government from the standpoint of an engineer, not as a practical politican. His first two goals were a tariff revision and farm relief. The Smoot-Hawley Tariff of 1920, however, raised the tariff levels to an all-time high; the Farm Board authorized relief measures but generally provided little help. Hoover's biggest problem began in October 1929 with the stock market crash and was known as the Great Depression. While Hoover was not responsible for the coming of the depression, his negative thinking did not equip him to adequately handle it. Eventually Hoover, the "Boy Wonder," became America's biblical Jonah.

Minorities in the 1920s

Although Harding, Coolidge, and Hoover brought business once again into politics, the legislative gains of the Progressive Era had become permanent policies. Minority groups, however, and in particular blacks, Indians, and Mexican-Americans, found that latent racial hostility lay behind the guise of unlimited prosperity. During the presidency of Woodrow Wilson, a great shifting of blacks occurred from the Southern farms to the urban centers of the North. The move from the rural South can be explained by many factors. Jim Crow laws in the South were becoming more dominant, and years of crop failures led to increased poverty. The North appeared to offer more opportunities. America's entry into World War I created new jobs in semiskilled and unskilled areas. But when blacks moved north they found resentment in the Northern cities. Whites resented competition for jobs and having blacks move into neighborhoods hitherto occupied only by whites. The growth of a national Ku Klux Klan helped to forment antiblack feeling.

1915
Klan reborn The reborn Klan was founded in 1915, near Atlanta, by William Simmons to be an exclusive fraternity for "the 100-percent American." The 100-percent American in this instance was the white Anglo-Saxon Protestant (WASP). Unlike the earlier klan, this new organization was more than just anti-black; it attacked all racial and religious groups that were out of the mainstream, particularly the blacks, Jews, and Catholics. By 1925 it had attracted five million members, and its appeal was truly national. Strong pockets of support were found in the cities of the North and West—the same cities that had received the migration of blacks from the South. Racial conflict seemed inevitable.

In 1919 growing tension broke into violence. More than 20 urban race riots occurred, the worst ones in Washington, D.C., and in Chicago. In Chicago, 3 days of fierce rioting left 33 blacks killed and more than 500 injured. Yet the blacks remained in the Northern cities.

Out of the frustration of the Northern ghettos emerged a new national leader who spoke of black pride; this was Marcus Garvey. Born in Jamaica, he came to New York City and formed the Universal Negro Improvement Association. This organization emphasized that black was beautiful: blacks should be proud of being black and join in league with all blacks from around the world. Garvey was particularly harsh with the white Americans, who had taken advantage of blacks for centuries. In his church angels were black and devils were white. In fact, he believed that the only real home for black people was Africa; he wrote, "The thoughtful and industrial of our race want to go back to Africa, because we realize it will be our only hope of permanent

Marcus Garvey offered black pride to the frustrated urban blacks of the eastern cities.

existence." His movement, with its emphasis on black pride and black na-tionalism, had mass appeal. He even proposed black economic control of blacks' own communities. His philosophy of black racial hatred was a chal-lenge to the growing white supremacy of the 1920s. In 1923 he was arrested for mail fraud and deported as an undesirable alien. His back-to-Africa cam-paign had found little success among American blacks, but his philosophy of black pride offered hope to blacks during a period of threatening racism.

Black pride also emerged among intellectuals during the Harlem Renais-sance movement of the 1920s. Black artists depicted life in the Northern cities in vivid terms. Black poets Claude McKay, Langston Hughes, and Countee Cullen were noteable writers of social protest. McKay wrote, "If we must die—let it not be like hogs . . ." These poets joined with other brilliant black artists, such as scholar Franklin Frazier, musician W. C. Handy, and actor Paul Robeson, to prove to America the worth of the black experience. But the grip of white Anglo-Saxon America was strong, and black culture would have to wait to receive any extensive acceptance.

The Red Scare and Immigration Quotas

The Red Scare and restrictions on immigration heightened antiminority feelings. After World War I, Americans feared that world communism was beginning to creep into the United States. Labor radicals and foreigners came under suspicion. At the height of this hysteria, Attorney General A. Mitchell Palmer instituted a series of raids to round up communists. A total of 6000 persons were taken into custody, and most of them were released. While the Red Scare subsided in the early years of the 1920s, it led the way to a quota system for immigrants. The American way had to be protected, or so reasoned even President Coolidge. Congress responded to this call with the passage of the National Origins Act of 1924, which restricted immigration to 150,000 total immigrants a year, depending on their place of birth. The act included an immigration quota for each foreign nationality based on the number of the same foreign-born in the United States as recorded in the 1890 census. This virtually closed immigration from Southern and Eastern Europe and forbade all immigration from the Orient. Such anticommunist and antiforeign feeling greatly added to the bigotry and racism of the 1920s and hurt most internal minority groups, such as the American Indian.

1924 National Origins Act

Indian Affairs

During this time the federal government continued to use the Dawes Act as the basis for Indian policy, but Secretary of Interior Albert Fall had other plans. He attempted, through the Omnibus Bill, to strip Indians of title to their land, title which had been granted by executive order. When this failed, he turned to the Bursum Bill, which would have taken away the titles to pueblos that the Pueblo Indians held through Spanish grants. This action failed only after the Pueblos put up a united front. Attempts also were made to use Flathead-Indian tribal land for a power plant and to transfer Walapai lands without compensation to the Santa Fe Railroad. Business continued to covet the Indians' diminishing lands. In 1924, however, Congress responded to the Indians' fine service in World War I by making all Indians United States citizens; most accepted this as a mixed blessing. Herbert Hoover's vice-president was Charles Curtis, a Kaw Indian, the first Indian ever elected to a high government post. Under Hoover's administration Ray Wilbur, secretary of interior, and Charles Rhoads, Indian commissioner attempted to improve Indian affairs. The Meriam Report, published in 1928, also proposed a radical departure from the policies of the Dawes Acts. A reform movement was building, but it was blunted by the effects of the depression. Mexican-Americans also suffered during the 1920s.

Migration from Mexico greatly increased in the early years of the twentieth century. Irrigation projects had opened new lands in the West; cotton was booming in Arizona and Texas. Railroads still were spanning the West. Workers were needed on the farms and railroads. With the exclusion of oriental immigration, the source of cheap labor had dried up. The agricultural industry, known as agribusiness, now began to actively recruit Mexican laborers. These workers were allowed to enter the United States during the busy season and then return to Mexico. The Mexican Revolution further stimulated Mexican immigration. During the period from 1910 to 1920 more than one million Mexicans came into the United States, but most of them returned to Mexico. Still, the question of Mexican immigration was causing a controversy. By World War I more businesses were setting up permanent camps for Mexican workers. The migrants who stayed in these permanent camps provided the nucleus for the growing urban Mexican-American population of today.

By the 1920s the issue of Mexican immigration began to be debated on a national level. Since the 1920s was a period of strong racial hatred, racial overtones influenced the debate. While the Immigration Act of 1924 placed quotas on immigrants, the Mexicans were exempted. But a border patrol was created, and a tax of $8 per person was instituted. This hardly stopped Mexican immigration. The Box Bill of 1926 attempted to apply a quota to Mexican immigration, but cheap labor was still needed. One Californian wrote, "We, gentlemen, are just as anxious as you are not to build the Civilization of California or any other western district upon a Mexican foundation. We take him because there is nothing else available to us." Although the bill was defeated, the controversy continued. And racism was evident, "Do you want a mongrel population, consisting largely of Mexicans?" Mexican immigrants received worse treatment than Mexican-American citizens already in the Southwest. They were treated as aliens, and with open contempt. Yet the Great Immigration of the first thirty years of the twentieth century created the basis for a growing Mexican-American minority in the Southwest.

Although very few minorities shared in the general prosperity of the 1920s, to the white masses it appeared that the good times would go on forever. But the bubble burst in 1929; the Coolidge boom ended with the Hoover crash. Theodore Roosevelt had brought progressive reform into the national political scene. While William Howard Taft took very unpopular stands on some explosive issues, he continued the progressive direction. But it was Woodrow Wilson who brought progressivism to new heights. The political and social reforms of Roosevelt, Taft, and Wilson were not discarded or forgotten in the 1920s, but they seemed buried beneath prosperity. The impetus toward progressivism was blunted when America entered World War I. The origins of that war and the rise of America as a world power are found in the diplomacy of the late 1800s, in the Spanish-American War, and in the foreign affairs of Roosevelt, Taft, and Wilson, all of which will be explored in Chapter 12.

Essay

The Democratic Party in the Progressive Age: From Bryan to Wilson

The Progressive Era started the nation on a new direction in national politics, and Republican President Theordore Roosevelt led the way. Big business could be regulated only by big government, he reasoned. Roosevelt believed that conservation had to become national policy, that further railroad regulation was necessary, and that standards needed to be set for goods and drugs. Roosevelt, head of the Republican party, led the way for progressive reform; in fact, he even handpicked his successor, William Howard Taft, to continue the momentum that he had started. Meanwhile, the Democratic party was in a state of disarray. The leadership of William Jennings Bryan reflected the outlook of rural, small town America at a time when America was moving toward urbanism. Who would bridge the gap between the rural and urban factions of the Democratic party? Would progressive reform become synonymous with the Republican party? These questions would be answered in the early years of the 1900s.

In 1896 the Democratic party turned to William Jennings Bryan, the choice of the rural West and South; he also was embraced as a candidate by the Populist party. Bryan had decidedly sectional appeal, but he tried to win the support of both farmer and laborer. He failed. Urban America moved away from the Democratic party. The Republican party now had the allegiance of the most populous, urbanized, and industrialized areas of the nation. The Democrats entered the Progressive Era with a severely crippled organization. Bryan, however, remained the voice and symbol of the Democrats. Still viewing politics as a form of crusade, he never tried to unite the party and actually caused it to further pull apart. At this time much of the Democratic party was on the wrong side of the progressive reform issue. Democratic politicans, however, had won favor with immigrant groups in Northern cities and had formed political machines based on these urban-immigrant coalitions. Many reforms during this time were directed at these political machines, but the reforms frequently were frustrated. It would be wrong, however, to think the Democratic party was entirely outside of progressive reform. Examples of Democratic reform were most evident in the South, which had become the stronghold of the party.

Southern progressivism urged reform in areas of social justice, honest government, and business regulation. Southern Democrats felt state government needed to intervene to restore dignity to the American scene. But the Democratic party's stand on racial issues in the South damaged the party's other progressive efforts there. Meanwhile, bloodletting was evident at the national level. In 1900 Bryan was again the candidate, and he again lost. Now publisher William Randolph Hearst attempted to seize power from Bryan. Although Hearst was a domestic re-

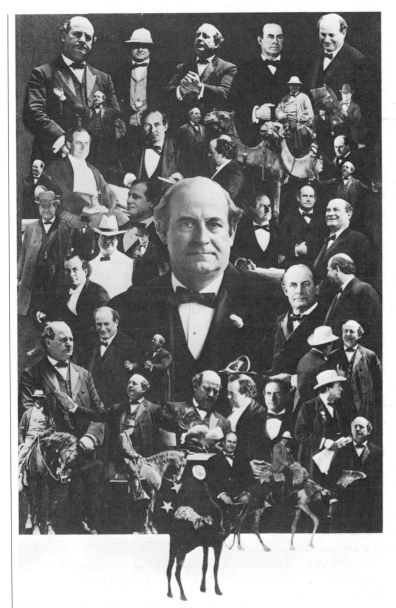

William Jennings Bryan, a three time loser for the office of president, symbolized the virtues of rural America.

Woodrow Wilson united many dissident elements in the Democratic party and led the way to the climax of the Progressive movement.

former, he was power hungry. The Democratic party's weakness at the time was evident in its choice in 1904 of Judge Alton B. Parker for president. The fact that he was so little known was the best thing in his favor. Parker's conservative stand failed, and the Democratic party suffered one of its worst defeats in history at the hands of Theodore Roosevelt.

The Democrats who had managed to win on state and local levels had done so on progressive reform platforms; this told the national party something important. The party now moved to a new focus—reform of state and local governments. Grassroots Democrats were on the rise, but Bryan was still in control of the national party. And his progressive program had been outflanked by Roosevelt. Much of the reform that Bryan had proposed in the 1890s, from his strident rural perspective, had been integrated into Roosevelt's own national progressive program. Bryan was nominated again for president in 1908, and, with the victory of Roosevelt's handpicked successor, Taft, Bryan became a three-time loser. He reminded too many voters of the Bryan of old.

Still, things were beginning to look up for the party. The state and local reforms were beginning to surface in national politics. The American Federation of Labor was moving to support the Democratic Party. Republican President William Howard Taft was losing the momentum that Roosevelt had created. In the 1910 congressional elections the Democrats won a landslide and again took control of the House of Representatives. Democrats now guided a series of social reform measures into law.

By 1912 the Democratic party needed to leave the vestiges of Bryan and Parker behind and turn to a new candidate who would unite the divergent rural and urban factions, as well as gather labor support, and would continue the party's growing role in progressive reform. The man who accomplished this near impossible task was Woodrow Wilson. On the forty-sixth ballot he had won the nomination, and now he began to form a national coalition. He introduced his own brand of progressivism in the New Freedom, which attempted to restore the free-enterprise system without expansion of federal regulation and yet by restoring normal economic competition.

His program frequently was filled with moralisms and ambiguities, but he did bridge the gap between the factions of the party and won the election of 1912—thanks largely to divisions within the Republican party. For eight years Wilson held together a still-divided party and moved from New Freedom to all-out social reform. The transition from the splintered Democratic party under Bryan seemed complete. Yet Wilson's unification of the party had not been permanent; by the 1920s the party once again fell into factionalism, not to reach strong unity until the days of Franklin D. Roosevelt. The Democratic party, however, did participate in the Progressive Era, and under President Woodrow Wilson it attained a climax of social reform with a temporarily united party. ∎

Suggested Reading

Two excellent overviews of the Progressive Era are *Rendezvous with Destiny* (1952) by ERIC F. GOLDMAN and *The Response to Industrialism, 1885–1912* (1952) by SAMUEL P. HAYS.

The best biographies on Roosevelt include *Power and Responsibility: The Life and Times of Theodore Roosevelt* (1961) by WILLIAM HENRY HARBAUGH and *The Era of Theodore Roosevelt* (1958) by GEORGE E. MOWRY.

The life of Taft is covered in the biography *The Presidency of William Howard Taft* (1973) by P. E. COLETTA.

JOHN MORTON BLUM gives a short biography of Wilson in *Woodrow Wilson and the Politics of Morality* (1956), while much more detail is found in the numerous works of ARTHUR S. LINK, which include *Woodrow Wilson and the Progressive Era, 1910–1917* (1954).

Two general surveys of the 1920s are WILLIAM E. LEUCHTENBURG's, *The Perils of Prosperity, 1914–1932* (1958) and PAUL A. CARTER's, *The Twenties in America* (1968).

ANDREW SINCLAIR has written an excellent biography of Warren G. Harding, *The Available Man: The Life Behind the Mask of Warren G. Harding* (1965). The life of Coolidge is described in DONALD R. McCOY's, *Calvin Coolidge* (1967). Another analytical study of these two men is available in *The Politics of Normalcy: Government Theory and Practice in the Harding-Coolidge Era* (1973) by ROBERT K. MURRAY.

CHAPTER 12

From One War to Another:
Rise of a World Power

Time Line

?—A.D. 1492	Migration and evolution of American Indian societies
1492	Christopher Columbus lands in West Indies—beginning of European exploration
1607–1732	Establishment of 13 English colonies
1775–1783	American Revolution
1776	Declaration of Independence
1789–1797	Presidency of George Washington
1812–1815	War of 1812
1816–1824	Era of Good Feelings
1846–1848	Mexican War
1861–1865	Civil War
1865–1877	Reconstruction
1875	Reciprocal trade treaty with Hawaii
1898	Annexation of Hawaii / Spanish-American War
1899	U.S. sends Open Door notes to major powers / Philippine Revolt
1900	Boxer Revolt
1901	Platt Amendment
1903	Panama Revolt and Treaty
1905	Roosevelt Corollary to the Monroe Doctrine
1914	American Intervention in Mexico
1915	Sinking of the *Lusitania*
April 1917	United States enters World War I
November 1918	Germany surrenders
1919	Versailles Treaty meeting
1920	Senate rejection of Versailles Treaty
1877–1900	Industrialization and urbanization
1900–1916	Progressive Era
1917–1918	World War I
1930s	Depression and New Deal
1941–1945	World War II
1945–1960	Post-war politics
1950–1953	Korean War
1950–1960	Civil rights movement
1961–1973	Vietnam War
1976	Bicentennial celebration

From One War to Another: Rise of a World Power

The United States now has diplomatic relations with China. American presidents have played a major role in Middle East negotiations and proposed settlements. Since the Vietnam War the nation has relied upon a volunteer army; still military preparedness is very evident. It is hard to imagine a time in our history when we were more concerned with domestic growth than with foreign affairs. With the conclusion of the Civil War, urban-industrial America emerged. There were no foreign wars, and Europe was concerned with its own internal problems. Of course, America was still filling in the West and fighting wars against American Indians. Still, foreign affairs did not play a prominent role. Some Americans did talk of expanding our capitalistic system and seeking new markets for our products. But there was little talk of seeking new land. By the time of the census of 1890, which signaled the closing of America's last frontier, a new Manifest Destiny arrived on the scene. Coupled with the desire for new markets, this imperialism sought new lands for the American way of life. Businessmen, politicians, and the military alike supported this idea, which became reality during the Spanish-American War of 1898. America was now a world power in word and in fact. During its rise as an imperial power, the American capitalistic system began to extend itself into foreign countries, especially in the Western hemisphere. That course which involved America in the affairs of other nations saw the United States become part of the European struggle known as World War I. After the war the United States found that it was one of the dominant countries in the world and could no longer deemphasize foreign policy. The origins of the new Manifest Destiny and of imperialism existed as early as the years after the Civil War, but became most evident in the late 1800s.

Early Expansionism

In 1895 Senator Henry Cabot Lodge wrote, "We have a record of conquest, colonization, and expansion unequaled by any people in the nineteenth century." Although our colonization policy remained internal until the Spanish-American War, economic expansion, or the seeking of foreign markets, was intense. Finding new foreign markets was one of the desires of Secretary of State William Seward, who acquired Alaska under President Abraham Lincoln. After the Civil War this search for markets continued. President Grant particularly coveted many islands of the Caribbean, especially Cuba, but his desire to purchase the island was thwarted. Under President Hayes, Secretary of State William M. Evarts sought expansion of our trade network in the Far East and even with Canada. Secretary of State Frederick Frelinghuysen worked under President Cleveland to establish trade relations with many countries, including Mexico, Cuba, and numerous islands of the Caribbean. The most active secretary of state was James Blaine, who served in 1881 under Garfield and again from 1889 to 1892 under Harrison. He was a true internationalist who believed that this country was destined to dominate the Far East, the Pacific, and especially Latin America. Blaine's expansionist policy was based largely on his belief that the United States needed foreign markets for surplus goods. He saw Latin America as the most likely source. Blaine was the driving force behind the modern Pan-American movement, although its roots were found in the Monroe Doctrine and in the Latin American policy of President John Quincy Adams. In 1889 the first Pan-American Congress convened here with nineteen nations being represented. The American delegates were anxious to show the economic potential of the United States, so they foolishly took the delegates on a 5400-mile railroad tour. Exhausted from travel, the delegates adopted few positive measures. They rejected Blaine's plan for a custom union, but they endorsed arbitration of disputes and established an International Bureau for the exchange of economic, scientific, and technical information. This conference revealed American interest in the affairs of the Western hemisphere.

Blaine also was involved in disputes with Great Britain, Italy, and Chile. The United States had owned the two Pribilof Islands, the breeding place of many seals, and had come to believe that it had the power to protect the seals even beyond the three-mile international limit. So ships from various countries were seized. An international court of arbitration in Paris in 1893 ruled that the Bering Sea was not an American sea and that America had violated the rights of Britain by seizing its ships. In 1891 in New Orleans, 11 Italians were lynched for murder. This caused diplomatic repercussions with Italy. Diplomatic relations were broken. The United States, however, in a gesture of peace agreed to pay $25,000 to the families of the victims. The crisis passed. Later it was found that only three of the murdered men were actually Italians. In 1891 in Chile, the United States had supported the losing side in a civil war, so when a party of American sailors went ashore at Valparaiso they were attacked by a mob, and two of them were killed. Americans were incensed, but war was averted, for the Chilean government finally apologized and paid an indemnity of $75,000. This event, however, did hurt the good feelings that had been created by the Pan-American Congress.

Pacific Relations

Blaine also found himself involved in foreign problems in the Pacific. In 1878 the United States was given a naval station and commercial coaling rights at

Pago Pago in the Samoan islands, as well as an interest in the future of the islands. By the 1880s the United States found itself involved in a commercial struggle with Germany and Britain over control of Samoa. In fact, in 1889 the Germans supported a new ruler, while America and Britain supported the old one—a fight seemed imminent. However, the three powers negotiated instead, establishing a tripartite protectorate over Samoa, which ended in 1899 with the United States and Germany dividing the islands. The United States received Tutuila with the harbor of Pago Pago. Meanwhile, trouble was brewing in the Hawaiian Islands.

Missionaries had been sent in the early 1800s to Hawaii, and they were soon followed by planters. As early as the 1840s the United States warned other countries to stay out of the affairs of the Hawaiian Islands. In 1875 Hawaii signed a treaty with the United States that permitted Hawaiian sugar to enter the United States duty-free; in return the islands were prohibited from making economic or territorial agreements with any other nation. In 1887 the United States was guaranteed a naval base at Pearl Harbor. The American planters in Hawaii became extremely prosperous, that is, until the passage of the McKinley Tariff Act in 1890, which gave benefits to domestic producers of sugar and caused sugar-export prices to drop. Furthermore Queen Liliuokalani, who had become ruler in 1891, was trying to oppose American annexation of the islands and to stop nonnatives from taking political control. In 1893 a revolt occurred with the help of John L. Stevens, an American foreign minister, Steven Dole, a pineapple planter, and the United States Marines. The rebellion was successful, and Queen Liliuokalani stepped down from her throne. A provisional government was established, and the islands were declared a protectorate of the United States. Although President Cleveland delayed annexation of Hawaii, it was eventually accomplished in 1898. And by that time America was involved in another dispute in Cuba.

Cleveland and Venezuela

America's continuing aggressive foreign policy also involved a boundary dispute between Venezuela and British Guiana. These two countries had been in a conflict over mutual boundaries for years; now gold had been discovered in the disputed area and Venezuela asked for United States aid—in the spirit of the Monroe Doctrine—to uphold Venezuela's valid claim. England asserted that most of the area belonged to British Guiana and that the Monroe Doctrine did not apply in such a situation. President Cleveland realized public opinion was strongly anti-British; while he was not an imperialist, he felt that he must act. So in 1895 he intervened on the side of Venezuela. England was angered over American involvement but, to avoid further controversy, submitted the matter to international arbitration. The international court ruled in 1899 that

90 percent of the disputed area belonged to British Guiana. While the United States had not won a direct victory, it had expanded the meaning of the Monroe Doctrine and its vision of foreign policy.

The Spanish-American War

Much of the reasoning behind the growth of an American overseas empire can be traced to the expansion of American industry, which wanted overseas bases for its products. Some leading writers of the time gave voice to these sentiments and even interpreted them in terms of Social Darwinism. If the ideas of Darwin could be applied to religion and society, why not to foreign affairs? Certain strong nations seemed destined to take control over weaker ones. The doctrine of the survival of the fittest was being argued in the international realm. Writers John Fiske and Josiah Strong contended that the Anglo-Saxon people were the fittest and would take over the world, both economically and socially; said one, "God is training the Anglo-Saxon race for its mission." Congress gave expression to many of these ideas; a congressman even wrote, "We must go abroad!" One of the most influential writers was Alfred Thayer Mahan, who, in his book *The Influence of Sea Power Upon History*, reasoned that American sea power was essential to its international commercial supremacy. He declared the need for a strong navy and even recommended the building of a canal across the Isthmus of Panama. The new international Manifest Destiny, which would make America prominent in world affairs, was being born. An influential group of politicians began to give voice to these ideas, but it was events in Cuba that gave reality to them.

By the early 1890s, Cubans were still under Spanish domination, which was often inconsistent and at times oppressive. A Free Cuba movement had existed since the late 1860s, but no rebellion had been successful. For many years the United States had been interested in obtaining Cuba; nothing had happened, but Americans still kept a close watch on Cuban affairs. The depression of 1893 caused the passage of the Wilson-Gorman tariff, which imposed a high duty on foreign sugar, Cuba's leading import. A depression on the island stimulated another attempt at revolution in 1895. The rebels attempted to destroy the sugar crop, the island's source of economic revenue for Spain. The Spanish responded by sending General Valeriano Weyler to put down the rebellion; he earned the nickname "Butcher" through his use of concentration camps, where more than 200,000 people died. Initial sympathy for the rebels was evident in America as was economic self-interest, for Americans had more than $100 million invested in Cuban sugar. Sensational journalism turned sympathy into mass support. The *New York World* of Joseph Pulitzer and the *New York Journal* of William Randolph Hearst ran atrocity stories of Weyler's tactics, although many of the stories were untrue. These examples of the yellow press, or sensational journalism, included pointed questions such as, "How long are the Spaniards to drench Cuba with the blood and tears of her people?" and "How long will the United States sit idle and indifferent within the sound and hearing of raping and murder?" American sympathy continued to rise, and the Cuban revolutionary junta established an office in New York to foster more support. When President William McKinley assumed office in 1897, the demand for American action had reached a fever pitch. But Weyler had now been removed by Spain, and McKinley stated, "We must avoid the temptation of territorial aggression." Two events in 1898, however, caused him to change his mind.

Both Presidents Cleveland and McKinley had offered to mediate the dispute, but their offers were rejected. A new diplomatic ministry in Spain in 1897 offered limited autonomy to Cuba, but the rebels refused this offer. Then appeared in the United States on February 9, 1898, the publication of a letter written by Dupey de Lome, Spanish minister to the United States, which described McKinley as a "cheap politican" and as "weak and a bidder for the admiration of the crowd." Many Americans had said virtually the same thing; even Theodore Roosevelt had claimed McKinley had a backbone like a "chocolate eclair." But this was a Spanish minister criticizing an American president, and Americans became incensed.

The second inflammatory incident was the sinking of the ship *Maine*, which occurred in the Havana harbor by an explosion on February 15, 1898. Two officers and 264 enlisted men were killed. American popular opinion believed the Spanish government was responsible. An American naval court of inquiry decided that the *Maine* had been sunk by a submarine mine, while the Spanish government reported that the explosion had been internal and accidental. A recent naval investigation overwhelmingly pointed to spontaneous combustion as the cause of the explosion. But most Americans in 1898 blamed the Spanish. Theodore Roosevelt said, "The *Maine* was sunk by an act of dirty treachery on the part of the Spanish." The slogan "Remember the Maine! To Hell with Spain!" could be heard throughout the country.

By April 1898, Spain had apologized for the de Lome Letter and had promised further concession and negotiation, but Spain refused independence for Cuba. McKinley could feel the public clamor for war; even the business community was beginning to espouse the cause for military action. Although

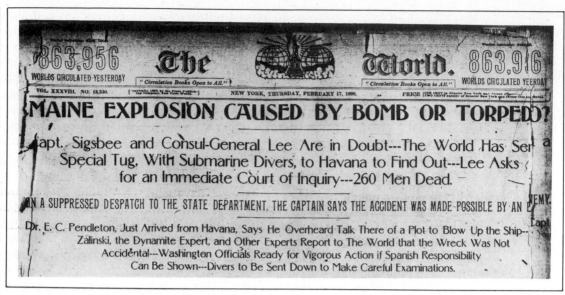

The World.

"Circulation Books Open to All."   "Circulation Books Open to All."

VOL. XXXVIII. NO: 13,330.   NEW YORK, THURSDAY, FEBRUARY 17, 1898.   PRICE (ONE CENT in Greater New York)

MAINE EXPLOSION CAUSED BY BOMB OR TORPEDO?

Capt. Sigsbee and Consul-General Lee Are in Doubt---The World Has Sent a
Special Tug, With Submarine Divers, to Havana to Find Out---Lee Asks
for an Immediate Court of Inquiry---260 Men Dead.

IN A SUPPRESSED DESPATCH TO THE STATE DEPARTMENT, THE CAPTAIN SAYS THE ACCIDENT WAS MADE-POSSIBLE BY AN ENEMY.

Dr. E. C. Pendleton, Just Arrived from Havana, Says He Overheard Talk There of a Plot to Blow Up the Ship---
Zalinski, the Dynamite Expert, and Other Experts Report to The World that the Wreck Was Not
Accidental---Washington Officials Ready for Vigorous Action if Spanish Responsibility
Can Be Shown---Divers to Be Sent Down to Make Careful Examinations.

Whatever the reason for the sinking of the *Maine*, Americans blamed the Spanish. This incident helped push the American public toward the Spanish-American War.

McKinley personally opposed war, he knew that it was a popular issue and that reelection was fast approaching. After Congress appropriated money for possible military action, McKinley announced that America must "act in the name of humanity, in the name of civilization, in behalf of the endangered American interests." Congress then adopted a resolution granting independence to Cuba, demanding withdrawal of Spain, authorizing the president to use army and naval forces to support the resolution, and promising that the United States would not annex Cuba.

American Involvement

Although the war was designed to liberate Cuba, the first action took place in the Philippines. Assistant Secretary of the Navy Theodore Roosevelt had warned Commodore George Dewey that in the event of war Dewey was to attack the Spanish fleet in the Philippines. On May 1, 1898, war was declared; one week later, Commodore Dewey's Pacific squadron destroyed the Spanish fleet in Manila Bay without the loss of one American ship or a single American life. With eventual army assistance the Philippines were seized, and officially surrendered on August 13, 1898. Imperialism was alive and well in the Pacific.

The Spanish-American War, referred to by some as that "splendid little war" and by others as "the dirty little war," was a ten-week war, with the actual fighting being brief. More Americans died from disease than from gunfire. War was declared in April; Spain was seeking a peace treaty by the middle of July. The major action on the island of Cuba focused on the city of Santiago, the Spanish stronghold. The most publicized battle in the early days of the war was the battle of San Juan Hill, in which the first Volunteer Cavalry Regiment proved their mettle with the help of two crack black regiments. The Rough Riders, composed of cowboys, ranchmen, athletes, and ex-convicts, were led by Lieutenant Colonel Theodore Roosevelt. This bloody encounter was described later by Roosevelt as "great fun." After the Americans blockaded the major port city of Santiago, the Spanish fleet attempted to openly confront the superior American Navy but was destroyed in a running battle along the Cuban coast; more than 500 Spanish were killed. "Don't cheer, men, the poor devils are dying," spoke one American officer. The war was short; the Americans victorious. In many ways the Americans were lucky, for the American war effort was a mess.

Generally the American public gloried in the war. People were singing,

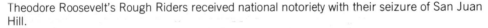

Theodore Roosevelt's Rough Riders received national notoriety with their seizure of San Juan Hill.

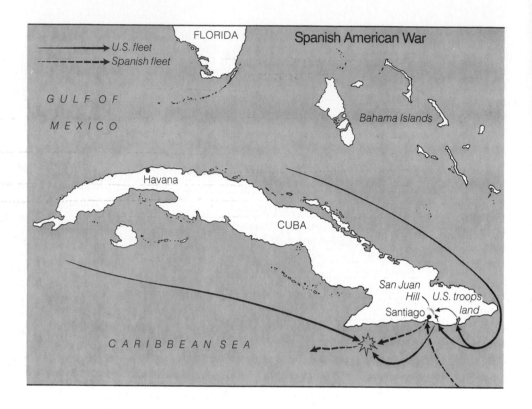

Spanish American War

- → U.S. fleet
- --→ Spanish fleet

FLORIDA

GULF OF MEXICO

Bahama Islands

Havana

CUBA

San Juan Hill

U.S. troops land

Santiago

CARIBBEAN SEA

"There'll be a Hot Time in the Old Town Tonight" and "Hail, Hail, the Gang's All Here." Meanwhile the soldiers found the war effort confused and inefficient. Administration was disorganized; the main departing area near Tampa, Florida, was extremely unsanitary. Soldiers received woolen uniforms for the tropical fight, ate "embalmed beef," and frequently lacked essential supplies. One soldier wrote:

> The other volunteers were at a hideous disadvantage, owing to their not having smokeless powder. General Shafter is too unwieldly to get to the front. I have not blanket or coat; I have not taken off my shoes even. I sleep in the drenching rain and drink putrid water.

Gout-ridden American General W. R. Shafter was fortunate that Spanish inefficiency was worse than American mistakes. When the smoke cleared, the mosquitos and dysentery had killed more Americans than Spanish bullets.

The Heritage of War

The Spanish-American War marked the beginning of America as a world power. When the war started, America claimed to have no overseas ambitions, but with the conclusion of the war the United States had achieved economic domination of independent Cuba and had acquired Puerto Rico, Guam, and the Philippines for $20 million. President William McKinley and others had strong reservations about taking the whole of the Philippines, but supposedly after prayerful consideration they found "there was nothing left for us to do but to take them all, and to educate the Filipinos, and uplift and civilize and Christianize them and by God's grace do the very best we could by them, as our fellow men, for whom Christ died." Most Americans had supported the war, but now a group of citizens known as the Anti-Imperialist League, including Cleveland, Carnegie, and Mark Twain, tried to stop the passage of the treaty. These men argued that imperialism violated the principles of the Declaration of Independence and risked war with Asian powers. They concluded that this imperialism was outright racism. A spirited debate occurred, but the Senate ratified the treaty with only one vote more than the necessary two-thirds majority. Now America took up "the white man's burden." American rule was imposed on peoples different in language, race, and customs. Many moralists such as President McKinley saw the expansion as part of God's destiny for America, while industrialists and bankers anticipated new markets for selling of surplus goods and investment of surplus funds.

The United States now had an overseas empire that included more than nine million foreigners. Rule over this empire was not an easy task. Puerto Rico was made a protectorate. Although the Teller Amendment had forbade American annexation of Cuba, military occupation of the island continued until a Cuban assembly wrote a constitution that included the Platt Amendment. This amendment guaranteed American domination through veto power over Cuban treaties, occupation of "naval stations" on the island, and the right to intervene militarily to preserve Cuban independence. American influence continued in Cuba. The Filipinos had welcomed American help against the Spanish, but, when they learned they merely were undergoing a change of masters, they rebelled. Under the leadership of Emilio Aguinaldo the rebels put up a formidable fight against overwhelming odds. Their use of guerilla warfare frustrated American soldiers; racial hatred rose, and atrocities were evident on both sides. This war to maintain an overseas empire ended in 1901 after two years of unpleasant fighting. Americans had learned that "bearing the white man's burden" could involve the use of force.

American expansion into the Philippines caused renewed interest in China. Since America was now an Asian power, businessmen once again became interested in the potentially lucrative Chinese trade, while missionaries became more involved in saving Chinese souls. But America was not the only nation interested in China. European imperialistic powers had begun to divide China into "spheres of influence." American-China trade was being threatened by these "spheres." In 1899 Secretary of State John Hay issued a statement in the form of an Open Door note to other major powers in China, telling them China was to be left open for all nations. Although there was little response, the United States announced that all the powers had accepted the open door policy. Just as this note was being issued, a group of Chinese nationalists known as the Righteous Fist of Harmony, or the Boxers, revolted against foreign intervention. This Boxer rebellion in 1900 was put down by an international army, which included 2500 American soldiers. Military invasion of China directly threatened Chinese independence, so Hay, to limit the extent of intervention and to help bring a swift conclusion to the war, issued a second Open Door note. This note demanded "impartial trade" in all parts of China, unrestricted by any "spheres of influence", and demanded the preservation of China's territorial integrity. This policy was adopted reluctantly by the other countries, and instead of a continued invasion the major powers exacted huge reparation payments from China. Although these notes lacked real enforcement, they did reveal America's interest in its overseas empire, as well as its moralism in foreign affairs.

American Power Expands under Three Presidents

Under McKinley an overseas empire had taken shape; the next two presidents, Theodore Roosevelt and William Howard Taft, now followed a course in foreign affairs known as *economic imperialism*. Roosevelt's program can be described as "Big Stick" diplomacy, based on his belief that in international affairs the United States should "speak softly and carry the big stick." Roosevelt believed that the United States now had a moral obligation to be active in world affairs and that the key to American leadership rested on sea power. Roosevelt echoed the ideas of writer Alfred Thayer Mahan by believing that the control of an overseas empire rested with a powerful navy. Roosevelt also saw the need for a Central American canal, which would connect the Atlantic and Pacific. He believed the United States now had risen to the status of an imperial power and should begin to act like one, using its influence in world councils and even helping solve world problems that were not of immediate concern to the American people. Here were the origins of our modern foreign policy.

This political cartoon pictures Theodore Roosevelt's "Big Stick" diplomacy toward Latin America.

Roosevelt's foreign policy was evident in his handling of the proposed canal. The Hay-Pauncefote Treaty of 1901 with England authorized the United States to build, operate, and fortify an Isthmian canal. Secretary of State Hay now attempted to obtain from Columbia a six-mile-wide canal zone across the Isthmus of Panama for a cash payment of $10 million and an annual rental fee of $250,000. Colombia rejected the agreement, for they wanted more money and more control over the canal zone. This rejection caused Roosevelt to describe the Colombians as "dagoes," "contemptible little creatures," "jack rabbits" and "homicidal corruptionists." "I want the canal built," he raged. If Colombia would reject a fair offer, another method of obtaining the land must be found.

While Roosevelt was prepared to ask Congress for the authority to seize the canal zone, plans were underway for a Panamanian insurrection. In November 1903, the rebellion occurred; a United States warship prevented Colombians from landing and putting down the Panamanian insurrection. A little more than an hour after receiving news of the rebellion, Roosevelt recognized the new, independent Republic of Panama. The only casualties in this "spontaneous" rebellion were a Chinese laundryman and a French poodle. Panama agreed to a treaty that gave the United States perpetual lease of a strip of land across Panama ten-miles wide and complete sovereignty within this zone. Roosevelt later boasted, "I took the canal." He wrote," ". . . I confidently maintain that the recognition of the Republic of Panama was an act justified by the interests of collective civilization." While Roosevelt was not responsible for the revolt, his big stick diplomacy did prevent Colombian intervention, a move which raises real questions about his motives.

American intervention in affairs of the Western hemisphere were further expanded by our involvement in the Dominican Republic. In the early 1900s the economy of the Dominican Republic was undergoing much chaos. Rumors arose of possible European intervention to collect long overdue debts. The possibility of such action caused Roosevelt in 1904 to issue a statement now known as the Roosevelt Corollary to the Monroe Doctrine. America was clearly to be the policeman of the Western hemisphere:

Chronic wrongdoing, or an impotence which results in a general loosening of the ties of civilized society . . . . may force the United States, however reluctantly, in flagrant cases of such wrongdoing or importance, to the exercise of an international police power.

This doctrine was used in 1905 when the United States managed the customs revenues and debt payments of the Dominican Republic. The Monroe Doctrine, which had warned against European intervention, now was being used to justify American intervention.

Roosevelt also acted as a mediator in a Far East war. In 1904–1905 Russia and Japan had fought a war over Manchuria. In 1905, at Portsmouth, New Hampshire, Roosevelt helped both parties to reach a truce. With the agreement Japan emerged as a major world power, while Roosevelt received the Nobel Peace Prize. Many critics today note that Roosevelt's involvement helped the Japanese win the war and led to increased Japanese militarism, anti-American feelings, and eventually to the events of Pearl Harbor. Of course, Roosevelt's Gentlemen's Agreement of 1907 helped foster anti-American feelings. Roosevelt at this time also sent a fleet of 16 warships around the world to demonstrate our naval superiority. This "Great White Fleet" became laughable when Congress cut off funds for it and it was forced to limp home.

Roosevelt not only believed in direct action in the Western hemisphere but also similar action in other parts of the world. His diplomatic interference in Morocco is an example of his involvement in European politics. In 1904 news reached the United States that a supposed American citizen, Ion Perdicaris, had been captured in Morocco and held for ransom. Ignoring evidence that he was not an American, Roosevelt demanded his release and sent a fleet to Morocco to hasten his freedom. Perdicaris, it was learned, turned out to be Greek. Tension also was rising between France and Germany over the control of Morocco. Germany asked Roosevelt to call an international conference to deal with this issue. In 1906 at Algeciras the United States participated in a conference that temporarily settled the Moroccan issue. Roosevelt's foreign policy had broadened the role of America as a nation in the world of nations. His successor, Taft, continued this involvement.

Taft and Dollar Diplomacy

Taft believed in economic imperialism, or that American investments should be encouraged abroad. His Secretary of State Philander C. Knox, a former corporation lawyer, placed great emphasis on expansion of American capitalism, particularly in Central America. American industry had money for overseas investments; this principle of "dollar diplomacy" was the heart of Taft's foreign policy. While the American investments became most evident in Honduras, Guatemala, and Haiti, dollar diplomacy faced a real challenge in Nicaragua. Possible political and economic chaos caused 2700 marines to be sent to Nicaragua to keep order and protect American business interests there. Dollar diplomacy ultimately required military intervention to insure stability for American investments. Distrust of the United States in the Western hemisphere began to grow. But dollar diplomacy was even directed to the Far East. Knox proposed the American purchase of a railroad in Manchuria as a key to American economic growth in China; this move was rebuffed. The United States now was following a policy of foreign economic and military intervention for the sake of American investors.

Wilson and Moral Meddling

When he became president, Woodrow Wilson attempted to move away from the economic imperialism of dollar diplomacy, yet he inaugurated a new era of moral meddling. This policy was most evident toward Mexico. Wilson judged foreign leaders and governments by his strict moral standards. He did not agree with the tactics of Victoriano Huerta, who had seized control of the Mexican government; Wilson referred to him as the leader of "a government of butchers" and refused recognition to his "government by murder." In 1914 Wilson openly supported rebel forces under Venustiano Carranza and Francisco "Pancho" Villa and allowed them to buy arms in the United States with congressional approval. Wilson decided to eliminate the Huerta government by occupying the city of Vera Cruz. Both Carranza and Huerta protested the invasion. Although Carranza came to power, Mexican politics continued to be in a turmoil, with the forces of Pancho Villa trying to overthrow Carranza. Villa's raid on Columbus, New Mexico, in March 1916 led to the death of 17 Americans. Demands for war rose. Wilson ordered a punitive expedition under Brigadier General John J. Pershing to hunt down Villa. Pershing pursued Villa in Mexico and barely missed capturing him. Carranza ordered Wilson to withdraw the troops; he refused. The United States and Mexico were on the brink of war. Pershing's forces twice came into contact with Carranza's troops. But both leaders desired peace, and war was avoided. Wilson's confused policy

Woodrow Wilson's moral meddling in Mexico led to General John J. Pershing's expedition against the forces of Mexican rebel Pancho Villa.

toward Mexico was complicated by his moralism in foreign policy; it created an anti-American hostility there that would last for years.

The demands of the time made Wilson the *moralist* into Wilson the *imperialist.* Wilson spoke of Pan-Americanism and a "good-neighbor policy," but he also encouraged American investment. During his presidency troops were sent to Santo Domingo, Cuba, and Haiti and a treaty was signed that gave the United States the right to naval bases in Nicaragua. But the events in the Western hemisphere were quickly becoming secondary to the happenings in Europe.

The Great War

By the early years of the 1900s, Europe was on the brink of war. Hatred between France and Germany was on the rise, while two alliance systems had emerged with Germany, Austria-Hungary, and Italy on one side and England, France, and Russia on the other. Within this precarious balance, Britain and Germany began to enter into much more open rivalry in areas of commerce and industry. Eventually, the two armed camps came into direct conflict over events in the Balkans. Russia and Austria were at odds over land in the Balkan peninsula. Few Americans understood the significance of the shooting of Arch-duke Franz Ferdinand, the heir to the Austrian throne, on June 27, 1914, by a Serbian nationalist. The events that followed the incident led to a world war. Austria demanded satisfaction from Serbia and eventually declared war. The domino-effect of the alliance system began. Russia helped Serbia, Germany aided Austria, while France and England entered on the side of Russia. Europe was at war.

The United States was not bound to any European country by alliances, nor did it see any advantage in entering the war. So it became the leading neutral. President Wilson asked for absolute impartiality "in thought as well as action." But this was difficult. America was emotionally and culturally tied to the nations of Western Europe. Skillful British propaganda, plus Germany's invasion of neutral Belgium, turned American opinion against Germany. The anti-German song "The Hun is at the Gate" became popular. Movies and the newspapers pictured German atrocities and dramatized the horror a German take-over of America would create. Still Wilson pushed for complete neutrality, even though he himself favored the British heritage. At the same time, American "merchants of death"—the munitions industry—were beginning to make a sizeable profit from the war. American capitalists also saw the Allied (Britain and France) need for money and began to make huge loans. By 1917 they had loaned the Allies $2.3 billion, while only loaning $27 million to Germany. The American bias was obvious.

Since Britain was the strongest naval power, the British initially violated American neutral rights on the seas. England, trying to establish a blockade of the European coast, stopped and searched American ships and confiscated American goods. America protested; England did realize the importance of American friendship and frequently paid for confiscated goods, but it continued the blockade policy. Germany now began to feel the effect of the blockade and sought a way to counter it through the use of a new weapon, the submarine, or U-boat. In February 1915 Germany announced that all vessels sailing into the war area around Britain would be sunk, and this even included neutral vessels. Taking a strong stand, Wilson warned Germany that America would hold them to a "strict accountability" for illegal destruction of American ships, goods, and lives.

A challenge to this "strict accountability" occurred on May 7, 1915. On that day a British passenger ship, the *Lusitania*, was sent to the bottom of the Irish Sea by a German U-boat; casualties included the loss of 128 American lives. One newspaper reported, "It was a deed for which a Hun would blush, a Turk be ashamed, and a Barbary pirate apologize." Although this ship had carried a cargo of munitions for the Allies, the loss of American lives caused

The sinking of the *Lusitania* with the loss of 128 American lives caused the Germans to change the focus of their U-boat warfare.

many Americans to demand war. But Wilson correctly read the mood of the nation and responded with words, not bullets. In defending his policy of continued nonintervention he said, "There is such a thing as a man too proud to fight; there is such a thing as a nation being so right that it does not need to convince others by force that it is right." In September 1915, Germany promised the United States that it would not sink passenger liners again without warning.

But the pledge would not be followed. In March 1916, the French liner *Sussex* was sunk with some Americans injured. Wilson issued another ultimatum and warned that if similar incidents occurred the United States would break off diplomatic relations with Germany. Germany again promised not to sink merchant ships without searching them for neutral passengers. Wilson did not know how long this pledge would be lived up to and felt that military preparedness was necessary. So he pushed through Congress compromise measures to strengthen the navy and army.

After his reelection in 1916, Wilson tried harder to bring the war to an end by asking both sides to clearly state their war aims. But both sides, as they had earlier, felt that victory was near at hand and refused to enter into any negotiations. Germany had practiced restricted submarine warfare for nine months. But in January 1917 Germany now decided to embark upon an all-out war, even if this meant involving the United States. Even as Wilson was asking for "Peace without victory," unrestricted submarine warfare was being resumed. Meanwhile, in March 1917, disclosure of the Zimmerman note aroused the nation. This note, written by the German foreign secretary to the German minister in Mexico, invited Mexico to attack the United States in the event of a general war. In return Mexico was promised its lost territory in Texas, New Mexico, and Arizona. Diplomatic relations with Germany were broken off. American merchant vessels were armed. But the German sea attacks continued; four American ships were sunk. On April 2, 1917, Wilson declared a state of war; the world he said, must be made "safe for democracy." He had wanted to maintain American neutrality, "but the right is more precious than peace, and we shall fight for which we have always carried nearest our hearts—for democracy—. . . . for the rights and liberties of small nations . . . ." America had entered the war.

Ever since the fateful day of April 6, 1917, when Congress voted for war, there has been no agreement as to why America entered the war. President Wilson declared that the United States had declared war because of the German U-boat policy, which had pushed the nation out of neutrality and into armed conflict. But Wilson's neutral policy was not really a "neutral" one. American hearts and minds—and pocketbooks—seemed to be on the Allied side. While the German U-Boat became the great menace, British ships continued to damage our commerce. But according to the propaganda, it was only Germany that represented a threat to America's democratic system—and to our Anglo-Saxon heritage. As with all wars, complex issues were at the heart of our involvement. But whatever the reasons were, America was finally committed to action.

American Involvement

While Americans were singing "I Didn't Raise My Boy to be a Soldier," the nation mobilized for war. It became obvious very soon that America would have to contribute supplies, money, and men to the Allied cause. Under the

By June, 1917, American troops in Europe were actively involved in the trench warfare of World War I.

command of General John J. Pershing, troops arrived in Paris by June 1917; they were known as the American Expeditionary Force. The Allies looked upon the American soldiers as reinforcements for their sagging armies, but Pershing wanted the American unit to remain separate. With the advent of the Russian Revolution, that country's new leaders entered into peace with Germany in early 1918. The Eastern front was closed. Germany now began an all-out effort to take Paris. By the spring of 1918 American troops were involved in an Allied counterattack to drive the Germans back from the area near Paris. After this objective was achieved, Pershing began the first independent American operation with offensive action in the Argonne Forest and along the Meuse River. After days of bloody encounters the German line of defense was broken, and the Allies advanced. This forced the Germans to retreat. Soon they would capitulate, signing an armistice on November 11, 1918. While the American troops had been involved in little more than six months of heavy fighting, they had boosted the morale of the Allies and had been a significant factor in bringing about Allied victory. Many Americans felt "they could not have won without us." American destroyers also were effective in limiting the U-boat tactics. By the end of the war more than

World War I in Europe

- - - - - - Battle Line, April, 1918
————— Battle Line, Armistice, Nov. 11, 1918

116,000 Americans of every ethnic and racial background had died, including many blacks.

With American entry into the war many blacks rushed to join the armed forces only to find that a quota had been set on black enlistees. After the passage of the Selective Service Act of 1917 blacks registered for the draft, and nearly 31 percent of those registered were drafted. Blacks suffered the same prejudice and discrimination that they had in past wars. Most blacks were considered unfit for combat duty and were assigned to labor and service units;

army officials noted that they were best fit for manual labor. This idea even applied to black doctors, who were drafted as privates. Officers' training programs for blacks were virtually nonexistent before the opening of a black-officers program at Fort Des Moines, Iowa. Blacks were not even allowed in the marine corps or coast guard. And along with discriminatory treatment in the armed forces, blacks continued to receive poor treatment on the home front too. There were many examples of racial prejudice in basic-training camps. In addition, race riots occurred in Houston, Texas, and Spartanburg, South Carolina. In Houston, black soldiers attempted to board a streetcar reserved for whites; violence occurred and 12 civilians were killed. As a result of the incident, 13 black soldiers were hanged and 41 more were sentenced to life imprisonment. Segregated facilities were maintained in training camps, service centers, and even aboard troop ships. Still, 371,000 blacks served admirably in the war and won much acclaim.

The Nation at War

Wilson had the inevitable duty of transforming a peacetime nation into a nation at war. Initially, the government relied on voluntary and cooperative efforts, but a modern war demanded total mobilization. So Wilson began to establish control over every important aspect of American economic life. First he faced the problem of financing the war. The war cost more than $46 million per day; to meet this fantastic expense, the Revenue acts of 1917 and 1918 raised tax rates. There were also luxury, excise, and excess-profit taxes, as well as a "victory surtax." The government also went into the business of selling government bonds, known as Liberty and Victory Loans. $11 billion dollars was raised through increased taxes, and $22 billion was raised from bond subscriptions.

Wilson then attempted to adjust and coordinate American industry to war production. Initially the Council of National Defense was established for the purpose of utilizing the resources of the nation for war, but it failed at its task. So, in 1917, the War Industrial Board was created. At first it had little authority or power, but in the next year Bernard Baruch, a wealthy businessman, was appointed chairman of the board and given power to determine priorities on production and deliveries, to fix prices, to promote industrial efficiency and eliminate waste, and to increase the volume of munitions output. The entire control of manufacturing facilities came under its auspices. Government justification for this control was that the economic life of the nation must be integrated with great care. The United States Shipping Board was created to buy, build, charter, and operate merchant ships. The entire railroad system

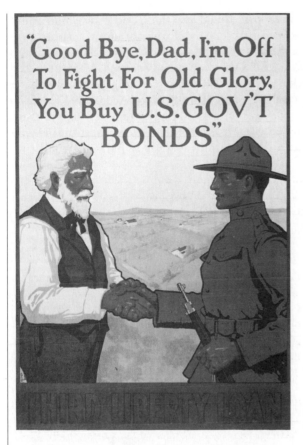

"Good Bye, Dad, I'm Off To Fight For Old Glory, You Buy U.S. GOV'T BONDS"

THIRD LIBERTY LOAN

One of the ways the government financed the war was through the sale of government bonds.

came under government control and was operated as a single system. Even with strict government supervision, the demand for industrial production was fantastic; guns, ships, shells, and other essential goods were made as quickly as possible. The production volume kept pace, and so did the profits.

This economic boom was a godsend to labor. Samuel Gompers of the A.F.L. pledged organized labor's full support to the war effort and made it clear that in return labor expected the government to enforce fair-labor standards and to include labor representatives on all defense agencies. Labor was represented on a host of public and regulatory agencies, and the National War Labor Board was set up to settle disputes in war-connected industries and to insure that workers had the right to organize in unions and to bargain collectively.

Farmers and housewives were mobilized by the Food Administration, headed by Herbert Hoover, who convinced Americans to adopt a voluntary-control program. A schedule of wheatless Mondays and Wednesdays, meatless Tuesdays, and porkless Thursdays and Saturdays was observed. Vegetable gardens appeared in the most unlikely places. After heated congressional debate, a mass army was recruited through the Selective Service Act of 1917, which stipulated that all men between the ages 21 and 30 had to register for the draft. On July 20, 1917, Secretary of War Newton D. Baker drew the number 258 from a bowl; this was the beginning of a draft system which eventually in-

This anti-German war poster was typical of the American propaganda campaign.

ducted 3 million men into the army. One of the most difficult tasks was to galvanize public opinion while at the same time preserving civil liberties. Wilson established the Committee on Public Information, whose job it was to mobilize public opinion by "selling" the war as a crusade of all that was good against all that was evil. Through massive propaganda tactics, the committee succeeded in getting the majority of Americans mentally behind the war effort. To add to this propaganda campaign, Congress passed the Espionage and Sedition acts. These acts were passed to limit criticism of the war and of American involvement in it. They outlawed "disloyal, profane, scurrilous or abusive language" concerning the government, the flag, or the Constitution, making illegal any action that interfered with the conduct of the war, the draft, or the sale of war bonds. Although both laws were obvious violations of civil rights, they were upheld by the Supreme Court. Hysteria gripped the country. Americans became overly suspicious. Citizens began to report their neighbors' unusual behavior. Radicals, socialists, and government critics were suppressed. Anything German was suspect. German music was not played; German language was not offered in the schools. German measles became "liberty measles," while sauerkraut became "liberty cabbage." A California newspaper demanded the dismissal of teachers who were "apathetic." A film entitled *The Spirit of '76* was withdrawn from circulation because it showed British atrocities during the American Revolution and, therefore, criticized our ally, England. Senator Robert La Follette commented upon the hysteria: "Any man who seeks to set a limit upon those rights, whether in war or peace, aimed a blow at the most vital part of our government." By the end of the war more than 1500 people had been convicted under the Espionage and Sedition acts.

Wilson's Fourteen Points

Although America itself may not have been made safe for democracy during the war, at war's end Wilson tried to make the world safe for democracy. In recent times it has been discovered that Wilson really believed American involvement in the world would thrust him into the position of world leader, allowing him to solve European problems and to bring European society to a new moral peak. He was sadly mistaken. Wilson viewed the war as a struggle of humanity and was most interested in proposing a solution that would bring true democracy to the countries of Europe. In January 1918, he proposed his Fourteen Points. This address listed the essential provisions of a permanent peace. They included: (1) open-peace convenants, (2) freedom of navigation on the seas, (3) elimination of tariffs, (4) reduction of arms, (5) self-determination of all peoples, (6) evacuation from Russia by Germany, (7) restoration of Belgium, (8) German evacuation of France, (9) a new frontier in northern Italy, (10) new national states in central Europe, (11) freedom for Serbia, (12) self-determination for the Turkish Empire, (13) a free Poland, and (14) formation of a general League of Nations to guarantee the political independence of all nations and to preserve international peace. One critic wrote of his speech, "Wilson has fourteen points, even God has only ten." The Fourteen Points were praised in both America and Europe, but the American nation did not share the crusading zeal of Wilson. This was evident in the election of 1918, which brought Republican majorities to both congressional houses. Still, the armistice with Germany included the Fourteen Points, and Wilson was optimistic that the final peace treaty would be based on them.

At the end of the war Wilson was at the height of his popularity, but from there until the end of his second term as president it was all downhill. His peace delegation to the treaty meeting at Versailles included no prominent Republicans nor any Senators, and he decided to personally attend the conference. No president had ever visited Europe while in office. Critics' voices began to be heard. Theodore Roosevelt wrote, "He is president of the United States, he is part of the treaty-making power, but he is only part." Still Wilson went to Versailles to remake Europe.

In Europe Wilson was greeted as the conquering hero. Crowds yelled "Wilson the Savior" and "Wilson the Just." But the charismatic charm that

Wilson went to Europe to negotiate a permanent peace. He is seen here (center) leaving the Peace Conference.

surrounded his arrival did not carry over into the peace meeting. The hard-line European diplomats David Lloyd George of England, Vittorio Orlando of Italy, and Georges Clemenceau of France did not accept the leadership role of Wilson nor the concept of the Fourteen Points. They saw the peace meeting as an opportunity to get revenge on Germany and to enact many of the secret treaties that had already been formulated. One by one the Fourteen Points were whittled away, until Wilson took a determined stand to preserve the heart of the points—the League of Nations. He felt that the League would overcome all the conflicts of the Versailles peace meeting and go on to arbitrate all future world problems. Meanwhile the other diplomats continued to carve up Europe and punish Germany. Germany had to pay harsh reparations for starting the war. Germany was left weak and angry; and a power vacuum was created in central Europe. Still, Wilson returned to America with a treaty that he felt would eventually bring world peace.

Defeat of the Treaty

The battle for the Versailles Treaty in the Senate would be Wilson's last. He had now made many political enemies, but he stood a fighting chance for ratification if he was willing to compromise. But he had compromised time and again in Versailles; he was no longer willing to budge. Factions in the Senate were divided, with the most adamant group being the "irreconcilables," who were against any form of a League. The "reservationists," who would only accept the treaty and the League with modifications, were led by the chairman of the Senate Foreign Relations Committee, Republican Henry Cabot Lodge. Lodge proposed fourteen reservations to counter Wilson's Fourteen Points and prepared a long session in committee to evaluate the treaty. Wilson became frustrated and took his cause to the people. Contrary to his doctor's advice, he staged a cross-country tour in support of the treaty. It was too much; in September 1919, after a speech in Pueblo, Colorado, he felt ill and returned to Washington. He had suffered a stroke and was near death. Meanwhile the discussion of the treaty continued. The major criticism fell upon Article X of the League of Nations Convenant, which states that the League would protect against external aggression "the territorial integrity and existing political independence of all members of the League." Lodge argued that this violated national sovereignty. Would Wilson allow reservations or compromise? "Never!" When the first vote was taken on an amended treaty backed by the reservationists, Wilson instructed his supporters to only vote for the treaty without amendments. The first vote defeated the amended treaty. Wilson refused to budge; the treaty would be accepted intact or rejected altogether.

In 1920, a coalition of irreconcilables and Democrats defeated the treaty for the last time. Wilson had suffered a major defeat. Europe was shocked. A joint resolution of Congress brought a legal end to the war. A League of Nations was created; but without the support of the strongest country in the world it was merely a shadow of what it would have been. The nation now turned away from war and the high moral goals of Wilson and went back to pursuing "normalcy" and peace.

1920 marks a temporary halt in America's rise as an imperial power; it also marks a new direction in foreign affairs. This was not a time of staunch isolation; the United States did recognize it had some obligation to help solve world problems—primarily out of self-interest—but not to the point of becoming entangled in military operations. From 1890 to 1920 the United States had fought two wars, a war of imperialism and a world war. It had entered a new period in foreign affairs and now became one of the leading nations of the world. Still, a deep disillusionment had developed in the nation with World War I. Thousands of Americans had lost their lives, and this would not be "the war to end all wars," as Wilson had promised. Progressivism and active imperialism both were curtailed during the 1920s. But with the stock-market crash of 1929, America again began to reevaluate its domestic policies and to carefully watch the troubles that were once again rising in Europe.

Essay

The Panama Canal: From Theodore Roosevelt to Jimmy Carter

In March 1978, two Panama treaties were ratified by the United States Senate. An old era ended and a new age began; the 1903 Panama treaty was now past history. For many Panamanians the ratification of the two treaties was a final triumph over that 1903 agreement, which has been referred to as "the treaty that no Panamanian ever signed." To many Americans it signaled a real retreat from world leadership and a defeat at the hands of a second-rate country. For Jimmy Carter it was a victory, which had come with quite a struggle. But all things considered, the treaty seemed to be a necessary step in the gradual evolution of America's foreign policy.

It all started during the presidency of Theodore Roosevelt. Roosevelt was interested in an Isthmus canal but found little cooperation from the government of Colombia, which then governed the region. So he helped to support a Panamanian revolt that had been brewing for years; American intervention stopped Colombia from suppressing the revolt, and, in "the interest of civilization," Roosevelt recognized the Republic of Panama. Quickly the Hay-Bunau Varilla Treaty was drawn up and ratified. This treaty is at the heart of the twentieth-century problems between the United States and Panama; it is the document that gave birth to the Panama Canal. According to the treaty a canal zone in Panama was created; a payment was given for the zone; and an annual fee of $250,000 was fixed. Panama's perpetual independence was guaranteed, but the United States emerged as the protectorate of that small nation. In the Canal Zone the United States had extensive power, which included judicial and commercial rights. In essence the United States exercised sovereignty over that territory.

Roosevelt, however, put the treaty in perspective: "We have not the slightest intention of establishing an independent colony in the middle of the State of Panama, or exercising any greater governmental functions than are necessary to enable us conveniently and safely to construct, maintain, and operate the canal, under the rights given us by the treaty." Work went ahead immediately to build the canal, and it was opened in 1914. During the next few decades Panamanian frustrations grew regarding their ruling oligarchy and the informal colonialism of the United States presence there. Americans in the Canal Zone were exerting more and more control over the economy, immigration, basic services, and foreign policy. American troops even intervened in Panamanian politics.

The Panamanian Revolt of 1931 resulted in an overthrow of the government and also focused frustrations on the Canal Zone. President Arias came into power as an avowed savior of the masses; in 1936 he was greatly responsible for the formulation of the Hull-Alfaro Treaty,

This cartoon pictures "Teddy Bear" Roosevelt overseeing the digging of the Panama Canal.

which made some basic changes in the 1903 agreement. United States intervention in Panamanian affairs came to an end. The annual payment for use of the Canal Zone was raised to $430,000. The United States could no longer seize additional lands outside the Canal Zone, as it could under the 1903 treaty, and American economic concessions in the zone were reduced. Panama emerged as an independent country and was no longer a legal protectorate of the United States. This was part of Franklin Roosevelt's Good Neighbor policy. But it did not solve the basic problem of American sovereignty in a foreign country. Frustration with the Canal Zone was lessened, but it did not disappear.

In the 1940s and 1950s President Arias moved in and out of power. While military bases in Panama were an essential part of the defense of the Western hemisphere during World War II, American determination to continue some of these installations after the war led to national riots in 1947. This was the birth of a massive nationalistic movement, and it was successful in thwarting United States policies. It was also the first time that students became involved in a mass protest. This defeat of an American proposal boded well for Panamanian power politics.

In 1931 the Panamanian oligarchy had been overthrown, but until 1968 the Panamanian government lacked real stability. The Panamanian military forces, or National Guard, were becoming more and more dominant. During the presidency of Dwight Eisenhower, Panamanian nationalism and dissatisfaction with the Canal Zone and Canal policies became more obvious. In 1955 another treaty was ratified, which raised the annual payment to $1.43 million; it also allowed the Panamanian government to tax employees in the Canal Zone who were Panamanian. Some land was returned, and businesses in the zone could sell only to United States citizens. But this treaty did not soothe the feelings of many militant nationalists. In 1959 some students tried to plant Panamanian flags in the zone; riots followed and anti-American feeling ran high.

A new watershed in tension and violence was reached with the riots of 1964. In January, after 4 days of rioting between Panamanian mobs and United States troops, 4 United States soldiers were killed and 85 were wounded, and 24 Panamanians were killed with nearly 200 wounded. The economic and social problems of Panama seemed integrally tied up with American control of the zone. Frustrations continued to mount. In 1967 Lyndon Johnson tried to formulate a new treaty; all attempts failed. The following year the National Guard came into power with a military coup, which brought into power Colonel Omar Torrijos Herrera. Torrijos first consolidated his power base and then focused on a new canal treaty, which would change the direction of Panamanian government.

In 1974 Henry Kissinger saw the inevitable approaching; for the avid supporters of the sovereignty concept as embodied in the 1903 treaty, what Kissinger then proposed was anathema. He suggested some changes that he felt better fit the political reality of the Western hemisphere in general and Panama in particular. These sug-

President Jimmy Carter and Panama leader Omar Torryos sign the Panama Treaties at the Pan American Union in Washington, D.C.

gestions included: a fixed termination date for the end of United States control of the zone; the end of the zone completely; the right of the United States to operate and defend the canal itself; and the payment to the Panamanian government of a just and equal share of the revenues. President Gerald Ford did not see eye to eye with the Kissinger proposal, and he took a very hard line on keeping control of the zone and the canal.

In 1977 President Torrijos, motivated by the declining Panamanian economy and incipient Panamanian nationalism, negotiated two treaties with President Jimmy Carter. The two treaties instituted major changes. By 1999 the canal will be turned over to Panama, which then will have complete territorial jurisdiction over the zone and the canal (in essence, the zone will be no more). Until 1999 all United States citizens in the zone will be employees of the United States government with no special privileges. In the year 2000, neutrality of the canal will take effect. This means that Panama will defend the canal after 2000 but that in case of an emergency the United States can still protect the region from outside or inside threats. For the present, Panama will be guaranteed a handsome financial return, and by 2000 all revenues will go directly to Panama. With the ratification of these two treaties the heritage of Theodore Roosevelt's diplomacy formally ended; the Good Neighbor policy became more than empty words, and the United States moved into a new era of realism in foreign affairs. ∎

Suggested Readings

The coming of the Spanish-American War and the American overseas empire is described in H. WAYNE MORGAN's *America's Road to Empire* (1965). An excellent study of the war itself is found in FRANK FRIEDEL's *The Splendid Little War* (1958).

The two opposing sides of the imperialist debate are found in JULIUS PRATT's *Expansionists of 1898* (1936) and in E. BERKELEY TOMPKINS's *Anti-Imperialism in the United States: The Great Debates, 1890–1920* (1970).

Roosevelt's big stick diplomacy is described in HOWARD K. BEALE's *Theodore Roosevelt and The Rise of America to World Power* (1956).

Wilson's moral outlook in foreign affairs is well depicted in *The Origins of the Foreign Policy of Woodrow Wilson* (1937) by HARLEY NOTTER.

E. H. BUEHRIG's *Woodrow Wilson and the Balance of Power* (1955) and ERNEST MAY's *The World War and American Isolation, 1914–1917* (1959) explain the origins of America's involvement in World War I.

ARTHUR LINK's numerous works on Wilson such as *Progressivism and Peace, 1916–1917* (1959) document his role in the war.

American war effort here and abroad is found in C. C. TANSILL's *America Goes to War* (1938) and in H. A. DE WEERD's *President Wilson Fights His War* (1968).

The problems of the Versailles Treaty are covered in two books by THOMAS BAILEY, *Woodrow Wilson and the Lost Peace* (1944) and *Woodrow Wilson and the Great Betrayal* (1945).

CHAPTER 13

The New Deal: Just Another Old Deal?

Time Line

?–A.D. 1492	Migration and evolution of American Indian societies
1492	Christopher Columbus lands in West Indies—beginning of European exploration
1607–1732	Establishment of 13 English colonies
1775–1783	American Revolution
1776	Declaration of Independence
1789–1797	Presidency of George Washington
1812–1815	War of 1812
1816–1824	Era of Good Feelings
1846–1848	Mexican War
1861–1865	Civil War
1865–1877	Reconstruction
1877–1900	Industrialization and urbanization
1900–1916	Progressive Era
1917–1918	World War I

October 1929	Stock-market crash
1930	Hawley-Smoot Tariff Act
1931	Reconstruction Finance Corporation created Norris-La Guardia Act
1932	Election of Franklin Delano Roosevelt
1933	The Hundred Days program Emergency Banking Act Agricultural Adjustment Act National Industrial Recovery Act Tennessee Valley Authority Public Works Administration

	Civilian Conservation Corps Federal Security and Exchange acts
1932	Indian Reorganization Act Gold Reserve Act National Resources Board National Housing Act
1935	Social Security Act Wagner Act Banking Act Works Progress Administration Wealth Tax Act Public Utility Holding Company Act Supreme Court rules N.R.A. to be unconstitutional
1936	Supreme Court invalidates A.A.A. Reelection of Roosevelt
1937	Roosevelt's court-reform plan proposed

1930s	Depression and New Deal
1941–1945	World War II
1945–1960	Post-war politics
1950–1953	Korean War
1950–1960	Civil rights movement
1961–1973	Vietnam War
1976	Bicentennial celebration

The New Deal: Just Another Old Deal?

There are many things that Americans today take for granted. Everyone has a social security number; in fact, for many college students this number is their identity. Few worry about the neighborhood bank collapsing and taking with it their life savings; the Federal Deposit Insurance Corporation insures bank deposits. It is not unusual for a couple to purchase a house through the Federal Housing Administration with an FHA loan. And, in this day of large, national unions, who would question the worker's right to organize. But social security, insured bank deposits, FHA loans, and a federal guarantee of the worker's right to organize were nonexistent in the 1920s. These programs came with Franklin Delano Roosevelt's New Deal—a direct response to the Great Depression of 1929 and a program that extended governmental powers and responsibilities more than ever before. Initially the New Deal was created to bring relief and recovery to the devastating effects of the depression. But it also brought permanent reform and greatly increased the federal government's role in Americans' daily lives. It made government much more responsive to minorities—in particular to American Indians, who saw the Dawes Act replaced by the Indian Reorganization Act, a step toward self-determination. The effects of the New Deal were not temporary. Today we are still living Roosevelt's New Deal.

The Great Depression

Economic prosperity, which had appeared during Harding's presidency, grew into the Coolidge and Hoover "Booms." While Americans were putting a chicken in every pot and two cars in every garage, the rich were getting richer. Still, the euphoria of the 1920s seemed to indicate that prosperity would reach new heights and continue on and on forever. But below the surface there was economic trouble brewing. Labor unions were becoming weak; labor was secondary to industrial expansion. Farm production began to drop, and farmers received less and less in the way of profit. The gap between rich and poor was ever increasing; one-third of all personal income was distributed to five percent of the population. Minorities and the poor were at the bottom of the economic ladder with little chance to rise above their miserable lot. American loans to European countries were not being repaid due to the slowness of industrial recovery in post-war Europe. More and more corporations were setting up interlocking directorates and creating one vast economic pyramid of American corporations. The fundamental business of the country was on an unsound basis.

Government policies did not help to solve the flaws. The Federal Reserve Board failed to limit the upward spiral of the rapidly inflating currency or to curb excessive borrowing. Treasury Secretary Andrew Mellon pushed the passage of tax laws that increased the gap between the rich and poor. Labor had few friends in government circles and watched as its bargaining power increasingly diminished. No coherent farm program was adopted. The federal government was caught up in the quest for more prosperity and saw little reason to risk limiting further economic growth. But even when the inequities in the system began to appear, no positive action was taken. In early 1929 the Federal Reserve Board came briefly to its senses and warned of the dangers of the inflated economy. The warning fell on deaf ears. During the summer of 1929 the nation experienced a severe recession in the building industry and a rapid decline in consumer purchasing power. These were signs that something was going wrong. But the worst was yet to come.

The prosperity of the 1920s had included the stock market boom. In the stock market, investors with abundant or even limited capital could speculate. Some Americans took their hard-earned capital and "played" the stock market. Stock prices became overinflated. By early September 1929, they had reached an all-time high. But now stock prices began to fall. Panic buying and selling increased. Then came that tragic day of October 29, 1929:

> Within half an hour of the opening, the volume of trading passed three million shares, by twelve o'clock it had passed eight million, by half past one it had passed twelve million, and when the closing gong brought the day's madness to an end the gigantic record of 16,410,030 shares had been set.

Stocks had dropped to a record low. Fortunes had been quickly lost. This stock-market crash marked the beginning of economic panic and a national depression. Business leaders now began to cut back on workers and production; they turned to banks for help but found that most banks had little available capital. Government leaders, such as Secretary of the Treasury Andrew Mellon, comforted business leaders with the old adage that the depression would quickly run its course and that the economy would automatically recover as it always had. Mellon advised, "Liquidate labor, liquidate stocks, liquidate the farmers . . . let the slump liquidate itself."

The bewildering years between 1929 and 1932 made Americans question prevailing economic theories. The economic collapse marked the end of finance capitalism and a loss of prestige and power for Wall Street. The crash undermined public faith in the philosophy of American business, in the ideas

The New Deal: Just Another Old Deal?

Crowds gather near the New York Stock Exchange on Wall Street to receive news of the stock market crash.

of laissez-faire, and in the working of natural economic laws, such as Social Darwinism. The Horatio Alger myth, with its image of the local boy making good and its condemnation of poverty as a lack of hard work and initiative, was quickly going out of style. The gospel of wealth and rugged individualism were lost in the growing bread lines of the cities. The bubble of unregulated prosperity burst. Americans now looked to their president, Herbert Hoover, for help. His efforts to stem the depression produced more government involvement than past presidents but were still not enough.

Hoover Fights the Depression

Hoover blamed the depression on Europe and felt that the key to recovery lay in increased industrial production. Still his basic philosophy of rugged individualism, with its emphasis on individual achievement without government intervention caused him to adopt only limited government policies. Hoover believed government should not directly interfere with business, although it should help limit the effects of the depression and lead the way to recovery. The Federal Farm Board was created with power to make loans to farm co-operatives and to buy up farm surpluses. Still the price of farm products declined, and the farm board made few noticeable changes. The Federal Reserve Board adopted a policy that made it easier for businesses to borrow money; still hundreds of banks had already closed their doors and many more were not far away from insolvency. Under pressure from manufacturers' lobbyists, Congress passed the Hawley-Smoot Tariff of 1930, which raised tariff levels to an all-time high. Hoover's economic advisers warned of the effects of the law, but Hoover, who believed that the American economy had been hurt by its close ties with Europe, signed the bill into law. And then he defended his actions: "I may repeat that this tariff bill was not passed until nine months after the economic depression began in the United States and also not until twenty other countries had already gone into the depression." This tariff further hurt the American consumer, creating a rapid escalation in the prices of foreign goods. It also deepened the depression in Europe. Meanwhile, Hoover held a series of conferences with business leaders to continue to push voluntary cooperation between business and government.

In 1930 Hoover naively reported, "We have now passed the worst." He was mistaken. Businesses and banks were still failing; unemployment was approaching seven million workers and rising. Homes and savings were being lost. Few remembered the Coolidge Boom; they now were reminded daily of the Hoover Depression. The effects of the depression were everywhere. One reporter wrote, "In the State of Washington I was told that the forest fires raging in that region all summer and fall were caused by unemployed timber workers and bankrupt farmers in an endeavor to earn a few honest dollars as firefighters." Shanties known as "Hoovervilles" sprang up. On city streets were shoe shiners and apple vendors. Hoover wrote of the apple sellers, "Many persons left their jobs for the more profitable one of selling apples." Men pulled out the empty pockets of their trousers and called them Hoover handkerchiefs. And across the nation the question could be heard: "Brother, can you spare a dime?"

Hoover's early relief policies had been little help. Voluntary cooperation between business and government had not worked. Local relief had proved inadequate. More federal action was necessary. His later policies included special bank loans for emergency credit, the encouragement of residential construction, and the creation of the Reconstruction Finance Corporation. This agency was authorized to lend money to banks, insurance companies, and railroads to forestall bankruptcy and lead to recovery. Even with the deep-

The effects of the Depression were felt across the nation and relocation became common.

Chart 13-1
Unemployment, 1929–1941

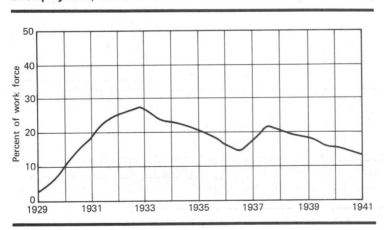

ening of the depression and the financial panic that swept over Europe in the spring and summer of 1931, Hoover continued to believe in government working through states and local governments and not directly with individuals. He had enlarged the role of the federal government, but he had not gone far enough to stem the tide. He offered little personal leadership when the nation needed a dynamic individual to turn to.

By 1932 the depression had deepened and labor's voice became more strident, but Hoover refused direct relief programs. The number of unemployed was between 11 and 17 million—roughly one-third of the nation's wage earners. The net income of industrialists fell from $11 billion to $2 billion. Businesses found their products difficult to sell, and by 1932 industrial production had fallen to one-half its 1929 level. Building contractors were doing one-fifth the volume of construction they had done in 1929. Hoover, who was becoming more and more unpopular, started to look like the national scapegoat. But he still defended his record: "Had it not been for the immediate and unprece-

The election in 1932 of Franklin Delano Roosevelt brought to the presidency a man with a "new deal" who would lead the nation out of the Depression.

dented actions of our government, things would be infinitely worse today."
By the election of 1932 voters were in a hostile mood and wanted a change.
The dissatisfaction was revealed in the words of disgruntled workers: "Mellon
pulled the whistle, Hoover rang the bell, Wall Street gave the signal—and the
country went to Hell!"

The Republicans once again turned to Hoover as their nominee, but with
no great enthusiasm. Hoover stood on his antidepression record and promised
a return to prosperity. The Democrats nominated on the fourth ballot the
governor of New York, Franklin Delano Roosevelt, who promised both a balanced budget and sweeping economic and social reforms with a "new deal for
the American people." The nation was more anti-Hoover than pro-Roosevelt,
and Roosevelt was swept into office. Now America waited for a change, and
change came.

Franklin Roosevelt and the New Deal

Born of wealthy parents in New York State, Franklin Delano Roosevelt was
much influenced by his domineering mother. He early enjoyed the advantages
of wealth, which included his yearly trips to Europe and his private tutors.
After graduating from private schools, he entered Harvard, majored in history,
and participated in rowing and football. He studied law, but, deciding that law
was not for him, he turned to politics. Unlike his cousin, Theodore Roosevelt,
Franklin joined the Democratic party, the party of his father. After being
elected to the state senate, he learned much valuable political experience but
fought against the party machine. His support of Wilson for president in 1912
led to his being appointed assistant secretary of the navy, a position he retained
during World War I. In 1920 he was nominated for vice-president on the Cox
ticket, but "normalcy" won the day, Harding was elected, and Franklin became vice-president of a surety-bonding firm instead. It was at this juncture
in his life that the world turned upside down. He became partially paralyzed
and was diagnosed as a victim of poliomyelitis. He nearly died, but he fought
back courageously. Still, the disease left him permanently crippled. Many
persons, including his mother, urged him to retire from politics, but he did
not. He returned to national politics when he made a dramatic presidential-
nomination address on behalf of Alfred E. Smith in 1924. In 1928 he was
elected governor of New York State and earned a national reputation for combatting the effects of the depression there. He set in motion programs for
unemployment relief, water-power development, a state-prison system, and

old-age pensions. By 1932 he was known nationally as an antidepression innovator and was nominated on the fourth ballot for president. He was the first candidate ever to accept the nomination before the national convention. To show the nation that he had overcome his physical handicaps he travelled to more than 38 states, preaching a "new deal" that would lead the nation out of the depression. With his election the nation began to sing "Happy Days are Here Again," eagerly waiting for the "new deal" to begin.

Roosevelt now moved toward a "rendezvous with destiny." He was a child of progressivism, born of Wilson's New Freedom and Theodore Roosevelt's New Nationalism. He believed that the federal government must be directly involved in the welfare of individual citizens: "That nation or state which is unwilling by government action to tackle new problems caused by the immense increase of population and the astonishing strides of modern science is headed for a decline and ultimate death from inaction." Specific programs must be designed to meet specific problems. And the president must take a strong leadership role in the process. Roosevelt did not have a completed list of programs that he expected Congress to enact; the New Deal was an experimental program, adopted after much debate and discussion, which attempted to give the federal government some control over the economic future of the nation. Roosevelt knew what must be done, but he didn't know exactly how to do it. He was surrounded by a group of advisers known as the "brain trust," which included men such as Adolf Berle, Jr., Rexford Tugwell, and Raymond Moley, who saw public control as essential to economic survival. His cabinet consisted of able individuals who frequently held a diversity of viewpoints, such as Cordell Hull as secretary of state, Henry Wallace as secretary of agriculture, Harold Ickes as secretary of the interior, and the first woman cabinet member, Frances Perkins, as secretary of labor. Roosevelt understood the subtleties of politics and, through his fight with polio, had acquired a real empathy for the underdog. He was ready to move with Congress and the people toward a permanent solution of the nation's worst economic problem in history—the Great Depression.

One Hundred Days

On March 4, 1933, the attention of the nation turned to a 51-year-old man with eyeglasses clipped to his nose and a cigarette holder in his mouth, who might be the possible savior of America. In his inaugural address he denounced the "money changers," meaning the business leaders who were responsible for the present crisis, and he tried to restore public confidence immediately with the words, "The only thing we have to fear is fear itself." Sensing a national bank crisis, on March 6, Roosevelt immediately declared a nation-wide bank holiday and called Congress into special session. The next "Hundred Days" (March 9–June 16, 1933) saw Congress rush through a series of massive relief and recovery measures that began the long road to recovery. Roosevelt initially believed that if confidence was restored in the banking system, the economy would mend itself. After the bank holiday, on March 9, the Emergency Banking Act was passed. This act required each bank in the Federal Reserve System to be inspected and licensed before it could reopen; the banking act also forbade the hoarding of gold and extended loans to banks. At the end of his first week in office, Roosevelt went directly to the people with his first "fireside chat." He began, "I want to talk a few minutes with the people of the United States about banking," and continued to explain the confusing economic picture and his banking policy. Banks now began to reopen, and the fear of immediate collapse disappeared. The New Deal was underway.

The Emergency Banking Act, however, was only looked upon as a stopgap measure. The Glass-Steagall Act of June 1933 separated commercial and investment banking to limit bank speculation; the Federal Deposit Insurance Corporation insured bank deposits up to $5000. The Federal Securities Act of May 1935 set standards for Wall Street in the issuance of new securities; the Securities Exchange Act of 1934 set up the Securities and Exchange Commission to supervise the activities of all stock exchanges and to protect the public against deceit. While these acts met with much hostility on Wall Street, they did help to restore public confidence in the stock market. With the idea in mind that an inflated dollar would help raise prices and solve the problems of the depression, Roosevelt moved away from the gold standard. The Gold Reserve Act of 1934 gave the president the authority to order the Federal Reserve banks to turn over their supply of gold to the United States Treasury in return for gold certificates. Roosevelt then devalued the dollar by cutting the amount of gold backing each dollar. An inflated currency would make it easier for groups, such as farmers, to pay their debts. The Banking Act of 1935 gave the Federal Reserve Board more power to limit the credit of the member banks, hence controlling their operations. This law brought more security and stability to American banks. These banking and financial measures had the result of creating a healthy economic climate.

To add a little cheer to his early legislation Roosevelt authorized the legalization of beer and other alcoholic beverages. But this did not solve one of the most basic problems of the depression—unemployment. Federal money needed to be used to help the unemployed. The Federal Emergency Relief Administration, in May 1933, provided federal money to states to combat

This Public Works Administration Project in Harlem was typical of the federal government's program to stem unemployment.

unemployment and to set up labor projects. The Public Works Administration, in June 1933, under Secretary of the Interior Harold Ickes, administered a fund of $3.3 billion to construct public-works projects such as highways, buildings, and dams. By 1935 there was some criticism of Ickes's handling of this program; many felt that the program was too slow and was not really reducing unemployment. In 1935 Congress created the Works Progress Administration under the direction of New York social worker, Harry L. Hopkins, who favored small, public projects. This program provided work-relief for nearly three million Americans, who participated in the building of airports and schools and the production of plays, maps, and books. Its critics called the jobs a "boondoggle." The W.P.A.'s most controversial projects were in the arts, giving writers, photographers, and theater groups a chance to get work. Roosevelt's conservation program also provided employment.

Conservation and the New Deal

Since Theodore Roosevelt, the conservation policies of the federal government had been virtually nonexistent. Franklin Roosevelt restored a needed concern for natural resources. He not only desired to withhold more land from public use but also worked to rejuvenate millions of wasted acres. This desire to reclaim wasted land was well demonstrated in the Tennessee Valley Authority, created in 1933. The Tennessee River Valley was a problem area with its poor soil, thin forests, floods, pockets of poverty, high unemployment, and lack of electricity. But the electric power sites at Muscle Shoals, Alabama, were among the most valuable in the country. During the 1920s there was a fierce debate in Congress over whether the government should operate the power sites. Roosevelt saw the Tennessee Valley as an opportunity to form a single development project that would deal with a variety of problems. So, in May 1933, the Tennessee Valley Authority Act created "a corporation clothed in the power of government but possessed of the flexibility and initiative of a private enterprise." This agency was empowered to develop the entire Tennessee River valley, solve its basic environmental problems, and bring better living conditions to its inhabitants. This government agency was unique in that it had the powers of a private corporation. The T.V.A. project more than accomplished its goal and provided a model for future programs.

The preservation of natural resources and relief for the unemployed came together in June 1933 with the creation of the Civilian Conservation Corps. This organization brought together men between the ages of 18 and 25 to work in the countryside and protect and develop forests and parks. Even though critics scoffed that the C.C.C. workers were "raking leaves in the wind," the program benefitted both human and natural resources.

In 1934 Roosevelt established a National Resources Board to inventory the nation's remaining natural resources. The report revealed the basic relationship between water, land, and mineral problems and demonstrated how soil erosion and forest depletion contributed to floods and drought. Public interest in conservation issues was again awakened. One result of this awareness was the creation of the Soil Conservation Service, which helped farmers to wisely use their land to its best advantage. The New Deal focused not only on basic economic issues but also made Americans aware again of their diminishing natural resources and the need for a cohesive conservation program.

Further Relief

The National Industrial Recovery Act of June 1933 played a major role in the government's program for industrial planning. This act attempted to balance supply and demand, as well as labor and business, through the formation of codes of fair competition. The National Recovery Administration (N.R.A.) under the direction of ex-cavalry officer, Hugh S. Johnson, oversaw the creation of voluntary codes, which made it necessary for employers to "comply with the maximum hours of labor, minimum rates of pay, and other conditions

The National Recovery Administration with its symbol of the blue eagle was a government attempt to control business and labor.

of employment approved or prescribed by the President." The symbol of the program was the Blue Eagle, which appeared on store windows, billboards, and even in a major New York parade.

One of the most controversial sections of the act was Section 7-A, which guaranteed the rights of workers. During the early years of the depression organized labor received little recognition, but Congress did pass the Norris-LaGuardia Act in 1932, which released labor from many legal encumbrances. The courts could no longer issue injunctions that outlawed strikes and other related strike activities. Labor disputes could no longer be interpreted, in terms of the Sherman Anti-Trust Act, as unlawful "combinations" in restraint of trade. Section 7-A guaranteed the workers' right to organize and bargain collectively through representatives of their own choosing and to receive maximum hours of labor and minimum rates of pay. This seemed to give a needed boost to organized labor, but employers frequently overlooked the requirement, which led to bitter strikes. The voluntary codes did not balance supply and demand. Prices rose much more quickly than wages. In some industries near-monopolies were created, while more than 100,000 violations were reported. Critics of the act became more and more vocal. The program was called the "National Run Around," and in 1935 the Supreme Court gave the program a death blow. "The blue eagle became the sick chicken," when the

Supreme Court, in the case of *Schecter Poultry Co.* v. *United States,* invalidated the N.R.A. code system as an unconstitutional delegation of the law-making power to the executive and a federal invasion of intrastate commerce. This noble experiment was over.

Another noble experiment was the Agricultural Adjustment Act of May 1933. One of the great tragedies of depression America was the surplus of farm products in the midst of starvation. This surplus had caused a decline in farm income and in turn had restricted farmers' purchasing power. A program was needed that would dispose of the surplus and at the same time would benefit the poverty-striken farmers. Secretary of Agriculture Henry Wallace's plan was embodied in the Agricultural Adjustment Act. The aim of the law was to restore the farmer to "parity" with industry by getting rid of the farm-product surplus and by paying farmers for limiting their production. This program would result in the rise of agricultural prices and, in turn, farmer income. For example, six million surplus pigs were killed and distributed to public institutions. This act met with mixed feelings; some felt that it was wasteful and unnecessary: "It just makes me sick all over when I think how the government

The Dust Bowl conditions of 1933 caused many farmers to abandon their farms and move West.

has killed millions and millions of little pigs, and how that has raised pork prices until today we poor people cannot even look at a piece of bacon . . ." But in spite of the critics, these reductions and the Dust Bowl conditions of 1933 caused farm prices and income to rise. In 1936 the Supreme Court brought an abrupt end to the A.A.A. when it ruled that the processing of tax regulated agricultural production was illegal.

Roosevelt's Critics

By the end of the Hundred Days, the maze of legislation had stunned the popular mind. Americans looked upon Roosevelt as the national hero, but statistics revealed that the depression was only slowing down. Critics of specific legislation were making their position known. And increasing attacks were coming from right-wing and left-wing sources. Business demanded a return to the days of the laissez-faire philosophy. Roosevelt appeared to be favoring the common people while handicapping industrial growth. The

Huey Long with his Share the Wealth program and Father Charles E. Coughlin, the radio priest, were two demagogues who rose to criticize Roosevelt's programs.

N.R.A. was a direct challenge to the free-enterprise system. The economic misery of the depression led to the rise of three popular demagogues: Huey Long, Father Coughlin, and Dr. Francis E. Townsend. A United States senator from Louisiana, Huey Long used simple arguments to solve all economic problems. Long's proposed redistribution of income would pay a guaranteed income of $5000 to every family in America and make "Every Man a King." This "Share the Wealth" program received considerable support and made Long a potential challenger for president in 1936. His folksy and racist ways made him a real man of the people during these frustrating days. His assassination in 1935 removed him as a potential threat to Roosevelt's support.

Father Charles E. Coughlin, "the Radio Priest," turned his weekly religious message from the subject of God to social reform. He claimed Roosevelt had failed and was now a great "betrayer." Coughlin warned his listeners of national dangers he believed were at hand, such as the nationalization of industry and the Jewish takeover of the New Deal. His campaign of "Social Justice" spread over the air waves and was listened to by millions. Dr. Francis E. Townsend, a retired physician, felt "We owe a decent living to the older people." So Townsend supported a plan that would give every citizen over age 60 a monthly income of $200, a sum which would have to be spent in the country. His appeal among senior citizens was particularly strong. Long, Coughlin, and Townsend, added to the attacks from business and industry, revealed to Roosevelt that his program had not gone far enough. So, in 1935, the New Deal moved into a phase of much more permanent reform.

The Second New Deal

Democrats were elected overwhelmingly in the congressional election of 1934 and helped lead the way to Roosevelt's Second New Deal. While many measures of this Second New Deal seemed radical to his critics, Roosevelt knew that his actions during the Hundred Days were merely stopgap measures and that permanent reform was needed. In fact, certain programs such as the N.R.A. and the A.A.A. had been invalidated by the Supreme Court. One of the most significant laws of the Second New Deal was the Social Security Act of 1935. This law took away much of the appeal of the Townsend proposals by guaranteeing a pension plan for the elderly, which was coupled with unemployment benefits for younger workers. Financing of the system would come from payroll taxes. Government responsibility to the aged, the unemployed, and eventually the dependent and disabled, was guaranteed. Poor farmers also were assisted by the Resettlement Administration, which extended credit to help settle them on better land, and by the Rural Electrification Administration, which extended electrical power to more farm families.

The Second New Deal also implemented the Federal Housing Administration, which authorized loans to homeowners for improving their homes and completing new ones. The Public Utility Holding Company Act of August 1935 restricted the concentration of economic power in the hands of a few electric and gas companies and struck against monopoly in business. The Wealth Tax Act of 1935 increased the tax burden for the wealthy with an excess-profits tax and raised income and estate taxes. One of the most noteworthy measures was the National Labor Relations Act, popularly known as the Wagner Act. This act harkened back to section 7-A of the National Industrial Recovery Act by clearly defining government's support of labor and labor's right to organize. It also provided for establishment of a National Labor Relations Board, which would protect employees' "right to self-organization, to form, join, or assist labor organizations, to bargain collectively through representatives of their own choosing, and to engage in concerted activities for the purpose of collective bargaining or other mutual aid or protection." The board also investigated illegal employer practices such as employer interference with unions or employer refusal to bargain collectively, and could issue cease and desist orders in such cases. The Recovery Act was one of the great victories for labor in America.

Formation of C.I.O.

Under this law union membership increased in the established unions. There was also a growing need for an organization for unskilled workers. The number of unskilled workers had increased dramatically with the introduction of assembly-line production in the 1920s; still, the A.F.L. remained an organization for skilled workers only. The Knights of Labor needed a revival, and a man named John L. Lewis was responsible for that rebirth. In fact, his father had been a member of the Knights and had taught his son the need for worker organizations serving both skilled and unskilled. John L. Lewis organized miners into the United Mine Workers and sought to find a place for his organization within the A.F.L. Lewis began to form other industrial unions, which he believed should exist within the structure of the A.F.L. too, but at the A.F.L. National Convention in 1935 recognition of these new industrial unions was voted down.

Lewis then began to form the Committee for Industrial Organization, an organization dedicated to the unionization of industrial workers, yet which would work within the framework of the A.F.L. William Green, then leader of the A.F.L., condemned this movement and forced the C.I.O. into an independent status. The C.I.O. now became the Congress of Industrial Organizations, elected Lewis president, adopted its own constitution, and became a bitter rival of the A.F.L. This new union began to attract many unskilled workers and some leftists and radicals. Due to this challenge, the A.F.L., for years deep in lethargy, now emerged again as a vigorous, active union in the tradition of Samuel Gompers.

The C.I.O. offered real hope to the mass-production workers and provided a challenge to some of the new industrial giants. It added a new dimension to the traditional labor-business fight when it fostered direct government assistance and intervention. In the mid-1930s it encountered formidable opposition when it attempted to organize workers in the automobile, steel, rubber, electrical, and meatpacking industries. A recession in 1936 and 1937 forced Lewis to use the technique of the sit-down strike against automobile and steel industries. The most noteworthy strike of this kind occurred in 1937, when autoworkers occupied a General Motors plant in Flint, Michigan, for six weeks. Describing the striker, one worker said,

> It was like we was soldiers, holding the fort. It was like war. The guys with me became my buddies. I remember as a kid in school readin' about Davy Crockett and the last stand at the Alamo. You know, Mister, that's just how I felt. Yes sir, Chevy No. 4 was my Alamo.

General Motors eventually gave limited recognition to the union, and the strike ended. Before the Supreme Court outlawed the sit-down strike, the C.I.O. had won many victories; but it now turned to more traditional labor tactics, which widened public support. The working person was being heard, and labor would play a decisive role in the next presidential election.

Election of 1936

In 1936 the Democrats turned to their man Roosevelt, who ran on his record of the New Deal. The Republicans were somewhat at a loss for a candidate, but they finally turned to the colorless Alfred M. Landon, governor of Kansas. Landon tried to portray the New Deal as radical and to appeal to America as another Coolidge. But America had been rescued from the depths of the depression by Roosevelt; they were going to stick with him. The election results gave Roosevelt a landslide with only two states going for Landon. Roosevelt's victory over Landon was an enthusiastic demonstration of his broad base of support and was proof of the nation's admiration toward a friend who had pursued an innovative course that had made America a better place in which to live.

The Third New Deal

Roosevelt now saw that the economy was on the upswing, but poverty still persisted. The New Deal must be further extended; but one thing stood in his way, and that was the Supreme Court. Over the previous few years, the Supreme Court had invalidated many New Deal programs, they were now threatening some of the legislation that had just been passed during the Second New Deal. Before moving ahead with more legislation, Roosevelt decided to attack the conservative members of the Supreme Court with his court-packing plan. This was a tactical error that lost him the momentum which he had built up and caused a split in his party. His plan was to replace all justices over 70 years old; if an elderly justice refused to voluntarily retire, the president could add a new justice—until the court had as many as 15 justices. After many weeks of acrimonious debate in Congress, Roosevelt withdrew his proposal. But the damage had been done. Never again would he have the same united support of his party.

Still, Roosevelt managed to get a few more New Deal laws passed. The Farm Tenancy Act provided government support for slum clearance and low-income housing. The Fair Labor Standards Act provided a minimum wage of 40 cents an hour, a 40-hour workweek by 1940, and federal child-labor controls. A new agricultural adjustment act introduced a soil-conservation program and provided subsidies to farmers who kept their production levels down.

[handwritten margin note: cause for split in his party]

This cartoon shows the furor that surrounded Roosevelt's plan for reform of the Supreme Court.

484

But Roosevelt's attempt to balance the budget by cutting back some of the relief programs had an adverse effect. A recession in 1937 brought back unpleasant memories of the depression. Unemployment rose, and the stock market was weakened. The New Deal was losing its momentum. In the congressional election of 1938, Republicans and Democratic opponents of Roosevelt cut into his support. The days of the New Deal were quickly coming to a close. It became increasingly difficult, however, to concentrate on domestic issues because of disturbing events in the Pacific and in Europe.

Minorities and the New Deal

The New Deal was not just a new deal for whites, it also affected American Indians, Blacks, and Mexican-Americans. Of course, the effects of the depression were particularly severe among these groups because they were already at the bottom of the economic ladder when the depression began. The Indians still were feeling the effects of the disastrous Dawes Act, which had been in existence since 1887. During the late 1920s the Meriam Report had appeared, which recommended the end of the Dawes Act and the restoration of tribal ownership of land. Little positive action was taken until the presidency of Roosevelt. He appointed as commissioner of Indian affairs, John Collier, an anthropologist who had worked for years for Indian rights. Collier's first annual report demanded an end to severalty or allotment and a return to "community ownership and control." Collier also proposed the shifting of Indian students from boarding schools to day schools, more Indian employment in the Bureau of Indian Affairs, direct financial aid to tribes, and more Indian self-government. One white critic of Collier's plan wrote that it was "A unique program of regimentation which is the most extreme gesture yet made by the administration toward a communistic experiment." After much heated debate and with substantive changes in Collier's original proposal, Congress responded to public pressure and in 1934 passed the Wheeler-Howard Act, known as the Indian Reorganization Act.

The act was based on the belief that Indians should be allowed to function as tribes and possess tribal land once again. Indians should not be forced to assimilate into white society; they should be given a choice to maintain their separate Indian society. The allotment system of the Dawes Act ended. Tribes again were allowed to acquire title to reservation land. Tribes also voted to decide whether they wanted to be a self-governing body or not. Confusion and lack of tribal unity caused only 70 percent of the tribes to become semi-independent groups eligible for federal funds. The act also allowed economic assistance for individual and tribal enterprises, improvement of reservations, and preferred hiring in the Bureau of Indian Affairs. This act marked the first time the federal government attempted to make reservations liveable. In essence, the act accentuated the trend toward self-determination and preservation of Indian culture. It was tragic that much traditional Indian culture already had disappeared by the 1930s. But Indian culture—especially arts and crafts—had a revival. During the first three years of the law more than $70 million in federal funds was poured into reservation programs. But this act did not bring complete self-determination because the federal government still had ultimate veto power over all the decisions of the tribes. Still, the process of forced assimilation was slowed, and American Indians could practice their religions in peace for the first time since the days of the Western wars.

Blacks and the New Deal

Blacks were unprepared for the depression, more so than whites, for their unemployment rate had already been high, and blacks already had been recently victimized by the extreme racism of the 1920s. Although they were included in many New Deal programs, their sorry plight continued. Democratic senators, such as Huey Long who frequently used the word "nigger," often were openly hostile to black Americans. Many welfare agencies did not deal with urban blacks; and the Conservation Corps adopted a strict segregationist policy, while the A.A.A. program left out Southern tenant farmers and sharecroppers.

But the New Deal did benefit many blacks. Roosevelt appointed Robert Weaver as adviser to the Department of the Interior and Mary M. Bethune as director of Negro affairs. Roosevelt's awareness of race relations and minority affairs was due greatly to his wife, Eleanor. Eleanor was openly sympathetic to the cause of minorities and was often called "nigger lover" because of this open support of black rights. Her husband appointed race-relations advisers to many federal departments and saw that blacks benefitted from many New Deal relief programs. Many blacks moved into low-cost homes. Blacks were employed by the W.P.A. and the C.C.C. Black policies paid off for Roosevelt; black voters shifted from the Republican to the Democratic party. Blacks had found a leader—with an enlightened wife—who would lead them to the beginnings of their civil rights movement.

Mexican-Americans in the Depression

Mexican-Americans suffered along with the general population. They lost jobs and saw the immigration from Mexico reduced to a trickle. Those in the cities

The New Deal: Just Another Old Deal?

were hardest hit. That is why it is ironic that the movement of Mexican-Americans from village to city increased so dramatically during the 1930s. Those who moved into the urban centers of the Southwest, such as Los Angeles and El Paso, believed that opportunities there would be much greater for them. They were mistaken. The main result of this migration was the growth of Mexican-American barrios, or ghettos. In the cities they found growing discrimination and open resistance. Some states, such as California, even tried to pass laws to limit their economic opportunities. And they found themselves competing with urban blacks and poor whites for the unskilled jobs that still remained.

The New Deal improved their lot somewhat. Federal agencies sprang up across the Southwest to reduce racial conflict and improve working conditions. The Farm Security Administration established migrant camps in rural areas. The Works Progress Administration also hired many Mexican-Americans, while many others took advantage of the low-income-housing programs. But the repatriation program nullified many of the gains. During the 1930s,

Mexican American migrant camps, like this one in Texas, shared in the general suffering from the depression.

there was increasing pressure to send Mexican-Americans "back where they came from"—and keep them there. One politician wrote,

> These people sleep by day and prowl by night like coyotes, stealing anything they can get their hands on, no matter how useless to them it may be. . . . Yet there are Americans clamoring for more of this human swine to be brought over from Mexico.

The repatriation program attempted to round up noncitizens and transport them back to Mexico. During the 1930s more than 500,000 Mexicans were deported; more than half of them had been born in the United States and were United States citizens. The repatriation program was also a shock to the Mexican government, which had a difficult time placing deportees back into society. The 1930s were difficult for white Americans, but they were tougher for American minorities.

By the 1940s prosperity had returned to America because the nation was at war. With his election in 1932, Franklin Delano Roosevelt had begun to directly combat the effects of the Great Depression and had begun a national policy of government intervention and supervision, which is evident today. While Roosevelt and his policies were much criticized then—and still are—he did provide dynamic leadership at a crucial time in our history. His New Deal programs did not solve all American problems, but they did achieve some measure of success and did point the way to welfare capitalism as part of the American experience. Belief in the American system had been restored. But Roosevelt's greatness lies not only in his direction of the New Deal; he also led the nation to victory and world supremacy in World War II.

Essay

Depression after Depression

The dictionary tells us that a "depression" is a period marked by a slackening of business activity, much unemployment, falling prices, and falling wages. Americans today assume that the fear of another Great Depression is unfounded. True, inflation may be running rampant, and presidents since World War II have warned of recessions. But the policies of the New Deal, which included permanent economic safeguards, have made depressions a phenomenon of the past. Throughout our history, depressions or panics have grown in severity and intensity, greatly altering the course of events. The climax to the depression cycle came with the stock market crash of 1929 and the Great Depression of the 1930s.

In the years after the American Revolution, trade and commerce entered into a most prosperous period. More and more ships were in operation and the establishment of banks allowed more stable capital to come into circulation. But in the year 1784, America's first economic depression hit. However, the effect on the economy of the incipient nation was minimal. There was little extensive unemployment, nor was there any terrible suffering. The overwhelming number of Americans were farmers, and most businesses were either family enterprises or small operations. The next, much more severe, depression would occur in 1819.

It was the Era of Good Feelings: James Madison was president. There was overspeculation in Western lands. The National Bank of the United States, with its branches, was loaning much of the capital for this speculation. A depression hit in 1819, and the National Bank responded by tightening credit, which caused many of the Western banks to fold. Bankers foreclosed numerous farm mortgages. Cities were growing in size, and unemployment was on the rise. The Panic of 1819, as it was called, forced the government to adopt a new policy toward the sale of Western lands and caused the federal-court system to adopt a new attitude toward debtors. However, America was still overwhelmingly rural. The Depression of 1819 dampened the ardent nationalism of the Era of Good Feelings and caused a temporary cessation to speculation in land, but generally, life went on as usual.

In 1832 Andrew Jackson had adopted a popular policy with his veto of the Second National Bank recharter. What he had done, however, was not fully realized until 1837; he had removed any effective curb on the nation's economy. Now speculation ran rampant. As in the period before the 1819 panic, there was wild purchasing of Western lands on borrowed money, which was backed by few reserves. Western banks allowed liberal loans with equally liberal repayment schedules; these loans generally were unsecured. Speculation was not only in land; there were also ventures in canal building and railroad constructions. Many slaves were purchased on very shaky credit. The economic base became even weaker when American wheat crops failed, raising grain prices to a new high. In 1836 President Andrew Jackson, recognizing the effects of his economic policies, issued the Specie Circular, which ordered the land office to accept only gold or silver in payment for federal lands. However, this policy only hastened a collapse that was already beginning to take place. In the spring of 1837 an economic depression began. The failure of some British banks abroad caused many British investors to withdraw from American speculation and had sounded the death knell. Hardship was evident. Prices dropped, and many factories closed their doors. Unemployment rose. The government, thinking the depression would run its course, took a hands-off policy. It was President Van Buren who became the victim of the Panic of 1837.

Another depression would not occur for 20 years. During that time the North and South were becoming increasingly different. With the end of the Mexican War, in 1848, slavery once again burst onto the national scene, and the next few years would involve political crisis after political crisis. In the midst of this situation, there was again economic overspeculation, this time in both railroads and Western land. In addition, the farming market was quickly drying up. When a depression came in 1857, it caused suffering in the industrial North and in the farming West, but in the South the cotton crops, which relied on the slave system, remained fairly stable. Once again bank collapses and rising unemployment

This cartoon satirizes Jackson's policy to remove deposits from the federal bank, an action that helped to foster speculation and led to the Depression of 1837.

were common. Although this financial depression was relatively brief, it helped to cause North and South to further split apart, leading closer to the Civil War.

In the midst of Ulysses Grant's second term as president, and following upon some of the nation's most severe public scandals, came the Depression of 1873, the deepest depression the nation had yet known. A series of financial disasters in New York prompted the panic. European investments suddenly were curtailed; speculation in land and railroads again were on a flimsy basis. The banking firm of Jay Cooke and Company collapsed under pressure. Railroads and businesses began to fail; factories closed their doors. More than half a million workers were unemployed. Wages dropped and farm prices declined. Farmers were unable to pay their mortgages, and their farms were confiscated. The reality of overexpansion had again hit hard. And the Depression of 1873 brought home another fact: the severity of the depressions appeared to be increasing with every new panic.

Big business was now on the rise; it was the age of the captains of industry. Large urban centers were springing up across the country, while the cities of the East Coast were becoming metropolises. The office of the presidency had passed from Grant to a series of mediocre leaders and now was in the hands of Grover Cleveland for the second time. The economic trends were no longer easy to read. Finance capitalism and control of big business by bankers were entering the scene. A leading railroad went bankrupt and the New York Stock Exchange entered upon a wild selling spree. Bank loans were called in, and credit became virtually unobtainable. Railroads, then banks, began to fail. The captains of industry cut back their labor force, and,

in some cases, shut down their factories. More than 15,000 businesses went bankrupt. Economic conditions in Europe further aggravated America's distress. The Depression of 1893 was on. As many as 3 million workers were unemployed. Neither city nor federal government offered much relief. Again the depression was allowed to run its course—but how long could that kind of negative response be tolerated?

The Panic of 1907 was quick and relatively painless. American productivity had created more supply than demand. Banks had again been involved in speculation, and they would again have to pay the price. In this moment of crisis, banker and financier J. P. Morgan endorsed a program involving a voluntary plan to save the threatened banks. His plan worked, and Theodore Roosevelt was saved from any worsening depression. This voluntary action showed the nation how inadequate the present banking safeguards were and led the way to banking reform with the creation of the federal reserve system in 1913.

The stock market crash of October 1929 led to the Great Depression, the nation's most severe and long-lasting panic. Throughout American history, many of the same factors that led to the Great Depression were present in virtually all the depressions. Most depressions were hastened by unstable economic conditions in Europe. Overspeculation, whether it be in Western lands or the stock market, was evident. Bank and factory failures were followed by rising unemployment and declining prices. The Great Depression led to permanent reform of our economic policy. It was a harsh lesson in economics that will not soon be forgotten. Because of it, the New Deal was born, and it is being reborn with each new economic crisis. ∎

Suggested Reading

The causes and course of the Great Depression are well examined in *The Great Crash of 1929* (1955). by JOHN KENNETH GALBRAITH.

An excellent biography of Herbert Hoover is *Herbert Hoover: Forgotten Progressive* (1957) by JOAN HOFF WILSON.

Two general studies of the life and times of Franklin Roosevelt are WILLIAM E. LEUCHTENBERG's *Franklin Roosevelt and the New Deal, 1932–1940* (1963) and ARTHUR M. SCHLESINGER, JR.'s *The Crisis of the Old Order, 1919–1933* (1957) (many other Schlesigner works are also valuable sources on Roosevelt).

Two of the better Roosevelt biographies are found in JAMES MacGREGOR BURNS's *Roosevelt: The Lion and the Fox* (1956) and FRANK FREIDEL's, *Franklin Delano Roosevelt* (1956–1974), in four volumes.

Huey Long (1969) by T. HARRY WILLIAMS presents a study of one of Roosevelt's greatest critics.

The cause of labor during the New Deal is examined in IRVING BERNSTEIN's *Turbulent Years: A History of the American Worker, 1933–1941* (1960).

The Tennessee Valley Authority is examined in D. E. LILENTHAL's *TVA: Democracy on the March* (1953).

The Indian's role in the New Deal is described in *Crusade for Indian Reform, 1920–1954* (1977) by KENNETH R. PHILIP and JOHN COLLIER.

CHAPTER 14

World Peace,
World War, and a Cold War

Time Line

?–A.D. 1492	Migration and evolution of American Indian societies
1492	Christopher Columbus lands in West Indies—beginning of European exploration
1607–1732	Establishment of 13 English colonies
1775–1783	American Revolution
1776	Declaration of Independence
1789–1797	Presidency of George Washington
1812–1815	War of 1812
1816–1824	Era of Good Feelings
1846–1848	Mexican War
1861–1865	Civil War
1865–1877	Reconstruction
1877–1900	Industrialization and urbanization
1900–1916	Progressive Era
1917–1918	World War I

1921	Washington Disarmament Conference convenes
1928	Kellogg-Briand Peace Pact
1930	Clark Memorandum
1931	Japan invades Manchuria
1933	Adolph Hitler becomes chancellor of Germany
1935	First Neutrality Act
1938	Munich Pact
1939	World War II begins in Europe
1940	Reelection of Roosevelt to third term

1941	Lend-Lease Act Pearl Harbor is attacked by Japanese U.S. enters World War II
1942	Executive Order 9066 begins internment of Japanese-Americans Battle of Coral Sea Battle of Midway Allied invasion of North Africa
1943	Zoot Suit riots in Los Angeles Allied invasion of Italy Teheran Conference
1944	D-Day landing on Normandy beaches Battle of the Bulge Reelection of Roosevelt to fourth term
1945	Yalta Conference Germany surrenders Death of Roosevelt Vice-president Harry S. Truman becomes president Potsdam Conference Dropping of atomic bomb on Hiroshima and Nagasaki Japan surrenders
1947	Truman Doctrine Marshall Plan
1948	Berlin Crisis

1930s	Depression and New Deal
1941–1945	World War II
1945–1960	Post-war politics
1950–1953	Korean War
1950–1960	Civil rights movement
1961–1973	Vietnam War
1976	Bicentennial celebration

Memories of World War II seem distant to many young Americans, yet veterans of that war frequently gather and share experiences. Many a late-night movie features John Wayne or other Hollywood stars fighting the Japanese or Germans and, of course, winning. Even Tarzan, in a few of his movies, fought off the Nazi threat in the far-off jungles of Africa. And "G. I. Joe" and his fighting friends are very much alive today in nearby toy stores. While the scars of World War II are slowly healing, that war, and the Cold War which followed it, are essential to an understanding of America's present foreign policy. World War I was supposed to be the war to end all wars. Its conclusion brought disillusionment both with war and with internationalism. America refused to join the League of Nations, yet it had become a world power. Although the United States could no longer withdraw from the world scene, it did adopt a policy of semiisolation and noninvolvement. By the 1930s we found ourselves again the world's leading neutral. Germany, Japan, and Italy were on the move; major nations were being threatened. The sudden attack on Pearl Harbor ended our neutrality and thrust America into the second world war. We now had to join the Allied military campaign and mobilize our nation for war. This war caused the federal government to adopt a very harsh policy toward Japanese-Americans in this country. With the end of the war a new struggle of ideology emerged in the Cold War between Russia and the United States. This Cold War caused our foreign policy to shift its priorities and form the basis for our present foreign outlook.

Foreign Affairs in the 1920s

With the repudiation of the League of Nations by the Senate and the election of Harding in 1920, America's role as an imperialist nation somewhat halted, and a new period of semiisolation began. This was a strange form of isolation, however, for the United States still recognized some responsibility to help solve world problems (primarily out of self-interest and never to the point of becoming involved in military action). Continued American internationalism was initially visible with the Washington Disarmament Conference. The world arms buildup was a major threat to world peace, but since the United States was not a member of the League of Nations, arms limitation had to be accomplished outside the League. In 1921–22 the Washington Naval Disarmament Conference was held to limit the naval-arms race and to discuss the problems of the Far East. The result of the conference was a series of agreements: Britain, the United States, Italy, France, and Japan agreed to reduce the number of their heavy warships to a fixed ratio. The United States, France,

Britain, and Japan also signed an agreement to respect each other's rights in the Pacific and to confer in case of trouble. All nations represented at the conference agreed to uphold the territorial integrity of China and observe the Open Door Policy. The countries involved now started to build smaller war ships, but Japan instead continued its military buildup, which was to lead to their dominance of the Western Pacific.

During the 1920s Americans were taken up with the notion of permanent peace. Peace societies were formed to discuss the permanent "abolition of war." Even the *Ladies Home Journal* offered a prize for plans to bring world peace. In the midst of this peace frenzy, an American effort to bring peace to the world emerged with the Kellogg-Briand Pact. Aristide Briand, the French foreign minister, feared possible war with the now resurgent Germany and suggested that the United States and France make an agreement outlawing war between the two nations. Frank B. Kellogg, secretary of state under Coolidge, suggested that the idea become multinational; he persuaded representatives of foreign nations to meet in Paris in 1928, where they signed an agreement "to condemn recourse to war . . . and renounce it as an instrument of national policy." This promise of prolonged peace eventually was signed by 60 nations. How foolish was this diplomacy of words. War could not be stopped by a moralistic pact of peace; within the next decade the high purpose that surrounded the peace agreement would quickly disappear.

Good Neighbor Policy

The American desire for peace led to a positive change in foreign policy toward Latin America. A series of American diplomatic actions show its gradual evolution toward the Good Neighbor policy: Cuba was granted more self-government, while Columbia was paid reparations for our 1903 involvement in the Panama revolt. American troops were removed from the Dominican Republic, and the United States helped negotiate a boundary dispute between Chile and Peru. These policies were a sharp departure from the days of the Roosevelt Corollary and dollar diplomacy. And President Herbert Hoover carried them one step further. After his election he made a goodwill tour of South America, and in 1930 he issued the Clark Memorandum, which renounced future American intervention in Latin America, except in cases of "national self-preservation," and completely repudiated the Roosevelt Corollary. In the spirit of this memorandum, Hoover withdrew the last marines stationed in Nicaragua. He had prepared the groundwork for Roosevelt's Good Neighbor policy.

In his first inaugural address Roosevelt announced to Latin America that he would follow "the policy of a good neighbor." At the Montevideo Conference of 1933, Secretary of State Cordell Hull voted for a resolution that outlawed war as a means of settling disputes in the hemisphere and that declared "no state has the right to intervene in the internal or external affairs of another." In 1933 America stayed neutral during a Cuban revolution, and in 1934 it threw out the Platt Amendment, which would have justified American intervention there. In 1936 Roosevelt personally attended a Pan-American Conference and further emphasized the Good Neighbor policy while there. Even when Mexico seized American oil properties, Roosevelt reaffirmed Mexico's right to do so; but he did request compensation to owners for the confiscated property. This policy of Hoover's and Roosevelt's was a sharp break from the earlier policies of Theodore Roosevelt, Taft, and Wilson and helped to create a friendship between the United States and Latin America that would be invaluable during World War II. While Roosevelt focused on a new policy toward Latin America, he spent many a day keeping a watchful eye on the deteriorating situation in Europe and the rise of Japan in the Far East.

World War II Approaches

While the United States remained aloof from the League of Nations, it still became involved in disarmament limitations, a peace pact, and the Good Neighbor policy. Meanwhile, world relations quickly deteriorated. The militarists had now taken over control of the Japanese government, and, in 1931, Japan invaded the Chinese region of Manchuria. This initial challenge to the post-war peace was in open violation of the Covenant of the League of Nations and of the Washington Disarmament Conference. But neither the League nor the United States acted to help China. President Hoover avoided a policy of economic sanctions; but Secretary of State Henry Stimson did announce that the United States would not recognize seizures made in violation of American treaty rights, a policy which became known as the Stimson Doctrine.

Meanwhile in Europe the Versailles Treaty had left many problems unsolved. Wilson's plan for permanent peace had turned into "grape juice diplomacy" in the form of the Versailles Treaty and the League of Nations, which was described in America as the "international smelling committee." The treaty had reconstructed European nations based on boundaries, not nationalities, and had left a power vacuum in Central Europe. In addition, Germany was still reeling under the burden of war reparations. Desperate conditions in Europe now led to the rise of totalitarian governments. Benito Mussolini and his fascist government rose to power in Italy. Adolph Hitler and his Nazi party in Germany took advantage of the chaos of the depression,

Adolph Hitler with his Nazi party began a military buildup that threatened the peace of Europe.

and Hitler became chancellor in 1933. These two men were destined to destroy the Versailles system and to eventually dominate Europe.

Hitler acted first when he announced in 1935 that he was instituting a military buildup in violation of the Versailles Treaty. Then Mussolini launched a brutal attack on Ethiopia. The League of Nations issued a strong protest but took no direct action. In Spain, in early 1936, fascist General Francisco Franco launched a war against the Republican government. The United States and the other democratic governments of Europe remained neutral, while Hitler and Mussolini provided Franco with soldiers and supplies. Franco was victorious. And Hitler was also now on the move. He again violated the Versailles Treaty in 1936 by seizing back the German Rhineland from France. In 1938 Hitler bloodlessly took over Austria. In the Far East, in 1937, Japan had invaded northern China; an American gunboat had been sunk, but the Japanese government had apologized. Britain and France were becoming increasingly uneasy, but they continued their appeasement policy with

Hitler { 1936 - German Rhineland
1938 - Austria

1937 Ching by Japan

World Peace, World War, and a Cold War

the signing of the Munich Pact in the fall of 1938, which gave Hitler the Sudetenland section of Czechoslovakia. By March 1939, Hitler had seized all of Czechoslovakia. A few months later news was released of a German non-aggression pact with Russia. The world crisis deepened when, on September 1, 1939, Hitler invaded Poland and violated an English-French agreement upholding Polish security. Two days later France and England declared war. World War II had begun. ← *Sept 3, 1939*

fall 1938 Sudetenland
march 1939 Czechoslovakia

American Neutrality

The rise of Italy, Germany, and Japan perturbed most Americans, but during the 1930s they were more concerned with taming the depression than with positive action against the rise of totalitarianism. Americans were more concerned with avoiding foreign conflict than with combatting foreign aggression. The reports of the Nye committee, which were publicized between 1934 and 1936, confirmed many Americans' suspicions that the real reason the United States had entered World War I was to benefit the munitions industry, "the merchants of death." Americans wanted safeguards against further involvement. In 1935, 1936, and 1937, a series of Neutrality Acts were passed that seemed to guard against further entanglement. These acts prohibited trade with belligerents, prohibited Americans from traveling on belligerent ships—except at their own risk—and prohibited them from making loans, selling munitions, or arming belligerent merchant ships. American isolationist forces were continuing to gather strength. They were determined that the United States would not go to war again as it had in World War I.

With the outbreak of war in Europe, Americans generally supported the Allied forces against the Axis powers but still were interested in noninvolvement. Roosevelt was coming slowly to the conclusion that American involvement might be necessary, but he knew that he had little support for that position. He also feared that the Neutrality Acts would hamper the Allied cause, so he called a special session of Congress, which resulted in passage of the Neutrality Act of 1939. This law allowed the sale of war supplies as long as the purchasers would come and get them on a cash-and-carry basis. This would avoid loans and credit problems, such as with Allied repayment. The Neutrality Act was really pro-Allies, however: since the Allied navies controlled the Atlantic, only they could participate in such a program. But limited American help was not enough.

Europe at War

The war opened in Europe with little actual fighting. While Hitler prepared for a strike against France, Russia occupied Finland. This period of "phony war," however, was only temporary. With his "lightning war," or *blitzkreig*, Hitler swept through Western Europe—Belgium, the Netherlands, Norway, and Denmark fell. By June 1940, France had fallen too. England was now alone. Winston Churchill had replaced passive Neville Chamberlain as prime minister, and he began to ready Britain for German invasion; it was the beginning of the Battle of Britain. Churchill's spellbinding oratory galvanized the nation with such immortal words as "We shall defend our island, whatever the cost may be, we shall fight on the beaches . . . we shall fight in the fields and in the streets. We shall fight in the hills; we shall never surrender." Still the continual bombing of England went on. England looked to America as its savior, but in America there was a fierce debate going on between the non-interventionists, known by their group name as "America First," and the internationalists, who believed that United States involvement was essential to world peace.

The fall of France and the Battle of Britain gave the internationalists an advantage. In September 1940, Congress instituted the first peace-time draft in our history, and by 1941 there was a standing army of 1.6 million. In September 1940, Roosevelt traded England 50 World War I destroyers for naval bases in Bermuda, Newfoundland, and the Caribbean. In the midst of this domestic and foreign turmoil, a national election was held. Roosevelt decided to break the two-term tradition and run for a third term. He told the American people that he desired retirement but that the crisis demanded his leadership. The Republicans, meanwhile, turned to a newcomer, Wendell Wilkie, a former Democrat. Both Wilkie and Roosevelt wanted to keep America out of war, and both supported assistance of the Allied war effort. Their differences revolved around New Deal policies; Wilkie referred to Roosevelt as a "dictator" and called the New Deal "inefficient." The people voted to stick with an experienced president in those trying times. Roosevelt was elected for an unprecedented third term.

After the election the United States was pushed closer to the brink of war. Britain, rapidly running out of available dollars for purchasing supplies in the United States, asked for a new policy of support without payment. Roosevelt hit upon a scheme of lending, or leasing war supplies, but one critic said that it would be like lending chewing gum—you would never want it back. Roosevelt responded, "We must be the great arsenal of democracy." A fierce debate over the proposed plan occurred in Congress. But with strong Democratic support, the Lend-Lease Act became law in March 1941. Still trying to avoid full-scale war, Roosevelt extended the lend-lease policy to Russia after Germany invaded Russia in June 1941. American involvement also was building on the seas. Lend-Lease shipments of munitions were attacked by German submarines in the Atlantic. Roosevelt ordered naval ships to escort these shipments. During the fall of 1941 Roosevelt adopted a "shoot on sight" policy, and American destroyers *Greer, Kearney,* and *Rueben James* all saw action. In November 1941 Roosevelt adopted a policy of arming merchant vessels. It appeared that the United States would soon enter the war. But the event that plunged the United States into war came not from Germany but from Japan.

Pearl Harbor

With its invasion of China, the Japanese government made it clear that it intended to establish complete domination over the Western Pacific. Further, Japan had formed an alliance with Germany and Italy to comprise three Axis powers. The United States was aiding China and restricting the flow of supplies to Japan. Diplomacy was not working. Neither side would negotiate their differences. The United States became a roadblock in Japan's road to military domination of the Far East. Japan now received word from Russia that Russia would remain neutral in event of war between Japan and the United States. And Germany and Italy promised mutual assistance in case of a war with the United States. The military was gaining more power in Japan, and in the fall of 1941 General Hideki Tojo became premier and planned for war. Officials in the United States became aware of the Pacific war threat, but they were not sure where it would begin. Warnings of an imminent attack were sent in late November to commanders at the naval bases in Pearl Harbor and in Manila. But these warnings were either not heeded or not correctly interpreted. December 7, 1941, was the date Japanese forces attacked the naval and air base at Pearl Harbor, devastating American installations and leaving 2000 men killed and more than 1200 wounded. The American battleship fleet was in ruin; the country was fortunate that its aircraft carriers were not in port. Since that tragic day historians have continued to ponder the question of why we were so unprepared for the attack. But no satisfactory answer has ever been found. Further Japanese attacks took place in the Philippines and other spots in the Pacific. The debate over involvement or noninvolvement was over. The following day, before Congress, Roosevelt sought war with Japan and sadly told of that "Day of Infamy." Germany and Italy declared war on the United States, and the United States made it mutual. The nation mobilized for war.

The American Military Mobilized

With the United States now in the war, Churchill came to Washington to meet with Roosevelt. They both concurred that Germany was the leading menace and must be defeated at all costs. Yet the defeat of Germany and victory over Japan would be no easy matter. In fact, during most of the first year of the war, it appeared to be an impossibility. German submarines were devastating Allied shipping, and German troops were still on the move, now in Africa and threatening to completely dominate the Mediterranean. The German invasion of Russia also was moving forward; German soldiers had reached the outskirts of Moscow. Meanwhile, Japanese forces overran Southeast Asia and defeated the Americans under the command of General Douglas MacArthur in the Philippines; Australia would be their next target. But then the American counteroffensive began.

In the Pacific, American naval forces stopped the Japanese advance with victories at the Battle of the Coral Sea, in May 1942, and near Midway Island, in June 1942. American victory at Midway Island was a major blow to Japanese expansion and placed the Japanese navy on the defensive for the remainder of the war. A combined sea and land force now moved slowly from one Pacific island to another toward Japan. After six months of bloody fighting, Guadalcanal fell in February 1942, to the Americans. In the spring of 1942 James Doolittle led a daring bombing raid on Tokyo, but with little effect. On the European front, American and English forces were used to drive Hitler's army out of North Africa. This strategy was unpopular with Joseph Stalin in Russia, who had wanted a direct attack on Germany in Northern Europe. But the Western Allies believed that such an attack at this point in the war would be at a failure. In late 1942 British troops under General Montgomery began to stop the advance of Hitler's *Africa Korps*, which was commanded by the dashing "Desert Fox," General Erwin Rommel, in Egypt and then began to push the *Korps* back to Tunisia. Amphibious landings along the coast of Northern Africa, under the command of General Dwight D. Eisenhower, gave the Allies an advantage, and the German forces in Africa eventually surrendered in May 1943.

With victories in both the Pacific and Atlantic theaters of war, the Americans now hastened their offensive action. From Africa, in mid-1943, Eisenhower led an invasion force to Italy. Strong internal opposition had developed toward Mussolini, and he was soon overthrown; but the German army still occupied Italy. With Italian assistance the Allied army began the long fight to liberate Italy; after eight months of intense combat, Rome was liberated in June 1944. The Allies now felt ready to open another front against Germany, and, on D-Day (June 6, 1944), the largest amphibious landing in history took place under the command of Eisenhower on the Normandy beaches of France. This Allied force now tried to unite with the other invading Allied army, which landed in August in southern France. On August 25, 1944, the city of

World Peace, World War, and a Cold War

The daring D-Day Invasion of June 6, 1944 led to the liberation of Paris two months later.

Paris had been liberated, but the European war was far from over. The Germans stepped up their bombing raids on England, using a devastating new weapon—the V-2 bomb. German forces also began a new land offensive in Belgium in the Ardennes Forest. In December 1944, they surprised the Allied forces there in Battle of the Bulge. But the Allied forces regrouped and moved inexorably toward the Rhine. Meanwhile, the Russian army was advancing toward Berlin. The Rhine was soon crossed, and Germany was on its knees. Internal political strife had racked German leadership during the last few months of the war. Just a few days after Hitler's suicide, Germany surrendered on May 8, 1945. The European war was over.

In the Pacific, the United States had launched a massive island-hopping campaign under the command of Admiral Chester Nimitz and General Douglas McArthur, who in 1942, after fleeing from the Philippines, had issued the immortal words, "I shall return." Island after island fell to American forces, but only after long and bloody fighting. By the fall of 1944, McArthur had

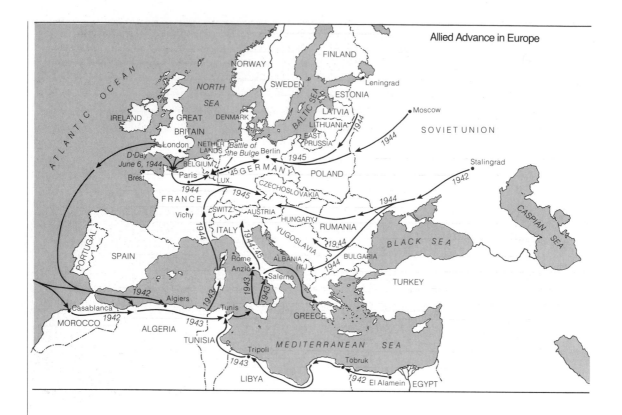

indeed returned to the Philippines, and in March and June 1945 the Japanese island strongholds of Iwo Jima and Okinawa fell. Recaptured islands were used as bases for bombing raids against Japan. The use of fire bombs had brought widespread devastation to the islands, but the Japanese fought on. Confronted with the prospect of a massive invasion of the home island, President Harry Truman, who had assumed the presidency with the death of Roosevelt in April 1945, now had to make a decision between risking millions of American lives or using a devastating new weapon on the Japanese—the atomic bomb. Roosevelt had authorized the development of an atomic weapon. The first successful test of the new weapon had just taken place in July, in White Sands, New Mexico. With Churchill's consent, Truman first asked for Japanese surrender, then dropped the bomb on Hiroshima on August 6, 1945 and on Nagasaki on August 9, 1945. This devastating attack brought almost immediate surrender. On August 14, 1945, Japan surrendered and World War II came to

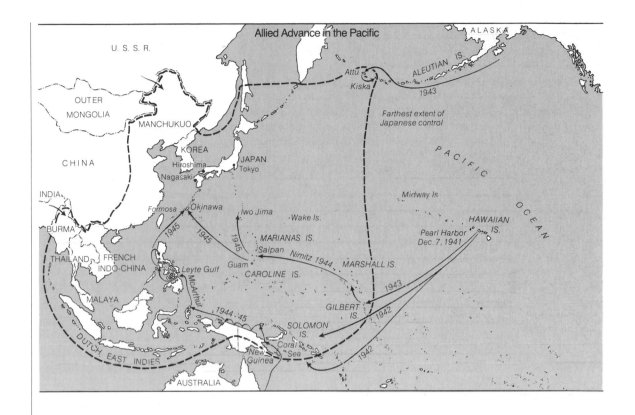

Allied Advance in the Pacific

Here is the aftermath of the dropping of the atomic bomb on Hiroshima.

<u>a close.</u> The need for the use of the atomic weapon was debated then and will continue to be debated for years to come.

America at War

America during World War II was similar to World War I America. But greater mobilization was needed and achieved. <u>More than 16 million people served in the armed forces, with more than 1 million casualties. Industrial production and advances were remarkable. Gross production of goods and services rose to $215 billion—twice the $92 billion of 1939.</u> United <u>States war production in 1943 was six times greater than military output in 1939.</u> Some economists have estimated that <u>by 1944 United States war production was twice that of the total output of Germany, Italy, and Japan.</u> As <u>with World War I,</u> however, <u>such industrial expansion was only made possible by direct federal control of a major portion of American industry.</u> The <u>War Production Board became responsible for the control of industrial output;</u> the <u>Office of Transportation directed domestic transportation;</u> while the <u>War Shipping Administration oversaw the merchant marine.</u> The <u>proliferation of war agencies led in 1943 to the establishment of the Office of War Mobilization under James F. Byrnes.</u> The <u>government also offered incentive programs, which virtually guaranteed</u>

Posters like this one helped recruit Americans for the armed services.

I'll give 'em HELL!

YOU GIVE ME THE *STUFF!*

profits; antitrust laws were even overlooked to create needed production. All segments of the economy benefitted, especially the munitions industry, while corporate profits rose to a total of $246 billion.

Labor reaction to the war was similar to that of World War I. Americans knew the dangers of war and the role that labor would have to play in the war effort. At the same time union leaders were aware of the need for government regulation and for cooperation between labor and management; still, they insisted, the rights of workers would have to be safeguarded. At a White House labor-management conference, representatives of labor reaffirmed their willingness to refrain from strikes and to submit disputes to the National War Labor Board. This board, created in January 1942 under the leadership of William H. Davis, was given authority to settle all industrial disputes that were likely "to interrupt work which contributed to the effective prosecution of the war." Labor and business were well represented in all war-production agencies. While labor contributed greatly to the war effort, some strikes occurred each year of the war. The strike with the most national impact was that of the coal miners under the direction of John L. Lewis, who continued his strike in defiance of Roosevelt and the War Board. Lewis was extremely callous in his repeated work stoppages and frequent strikes. While both labor and industrial leaders could have taken advantage of the war situation to gain benefits, few availed themselves of this opportunity. Congress, however, reflected growing antiunion feelings in the Smith-Connally War Labor Disputes Act, which authorized the National War Labor Board to seize strike-bound war industries and levy criminal penalties against persons who promoted strikes in government-operated plants or mines. Labor, nevertheless, made an invaluable contribution to the winning war effort.

Black Involvement

More than 30 million men registered for the draft, and more than 15 million served; many of those were from minority groups. In fact, more than 1 million blacks served in the armed forces, while 2 million more worked in defense-related industries. When the United States entered the war, blacks were reluctant to join the war effort, for they remembered the discrimination blacks had faced during World War I. Job discrimination in the defense industry was particularly evident, and black leaders urged Roosevelt to issue Executive Order 8802, which affirmed the government's policy of nondiscrimination in employment. A Committee on Fair Employment Practices eventually was formed to investigate violations of this order. However, those blacks who served in the armed forces, whether officers or enlisted men, once again were

More than one million blacks participated in the armed services.

victims of segregation. While certain barriers slowly were breaking down, segregation was still the rule.

Nevertheless, Roosevelt brought some equality to the black man and woman fighting and working for freedom. Eventually the navy began to accept blacks into general services, as did the marines and coast guard. Colonel Benjamin O. Davis, Sr., became the first black general in the nation's history when he was promoted to brigadier general. Black troops served on all fronts and performed valiantly; those who were employed in defense-related industries helped the nation's mobilization for war.

As during World War I, an exodus from the South occurred, and racial tension again raised its ugly head. Riots broke out in New York, Chicago, Los Angeles, and Detroit. The riot in Detroit, in June 1943, was the most severe; 34 people were killed and property losses exceeded $2 million. Yet despite all the setbacks, blacks were beginning to make some improvements in civil rights.

Indians and World War II

World War II marked a turning point in the relationship of the American Indian to white society. More than 25,000 Indians served in the armed forces, and many more worked in defense industries. Unlike blacks, Indians served in integrated units. They served on all fronts. Often Indians found a place in communications, for the Indian language was a difficult code for the enemy to break. Many were decorated for bravery, and one received the Congressional Medal of Honor. Ira Hayes, a Pima Indian, was one of a group of marines photographed raising the United States flag atop Mount Suribachi on Iwo Jima. Hayes became a hero after the war, but he turned to alcoholism. One night in 1955 he died in a corn field on the Gila River Indian Reservation in Arizona. To many whites, Ira Hayes had been the symbol of the modern Indian; he came to a tragic end.

During the war many Indians moved away from their tribes and into white society for the first time. This contact frequently brought with it obvious discrimination. Off-reservation sale of liquor to Indians was outlawed; certain Western states restricted off-reservation Indians from voting. With the end of the war, the urban Indian became an American phenomenon. Although Indians had difficulty living in "the cement prairie," they often remained there, and they were becoming America's forgotten people. More and more Indians continued to move into the cities of the West, creating their own urban ghettos. The Indian Reorganization Act was still in effect, but the war had depleted many of its programs. World War II ironically had done what many whites had wanted over the years; it had hastened the process of assimilation into white society.

Mexican-Americans and World War II

Mexican-Americans also served America well during the war. In fact, more than 30,000 of them were members of the armed forces. Since the armed forces seemed to offer minorities a chance for a better life, many willingly joined the army; others were drafted. For Mexican-Americans, who were often noncitizens, military duty meant instant citizenship.

Mexican-Americans were the forgotten soldiers of World War II. They were the most decorated and yet the least recognized. But the war did bring many of them more money, citizenship, and a better position in society; and they shared in many veteran programs after the war. As with other minorities, wartime life at home was often unpleasant.

Racial tension between Mexican-Americans and whites was most obvious in the pachuco riots. A "pachuco" was a Mexican-American youth who had joined the youth gangs of East Los Angeles. Pachucos were easily recognized by their tattoos and baggy pants with suspenders (a "zoot suit"). These second-generation Mexican-Americans were members of barrio groups with names like the Happy Valley gang or the Alpine Street gang. Many felt lost between two worlds: the white society refused to accept them, but they were no longer

Mexican either. By the 1940s their frustrations often led to violent confrontations with other nearby gangs.

In August 1942, in the Sleepy Lagoon section of East Los Angeles, Jose Diaz was found dead. The entire Thirty-eighth Street gang was jailed and found guilty. The prosecution ruled that Mexican-Americans were basically Aztecs, and Aztecs had sacrificed human beings. Although a high court overturned the decision because the lower-court judge was biased, racial tension began to build. Sailors and soldiers on leave in Los Angeles frequently looked for "action" and found it among the pachuco gangs. The elements for a race war between servicemen and Mexican-Americans were coming to a head.

In June 1943, sailors came into the barrios of East Los Angeles looking for war. Fights broke out: pachucos had their clothes ripped off them; a black had his eyes gouged out. Full-scale riots broke out on several occasions, terrorizing the East Los Angeles community. Mexican-Americans were arrested for causing the riots, while Los Angeles newspapers ran emotion-charged headlines such as "Zoot Suit Chiefs Girding for War on Navy" and "Zoot Suiters Learn Lesson in Fight with Servicemen." Surely the violence and terror would have continued if the armed forces had not declared that area off limits for servicemen and if the Mexican government had not directly intervened in the trouble. Still, white society blamed Mexican-Americans for the riots; the whites' one-sided viewpoint strengthened their stereotype of Mexican-Americans as dangerous and violent people. The United States eventually investigated the pachuco riots and found that white racism was the cause of the incident. Like other minority groups, Mexican-Americans suffered in both the military and at home; but no minority group suffered as blatant a violation of civil rights as the Japanese-Americans.

Japanese-American Relocation

During the second world war, 110,000 West Coast Japanese, two-thirds of whom were American citizens, were placed in relocation camps. Many historians have justified this action in terms of wartime hysteria, but it can best be explained by racism toward Japanese-Americans. Hostile feelings toward the Japanese had been building in America for years. Cruel stereotypes pictured them as sly, treacherous, and desirous of white women. California had passed legislation that prevented them from owning property, purchasing power motors for use in their work, and hiring white women. Many Americans felt that Japanese-Americans had ties with their mother country, Japan, and now that Japan was on a militaristic course, Japanese-Americans must come under suspicion. Nor did it help the situation that in California, during the

1920s, many Japanese-Americans had prospered, becoming successful fishermen, cannery workers, and farmers.

The specter of war with Japan further raised the issue of Japanese-American security. The California legislature responded to the war scare with a series of anti-spy laws. But then the Pearl Harbor attack actually occurred—What would happen to the Japanese in America now? The *Issei* were the first-generation Japanese-Americans, born—and frequently raised—in Japan; they were noncitizens and were labeled as enemy aliens. The second generation were the *Nisei*, born in the United States; they were United States citizens, so they could not be labeled as foreigners. With the outbreak of war with Japan, the Nisei began to be rounded up. Meanwhile the war, coupled with racism, brought out increased anti-Japanese feelings; said one popular slogan, "All Japanese are traitors."

American organizations, such as the American Legion and the national Chamber of Commerce, demanded close surveillance of Japanese-American activities. One newspaper reporter wrote, "The stories of arrows in cane fields pointing toward Pearl Harbor, and the yarns about the Jap vegetable trucks blocking the roadway to Pearl Harbor that day, are all unadulterated bunk." But his feelings were not those of the majority: "Personally I hate Japanese, and that goes for all of them. . . . If all the Japs were removed tomorrow, we'd never miss them." When one Japanese submarine attacked a wooden jetty near Santa Barbara, panic ensued. Unfounded stories were circulated of a Japanese airstrike on Los Angeles. Japanese invasion was imminent, reasoned many West Coast residents. Federal action against all Japanese in America was thought to be necessary.

The federal government acted. In January 1942, Attorney General Francis Biddle ordered all enemy aliens to be removed from security areas along the West Coast. This action was not enough. West Coast pressure continued to build for the removal of all Japanese, citizens or not. The public feared that Japanese-Americans were still bound to Japan and that, living in the United States, they were too close to military establishments, inviting potential sabotage. No evidence existed of sabotage or disloyalty by any Nisei, but the sentiments for removal gathered strength. Lieutenant General John L. DeWitt, commander of the Western Defense Command, led the campaign for the removal of all Japanese from the Pacific Coast. Before a congressional committee he testified:

> *Once a Jap, always a Jap. They are a dangerous element. There is no way to determine their loyalty. . . . It makes no difference whether he is an American citizen; theoretically he is still a Japanese and you can't change him. . . . You can't change him by giving him a piece of paper.*

DeWitt was not alone. California Attorney General Earl Warren pushed hard for evacuation with some consideration given to American citizens of Japanese ancestry; meanwhile Secretary of War Stimson drew up a plan of evacuation. Pressure continued to build, and now it focused on Roosevelt.

In February 1942 Roosevelt succumbed to public pressure and signed Executive Order 9066, which set up evacuation areas and authorized the building of "relocation" centers for the evacuees. This legalized the removal of more than 110,000 West Coast Japanese, two-thirds of whom were American citizens. DeWitt issued orders to begin the evacuation. Posters were put up in Japanese communities that explained the evacuation procedure. Little time was given for preparation; entire families had to leave their homes and frequently were forced to sell them. Most possessions were abandoned; the only possessions the evacuees could take were those that fit into a suitcase. Overnight, Japanese were forced to abandon what they had worked long and hard for; property losses exceeded $365 million. It is surprising to many that the Japanese-Americans accepted the orders and quietly gathered at bus stations to be shipped to temporary quarters. By late summer of 1942 the evacuation was well under way. Temporary quarters were set up in some of the strangest places, such as the Santa Anita racetrack. From the temporary quarters the Japanese were then transferred to permanent quarters.

Relocation of thousands of American citizens shocked Nisei more than it did the rest of American society. One child of a Nisei family sadly noted,

Executive Order 9066 authorized the removal of West Coast Japanese, citizens and noncitizens alike, to relocation camps.

"I don't like Japan, Mommy. I want to go back to America." Permanent camps were established at Manzanar and Tule Lake in California, Poston and Gila Rivers in Arizona, Minidoka in Idaho, Heart Mountain in Wyoming, Granada in Colorado, Topaz in Utah, and Rohwer and Jerome in Arkansas. While these were officially called "relocation camps" (under the direction of the War Relocation Authority), they were crowded, cramped concentration camps with barbed wire and armed guards. The entire process of relocation had been accomplished with only one minor incident of violence. By the end of 1942 Japanese relocation was complete, and the government now directed the inhabitants of the camps to live a "normal life."

Dillon Meyer, director of the War Relocation Authority, was anxious to get the Japanese back into the mainstream of American life. A screening process was established and the "safe" Japanese were then sent to the Midwest or East Coast, usually never again to return to the West. By the end of 1943 more than 35,000 Japanese were out of the camps and back into American society. Needless to say, normal life in the camps was difficult. Most families were left with only memories of their material possessions, which they worked so hard to acquire. After the war they would have to start all over again. Traditional cultural patterns were changed: respect for the elderly and domination of the Japanese by the Issei diminished; the Nisei controlled the camps, frequently coming into conflict with the Issei; and family roles were broken forever. It is ironic that Japanese-Americans were allowed to enter the armed services and saw action on all fronts; the all Japanese-American 442nd Regimental Combat Team won glory and praise. It is also difficult for many to understand why, when the war ended, relatively few Japanese returned to Japan. These people were Americans, and, no matter what had happened, they would remain Americans.

While few Japanese resorted to violence, some did challenge the relocation process on the grounds that they were United States citizens. In the *Gordon Hirabayashi* case involving military curfew, the Supreme Court ruled: "We cannot close our eyes to the fact, demonstrated by experience, that in time of war residents having ethnic affiliations with an invading enemy may be a greater source of danger than those of a different ancestry." It was not until December 1944 that the Supreme Court ruled in the *Endo* case that the federal government could not legally detail American citizens in relocation camps. The period of relocation then came to an end. But it had already brought untold misery and suffering to American citizens who had committed only one crime; they were of the same race as our enemy. The Japanese-American relocation experience will remain forever one of the darkest blots in our nation's history.

Wartime Diplomacy

In the early stages of the war, the leading planners of a reconstructed postwar world were Winston Churchill and Franklin Roosevelt. In August 1941, Roosevelt and Churchill met off the foggy shores of Newfoundland and drafted the Atlantic Charter, which enumerated the goals for a post-war world. With the German invasion of Russia in June 1941, Joseph Stalin found Russia on the Allied side and was eager for Allied support. With American entrance into the war, Russia pushed for a two-front war, while slowly driving German troops off its own soil. In January 1943, in Morocco, Roosevelt and Churchill met and discussed Russian participation in the war effort. They felt that Russia needed assurances about their commitment to victory and their basic intentions. There in Morocco the two leaders proclaimed the policy of "unconditional surrender," which meant "not the destruction of the German populace, nor the Italian or Japanese populace" but surrender without conditions. Although this statement may have stiffened the Nazi will to fight, it helped to make Russia willing to participate in Allied diplomacy.

Secretary of State Cordell Hull visited Moscow, talked with Stalin, and was very much impressed with him. In fact, Stalin was receiving very favorable press in America. *Time* magazine had named him Man of the Year. Books and films pictured him as a gentle grandfather with "deep brown eyes" and a dog on his lap. After Hull's visit had cleared the way for a meeting of Allied leaders, Stalin, Roosevelt, and Churchill met for the first time in November 1943, in Teheran, Iran. While the Teheran conference brought few specific results, it was important that these three world leaders meet, remove doubts about each other, and discuss general war strategy. Roosevelt felt it was essential to involve Stalin (and Russia) in postwar planning. A future world organization was talked about, and Stalin promised to enter the war against the Japanese after the defeat of Germany. Roosevelt promised to start a second front in the war against Germany. All three leaders seemed willing to compromise on issues, and a spirit of friendliness permeated the conference. On leaving Iran, Roosevelt cheerfully wrote, "We are going to get along very well with him and the Russian people—very well, indeed." But one American participant saw sinister motives behind Stalin's smile, predicting that after the war the Soviet Union would become ". . . the only important military and political force on the continent of Europe. The rest of Europe would be reduced to military and political impotence."

In the midst of these negotiations and the war itself, a national election was held in 1944. The Republicans turned to the governor of New York, youthful Thomas E. Dewey, who ran on continued prosecution of the war and the formation of a permanent world peace-keeping body. The Democrats had little

Churchill, Roosevelt, and Stalin during their meeting at Yalta.

choice; they turned for a fourth time to their aging president, who had little time to campaign or make speeches. In spite of his noticeable failing health, Roosevelt was again swept into office. He turned immediately to the conclusion of the war and to plans for continued foreign diplomacy with Churchill and Stalin.

Yalta

Three months before the final surrender of Germany, the Big Three (Churchill, Roosevelt, and Stalin) met at Yalta in the Crimea to work out many of the issues that had been discussed at Teheran. Russia wanted reparations from Germany; the sum would be decided upon later. Russia wanted a guarantee that Germany would never be capable of military aggression again. It was decided that the three powers, plus France, would divide Germany into occupied zones. Roosevelt, very sick and weak, was able to get Russian support for a world organization, the United Nations, which would be successor to the old League of Nations. Russia, China, the United States, France, and England were all to have veto power in the Security Council of this new organization. Russia agreed to enter the war against Japan three months after the surrender of Germany; in return, Russia was given territorial concessions in Manchuria and some northern Japanese islands. The issue of gravest concern was the future of Eastern Europe. It was obvious that Russia wanted dominance in this area, but Roosevelt and Churchill wanted Stalin to agree to allow these people self-determination. And it appeared that they won a victory when Stalin agreed to "free elections of governments responsive to the will of the people" in Poland and the rest of Eastern Europe. Stalin was in a very strong bargaining position, for the Russian army now already occupied most of Eastern Europe, but it appeared that he had given his support to freedom of expression in this region. The conference ended with high hopes. Roosevelt was now extremely weak and ill. It was not long after the decisions of Yalta were made public that critics wrote, "Yalta was the most cynical and immoral international transaction to which the United States was ever a partner." But Roosevelt, as sick at the time as he was, had done his best to guarantee a better postwar world. Critics have described the Yalta agreement as a sell-out, but it merely confirmed the reality of the military situation in Europe. The Russians, however, would never live up to all the promises made there.

Roosevelt now returned to the United States to rest. On April 12, 1945, during a sitting for a painting at Warm Springs, Georgia, he slumped over and died of a massive cerebral hemorrhage. A shocked Harry Truman became president. So ended the career of one of America's truly great presidents. His life was a testimony to the underdog. Although born wealthy, he fought valiantly to overcome polio and remain a viable political leader. Elected to the presidency in the midst of our worst national depression, he experimented with a New Deal, which brought more Americans a real share of the American dream. Then he faced a world war on two fronts against two formidable enemies. Franklin Roosevelt was a human being with faults and foibles. His New Deal had its failures, as did his handling of the nation at war. But he spent most of his presidency making America a good place to live, for now and for the future, and in making the world a world at peace. Since his presidency, the role of the federal government at home and abroad has never been the same. This is the heritage of Franklin Delano Roosevelt.

The Presidency of Truman

Little known Harry S. Truman now became president. Truman's background gave him little practical experience for the difficult road that lay ahead. Son of a mule trader, Truman's early life in Missouri involved a high school education, work as a timekeeper for the Santa Fe Railroad, and farming. During World War I, he served as an artillery captain and later became a reserve colonel. After the war he invested his life savings in a men's clothing store, which failed. Turning to politics, he won the support of "Big Tom" Pendergast, one of the most powerful Democratic city bosses who helped get Truman elected county judge, a position he held for many years. With Pendergast's support, he was elected to the United States Senate in 1934; but once Pendergast's corrupt dealings had been made public, Truman was able to stand

With the death of Roosevelt, Harry Truman became president.

alone on his record and was reelected in 1940. He got national publicity for his role in trimming defense waste and speeding war production. As a compromise candidate for vice-president in 1944, he won the nomination on the second ballot. After only 83 days in the vice-presidential office, Roosevelt died, and Truman was thrust into the presidency. Harry S. Truman seemed to be an average American, with his thick glasses and happy grin. He had only a high school education, was a poor speaker, and had a bad temper. But he was a practical man who was willing to tackle any problem, no matter how large. On his inaugural day he admitted, "I feel as if a load of hay has fallen on me." That "load" would continue to get heavier.

Truman watched as the war effort, which Roosevelt had worked so hard to get in motion, led to the end of the war. Some of the decisions undertaken at Yalta also now were coming to pass. In April of 1945 in San Francisco, the United Nations Conference established the United Nations Charter. This organization was to consist of a General Assembly open to all nations and of a Security Council composed of 11 members, of which 5 would be permanent, including the United States, China, Russia, Great Britain, and France. A secretariat, headed by a secretary-general, was to handle all administrative duties of the organization. The power of the new world organization was weak in several ways: member-states maintained complete national sovereignty, so the U.N. could never be a "world government"; unanimous agreement among the five permanent Security Council members was required for any action; and any of the five could exercise a veto power. Still, a world forum was formalized.

Potsdam and the Cold War

In July 1945, Truman met with Stalin and Churchill at Potsdam, near Berlin, in the final war meeting of the three powers. Already Truman and Stalin had become suspicious of each other's motives. There at Potsdam, Stalin reaffirmed his country's commitment in the war with Japan, while the United States and Great Britain issued an unconditional-surrender ultimatum to Japan, which demanded complete disarmament. The conference also reconfirmed the division of Germany into four occupation zones. Although this division and occupation appeared to be only temporary, this issue never was settled completely. Truman was unable to get a firm commitment from Russia on the fate of Eastern Europe. While Potsdam ended on a cordial note, dissension was becoming increasingly evident. And within a few months the Communist domination of Eastern Europe became more obvious. Now that Germany had been defeated and Japan finally had surrendered, Russia loomed as a major threat to American security.

The emerging Cold War, which was a power struggle between Russia and the United States over world dominance, was created by both countries. It was a response to the potential power of each and to the possible danger to either country's security by threat from the other. In a speech in Missouri in 1946, Churchill talked of an "iron curtain" that was spreading across Europe. Creative diplomacy seemed a necessity. George F. Kennan, a State Department expert on Soviet affairs, outlined a policy to combat the Russian plan for taking over the world and destroying capitalism. His policy was based on "a long-term, patient, firm, and vigorous containment of Russian expansive tendencies." This policy would stop the communistic menace and preserve freedom for democratic nations.

While Kennan was outlining his policy of containment, Truman was already on the offensive. War-torn Europe was ripe for Communist takeovers. Depleted Britain announced that it could no longer support the "rightist" government of Greece against Communist guerillas. If Greece fell, Turkey and

Atlee, Truman, and Stalin discussed the postwar world at Potsdam.

the rest of the eastern Mediterranean might not be far behind. Truman sought $400 million from Congress for military and economic assistance to Greece and Turkey. In his Truman Doctrine, presented before Congress on March 12, 1947, he stated, "We shall not realize our objectives, however, unless we are willing to help free peoples to maintain their free institutions and their national integrity against aggressive movements that seek to impose upon them totalitarian regimes." The new direction in foreign policy had been enunciated. The acceptance of this program revealed the extent of the belief in the potential Communist take-over of the world. The United States now pledged itself to support free government anywhere in the world. The Monroe Doctrine now became a world doctrine. But this was merely step one in the cold war.

Kennan's containment ideas became reality in the Marshall Plan. European recovery was slow; countries of Western Europe were still ripe for internal communism. America must act. Secretary of State George Marshall, in June 1947, formulated a plan that would offer direct economic aid to the ailing nations of Europe. This would bring them recovery and allow them to fight off communism. Although this plan initially was much criticized, the Communist take-over of Czechoslovakia led to its passage. By the early 1950s more than $12 billion in economic aid had been given to 12 European nations.

The greatest threat to post-war peace was the Berlin crisis of 1948. France, England, and the United States had decided to unify their occupation zones and create a West German republic. Stalin protested this action and talked of the creation of a Communist East German republic. Of course, Berlin was situated in the Russian section; Russia decided to close off the city. Truman and the Western powers faced a real crisis, but they met it head-on. They decided to airlift supplies to the people of the non-communist sectors of the city. Russia allowed the airlift and recognized in it the determination of the United States. In May 1949 the airlift was ended. A moral victory had been achieved. But this would not be the last power play in the Cold War. It was not long before two independent German governments were formed: Communist East Germany and democratic West Germany.

The Berlin blockade caused the United States to discuss a possible military alliance with the countries of Western Europe to limit Soviet expansion. In April 1949, a 12-nation alliance was formed, including the United States, which was called the North Atlantic Treaty Organization. NATO members pledged that an attack on any one member would be an attack on all. An international military force was created as a deterrent to Soviet aggression, and General Dwight D. Eisenhower was appointed first commander of the NATO forces. This peacetime military alliance showed American commitment against potential Soviet aggression.

World War I had proved not to be the war to end all wars. Already suspicious of this, and not anxious to enter another such war, caution marked American foreign policy in the 1920s and 1930s. But international tensions were drawing the United States ever closer to war. Pearl Harbor pushed America into World War II, a true world war in which American military units fought in seemingly every corner of the globe. Faced with difficult obstacles, American troops won the war on all fronts, while the nation again mobilized successfully. Minorities had problems both abroad and at home, with the Japanese-Americans suffering most. Nor was World War II the war to end all wars, either. The United States did participate in the restoration of the postwar world much more than it had after World War I. But now it faced a new enemy—Communist Russia. The struggle between these two countries pitted two seemingly opposing systems in a cold war. In response to the Communist threat, President Truman changed the direction of our foreign policy and introduced a doctrine of positive containment and foreign aid. Neutrality and isolation were policies of the past. Truman now led the way toward a new postwar America, beset with troubled domestic and foreign policies.

Essay

Pearl Harbor—Why?

At 7:55 A.M. December 7, 1941, the first bombs began to fall on Pearl Harbor. Approximately 360 Japanese planes had attacked the Pacific Fleet, the naval base, and army aircraft at Hickam Field. The assault lasted two hours. The Pacific Fleet lost eight battleships, three light cruisers, three destroyers, and four other vessels. The final American casualties were 3700. This surprise attack propelled the United States into World War II. This was a day of infamy.

The remains of the *USS Arizona* lie in the waters of Pearl Harbor as a tragic reminder of that "day of infamy."

Why did it happen? The frenzy of World War II postponed a possible answer to that question. Before the war, isolationists and interventionists had struggled to steer America's course. The attack on Pearl Harbor thrust America into World War II and caused the two groups to present a united front. With the end of the war, questions again were asked about that horrible surpise attack. Who was responsible? Why were the American forces so unprepared?

Critics of Franklin Roosevelt pointed at him and his prewar foreign policy. Clare Boothe Luce, for example, wrote, "He lied the American people into war because he could not lead them into it." These critics felt that Roosevelt was out of touch with the majority of Americans, who were actually isolationists. He had been reelected by the crucial votes of isolationists, who had believed him when he vowed to stay out of the war. But soon after the election he followed a course that led directly to war; by supporting the Lend-Lease Act, he put America on a collision course with Germany. Roosevelt's duplicity involved his public stand on noninvolvement and his private desire to get America into war as soon as possible. In 1940 and 1941 Roosevelt moved from decision to decision and accomplished his goal— America entered World War II.

Other critics of Roosevelt focused on America's prewar relationship with China and Japan, which they claimed had been unrealistic and foolish. They felt that Roosevelt had viewed a clash with Japan as a way of getting into the European war; he knew that Britain needed help, and he would do almost anything to get assistance to that faltering country. Although Roosevelt was talking peace with Japan in the fall of 1941, he knew that relations with the Japanese government were deteriorating to the point of war. Japan had even proposed a Pacific confer-ence, but Washington rejected such a suggestion. The die had been cast.

Supporters of Roosevelt apply a much different interpretation to the events of 1940 and 1941. They insist Roosevelt did all in his power to avoid war and to give America needed time to prepare. For example, he had made ample gestures to the Japanese ambassador, Admiral Nomura, to convey America's concern over Japanese militarization and our commitment to peace. The Japanese government had its mind set on expansion and war and these plans included the United States. Roosevelt's Lend-Lease plan was necessary to keep Britain alive and give America more time to prepare for what seemed to be an unavoidable involvement. Roosevelt's supporters believe that he steered a course of collective security in foreign affairs and that he was honest and straight forward to the American public.

To both critics and supporters of Roosevelt's course of action in the years before American involvement, the surprise attack on Pearl Harbor and American unpreparedness still remains a mystery. Admiral Husband E. Kimmel, commander of the Pacific Fleet at the time, placed the blame on the lack of communication within the Navy and on impassioned politics. He believed that the Navy Department in Washington had intercepted and decoded certain Japanese messages that pointed directly to the Pearl Harbor attack, information which was never forwarded to him. Admiral Robert Theobold agreed with Kimmel and noted that the Pacific Fleet, stationed in Hawaiian waters, was an invitation to Japanese attack. In essence, key information had been withheld.

With all the evidence at hand *after* the war, their conclusions seem reasonable; but not all evidence was available in those dark days prior to the attack. The best intelligence available listed potential Japanese targets in the Pacific, but these circulated lists of targets did not include Pearl Harbor. And in defense of naval intelligence much of the decoding of the Japanese messages involved what was sophisticated guesswork at best. Commanders of the military bases at Pearl Harbor seem to have been given the best available information. Hindsight tells us that information was not good enough to avoid the tragedy of December 7.

The debate over Roosevelt's course of action in 1940 and 1941 continues. The question of why the attack took place and why the American forces were so unprepared causes Americans to search for an answer and frequently shake their heads in frustration. Historian Robert Sherwood reflected on the mystery of Pearl Harbor:

> Millions of words have been recorded by at least eight official investigating bodies, and one may read through all of them without arriving at an adequate explanation of why, with war so obviously ready to break out somewhere in the Pacific, our principal Pacific base was in a condition of peacetime Sunday-morning somnolence instead of Condition Red. ∎

Suggested Reading

The coming of World War II and America's changing neutrality are described in *From Isolation to War, 1931–1941* (1968) by J. E. WILTZ and in *The Reluctant Belligerent* (1965) by ROBERT A. DIVINE.

The controversy surrounding the attack on Pearl Harbor is brought to life in ROBERTA WOHLSTETTER's *Pearl Harbor: Warning and Decision* (1962).

A. RUSSELL BUCHANAN, in *United States and World War II* (1964) (2 volumes), presents a detailed study of the military action of the war.

The home front is examined in JOHN M. BLUM's *V Was For Victory: Politics and American Culture During World War II* (1976).

The Japanese-American experience is described in *Nisei: The Quiet Americans* (1969) by BILL HOSOKAWA.

Wartime diplomacy is examined in GADDIS SMITH's *American Diplomacy During the Second World War, 1941–1945* (1965), while Roosevelt's role as a diplomat is explored in JAMES MCGREGOR BURNS's study, *Roosevelt: Soldier of Freedom* (1970).

M. SHERWIN discusses the controversy surrounding the Atomic bomb in *A World Destroyed: The Atomic Bomb and the Grand Alliance* (1975).

The evolution of the Cold War is found in *The Cold War and Its Origins, 1917–1960* (1961), (2 volumes), by D. L. FLEMING.

CHAPTER 15

The Fair Deal to Camp David:
From Truman to Carter

Time Line

?–A.D. 1492	Migration and evolution of American Indian societies
1492	Christopher Columbus lands in West Indies—beginning of European exploration
1607–1732	Establishment of 13 English colonies
1775–1783	American Revolution
1776	Declaration of Independence
1789–1797	Presidency of George Washington
1812–1815	War of 1812
1816–1824	Era of Good Feelings
1846–1848	Mexican War
1861–1865	Civil War
1865–1877	Reconstruction
1877–1900	Industrialization and urbanization
1900–1916	Progressive Era
1917–1918	World War I
1930s	Depression and New Deal
1941–1945	World War II
1945–1960	Post-war politics
1948	Election of Harry S. Truman
1950	Senator Joseph McCarthy institutes anti-Communist campaign
1950	Start of Korean War
1951	Truman removes General MacArthur from command
1952	Election of Dwight Eisenhower
1953	Truce ends Korean War
1955	Geneva Conference Merger of AFL–CIO

1956	Reelection of Eisenhower Suez Crisis
1957	Eisenhower Doctrine Launching of Sputnik I
1960	Election of John Kennedy
1961	Bay of Pigs Invasion
1962	Cuban Missle Crisis
1963	Assassination of Kennedy Johnson becomes president
1964	Election of Johnson
1965	Civil Rights Act Bombing attack on North Vietnam begins in earnest
1968	Election of Richard Nixon
1969	Moon Landing
1970	Cambodian Campaign Nixon visits Peking
1972	Reelection of Nixon
1973	Vietnam armistice
1974	Resignation of Nixon Gerald Ford becomes president
1975	*Mayaguez* incident
1976	Bicentennial celebration Election of Jimmy Carter
1977	Department of Energy created
1978	Panama Canal treaties
1979	Diplomatic relations restored with China Middle East settlement Iranian hostage crisis
1950–1953	Korean War
1950–1960	Civil rights movement
1961–1973	Vietnam War
1976	Bicentennial celebration

It seems such a long time since the days of World War II and President Harry Truman. The years between Presidents Truman and Carter were filled with events both here and abroad that are only dim memories to some Americans, but very vivid to many others. Truman's domestic problems were frustrating ones indeed. The Korean War, was a different conflict from earlier American wars; it was a war of containment and marked a new beginning in foreign affairs. Dwight D. Eisenhower, a military hero who became president, also had to deal with the Korean War, as well as sticky domestic issues. In foreign policy, he added the Eisenhower Doctrine to our growing world commitments. John Kennedy's brief presidency saw our involvement in Vietnam really begin; his "quest for the impossible dream" led to a rekindling of the spirit of the New Deal. Lyndon Johnson brought with him a Great Society, whose greatness was marred by our growing involvement in the Vietnam quagmire. Richard Nixon's presidency seems synonymous with Watergate; his attempts to control runaway inflation and his breakthroughs in foreign affairs are diminished by the memory of America's greatest political scandal. The resignation of Nixon led to the brief tenure of Gerald Ford, with his conservative policies and emphasis on honesty and openness. Ford was president when America celebrated its two-hundredth anniversary. The election of 1976 brought Jimmy Carter to Washington. A moralist with strong humanitarian sentiments and a feeling for the masses, he entered an age of rampant inflation, growing energy problems, and increased foreign demands. His handling of the Panama Canal Treaty, the opening of diplomatic relations with China, and his influence in the Middle East settlement mark his presidency. American politics since World War II have seemed to offer something for everyone: war, anti-Communist campaigns, and crises in Cuba and the Middle East, assassinations, Watergate, and China. This complex modern era began with the presidency of Harry S. Truman.

The Truman Years

With the end of World War II, Truman had to face the monumental problem of reconverting the nation to a peacetime economy and, at the same time, decide whether to continue or even to expand the New Deal. World War II had involved the greatest mobilization of men and materials in our history, so the reconversion process was a difficult one. Some Democrats and many Republicans feared both a postwar depression and a return to an expanded New Deal. Truman proved to be a liberal; his plans for New Deal programs included expansion of social security benefits, a health-insurance plan, and another T.V.A. project. This stance, plus his belief that wartime controls should only gradually be eased, led to a bitter dispute with Congress. The postwar recession did not materialize, but spiraling inflation appeared instead. Many goods had been in short supply during the war; now, with controls off, consumers went wild. Many prices rose more than 33 percent in one year. Truman anticipated that the rapid increase of prices would lead to an escalation of wages. He asked for controls from Congress to stop this inflationary threat, but Congress refused to grant them to him.

In the midst of the price increases, labor began to ask for substantial raises. Lacking power to control prices, Truman felt that his hands were tied. Labor saw that Truman was not going to be much assistance; they felt that the only viable weapon they had left was the strike. It is true that the government had passed the Full Employment Act of 1946 to guarantee full employment conditions; but it was a hollow law, and unemployment was on the rise. Strikes now broke out. The General Motors strike, 112-days long, came first. When John L. Lewis led the United Mine Workers out on strike, Truman called the coal shortage a national disaster and brought in troops to run the mines. This precipitated a settlement. The Railway Workers Union struck; Truman asked Congress for emergency powers to break strikes that in any industry was essential to the national welfare and to draft the strikers into the army. Labor was angered at Truman's tactics; it appeared that he was taking away labor's only real weapon in the fight against inflation. High prices, low wages, and labor's lack of faith in the president led to the election of a Republican majority in Congress in 1946.

The Republican Congress now stood ready to wage battles with the president over government spending. One of its first acts was the passage of the Taft-Hartley Act of 1947. This act was directed at the growing power of unions, which had been given a real boost by the Wagner Act. The Taft-Hartley Act outlawed the closed shop, which had made it illegal for employers to hire nonunion workers; it also restricted union activities, such as coercion of employees, excessive membership fees; it also restricted unions from refusing to bargain in good faith. One of the most controversial sections of the law was the stipulation that in case of a strike which threatened the national welfare, the attorney general was authorized to secure an injunction ordering workers back to work for an 80-day "cooling off period," during which time the federal government would attempt to reach a settlement. Unions now had to issue financial statements and could no longer contribute to political parties. The National Labor Relations Board was increased to five members, with power to administer the act. Truman had vetoed the act, noting that "It would go far towards weakening our trade-union movement." Congress, however, overrode the veto; and a repeal movement by labor failed.

The Election of 1948

Truman's chances for reelection in 1948 appeared rather slim. The <u>Republicans again turned to Thomas Dewey of New York</u>, who announced that it was time for a change. Dewey planned to run a low-key, confident campaign. <u>Few Democrats were "wild about Harry,"</u> as the slogan said, yet Truman felt that the nation wanted him to continue the policies of Roosevelt. But he did not have a united party behind him. <u>Southern Democrats were offended by the strong civil-rights plank that was inserted into the platform; they left the convention and nominated Strom Thurmond of South Carolina</u> as the "Dixiecrat" candidate for president. The <u>radical New Dealers, known as Progressives, nominated Henry Wallace, former secretary of commerce</u>. Things looked glum for the Democrats. Few Americans thought that Truman could win, but Truman was one of those true believers. While Dewey appeared confident and arrogant, <u>Truman took his campaign to the people and really put on a show. His whistle-stop tactics were centered around his "Give 'em Hell" oratory. He was beginning to emerge as a real man of the people, not a plastic politician. But the polls predicted a sure Dewey victory, as did the *Chicago Daily Tribune*, which printed the headline "DEWEY DEFEATS TRUMAN"</u> the morning after the election. Pollster George Gallup and the newspapers were wrong. <u>Truman won by more than 2 million popular votes.</u> The

This newspaper was wrong, as were most polls;
Truman won the election of 1948.

Democrats again took control of Congress. Truman saw this victory as a mandate for the continuation of the New Deal in a new form, which he called the "Fair Deal."

The Fair Deal was based on the premise that "our economic system should rest on a democratic foundation and that wealth should be created for the benefit of all." It included an expanded T.V.A. program, a higher minimum wage, price supports for farmers, housing reforms, an extension of social security, and a repeal of the Taft-Hartley Act. While the Fair Deal met many roadblocks, it also had some important successes. Congress passed a housing act providing for low-income public housing, slum clearance, and urban renewal; it also improved the Social Security system and increased the minimum wage. The philosophy of the New Deal was becoming permanent government policy.

The Korean War

Truman's foreign policy was based on America's willingness to fight communism anywhere in the world, usually through economic and military aid. But the spectre of communism appeared to be growing. News reached America in the fall of 1949 that the Soviet Union had exploded an atomic bomb; nuclear war now became a possibility. The shock of this news had not worn off before Americans learned that the Communists had taken over mainland China and that the Nationalist government of Chiang-Kai-shek had fled to the island of Formosa (Taiwan). Meanwhile the Cold War was heating up in Korea. Russia and the United States had jointly occupied Korea at the end of World War II, and each had established governments friendly to themselves. The Communists were in North Korea, while the Republic of Korea, under the leadership of Syngman Rhee, occupied the South. When Russia and the United States had ended their occupations, they had left behind a divided country. Both sections of the country prepared for armed conflict; and, in June 1950, the North Koreans crossed the thirty-eighth parallel, which had divided the peninsula, and invaded South Korea, moving toward the capital of Seoul. While invasion did not directly threaten the security of the United States, it was perceived as another advance for world communism. The United Nations condemned North Korea's actions and ordered a "police action" against North Korea, under the leadership of General Douglas MacArthur. Without the authorization of Congress, Truman already had ordered American aircraft to support South Korean forces; he now ordered two divisions of troops to move into South Korea. United States forces comprised the major contingent in this United Nations police action. It was an American war of containment under the guise of a United Nations action.

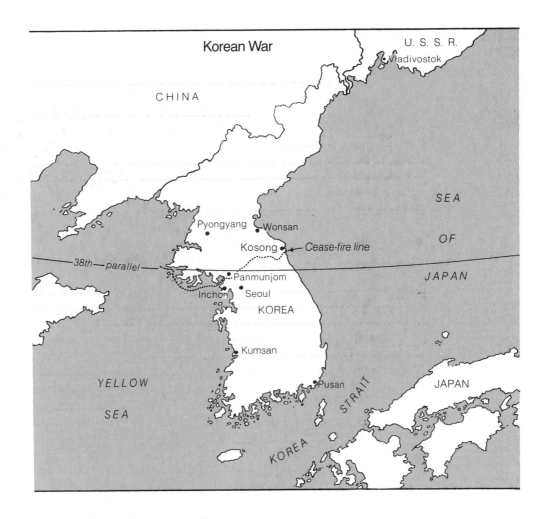

Korean War

CHINA

U. S. S. R.

•Vladivostok

SEA

OF

JAPAN

Pyongyang• •Wonsan

Kosong• ←Cease-fire line

—38th—parallel—

•Panmunjom

Inchon Seoul

KOREA

•Kumsan

YELLOW

SEA

•Pusan

JAPAN

KOREA STRAIT

Although most Americans initially seemed unwilling to enter another foreign war, our involvement in the Korean War received little opposition. It was felt that the threat of communism had to be stopped and that Americans should be willing to do the fighting. But we began to worry when American forces were unable to stop the North Korean army; American troops retreated into the southeastern corner of the Korean peninsula. But then Douglas MacArthur made a daring move. In September 1950 he launched a surprise amphibious attack on Inchon and drove the North Koreans back. Once the North Koreans had retreated back across the thirty-eighth parallel, Truman

American troops in Korea, as part of United Nations police action, here pass by fleeing refugees.

had to make the decision whether to invade North Korea or to try negotiating a truce. With the advice of the National Security Council and the backing of the United Nations, MacArthur invaded North Korea, headed for the Yalu River, which is the border between North Korea and China, and invited possible Chinese intervention. At a meeting on Wake Island Truman and MacArthur assessed the situation and came to the conclusion that the war would soon be over and that no Chinese troops would enter the conflict. Both men were wrong. In November 1950, Chinese troops were sent into North Korea and drove the Americans back across the thirty-eighth parallel.

MacArthur was becoming increasingly dissatisfied with a limited war. He saw that a total victory in Asia must involve a war against China. He said, "In war, there is no substitute for victory." MacArthur's plans included the strategic bombing of China and even the use of the atomic bomb. Truman disagreed with his line of thinking: Korea was a limited war; America was not willing to enter into a major Asian conflict. But MacArthur continued to make his demands known and to publicly criticize the President. He even wrote to Joseph W. Martin, Republican leader in the House, and asked for support to escalate the war against China. Truman had no choice; he replaced MacArthur with General Matthew Ridgway. Criticism of Truman now reached a fever peak. One headline reported, "A Five-Star General has been fired by a two-bit President." Truman defended his action:

> There are things a military officer is not likely to learn in the course of his profession. The words that dominate his thinking are 'command' and 'obedience' and the military definitions of these words are not definitions for use in a republic. It was my duty to act.

While the Korean War became a stalemate near the thirty-eighth parallel, MacArthur returned to America as a military hero. He toured the country and spoke before Congress. The nation accepted his word and found it hard to understand that he had challenged the President's authority over the armed forces and invited a major war. The frustrations of fighting a limited war against the Communist threat continued to build. Much of this frustration was evident in a witch hunt for Communists in this country.

The Communist Scare

The period after World War II was hardly a return to normalcy. Domestic issues, such as rising prices and labor disputes, caused much discontent; meanwhile Communists were registering victories all over the world: in Europe, in China, in Korea. It was suspected that Communists were infiltrating foreign governments. The press now began to imply that Communists were in America, maybe even in government positions. Truman ordered an investigation of possible government subversion, and the report indicated that such subversion was going on. Truman set up a federal loyalty program. The House Committee on Un-American Activities began to search for Communists. Under the leadership of Congressman Richard Nixon of California, Alger Hiss, an employee of the State Department, was accused of releasing government secrets. Hiss pleaded his innocence, but a court found him guilty of perjury and sentenced him to five years in prison. Truman's defense of Hiss fell on deaf ears, and the conviction of Hiss lost Truman much popularity. In 1950 the McCarran Internal Security Act was passed, which required all Communists and Communist-controlled organizations to register with the attorney general; it also stipulated that "subversive Americans" could be put into camps in case of war. The witch hunt now intensified.

In the midst of this turmoil there arose to power an opportunistic Republican senator from Wisconsin, Joseph McCarthy. He used the Communist fear to gain publicity and further his career. In 1950 he made a speech in which he claimed that there were 205 card-carrying Communists in the State Depart-

Joseph McCarthy's televised hearings against the army destroyed his credibility with the American public and led to his decline.

ment. While his allegations were never proven, he further intensified the anti-Communist campaign. Now he began to criticize Truman, Secretary of State Dean Acheson, and many other prominent government leaders of being "soft on communism." Coupled with McCarthy's accusations were increased anti-Communist activities across the nation. Textbooks with references to Russia were burned. Gumballs with a picture of Russia were banned. National witch hunts were paralleled by local witch hunts. The confrontation with Mac-Arthur, the frustrating domestic problems, the war in Korea, and now the anti-Communist crusade, brought Truman to a new low in popularity.

It is not surprising that in 1952 Truman sensed his political future was limited and declined to run for president. He had been a "common man," who had risen to the demands of the presidency. His election victory in 1948 against overwhelming odds was both a triumph for the New Deal as well as for Truman, the "Man of the People." While his domestic policies were frustrated by a Republican Congress and complex economic problems, his foreign policy was committed to a firm stand against world Communism, even if this involved using American military might. His removal of General Douglas MacArthur was unpopular but necessary. He avoided political excesses in his own investigation of possible Communist subversion. Although in 1952 the nation wanted Truman out of office, today he stands as a man who ably led America through very difficult times.

Eisenhower: the President of the 1950s

In 1952 the Democratic Party turned to a liberal intellectual, Adlai Stevenson, governor of Illinois. The Republicans turned to an old winning formula and nominated a military hero, Dwight David Eisenhower. Eisenhower, the conquering hero of World War II, had tremendous personal popularity and offered an image of confidence at a time when the nation wanted firm, conservative leadership. Stevenson's image as an "egghead" and Truman's unpopularity virtually guaranteed Eisenhower's victory. Eisenhower's only stumbling block was his vice-presidential candidate, Richard Nixon, who allegedly had received money from business interests that he had put into a private account. But Nixon defended himself in his emotional "Checkers" speech, in which he pledged complete honesty and even referred to the family dog, Checkers; Eisenhower kept him on the ticket and steamrolled to victory in 1952. The election of 1956 was a virtual repeat performance, with Eisenhower winning over Stevenson even more decisively. From 1953 to 1961 the general was president.

Born in Texas, Dwight David Eisenhower was raised in poverty in Abilene, Kansas. Nicknamed "Ike" as a child, he struggled through high school and was accepted to West Point. From then until his election in 1952 he remained Eisenhower, the soldier. His career in the army ranged from commander of tank-training centers during World War I, to executive director in the Panama Canal Zone, to aide to General Douglas MacArthur, to head of Operations Division in the War Department. Due to his outstanding record, he became commanding general of American forces in the European theater. His achievements in Africa, Italy, and on the Normandy beaches have become legendary. With the end of the war he retired from active duty and was appointed to the presidency of Columbia University. But the military lure was too great, and in 1950 he was appointed supreme commander of the North Atlantic Treaty Organization. After the war, both political parties had tried to lure him into politics, but the attempts had failed. Finally in 1952 the Republican party convinced him to run, and he became the party nominee. He promised "to clean up the mess in Washington." His subsequent win gave him the opportunity to try. Eisenhower had absolutely no political experience. His goal was to run the country with moderation and through compromise. Since his experiences were military, he tried to apply as many of them as possible to politics. Cabinet members were like his military advisers; they were to handle all the detailed work and report to him. The President would then make the final decision. As in the Army, he needed a chief of staff to help handle his duties. His choice was Sherman Adams, a businessman and former Governor of New Hampshire; Adams was his link with Congress and the cabinet. Eisenhower's middle-of-the-road politics frequently pleased few politicians, but it did bring a needed calm to the nation after a long period of drama that included the New Deal, with its rapid social changes, and two wars, World War II and the Korean War. Eisenhower seemed to be just what America needed in the 1950s.

Eisenhower and Foreign Affairs

While Eisenhower talked of a new approach to foreign affairs, his policies did not differ greatly from those of Truman. Containment continued but with one important innovation: the doctrine of instant and massive retaliation. Secretary of State John Foster Dulles clearly described this "new look" in foreign policy. The United States must avoid long, drawn-out wars, such as the one in Korea. America must now meet aggression "vigorously at places and with means of its own choosing." "Massive retaliation" meant using nuclear weapons rather than conventional ones. Nuclear arms would be a greater deterrent to Communist expansion, although this tactic risked possible nuclear war.

Still the policy of containment was followed. The fear of Communist expansion in Asia led to the support of Ngo Dinh Diem in South Vietnam, the signing of a mutual-defense treaty with Formosa, and the creation of the Southeast Asia Treaty Organization (SEATO). This agreement was similar to NATO in that an attack on any of the members would be an attack upon all. But there was no joint military force to police the agreement; the United States, with its military might, was the solitary policeman.

Eisenhower's foreign policy featured an improvement in Soviet-American relations and American involvement in the Middle East. Before the 1950s American interest in the Middle East had been minimal. But the creation of the state of Israel and its conflict with the Arab countries caused the United States to play a much more active role. America was friendly to Israel, but at the same time America did not want to alienate the oil-rich Arab nations and force them into the Russian camp. So the United States tried to befriend both sides through economic and military aid to Israel and economic assistance to Egypt, where President Gamal Abdel Nasser ruled as the dominant leader of the Arab nationalist movement. When Nasser adopted policies that seemed to move Egypt closer to Russia, America withdrew its promised economic assistance. In retaliation, Nasser seized the Suez Canal, purportedly to obtain money for the building of the Aswan Dam on the Nile. The seizure of the canal cut off oil supplies to Europe. In return, Israeli, British, and French forces attacked the canal zone in October 1956. The United States led a United

Nations protest against the attack and pressured the countries to issue a cease-fire. A United Nations force was sent to the region to monitor the cease-fire and uphold an uneasy truce.

Eisenhower now clarified his Middle East position with his Eisenhower Doctrine. In 1957 he asked for authority from Congress to use military and economic aid "to secure and protect the territorial independence" of Middle Eastern nations "against overt armed aggression from any nation controlled by international communism." Congress supported the doctrine, and it was soon invoked. Aid was sent to King Hussein of Jordan to put down a Nasser-inspired rebellion, and troops were sent to Lebanon for the same reason. The Eisenhower Doctrine did not defuse the powder keg of the Middle East, but it did clearly define America's position there.

The death of Stalin in 1953 brought a marked improvement in Soviet-American relations. Under the leadership of Georgi Malenkov and Nikita Khrushchev, Russia recognized the growing danger of a possible nuclear war and decided upon a course of "peaceful coexistence." While Eisenhower and Dulles questioned Russian motives, the United States also was interested in improved relations. In July 1955, Khrushchev, Eisenhower, and the prime ministers of Britain and France met at Geneva to discuss mutual issues. While nothing concrete was accomplished, this meeting did go a long way toward improving relations. While some talked of the "Spirit of Geneva" leading the way to the end of the Cold War, their optimism was premature. The launching of the Soviet satellite Sputnik I in late 1957 shocked America into the realization that it was behind Russia in certain scientific achievements. Khrushchev tried to take advantage of this superiority by pushing for American concessions in Germany. He was not successful. In 1959 he toured the United States amidst a spirit of friendship; in fact, the only unpleasant incident of the entire trip occurred when the officials at Disneyland refused to allow him entrance. This trip led to the scheduling of another summit meeting in 1960. Only days before the scheduled opening of that conference, a United States U-2 spy plane was shot down over the Soviet Union. After repeated denials of responsibility by United States officials, Eisenhower eventually took personal blame. This incident caused hard feelings on both sides and was a real setback to improved relations.

Eisenhower saw other problems developing in foreign affairs. New nations were being formed in Africa through rebellion against colonial powers. Fidel Castro had ousted pro-American Batista and was receiving Soviet aid. Relations with Latin American countries were deteriorating, and Vice-president Nixon's goodwill tour there (which saw much ill will) was evidence of Latin American disenchantment with the United States. European countries were becoming less dependent upon America and more critical of NATO. Eisenhower's real achievement in foreign affairs was the temporary improvement in relations between the United States and Russia, but even that relationship was in jeopardy.

Domestic Problems

Eisenhower's domestic programs were marked by inconsistency. He wanted to limit inflation and balance the budget, but he also wanted to expand some of the New Deal programs. The economy was generally prosperous through most of Eisenhower's eight years, but in 1957–58 a recession occurred, which Eisenhower combatted by supporting greater appropriations for defense and public works, hoping to stimulate economic recovery. He also loosened credit to encourage purchasing, cut taxes, and increased government benefits. While legislation generally lagged, certain administrative policies did materialize. A Department of Health, Education and Welfare was established; the National Defense Education Act, which aided colleges and universities, passed; and Social Security was expanded. Alaska and Hawaii became states. Still, Eisenhower basically opposed further expansion of social welfare legislation.

On February 9, 1955, an important event took place when the A.F.L. and C.I.O. ended their internecine dispute and merged. Craft unions and industrial unions were both needed, but disunity had been disastrous to the cause of organized labor. This merger led to the formation of one strong, united organization. It did not, however, silence the critics who demanded the investigation of labor corruption. The new AFL-CIO had established an in-house committee to examine charges of corruption, but Congress felt that the federal government should have a say in that investigation. In 1957, a Committee on Improper Activities began to hold a series of public hearings to deal with the issue of union corruption. Labor in general now came under the microscope and corruption was found. Stories of illegal activities involving Teamster president Dave Beck and James Hoffa were revealed. Beck had taken funds from the union for his personal use; he eventually was convicted on charges of tax evasion and grand larceny. James Hoffa was charged with having suspect business connections; he eventually was found guilty of tampering with a jury. The AFL-CIO placed the Teamsters and all guilty unions on probation; then, in 1957, the Teamsters were expelled officially. Public agitation against illegal union activities led Congress to pass the Landrum-Griffin Act in 1959. This act attempted to restrict the power of labor-union leaders and to demand that unions' financial reports be made public. Certain restrictions also were placed on picketing. Labor had received a real setback in the 1950s.

The years under President Dwight Eisenhower offered Americans a time of relative peace and tranquility. As the first Republican president in 20 years, he followed an inconsistent pattern in both foreign and domestic policies. His desire for a balanced budget did not always agree with his continuation of some of the New Deal programs. In foreign affairs he perceived many problems but did little to solve them. He was not an experienced politician; he was a military hero who felt that it was his duty to serve the nation, both in war and in peace. He did the best he could with his limited experience, but he left his successors a myriad of problems that he had not begun to solve.

The New Frontier and the Great Society

The election of 1960 featured two men with differing philosophies and styles and presented a tough challenge to the Republican party. Eisenhower's eight years in office had left many unsolved problems; in addition, the Democrats had done well in the congressional election of 1958. The Republican nominee was Richard Nixon, Eisenhower's vice-president, who had been much in the limelight during his second term. Nixon offered the voters a continuation of Eisenhower's middle-of-the-road politics, with perhaps a little more conservatism. The Democrats turned to a youthful millionaire from Massachusetts, John F. Kennedy. Kennedy was a liberal and a Catholic. He sharply criticized the Eisenhower presidency as the 'do-nothing' years and pushed for a change. His religion and his youth hurt him, but the television debates between the candidates were to his advantage. While Kennedy appeared relaxed and confident, Nixon, whose "make-up man was a mortician," looked tense and uptight. Kennedy needed all the advantages he could get. On election night the decision was in doubt; in fact, it remained in doubt well into the next day. Kennedy barely won by a margin of about 112,000 popular votes. John F. Kennedy now led America away from the mediocre politics of the 1950s and into the challenging decade of the 1960s.

The Kennedy Style

John Fitzgerald Kennedy was the youngest man ever elected to the presidency. Born of wealthy parents in a Boston suburb, he received his early education in New England, graduated from Harvard, and enlisted in the U.S. Navy. His exploits on a PT-boat in the Pacific earned him a Purple Heart and the Navy and Marine Corps Medal. After a brief career as a journalist, he entered politics and was elected to the House of Representatives. After six years in the House, he upset Henry Cabot Lodge, Jr. to win the Senate seat from Massachusetts. His years in the Senate were characterized by continual criticism of Republican policies and his constant desire for a new foreign policy that would give aid to underdeveloped countries. After winning seven primaries, he captured the Democratic nomination for president and went on to win a close race. This youthful intellectual, with his wit, good looks, and charming wife, now replaced the oldest outgoing president and offered the nation a New Frontier.

John Kennedy's New Frontier was a fresh approach to domestic and foreign problems. In his inaugural address he set the tone when he referred to a "new generation of Americans" who had taken over the country. Americans must now "pay any price, bear any burden, meet any hardship, support any friend, oppose any foe, to assure the survival and success of liberty." And, in his most-quoted words, he told Americans, "Ask not what your country can do for you—ask what you can do for your country." He was expressing his sense that foreign problems were more pressing than domestic ones when he stated that "The die of events" were running out and that time had "not been our friend." He then introduced two innovations, the Peace Corps and the Alliance for Progress, which promised more than they accomplished. The Peace Corps recruited young Americans to go into underdeveloped countries and teach people the benefits of technology while, at the same time, instilling them with the doctrine of democracy. Thousands of Americans brought idealism into foreign lands, only to return home filled with disappointment. The Alliance for Progress, introduced in 1961, was a program of economic aid for Latin America. The goal of the program was to raise the living standards of the people in these countries; more than a billion dollars a year was to be poured into Latin America. But over the years, the Alliance provided little progress, and democracy took a back seat to the rise of military dictatorships. While these two new programs did not live up to their expectations, they did not cause as much dissatisfaction as Kennedy's policy toward Cuba.

Bay of Pigs and the Cuban Missile Crisis

During Eisenhower's presidency, a group of Cuban exiles, with the assistance of the United States Central Intelligence Agency (CIA), began to plan for an invasion of Cuba and the overthrow of Fidel Castro. When Kennedy began as president, he continued the plans, and, in April 1961, more than 1200 rebels landed at the Bay of Pigs; they were easily defeated by Castro's forces. The collapse of the invasion was an embarrassment to the administration; Kennedy personally bore the responsibility for its failure. This incident pushed Cuba ever closer to Russia. In the eyes of Russia, Kennedy began to appear indecisive and weak; Khrushchev now made plans to take advantage of the situation.

In June 1961, not long after the Bay of Pigs failure, Khrushchev and Kennedy met in a summit conference in Vienna and Khrushchev took the initi-

Bay of Pigs

The Fair Deal to Camp David: From Truman to Carter

ative. He refused to limit Russian armaments in any way and demanded that the occupation of Berlin be ended in six months. A Berlin crisis seemed imminent; reserve units were put on alert. Fallout shelters were built across the nation to prepare for a possible nuclear war. While no crisis developed, the East Germans did erect a Berlin Wall to halt the flood of refugees from East Germany to West Germany. This wall stood as a symbol of the Communist presence in Germany and became the "iron curtain" in concrete. But the Western powers made no move to tear it down, and the Berlin issue died away.

Khrushchev still felt he could take advantage of Kennedy, so, during the summer and fall of 1962, Russians installed Soviet medium-range ballistic missiles and bombers in Cuba. Spy-plane aerial photographs revealed to the Americans that missile bases existed on the nearby island. The situation was serious. Kennedy pondered a course of action. He decided an immediate invasion or air strike would be foolish. In a tense public announcement, he announced that a naval blockade of the island would be enforced to prevent further Soviet military aid; then he warned that if Russia did not remove the missiles the United States would do it. He told America, "One path we will never choose, and that is the path of surrender or submission". The world and the nation nervously waited. Khrushchev backed down, informing Kennedy that the missiles would be withdrawn if the United States promised not to invade Cuba. The promise was given. Kennedy's strong stand had paid off, and both he and the United States scored a concrete victory in what was the most serious confrontation of the Cold War. Not long after the Cuban Missile Crisis, a "hot-line phone" was installed so Washington, D.C., and Moscow always could have a quick exchange of views to avoid a nuclear war. In 1963, Kennedy and Khrushchev signed a Nuclear Test-Ban Treaty, which limited nuclear testing. Relations between Russia and the United States again improved, but the two countries were still a long way from a genuinely cordial relationship.

Domestic Policies

Kennedy promised a lot in domestic affairs, but his legislative record was far from dynamic. Initially worried by an economic recession, he urged labor and business to keep wage increases within the limits of advances in productivity. He also worried about inflation, but business did not always cooperate with his wishes. The steel industry ignored Kennedy's demand for price stability and began to raise prices, which caused Kennedy to assert, "My father always told me that all businessmen were sons of bitches, but I never believed it until now." Still prices continued to climb. Despite a stock-market slump in 1962, Kennedy utilized increased spending, control of interest rates, and tax cuts to stimulate the economy. He also planned for federal deficits meant to stimulate the economy as well. These measures led to the longest peacetime expansion of the American economy in the recorded history of business-cycles. He also was responsible for the initial appropriations for a man-on-the-moon program. The Russians had taken the lead in space; in April 1961, Yuri Gagarin had become the first human in space. Kennedy answered, "I believe this nation should commit itself to achieving the goals, before the decade is out, of landing a man on the moon and returning him safely to earth." During his presidency, Alan Shepard and Virgil "Gus" Grissom were hurled into space, and John Glenn became the first American to orbit the earth.

Since the nation was generally prosperous, few shared Kennedy's desire for more social-welfare legislation. The high points of his legislative achievements were a housing act, which appropriated 5.6 billion dollars for public housing—with emphasis on urban renewal—an Area Redevelopment Act, which helped stimulate economic growth in chronically depressed regions of the nation, a new minimum-wage law, and an expanded Social Security program. One of his most important acts was the Trade Expansion Act, which gave the president power to reduce tariffs by 50 percent on some items and by 100 percent on others whenever the president thought lowering barriers would stimulate trade. But Kennedy's tragic assassination on November 22, 1963,

Area Redevelopment Act

Trade Expansion Act

The Kennedy motorcade photographed at the moment the president was shot.

cut short his accomplishments and evoked an outpouring of grief both here and abroad. Americans could not deny that his assassination removed from the office of the presidency a youthful, energetic man with a sparkling wit and a desire to change America. Although he had accomplished relatively little, he did cause a redirection in both domestic and foreign policies that would reach some fruition under his successor, Lyndon Johnson.

L.B.J. and the War on Poverty

Ninety-eight minutes after the death of John F. Kennedy, Lyndon Johnson was sworn in as president of the United States. But Johnson was no accidental President, such as John Tyler or Chester Arthur. He was a president in his own right. Born in a farmhouse in central Texas, Johnson graduated from high school and then headed for California, where he held a series of odd jobs. Returning to Texas, he became tired of "working with my hands," so he attended Southwest Texas State Teachers College. After graduation, he taught at a rural elementary school before he became speech and debate teacher at a Houston high school. His first encounter with Washington politics came during his job as administrative assistant there; after his marriage to Lady Bird, he became Texas state administrator of Roosevelt's National Youth Administration program, and, as a Congressman, Johnson became one of Roosevelt's best supporters of New Deal legislation. During World War II he served in the Pacific and was awarded a Silver Star for gallant action. Elected to the Senate, he eventually became the youngest majority leader of either party in Senate history. There in the Senate he became a congressional master at the art of legislative manipulations. He intimately knew power politics. He proved his commitment to the "space race" by sponsoring the law that created the National Aeronautics and Space Administration. He also pushed for civil-rights legislation. He was a liberal, yet business liked him. He tried for the presidency in 1960 but was given second place on the ticket. The six-foot-three-inch tall vice-president, known lovingly by many as "L.B.J.," shared the shock of the nation as he assumed the office of president following Kennedy's death.

Lyndon Johnson, the Texas politician, was now president. He had been weaned on political maneuvers and had played the game adeptly. On first appearance, he was open, warm, outgoing, and folksy; but later in his presidency his image was one of slyness, mistrust, and aggressiveness. Congress responded to Kennedy's death and Johnson's plea "Let us continue" with numerous legislative enactments. A Revenue Act, which reduced taxes, a Civil Rights Act, and the Economic Opportunity Act, which established numerous

Lyndon Johnson as president led a War on Poverty with his Great Society programs.

antipoverty programs, were essential parts of Johnson's War on Poverty. Johnson's program for ending poverty and discrimination, fighting pollution, caring for the aged, and reviving the cities was aimed at carrying the nation closer to his dream of a Great Society: a place "where the city of man serves not only the needs of the body and the demands of commerce but the desire for beauty and the hunger for the community." This was his platform when he was nominated for President in 1964.

In 1964 the Republicans moved to the extreme right, nominating a conservative candidate, Barry Goldwater from Arizona, who was a political romantic ready to go back to America's golden past. One wit noted that in case of nuclear attack Goldwater would "tell the wagons to form in a circle." Goldwater was blunt speaker, and he scared many Americans with his talk of nuclear attacks. The nation was not ready to return to Republican "normalcy," especially Goldwater's kind, and he was soundly defeated. Johnson was swept into office by the largest majority in American history. Now he continued his plans for building his Great Society.

Aided by large Democratic majorities in both houses of Congress, Johnson was extremely successful in 1965 and 1966 in getting his proposals enacted into law. In fact, Johnson's Eighty-Ninth Congress was the most productive Congress since the days of the New Deal. Congress passed the Appalachia poverty program; the School Aid Bill, which increased federal aid to education; Medicare, which provided subsidized hospitalization and other medical assistance for the elderly; a major housing program that included rent subsidies for low-income groups; a Department of Transportation program; a model-city program; and a major antipollution measure. Further cuts in excise taxes and stronger safety measures for automobiles were enacted. The cabinet post of Housing and Urban Development was created, and numerous urban-renewal projects were undertaken. Many of these programs forced the federal government to provide more tangible benefits for millions of aged and impoverished people. The Great Society intensified the New Deal.

But by 1967 the Great Society slowly seemed to be unraveling at the seams, and the major reason was Johnson's foreign policy. Johnson's skills in domestic affairs were not matched in foreign matters. Johnson was a tough diplomat, and he believed in the psychology of the Cold War—that communism was a global menace which the United States had to contain, wherever it threatened peaceful states and peoples. His toughness was especially noticeable in his Latin American policy. In April 1965 America again intervened in the Dominican Republic, which was in the midst of a civil war. Johnson, who said he was attempting to stem communism in the Western hemisphere, ordered 25,000 marines to the island to restore order. This action caused much criticism here and abroad; but the forces still remained for over a year, until peace had been established and free elections were held. The Middle East also heated up, erupting in the Six-Day War in 1967. And Charles de Gaulle, in France, also proved to be a less friendly ally. But Johnson's greatest frustration was his Vietnam dealings.

The Vietnam Quagmire

It is true that the scars of the Vietnam War are healing, and many college students today remember little about the war and the tension that surrounded it. Still, interpretations of the war today continue to depend very much upon your political outlook. This war has been looked upon in many different ways:

some considered it an essential step in the continuing Cold War; others felt that our involvement in Southeast Asia was part of the SEATO alliance; still others believed the Vietnam War was an example of "American Imperialism for the benefit and protection of American corporate and military interests"; minorities interpreted the war as white America's plan to wipe out minorities and minority gains. Originally, the involvement in Southeast Asia began with the Cold War perspective in foreign affairs, which started under Eisenhower and led to Johnson's undoing.

During the 1950s the United States vainly had supported French forces who were attempting to retain a foothold in Southeast Asia. With the ouster of the French and the division of Vietnam along the seventeenth parallel in 1954, in accordance with a Geneva agreement, President Eisenhower continued to commit money, arms, and noncombatant advisers to Ngo Dinh Diem, President of South Vietnam, who was fighting to combat Communist incursions from the North. President Kennedy, who took office in 1961, subscribed to the domino theory in Southeast Asia: if one nation fell to the Communists, the others would follow suit. So he increased military advisers in South Vietnam and Laos to more than 15,000 by 1963. More and more of a commitment was being made. In fact, when Johnson became President, 60 American soldiers already had been killed there. But by then the corrupt regime of Diem had been overthrown and things were looking up.

During the 1964 election campaign Johnson promised that American soldiers would not be sent to Vietnam; he did not keep his word. In fact, he

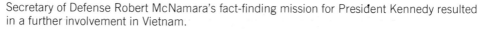

Secretary of Defense Robert McNamara's fact-finding mission for President Kennedy resulted in a further involvement in Vietnam.

actually was creating a "credibility gap" to gather support for increased involvement there. While reports in early 1964 seemed to indicate that the Saigon government was achieving some measure of stability, actually the American government knew the Viet Cong—South Vietnamese pro-Communist rebels—and the North Vietnamese were planning new attacks. In fact, the *Pentagon Papers,* which were made public in 1971, indicated that the United States already was launching attacks against the North in early 1964. In August of that year there were reports of two separate attacks on American destroyers, which the North Vietnamese described as spy ships. Johnson pictured the attacks as unprovoked and asked Congress for power "to take all the necessary measures to repel any armed attack against the forces of the United States and to prevent further aggression." Congress approved, and the Tonkin Gulf Resolution provided the groundwork for increased American involvement in Vietnam.

By 1965 Johnson had come to the conclusion that an increase in American forces was essential to bring North Vietnam to the bargaining table. In addition, Johnson linked the Viet Cong and North Vietnamese with a general world movement of communism to take over the free world. If Southeast Asia fell to the Communists because America had failed to help militarily, what would be the next step in world conquest? Johnson, listening more and more to his military advisers, slowly increased the numbers of American combat troops and then ordered the bombing of North Vietnam. All these actions were geared to bring North Vietnam to the bargaining table. But they did not seem to work. The determination of the Viet Cong and the North Vietnamese was strong. American troops now used chemical weapons, such as napalm. The numbers of American troops killed, wounded, and disabled for life increased. By 1968 more than 533,000 American troops were on Vietnamese soil; more troops than at the high point of the Korean War. More and more critics of the war asked the question, "What are we doing there? When will the war end?"

Johnson talked of "guns and butter," but Americans saw on the nightly news pictures of the growing atrocities of the war and thought only of the guns. Still Johnson, his Secretary of Defense Robert McNamara, and General William Westmoreland, continually made optimistic predictions about the course of the war and its swift conclusion. But growing casualties caused increased disillusionment. Student marches led to riots and violence. Antiwar critics rose throughout the country to demand American withdrawal. A group called the doves, who sought eventual withdrawal, debated with hawks, who favored a quick, decisive end to the war. Millions of Americans now asked the question, "Was the Cold War worth the loss of American lives in a far-off country?"

Vietnam War

Troubles continued to mount for Johnson at home. Republicans were elected to Congress in large numbers in 1966 and stymied Johnson's War on Poverty and Great Society plans. Americans were beginning to doubt all statements by officials on the progress of the war. Meanwhile, Johnson's feud with the Kennedy family grew more intense. First Senator Eugene McCarthy, then

The Fair Deal to Camp David: From Truman to Carter

Senator Robert Kennedy, announced that they would oppose Johnson for the Democratic nomination. On March 31, 1968, Johnson surprised the nation with the announcement that he would not run again for president, that American aircraft would stop bombing North Vietnam, and that diplomatic representatives of all combatants would soon meet in Paris to formulate a plan for peace. Now the career of Johnson was over. When he left office he was cursed as the president who committed the nation's youth to a senseless war. He became the symbol of national frustration, the scapegoat of the bewildering years of the 1960s. Few remembered the progress he made in social welfare and his war on poverty. In light of the Vietnam War, his Great Society appeared not very great. Yet his revolution in social welfare was the first breakthrough in this area since the New Deal. Lyndon Johnson still is remembered today as the president who dragged America through the Vietnam War, but future generations may judge him more kindly.

Nixon as President

The assassination of Robert Kennedy in June 1968 threw the race for the Democratic nomination wide open. In the midst of antiwar demonstrators and violence, the Democrats met in Chicago and chose party stalwart Hubert Humphrey of Minnesota. The Republicans turned to a man who had left politics a few years before but who had worked for Republican candidates in 1964; he was repaid for his party loyalty with the presidential nomination on the first ballot. This was Richard Nixon. Nixon's campaign promised an end to the Vietnam War and the return to "law and order." Humphrey, who had been Johnson's vice-president, was hurt by his association with Johnson's unpopular policies. In addition, the Democratic party had been torn asunder and was having problems putting itself back together. Humphrey eventually broke from Johnson's Vietnam policy and became his own man, expressing progressively stronger antiwar sentiments, but this happened too late in the campaign. Still, the election was extremely close. By less than 1 percent of the total vote, Richard Nixon was elected president.

Richard Nixon's remarkable political comeback had won him the highest office in the land. Born of a Quaker family near Los Angeles, he attended school and worked at odd jobs in Whittier, California, jobs which ranged from bean picker to janitor to sideshow barker. Graduating from Whittier College, where he had been a history major and a football player, he attended Duke University law school and graduated with honors. After being rejected by the Federal Bureau of Investigation, he served in a Whittier law firm, married

Patricia Ryan, and was in a Naval Air Transport Unit in World War II. Asked to run against a liberal Democrat for Congress in 1946, Nixon used his skills as a champion debater to good use; using another tactic, he accused his opponent of being "soft on communism," which won him much support and probably the election. In Congress he continued to fight against communism as a member of the House Un-American Activities Committee. His tireless fight in the Alger Hiss case brought him national recognition as one of America's freedom fighters. After a bitter political fight for the Senate seat from California in 1950, he became much more active in the affairs of the Republican party and was nominated for vice-president in 1952. During the campaign it was disclosed that Nixon had received some questionable campaign funds; his place on the Republican ticket was in jeopardy. He went before a television audience with his famous "Checkers" speech, defending himself in part by claiming he was a man of modest income: "Pat doesn't have a mink coat. But she does have a respectable Republican cloth coat." He was vindicated and stayed on Eisenhower's ticket, soon beginning his eight-year term as vice-president. During these Eisenhower years, Nixon picked up invaluable experience by presiding over cabinet meetings and serving America abroad. As presidential nominee of the Republican party in 1960, he lost by a slim margin and returned to California. Friends convinced him to run for governor against Democrat Edmund Brown; Nixon lost. He now savagely turned against the media of California and, in a tense news conference, announced that they would ". . . not have Nixon to kick around anymore," because he was retiring from politics. This retirement, however, was not permanent. He moved to New York and prospered as a corporation lawyer there, while he continued to support Republican candidates. The overwhelming defeat of Goldwater thrust Nixon back into politics as the one man who could unite the Republican party. With real grass-roots support, he quickly captured the Republican nomination in 1968 and barely won the election. The old Communist fighter became President. But over the years his image had changed from the harsh, bitter politician to the peacemaker and friend of all Americans. He attempted to unite the entire nation, but frequently reverted to his old ways by name calling and threats. Still, he did know his priorities. In his first inaugural address he said, "The greatest honor history can bestow is the title of peacemaker. This honor now beckons America."

Nixon in Foreign Affairs

Although Nixon had thrived on the rhetoric of the Cold War, as President he believed that a new day had arrived when the United States should recognize the existence of Communist nations in the world and should try to deescalate the threat of nuclear war. His Nixon Doctrine stated that the United States would no longer "conceive all the plans, design all the programs, execute all the decisions and undertake all the defense of the free nations of the world." Foreign policy now shifted away from the Truman Doctrine to a period of increasing detente with Russia, new friendships with European countries, improved relations with Red China, and gradual withdrawal from the frustrating war in Vietnam.

It was clear to Nixon that Vietnam withdrawal had top priority. And "Vietnamization" (reversing of the escalation of the five previous years and returning control of the war to South Vietnam) became the answer. In July 1969 Nixon announced the first withdrawal of 25,000 American troops and elaborated upon his goal to build up South Vietnamese military forces so that they could sustain their own independence. The policy of Vietnamization was under way and the antiwar critics were temporarily silent.

In 1970 news of the massacre of civilians at My Lai caused Americans to question more intensely the value of American involvement. Meanwhile Cambodia was in the midst of a civil war; the Viet Cong now began operations there. In April 1970 Nixon announced that he was using American troops to drive the Communists from Cambodia in order to further protect South Vietnam. He reasoned that the Communists were making drives into South Vietnam from Cambodia, which he believed had to be stopped. Contrary to his Vietnamization program, this action seemed to be an escalation of the war.

Death at Kent State.

Hostile voices were again heard. Deaths of college-student protestors at Kent State University and Jackson State hardened the opposition. Nixon's support in Congress was diminishing; in the summer of 1970 the Tonkin Gulf Resolution was repealed.

In the midst of this ground-fighting escalation, Nixon increased bombing of North Vietnam, Laos, and Cambodia. At the same time, more soldiers returned home. In early 1972 he announced that he had submitted to the Communists an eight-point program to end the war. But peace talks in Paris accomplished little. To speed up negotiations, and in response to a new North Vietnamese assault, Nixon announced in April that North Vietnamese ports would be mined and land and sea routes to North Vietnam blockaded to cut off military supplies. Then, in December, a new bombing of Hanoi was instituted.

In early 1973 the Paris peace talks finally produced a settlement. North Vietnam and the United States agreed on a cease-fire. All American troops were to be withdrawn from Vietnam, Laos, and Cambodia, and American prisoners of war were to be released. A formal agreement was signed on January 27, 1973. The Vietnam War was over. So ended a war that had cost America 56,000 dead and more than $141 billion. And for what? In April 1975 South Vietnam fell to the North; Laos and Cambodia fell to Communist rebels. In late 1978 Vietnamese troops moved into Cambodia and threatened a complete take-over; Communist forces were now pitted against each other. Henry Kissinger, secretary of state under Nixon, commented on the war, "However we got into Vietnam, whatever the judgment of our actions, ending the war honorably is essential to the peace of the world." Peace took a long time to come to Southeast Asia, and it is still not complete. Meanwhile, the scars from the Vietnam conflict run deep and will not easily be erased.

While the Nixon Doctrine favored a closer relationship with America's allies and friends, it also involved detente with Russia. To allay the fears of many countries, Nixon reassured them that the United States would honor its treaty commitments and would still stand ready to cope with any communist attack upon a country deemed vital to the security of the United States. In 1969 the United States and Russia began strategic-arms limitation talks; in May 1972 Nixon kept his promise to visit Moscow, where he conferred with Communist party leader, Leonid Brezhnev. The Cold War further thawed. The meeting of these two leaders produced a series of agreements on joint cooperation in space flight, medicine, health, and the environment. In June 1973 Brezhnev reciprocated by visiting the United States and continuing to develop the spirit of detente.

Nixon also moved toward improved relations with the People's Republic of China. Embargos were relaxed on Chinese goods. In 1971 an American table tennis team was invited to tour the country; this "ping-pong diplomacy" seemed to indicate that China was willing to normalize relations. After Henry Kissinger's secret visit to Peking, Nixon revealed publicly that he would visit China. This was a major breakthrough. In February 1972 came Nixon's historic visit to China. A new era was now on the horizon. But normalization of relations would be a gradual process. Trade ties first were strengthened, then members of Congress were invited to China. Talks began for a possible exchange of diplomats. China now was admitted to the United Nations. Some critics felt that America had sold out Taiwan, but the recognition of China as a world power seemed inevitable.

Nixon's policy toward Europe was known as a "new Atlantic Charter." Its development involved a series of summit conferences between Nixon and the heads of key nations in NATO. Meetings with the leaders of Britain, Germany, Italy, and France paved the way for a Nixon tour of Europe and a new era of friendliness. In April 1974 Nixon personally attended the funeral of French President Pompidou and continued to talk with European leaders. Meanwhile, the delicate Middle East situation blew up again, escalating into a full-scale war in October 1973. Israel and the Arab nations were in a power struggle. Arab nations now began to withhold oil from the United States to get support for their cause. But even without a permanent settlement in the Middle East, Nixon's foreign policy went much smoother than his domestic affairs.

Nixon's Domestic Program

Nixon promised "Peace with Prosperity"; but his economic policies were controversial, and their effects are still questionable today. On August 15, 1971, he announced a far-reaching new economic policy designed to check the rise in prices and wages, strengthen the nation's external economic position and stimulate economic activity at home. Acting under the authority of the Economic Stabilization Act of 1970 to curb the rate of inflation, the president subjected prices, wages, and rents to a 90-day freeze, which was followed by a comprehensive but more flexible system of mandatory controls. The challenge was to hold down runaway inflation without bringing the economy to a halt—but could it be done? Nixon did not succeed in either reducing inflation or stimulating the economy. Nixon's economic problems were complicated further by an energy crisis in 1974, which helped to drive many prices up, caused long gas lines, and brought sharp criticism of government planning. William Simon, Nixon's energy czar, attempted to coordinate energy efforts and to avoid harsh measures, such as gas rationing. The easing of the Arab oil embargo, which was imposed during the Middle East war, eased the energy crisis, but the critical shortage of American natural resources remained a problem.

Nixon also tried hard to win support in the South with his Supreme Court nominations, some of whom the Senate considered unqualified, and with his stand against forced school bussing. He tried in vain to push the supersonic transport plane through Congress. And he declared a victory for mankind when, on July 20, 1969, astronaut Neil A. Armstrong became the first human to walk on the surface of the moon. But the Armstrong walk did not end our Apollo program. From July 1969 to December 1972, six more Apollo missions were sent before the Apollo program was completed. It was followed by Skylab, the first manned orbital space station.

In many ways Nixon tried to be everything for everyone; at times he was a liberal, at others, a conservative. He backed the lottery system for the draft, then instituted an all-volunteer army. He even backed the vote for 18-year-olds. A revenue-sharing program between states and the federal government was enacted, and an independent Post Office was created. He also proposed a national welfare program that would guarantee a minimum income of $1600 per family of four, and he increased federal money to colleges and universities. The President was exerting his authority in formulating both domestic and foreign policies, but Nixon was becoming increasingly sensitive to criticism. His hatred of the media became more obvious. Still, he appeared to be an unbeatable candidate in 1972.

The Democrats were torn over the choice of a candidate. Hubert Humphrey was willing to run, and Edmund Muskie of Maine had been involved in some of the primaries. However, the composition of the Democratic convention was much more liberal than it had been in past years, particularly with its increased representation from women and minority groups. George McGovern of South Dakota had built a strong organization, had won some important primaries, and was the overwhelming choice of the liberal convention on the first ballot. Nixon and Spiro Agnew were again nominated at the Republican convention. The final November election results were one-sided. McGovern did not really represent most Democrats; in addition, he was inconsistent on important issues such as tax reform and welfare. He supported his vice-presidential candidate, Thomas Eagleton of Missouri, even after word was released that he had undergone psychological treatment. Under continuing pressure, McGovern turned to Sargent Shriver as the replacement candidate for vice-president. Near the end of the campaign the nation learned of a break-in at the Democratic national headquarters in Washington, D.C., at the Watergate apartment complex. McGovern voiced suspicions of a possible Watergate connection to the White House, but it was too little and too late.

554

Nixon was swept into office again. He saw his landslide victory as a popular mandate to increase the power of the president. But the Watergate break-in would become his undoing.

Watergate to Resignation

By the end of his first administration, Nixon had become "absolutely paranoid about criticism." He had even drawn up an "Enemies List" to get information to "screw our political enemies." His planned tactics included bugging, wire tapping, and other techniques forbidden by law. When F.B.I. Director J. Edgar Hoover learned of his plans, he pressured Nixon to abandon them. So Nixon then formed the "plumbers," a secret White House group, to use any tactics necessary, to be justified in the name of national security. Two *Washington Post* reporters discovered that this unit even helped institute a series of "dirty tricks" to bring his Democratic opponents into disrepute; these activities were done under the supervision of H. R. Haldeman, one of Nixon's trusted aides. On June 17, 1972, five of the "plumbers" were arrested in the offices of the Democratic National Committee at the Watergate apartments. After Nixon's election the question began to be asked whether he was responsible for the break-in or knew of it in advance.

In early 1973 the Watergate grand-jury trial began, but Judge John J. Sirica felt that there was more to the case than a simple break-in and called for further investigation. The Senate responded by setting up a special committee under the leadership of Senator Sam Ervin of North Carolina to investigate a possible connection between the White House and Watergate. More and more evidence surfaced. A major break occurred when White House counsel John Dean testified that the White House was involved. Nixon's two most trusted aides, H. R. Haldeman and John Erlichman, resigned, as did John Dean and Attorney General Richard Kleindienst. When Nixon announced the resignations, he assured the nation that he knew nothing about the cover-up. The Ervin committee now began its public hearings; acting Attorney General Elliot Richardson named Archibald Cox as special Watergate prosecutor. Initially Nixon cooperated with Ervin's committee; when the committee learned in July 1973 that every conversation in the White House since 1971 had been taped, Nixon became uncooperative, refusing to release the tapes or transcripts of the tapes. He defended this action by citing the right of "executive privilege."

Former Attorney General John Mitchell and Maurice Stans, former secretary of commerce and chief fund-raiser for the President's reelection campaign, were indicted for conspiring to block a fraud investigation. Vice-Presi-

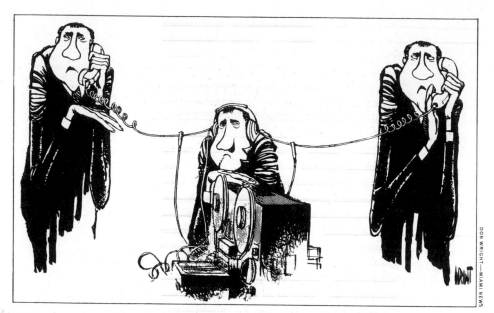

This cartoon shows Nixon's involvement with tapes and wiretapping.

dent Agnew was accused of bribery during his time as governor of Maryland and also as vice-president; as a bargain, Agnew, on October 10, 1973, agreed to resign and plead "no contest" to charges of tax evasion. Gerald Ford, Republican minority leader in the house, was appointed to replace him. Nixon now demanded the firing of Special Prosecutor Cox by Richardson; the acting attorney general refused, so Nixon found someone in the Justice Department to do the dirty deed. Richardson resigned. This "Saturday Night Massacre" on October 20, 1973, stirred public indignation. The nation demanded Nixon's resignation; the House of Representatives began impeachment proceedings. While Nixon pursued a new policy he called "Operation Candor" to convey to the American people his innocence and truthfulness, reports of erased tapes, and missing records all undermined his attempts. To add to his misfortunes, the I.R.S. reported that he owed more than $400,000 in back taxes. This was the beginning of the end.

In late October 1973 the House Judiciary Committee, under the chairmanship of Peter Rodino of New Jersey, began to consider if there were sufficient grounds for impeachment. As the proceedings continued, Nixon at-

Under threat of impeachment, Richard Nixon became the first American president to resign.

tempted to defend himself; "I'm not a crook," he noted. When transcripts of the tapes were released in April 1974, they revealed Nixon as an insecure, mean, foul-mouthed individual. Still, there were many blank spots, and Nixon's guilt was in question. The evidence continued to mount against the President. In July 1974 the House Committee voted three articles of impeachment, charging Nixon with obstruction of justice, abuse of presidential power, and unconstitutionality in defying subpoenas. After a Supreme Court ruling Nixon turned over three additional tapes which left no doubt that he had planned the cover-up. His support in the Senate vanished. On August 9, 1974, Richard Nixon became the first American president to resign in office; but even to the last he did not admit to any guilt, he only stated that he had lost "a strong enough political base in Congress" to enable him to continue. Richard Nixon became the focal point of America's greatest political scandal. Nixon's presidency will be long remembered for his abuse of the office. His dramatic visit to China, his increased detente with Russia, and his Vietnamization program all fade in the face of the Watergate scandal and cover-up. Since the days of Franklin Roosevelt, the office of the president had become increasingly powerful; while power does not necessarily corrupt, it did for Richard Nixon. Many writers refer to the days of Nixon's Imperial Presidency; this is not too far from the truth. If the *Washington Post* reporters had not been so persistent, if the tapes had not existed, if the Watergate burglars had not been caught, maybe Richard Nixon would have left office in 1976 as one of America's greatest presidents. But the nation would have had a disservice done to it. Gerald Ford now became president; his chief task was to restore some faith in government.

Ford: A New Thrust of Leadership

Gerald Ford offered a form of leadership that was a drastic change from Nixon. Born in Omaha, Nebraska, he was well known as a star center on the Uni-

Vice-president Gerald Ford succeeded Nixon as president and was met by problems such as inflation, the energy crisis, and the Middle East.

versity of Michigan football team. After graduating from Yale Law School, he practiced law in Grand Rapids, Michigan, and was elected to the House as a Republican in 1948. There he served the nation well for many years and gained public attention as one of the chief opponents of Johnson's Great Society programs. In 1965 he became minority leader in the House and held that position until Nixon appointed him vice-president. Unlike Nixon, he was an open and warm individual, who was a political conservative. While his critics felt that he was not too bright, nor a great speaker, he seemed to be what the nation needed after the dark days of Watergate. He planned to work closely with Congress and to follow the policy of "continuity and stability."

Ford was not a New Deal president; he did not believe in social-welfare programs. But he believed that the government should adopt policies if they were necessary to the public good. Some of his initial measures met with mixed success. He chose Henry Kissinger as secretary of state to continue Nixon's foreign policy of detente with Russia and closer relations with China. And he offered conditional amnesty to those who had evaded the draft or left the country during the Vietnam War. But his unconditional pardon to Nixon for all federal crimes, which Nixon "committed or may have committed or taken part in," caused an uproar. It did not help that Nixon accepted the pardon and declared that he was "wrong in not acting more decisively and more forthrightly in dealing with Watergate." Rumors rose of a possible deal; Ford's press secretary resigned. Congress voted to give the federal government permanent custody of the tapes, but this matter was still unresolved. Ford saw inflation as the most crucial domestic issue, but he did not plan to impose wage and price controls. He instituted a voluntary economic program of limited federal spending, which included his "WIN" buttons, referring to the slogan, "Whip Inflation Now."

Through most of 1975 Ford and the Congress struggled over the issues of a national energy policy, inflation, and foreign affairs. Ford's plans for energy independence included removal of price controls from domestic oil and natural gas and a tax on all imported crude oil. Late in 1975, price rollbacks and price controls were authorized by Congress. In addition, Congress responded to increased unemployment and rampant inflation by passing more social-welfare legislation; by late 1975 Ford had vetoed 40 of these measures, much to the frustration of the Democratic Congress. But Congress did agree with the president that a tax cut was needed; they passed legislation cutting the budget by $22.8 billion.

While Ford's foreign policy continued the tradition of Nixon, he saw little success. Communist forces were beginning to completely take over Southeast Asia by early 1975. Ford went to Congress and demanded emergency military aid, but memories of Vietnam were still fresh, and Congress refused his demand. South Vietnam and Cambodia fell to the Communists; the United States did offer asylum for those South Vietnamese who wished to come to this country. The *Mayaguez* incident, however, showed Ford's determination to take a strong stand in foreign affairs. The American merchant ship *Mayaguez* and its crew were seized by Cambodian naval forces; Ford ordered a marine attack on the island where the vessel was held. The vessel and its crew were freed, but there were numerous American casualties. Many Americans thought the president had overreacted, while others praised his decision. A later General Accounting Office report revealed that Ford had not exhausted all diplomatic channels before he had ordered the marines to land.

Detente between the United States and Russia was continued under Kissinger but with few important results. The two countries were involved in a joint space-docking mission, and the United States agreed to continue to send wheat to Russia. Ford's visits to China and Russia achieved nothing concrete. In fact, Cuban-Soviet aid to Angola in Africa brought into question our new relationship with Russia and indicated that the Soviets were still intent on expanding their power base in the world. Meanwhile, the Middle East remained a trouble spot, and the killing of six American soldiers in Korea caused a temporary crisis. During Ford's brief administration he did try to bring Nixon's foreign policy to a climax; but he did not quite succeed.

1976: The Bicentennial

Inflation continued into 1976, and Ford continued a conservative economic policy stressing limited spending. By the time he left office he had vetoed 66 congressional measures and frustrated Congress's attempt to expand the government role in social welfare. The election of 1976 was drawing close, but on July 4, 1976, the nation stopped its political bickering and turned for a moment to celebrate its two hundredth anniversary with a Bicentennial festival. Actually the celebration, which climaxed on July Fourth with the ringing of bells, parades, bands, fireworks, and local events, had been building all year. St. Louis Cathedral in New Orleans and the Alamo in San Antonio had been restored. The Freedom Train toured America with its memorabilia from America's past. Ethnic groups developed oral histories of their traditions. Foreign countries gave special gifts ranging from bonsai trees to a replica of the Liberty Bell. But it all culminated on July Fourth: Operation Sail in the New York Harbor attracted more than six million onlookers to its passing flotilla of "tall ships." Washington, D.C., featured music, speeches, fireworks, and parades. Birthday cakes, some large, others small, were baked and eaten. Churchgoers gathered to pray for the nation—past, present, and future. Flags flew everywhere. But by nighttime the party was over, and the nation went back to its day-to-day business. The election of 1976 would be at hand in a few months.

Ford had announced his candidacy for the Republican nomination more than a year before the convention, but he received a strong challenge from Ronald Reagan, who represented the right wing of the party. The fight for the nomination was nip and tuck, but Ford became the party choice. The Democratic field for the presidency was cluttered; but Georgia's Governor Jimmy Carter, who ran long and hard in most of the primaries, began to pull ahead. His hard work and his platform of government responsiveness won him the nomination. Both Ford and Carter saw inflation and unemployment as major problems and engaged in three television debates, none of which either won decisively. The election was as close as the campaign, and Carter won by only 56 electoral votes. The shadow of Nixon may have stopped Ford from getting elected as a legitimate president. But Ford did restore dignity to the office of the presidency and, as a consistent economic conservative, helped slow the tide of inflation. As he saw it, the nation needed a decent, honest man who felt that limited government spending was better for America than another spate of New Deal legislation. The peanut farmer now became president.

Carter and the Challenge of Modern America

Jimmy Carter became the first president from the deep South since Zachary Taylor. As a peanut farmer, businessman, naval officer, and governor of Georgia, he brought with him administrative experience, a liberal outlook, and a strong religious sense. He promised a "fresh faith in the old dream." He was not from the congressional establishment, but this worked to his advantage. He had not been tainted by the memory of Watergate. Yet he did not always understand the inner workings of Washington politics and found that many parts of his program were stymied. For example, in his first year as president he and Congress debated long and hard over the passage of a comprehensive energy program to solve the energy crisis. Congress did at least establish a Department of Energy. He also proposed tax reform, electoral reform, and a new welfare system. Carter's solution to inflation was continued government spending; this approach worried the nation because inflation was now seemingly beyond control. Business began to feel that Carter lacked a firm direction in economic planning. Still he was able to get a major urban aid and housing law through Congress and a revision of the social security system. Actually,

Jimmy Carter brought to the office of the presidency a strong religious bent.

his first major domestic crisis centered around his friend, Bert Lance, the White House budget director, who was forced to resign.

In foreign affairs, Carter's strong position on human rights endangered our detente with Russia. Carter began to issue statements on the treatment of Soviet dissidents; these statements angered the Russians. Carter also admonished some Latin American and African countries for violations of human rights, even suggesting that foreign aid be withheld from them.

One of his early controversial measures in foreign affairs was the Panama Canal treaties (signed in September 1977), which turned over United States control of the Canal Zone to Panama by the year 2000 and which guaranteed

The Fair Deal to Camp David: From Truman to Carter

its permanent neutrality. Conservatives strongly criticized the president's action; and he still had to get Senate ratification the following year, which provided him a real challenge.

After Carter's first year in office his accomplishments were not noteworthy, and his popularity began to slip in 1978. But Carter took the initiative. After heated debate and much compromise, Congress at last passed revised forms of Carter's energy and tax laws that promised to bring some relief. In spite of vocal opposition, the Senate ratified the two Panama Canal treaties; Carter and Panama's Chief of Government Omar Torrijos Herrera signed them on June 16, 1978. Carter's personal involvement in Middle East negotiations at Camp David provided the necessary groundwork for an Israeli-Egyptian settlement. After three days of intense meetings Carter, Egyptian President Anwar Sadat, and Israeli Premier Menachem Begin, emerged with two agreements that appeared to hold the solution to the Middle East controversy, which had raged for three decades. Never have such intense negotiations taken place under the guidance of an American president. Still, major stumbling blocks had to be removed before a permanent peace could emerge. Carter's bombshell in foreign affairs came late in 1978 when he announced that full diplomatic relations would be restored with China on January 1, 1979, and that, by March 1979, embassies would open in the two capitals. Chairman Hua Kuo-feng and Carter moved toward a new detente. Nixon's dream had now reached reality. Critics charged Carter with a sell-out of Taiwan and threatened to challenge the constitutionality of breaking the treaty with Taiwan in the courts. But Carter now stood on a new threshold of popularity. Although the Middle East talks between Egypt and Israel were not living up to expectations, Carter's foreign policy expanded the Nixon Doctrine and featured him as a real groundbreaker in world politics.

Foreign and Domestic Problems

In 1978 the American people became fed up with increased taxes, federal spending, and inflation. This was most obvious with the passage of Proposition 13 (June 1978) in California. The proposition placed a limit on property taxes. This uprising against property taxes signaled a national revolt against government spending and inflation. Other states introduced less harsh but similar measures. Many looked upon the tax revolt as a time to rethink the New Deal approach. Even liberal Carter took a new tack; his fight against inflation involved a wage–price-guideline program, plus promises of slimmer budgets and a defense of the slipping American dollar. Carter reacted to the feelings rising across the country with his economics of austerity.

1979 was a year of achievements in foreign affairs and frustrations in domestic policy. The signing of the historic Middle East peace treaty in Washington, D.C., by Egyptian President Anwar Sadat and Israeli Premier Menachem Begin in the spring of 1979 brought an uneasy peace to the Middle East. Carter's six-day mission to Cairo and Jerusalem capped this historic event and brought momentary praise to the Carter presidency.

In June 1979 Carter and Soviet Communist Party Chief Leonid Brezhnev held their first summit conference in Vienna and signed the Strategic Arms Limitation Treaty, known as SALT II. This treaty, which Carter described as lessening "the danger of nuclear destruction, while safeguarding our military security in a more stable, predictable, and peaceful world," has become the focus of a national debate on arms limitations and of a fierce battle in the Senate for ratification. At the heart of the treaty is an agreement to limit the numbers of strategic arms and to put restrictions on missile size. It would have taken dynamic leadership to have gotten this treaty approved by Congress; but in light of world events in early 1980 and the United States boycott of the summer Olympics in Moscow, its demise appears imminent.

Rampant inflation, a new energy crisis—which surfaced in 1974 with long gas lines and odd-even plans—an emerging recession, and low ratings in opinion polls, caused Carter to reevaluate his presidency. In July 1979 Carter took a self-imposed six-day retreat at Camp David, where he conferred with leaders from all phases of American society and even with some private citizens. Emerging from this historic self-examination Carter went before the public to tell them that the heart of the American malaise was "the crisis of the American spirit." He then proposed cutting our dependence on foreign oil and undertaking a drastic energy program, which would rely on developing alternative sources of energy.

On the heels of this well-directed message to the American people, Carter shocked the nation by demanding the resignations of his top 34 cabinet and staff aids. Heads began to fall, five cabinet members were replaced, and the title "Chief of Staff" went to his top aide, 34-year-old Hamilton Jordan. Carter then took his promise for a renewed drive to solve American problems to the people themselves. At the same time he was beginning to gear up for the election campaign of 1980 with renewed vigor, because Senator Edward Kennedy had announced his candidacy for president. Carter's economic problems still seemed insurmountable, and there remained the question of whether he could provide the necessary national leadership to overcome them.

In November of 1979 Carter faced a new challenge in foreign affairs. Student militants in Teheran, Iran, seized 50 American hostages at the United States Embassy. The students demanded that the former Shah Mohammed

Americans wait for gas in 1979.

Reza Pahlevi, who had sought medical assistance in New York City, be turned over to them. They had the support of the ruling religious leader, Ayatollah Ruhollah Khomeini. Americans became incensed; Carter's presidency received a much needed boost. All diplomacy failed. Even with the backing of the United Nations Security Council and the International Court, the United States was unable to break the stalemate. The Shah's leaving the United States for asylum in Panama had little effect on the militants' demands. 1980 opened with the hostages still in the hands of the student militants, who were preparing to try them as spies. As the United States considered economic sanctions—or even military action—another world crisis emerged that threatened the Salt II treaty and detente.

Claiming that Afghanistan authorities had asked for Soviet military aid to put down "counterrevolutionary gangs," the Soviet Union invaded Afghanistan in one of the most obvious acts of Communist aggression since the

Korean War. This invasion not only seriously threatened the relationship between the United States and the Soviet Union, it also provided a threat to the control of the oil-rich Persian Gulf region. In a televised address Carter indicated a new stand: "Neither the United States nor any other nation which is committed to world peace and stability can continue to do business with the Soviet Union." Carter imposed a limited embargo on grain shipments, barred the sale of high-technology items, and cancelled cultural exchanges. A *Newsweek* cover story told of the return of the Cold War. The economy, the energy crisis, and trouble in Iran and Afghanistan—coupled with an approaching re-election campaign—ushered in 1980 as a critical year for President Jimmy Carter.

Presidents from Truman to Carter have helped shape the post-World War II world of today. Since 1945 American foreign affairs have included two wars of containment—one in Korea and one in Vietnam—and a general policy which gradually emerged from the icy grip of the Cold War to culminate in the days of detente, of more creative and realistic outlooks; and which has since slid back closer to Cold War. Domestic programs have ranged from the Fair Deal to the New Frontier to the Great Society. The Watergate incident and the subsequent resignation of President Richard Nixon brought a real crisis in leadership to the surface and cast a large shadow over Presidents Gerald Ford and Jimmy Carter. Since World War II the New Deal has been transformed and expanded, but the problems of energy and inflation may bring America to a new plateau of government planning and regulation, which will even eclipse the philosophy of the New Deal.

Essay

Containment and the Eisenhower Doctrine

After World War II the Cold War emerged on the scene and containment of communism became the basis for American foreign policy. According to the Cold War view, world communism was out to destroy the free world; United States policy involved "long-term, patient, firm, and vigorous containment of Russian expansive tendencies." This would limit world communism and cause a drastic shift in Russian policies. During the presidency of Harry Truman containment became policy with the Truman Doctrine, with the Marshall Plan, with the formation of the North Atlantic Treaty Organization, and with our involvement in Korea. Many Republican leaders attacked our involvement in the war and the general principles of containment. With the election of Dwight Eisenhower in 1952 many Americans wondered whether the containment policy would end and a new foreign emphasis begin.

Eisenhower initially was ambiguous about containment; he made policy statements that seemed at the same time to both criticize and embrace that policy. A plank in the Republican platform, however, was quite clear in condemning containment as "negative, futile, and immoral." Also, Eisenhower's Secretary of State John Foster Dulles described containment as a treadmill policy that would go nowhere. Eisenhower was a military man; surely he would do more than just contain the spread of communism. Many Americans wanted him to liberate those poor souls from Communist dominion.

President Eisenhower was surrounded by leading Republicans who were fiscally conservative. They wanted a balanced budget, and that included the defense budget. An aggressive program of liberation fought directly against the Communist nations cost money. That was not very realistic. Eisenhower had promised to get America out of the limited and frustrating war in Korea. It was hardly a time to go out and fight for liberation. Although the containment policy was criticized in the election of 1952, in reality Eisenhower and Dulles continued that policy with few changes. Still, it would be positive containment rather than merely a negative approach.

Eisenhower's "New Look" became his brand of containment. It was based on the fact that the United States now had overwhelming superiority in nuclear weapons and in the means of delivering them. Thus was born the doctrine of instant and massive retaliation. Dulles believed that the United States should no longer get involved in frustrating wars of containment, such as the one in Korea. Aggression must be met "vigorously at places and with means of its [America's] own choosing." Nuclear weapons in the hands of the United States would be the savior of the free world. The next war would not be like Korea or World War II; it would be a war of tactical nuclear weapons. Containment would be implemented by maintaining our nuclear advantage over the Soviet Union. The Soviet Union began to develop their own nuclear weapons during the 1950s, but America kept up its striking force with its potential to destroy the Soviet Union.

In the hands of Eisenhower and Dulles the threat of massive retaliation became the main

Secretary of State John Foster Dulles was greatly responsible for the policy of massive retaliation.

weapon of their containment policy. Crises in Korea, Vietnam, and Formosa prompted the use of this New Look, but with mixed success. Eisenhower visited Korea and tried to get the truce talks completed. But these talks were stalled on the question of prisoner-of-war repatriation. Word got to China that the stalemate must be broken or the United States would use massive retalia-

tion. The prisoner-of-war question was resolved, and the truce was signed.

However, the threat of massive retaliation did not work with Vietnam. The French had now fallen, and the Communists held a sizeable portion of the country; America's nuclear weapons didn't seem to cause any changes in the status quo there. So a new innovation was added. In

1954 a group of countries in Southeast Asia formed with the United States the Southeast Asian Treaty Organization: it was to be a united front against Communist aggression. The containment policy of NATO was being applied to the Asian front.

The shelling of the islands of Quemoy and Matsu and the threat to Nationalist China on the island of Formosa again caused the New Look of aggressive containment to rise to the challenge. Eisenhower felt that the loss of the two Formosan islands to mainland China would eventually lead to the end of Formosa and the spread of communism throughout the Pacific islands. The Eisenhower administration now seriously debated whether they should drop nuclear weapons on the Chinese mainland. But the danger subsided. This brand of nuclear politics was a grave danger to the survival of two major world powers and, possibly, to the survival of the world itself.

Eisenhower's meeting with Russian leaders in Geneva was a major departure from the New Look and signaled, in "the spirit of Geneva," the beginning of modern detente. The Cold War was still quite frigid, yet the United States and Russia were beginning to see the potential danger in the use of nuclear weapons and in meeting massive retaliation with more massive retaliation. It is unclear whether Eisenhower's policy of massive retaliation was just Cold War rhetoric or a real tactic that would be employed if necessary. While Dulles and Eisenhower talked of the liberation of peoples under Communist domination, they never seriously threatened massive retaliation to accomplish that end.

The Truman Doctrine of containment had been superseded by the Eisenhower Doctrine. In 1957 Eisenhower received from Congress authority to use military and economic aid "to secure and protect the territorial independence of Middle Eastern nations against armed aggres-

Tactical weapons necessary to the policy of massive retaliation.

sion from any nation controlled by international communism." This sounded much like the Truman Doctrine. It is true that the containment policy, which was formulated by George Kennan during the Truman presidency, was continued through the 1950s. But Eisenhower and his Secretary of State Dulles went beyond limited military and economic aid to threaten massive retaliation with nuclear weapons. As the 1950s faded, the spirit of Geneva was bringing about an improved relationship with the Soviets, but containment still seemed necessary to keep the United States the leader of the free nations and to stave off the Soviet threat of world communism. ■

Suggested Reading

Two general studies of the postwar period are ERIC GOLDMAN's *The Crucial Decade and After America, 1945–1960* (1956) and WILLIAM MANCHESTER's *The Glory and the Dream: A Narrative History of America, 1932–1972* (1973).

The Truman presidency is covered in CABELL PHILLIPS' *The Truman Presidency* (1966). The Korean War is the subject of DAVID REES's book, *Korea: The Limited War* (1964).

Two views of the Eisenhower presidency are found in HERBERT S. PARMENT's *Eisenhower and the American Crusades* (1972) and G. W. REICHARD's *The Reaffirmation of Republicanism: Eisenhower and the 83rd Congress* (1975).

THEODORE C. SORENSON, in *Kennedy* (1965) and H. FAIRLIE, in *The Kennedy Promise* (1973), both cover the Kennedy years.

ROBERT SHERRILL, *The Accidental President* (1967), and ERIC GOLDMAN, in *The Tragedy of Lyndon Johnson* (1969) analyze the Johnson presidency.

The presidency of Richard Nixon is explored in *The Imperial Presidency* (1973) by ARTHUR M. SCHLESINGER, JR., and *Nixon in the White House: The Frustration of Power* (1971) by ROWLAND EVANS, JR., and ROBERT NOVAK (1976). ROBERT BERNSTEIN and CARL WOODWARD, in *Final Days*, document the Watergate crisis.

The Vietnam War is the subject of *The Abuse of Power* (1966) by THEODORE DRAPER and *The Bitter Heritage* (1967) by ARTHUR M. SCHLESINGER, JR.

The days of Gerald Ford as president are covered in R. REEVES's *A Ford not a Lincoln* (1975), while DAVID KUCHARSKY covers the Carter presidency in *The Man From Plains* (1976).

CHAPTER 16

Minorities in
Post-World War II America

Time Line

?–A.D. 1492	Migration and evolution of American Indian societies
1492	Christopher Columbus lands in West Indies—beginning of European exploration
1607–1732	Establishment of 13 English colonies
1775–1783	American Revolution
1776	Declaration of Independence
1789–1797	Presidency of George Washington
1812–1815	War of 1812
1816–1824	Era of Good Feelings
1846–1848	Mexican War
1861–1865	Civil War
1865–1877	Reconstruction
1877–1900	Industrialization and urbanization
1900–1916	Progressive Era
1917–1918	World War I
1930s	Depression and New Deal
1941–1945	World War II

1946	Indian Claims Act Committee on Civil Rights established
1954	*Brown* v. *Board of Education of Topeka*
1955	Formation of Southern Christian Leadership Conference
1957	Little Rock crisis
1962	Formation of National Farm Workers Association
1963	March on Washington

1964	Civil Rights Act
1965	Murder of Malcolm X Watts Riot
1967	Tijerina leads raid on county courthouse in New Mexico
1968	Assassination of Martin Luther King, Jr.
1969	Indians seize Alcatraz Island
1973	Wounded Knee occupation
1975	Indian Self-Determination Act
1978	Longest Walk

1945–1960	Post-war politics
1950–1953	Korean War
1950–1960	Civil rights movement
1961–1973	Vietnam War
1976	Bicentennial celebration

The years from Truman to Carter were filled with domestic struggles, foreign frustrations, and a bloodless revolution—the minority revolution. Throughout our history black Americans were a large minority but a subjugated one. In the early years most blacks were slaves; some were free but with an inferior social position. After the Civil War, freedom was extended to all blacks, but their place in society was still a very low one. Leaving the Jim Crow laws behind, in the twentieth century they moved North and West, but there they found open resistance too and in some cases violence. With the end of World War II, the presidents, the courts, and black leaders themselves moved toward an era of civil-rights struggles. Meanwhile, Mexican-Americans, by the twentieth century had begun to form large urban communities, concentrated mainly in the Southwest; for years many of them had had fears of repatriation, but now they were American citizens. In the 1960s they too began to demand equal rights and to form regional organizations with regional leaders. The American Indians—the only true Native Americans—had seen their land and culture taken from them. The Dawes Act of 1887 attempted to remold them in the image of the white farmer, but this act only created poor Indians plagued by ill health and with little land. The Reorganization Act of 1934 attempted to reverse this trend, but the damage had been done and little traditional Indian culture remained. The American Indian also began to organize and demand equality in the 1960s; organizations were formed and tribes became active. The black, brown, and red revolutions are part of the post-war world.

Black Americans and Civil Rights

The black revolution in civil rights received its first government push from President Franklin Roosevelt but got its major momentum from President Truman. In 1946 Truman established a President's Committee of Civil Rights to investigate the status of civil rights in America; that committee recommended certain essential changes in voting laws and lynch laws, in discrimination in the armed forces, and in Southern "separate but equal" measures. While Congress studied these recommendations, Truman took the initiative with two executive orders that ended racial segregation in the armed forces and stopped discrimination in the federal civil service through the creation of the Fair Employment Board. Truman had led the way in civil rights and now passed the ball to Congress. Congress remained inactive, but the Supreme Court did not.

During the 1940s the Supreme Court became more responsive to the cause of blacks in the South. Jim Crow laws were slowly overturned. The National

National Association for the Advancement of Colored People was the organization that had been most responsible for these legal victories. By the early 1950s a series of suits were instituted to end segregation in public schools. These cases came to a climax on May 17, 1954, when the Supreme Court ruled in the case of *Brown* v. *Board of Education of Topeka* that segregation of children in public schools on the basis of race was unconstitutional. Not long after this monumental decision the court ordered that desegregation should proceed with "all deliberate speed." It was up to the Eisenhower administration to implement this decision.

Little resistance to desegregation at first appeared in the District of Columbia or the border states, but trouble began to brew in the deep South. The Ku Klux Klan was revived to "protect" the white Americans there, and white citizens' groups were formed. In March 1956, a group of 19 Senators and 81 House members from the South issued a "Southern Manifesto" praising "the motives of those states which have declared the intention to resist forced integration by any means." White parents began to send their children to private schools. Black organizations came under open attack. The first real resistance occurred in September 1957, in Little Rock, Arkansas. That fall a few black students were to be admitted to all-white Central High School. Governor Orval Faubus took a militant stand, appearing on television to announce his policy against "forced integration" and calling out the Arkansas National Guard to prevent the integration. In the face of a federal court order, the National Guard blocked the entrance of nine black students. After a direct confrontation with Eisenhower, Faubus withdrew the National Guard, but tension continued throughout the year. And the next year the black students went to another high school.

Southern antagonism toward desegregation continued into the 1960s. In 1962 President John F. Kennedy ordered regular army troops to Oxford, Mississippi, to protect black student James Meredith's right to enroll in the university there. Kennedy commented, "It ought to be possible for American students of any color to attend any public institution they select without having to be backed by troops." But desegregation was not really moving with all "deliberate speed." Most white schools still were totally segregated by the mid-1960s. While segregation in public schools was illegal, *defacto* school segregation through neighborhood segregation was becoming increasingly prevalent. The black schools were usually inferior to the mdidle-class white schools. The Supreme Court now ruled that school bussing was one way to desegregate schools. Bussing eventually became unpopular among white and blacks alike. But it proved to be the most common way of desegregating neighborhood schools. By the 1970s school bussing spread across the nation. Nixon

The Little Rock crisis was the first instance of Southern resistance to school desegregation.

and Ford both expressed their opposition to it. In regard to the Boston desegregation process, Ford felt that bussing was "not the best solution to quality education in Boston." The Supreme Court in the 1970s was making certain decisions that limited desegregation, such as in cases involving Detroit and Memphis. In 1975 Louisville, Kentucky, became the first metropolitan area to carry out court-ordered, cross-district bussing of children to establish racial balance in the public schools. The federal government then added a new weapon to its desegregation fight by withholding federal funds from segregated schools. The Supreme Court expanded the fight when it ruled in 1976 that private, nonsectarian schools may not exclude black children because of their race. School desegregation and school bussing still remain burning civil-rights issues.

Martin Luther King, Jr.

The heart of the civil-rights movement now grew from a grass-roots movement started in 1955 in Montgomery, Alabama. One day in December a black seamstress, Rosa Mae Parks, boarded a bus, sat down in the whites-only section, and refused to move. Her arrest fired a black protest movement, which was led by a Baptist clergyman, Martin Luther King, Jr. King organized the Montgomery blacks into the Montgomery Improvement Association and set up a boycott of the bus lines. The goals of the boycott were courteous treatment of black riders and the hiring of black bus drivers; it was effective. King also took his case to the Supreme Court. When the Court ruled that segregated buses were unconstitutional, the civil-rights movement had been given a beginning. "Praise the Lord, God has spoken from Washington, D.C." King now became a national black leader and formed the Southern Christian Leadership Conference, or S.C.L.C., a group of 100 Southern clergymen who felt that the civil-rights movement must be led by churches and church leaders. This organization dedicated itself to voter registration and nonviolent demonstrations against Jim Crow laws. It became one of the most effective black organizations in the movement for black equality, and for years its guiding light was Martin Luther King, Jr.

Born in the slums of Atlanta, King grew up as a second-class citizen. He saw that blacks were victims of discrimination in both North and South and that the federal government offered little legal opportunity for equality. Personally, he felt he could better change society through his career as a Baptist minister; he also became imbued with the ideas of Henry David Thoreau and Mahatma Gandhi on nonviolent, passive resistance. Through the S.C.L.C. he used nonviolent protest to achieve remarkable gains for black Americans. During the 1950s and 1960s King became the real soul of the black protest movement.

After the Montgomery bus boycott, King turned to Birmingham, which was considered the most racist city in the South. The Birmingham protests of 1963 marked the climax of nonviolent protest in the South. America turned to the nightly news and saw blacks beaten, set upon by police dogs, and knocked down by water from high-pressure hoses. King wrote: "The eyes of the world are on Birmingham. We're going on in spite of dogs and firehoses. We've gone too far to turn back." After six weeks of demonstrations the nation could take it no longer. Pressure came to bear on Birmingham's city fathers. Americans now began to ask the question: Is there racism in America? The obvious answer was, "Yes."

The largest civil rights rally took place in August 1963 under the direction of King. This march on Washington for "Jobs and Freedom" attracted 300,000 Americans, who asked that President Kennedy establish a federal fair employment commission and that Congress enact major civil-rights legislation. It was here at this rally that Martin Luther King, Jr., enunciated his

Martin Luther King, Jr., was the most successful black civil rights leader.

dream: "I have a dream, that my little children will, one day, live in a nation where they will not be judged by the color of their skin, but by the content of their character . . . With this faith, we will be able to hew out of the mountains of despair a stone of hope." His dream came closer to reality with the passage of the Civil Rights Act of 1964. The act outlawed discrimination in all public facilities and accommodations, gave the attorney general authority to file suits to speed integration, made discrimination in all areas of interstate commerce illegal, denied states that practiced discrimination federal funds, and established a commission on civil rights. Civil rights received a major boost.

Now King turned to the issue of black voting rights. Black voting registration drives were undertaken. King marched twice from Selma to Montgomery, Alabama, to protest voting-rights restrictions; both times he was stopped by state troopers and violence occurred. A white minister was beaten to death;

a civil rights worker and a black youth were shot and killed. President Lyndon Johnson declared, "It is not just Negroes, but it is all of us, who must overcome the crippling legacy of bigotry and injustice. And we shall overcome." Federal troops protected the marchers. Injustices at Selma had stirred the national conscience; in August 1965 the Voting Rights Act was passed, which abolished literacy tests and other discriminatory devices. Protection was extended to civil-rights workers and persons seeking the right to vote. The meaning of equality was again expanded.

From 1965 to 1968 King turned to discrimination and injustice in the North. He protested vehemently against the Vietnam War and the conditions of blacks in Northern ghettos. But his life was cut short in Memphis, Tennessee, on April 4, 1968, when he was struck by a bullet from James Earl Ray's gun. Whether his assassination was the work of Ray or a conspiracy makes little difference. King is gone. He tried every day to bring his dream to reality and to allow black Americans to share in the American experience. He was the spirit behind the civil-rights movement of the 1960s and was consistently a believer in nonviolent protest. It is a great tragedy that he did not live to see the advances blacks have made in America since his death.

From Sit-ins to Black Power

But King and the S.C.L.C. were not alone in the black protest movement of the 1960s and 1970s. In 1960 a group of students in North Carolina introduced a technique that soon spread throughout the South: the sit-in. During the next few years thousands of young people were arrested for sitting-in at segregated public facilities. Publicity was achieved, and the actions helped pressure the passage of the Civil Rights Act of 1964. The organization that arose during these activities was the Student Nonviolent Coordinating Committee, or S.N.C.C. In 1961, James Farmer, a national director of the Congress of Racial Equality, or C.O.R.E., undertook freedom rides to desegregate interstate buses and bus terminals. C.O.R.E. had been in existence since the 1940s, but it came into its own with the freedom rides. By the 1970s, black organizations had expanded from the N.A.A.C.P. and the Urban League to include S.C.L.C., S.N.C.C., and C.O.R.E. While these groups seemed to perform different functions, they were often at odds for both money and support. It was also by this time that a split developed among these groups over the concept of black power and the increasing racial violence in the cities.

During the 1960s the slogan "Black Power" became a rallying cry for black Americans. To some white Americans it meant the destruction of the white man and his society. It became visible in raised black fists in the 1968 Olympic Games in Mexico, among the Black Muslims and Black Panthers,

Black sit-ins, such as this one in a drugstore in Jackson, Mississippi, gave national publicity to segregated public facilities throughout the South.

and on television with the emphasis on "Black is Beautiful." The Black Muslims are a little known and little understood group. Their founder was the mysterious man W. D. Fard, who appeared in the Detroit ghettos in the early 1930s. He arrived in Detroit to preach a black religion of pride; the white man was the enemy. Before his disappearance, he left blacks in Detroit a sacred literature, a university, a military organization, and a Temple of Islam. His chief lieutenant, Elijah Muhammad, formerly Elijah Poole, took over the leadership of this black-nationalist movement. During the depression it had great appeal with its anti-white overtones and religious beliefs. By the 1940s the movement became centered in Chicago, where Elijah Muhammad set up a new headquarters and began a national membership drive. Its appeal was now to the frustrated blacks of the Northern and Western ghettos. But it was not easy being a Black Muslim. All Muslims were forbidden to eat pork, gamble, drink, smoke, overeat, or buy on credit. Each Muslim gave a fixed percentage of his or her income and also contributed extra on special holy days.

Critics of the Black Muslims have pictured them as being a violent organization. Yet while most of their members were young, frustrated blacks who believed that violence should be met with violence, they were a very disciplined group. Their organization found only narrow acceptance by either

Malcolm X was the voice of the Black Muslims until his split with Elijah Muhammad.

black or white society, and by the 1960s they faced an internal crisis. Malcolm X became the central figure of this controversy. Born in the ghettos of Omaha, Nebraska, while in jail he became a convert to—and eventually the most effective spokesman of—black nationalism and race separatism. But after his trip abroad to Mecca, the religious capital of the Muslim faith, he began to change his belief that all whites were really "devils"; he split from Elijah Muhammad and established Muslim Mosque, Inc. On February 21, 1965, during a speech in Harlem, Malcolm X was shot 16 times; the persons responsible for his murder were never discovered. Later, with the death of Elijah Muhammad, power passed to his son, Wallace D. Muhammad. In 1976 the entire direction of the Black Muslims changed when Wallace Muhammad made the name of the organization the World Community of Islam in the West, announcing, "We are not Black Muslims and never have been. We're not black separatists. We're a world community, a community that encompasses everybody." Blacks and whites alike are in the organization now, and the impetus that made it a leader in black nationalism is gone forever.

The Black Panthers are another misunderstood black fringe group. Formed in Oakland, California, in 1966 by Huey Newton and Bobby Seale, the Black

Panthers were initially a revolutionary black political party dedicated to the improvement of blacks in the ghetto. They adopted a ten-point program, which had some conservative elements as well as radical ones. One of the major enemies the Black Panthers singled out in their program was the "white cop in the ghetto." They challenged white authority in their neighborhoods by using California gun laws, which then allowed guns to be carried, to their advantage. With the support of Eldridge Cleaver as their publicity minister they challenged white police and were met with increasing resistance. By the late 1960s Cleaver had fled to Algeria, and Newton and Seale were in jail. The party suffered an internal crisis and lost its initial momentum. Eldridge Cleaver, a reborn Christian, subsequently returned to this country to face criminal charges; Newton and Seale have both dabbled in traditional politics. In the 1970s the Black Panthers have become more of a social-action group. They now work among the poor in the black ghettos and attempt to improve black conditions there. They have come a long way from the revolutionary rhetoric of the 1960s.

Race Riots and Beyond

The frustrations that were evident in the strivings of black people in the 1960s were most noticeable in the urban riots of the decade's second half. What exactly caused the black riots of the period will never be determined, but they started in August 1965 with a disturbance in the Watts area of Los Angeles. Rising unemployment, summer heat, and white police brutality burst into six days of rioting. By the end of the sixth day, 34 blacks were dead, and property damage was in excess of $40 million. In 1965 and 1966, summer riots continued; the violence peaked in 1967 with more than 150 urban riots. President Lyndon Johnson appointed a Commission on Civil Disorders, headed by Governor Otto Kerner of Illinois, to investigate the riots. In 1968 the Kerner Commission reported that the riots were caused by racism in America and that America was growing into two nations: "Our nation is moving toward two societies, one black, one white—separate and unequal."

By the 1970s this bleak prophecy did not seem as real as it had in the midst of the black revolution of the 1960s. Blacks played a greater role in American society, from music to athletics to government to business. The black middle class continued to rise. Still problems existed. Black politicians felt that the major political parties were no longer interested in the civil-rights movement; fewer black delegates appeared in the national conventions in 1976. Today, leading blacks include Ralph Abernathy of the S.C.L.C., Benjamin Hooks of the N.A.A.C.P., Jesse Jackson of Chicago's Operation P.U.S.H.,

The Watts riot in Los Angeles in 1965 was one of more than 150 urban riots during the 1960s.

and Vernon Jordan of the Urban League. All these organizations went through a financial crunch and a decline in membership in the late 1970s. Some blacks felt that the Allan Bakke case, in which the Supreme Court made a very vague ruling on reverse discrimination, was a partial victory for black equality during this period. The turbulent days of the 1960s are gone; the civil-rights revolution has achieved much success. The 1970s were a time of quiet expansion of those victories. But the blacks were not the only minority in revolution.

Mexican-Americans

Mexican-Americans joined blacks in the minority revolution, but their movement has been basically regional, with regional goals and leaders. Today they are lumped together with Puerto Ricans and Cubans to comprise the Hispanic population. Much of their success since World War II can be attributed to Cesar Chavez, who brought them national publicity. Chavez had one answer to the Mexican-American problem: "Money will break the cycle of poverty." He attempted to put this idea into action through the unionization of migrant farm workers.

Cesar Chavez and Tijerina

Cesar Chavez himself rose from humble origins as a migrant worker; in 1962 he formed the National Farm Workers Association to unionize the farm workers, raise their living standard, and solve many of their related social and economic problems. As with King, his major technique was the use of nonviolent protest, or passive resistance. His first action against the rose growers of McFarland, California, was successful; so he joined with the Agricultural Workers Organizing Committee, a Filipino union, to strike against the grape growers of Delano, California. "Huelga"—strike—became the weapon of Chavez to achieve his goals. With their red flags with a black eagle in the center, migrant workers picketed the large grape farmers of the Delano area; their demands were simple: $1.40 an hour or $.25 a box. The chances for Chavez and his new union to beat the powerful forces of agricultural business were slim indeed. Chavez knew that he needed support of white America, so he invoked the white conscience and called for a national boycott of table grapes. His timing was excellent; the black revolution had peaked and liberals sought a new cause. Eventually more and more whites supported the farmworkers' movement. During the course of the strike the two unions united and formed the United Farm Workers Organizing Committee, U.F.W.O.C., with Chavez as its leader. Public sympathy grew. In 1965 the AFL-CIO supported the strike; in 1966 Chavez and his supporters led a 300-mile pilgrimage to Sacramento to plead for state assistance. The national media now covered the strike and Chavez became a well-known figure. During Lent in 1968, Chavez fasted "to the sin and suffering of the farm workers." When the fast was over, Senator Robert Kennedy broke bread with him. The boycott had worked. One by one the grape growers signed with Chavez union. Chavez had become the first Mexican-American leader to organize migrant laborers and achieve an economic breakthrough. The years of the 1970s were rough ones for Chavez and his union. Not only did he face a union struggle with the Teamsters, but additional strikes against other California growers were met with stiff opposition. Chavez's drive for a better existence in America for migrant laborers is far from over; yet already he has achieved victories which most Americans thought were impossible. But Chavez provided only one answer to the Mexican-American plight.

Reyes Lopez Tijerina saw the land as essential to Mexican-American existence. In land is found Mexican-American power and pride; he wanted land stolen by whites to be given back to the rightful owners. Also born a migrant, Tijerina studied the history of the Mexicans in America and saw that from the earliest days of the Spaniards, land was illegally taken from them. He researched old Spanish and Mexican land grants, the Treaty of Guadalupe

Cesar Chavez through his farm workers' union has achieved success in raising the living standard of the migrant workers.

Hidalgo, and the Private Court of Land Claims. "I dedicated my life to research to make sure these land grants were legal." In February 1962 he founded the Alianza Federal de Mercedes to fight for land in New Mexico. This organization was based on the belief that land had been stolen from the original inhabitants. Law after law, treaty after treaty had been violated. The Treaty of Guadalupe Hidalgo of 1848 guaranteed the property rights of the inhabitants, yet the Private Court of Claims took away most of the land. If the land was returned, he knew that Mexican-American pride and culture would also be renewed. He said, "We are angry because they have stolen our lands and language; they gave us the 'freedom' a man gives to a bird in a cage. They took the scissors and clipped both wings." The Alianza began to preach these ideas throughout New Mexico and to stir the Mexican-Americans to demonstrate for their lost land.

Tijerina's appeal was to the rural Mexican-Americans of New Mexico. Most Mexican-Americans felt that he was too radical in his drive to reacquire the land. But he began to gather supporters, and in 1966 he marched upon the Governor's house in Santa Fe. "We want justice, not powdered milk," he demanded. Next, he and his followers made a citizens' arrest of two forest rangers in the Carson National Forest, the site of the old San Joaquin del Rio de Chama land grant. The forest rangers were tried in a picnic area, found guilty and released, but their jeeps were confiscated. Newspapers reported the incident with tongue in cheek. Tijerina was described as everything from the Mexican Elmer Gantry to the jet-age Pancho Villa. Meanwhile, his group was making little real headway.

The high point of the Tijerina movement came in 1967 when his men made a raid on the country courthouse in Rio Arriba county to arrest State Attorney General Alfonso Sanchez and release some of Tijerina's followers. The state of New Mexico called out a small army of 200 state troopers, 2 armored vehicles, helicopters, and 400 national guardsmen to capture Tijerina. As bait, General Jacob Jolly placed 50 Mexican-Americans, men, women, and children, in a sheep pen for 36 hours (without legally arresting them). Tijerina was captured, charged with 54 criminal acts, and went through two trials. In jail he had a vision that he should be the official United States representative to the Middle East to end the tension there. After his release he was ordered to disband the organization. While Tijerina holds little power in New Mexico today, he did shake the white establishment and offered some hope to the poor, rural Mexican-Americans.

The Future

Some Mexican-American leaders feel that Mexican-Americans must begin to form political organizations, either separate ones or units within the two major parties. Rodolfo "Corky" Gonzales has been trying to instill cultural pride in his people from his base in Denver. His Crusade for Justice has attempted to reform the courts and to offer better education and employment opportunities. The answers to Mexican-American problems are many and usually regional. Some regional victories have been accomplished but more are needed.

Today there is a movement afoot to unite all Hispanic-American groups into an organization such as the National Council of La Raza under the direction of Raul Yzaguirre. There are now 12 million Hispanic people in the United States; 7.2 million of them are Mexican-Americans. Now in the 1980s Hispanic-Americans are becoming the largest minority in the United States. As the fastest-growing minority group, they are receiving much-deserved recognition. Most of the early activist Hispanic groups of the 1970s have become less active and have been replaced with groups such as the Southwest Voter

Registration Education Project. There are five Mexican-Americans in Congress today; in California Mario Obledo is secretary of health and welfare under Governor Jerry Brown. There are now 27 Mexican-American judges in California. Many Mexican-Americans look forward to the Hispanic-American's potential power, and they hope, as one leader said, "The 1980s will be the decade of the Hispanics."

The American Indian

The American Indians, who today number more than 800,000 are a unique minority. Many of them left their reservations after World War II and became assimilated into white society; these Indians wanted a greater share in white America. Others, with their emphasis on traditional ways, wanted increased self-determination. The Indian Reorganization Act of 1934 slowed the process of assimilation and attempted to restore tribal culture and improve the reservation. But many thousands of Indians continued to leave the reservation for the city after World War II, as they still do today. To make matters worse, American taxpayers by the 1950s were unhappy with the Indian Reorganization Act because they felt they were financing a way of life that was not in the American mainstream. During that decade certain measures were enacted that again threatened Indian existence and forced Indian assimilation. In 1953 off-reservation drinking was legalized; this decision affected Indian drinking habits hardly at all. Alcoholism has been for years the number one social problem among American Indians. The government then passed Public Law 280, which authorized certain states to assume jurisdiction over criminal and civil matters on reservations without approval by the tribes, even though the reservations remained federal trust land. But since 1953 many exceptions to the law have arisen. In fact, there are many Indians today who would like the federal government to again assume civil jurisdiction over reservations because state and local governments have been burdening them with zoning laws, ordinances, and similar restrictions. But Public Law 280 today still remains vague and confused. Some tribes are now trying to extend their jurisdiction over non-Indians on their reservations.

Modern Policy

The most disastrous action of the 1950s was the termination policy. It was an attempt to assimilate Indians by withdrawal of federal trusteeship and was under the guidance of Senator Arthur Watkins of Utah and Secretary of the Interior Fred Seaton. Simply put, certain tribes were chosen to be terminated;

the process involved cutting the tribe off from federal jurisdiction and turning it over to the state. During the 1950s about 10,000 Indians were terminated. And in virtually every case, termination caused suffering and hardship. The Klamaths of Oregon had their reservation sold, while the Paiutes of Utah had their reservation placed in the hands of a guardian. The Menominees of Wisconsin were one of the most prosperous tribes of the 1950s; they had owned and operated a profitable commercial forest. When they were cut off from the federal government, the state of Wisconsin made them a county and forced them to finance county services. Almost overnight personal and tribal savings and tribal lands were lost. The State of Wisconsin then found that it had a huge increase in its welfare rolls and turned to the federal government for help. The Menominee Tribe, however, fought back and they were restored to tribal status by the Supreme Court in 1968. Termination was deemphasized in the late 1950s, but was not abandoned as a government policy until the arrival of President Kennedy, who agreed with many Indian leaders that it was another attempt to make Indians white. But many Indian leaders today feel termination is still a potential threat that the government could use at any time.

In the late 1950s the policy of relocation was instituted. Relocation was another attempt to hasten assimilation by taking Indians from reservations and bringing them into the cities. The result, supposedly, would be a well-adjusted urban Indian. Indians were chosen, taken off reservations, and brought to relocation centers. At these centers they received a little job training and then they were on their own. Many returned to the reservations, others remained in the cities as poor, urban Indians. Although Indians may not be suited to city life, the relocation program has been refined and continued up to today. Relocation centers are found in Los Angeles, San Francisco, Chicago, Phoenix, and Minneapolis. The 1950s posed a real threat to Indian life.

One positive policy of postwar America was the passage in 1946 of the Indian Claims Act. This act attempted to allow the Indian tribes to get some sort of fiscal settlement for the damages that they had suffered because of broken treaties and loss of land. Tribes could now file a suit against the federal government, which was heard by a special Indian Claims Commission. On paper it appeared that retribution was being made, but in action, it was a long, tedious, and confusing process for most tribes. While the government did settle some substantial Indian claims during the 1960s and 1970s, the effects of these claims, which were only paid in money, not land, brought few changes. Often much of the money went for the cost of the court case, while a large portion continued to be held in trust by the Bureau of Indian Affairs until the tribe decided how the money should be distributed. Real justice was not doled out by the Indian Claims Commission.

Presidents since Kennedy have often included the American Indian in their general philosophy of government. Kennedy, for example, was interested in social-welfare legislation and introduced new programs for education, housing, and economic development of reservations. Lyndon Johnson attempted to include Indians in his War on Poverty, since they were among America's poorest citizens. He appointed Robert Bennett, an Oneida Indian, Commissioner of Indian Affairs, and helped to speed up the economic development of reservations. Nixon's general decentralization of government powers slowed Indian programs. Although he spoke of Indian self-determination, he seemed to speak with a "forked tongue," because he did little in this direction. Termination was again talked about, and the Bureau of Indian Affairs was weakened. It is surprising that Ford, who pursued a balanced budget and limited government spending, greatly increased spending for Indian programs. The Indian Self-Determination Act of 1975 increased tribal governments' desires for self-sufficiency. The Indian Education Act placed much more emphasis on bilingual programs and tribal input. Indian programs in many departments of the government were expanded. Carter's Indian policy is still unclear. He has talked of working with the "full consent of tribal representation," but beyond an American Indian Policy Review Commission Report little has changed. Indian Affairs, however, were given a boost when Forrest J. Gerard became Interior assistant secretary for Indian affairs.

Prior to 1944, Indian organizations were small and regional. But it must be remembered that Indians already had their tribes, and tribes frequently hindered national Indian development. In 1944, in Denver, the National Congress of American Indians was formed; this, the oldest Indian organization, has frequently tried to help Indians adjust to white society, and it has become the lobby of American Indians in Washington. The National Indian Youth Council was formed in 1961; as a more active group they have been directly involved in hunting and fishing controversies, strip mining, and other related issues. During the 1960s and 1970s Indians across the country have formed a variety of regional organizations. One of the newest, and with a powerful weapon, is the Council of Energy Resources Tribes, which is attempting to utilize natural resources on Indian land. Today 50 percent of all uranium deposits are found on Indian land. These groups are usually directed at solving specific problems in economics, education, law, or business.

Red Power

Many of these organizations have become very much involved in an Indian revolution known as "red power." Red power is the movement of angry Indians striving for recognition in white society. Red Power activities since the early 1960s have involved fish-ins, the seizure of Alcatraz Island, blockades, marches, demonstrations, and sit-ins. Many of the successful techniques of black power have been adopted by modern Indian leaders. Red power first appeared when the Indians of Western Washington had a running battle with the State of Washington over their fishing rights and staged a fish-in. Tribes from all over the country, and white liberals, came to the shores of the Nisqually River to participate in the fish-in. National media coverage brought the event to television viewers, and white America began to realize that modern Indians were demanding their rights. The seizure of Alcatraz Island in November 1969 also made national headlines. Nearly 100 Indians, led by Lehman Brightman, used the Sioux treaty of 1868 to justify the seizure of the famous 12-acre rock in the middle of San Francisco Bay. For one and a half years the island became the Indians' Statue of Liberty. Flaming arrows were shot in the direction of tour boats; a totem pole was erected, and those on the island wore red armbands. In violation of an agreement with the government, the remaining occupants of the island were arrested and Alcatraz became federal property again. The occupying Indians had had plans for an Indian museum and national cultural center, but the plans were never put into action. Today the only visible residue of Indian occupation is a huge sign painted on one building that reads, "Red Power."

With the appearance of Dee Brown's book, *Bury My Heart at Wounded Knee* (1970), the white conscience became sympathetic to the Indians' plight. This movement was evident in books, movies, songs, and plays that appeared in the next few years. Movies such as *Soldier Blue, Little Big Man, Man Called Horse*, featured a new sympathetic perspective of Indian history. Indian jewelry became a popular commodity. National and local newspapers and magazines now covered Indian news. While most Americans felt sorry for the Chief Josephs of America's past, they still knew little about the modern Indian. In fact, many Americans still viewed Indians as a vanishing breed.

To bring to white America the aspirations of the modern Indian, red power continued. Red power leaders still believed that positive achievement could be accomplished only through publicity; and publicity was achieved by activities that were unusual, violent, or involved great numbers of people. Tribes continued to become active. The Pit River Indians of northern California attempted to take back the land which had been taken away from them. The Makah Indians of Washington State closed their beach front to the public. During the early 1970s the organization that captured national headlines was the American Indian Movement (A.I.M.), which was formed by Russell Means and Dennis Banks in 1968.

After some demonstrations in Custer, South Dakota, the organization sponsored a caravan to Washington called the Trail of Broken Treaties to present a 25-point program to President Nixon. In November 1972 they occupied the Bureau of Indian Affairs office, caused some damage, and were arrested and released. Later it was discovered that most of the destruction was done after they had left the building. On February 27, 1973, militants seized the tiny hamlet of Wounded Knee on the Pine Ridge Reservation in South Dakota. This occupation lasted from February 27 to May 8. During that period they attracted the attention of the country to their demands for a Senate investigation of the Bureau of Indian Affairs, a review of all treaties, and the ouster of Richard Wilson, who was then president of the Oglala Sioux tribe. While most Indians did not agree with the tactics of the A.I.M. group, they concurred with the basic goals of self-determination and preservation of Indian culture.

During the last few years Indians have continued to win some victories over white society. The charges against Russell Means and Dennis Banks stemming from the Wounded Knee occupation were dismissed. U.S. District Court Judge George Boldt ruled that the Washington Indians were entitled to

The Wounded Knee occupation of 1973 dramatized the plight of the modern American Indian.

exactly half the catch of salmon and steelhead trout yearly in the state. Leases with the Northern Cheyenne for strip mining of coal on their reservation were renegotiated to the tribe's benefit. In 1976 the Supreme Court ruled that Public Law 280 did not give the states the power to tax reservation Indians. The Passamaquoddy and Penobscot Indians of Maine have Department of Justice backing in their suit for more than one-fourth of the State of Maine. Other East Coast tribes have instituted similar suits. A Maine settlement has not yet been reached. In 1978 a group of nearly 200 Indians undertook the Longest Walk, traveling by foot about 3000 miles from San Francisco to Washington, D.C., to bring Indians together nationally and to protest the number of anti-Indian bills before Congress. These Indians and their supporters arrived in Washington, D.C., and held a week-long series of meetings.

But the white backlash has begun. The era of white conscience is over; Indian victories have caused congressional representatives to try to stem the advance of red power. Laws before Congress pose a real threat to Indians across the country. These laws would limit hunting and fishing rights, virtually take away any water rights, force termination of all tribes, limit suits against the federal government and states for land, and virtually stop Indian demonstra-

The Longest Walk of 1978 attempted to focus attention on anti-Indian legislation before Congress.

tions and protests. Considering the number of Indians in America, the Indian revolution has been successful. Yet Indians still suffer from the paternalism of the B.I.A. and from the shock of living in white America.

From the days of the Birmingham protests to the Indians' Long Walk, post-World War II America has been the scene of a movement toward minority awareness. Cries of racism and discrimination have been heard across the land and have been followed by national organizations with national leaders and programs. Successes have been achieved by all minorities; and while America is still a long way from being a melting pot, America the cultural mosaic is slowly becoming a reality. The majority culture here in America does not well accept the minority cultures; still majority and minority alike share in a mass American culture that has burgeoned in the twentieth century.

Essay

Helen Hunt Jackson and Dee Brown: Writers of Indian Sympathy

It was the end of the period of the Indian wars in the West; most of the Indians were now on reservations. Their culture was starting to quickly erode. The white man had pushed them from the East Coast to their entrenched, isolated ghettos throughout the West. The struggle between two cultures had come to an end. Newspapers carried reports of the Nez Perce War of 1877, in which Chief Joseph attempted to take his section of the tribe and flee to Canada. His ingenious retreat and the blunders of the United States Army made front-page news. His trek, however, was for naught; he was captured, and with the memorable words, "I will fight no more forever" surrendered. White society began to feel sorry for such a courageous warrior. At the same time, the Northern Cheyenne, who had been put on a reservation in Indian Territory (in what is today Oklahoma), left and headed for their homeland in the northern Plains. They were also pursued, and the American public again wondered why such wrongs were perpetuated against these people.

A writer, Helen Hunt Jackson, became as interested as many other Americans in the plight of "the noble red man." Tribe after tribe had been decimated or moved from place to place. She began to study more about the history of Indian policy and to investigate, in particular, the plight of the Poncas. Her research moved her pen to action, and in 1881 *A Century of Dis-*

honor appeared. It was the first detailed indictment of Indian policy, and it won wide public acceptance. Critics today tell us that her impassioned pleas may have distorted some facts of history, but, whatever the case, white society began to be moved to action. A white-conscience movement appeared. It was evident in national organizations and in conventions and meetings, which all focused on the plight of the Western Indians, trying to find a solution for their problems.

Most of the organizations that appeared in the 1880s were filled with sympathetic whites who truly felt they could help Indians in some way. They were all seeking some sort of answer to the Indians' problems, but few of them thought to ask the Indians what they really wanted. The National Indian Association was a female organization that was started in Philadelphia and then spread through the East. It decided to sponsor missions to the Indians and to lobby in Washington for better treatment. The Indian Citizenship Committee, which was centered in Boston, saw citizenship and political rights as the answer to the Indians' dilemma. The Indian Rights Association, which is still in existence, also emerged out of Philadelphia and was one of the most effective of the national organizations. It did detailed studies of the violation of Indian rights, which appeared in article and pamphlet form. One of the mainstream was the

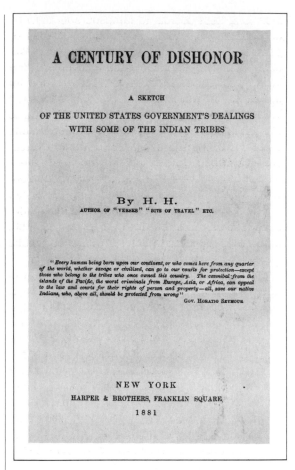

A CENTURY OF DISHONOR

A SKETCH

OF THE UNITED STATES GOVERNMENT'S DEALINGS
WITH SOME OF THE INDIAN TRIBES

By H. H.

AUTHOR OF "VERSES" "BITS OF TRAVEL" ETC.

"*Every human being born upon our continent, or who comes here from any quarter of the world, whether savage or civilised, can go to our courts for protection—except those who belong to the tribes who once owned this country. The cannibal from the islands of the Pacific, the worst criminals from Europe, Asia, or Africa, can appeal to the law and courts for their rights of person and property—all, save our native Indians, who, above all, should be protected from wrong*"

Gov. Horatio Seymour

NEW YORK
HARPER & BROTHERS, FRANKLIN SQUARE
1881

Helen Hunt Jackson's book was responsible for a white sympathy movement in the 1880s.

National Indian Defense Association, which attempted to get answers from the Indians themselves about their needs. Most of the organizations felt that the Indians' major problem was their native culture; if Indians could be mainstreamed into white society, their problems would be solved. The National Indian Defense Associ-

ation foresaw the need to protect Indian life and culture. Needless to say, in the 1880s this was not a very popular stand.

This decade also featured many national meetings with leading religious leaders and politicians who debated the alternatives facing the Indians and again sought solutions. The annual Lake Mohonk Conference of Quaker Albert K. Smiley was one of the significant meetings of this type; each year the meeting attracted leading Americans who came forth with new programs. Many of these suggestions were listened to very carefully in the halls of Congress. While there was a white-conscience movement in the late 1870s and 1880s, and while Jackson's book did much to publicize the plight of the American Indian, few Indians had input into programs for their future. The climax to this reform movement eventually came from Congress with the passage of the Dawes Act of 1887. The new law attempted to force assimilation upon Indians through the allotting of individual plots of land. The major result of this act, which lasted until 1934, was not the creation of a white Indian but the creation of a poor, ill-housed, and ill-fed Indian. The Dawes Act caused this first white-conscience movement to slowly fade into history.

Throughout much of the twentieth century white Americans thought little of, and cared less for, the American Indian. They still were isolated from white society; except during periods of wars there was little contact. After 1945 Indians began to leave reservations in large numbers, giving birth to an urban population that still is increasing rapidly in size and strength. After World War II Indians also began to form national groups and to lobby for Indian causes. Some of the most effective groups were organized in the 1960s and were part of a movement called red power. Politically active Indians made national headlines with a fish-in in Washington State and the seizure of Alcatraz Island. But many Americans equated these movements with black power and brown power and paid little attention.

In 1970 a book appeared that caused quite a stir among the American public. Dee Brown, a librarian and a writer on Western themes, presented an Indian history of the West in *Bury My Heart At Wounded Knee.* It was the story of the Wars of the West from a supposed Indian perspective, which focused sympathetically on the Warrior's last stand. The book became a best seller and was at the top of the chart for months. White America, which had heard of the Indian movement of the 1960s and had seen a few Hollywood movies, now once again was moved to sympathy for the Indian in American history; another white-conscience movement began to form.

But this movement was unlike the early movements of the 1800s; it was not limited to white society but had instead a parallel side in the idea of red power. This modern awakening to the mistreatment of Indians was much more commercialized than the first movement had ever been. Hollywood movies continued to appear and to portray the Indian as the victim of white aggression. Indian jewelry became increasingly popular. Songs such as "Cherokee Reservation" and "Half Breed" were at the top of the charts. Not only white singers but Indian singers like Buffy St. Marie received acceptance for their Native-American themes. The media featured stories on past Indian leaders and on the modern movement. A growing list of books were written on Indian subjects which ranged from interviews with elderly Indians who told their long kept secrets to fantastic speculations on possible visits to ancient Indian societies by people from outer space. Meanwhile red power continued. The American Indian Movement rose in the Midwest and took a very active stand for Indian rights. Not long after the Trail of Broken Treaties trek to Washington, D.C., which led to the occupation of the Bureau of Indian Affairs office there, the site of the 1890 Indian massacre—Wounded Knee, located on the Oglala Sioux reservation of Pine Ridge—was occupied. When one of the occupation leaders was asked why they had chosen Wounded Knee for the occupation, he referred to Dee Brown's book, which had done so much to influence public feeling about the American Indian.

As with the white-conscience movement of the 1880s, the movement of the 1970s was not long lasting. By the late 1970s a white backlash was developing in response to the victories Indians were achieving over white society. Maine Indians had won back their ancestral land; other Indians had won important court fights over commercial-fishing rights. Indian claims settlements arising from past damages were giving some tribes sizeable treasuries. Some members of Congress began to introduce legislature that would limit such Indian activity and return to the past status quo.

Helen Hunt Jackson and Dee Brown are both writers who were catalysts of a movement of white conscience. Both recognized the way that Indians had been treated and described their treatment as they saw it. Their books became influential and caused Americans to once again reexamine their past and perhaps apply those past lessons to the present. ■

Suggested Reading

LOUIS E. LOMAX gives a general treatment of the civil-rights movement in *The Negro Revolt* (1963). An insight into black militancy is found in MALCOLM X's *The Autobiography of Malcom X* (1966). MARTIN LUTHER KING, JR., in *Why We Can't Wait* (1964), tells of the struggles of the 1960s, while S. A. LEVITAN, in *Still a Dream: The Changing Status of Blacks Since 1960* (1975), updates the black movement.

A general overview of the Mexican-American movement is available in *The Chicanos* (1972) by MATT S. MEIER and FELICIANO RIVERA and *La Raza* (1970) by STAN STEINER. JOHN GREGORY DUNNE in *Delano* (1971) and PETER MATTHIESSEN in *Sal Si Puedes: Cesar Chavez and the New American Revolution* (1969) cover the rise of Cesar Chavez.

STAN STEINER discusses the rise of red power in his book *The New Indians* (1968). Editor ALVIN JOSEPHY presents an excellent collection of documents in his book *Red Power* (1971). EDGAR CAHN examines various aspects of the American Indian in modern society in *My Brother's Keeper* (1970). VINE DE LORIA, JR., offers a critique of the modern Indian movement in *Custer Died For Your Sins* (1969).

CHAPTER 17

Mass Culture for a Mass Society: Twentieth-Century American Culture

Time Line

?–A.D. 1492	Migration and evolution of American Indian societies
1492	Christopher Columbus lands in West Indies—beginning of European exploration
1607–1732	Establishment of 13 English colonies
1775–1783	American Revolution
1776	Declaration of Independence
1789–1797	Presidency of George Washington
1812–1815	War of 1812
1816–1824	Era of Good Feelings
1846–1848	Mexican War
1861–1865	Civil War
1865–1877	Reconstruction
1877–1900	Industrialization and urbanization
1900–1916	Progressive Era
1917–1918	World War I
1919	Nineteenth Amendment ratified
1925	Scopes Trial
1927	Publication of *Middletown* Charles Lindbergh's crossing of the Atlantic
1928	*The Jazz Singer* brings talking movies to the silver screen
1939	*Gone with the Wind* achieves new technical breakthroughs in moviemaking
1949	Housing Act is passed
1950	Formation of the National Council of Churches

1955	Development of Salk vaccine
1960	*Silent Spring* appears
1961	President's Commission on the Status of Women is established
1969	First Moon Landing achieved by Americans
1970	Earth Day celebration National Environmental Policy Act
1976	*Viking* landing on Mars
1977	Mini-series *Roots* attracts largest television audience in history
1930s	Depression and New Deal
1941–1945	World War II
1945–1960	Post-war politics
1950–1953	Korean War
1950–1960	Civil rights movement
1961–1973	Vietnam War
1976	Bicentennial celebration

Mass Culture for a Mass Society: Twentieth-Century American Culture

One night at a party in suburban America, two men got in a very heated discussion over what constituted modern American culture. If these men had only taken a careful look at themselves they would have come very close to an answer. Both men work downtown and commute to their jobs in new compact cars; they frequently eat out at fast-food restaurants, and one of the men even attends a drive-in church. When they bank, they always use the drive-up window. They constantly complain about the frustration of their growing metropolis, which is getting larger each year. In fact, just last week the city issued another smog alert. On the way to work yesterday one of the men drove past a group of Hare Krishna followers who were having a fierce debate with some Jesus people. Both men are college graduates and expect their children to attend college. Much of their time at home is spent watching television, reading newspapers, or reading paperback best sellers dealing with sex, dieting, and politics. On weekends they take their wives to a movie, play, or a sporting event. Their wives both hold part-time jobs and are very active in church groups and the school P.T.A. Just before Christmas, the wives debated whether to get a new videorecorder, a microwave oven, or please the children with the newest electronic game. And there these men were in the midst of a party in twentieth-century America trying to define modern culture.

Modern American culture is many things to many people. It is the large corporation, which virtually has engulfed small businesses and has standardized consumer tastes. It is the metropolis, which is quickly becoming a megalopolis. Pollution fills the air and the streams. The women's movement is concerned with the Equal Rights Amendment, but that is not their only concern. Religion is a polyglot of traditional and nontraditional faiths, all seeking that path to ultimate happiness. Science has improved our daily lives and even led us to the moon and beyond. Mass education is coming under severe stress; money for education is increasingly scarce, while college graduates no longer are automatically assured the careers and goals they dream of. Serious and popular literature is available for all groups on any subject ranging from racquetball to sex therapy. And with our increased leisure time, mass amusements play a major role in our lives. Movies, theater, music, television, games, spectator sports, participant sports, vacations, miniature golf, horseback riding, all bombard our senses and compete for that all-important dollar, which has made mass amusements big business. The evolution of American culture in the twentieth century is the growth of a mass culture for a mass society.

The Corporate State

At the heart of modern culture is the American corporation. Small businesses now represent a very small percentage of our national income and productivity. Of course, most corporations are very much attuned to modern consumers, who spend more of their income on cars than on state and local governments. The trend toward the corporate state really began in the 1920s with the restructuring of corporate administrations, technological advances, and specialization. Henry Ford brought assembly-line production to America in 1913, and it has been with us ever since. Off the assembly line came the Model-T Ford—in any color, as long as you wanted black. While Ford brought a new form of industrial mobility to corporations, the automobile brought a new mobility to the masses. After the automobile revolution of the 1920s, American life would never be the same. Think of all the related businesses today directly tied to the automobile. From road building to gas stations to motels to auto shops to tire dealers, the list could go on and on. It is amazing how quickly the automobile caught on. A product that most Americans would soon be able to afford, by 1928 Hoover was already promising a day when every American would own two cars. By 1930 there were over 26.5 million cars. All across America the landscape became dotted with highways, traffic signals, drive-in restaurants, drive-in banks, drive-in theaters, and, in California, drive-in churches. Of course, the changes in society had a tremendous impact: the flight to the suburbs was increased, courting moved from the front porch to the automobile, Sunday drives were commonplace, and the desire for vacations heightened.

The automobile industry was not the only industry that participated in the consumer revolution of the 1920s. Homes now contained vacuum cleaners, washing machines, electric refrigerators, and radios. And the credit card came into its own; Americans purchased items on the installment plan: a low down-payment and small monthly payments plus concurrent interest. The credit-card society was taking root. Along with mass production and mass sales came advertising. Before the 1920s mass advertising was virtually nonexistent; now advertising agents sprang up to convince willing Americans to spend money and then spend some more. Would you want to be the only one in your neighborhood without a vacuum cleaner? How about keeping up with the Joneses? or Smiths? or Johnsons? Flyers featuring girls in bathing suits told of property in Florida. Advertising came at a good time because it provided employment for many writers, models, and photographers, and it also kept many magazines and newspapers publishing. The end result was a revolution of rising expectations that made the luxuries of yesterday the necessities of today. More and more control of the market came into the hands of the large corporations.

Needless to say, the 1930s and the Great Depression were not the best time for American business, but World War II brought a new prosperity. After

Mass advertising appeared in the 1920s and a
consumer revolution was born.

the war big business became bigger and "affluent America" was just around
the corner. Production rose drastically, as did prices, but wages frequently
lagged behind. By the 1950s and 1960s self-employed persons were quite unusual; the majority of workers were employed by large corporations. By the
late 1950s the income of more than eight corporations exceeded that of any
state or city government in America. By the end of the next decade 4 percent
of the corporations controlled nearly 74 percent of all corporate income. The
bigness of business was almost overwhelming. American Telephone and Telegraph employed more individuals than the combined total of 29 state governments, while General Motors had more income than 30 states. The dominant growth industries at any given time have varied from airplanes to
electronics to computers. American Airlines, United Airlines, R.C.A., Zenith,
Sony, I.B.M., all have become household words that hold a prominent place
on the stock market charts. Americans frequently see the positive side of
corporate largeness: more selection of products, new technology, and a variety
of marketing techniques. But there is also a negative side: automation, infe-
rior-quality products, and planned obsolescence. Lifetime guarantees are vir-

tually a thing of the past. New models in automobiles appear yearly. New gadgets are added to electronic equipment. You are programmed to keep up with the new styles and new gadgets—and spend money doing so.

What happened to the old gospel of wealth? Well, it was replaced with a new gospel of wealth. Large corporations frequently are looking for tax write-offs; foundations are created and funds are provided for medical research, science, and education. Consider the Ford foundation: more than $160 million each year is spent for these types of projects. But the amount of generosity has varied with the changes in the tax laws. Other new features of the modern corporation are the separation of ownership from management and the evolution of the corporate executive. Carnegie was a local boy who made good; today the local boy (or girl) is one who went to college, graduated with a degree in business administration, and worked his way up the administrative ladder. Once at the top, the corporate executive's influence over the habits and tastes of American consumers is extraordinary. Television-network executives, for example, experiment with popular taste. In the early 1970s "All in the Family" seemed to be a bold experiment; today the program choices run from "Charle's Angels" to "Alice" to "Good Times" to "Soap." Along with foundations and corporate executives came increased installment buying. Master Charge, American Express, and VISA have become the cash of today. Buy today and pay tomorrow has become the slogan of most Americans. Since World War II installment sales have increased over 500 percent. More sophisticated advertising with fewer racial stereotypes and sexist overtones has persuaded millions of Americans to buy this or that. Vance Packard in the book *Hidden Persuaders* even exposed the use of subliminal advertising, while other writers have analyzed magazine ads and found in a glass of scotch everything from a hidden vestal virgin to a secret four-letter word.

Critics of Modern Business

John Kenneth Galbriath, in his books *The Affluent Society* and *The New Industrial State*, has shown the influence of modern corporations. There is no doubt that America is under their domination. Franchises of successful businesses have become a common form of national expansion. Hamburger chains, ice-cream stores, 24-hour convenience stores, and more are springing up. Large supermarkets, chain stores, and discount stores are becoming more and more a part of normal living. Many Americans are asking what responsibility these corporations have to American citizens and what restraints should government place on them. Many of these corporations are responding to these questions with new technology geared to the modern environment. General Electric is experimenting with windmills as alternate sources of energy. Goodyear Tire is experimenting with tires that will reduce fuel consumption. Union Carbide is attempting to convert coal into oil. Ralph Nader and his "raiders" have been the most effective modern muckrakers in their attempts to protect American consumers. For years Nader has pointed out business malpractices and demanded investigations. When William C. Coleman, Jr., President Ford's secretary of transportation, delayed the installation of air bags for automobile safety, Nader called the decision "irresponsible and horrendous" and attempted to get congressional action. In 1977, however, Nader suffered one of his greatest defeats when Congress refused to establish a national consumer agency, which he had been fighting for throughout the 1970s.

Other critics of corporate America have claimed the existence of "power elite" and talked of a "military-industrial complex." It is true that in recent years defense spending has taken a sizeable chunk of the national budget and that business prospers in time of war. But the presidents of the 1970s have listened more carefully to the corporate critics and have been much more critical of increased defense spending and defense research. In fact, over the last few years defense spending has occupied a smaller percentage of the Gross National Product.

One of the newest trends in American business is the formation of the multinational corporation. Many American industrial giants have spread to all corners of the world. Often foreign countries resent the intrusion, but the increased prosperity which is the result of such foreign expansion is well accepted. Many American corporations are using foreign labor. Even certain Saturday-morning cartoons are being drawn abroad. Since the 1950s, the cost of American labor has risen to such a point that corporations find their profit margin declining and feel forced to turn elsewhere for a cheap supply of labor. Powerful national unions and their potent strike weapons have brought about wage increases plus numerous employee benefits. Business and the products of business are everywhere you turn. Computers control scoreboards at sporting events; computers are used for most college registrations. New computerized cash registers are used at food markets. This domination of American life by industrial giants has gone hand in hand with the growth of the twentieth-century city.

Cities and Urban Politics

The census of 1920 revealed that most Americans now lived in cities. The census of 1890 had signaled that the frontier was closed; 30 years later America emerged as a land of cities. The farm heritage of America, however, was difficult to leave behind. For years stories were circulated of sin in the cities and of the innocence of country people. But the traditional, agrarian way of life was on the way out. The 1920s even saw the decline of the small farm and the rise of agricultural business. The new technology and consumer revolution coupled with the widespread use of the automobile further changed the composition of the growing city. Patterns of settlement changed. The flight to the suburbs brought with it the accompanying move of stores and industry. For example, the Country Club Plaza Shopping Center in Kansas City became the model for the suburban shopping center. City planners now had to facilitate movement from the suburbs to the city more easily. Speed limits were introduced; traffic lights became widespread. Parking spaces were added; highways became a national and state concern. Fast-growing suburbs, such as Beverly Hills and Inglewood near Los Angeles and Elmwood Park near Chicago, demanded city services; eventually new metropolitan districts were formed combining the city and its surrounding suburbs. Meanwhile downtown property began to rise in value; it became too expensive and wasteful to build simple structures in those areas. The 1920s saw the birth of skyscrapers, which soared upward to the sky and brought to city fathers a sense of civic pride.

The Great Depression brought an immediate end to city prosperity and, in many cases, caused city bankruptcy. The city of Atlanta began to print its own script to pay its public employees. The demand for increased economy was met through consolidation; in many cities, departments of parks and recreation were merged. In other cities, county and city administrations became one. Relief was difficult, for cities were running out of funds. Cities for the first time in history looked to the nation's capital for help, but President Hoover offered little. President Roosevelt, however, accepted the fact that large urban centers were the American way of life and that many of his programs should be geared to relief and recovery for urban dwellers. The federal government's efforts at city planning were also renewed.

Out of the New Deal came a national urban policy. The old functions of the city bosses, which included creating jobs through public projects, now were assumed by city and federal governments. Many city mayors became social reformers. Fiorello LaGuardia, mayor of New York, started programs for public works and slum clearance. By the 1930s the federal government was involved in a federal study of urban life, which urged the federal government to pay more attention to urban citizens and proposed public housing for low-income groups, more welfare services, abolition of slums, and more responsive local government. By the 1940s the federal commitment to the cities was growing; but two major problems were on the horizon: (1) the middle class exodus to the suburbs, and (2) the growing decay of the inner or "core" city.

By the 1970s more Americans lived in suburbs (76 million) than in cities (64 million). Since World War II, the growth of suburban America has been incredible. The demand for suburban housing and the availability of liberal housing loans for a time created a construction boom, which still is underway in many major metropolitan areas. Businesses and services have followed the movement outward. Shopping malls and plazas have hurt the tradition of shopping in the downtown area. City and county offices and financial centers often are still downtown; but retail-shopping facilities now are found in modernistic malls with franchised shops, which offer a wide range of products at a wide range of prices. But the dream of modern America—a land of suburbs and exciting living—has not really been fulfilled. The man in the gray flannel suit may have changed his suit to tweed, but he still complains about the sterility of life in the suburbs (where you can open your back door and hit the front of a house behind you). In many major cities, land developers have made

The majority of Americans now live in suburbs instead of cities.

tremendous profits at the cost of crowded suburbs with few parks, recreation areas, or green belts.

With the movement of the masses to the suburbs, the central city was left to minorities and the poor. In 1968 the National Advisory Commission on Civil Disorders stated that by 1985 more than 13 cities would have populations with blacks in the majority and that 10 other cities would have black majorities in the schools. The obvious trend is toward black central cities surrounded by white suburbs or satellite cities. This poses immense problems for city planners, who now seek to integrate schools and revive downtown regions.

Problems of Modern Cities

Public housing and urban renewal are attempts to change the picture of the deteriorating central city. The Housing Act of 1937 authorized local housing authorities to demolish slum buildings and build public housing for low rentals, with the federal government supplying rent subsidies. The Housing Act of 1949 continued the process and provided public-housing money and moving expenses for persons displaced by slum clearance. Slum clearance and urban renewal go hand in hand. Urban renewal has involved programs of local, state, and federal governments to increase low-cost housing, eliminate slums, and revitalize the central city. This has been a major undertaking with some results. In the 1960s, cities such as Pittsburgh proved that downtown renovation was possible. In the 1970s, urban renewal has been coupled with a growing middle-class disillusionment with the suburbs and a slow movement back to the central city. While this movement back is not overwhelming, it is noticeable. In Baltimore and Washington, D.C., home buyers' demands for downtown property have increased. In addition, many cities are undergoing substantial building booms in downtown areas. Chicago has constructed two-dozen new skyscrapers, while the Renaissance Center in Detroit, an impressive business-hotel-shopping complex, is a sight to behold. New statistics reveal that while increasing real-estate costs in the suburbs have pushed many white-middle-class people back to the city, the rising black middle class has begun to leave the city in large numbers. What this will mean for the central city in the 1980s is difficult to predict.

Since World War II the federal government's basic position toward the city has been inconsistent. Federal policies have wavered between encouraging cities to solve their own problems and assuming federal responsibility for urban affairs. Eisenhower in the 1950s stimulated city-controlled programs combined with some federal assistance: he also initiated the building of interstate highways with federal aid. Now the federal government is paying

Mass Culture for a Mass Society: Twentieth-Century American Culture

Urban renewal has involved the revitalization of the central city.

more than 90 percent of freeway construction costs. Presidents Kennedy and Johnson both mounted a direct attack on urban problems with some measure of success. Nixon once again reduced the role of the federal government in the city; he slashed the programs of the two previous Democratic administrations. Nixon's philosophy was New Federalism—the return of policy decision-making to state and local levels with revenue sharing, the distribution of federal funds, going directly to local governments. Although the plan did not fulfill its expectations, the program has been extended.

But a new problem has plagued the cities, and that is possible bankruptcy. New York City, weighed down by billions of dollars in debts, barely escaped bankruptcy in 1975; the federal government under Ford came to the rescue with $2.3 billion in short-term loans to the city. New York's problem then spread to Cleveland. In late 1978 the city defaulted on loans amounting to $15.5 million. Cleveland has continued to teeter on the verge of bankruptcy— the first city to default since the depression. Other cities fear Cleveland's fate, but they expect little further help from the federal government. President Carter has indicated very clearly that cities cannot count on the federal government to bail out their deficits. Yet Carter has not been completely inactive. His Urban Development Action Grant plan has stimulated more than $3 billion in private investment in the cities.

While urban analysts foresee the growth of future megalopolises, which will encompass super-cities such as two that may stretch from San Francisco to San Diego and from Boston to Washington, D.C., the problems of the cities mount. Many of the problems of the central city followed the middle-class exodus to the suburbs. Urban wealth has become increasingly concentrated there (with rising suburban-crime rates as a spin-off). Cities are now talking of cutting necessary services, laying off more workers, and putting off essential city repairs. Many Americans are now beginning to ask the question: Is the city really the best place to live? But the alternative is not clear. In the 1960s and early 1970s, youth groups known as communes attempted projects in experimental living outside the city, but few of these groups now remain. One of the major problems with the urban environment has been pollution; the ecology movement has attempted to counter this evil.

Ecology

The roots of the ecology movement are found among the conservationists. Ecology activists believe that all nature must be in balance and that all living things on this earth have a definite relationship to the environment and each other. This delicate balance must be preserved; severe imbalance can lead to the destruction of the natural cycle and even to the end of mankind itself. Conservationists George Marsh and Aldo Leopold saw the importance of the balance between man and nature. Marsh, in his book *Man and Nature*, referred to man's wasteful policies, which are threatening the survival of the environment. Leopold, a naturalist, argued for more than just a policy of conserving the natural environment; he felt a new national ethic toward the entire environment must be adopted.

The conservation movement lost its momentum during World War II. Truman and Eisenhower did little to restore that momentum. Truman had plans to expand the T.V.A. to other areas; but Congress frustrated that goal. Eisenhower spent little time trying to define a consistent conservation policy, but Congress did authorize the creation of the St. Lawrence Seaway under his leadership. In 1960, Rachael Carson published *Silent Spring*, a damaging indictment of the pesticide industry and its effects on the environment. The public at first did not respond to this attack, but then the pesticide industry rose to defend itself. A new crusade was on and this book proved to be the catalyst.

The transition from conservation to the ecology movement really began during the 1960s. President Kennedy began to deliver conservation speeches warning of environmental decay. Initially these speeches brought a yawn from the audience, but then they slowly began to take notice. By 1968 the environment had become a campaign issue, but not a very hot one. It was not really until Nixon's state of the union address in 1970, in which he referred to the environment as one of the major issues of the 1970s, that Americans began to jump on the ecological bandwagon.

While the federal government began to deal with the issue of the environment in the 1970s, ecology went beyond the federal government. It touched upon the quality of life of every American; and by the 1970s the results of environmental decay were everywhere—smog made your eyes water, food was filled with preservatives and pesticides, even diet drinks were no longer safe, smells of industrial smoke or automobile exhaust filled the air, and the noise of traffic, jet airplanes, and the nearby disco constantly bombarded the ear. The environment became a major social priority. One California Democrat noted in the early 1970s that "ecology" had become "the political substitute for the word 'mother'." On April 22, 1970, Americans gathered to celebrate the first Earth day, a day for serious discussion of environmental problems, filled with lectures, seminars, and community-action programs. One critic wrote, "If Nixon's war on pollution is as successful as Johnson's war on poverty, we're going to have an awful lot of dirty people around." But the nation

Clean air is the goal of the ecology movement, but this view of Chicago shows that air pollution will not easily be eradicated.

did take the ecology movement to heart. Popular literature pictured the human being's ultimate demise; *Time* magazine introduced to its format an environmental section. Paul Ehrlich and his Zero Population Growth group believed that it was irresponsible to bring more than two children into this decaying world. Increasing technology was leading to a world where, someday, the last man on earth would unplug his videorecorder, shut off the microwave, put his electronic car in the garage, and then breathe his last dirty breath.

An Energy Program

By the 1970s ecology was an issue which both right and left could espouse. And since Nixon's presidency, it has been an issue over which the president and Congress have constantly waged war. In 1970 Nixon signed the National Environmental Policy Act, which established as national policy the encouragement of environmental protection and the preservation of natural resources. Ecology had now become federal policy; while it encompassed the conservation movement, it was one step beyond. This act also created a three-member council of environmental advisers to constantly keep abreast of the state of the environment and make recommendations. Nixon continued to talk of necessary laws for water and land control, solid waste management, and park and public recreation lands. Congress also began to point the finger at the automobile and the automobile industry as major offenders in fouling the air.

The Environmental Protection Agency saw to it that automobile manufacturers were required to meet certain emission standards. While manufacturers protested, emission controls became standard equipment on all new automobiles. The Federal Water Pollution Control Act also regulated the discharging of materials into bodies of water and began to prove effective. But the ecology movement met a real stumbling block in the energy crisis of 1973. For years Americans had believed that low-cost energy was endless; this belief came to a quick halt when Nixon announced an energy shortage and proposed voluntary and congressional action to conserve energy. The 55-mile-an-hour speed limit was imposed upon the nation's freeways; Americans were told to turn their thermostats down; and millions of Americans waited in long lines at gasoline stations. The strict environmental standards that were being imposed helped stimulate the energy crisis. As energy conservation became a national campaign, many ecologists felt that they had been sold out.

Ecologists continued to criticize government environmental policy under President Ford. Ford felt that the energy crisis could be met through economic and industrial growth, which threatened to compromise the environmental standards of the early 1970s. Ford did propose Project Interdependence, which was a world program of energy conservation, and he formed the Energy Resources Council to determine the national energy policy. He further proposed that the federal government spend more than $100 billion to develop new energy resources.

The fight between ecologists and energy developers continued. In 1977 a proposition in California that would have expanded the development of nuclear power was defeated. The building of the Alaska oil-pipeline came under constant criticism for environmental destruction. The Council on Environmental Quality announced in 1977 that air pollution was being successfully cleaned up, but water-pollution progress still lagged far behind. Yet many Americans have changed their basic wasteful habits already, and new projects are now coming under constant scrutiny.

Carter's creation of the Department of Energy showed that the federal government had finally made a serious commitment toward the environment. Carter proposed further strong conservation measures, including restrictions on large automobiles and a reduced use of energy. His environmental message to Congress promised a stricter enforcement of existing laws and new controls to improve air and water pollution. One listener wrote that this report "represents the sharpest shift in policy on environmental matters since Teddy Roosevelt." The United States has a long way to go to balance energy needs, industrial growth, new technology, and conservationist demands, but it is on the road to recovery.

The Modern Woman

Progressivism had involved a philosophy of change under the direction of the federal government. One area that needed drastic revision was that of the woman's role in society. The breakdown of the values of the late 1800s and the search for new answers to age-old problems led to the rise of the womens' suffrage movement and to certain women reformers. Mary Baker Eddy, Charlotte Perkins Gilman, and Margaret Sanger each viewed the problems of twentieth-century America in terms of the modern woman. Mary Baker Eddy was responsible for the formation of a new American church known as the church of Christian Science. Charlotte Perkins Gilman wrote critical attacks on the traditional role that women play in America; she was forerunner of the modern feminist movement. Margaret Sanger was a leader in the campaign for birth control. She wrote about the tragedy of unwanted children and unwanted motherhood, but she was too far ahead of her time and achieved little success.

In 1890 the National American Women's Suffrage Association was formed. Under the leadership of Susan B. Anthony, Carrie Chapman Catt, and Anna Howard Shaw this organization concentrated on getting women's suffrage laws passed on state levels. While their initial victories were few, they persisted in attracting women from all walks of life and in forming a potent political organization. By 1912 nine Western states had allowed women to vote. A split in the original women's suffrage organization caused the formation of the National Women's Party under the leadership of Alice Paul. Now a twofold drive was being pressed. Pressure continued on states for passage of women's suffrage laws, while the National Women's Party attempted to bring direct pressure on President Wilson that would lead to the passage of a federal amendment to the constitution.

Women's pickets appeared around the White House. Representative Jeannette Rankin from Montana became the first woman in Congress. With America at war, the pickets continued to march. The women's lives were threatened, and women were arrested. In jail they resorted to hunger strikes to keep up the attention from the media; the arrests were finally invalidated by the courts. During this time women across America once again contributed to the war cause, stepping into jobs that would have been unavailable to them in peacetime. The involvement of women in the war effort coupled with increased militant activity caused a change in public opinion. In 1918 Wilson endorsed a federal amendment that would give women the right to vote; it passed the House and went to the states for ratification in 1919. In 1920 the necessary 35 states had ratified and suffrage had been won. It had been a long, hard fight, but one which brought an important advance in women's rights.

The women's vote, however, did not bring immediate changes to women's roles in society; in fact, relatively few women voted, and, when they did, they voted along party lines. (Even today relatively few women hold political offices.) The real changes in the feminist movement came in the years after World War II. During that war women helped with the mobilization of the nation and held many crucial jobs. Still, when the nation went back to peacetime, women went back to the homes.

The ideal woman of the 1950s was the mother who waited at home for her man. She was supposed to enjoy doing the housework, the cooking and sewing, and to feel she was put on this earth to please her husband to to care for her children. But the ideal dream came under attack with the publication of Betty Freidan's book *The Feminine Mystique* (1963), which attacked society's treatment of women as second-class citizens. While the National Woman's Party was still in existence, a group of women in 1966 joined with Freidan to form the National Organization for Women (N.O.W.). This feminist

Chart 17-1
The Working Woman

Year	Number Working	Percent of Working Force
1950	17,795,000	31.4%
1960	22,516,000	34.8%
1970	31,233,000	42.6%

group initially was considered militant because of its opposition to sex discrimination in all walks of American life. And it saw some successes in the 1960s (see Chart 17-1).

John Kennedy in 1961 established the President's Commission on the Status of Women, which issued a report on the economic and legal discrimination of women, but which did not recommend that the Democratic party push for an equal rights amendment. An equal rights amendment had been the goal of many women's groups since the 1920s and was now again an active issue in the 1960s. Kennedy did react to the report with the establishment of the Citizens' Advisory Council on the Status of Women, whose recommendations have not always been listened to. The Equal Pay Act of 1963 required the same pay for men and women for equal work performed. And the Civil Rights Act of 1964 prohibited discrimination in employment on the basis of sex. Under these new measures, women made some gains, achieving increased wages and entering fields usually only occupied by men such as telephone installation, police work, and sports such as basketball and race-car driving.

While women's groups continued to push for the Equal Rights Amendment, the N.O.W. organization organized a strike for equality in 1970 with the slogan, "Don't Iron while the Strike is Hot!" Still, the N.O.W. group seemed to be attracting a majority of professional women, who were attempting to bring change by working within the system. Other militant groups began to appear. More open attacks on "all-male" clubs were instituted. In 1972 writer Gloria Steinem, with assistance from the Ford Foundation, was able to publish the magazine *Ms.*, which stressed feminist reporting. This magazine gave new hope to women; it also made increasingly popular the term "Ms." rather than "Mrs." The magazine featured women's awareness articles, and it continually exposed sexist advertising, which still was evident. Feminists believed they had the right to make their own decisions about their own bodies, including the choices of birth control and abortion. In 1973 the

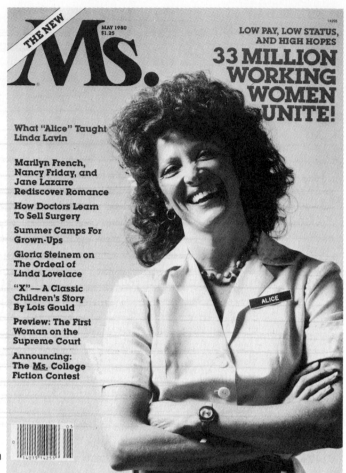

Ms magazine provides a feminist approach to news.

Supreme Court ruled—in a significant case for the women's movement—that state abortion restrictions were illegal. In 1978 a woman in Salem, Oregon, sued her husband for rape; while the man was found innocent, this was another step in the growing feminist awareness.

Even with rapidly growing radical fringe groups, N.O.W. was able to pressure Congress into passing the Equal Rights Amendment, which stated that "equality of rights under the law shall not be denied or abridged by the United States or by any State on account of sex." But congressional approval was only one hurdle. Ratification by three-fourths of the states was also required. While

The ERA supporters received an extension in their ratification fight, but victory is still a long way from being achieved.

the ratification struggle was easy in some states, the amendment eventually bogged down and was stalled. But advocates of the amendment got an extension in 1978 from Congress to continue the ratification fight. Supporters of the amendment, however, today admit that ratification may be an impossible dream.

Since the early days of the twentieth century the position of women in American society has changed dramatically. The suffrage struggle created a new feminist militancy, which was renewed in the 1960s and is continued today. The traditional role of women has come under severe pressure. Some critics of the feminist movement fear the possibility of women being drafted during wartime; but overall, with the victories that have been achieved, the future looks bright for equality of the sexes.

Modern Religion

Religion in twentieth-century America has undergone many transformations. Although churches indicate that memberships have grown substantially in this period, active church participation has declined. Sunday is no longer a day reserved for religion. It is now a family day filled with outings, picnics, drives in the country, and television sports. Events of the twentieth century—including two world wars, the birth of the atomic age, increasing divorce rates, and changing moral standards—have challenged traditional religion. Yet religion has held its own and attempted to respond to these changes.

The struggle between religious traditionalists and liberals, which started with the writings of Darwin, intensified in the 1900s. The liberals, or modernists, attempted to reconcile religion with modern thought; the conservatives, or fundamentalists, insisted that religion must not change, even though society had. During World War I the fundamentalists formed the World Christian Fundamental Association in Philadelphia, which called for a complete ouster of all modernist doctrine and a more careful scrutiny of religious leaders and their preaching. This organization further flamed the controversy, which affected all denominations but was most evident among Baptists and Presbyterians.

One focus of this controversy was the teaching of evolution in high school science classes. This controversy reached a climax with the Scopes trial of July 1925. John Scopes, a young biology teacher in Dayton, Tennessee, had taught the theory of evolution in his high school biology class in violation of a Tennessee law that banned such a practice. William Jennings Bryan, three-time loser for president, who was prosecuting the case became the voice of fundamentalism, while able Clarence Darrow defended Scopes. The trial became a struggle between Darrow and Bryan. Arrogant Darrow forced Bryan to adopt such a literal interpretation of the Bible that it made Bryan's brand of religion look silly. While the fundamentalists technically won this particular case and also forced the passage of a few antievolutionist laws in other states, they were the ultimate losers. Millions of Americans now questioned traditional religion and the fundamentalist viewpoint. The controversy was stilled during the depression and World War II, but fundamentalist Protestantism and organized religion in general had suffered a real blow.

The Scopes Trial featured a struggle between the modernist and fundamentalist approach to religion.

During the depression many Americans turned to God as an answer to their problems. All religions saw an increase in membership and a growth in active participation. It also was during the 1930s that a theological revival was taking place that redefined man's relationship to God. Swiss theologian Karl Barth saw Jesus Christ as the major source of God's message to man, while Paul Tillich stressed the importance of religion to human existence. Key theological issues again were raised and debated. These controversies continued to stimulate interest in organized religion. More and more Bible-study groups were formed, and after World War II America entered a period of real religious awakening.

The Great Depression, World War II, and the atomic bomb caused Americans to seek answers, and these answers were found in churches. Evangelists who considered themselves fundamentalists helped lead this revival. The National Association of Evangelicals and Youth for Christ were active. The Youth for Christ had recruited an itinerant evangelist named Billy Graham, who became a national personality by the 1950s. He offered to religion what Eisenhower had offered to politics, a moderate, conservative approach. Americans had not yet recovered from the shock of the war and the dawning atomic age, when the Korean War was upon them, and Joseph McCarthy was urging them to look under beds for Communists. Graham offered them a new peace of mind, he stated, "If you would be a true patriot, then become a Christian." Religion became patriotic. Graham was one of the first religious leaders with mass appeal to take advantage of the electronic media: radio and television. His "Hour of Decision" programs were heard by millions of Americans.

During this time, the Pledge of Allegiance was amended to include the words "under God." Meanwhile the National Council of Churches offered "go to church" campaigns. Another high priest of the fifties was evangelist Norman Vincent Peale. His book *The Power of Positive Thinking* preached his basic message: "Think positively and think Christian, and through belief in God you can be what you want to be." Conservative politics now went along with conservative religion.

Another high point of the 1950s came with the formation of the National Council of Churches of Christ in 1950. This American organization consisted of 25 Protestant and 4 Eastern Orthodox groups, which combined numbered over 31 million members, who had joined to coordinate their efforts here and around the world. This unusual Protestant unity helped reduce the barriers between churches and soften the fight between liberals and conservatives.

The social gospel, which had been preached in the late 1800s and which reappeared during the depression, once again became evident during the civil-rights movement and the Vietnam War protests of the 1960s. Mentioned earlier, the Southern Christian Leadership Conference, under Martin Luther King, Jr., was a black organization of Southern ministers that led the demand for black equality. The National Council of Churches created a Commission on Religion and Race to participate in the civil-rights movement. Religious leaders took part in the sit-ins, demonstrations, the Selma march, and the March on Washington in 1963. The Berrigan brothers were active antiwar activists, who felt that Catholic priests should take responsibility for the morality of American society. Religion was becoming more relevant.

The Variety of American Religion

America has always been a place where new religions could prosper. In the twentieth century Judaism, Pentecostals, and Eastern Orthodoxy all rose to prominence. American Jews have been evident since the colonial days, but they have never had sufficient numbers until the late 1800s to warrant much attention. Three forms of American Judaism are present in the Orthodox, Reform, and Conservative beliefs. Over the years their vocal support of Israel has become increasingly significant. While they are labeled the largest white minority, they have assimilated well into the system and have achieved success, particularly in communications and entertainment. Today important issues facing American Jews include Zionism, black animosity in the ghettos, and the continuing Middle East controversy. While most Jews are nonmilitant, the Jewish Defense League is a fringe group that has been vocal in their anti-Soviet stands.

The Pentecostal movement is composed of many sects, which include the Church of God, the Free Methodists, and the Church of the Nazarene. Their search for perfect holiness involves faith healing and the baptism of the Holy Spirit. One of their preachers who achieved national publicity was Aimee Semple McPherson, who, from her temple in Los Angeles, preached faith healing and the imminent return of Christ. The Jehovah's Witnesses also subscribed to the imminent coming. Under the leadership of Charles Russell, this group spread their word through their magazine the *Watchtower*. With the rapid changes in American society, the Pentecostal movement grew among those who were seeking a fairly simple answer. After World War II Eastern Orthodox churches also became more noticeable. With the influx of immigration from Eastern Europe, these churches eventually boasted more than three million followers.

The rise of the "youth culture," with its hard rock, drugs, and alienation gave rise to other religious organizations. Some have turned to Zen Buddhism and Yoga, while others have sought answers in Khrisna Consciousness. On American streets often appear individuals robed in yellow with shaven heads and pigtails. They sway and chant "Hare Krishna, Hare Rama," while seeking money for their cause. What they believe in is a form of Hindu religion with American overtones.

In 1967, on the streets of San Francisco, was born the Jesus Movement, another attempt to seek answers to rapid social change. Led by young evangelists, these followers of Jesus seek a common experience through the Bible and follow a strict view of morality. Jesus is here and now for them and is a real force in their lives. Their awakening rose from the youth culture's reaction to the drugs and violence of the 1960s. Their movement is carried to college campuses through the Campus Crusade, which preaches conversion and an intense commitment to Jesus Christ. Bible-study seminars are being introduced; classes on the Bible as literature are popular ones. While the movement has become commercialized through Bible sales and the movies *Godspell* and *Jesus Christ Superstar*, it has definitely made an impression on modern American religion.

During the 1970s the variety of American religion was hard to keep up with. Traditional religion, nontraditional religion, the Jesus movement, Hindu religion—there was something for everyone. Of all the traditional groups, the Catholic church went through the most internal stress when many of its

The movie *Jesus Christ Superstar* commercialized the new-found interest in Christ and the Bible.

members questioned the Pope's stand on certain moral questions such as birth control. In 1978 Catholics also faced the shock of two Popes in one year with the election of John Paul II and John Paul III, who, being of Polish ancestry, was a surprise choice. *The Living Bible* became a best seller; while 15-year-old Maharaj Ji traveled the United States, welcomed by throngs of people interested in transcendental meditation. But two years later Maharaj Ji would be removed from his post by his mother because he was "a spiritually imperfect playboy." Sun Myung Moon and his Unification Church also gathered American followers. But it did not take long for Congress to authorize an investigation of Moon for his questionable financial practices. While some Americans were accusing Moon, the Hare Krishnas, and other groups of brainwashing their children, America was shocked in late 1978 when the would-be messiah Reverend Jim Jones ordered his Peoples Temple followers to drink from a tub of poison at the cult's commune in Guyana; more than 900 cult followers died.

Modern Science

American science has come a long way in the twentieth century, but its most remarkable triumph came with the moon landing on July 20, 1969. Sputnik I caused America to fear that it might be behind Russian science and to realize it needed a real scientific revolution to gear up for the space race. Our space program was accelerated and slowly we advanced.

Commanders Alan Shepard and Virgil Grissom were sent into space; in 1962 John Glenn became the first American to orbit the earth. Experiments during the Gemini phase of space flights provided the ground work for a moon landing. The Apollo Projects, under the auspices of the National Aeronautics and Space Agency (N.A.S.A.), were more dramatic. Apollo 7 carried three men around the earth, while Apollo 8 carried three men around the moon. Apollo 9 and 10 continued experimentation with a lunar-landing craft. By 1969 Apollo 11 was ready. On July 20, Neil Armstrong and Edwin Aldrin had guided their lunar module, the *Eagle*, to a moon landing; Armstrong, descending from the craft, made the dramatic statement, "That's one small step for man, one giant leap for mankind."

With the moon landing, the United States appeared to have won the expensive race for space, but exploration of space was not over. Future Apollo landings continued to explore the surface of the moon. Apollo 17 in December 1972 was the last of the manned moon explorations. Astronauts Eugene Cernan and Harrison Schmitt took one final look at the bleak moon surface and left a plaque that read, "Here man completed his first exploration of the moon, December, 1972 A.D. May the spirit of peace in which we came be reflected in the lives of all mankind." The Apollo program ended, but the United States was not about to give up space exploration or lose its momentum toward future scientific finds.

In 1973 and 1974 the United States now tested the effects of living in space with a nine-month experiment in the orbiting space laboratory *Skylab*. Plans also went ahead for a joint American-Soviet space docking. Unmanned spacecraft were sent toward Venus and Mercury to bring back knowledge of these planets. In 1976 two United States *Viking* spacecraft made the first

The moon landing was a victory for American exploration of space.

landings on Mars and sent back spectacular pictures of the Martian surface. These landings revealed little life on Mars, destroying a myth popular to many. Future space missions will involve more unmanned spacecraft, the first women astronauts, and the *Enterprise*, a new spacecraft built to rocket into orbit but land like a plane. While the investigation of space goes on, American scientists have been involved in other research that has made remarkable medical advances.

Scientific Achievements

Experimental operations in the 1920s led to brain surgery; in the sixties, new experiments led to heart transplants. In 1968 Christian Barnard of South Africa performed the first successful heart transplant; American Dr. Denton Cooley continued this pioneering breakthrough. Organ transplants and limb transplants are now being tried. New drugs are being discovered. In the 1930s penicillin was used widely against many dreaded diseases, including venereal diseases. In 1955 Dr. Jonas Salk developed a successful polio vaccine that has reduced substantially the cases of polio in the United States. Vaccinations against smallpox and immunizations for measles, diptheria, and tetanus are now common preventatives. During the 1960s and 1970s different outbreaks of flu were met with vaccines to combat the spread of these dreaded illnesses.

Mass Culture for a Mass Society: Twentieth-Century American Culture

Research goes on for cancer cures and for relief for arthritis victims. Heart disease is still a major killer. With the birth of a test-tube baby in 1978, certain moral questions were raised, but the impressiveness of this scientific achievement cannot be questioned. Researchers also are continuing to work on genetic research, which may lead to control of cell changes and longer life. Although Americans constantly complain about the rising cost of medical care, science continues its work to keep Americans healthier and living longer.

Science has been greatly responsible for the rise of big business, contributing to industry certain technological advances, such as assembly-line production, automation, and the invention of new products that can be developed and sold. Since World War II the computer produced major changes in our way of doing things. Of course, the computer has caused many Americans to ask the question: Can man be replaced by the machine? The Hollywood movie *2001: A Space Odyssey* answers the question in the affirmative; as does the science of cybernetics, which goes one step further and concludes that humans can even become machines. Computers also have helped social scientists to take a more experimental view of humans and their universe.

Science and Thought

Man's psychological study of himself has been much influenced by science. Sigmund Freud was the founder of psychoanalysis, who took a scientific approach to the study of the mind; his writings were extremely popular during the 1920s and helped to justify the sexual revolution that was occurring. Americans Karen Horney and Eric Fromm have both been responsible for a neo-Freudian revival. Horney explained how anxiety over the changes in American society can lead to personal tension; Fromm looked at American society and recognized a vast need for love. Both these individuals were in the Freudian tradition; but instead of explaining most basic human drives in terms of sex, they viewed human frustrations in terms of the problems of American society. Other writers, such as Erik Erikson, told of man's need for personal identity, while Norman O. Brown explained human anxiety in terms of fear of death. Science has greatly effected the study of psychology, but has not as yet provided one ultimate answer.

Science has also attempted to explain the reasons for the turmoil of the twentieth century. Political scientists have attempted to measure public opinion and political sentiments. George Gallup and others have applied political polls to political preferences. Sometimes these polls change public opinion rather than merely report them. And of course Harry Truman could tell Gallup that the polls are not always correct. The Nielsen organization has applied similar scientific methods to sampling the preferences of television viewers. Historians have been utilized this new science; James Harvey Robinson in 1912 wrote *The New History*, which attempted to relate history to the other social sciences. Robinson's search for new interpretations led in 1913 to Charles Beard's economic explanation of the Constitution, but few other new trends emerged. Many twentieth-century historians have analyzed American history from a liberal viewpoint, highlighting periods of reform in history. These writers were challenged after World War II by a group of neo-conservative historians such as Russel Kirk, *The Conservative Mind*, and Clinton Rossiter, *Conservatism in America*, who saw the real heroes as the conservatives. The continuity of history has been stressed by "consensus" writers, such as Louis Hartz and Daniel Boorstin, who have minimized differences and stressed the social patterns that have been repeated over and over. With the Vietnam War, leftist historians began to view American history from a new radical viewpoint. By the 1970s the focus of historians had turned to more interdisciplinary studies, minority histories, and histories of women.

Sociology and anthropology also have been influenced by modern science. In-depth research on groups in the city have revealed the attitudes of urban dwellers. Robert and Helen Lynd, in 1927, established a model for such studies with their book *Middletown*, a detailed work on the attitudes of a Midwestern community. Other works, such as those by Lloyd Warner, have revealed a class struggle in the cities. Sociologists have continued to investigate the arrival of the computer age and its effect on humankind. David Reisman revealed the impersonal nature of modern society in his classic work *Lonely Crowd* (1950). Many cultural anthropologists such as Margaret Mead have applied new methods to study the societal ways of people here and abroad. The growing use of scientific methods has revealed a new perspective on Americans past, present, and future.

Modern Education

Since the early 1900s American education has undergone rapid change. The movement toward mass education, which really started with the reforms of Horace Mann in the 1800s, has slowly inched toward reality. But now the specter of an over-educated society is being raised. By the late 1970s more than 11 million Americans were attending college, but the growing job shortage for college graduates, especially in education, continued. Three out of every ten persons in the United States are connected somewhere in the educational process, either as students or teachers or employees. Education has become "big business," but it is no key to success in the real business world. By the late 1970s there were over 2500 unemployed Ph.D.s and M.A.s in the field of history with bleak prospects for future jobs.

By the 1960s the alienation of youth was becoming more obvious. The assassination of Kennedy, the civil-rights movement, and the Vietnam War threatened their traditional values; the drug scene and hard rock music allowed them some escape, but they needed an avenue for organized protest. On college campuses groups on both the right and left offered them an opportunity to join and vent their frustrations. In the year 1964 began a series of student demonstrations that lasted until 1970. These demonstrations were directed

The youth culture of the 1960s was characterized by life-styles and dress.

against certain ills in our society and questioned the direction in which our government was moving. Students asked: Why should we have to fight in far-off Vietnam? And they complained: R.O.T.C. training doesn't belong in an academic institution! The Students for a Democratic Society was the most active of the campus organizations. While these activities caused negative publicity for colleges and college students alike, they did focus on the problems of society at the time: The Vietnam War, civil rights, and the environment. By the 1970s the campuses became quiet, but the colleges had been scarred by the demonstrations and a new, conservative backlash was building. The radicals of the 1960s became the middle-class Americans of the 1970s. Meanwhile the backlash effect of the demonstrations threatened funding for all levels of education.

Today American education feels financial pressure from a voters' rebellion and from declining school enrollment. Almost half the college and universities today are facing a severe economic crunch, and more and more private colleges are closing their doors. Meanwhile student tests scores are beginning to decline, and the school systems are blamed. From forced integration to reduced funding to teachers' strikes, modern education is at the crossroads.

Modern Literature

American literature also reflected the turmoil of the twentieth century. Many writers in the 1920s expressed disillusionment with America as it evolved after the Great War, the war that was supposed to end all wars. This feeling was expressed in the literature both of those who remained in America and those expatriates who chose to live abroad. This was a time for the writers of "The Lost Generation." T. S. Eliot in England wrote of the hollow men who lived in modern civilization; his poem *The Waste Land* (1922) was a dark study of the lost glory of times past. Ernest Hemingway, master of the modern prose style, wrote in *The Sun Also Rises* (1926) of Americans in Spain and Paris who had lost their joy in life and felt wasted. His *Farwell to Arms* (1929) is another work that reflected the growing disillusionment with war. Sinclair Lewis wrote critical studies of America in the 1920s and of the decline of the small town. Ezra Pound filled his poetry with negative views of the world, while F. Scott Fitzgerald, in *The Great Gatsby* (1925) rejected the values of wealth and high society and depicted the dangers of such living. Archibald MacLeish returned to America and became the "poet laureate" of the Roosevelt administration by eloquently summoning writers to support democracy here and abroad.

In the 1930s many writers also pictured the complexities of life in America. John Steinbeck, in *The Grapes of Wrath* (1939), described the plight of a family in the dustbowl of Oklahoma and of their trek westward to California. John Crowe Ransom and Robert Penn Warren wrote about the values of Southern society. James Farrell's *Studs Lonigan* (1934) traced the failure of a young Irish-American in Chicago, while Richard Wright in *Native Son* (1940) showed how destructive the city could be to American blacks. Poets such as William Carlos Williams and Robert Frost were writing about the beauty and grandeur of the American scene. Frost's popularity reached a climax when he read his poetry at Kennedy's inauguration. The trends of the previous two decades continued into the 1940s when both the American nation and the American mind were concerned with a war for survival.

After World War II many novels appeared that commented upon the past military struggle. Norman Mailer's *The Naked and the Dead* (1948) condemned war, while Herman Wouk's *The Caine Mutiny* (1951) focused on military obedience. Naturalism continued with Mailer's *Miami and the Seige of Chicago* (1968), Truman Capote's *In Cold Blood* (1966) and William Styron's *The Confessions of Nat Turner* (1967). Realism was found in Saul Bellow's *Herzog* (1964) and Bernard Malamud's *A New Life* (1961). Meanwhile in the 1950s, a literary revolution was taking place in San Francisco, led by Poet Lawrence Ferlinghetti. This movement, known as the San Francisco Renaissance, soon fell under the spell of the "beat generation," exemplified by writers like Jack Kerouac and Allen Ginsberg.

A new ethnic literature emerged in the 1960s and 1970s. Dee Brown's history of the American West *Bury My Heart at Wounded Knee* (1971) led the way for a series of books on the American Indian. Philip Roth's books on the Jewish experience allowed non-Jewish Americans to share their frustrations. Ralph Ellison, LeRoi Jones, James Baldwin, and Eldredge Cleaver were just some of the outstanding black writers of the period. But it was Alex Haley's epic story of the black experience *Roots* (1976), and the book's subsequent television special, that caused white America to stop and investigate its past sins. The rise of national book clubs and the paperback revolution also have caused an increased interest in modern writers. The sexual revolution of the 1960s and 1970s was evident in clinical studies of sexual responses and sexual intercourse in books such as the *Joy of Sex* (1972) while novelists, such as Gore Vidal in *Myra Breckinridge* (1976), questioned traditional morality. James Michener's popularity has continued with his books *Centennial* (1974) and *Chesapeake* (1978); while new writers such as Richard Yates, *A Good School* (1978), and Mary Gordon, *Final Payments* (1978), have come upon the scene. In recent years the search for a best seller has turned to Watergate, diets, and even Erma Bombeck sitting in her bowl of cherries.

Mass Amusements

Mass society is most evident in the expansion of popular culture and mass amusements. Technology brought with it new products and, at the same time, more leisure to enjoy the new land of plenty. More and more Americans turned from a nation at work to a nation at play. Play became an essential part of the American experience, and the American imagination expanded the horizons of recreation. The Romans had their circuses and carnivals; Americans had much, much more.

It was the motion picture which first satisfied the American desire for mass entertainment. From its early origins in the 1890s as the nickelodeon, the motion picture spread to movie theaters and served more than 10 million Americans weekly in the period before World War I. These early silent films dealt with universal themes such as love and hate, cowboy versus Indian, and black versus white. They tried to capture the hearts and purse-strings of Americans with dashing heroes such as Douglas Fairbanks or passionate lovers such as Rudolph Valentino. The greatest director of silent films was D. W. Griffith, who achieved new technical dimensions in his unfortunately racist movie *The Birth of a Nation*, which featured the Ku Klux Klan as the good guys. World War I newsreels attempted to portray the action in Europe, while Mack Sennett tried to keep them laughing by featuring a little man who wore baggy pants, carried a cane, and walked with an unusual gait—Charlie Chaplin. More and more people went to the theaters, and now serials were introduced to entice audiences to return again.

By the 1920s motion pictures were big business, and the stars, who included Chaplin, Fairbanks, Harold Lloyd, Mary Pickford, Gloria Swanson, and Valentino, continued to pack them in. Hollywood was always publicity conscious, and the star system was a natural. Love meters were put on girls' arms to test the reaction of a Valentino kiss upon the audience; a near riot occurred at his funeral in the midtwenties. The popular epics of the time included *Ben Hur*, *The Thief of Bagdad*, and *The Three Musketeers*. Now movies were turned out quickly to satiate the public appetite, and the quality declined. Censors began to question some of the torrid scenes; for example, the movie *Flaming Youth* in which scenes were said to include "neckers, petters, white kisses, red kisses, pleasure-mad daughters, sensation-craving mothers. . . ." No, that movie is not playing today at local theaters; it was a cinema sensation during the twenties. With 20,000 theaters across the country, mass entertainment definitely had arrived, but the best was yet to come.

In 1928 Warner Brothers added sound to the new movie *The Jazz Singer*, starring Al Jolson; soon color was being added, and modern movies were here.

Mass Culture for a Mass Society: Twentieth-Century American Culture

Charlie Chaplin was the leading comedian of the silver screen in the 1920s and 1930s.

By 1929 more than 110 million people were seeing movies weekly; after the depression hit, however, the public became more selective in seeking forms of entertainment. But the movies of the 1930s had something for everyone: musicals, murder mysteries, adventures, Westerns, comedies, gangsters, prison tales, and even cartoons flashed across the screen. Stars included Mickey Mouse, Greta Garbo, Zazu Pitts, James Cagney, George Raft, and W. C. Fields. The appearance in 1939 of the technically advanced *Gone with the Wind* caused long lines to appear in front of movie houses.

Hollywood's glamorous view of the Civil War became absolute truth to millions of Americans. Censorship, however, continued to be a problem. In 1923, William Hays, who had become head of Motion Picture Producers and Exhibitors of America, tried to place some sort of moral standards on films. By the 1930s a uniform production code was instituted. Violence was curtailed; high morals were the norm. But censorship still remained an issue. By World War II movie popularity had reached a new high, but a serious threat to movie going was on the horizon. It was a new form of mass entertainment that could enter right into the home, and it became known as television.

Many theaters were forced to close, and only half as many people were going to movies in the 1950s as they had in the 1940s. Television had made its inroads. While some films were trying now to make social commentary on society, the money makers were those that still had mass appeal such as a new version of *Ben Hur*, as well as the films *Cleopatra*, *The Sound of Music*, and *The Godfather*. During the next three decades the stars included Spencer Tracy, Marilyn Monroe, James Dean, Paul Newman, Jane Fonda, and Clint Eastwood. By the 1970s movies were taking a nostalgic look at America (and at moviemaking itself) with movies such as *American Grafitti* and *Paper Moon*. Also, disaster films came into vogue with *Earthquake*, *The Towering Inferno*, and *The Poseidon Adventure*. The sexual revolution surfaced in pornography, with such clinical studies as the x-rated *Deep Throat*. The 1970s also saw a real resurgence among theater goers, led by the youth. Theater revenues in 1978 grossed over $2.5 billion. *Star Wars* was the talk of 1978, while *Kramer* v. *Kramer* and *The China Syndrome* were the hits of 1979. With sequels to many successful shows being made, such as the movie version of *Star Trek*, the future of films seems to lie in their offer of better escapism from modern society.

Radio

Home mass entertainment can be initially found in the birth of radio. Before the 1920s some radio experiments had produced favorable results, but commercial radio did not begin until radio station KDKA's first broadcast on November 2, 1920. Instant success was the result. Radio stations were set up and radio sales skyrocketed overnight. By 1924 the presidential election results were being broadcast. Radio featured entertainment similar to the movies, but with live action and up-to-date news. Sporting events, special events, music, speeches, the news—all these and more filled the air waves. President Warren G. Harding bought a radio for the White House. Entertainment was no longer down the street at the neighborhood theater, it was coming out of the little box in your own home. Through the twenties and thirties the radio boom continued. Millions of Americans tuned in to their favorite series such as "Superman," "Amos and Andy," "Buck Rogers," and "The Jack Benny Show." The activities of the Shadow and the Green Hornet became the talk of the town. The ear of America turned to radio. Franklin Roosevelt reached Americans with his "fireside chats" as no other president had ever done. But radio was a limited medium; the age of television was not long in coming.

Television

In 1939 at the New York World's Fair a demonstration of television was held. During the 1940s networks were established and television sets began to be sold. But radio still monopolized the entertainment industry in the forties.

Radio stations now claimed that more than 98 percent of Americans were tuned in nightly. Innovations such as FM stations improved reception, and car radios helped radio hold its monopoly. Jack Benny was joined on radio by Bob Hope; "Truth or Consequences" became the hit of the era, a show which offered $20,000 for identifying the voices of popular personalities. But the improvement of television sets and the expansion of viewing time began to make inroads into radio.

Television replaced radio in the 1950s. The networks—CBS, NBC, and ABC—improved viewing time; sets were larger, and more than 700 stations across the country were now broadcasting. Television picked up where radio left off. The same types of mass-entertainment programs were exploited and expanded: situation comedies, Westerns, detective dramas, variety shows, cartoons, soap operas, and movies were popular. The hit of the early 1950s was "The Saturday Night Review" with Ed Wynn, Fred Allen, Jack Benny, and Jimmy Durante, but "I Love Lucy" took over the top position in the mid-fifties and stayed there during much of the next decade. Other popular features were "Dragnet," "Gunsmoke," "Lawrence Welk," "Bonanza," "The Perry Mason Show," and "The Danny Kaye Show." While critics looked at these popular shows and called television a "vast wasteland," its potential brought Americans a new dimension.

During the 1970s the public taste began to change. Favorites like "Mission Impossible" and "Laugh-in" were replaced by family dramas such as "The Waltons" and black detective dramas such as "Shaft." In the early 1970s "All in the Family" was the number-one show, followed by "Maude," "The Mary Tyler Moore Show," and "Chico and the Man." Spin-off of popular shows continued with "Maude" being a spin-off from "All in the Family" and "Good Times" being a spin-off from "Maude." In the mid-1970s the "Six Million Dollar Man" joined the top ten shows. In 1976 nostalgia reached television with programs such as "Happy Days," featuring "the Fonz," and "Laverne and Shirley," about two bottle-cappers in Milwaukee. A little sex entered the scene with the introduction of "Charlie's Angels." In 1977 the dramatization of the best seller *Roots* attracted 130 million Americans—the largest audience in television history. Television was finally reaching its potential. News programs, specials, and election coverage drew increasingly larger audiences. But the quality of popular shows continued to rise and fall. Critics still complain about the excessive violence and lack of morals on television. Public television has offered some real alternatives to commercial television; its varied programming ranges from "Sesame Street" to serious drama. But public television has relied largely upon government funding and still is limited in its offerings. While commercial television may be a "vast wasteland" for the mindless, it still has revolutionized mass entertainment.

The dramatization of the book *Roots* was viewed by more Americans than any other television production.

Mass Sports

The twentieth century also witnessed the rise of mass-spectator sports. The major sports included football, baseball, basketball, hockey, boxing, and horse racing. By the 1970s these sports were multimillion-dollar operations that drew thousands of fans yearly to stadiums and arenas, in addition to the millions who were glued to their television sets. Of course, the sports heroes have changed over the years. In the 1920s they were Babe Ruth ("the Sultan of Swat"), the Four Horsemen of Notre Dame, who were noteable college-football players under the tutelege of Knute Rockne, as well as Gene Tunney and Jack Dempsey in boxing, Bill Tilden in tennis, and Bobby Jones in golf. The American heroes of the twentieth century have been, with few exceptions, athletes.

In the twenties, Charles Lindbergh, who made a solo crossing of the Atlantic in 1927, grasped the American imaginaton. But after Lindbergh the names of American heroes consist of sports greats. Over the years the predominance of professional baseball has been rivaled closely by professional football, basketball, and hockey. Many colleges survive today because of revenues their sports teams bring in. Today's heroes include Pete Rose in baseball, Ken Stabler, Bob Griese, and Roger Staubach in football, Jimmy Connors in tennis, and Lloyd Free and Kareem Jabbar in basketball. With the free-agent decision by the courts, which allowed athletes to negotiate better contracts with other teams when their original contracts had expired, professional athletes have become business-minded too. Their contracts are now up to the highest bidders. Individuals such as Pete Rose bargain for multimillion-dollar contracts, with fringe benefits added. Team loyalty gives way to the almighty dollar. still Americans wait in long lines to get tickets to important games; during football season Sundays are national television days. Now Monday Night Football has become an accepted part of America's leisure time. In bars and at parties the crucial questions are not about the economy or politics but who will win the game next week.

Spectator sports are for the masses, but this does not mean that Americans are not interested in participant sports too. By the 1970s Americans were becoming obsessed with an exercise craze. Jogging has become an American religion. Golf is a sport for the business-oriented, while swimming and tennis are more strenuous. Fishing and hunting have also remained popular outdoor sports. Many adults join bowling leagues or play softball. In southern California racquetball achieved instant popularity and now has spread across the country. In America, sports have a firm hold upon the modern man, woman, and child.

In America today corporations produce products for mass consumption. Metropolitan areas are approaching unmanageable size. The side-effects of living in a mass society are air, water, and noise pollution. The feminist movement sees a victory in the hoped-for passage of the Equal Rights Amendment. American religion offers a variety of answers to society's ills, from Hinduism to fundamentalist faith. Science took America to the moon and beyond. American literature is as varied as American taste. Movies provide escapism for the masses; television provides that same escapism, but at a lower price. American sports feature modern heroes pitted against each other before thousands of willing spectators. This is all part and parcel of modern American culture. Americans today are products of their past. Over the years we have become a vibrant, exciting nation with a rich heritage and, hopefully, a bright future.

Essay

From Milton Berle to Mork and Mindy: A Panoramic View of American Television

When did television begin? There are so many historic monuments to the origins of American television that it is very difficult to answer this question. In 1925 both John Logie Baird and Charles Francis Jenkins, working on either side of the Atlantic, provided weak and blurry images on a screen. In 1930 the National Broadcasting Company (NBC) operated an experimental television transmitter in New York. By 1932 there were an estimated 7500 television sets that picked up the Columbia Broadcasting System's (CBS) report on the presidential election. In 1939 the presentation of a Princeton-Columbia baseball game was the pioneer sportscast. Advertising broke into the airwaves in 1941 with the appearance of the first commercial—announcing a Bulova Clock priced at $9—during the telecast of a Dodgers-Pirate game from Ebbetts Field. Immediately after the war, in 1945, VE-Day celebrations were telecast, as were the Army-Navy games.

It is 1947, and there are over 14,000 sets across the country. This year, regular television programs begin. They include some of the following: "Juvenile Jury," "Leave it to the Girls," "Kukla, Fran, and Ollie," "Meet the Press," "Howdy Doody," and the first soap opera, "A Woman to Remember."

Some of the programs in those years have become media classics. "Howdy Doody," the first popular children's show, featured Buffalo Bob Smith, his puppet friend Howdy Doody, a clown called Clarabell who communicated by a horn, Mister Blister—a real meany—and a gang of kids who usually sat in the peanut gallery. "Roller Derby" was also a television pioneer; turn on any independent station and you still are likely to see the same hitting, pushing, and hard action as it appeared first in 1947. Bert Parks appeared in "Break the Bank" and, until the 1980s, was seen every September as the host of the "Miss America Pageant." Gene Autry, the first television Western hero, was seen with his horse Champion and his sidekick Pat Buttram. Television was off and running.

By 1948 there were 190,000 sets and "T.V." was really becoming a mass media. The hit of 1948—and for many years after—was Milton Berle, the king of early television comedy, who, dressed in outrageous costumes on his "Texaco Star Theater," was lovingly known as Uncle Miltie. Ed Sullivan with his "really big show" hit the tube, as did Arthur Godfrey and Ted Mack with their talent searches. Allen Funt today is still lurking unsuspecting guests before the camera with his "Candid Camera"; in the old days it was "Candid Microphone." 1948 was also the year that the Lone Ranger and his pal Tonto, joined Gene Autry, as did William Boyd as "Hopalong Cassidy." National wrestling featured attractions such as Gorgeous George, who wore gold hairpins. There was now a little something for everyone.

During the 1950s television began to take

Milton Berle, here pictured with Ed Wynn, was the most popular comedian in the early years of television.

form as the enduring American institution it has since become. The careers of well-known comics blossomed during this decade; take Jack Benny, Burns and Allen, Ken Murray, Eddie Cantor, Bob Hope, and Garry Moore. Or look to the sky and see "Superman," "Buck Rogers," and "Tom Corbett, Space Cadet." Quiz shows such as "What's My Line," and Groucho Marx in "You Bet Your Life" also appeared. In 1951 "I Love Lucy" makes its debut and loses its first sponsor because it doesn't sell enough cigarettes. But this situation comedy will become a classic of early television, and reruns of it today are still found early in the morning or late at night. Racist "Amos 'n Andy" may be a long way from "The Jeffersons" but it found its way into America's hearts nonetheless. "Ozzie and Harriett" became the favorite family comedy, lasting for many years. Laughter also rang out over "The Life of Riley," with William Bendix as a lame-brained Riley, and Danny Thomas in "Make Room for Daddy." Doctors began to enter the homes of many Americans, but not for house calls, in shows such as "Medic" starring Richard Boone as Dr. Konrad Styner. "Disneyland" made its appearance in 1954 and still holds strong as Sunday family fare. "Lassie" and "Father Knows Best" also appeared in the mid-1950s. "Rin Tin Tin," who was the German Shepherd mascot of Fort Apache, never had the same canine appeal as Lassie.

In 1955 American television viewers walked into the Long Branch Saloon with "Gunsmoke," starring James Arness as Marshall Matt Dillon. Serious drama was not forgotten: "Kraft Theater" and "Studio One" were among the offerings. But these shows drew very few viewers compared to family comedies, quiz shows, Westerns, and variety shows. The remaining years of the 1950s featured perennial favorites such as "The Price is Right," "Queen for a Day," "Maverick," "Wagon Train," "Leave it to Beaver," "The Rifleman," "Sea Hunt," "Bonanza," and the "Twilight Zone." Television in the 1950s was much more than a mere entertainment vehicle. The televised Army-McCarthy Hearings allowed the nation to view the man who was leading the greatest witch hunt in American history. Television viewers did not like what they saw, and these hearings led to McCarthy's downfall. Nearly 40 million television sets were now in American homes. Television commercials were big business. How can one forget "You'll wonder where the yellow went," "Leave the driving to us," and "Winston tastes good like a cigarette should"?

The 1960s opened with four debates fea-turing the presidential candidates; television from now on would play a central role in the election of the president. The turbulent sixties were also turbulent ones for television viewers. Luci and Desi Arnez split up. Jack Parr walked out of his talk show. Milton Berle lost his king midas touch and began hosting "Jackpot Bowling." But popular series still abounded. "My Three Sons" featured a father, Fred MacMurray, as head of a motherless family. "The Andy Griffith Show" pictured the life of a small-town sheriff. The doctor again appears; this time it is "Ben Casey" with Vincent Edwards. He is joined by "Dr. Kildare." "The Dick Van Dyke Show" and "Mister Ed" will leave viewers laughing for many years. Rural humor was found in "The Beverly Hillbillies."

Television viewers paused to reflect about the direction of American society with the assassination of President John Kennedy and the televised shooting of Lee Harvey Oswald. "The Fugitive" would run for many years, always looking for that one-armed man. "The Man from U.N.C.L.E." brought spy thrills to the television screen. "The Munsters" and "The Adams Family" brought family comedy into a new perspective, focusing on two families of monsters. "F Troop" portrayed the West in such a crazy way that no viewer really knew what the West was really like. Novelty hit the screen in 1966 with "Batman." "Star Trek" created a loyal following of space adventurers, who still look for the revival of this long defunct series.

Sports hit a high point in the 1960s with the broadcasting of Super Bowl I. "Ironside" confined Raymond Burr to a wheel chair; his hit series "Perry Mason" continued as well in syndication. Niceness abounded with "Gentle Ben," about a boy and his bear, and "The Flying Nun," about a Catholic sister who did just that. "Laugh-In" created a new form of topical humor in the late 1960s. And the decade ended with the dim, blurry, but historic picture of Neil Armstrong moving out of his lunar module to set his foot on the moon.

Relevance and irreverance were featured on television in the 1970s. Audiences kept laughing with "Flip Wilson," "Here's Lucy," "The Odd Couple," and "The Partridge Family." 1971 would be the year of the television bigot, beginning with the first broadcast of "All in the Family." This show created new topics for television, such as ethnic and sexual themes, that formally had been taboo for television. Television of the 1970s also would feature an abundance of spin-offs as competing networks attempted to keep the success formula intact. "All in the Family" would give birth to "Maude" and "The Jeffersons." In 1977 more viewers watched "Roots" than ever before in television history. In 1978 "Mork and Mindy," about an Orkan who comes to Boulder, Colorado, became the hit of the year.

"All in the Family" is no more and "Archie Bunker's Place" has replaced it; all that is left of the original cast is Carroll O'Connor. "The Love Boat" continues to sail with guest stars and more love. "Three's Company," which pictures a live-

All in the Family, with the emphasis on social and racial relationships, led the way to a new morality for modern television.

in relationship between a man and two women sees its apartment manager start his own series "The Ropers." The era of the 1980s opened with the same varied fare that ended the 1970s.

Television has come a long way since the days of Uncle Miltie and the horn of Clarabelle the clown; it has emerged as a media that features public television, movies made especially for television, and news specials, as well as soap operas, family comedy, Westerns, and detective shows—and those annoying commercials. But a look at television can never be complete without a quick glance back at that little girl who screamed, "See Daddy, no cavities!" ∎

Suggested Reading

A good general survey of twentieth-century culture is FREDERICK LEWIS ALLEN's *The Big Change* (1952), while RONALD BERMAN offers a study of the turbulent decade of the 1960s in *America in the '60s* (1968).

BLAKE MCKELVEY, in *The Emergence of Metropolitan America, 1915–1966* (1968), gives an overview of the evolution of the modern city.

HERBERT WALLACE SCHNEIDER, in *Religion in 20th Century America* (1963), documents the changes in modern religion.

The changing economic picture is found in JOHN KENNETH GALBRAITH's *The Affluent Society* (1968) and HERMAN MILLER, in *Rich Man, Poor Man* (1971), examines the distribution of wealth.

The rise of the women's movement is found in WILLIAM HENRY CHAFE's *The American Woman: Her Changing Social, Economic and Political Roles, 1920–1970* (1972).

Twentieth century writers are examined in MAXWELL GEISMAR, *Writers in Crises: The American Novel, 1925–1940* (1942) and in *City of Words* (1971) by TONY TANNER.

The reasons for the growth of the ecology movement are described in ALDO LEOPOLD's *Sand Country Almanac* (1949) while RODRICK NASH in *The American Environment: Readings in the History of Conservation* (1968) shows the evolution from conservation to the ecology movement.

LEO BOGART presents a history of television in *The Age of TV* (1958); ARTHUR KNIGHT does the same for the movies in *The Liveliest Art: A Panoramic History of the Movies* (1957).

HAL HIGDON, in *Professional Football, U.S.A.* (1964), examines the influence of that sport upon the American mind.

Mass Culture for a Mass Society: Twentieth-Century American Culture

CHAPTER 18

The Future:
The Past Revisited?

Time Line

?–A.D. 1492	Migration and evolution of American Indian societies
1492	Christopher Columbus lands in West Indies—beginning of European exploration
1607–1732	Establishment of 13 English colonies
1775–1783	American Revolution
1776	Declaration of Independence
1789–1797	Presidency of George Washington
1812–1815	War of 1812
1816–1824	Era of Good Feelings
1846–1848	Mexican War
1861–1865	Civil War
1865–1877	Reconstruction
1877–1900	Industrialization and urbanization
1900–1916	Progressive Era
1917–1918	World War I
1930s	Depression and New Deal
1941–1945	World War II
1945–1960	Post-war politics
1950–1953	Korean War
1950–1960	Civil rights movement
1961–1973	Vietnam War
1976	Bicentennial celebration

The Future: The Past Revisited?

People today believe that history is exclusively a study of the human past and that history books should end at the present. Yet today's present will be tomorrow's past—and may even be tomorrow's *future*. Time seems to move forward so quickly that today's facts, fashions, and events comprise tomorrow's history. Modern American society is changing quickly and moving in numerous directions all at once. We are everywhere and everything in an instant. American mobility is increasing. What will our future hold?

Throughout history writers have pondered the future. In this century, these individuals were usually labeled science-fiction writers, yet many of the things they wrote of have taken place. Perhaps they are really prophets. Edward Bellamy, author of *Looking Backward* (1888), described what he believed society would be like in A.D. 2000—a technologically advanced urban society complete with credit cards, radios, and air transportation. When his novel appeared, many critics deemed Bellamy an idiot; few talked of him as a real prophet. They said such a society could not exist in America. Bellamy's world of the future was a very rigid and authoritarian one. In it, labor is performed by an industrial army composed of all citizens, men and women, who serve until they are 45 years old. After 45 they can then begin to lead their own lives. Some aspects of Bellamy's state have some interesting relevance today. In his world credit cards replaced money, and the state ran the lives of most citizens. In the 1950s Arthur C. Clarke wrote a series of books on future life, including *The City and the Stars* and *2001: A Space Odyssey*. In these books Clarke describes the world of the future as a world of machines that control human life. In this sterile, static world free will is nonexistent; humans have become like the machines they have created.

In the 1960s and 1970s appeared two best sellers, Charles A. Reich's *The Greening of America* and Alvin Toffler's *Future Shock*. Both these books analyze present society and describe future trends. Reich describes the various levels of consciousness that have appeared throughout history. According to his system, Consciousness I was the age of individualism; Consciousness II is the corporate state; and we are now moving into an age of self-realization, or the Consciousness III level, a reaction to the impersonal ways of the corporate state and a return to individualism. On the other hand, Toffler recognizes the pace of change in modern society and warns that changes are taking place faster than Americans can adapt to them. He believes Americans must develop new methods of adaptation and a strategy of "social futurism"; planners must open their eyes and develop more creative planning. His descriptions of the modular man, of the cyborg-man-machine, and of the "plastic society" show how modern American life is outpacing itself.

Life in the Future

While many Americans view writers of the future with much scepticism and question their pictures of cyborgs, computer societies, and credit-card economies, many Americans in the year 1900 would have had similar responses to stories about hydroplanes, televisions, microwave ovens, trips to the moon, and communication satellites. Technology has continued to make life easier, but it has also made life more complex. The American future will be an electronic age of advanced technology. Homes will be run by a computer, preprogrammed to control the vital functions of normal living. Many homes will have solar lighting, microwave ovens, and television screens that flash computer readouts of shopping lists, children's homework, and the sports scores from last night. The environment may be more liveable because some

The computer world of tomorrow may be a reality by the year 2000.

suburbs will be protected by giant domes, or the environment may be constantly monitored by a spacelab, which daily passes over the cities.

For a moment, imagine you are in this world of the future: the coastline is now free of all buildings and houses and is slowly returning to its pristine beauty. Public monorails crisscross the land where thousands of automobiles once traveled. Those few wealthy individuals who own automobiles now operate electronic cars, which can travel for one month after a charge. A National Advisory Board now deals with all energy problems and has solved the energy crisis through the use of solar energy and the recycling of waste matter. "Population Zero" is fast approaching, and bonuses are given now to families who have more than two children. A national employment policy, coupled with a national welfare policy, has brought increased economic benefits to all Americans.

The city of the future could be a floating one.

Colleges and universities that could not afford to stay open are being relocated in isolated parts of the country and new college-cities are springing up. Organized sports have lost much of their appeal; Americans now spend money on the building of minds, not bodies. Thousands of Americans stand in line to get tickets for a debate between two religious leaders. And drive-in restaurants offer in-home service, so, after a hard day at the office, the food is right on your door step.

Yet certain problems still remain. Many animals are becoming extinct. Racial tension and religious strife are still evident. Prices are rising continually, a newspaper now costs three dollars per issue. Crime and taxes are also on the rise; taxpayers are talking of a tax strike. A foreign war has just been completed in Portugal, and another crisis looms on the horizon. Our president broadcasts her daily message on our car television, while we cruise home. She talks of problems of the environment, foreign affairs, rising prices, and her political opponents. Can this description be life in the future? Or is this life beginning tomorrow in America?

Future Trends

While this description of life in the future may be far-off or completely unlikely, we still can analyze some future trends that are beginning to take place now in our society. Racial minorities have gained more of a share in the American dream, but many of them are still dissatisfied. The black revolution, the brown revolution, and the Indian revolution have tapered off, but the aspirations of minorities continue to challenge the image of America as a "melting pot." White-conscience movements have given way to minority progress. While America may never be a complete melting pot, it is a conglomeration of peoples from all over the world.

Presidents are at the center of American politics. Certain presidents we consider almost as gods, while others have been condemned to a political limbo forever. The pressure of American society and world problems will continue to be the albatross around our future presidents' necks. The job of president is becoming increasingly more difficult and more trying. Some analysts have speculated on the value of having two people sharing the job; but that is a long way in the future. Presidents will have to become more and more aware of the media revolution, which burst upon our country in the 1960s and which has gripped the popular imagination. Will inflation ever be a problem of the past? Most economists say no to this question: they agree that inflation is now a permanent part of American life that can be controlled but never changed. How long can inflation rise without a possible revolution? A 1978 taxpayers' revolution in California may be just the tip of the iceberg.

The role of the United States is crucial to the balance of power in the world. The Cold War moved into a hot war in Vietnam and now has settled into a power struggle between the United States, Russia, and China. The Middle East has boiled with tension for years. Peace or a world war—some event will have to break the stalemate in that part of the world. Presidents are now world diplomats with one ear on the domestic problems at home and another ear on the foreign problems abroad. The next trouble spot in the world is uncertain—Southeast Asia, the Middle East, Africa, Latin America—isolation and noninvolvement have been put on the shelf forever. The world is now truly a world of nations with the United States very near the center; but even this could change.

American culture is moving so quickly it is difficult to determine what the future will hold. Mass amusements have taken a strong grip on American life: videorecorders enable viewers to replay their favorite programs over and over again. Videodiscs are not far behind. Movies will continue to appeal to the masses, mentally transporting them to a far-off galaxy or soaring them through the air with Superman. Both television and movies seem to have lost their moral standards. Is sexual prohibition in the future?

Religion, too, is changing. Perhaps the Jesus people of the sixties and seventies will become the future's orthodox faith. America has been the home for such religious variety that it is difficult to describe the mainstream experience. Protestantism and Catholicism are the majority religions, but changes are occurring within both groups. Meanwhile, religion becomes increasingly commercialized; religious books, games, statues, and pictures have become big business.

Science has offered the world a test-tube baby; scientists talk seriously about plastic bodies, longer life expectancy, skin-color changes, and other future experiments. Not all this is empty speculation, for we know what science already has achieved so far in the twentieth century; as we approach the twenty-first century, we will have a difficult time keeping up with scientific innovation.

Life for the future American will not be so different from what it always has been. Sleeping, eating, drinking—these activities occupy and will occupy a great deal of time. Yet life will be easier; more conveniences will come into vogue. Even now many Americans don't have to open their own garage doors, a gadget called a garage-door opener does it. Machines have brought a real revolution to the average American, and, thanks to the ad men, average Americans will keep trying to keep up with the Johnsons and the Smiths.

Further exploration of space may lead to space
colonies such as this one.

As we approach the twenty-first century we look back at our history. We
see the successes, and we note the failures. Our history has been a relatively
short one in terms of years, but we have made noticeable progress. We have
merged peoples from all over the globe into a dynamic nation that emerged
from a revolution, developed a national culture, and burst into the twentieth
century with innovative technology. We as a people now look over the horizon
to the future and hope that we will continue as a country to meet our challenges and overcome them.

Essay

Jules Verne:
Prophet or Dreamer?

Captain Nemo was a mad sea captain who cruised beneath the oceans in a fantastic submarine; moviegoers probably remember him from the adventure tale "Twenty Thousand Leagues Under the Sea." Another popular movie was "Around the World in Eighty Days," which featured the adventures of Phileas Fogg, who traveled around the world in the unheard of time of 80 days, just to win a bet. And win a bet he surely did. Another Hollywood adventure was "A Journey to the Center of the Earth," which related the tale of an underground trail to a world long forgotten. All these movies were based on the writings of the French novelist, Jules Verne (1828–1905) who was the first writer of science-fiction tales.

After studying law, he decided to take up writing, and, in an age of science, he predicted many future inventions, such as the airplane, submarines, television, guided missiles, and

The dome at Expo '67 revealed the possible shape of the future world.

man-made space satellites. It is amazing that he was so accurate in his predictions—much like a nineteenth century seer. His incredible tales were filled with adventure and fantastic machines. Who, in the late 1800s, would have really believed that someday there would be a craft that could transport humans to the moon? In 1969 America and the world believed it: Jules Verne's future has become today's present.

Numerous science-fiction writers, such as Ray Bradbury, write today about life on other planets and life in outer space. However, with space probes of Mars and Venus now reality, Americans have found it more and more difficult to accept the possibility of life on other planets. For years *Buck Rogers* and *Flash Gordon* were popular movie serials. These movies seem far less believable now, yet *Buck Rogers in the 25th Century* drew quite an audience to the movie theaters of today.

Perhaps Jules Verne was just a very fortunate science-fiction writer. He came at a time, during the rising age of science, when he could see many of the possible inventions that later would become actualities. Perhaps he was not a prophet but was just a very astute observer of modern science. Are modern science-fiction writers as astute as Verne? Or are they merely exploiting the American interest in a good adventure story?

What will the future hold? Jules Verne is gone; Ray Bradbury and other writers are here today. Should we ask them? Or should we just wait until the year 2000 and see for ourselves?∎

Suggested Reading

Two views of the last few decades and their emerging trends are found in CHARLES A. REICH's *The Greening of America* (1970) and ALVIN TOFFLER's *Future Shock* (1970).

A Victorian view of future life in America is the subject of EDWARD BELLAMY's *Looking Backward: 2000–1887* (1888). Many of the works of ARTHUR C. CLARKE, which include *The Promise of Space* (1962) and *2001: A Space Odyssey* (1968), also explore America's future.

Economics and social trends of the future are the subject of *Doomsday Syndrome* (1972) by JOHN MADDOX and of *Mankind at the Turning Point* (1974) by M. MESAROVIC and EDWARD PESTE.

APPENDIX A

The Declaration of Independence

When in the course of human events, it becomes necessary for one people to dissolve the political bonds which have connected them with another, and to assume among the Powers of the earth, the separate and equal station to which the Laws of Nature and of Nature's God entitle them, a decent respect to the opinions of mankind requires that they should declare the causes which impel them to the separation.

We hold these truths to be self-evident, that all men are created equal, that they are endowed by their Creator with certain unalienable Rights, that among these are Life, Liberty and the pursuit of Happiness. That to secure these rights, Governments are instituted among Men, deriving their just powers from the consent of the governed, That whenever any Form of Government becomes destructive to these ends, it is the Right of the People to alter or to abolish it, and to institute new Government, laying its foundation on such principles and organizing its powers in such form, as to them shall seem most likely to effect their Safety and Happiness. Prudence, indeed, will dictate that Governments long established should not be changed for light and transient causes; and accordingly all experience hath shown, that mankind are more disposed to suffer, while evils are sufferable, than to right themselves by abolishing the forms to which they are accustomed. When a long train of abuses and usurpations, pursuing invariably the same Object evinces a design to reduce them under absolute Despotism, it is their right, it is their duty, to throw off such Government, and to provide new Guards for their future security.—Such has been the patient sufferance of these Colonies; and such is now the necessity which constrains them to alter their former Systems of Government. The history of the present King of Great Britain is a history of repeated injuries and usurpations, all having in direct object the establishment of an absolute Tyranny over these States. To prove this, let Facts be submitted to a candid world.

He has refused his Assent to Laws, the most wholesome and necessary for the public good.

He has forbidden his Governors to pass Laws of immediate and pressing importance, unless suspended in their operation till his Assent should be obtained; and when so suspended, he has utterly neglected to attend to them.

He has refused to pass other Laws for the accommodation of large districts of people, unless those people would relinquish the right of Representation in the Legislature, a right inestimable to them and formidable to tyrants only.

He has called together legislative bodies at places unusual, uncomfortable, and distant from the depository of their Public Records, for the sole purpose of fatiguing them into compliance with his measures.

He has dissolved Representative Houses repeatedly, for opposing with manly firmness his invasions on the rights of the people.

He has refused for a long time, after such dissolutions, to cause others to be elected; whereby the Legislative Powers, incapable of Annihilation, have returned to the People at large for their exercise; the State remaining in the mean time exposed to all the dangers of invasion from without, and convulsions within.

He has endeavoured to prevent the population of these States; for that purpose obstructing the Laws of Naturalization of Foreigners; refusing to pass others to encourage their migration hither, and raising the conditions of new Appropriations of Lands.

He has obstructed the Administration of Justice, by refusing his Assent to Laws for establishing Judiciary Powers.

He has made Judges dependent on his Will alone for the tenure of their offices, and the amount and payment of their salaries.

He has erected a multitude of New Offices, and sent hither swarms of Officers to harass our People, and eat out their substance.

He has kept among us, in times of peace, Standing Armies without the Consent of our legislature.

He has affected to render the Military independent of and superior to the Civil Power.

He has combined with others to subject us to a jurisdiction foreign to our constitution, and unacknowledged by our laws, giving his Assent to their acts of pretended legislation:

For quartering large bodies of armed troops among us:

For protecting them, by a mock Trial, from Punishment for any Murders which they should commit on the Inhabitants of these States:

For cutting off our Trade with all parts of the world:

For imposing taxes on us without our Consent:

For depriving us in many cases, of the benefits of Trial by Jury:

For transporting us beyond Seas to be tried for pretended offences:

For abolishing the free System of English Laws in a neighbouring Province, establishing therein an Arbitrary government, and enlarging its Boundaries so as to render it at once an example and fit instrument for introducing the same absolute rule into these Colonies:

For taking away our Charters, abolishing our most valuable Laws, and altering fundamentally the Forms of our Governments:

For suspending our own Legislature, and declaring themselves invested with Power to legislate for us in all cases whatsoever.

He has abdicated Government here, by declaring us out of his Protection and waging War against us.

He has plundered our seas, ravaged our Coasts, burnt our towns, and destroyed the lives of our people.

He is at this time transporting large armies of foreign mercenaries to compleat the works of death, desolation and tyranny, already begun with circumstances of Cruelty & perfidy scarcely paralleled in the most barbarous ages, and totally unworthy the Head of a civilized nation.

He has constrained our fellow Citizens taken Captive on the high Seas to bear Arms against their Country, to become the executioners of their friends and Brethren, or to fall themselves by their Hands.

He has excited domestic insurrections amongst us, and has endeavoured to bring on the inhabitants of our frontiers, the merciless Indian Savages, whose known rule of warfare, is an undistinguished destruction of all ages, sexes and conditions.

In every stage of these Oppressions We have Petitioned for Redress in the most humble terms: Our repeated Petitions have been answered only by repeated injury. A Prince, whose character is thus marked by every act which may define a Tyrant, is unfit to be the ruler of a free People.

Nor have We been wanting in attention to our British brethren. We have warned them from time to time of attempts by their legislature to extend an unwarrantable jurisdiction over us. We have reminded them of the circumstances of our emigration and settlement here. We have appealed to their native justice and magnanimity, and we have conjured them by the ties of our common kindred to disavow these usurpations, which, would inevitably interrupt our connections and correspondence. They too have been deaf to the voice of justice and of consanguinity. We must, therefore, acquiesce in the necessity, which denounces our Separation, and hold them, as we hold the rest of mankind, Enemies in War, in Peace Friends.

We, therefore, the Representatives of the United States of America, in General Congress, Assembled, appealing to the Supreme Judge of the world for the rectitude of our intentions, do, in the Name, and by Authority of the good People of these Colonies, solemnly publish and declare, That these United Colonies are, and of Right ought to be Free and Independent States; that they are Absolved from all Allegiance to the British Crown, and that all political connection between them and the State of Great Britain, is and ought to be totally dissolved; and that as Free and Independent States, they have full Power to levy War, conclude Peace, contract Alliances, establish Commerce, and to do all other Acts and Things which Independent States may of right do. And for the support of this Declaration, with a firm reliance on the Protection of Divine Providence, we mutually pledge to each other our Lives, our Fortunes, and our sacred Honor. ★

APPENDIX B

The Constitution of the United States

We the people of the United States, in Order to form a more perfect Union, establish Justice, insure domestic Tranquility, provide for the common defence, promote the general Welfare,and secure the Blessings of Liberty to ourselves and our Posterity, do ordain and establish this CONSTITUTION for the United States of America.

ARTICLE I

Section 1. All legislative Powers herein granted shall be vested in a Congress of the United States which shall consist of a Senate and House of Representatives.

Section 2. The House of Representatives shall be composed of Members chosen every second Year by the People of the several States, and the Electors in each State shall have the Qualifications requisite for Electors of the most numerous Branch of the State Legislature.

No Person shall be a Representative who shall not have attained to the Age of twenty-five Years, and been seven Years a Citizen of the United States, and who shall not, when elected, be an inhabitant of that State in which he shall be chosen.

Representatives and direct Taxes shall be apportioned among the several States which may be included within this Union, according to their respective Numbers, which shall be determined by adding to the whole Number of free Persons, including those bound to Service for a Term of Years and excluding Indians not taxed, three fifths of all other Persons. The actual Enumeration shall be made within three Years after the first Meeting of the Congress of the United States, and within every subsequent Term of ten Years, in such Manner as they shall by Law direct. The Number of Representatives shall not exceed one for every thirty Thousand, but each State shall have at Least one Representative; and until such enumeration shall be made, the State of New Hampshire shall be entitled to chuse three, Massachusetts eight, Rhode-Island and Providence Plantations one, Connecticut five, New-York six, New Jersey four, Pennsylvania eight, Delaware one, Maryland six, Virginia ten, North Carolina five, South Carolina five, and Georgia three.

When vacancies happen in the Representation from any State, the Executive Authority therefore shall issue Writs of Election to fill such Vacancies.

The House of Representatives shall chuse their Speaker and other Officers; and shall have the sole Power of Impeachment.

Section 3. The Senate of the United States shall be composed of two Senators from each State, chosen by the Legislature thereof, for six Years; and each Senator shall have one Vote.

Immediately after they shall be assembled in Consequence of the first Election, they shall be divided as equally as may be into three Classes. The Seats of the Senators of the first Class shall be vacated at the Expiration of the second Year, of the second Class at the Expiration of the fourth Year, and of the third Class at the Expiration of the sixth Year, so that one-third may be chosen every second Year; and if Vacancies happen by Resignation, or otherwise, during the Recess of the Legislature of any State, the Executive thereof may make temporary Appointments until the next Meeting of the Legislature, which shall then fill such Vacancies.

No Person shall be a Senator who shall not have attained to the Age of thirty Years, and been nine Years a Citizen of the United States, and who shall not, when elected, be an inhabitant of that State in which he shall be chosen.

The Vice President of the United States shall be President of the Senate, but shall have no vote, unless they be equally divided.

The Senate shall chuse their other Officers, and also a President pro tempore, in the absence of the Vice President, or when he shall exercise the Office of the President of the United States.

The Senate shall have the sole Power to try all Impeachments. When sitting for that purpose, they shall be on Oath or Affirmation. When the President of the United States is tried, the Chief Justice shall preside: And no person shall be convicted without the Concurrence of two thirds of the Members present.

Judgment in Cases of Impeachment shall not extend further than to removal from Office, and disqualification to hold and enjoy any Office of honor, Trust, or Profit under the United States: but the Party convicted shall nevertheless be liable and subject to Indictment, Trial, Judgment, and Punishment, according to Law.

Section 4. The Times, Places and Manner of holding Elections for Senators and Representatives, shall be prescribed in each state by the Legislature thereof; but the Congress may at any time by Law make or alter such Regulations, except as to the Places of Chusing Senators.

The Congress shall assemble at least once in every Year, and such Meeting shall be on the first Monday in December, unless they shall by Law appoint a different Day.

Section 5. Each House shall be the Judge of the Elections, Returns and Qualifications of its own Members, and a Majority of each shall constitute a Quorum to do Business; but a smaller number may adjourn from day to day, and may be authorized to compel the Attendance of absent Members, in such Manner, and under such Penalties, as each House may provide.

Each House may determine the Rules of its Proceedings, punish its Members for disorderly Behavior, and, with the Concurrence of two thirds, expel a Member.

Each House shall keep a Journal of its Proceedings, and from time to time publish the same, excepting such Parts as may in their Judgment require Secrecy; and the Yeas and Nays of the Members of either House on any question shall, at the Desire of one fifth of those Present, be entered on the Journal.

Neither House, during the Session of Congress, shall, without the Consent of the other, adjourn for more than three days, nor to any other Place than that in which the two Houses shall be sitting.

Section 6. The Senators and Representatives shall receive a Compensation for their Services, to be ascertained by Law, and paid out of the Treasury of the United States. They shall in all Cases, except Treason, Felony, and Breach of the Peace, be privileged from Arrest during their Attendance at the Session of their respective Houses, and in going to and returning from the same; and for any Speech or Debate in either House, they shall not be questioned in any other Place.

No Senator or Representative shall, during the Time for which he was elected, be appointed to any civil Office under the Authority of the United States, which shall have been created, or the Emoluments whereof shall have been increased, during such time; and no Person holding any Office under the United States shall be a Member of either House during his continuance in Office.

Section 7. All Bills for raising Revenue shall originate in the House of Representatives; but the

Senate may propose or concur with Amendments as on other bills.

Every bill which shall have passed the House of Representatives and the Senate, shall, before it becomes a Law, be presented to the President of the United States; If he approve he shall sign it, but if not he shall return it, with his Objections, to that House in which it shall have originated, who shall enter the Objections at large on their Journal, and proceed to reconsider it. If after such Reconsideration two thirds of that House shall agree to pass the bill, it shall be sent, together with the objections, to the other House, by which it shall likewise be reconsidered, and if approved by two thirds of that House, it shall become a Law. But in all such Cases the Votes of both Houses shall be determined by Yeas and Nays, and the Names of the Persons voting for and against the Bill shall be entered on the Journal of each House respectively. If any Bill shall not be returned by the President within ten Days (Sundays excepted) after it shall have been presented to him, the Same shall be a Law, in like Manner as if he had signed it, unless the Congress by their Adjournment prevent its Return, in which Case it shall not be a Law.

Every Order, Resolution, or Vote to which the Concurrence of the Senate and House of Representatives may be necessary (except on a question of Adjournment) shall be presented to the President of the United States; and before the Same shall take Effect, shall be approved by him, or being disapproved by him, shall be repassed by two thirds of the Senate and House of Representatives, according to the Rules and Limitations prescribed in the Case of a Bill.

Section 8. The Congress shall have Power To lay and collect Taxes, Duties, Imports, and Excises, to pay the Debts and provide for the common Defence and general Welfare of the United States; but all Duties, Imposts, and Excises shall be uniform throughout the United States;

To borrow money on the credit of the United States;

To regulate Commerce with foreign Nations, and among the several States, and with the Indian Tribes;

To establish an uniform Rule of Naturalization, and uniform Laws on the subject of Bankruptcies throughout the United States;

To coin Money, regulate the Value thereof, and of foreign Coin, and fix the Standard of Weights and Measures;

To provide for the Punishment of counterfeiting the Securities and current Coin of the United States;

To establish Post Offices and post Roads;

To promote the Progress of Science and useful Arts, by securing for limited Times to Authors and Inventors the exclusive Right to their respective Writings and Discoveries;

To constitute Tribunals inferior to the Supreme Court;

To define and punish Piracies and Felonies committed on the high Seas, and Offences against the Law of Nations;

To declare War, grant Letters of Marque and Reprisal, and make Rules concerning Captures on Land and Water;

To raise and support Armies, but no Appropriation of Money to that Use shall be for a longer Term than two Years;

To provide and maintain a Navy;

To make Rules for the Government and Regulation of the land and naval forces;

To provide for calling forth the Militia to execute the Laws of the Union, suppress Insurrections and repel Invasions;

To provide for organizing, arming, and disciplining the Militia, and for governing such Part of them as may be employed in the Service of the United States, reserving to the States respectively, the Appointment of the Officers, and the Authority of training the Militia according to the discipline prescribed by Congress;

To exercise exclusive Legislation in all Cases whatsoever, over such District (not exceeding ten Miles square) as may, be Cession of particular States, and the acceptance of Congress, become the Seat of Government of the United States, and to exercise like Authority over all Places purchased by the Consent of the Legislature of the States in which the Same shall be, for the Erection of Forts, Magazines, Arsenals, dock-Yards, and other needful Buildings;—And

To make all Laws which shall be necessary and proper for carrying into Execution the foregoing Powers, and all other Powers vested by this Constitution in the Government of the United States, or in any Department or Officer thereof.

Section 9. The Migration or Importation of such Persons as any of the States now existing shall think proper to admit, shall not be prohibited by the Congress prior to the Year one thousand eight hundred and eight, but a tax or duty may be imposed on such Importation, not exceeding ten dollars for each Person.

The privilege of the Writ of Habeas Corpus shall not be suspended, unless when in Cases of Rebellion or Invasion the public Safety may require it.

No Bill of Attainder or ex post facto Law shall be passed.

No capitation, or other direct, Tax shall be laid unless in Proportion to the Census or Enumeration herein before directed to be taken.

No Tax or Duty shall be laid on Articles exported from any State.

No Preference shall be given by any Regulation of Revenue to the Ports of one State over those of another: nor shall Vessels bound to, or from, one State, be obliged to enter, clear, or pay Duties in another.

No Money shall be drawn from the Treasury, but in Consequence of Appropriations made by Law; and a regular Statement and Account of the Receipts and Expenditures of all public Money shall be published from time to time.

No Title of Nobility shall be granted by the United States: And no Person holding any Office of Profit or Trust under them, shall, without the Consent of the Congress, accept of any present, Emolument, Office, or Title, of any kind whatever, from any King, Prince, or foreign State.

Section 10. No State shall enter any Treaty, Alliance, or Confederation; grant Letters of Marque and Reprisal; coin Money; emit Bills of Credit; make any Thing but gold and silver Coin a Tender in Payment of Debts; pass any Bill of Attainder, ex post facto Law, or Law impairing the Obligation of Contracts, or grant any Title of Nobility.

No State shall, without the Consent of the Congress, lay any Imposts or Duties on Imports or Exports, except what may be absolutely necessary for executing its inspection Laws: and the net Produce of all Duties and Imposts, laid by any State on Imports or Exports, shall be for the Use of the Treasury of the United States; and all such Laws shall be subject to the Revision and Control of the Congress.

No State shall, without the Consent of Congress, lay any duty of Tonnage, keep Troops, or Ships of War in Time of Peace, enter into any Agreement or Compact with another State, or with a foreign Power, or engage in War, unless actually invaded, or in such imminent Danger as will not admit of delay.

ARTICLE II

Section 1. The executive Power shall be vested in a President of the United States of America. He shall hold his Office during the Term of four years, and, together with the Vice-President, chosen for the same Term, be elected, as follows:

Each State shall appoint, in such Manner as the Legislature thereof may direct, a Number of Electors, equal to the whole Number of Senators and Representatives to which the State may be entitled in the Congress; but no Senator or Representative, or Person holding an Office of Trust or Profit under the United States, shall be appointed an Elector.

The Electors shall meet in their respective States, and vote by Ballot for two persons, of whom one at least shall not be an Inhabitant of the same State with themselves. And they shall make a List of all the Persons voted for, and of the Number of Votes for each; which List they shall sign and certify, and transmit sealed to the Seat of the Government of the United States, directed to the President of the Senate. The President of the Senate shall, in the Presence of the Senate and House of Representatives, open all the Certificates, and the Votes shall then be counted. The Person having the greatest Number of Votes shall be the President, if such Number be a Majority of the whole Number of Electors appointed; and if there be more than one who have such Majority, and have an equal Number of Votes, then the House of Representatives shall immediately chuse by Ballot one of them for President; and if no Person have a Majority, then from the five highest on the List the said House shall in like Manner chuse the President. But in chusing the President, the Votes shall be taken by States, the Representation from each State having one Vote; a quorum for this Purpose shall consist of a Member or Members from two-thirds of the States, and a Majority of all the States shall be necessary to a Choice. In every Case, after the Choice of the President, the Person having the greatest Number of Votes of the Electors shall be the Vice President. But if there should remain two or more who have equal votes, the Senate shall chuse from them by Ballot the Vice-President.

The Congress may determine the Time of chusing the Electors, and the Day on which they shall give their Votes; which Day shall be the same throughout the United States.

No person except a natural-born Citizen, or a Citizen of the United States, at the time of the Adoption of this Constitution, shall be eligible to the Office of President, neither shall any Person be eligible to that Office who shall not have attained to the Age of thirty-five years, and been fourteen Years a Resident within the United States.

In Case of the Removal of the President from Office, or of his Death, Resignation, or Inability to discharge the Powers and Duties of the said Office, the same shall devolve on the Vice President, and the Congress may by Law provide for the Case of Removal, Death, Resignation, or Inability, both of the President and Vice President, declaring what Officer shall then act as President, and such Officer shall act accordingly, until the disability be removed, or a President shall be elected.

The President shall, at stated Times, receive for his Services a Compensation, which shall neither be increased nor diminished during the Period for which he shall have been elected, and he shall not receive within that Period any other Emolument from the United States, or any of them.

Before he enter on the execution of his Office, he shall take the following Oath or Affirmation:—"I do solemnly swear (or affirm) that I will faithfully execute the Office of President of the United States, and will, to the best of my Ability, preserve, protect, and defend the Constitution of the United States."

Section 2. The President shall be Commander in Chief of the Army and Navy of the United States, and of the Militia of the several States, when called into the actual Service of the United States; he may require the Opinion, in writing, of the principal Officer in each of the executive Departments, upon any subject relating to the Duties of their respective Offices, and he shall have Power to Grant Reprieves and Pardons for Offences against the United States, except in Cases of Impeachment.

He shall have Power, by and with the Advice and Consent of the Senate, to make Treaties, provided two thirds of the Senators present concur; and he shall nominate, and by and with the Advice and Consent of the Senate, shall appoint Ambassadors, other public Ministers and Consuls, Judges of the supreme Court, and all other Officers of the United States, whose Appointments are not herein otherwise provided for, and which shall be established by Law: but the Congress may by Law vest the Appointments of such inferior Officers, as they think proper, in the President alone, in the Courts of Law, or in the Heads of Departments.

The President shall have Power to fill up all Vacancies that may happen during the Recess of the Senate, by granting Commissions which shall expire at the End of their next Session.

Section 3. He shall from time to time give to the Congress Information of the State of the Union, and recommend to their Consideration such Measures as he shall judge necessary and expedient; he may, on extraordinary occasions, convene both Houses, or either of them, and in Case of Disagreement between them, with respect to the Time of Adjournment, he may adjourn them to such Time as he shall think proper; he shall receive Ambassadors and other public Ministers; he shall take Care that the Laws be faithfully executed, and shall Commission all the Officers of the United States.

Section 4. The President, Vice President and all Civil Officers of the United States, shall be removed from Office on Impeachment for, and Conviction of, Treason, Bribery, or other high Crimes and Misdemeanors.

ARTICLE III

Section 1. The judicial Power of the United States, shall be vested in one supreme Court, and in such inferior Courts as the Congress may from time to time ordain and establish. The Judges, both of the supreme and inferior Courts, shall hold their Offices during good Behaviour, and shall, at stated Times, receive for their Services, a Compensation, which shall not be diminished during their Continuance in Office.

Section 2. The judicial Power shall extend to all Cases, in Law and Equity, arising under this Constitution, the Laws of the United States, and treaties made, or which shall be made, under their Authority;—to all Cases affecting ambassadors, other public ministers and consuls;—to all cases of admiralty and maritime Jurisdiction;—to Controversies to which the United States shall be a Party;—to Controversies between two or more States;—between a State and Citizens of another State;—between Citizens of different States,—between Citizens of the same State claiming Lands under Grants of different States, and between a State, or the Citizens thereof, and foreign States, Citizens or Subjects.

In all Cases affecting Ambassadors, other public Ministers and Consuls, and those in which a State shall be Party, the supreme Court shall have original Jurisdiction. In all the other Cases before mentioned, the supreme Court shall have appellate Jurisdiction, both as to Law and Fact, with such Exceptions, and under such Regulations as the Congress shall make.

The trial of all Crimes, except in Cases of Impeachment, shall be by Jury; and such Trial shall be held in the State where the said Crimes shall have been committed; but when not committed within any State, the Trial shall be at such Place or Places as the Congress may by Law have directed.

Section 3. Treason against the United States, shall consist only in levying War against them, or in adhering to their Enemies, giving them Aid and Comfort. No Person shall be convicted of Treason unless on the Testimony of two Witnesses to the same overt Act, or on Confession in open Court.

The Congress shall have power to declare the Punishment of Treason, but no Attainder of Treason shall work Corruption of Blood, or Forfeiture except during the Life of the Person attainted.

ARTICLE IV

Section 1. Full Faith and Credit shall be given in each State to the public Acts, Records, and judicial Proceedings of every other State. And the Congress may by general Laws prescribe the Manner in which such Acts, Records and Proceedings shall be proved, and the Effect thereof.

Section 2. The Citizens of each State shall be entitled to all Privileges and Immunities of Citizens in the several States.

A Person charged in any State with Treason, Felony, or other Crime, who shall flee from Justice, and be found in another State, shall on demand of the executive Authority of the State from which he fled, he delivered up, to be removed to the State having Jurisdiction of the crime.

No Person held to Service or Labour in one State, under the Laws thereof, escaping into another, shall, in Consequence of any Law or Regulation therein, be discharged from such Service or Labour, but shall be delivered up on Claim of the Party to whom such Service or Labour may be due.

Section 3. New States may be admitted by the Congress into this Union; but no new State shall be formed or erected within the Jurisdiction of any other State; nor any State be formed by the Junction of two or more States, or parts of States, without the Consent of the Legislatures of the States concerned as well as of the Congress.

The Congress shall have Power to dispose of and make all needful Rules and Regulations respecting the Territory or other Property belonging to the United States; and nothing in this Constitution shall be so construed as to Prejudice any Claims of the United States, or of any particular State.

Section 4. The United States shall guarantee to every State in this Union a Republican Form of Government, and shall protect each of them against Invasion; and on Application of the Legislature, or the Executive (when the Legislature cannot be convened) against domestic Violence.

ARTICLE V

The Congress, whenever two-thirds of both Houses shall deem it necessary, shall propose Amendments to this Constitution, or, on the Application of the Legislatures of two-thirds of the several States, shall call a Convention for proposing Amendments, which, in either Case, shall be valid to all Intents and Purposes, as part of this Constitution, when ratified by the Legislatures of three-fourths of the several States, or by Conventions in three-fourths thereof, as the one or the other Mode of Ratification may be proposed by the Congress; Provided that no Amendment which may be made prior to the Year One thousand eight hundred and eight shall in any Manner affect the first and fourth Clauses in the Ninth Section of the first Article; and that no State, without its Consent, shall be deprived of its equal Suffrage in the Senate.

ARTICLE VI

All Debts contracted and Engagements entered into, before the Adoption of this Constitution, shall be as valid against the United States under this Constitution, as under the Confederation.

This Constitution, and the Laws of the United States which shall be made in Pursuance thereof; and all Treaties made, or which shall be made, under the Authority of the United States, shall be the supreme Law of the Land; and the Judges in every State shall be bound thereby, any Thing in the Constitution or Laws of any State to the Contrary notwithstanding.

The Senators and Representatives before mentioned, and the Members of the several State Legislatures, and all executive and judicial Officers, both of the United States and of the several States, shall be bound by Oath or Affirmation to support this Constitution; but no religious Test shall ever be required as a qualification to any Office or public Trust under the United States.

ARTICLE VII

The Ratification of the Conventions of nine States shall be sufficient for the Establishment of this Constitution between the States so ratifying the same.

Done in Convention by the Unanimous Consent of the States present the Seventeenth Day of September in the Year of our Lord one thousand seven hundred and Eighty seven, and of the Independence of the United States of America the Twelfth. In Witness whereof We have hereunto subscribed our names.

Articles in Addition to, and Amendment of, the Constitution of the United States of America. Proposed by Congress, and Ratified by the Legislatures of the Several States, Pursuant to the Fifth Article of the Original Constitution.

AMENDMENT I [1791]

Congress shall make no law respecting an establishment of religion, or prohibiting the free exercise thereof; or abridging the freedom of speech, or of the press; or the right of the people peaceably to assemble, and to petition the Government for a redress of grievances.

AMENDMENT II [1791]

A well regulated Militia, being necessary to the security of a free State, the right of the people to keep and bear Arms shall not be infringed.

AMENDMENT III [1791]

No Soldier shall, in time of peace, be quartered in any house, without the consent of the Owner, nor in time of war, but in a manner to be prescribed by law.

AMENDMENT IV [1791]

The right of the people to be secure in their persons, houses, papers, and effects, against unreasonable searches and seizures, shall not be violated, and no Warrants shall issue, but upon probable cause, supported by Oath or affirmation, and particularly describing the place to be searched, and the persons or things to be seized.

AMENDMENT V [1791]

No person shall be held to answer for a capital or otherwise infamous crime, unless on a presentment or indictment of a Grand Jury, except in cases arising in the land or naval forces, or in the Militia, when in actual service in time of War or public danger; nor shall any person be subject for the same offence to be twice put in jeopardy of life or limb; nor shall be compelled in any criminal case to be a witness against himself, nor be deprived of life, liberty, or property, without due process of law; nor shall private property be taken for public use, without just compensation.

AMENDMENT VI [1791]

In all criminal prosecutions, the accused shall enjoy the right to a speedy and public trial, by an impartial jury of the State and district wherein the crime shall have been committed, which district shall have been previously ascertained by law, and to be informed of the nature and cause of the accusation; to be confronted with the witnesses against him; to have compulsory process for obtaining witnesses in his favor, and to have the Assistance of Counsel for his defence.

AMENDMENT VII [1791]

In suits at common law, where the value in controversy shall exceed twenty dollars, the right of trial by jury shall be preserved, and no fact tried by a jury, shall be otherwise reexamined in any Court of the United States, than according to the rules of the common law.

AMENDMENT VIII [1791]

Excessive bail shall not be required, nor excessive fines imposed, nor cruel and unusual punishments inflicted.

AMENDMENT IX [1791]

The enumeration in the Constitution, of certain rights, shall not be construed to deny or disparage others retained by the people.

AMENDMENT X [1791]

The powers not delegated to the United States by the Constitution, nor prohibited by it to the States, are reserved to the States respectively, or to the people.

AMENDMENT XI [1798]

The Judicial power of the United States shall not be construed to extend to any suit in law or equity, commenced or prosecuted against one of the United States by Citizens of another State, or by Citizens or Subjects of any Foreign State.

AMENDMENT XII [1804]

The Electors shall meet in their respective States and vote by ballot for President and Vice-President, one of whom, at least, shall not be an inhabitant of the same State with themselves; they shall name in their ballots the person voted for as President, and in distinct ballots the person voted for as Vice-President, and they shall make distinct lists of all persons voted for as President, and of all persons voted for as Vice-President, and of the number of votes for each, which lists they shall sign and certify, and transmit sealed to the seat of the government of the United States, directed to the President of the Senate;—The President of the Senate shall, in the presence of the Senate and House of Representatives, open all the certificates and the votes shall then be counted;—The person having the greatest number of votes for President, shall be the President, if such number be a majority of the whole number of Electors appointed; and if no person have such majority, then from the persons having the highest numbers not exceeding three on the list of those voted for as President, the House of Representatives

shall choose immediately, by ballot, the President. But in choosing the President, the votes shall be taken by states, the representation from each state having one vote; a quorum for this purpose shall consist of a member or members from two-thirds of the states, and a majority of all the states shall be necessary to a choice. And if the House of Representatives shall not choose a President whenever the right of choice shall devolve upon them, before the fourth day of March next following, then the Vice-President shall act as President, as in the case of the death or other constitutional disability of the President.—The person having the greatest number of votes as Vice-President, shall be the Vice-President, if such number be a majority of the whole number of Electors appointed, and if no person have a majority, then from the two highest numbers on the list, the Senate shall choose the Vice-President; a quorum for the purpose shall consist of two-thirds of the whole number of Senators, and a majority of the whole number shall be necessary to a choice. But no persons constitutionally ineligible to the office of President shall be eligible to that of Vice-President of the United States.

AMENDMENT XIII [1865]

Section 1. Neither slavery nor involuntary servitude, except as a punishment for crime whereof the party shall have been duly convicted, shall exist within the United States, or any place subject to their jurisdiction.

Section 2. Congress shall have power to enforce this article by appropriate legislation.

AMENDMENT XIV [1868]

Section 1. All persons born or naturalized in the United States, and subject to the jurisdiction thereof, are citizens of the United States and of the State wherein they reside. No State shall make or enforce any law which shall abridge the privileges or immunities of citizens of the United

States; nor shall any State deprive any person of life, liberty, or property, without due process of law; nor deny to any person within its jurisdiction the equal protection of the laws.

Section 2. Representatives shall be apportioned among the several States according to their respective numbers, counting the whole number of persons in each State, excluding Indians not taxed. But when the right to vote at any election for the choice of electors for President and Vice-President of the United States, Representatives in Congress, the Executive and Judicial officers of a State, or the members of the Legislature thereof, is denied to any of the male inhabitants of such State, being twenty-one years of age, and citizens of the United States, or in any way abridged, except for participation in rebellion, or other crime, the basis of representation therein shall be reduced in the proportion which the number of such male citizens shall bear to the whole number of male citizens twenty-one years of age in such State.

Section 3. No person shall be a Senator or Representative in Congress, or elector of President and Vice-President, or hold any office, civil or military, under the United States, or under any State, who, having previously taken an oath, as a member of Congress, or as an officer of the United States, or as a member of any State legislature, or as an executive or judicial officer of any State, to support the Constitution of the United States, shall have engaged in insurrection or rebellion against the same, or given aid or comfort to the enemies thereof. But Congress may by a vote of two-thirds of each House, remove such disability.

Section 4. The validity of the public debt of the United States, authorized by law, including debts incurred for payment of pensions and bounties for services in suppressing insurrection or rebellion, shall not be questioned. But neither the United States nor any State shall assume or pay any debt or obligation incurred in aid of insur-rection or rebellion against the United States or any claim for the loss or emancipation of any slave; but all such debts, obligations, and claims shall be held illegal and void.

Section 5. The Congress shall have the power to enforce, by appropriate legislation, the provisions of this article.

AMENDMENT XV [1870]

Section 1. The right of citizens of the United States to vote shall not be denied or abridged by the United States or by any State on account of race, color, or previous condition of servitude—

Section 2. The Congress shall have power to enforce this article by appropriate legislation.

AMENDMENT XVI [1913]

The Congress shall have power to lay and collect taxes on incomes, from whatever source derived, without apportionment among the several States, and without regard to any census or enumeration.

AMENDMENT XVII [1913]

The Senate of the United States shall be composed of two Senators from each State, elected by the people thereof, for six years; and each Senator shall have one vote. The electors in each State shall have the qualifications requisite for electors of the more numerous branch of the State legislatures.

When vacancies happen in the representation of any State in the Senate, the executive authority of such State shall issue writs of election to fill such vacancies: *Provided,* That the legislature of any State may empower the executive thereof to make temporary appointments until the people fill the vacancies by election as the legislature may direct.

This amendment shall not be so construed as to affect the election or term of any Senator chosen before it becomes valid as part of the Constitution.

AMENDMENT XVIII [1919]

Section 1. After one year from the ratification of this article the manufacture, sale, or transportation of intoxicating liquors within, the importation thereof into, or the exportation thereof from the United States and all territory subject to the jurisdiction thereof for beverage purposes is hereby prohibited.

Section 2. The Congress and the several States shall have concurrent power to enforce this article by appropriate legislation.

Section 3. This article shall be inoperative unless it shall have been ratified as an amendment to the Constitution by the legislatures of the several States, as provided in the Constitution, within seven years from the date of the submission hereof to the States by the Congress.

AMENDMENT XIX [1920]

The right of citizens of the United States to vote shall not be denied or abridged by the United States or by any State on account of sex.

Congress shall have power to enforce this article by appropriate legislation.

AMENDMENT XX [1933]

Section 1. The terms of the President and Vice-President shall end at noon on the 20th day of January, and the terms of Senators and Representatives at noon on the 3d day of January, of the years in which such terms would have ended if this article had not been ratified; and the terms of their successors shall then begin.

Section 2. The Congress shall assemble at least once in every year, and such meeting shall begin at noon on the 3d day of January, unless they shall by law appoint a different day.

Section 3. If, at the time fixed for the beginning of the term of the President, the President elect shall have died, the Vice-President elect shall become President. If a President shall not have been chosen before the time fixed for the beginning of his term, or if the President elect shall have failed to qualify, then the Vice-President elect shall act as President until a President shall have qualified; and the Congress may by law provide for the case wherein neither a President elect nor a Vice-President elect shall have qualified, declaring who shall then act as President, or the manner in which one who is to act shall be selected, and such person shall act accordingly until a President or Vice-President shall have qualified.

Section 4. The Congress may by law provide for the case of the death of any of the persons from whom the House of Representatives may choose a President whenever the right of choice shall have devolved upon them, and for the case of the death of any of the persons from whom the Senate may choose a Vice-President whenever the right of choice shall have devolved upon them.

Section 5. Sections 1 and 2 shall take effect on the 15th day of October following the ratification of this article.

Section 6. This article shall be inoperative unless it shall have been ratified as an amendment to the Constitution by the legislatures of three-fourths of the several States within seven years from the date of its submission.

AMENDMENT XXI [1933]

Section 1. The eighteenth article of amendment to the Constitution of the United States is hereby repealed.

Section 2. The transportation or importation into any State, Territory, or possession of the United States for delivery or use therein of intoxicating liquors, in violation of the laws thereof, is hereby prohibited.

Section 3. This article shall be inoperative unless it shall have been ratified as an amendment to the Constitution by conventions in the several States, as provided in the Constitution, within seven years from the date of the submission hereof to the States by the Congress.

AMENDMENT XXII [1951]

No person shall be elected to the office of the President more than twice, and no person who has held the office of President, or acted as President, for more than two years of a term to which some other person was elected President shall be elected to the office of the President more than once.

But this Article shall not apply to any person holding the office of President when this Article was proposed by the Congress, and shall not prevent any person who may be holding the office of President, or acting as President, during the term within which this Article becomes operative from holding the office of President or acting as President during the remainder of such term.

AMENDMENT XXIII [1961]

Section 1.   The District constituting the seat of Government of the United States shall appoint in such manner as the Congress may direct:

A number of electors of President and Vice President equal to the whole number of Senators and Representatives in Congress to which the District would be entitled if it were a State, but in no event more than the least populous State; they shall be in addition to those appointed by the States, but they shall be considered, for the purposes of the election of President and Vice President, to be electors appointed by a State; and they shall meet in the District and perform such duties as provided by the twelfth article of amendment.

Section 2.   The Congress shall have power to enforce this article by appropriate legislation.

AMENDMENT XXIV [1964]

Section 1.   The right of citizens of the United States to vote in any primary or other election for President or Vice President, for electors for President or Vice President, or for Senator or Representative in Congress, shall not be denied or abridged by the United States or any State by reason of failure to pay any poll tax or other tax.

Section 2.   The Congress shall have the power to enforce this article by appropriate legislation.

AMENDMENT XXV [1967]

Section 1.   In case of the removal of the President from office or his death or resignation, the Vice President shall become President.

Section 2.   Whenever there is a vacancy in the office of the Vice President, the President shall nominate a Vice President who shall take the office upon confirmation by a majority vote of both houses of Congress.

Section 3.   Whenever the President transmits to the President pro tempore of the Senate and the Speaker of the House of Representatives his written declaration that he is unable to discharge the powers and duties of his office, and until he transmits to them a written declaration to the contrary, such powers and duties shall be discharged by the Vice President as Acting President.

Section 4.   Whenever the Vice President and a majority of either the principal officers of the executive departments, or of such other body as Congress may by law provide, transmit to the President pro tempore of the Senate and the Speaker of the House of Representatives their written declaration that the President is unable to discharge the powers and duties of his office, the Vice President shall immediately assume the powers and duties of the office as Acting President.

Thereafter, when the President transmits to the President pro tempore of the Senate and the Speaker of the House of Representatives his written declaration that no inability exists, he shall resume the powers and duties of his office unless the Vice President and a majority of either the principal officers of the executive departments, or of such other body as Congress may by law provide, transmit within four days to the President pro tempore of the Senate and the Speaker of the House of Representatives their written declaration that the President is unable to discharge the powers and duties of his office. Thereupon Congress shall decide the issue, assembling within 48 hours for that purpose if not in session. If the Congress, within 21 days after receipt of the latter written declaration, or, if Congress is not in session, within 21 days after Congress is required to assemble, determines by two-thirds vote of both houses that the President is unable to discharge the powers and duties of his office, the Vice President shall continue to discharge the same as Acting President; otherwise, the President shall resume the powers and duties of his office.

AMENDMENT XXVI [1971]

Section 1.   The rights of citizens of the United States, who are eighteen years of age or older, to vote shall not be denied or abridged by the United States or any state on account of age.

Section 2.   The congress shall have the power to enforce this article by appropriate legislation. ⋆

Index

National Conservation Commission, 407
National Consumers League, 381
National Council of Churches of Christ, 618
National Council of La Raza, 585
National Defense Education Act, 538
National Environmental Policy Act, 610
National Indian Association, 593
National Indian Defense Association, 342, 594
National Indian Rights Association, 342
National Indian Youth Council, 588
National Industrial Recovery Act, 477
National Labor Reform Party, 370
National Labor Relations Act, 482
National Labor Relations Board, 528
National Labor Union, 370
National Molders' Union, 369
National Municipal League, 400
National Origins Act of 1924, 426
National Organization for Women, 612
National Recovery Administration, 477
National Resources Board, 477
National War Labor Board, 455
National Women's Party, 612
Native Son, 627
Natives of the Southeast, 11
Nativism, 216
Naturalism, 389
Navigation Acts, 99
Nellie, the Beautiful Cloak Model, 391
Neutrality Act of 1939, 499
New Amsterdam, 44
"New Atlantic Charter," 553
New Deal, 473–481
    Second, 481–483
    Third, 484–488
New England Anti-Slavery Society, 226
New England colonies, 39

New England Primer, 83
New Federalism, 607
New Freedom, 415, 418
New Frontier, 540
New gospel of wealth, 602
New Hampshire, 43
New History, 624
New immigrants of the 1880s, 377
New Industrial State, 602
New Jersey Plan, 144
Newlands Reclamation Act of 1902, 407
New Life, 627
New Nationalism, 418
New Orleans, battle of, 189
New Sweden, 44
New York, city of, 250, 251, 607
New York, colony of, 44
New York Tenement House Law, 377
Newman, Paul, 630
Newton, Huey, 580
Nez Perce War, 337
Niagara Movement, 410
Nicaragua, 447
Nimitz, Chester, 503
Nixon, Richard, 173, 174, 355, 533, 535, 539, 610
Nixon Doctrine, 551
    as President, 549–566
Niza, Fray Marcos de, 26
Nonintercourse Act, 180, 182, 229
Norris, Frank, 399
Norris-LaGuardia Act, 478
Norse exploration and settlement, 16
North Atlantic Treaty Organization, 520
North Carolina, 44, 292
Northern Cheyenne, 339
Northern Farmers' Alliance, 348
Northern Pacific Railroad, 360
Northern Security Company, 402
Northwest Ordinance of 1787, 138, 153, 218, 239
Northwest Passage, 21
Noyes, John Humphrey, 237
Nuclear Test-Ban Treaty, 541
Nueces, 270

Nullification, 203
Nye committee, 499

Obledo, Mario, 586
O'Connor, Carroll, 637
The Ocoopus, 399
"Odd Couple," 637
Office of Indian Affairs, 204
Office of Transportation, 506
Office of War Mobilization, 506
Oglethorpe, James, 46
Ohio Gang, 420
Old field system, 80
Oliver, King, 392
Olmstead, Frederick Law, 405
Olney, Richard, 376
Omnibus Bill, 426
One hundred days, 474
On the Origin of Species, 382
O'Neale Scandal, 202
Opechancanough, 36
Open Door note, 444
"Operation Candor," 556
Operation Sail, 560
Orders in Council, 178
Oregon question, 267
Oregon Treaty, 268
Orlando, Vittorio, 459
Oriskany, battle of, 123
Osceola, 206
Osgood, Samuel, 150
Ostend Manifesto, 278
Owen-Keating Act of 1916, 418
"Ozzie and Harriet," 636

"Pachuco," 509
Pacific Borderlands, 4, 6
Pacific Northwest Indians, 10
Packard, Vance, 602
Pago Pago, 437
Pahlevi, Mohammed Reza, Shah of Iran, 564–565
Paine, Thomas, 120, 234
Paiutes, 587
Pakenham, Edward, 189
Palmer, A. Mitchell, 426
Panama Canal, 445, 461
Panama Canal Treaties, 461–464, 562

Panamanian insurrection, 445
Panamanian Revolt of 1931, 461
Pan-American Congress, 436
Panic of 1819, 92, 193
Panic of 1873, 332
Panic of 1907, 491
Paris Treaty of (1763), 105
Paris Treaty of (1783), 124
Paris peace talks, 552
Parker, Alton B., 404, 430
Parks, Bert, 634
Parks, Rosa Mae, 576
Parr, Jack, 636
"Partridge Family," 637
Passamaquoddy, 591
Pathfinder, 246
Paul, Alice, 612
Peace Corps, 540
Peale, Norman Vincent, 618
Pearl Harbor, 501, 522
Pendleton Civil Service Act, 344
Penn, William, 44
Pennsylvania Society for the Encouragement of Manufactures and the Useful Acts, 228
Penobscot, 591
Pentagon papers, 547
Pentecostal movement, 619
Peoples Temple, 621
Pequot tribe, 42
Perkins, Frances, 474
"Perry Mason Show," 631, 636
Perry, Oliver Hazard, 186
Pershing, John J., 447, 452
Pet Banks, 207
Philadelphia, 250, 252
Philip (King Philip), 42
Phips, William, 101
Pickering, John, 170
Pickford, Mary, 628
Pierce, Franklin, 277
Pike, Zebulon, 242
Pilgrims, 39
Pillsbury, Charles A., 363
Pinchot, Gifford, 406
Pitcairn, John, 131
Pit River Indians, 589

Pitt, William (The Elder), 105
Pitts, Zazu, 629
Pittsburgh, 371
Plains Indians, 11
Plantation slaves, 219
Platt Amendment, 497
Plessy v. *Ferguson*, 287, 408
Pocahontas, 35
Poe, Edgar Allen, 246
Polk, James, 266–273
Poker Flats California, 275
Polo, Marco, 18
Ponce de León, Juan, 21, 24
Pontiac, 107
Poole, Elijah, 579
Poor, Salem, 127
Pope, 29
Populism, 348
Poseidon Adventure, 630
Poston River, 513
Potsdam Conference, 518
Pound, Ezra, 626
Powderly, Terence, 373
Powell, John Wesley, 405
Power of Positive Thinking, 618
Power of Sympathy, 246
Powhatan, 35
Pre-Columbian explorers, 15–17
President's Commission on the Status of Women, 613
President's Daughter, 421
Prester, John, 22
Preuss, Charles, 243
Prevost, George, 188
Pribilof Islands, 436
"Price is Right," 636
Prigg v. *Pennsylvania*, 286
Prince Henry (the Navigator) of Portugal, 22
Princeton, 120
Proclamation Act of 1763, 109, 156
Progress and Poverty, 386
Progressivism, 399–401
Promise of American Life, 400
Promontory Point, Utah, 360
Prophet, 183
Prophet Town, 183
Proposition 13, 563

Prosser, Gabriel, 222
Public Law 280, 586
Public Utility Holding Company Act, 482
Public Works Administration, 476
Pueblo Revolt of 1680, 29
Pujo committee, 416
Pulitzer, Joseph, 439
Pullman Palace Car factory, 375
Pullman strike, 350, 375
Pure Food and Drug Act, 404
Puritans, 39, 42, 73–77, 80

Quaker policy, 327
Quay, Mathew, 346
Queen Anne's War, 101
"Queen for a Day," 636
Quebec, battle of, 105
Quebec Act, 108, 116
Quemoy and Matsu, 569
Queue Ordinance, 331
Quock Walker case, 129–130, 218, 286

Radcliffe College, 379
Radical Republicans, 311, 323
Raft, George, 629
Railroad expansion, 360–363
Raleigh, Sir Walter, 34
Ramirez, Francisco P., 335
Randolph, Edmund, 150
Randolph, John, 185
Rankin, Jeannette, 612
Ransom, John Crowe, 627
Rapp, George, 94
Rauschenbusch, Walter, 382
Ray, James Earl, 578
Realism, 388
Reason, the Only Oracle of Man, 234
Rebate, 362
Reconstruction, 310–317
Reconstruction Finance Corporation, 470
Red Badge of Courage, 389
Red Cloud, 338, 339
Red scare, 426
Reed, Thomas B., 347